Maharashtra and the Marathas: Their History and Culture

A Bibliographic guide to western language materials

Datta Shankarrao Kharbas

G. K. HALL & CO., 70 LINCOLN STREET, BOSTON, MASS.

Library of Congress Cataloging in Publication Data

Kharbas, Datta Shankarrao.
    Maharashtra and the Marathas, their history and
culture.

    Bibliography: p.
    Includes index.
    1. Maharashtra, India (State)--Bibliography.
2. Marathas--Bibliography. I. Title.
Z3207.M33K5 [DS485.M34]   015'.54'792   75-15929
ISBN 0-8161-1186-3

To Judith, Anna and Vijay

Foreword

"Maharashtra and the Marathas: Their History and Culture -- A Bibliographic guide to western language materials" is to our knowledge the first work of its kind on a region within South Asia. The guide is the result of several years of research and compilation by Mr. Datta Shankarrao Kharbas, Head Librarian of the Asian Library of the University of Rochester.

Mr. Kharbas was born and brought up in Maharashtra and holds a B. A. in History with a specialization in Maratha History from Poona University. He has a masters degree in Political Science with a specialization in government and politics of South Asia from the University of Michigan, and he is presently working for his Ph.D. in Political Science.

The initial work on the guide was made possible through the support of the University of Rochester's South Asia program, the Rush Rhees Library and, in part, through funds from the U. S. Office of Education under the provisions of the National Defense Education Act, Title VI.

Given the fact that the bulk of South Asian periodical literature has not been previously indexed, given the linguistic plurality and the vastness and cultural diversity of the region, we believe that Mr. Kharbas's work is a major contribution to the establishment of bibliographic control over South Asian research materials. Hopefully other works of this kind will follow covering other specific regions of South Asia in order to give the much needed bibliographic coverage of such a large and important world area.

ROBERT B. HALL, JR.
Director, Asian Studies Center
University of Rochester
Rochester, New York

Contents

Introduction

It is hoped that this guide to Western language materials on Maharashtra will be useful to scholars specializing in that area as well as to those who are concerned with the Marathas' broader role in Indian history. Maharashtra and the Marathas covers not only the political, cultural, and linguistic region of western India but also those parts of India where Maharashtrian influence has been predominant, particularly in disputed border areas between Maharashtra, Mysore, and Goa. The term "Marathas" is not used here in the sense that it is understood within Maharashtra among Maharashtrians -- a person belonging to a particular caste. Rather, it is used in the broadest possible sense to convey the meaning of being Maharashtrian -- a person from Maharashtra. In this context the terms "Maharashtrian" and "Maratha" could be used interchangeably.

In order to keep the size of the work to manageable proportions, it was decided at the outset to exclude articles from newspapers and weekly or biweekly journals. Afer a preliminary survey of government documents, it was found that they were too numerous to list in their entirety. Hence a decision was made to list them only on a selective basis. After close examination certain periodical articles (i.e. articles from Punjabi notes and queries, etc.) were considered unacceptable due to their brevity or the nature of their contents. Monographic publications with significant yet inseparable portions on Maharashtra or the Marathas have been included as are articles from commemorative volumes. Works on the Marathi and Konkani languages are included along with works dealing with the Parsis, but items on Gujarati language and literature are not. Translations from original Marathi or other Indian languages or fictional literature reflecting the social and economic conditions of the region have been chosen for inclusion. Items dealing with the activities of the Marathas and Maratha princely states outside Maharashtra till the end of the East India Company rule (1858) will also be found here. Works dealing with the Maratha princely states outside Maharashtra after the mutiny have been chosen sparingly. Unpublished Ph.D. dissertations have been included with a symbol (*) after the entry. In all, the guide lists 5809 items.

The guide is divided into 18 main sections, each of the main sections being further subdivided into several subject categories. The number of entries in each section has determined the specificity in classification. Although the emphasis of the guide is on the social sciences and humanities, there are a few entries on other subjects. Subject bibliographies and reference works are listed at the beginning of each subject section. General bibliographies and bibliographies covering more than one subject or section of the guide are listed under section A -- Bibliography and Reference. Each item is listed only once, and within each subdivision the arrangement is by alphabetical order. Library of Congress rules in regard to Indian names are followed, with Indian writers who flourished prior to the middle of the 19th century listed under their first names and modern authors entered under their last names. Whenever possible a serious attempt has been made to give as complete information (including dates) as possible about the authors. Citations for monographic publications include the total number of pages (i.e. 227p. instead of vi, xi, 210) and for periodical articles, the volume number and year.

I wish to thank the Director and Associate Director of the University of Rochester Libraries, Ben C. Bowman and Sul H. Lee, for their support and encouragement of this project. I am also very grateful to Dr. Robert B. Hall, Jr., Director of the Center for Asian Studies, for his wholehearted support and for writing the Foreword to this guide and to Dr. Brijen K. Gupta, Professor of South Asian History at the University of Rochester for his encouragement and advice from which the work has benefited considerably. I am also indebted to several staff members of the Rush Rhees Libraries who helped me during the various stages of the work, and to Mrs. Linda Fowler, Mrs. Carol Smith and Mrs. Naomi Lopatin, who worked as research assistants during the preparation of this guide. Finally I would like to thank the staff of the Asia Library, especially Mrs. Virginia Bartholomay and Dr. Robert Compton for their assistance.

Abbreviations and Symbols

b.	year of birth, born
comp.	compiler, compiled by
d.	died, year of death
ed.	editor, edited by
fl.	flourished
n., no.	number
n. d.	no date given or found
p., pp.	page, pages
pref.	preface
pseud.	pseudonym
tr., trans.	translator of, translated by
v.	volume(s)
*	unpublished Ph.D. dissertation

List of Abbreviations
of Periodicals Indexed

AA	Arts Asiatiques. Paris
AAR	Asiatic annual register. London
AB	Asian beacon. Selangor, Malaysia
ABORI	Annals of the Bhandarkar Oriental Research Institute. Poona
ActaH	Acta haematologie. Basel
AGMG	Acta Geneticae Medicae et Gemellologiae. Rome
AH	Agricultural history. Baltimore, Md.
AHG	Annals of human gentics. London
AI	Ancient India. Delhi
AICCER	All India Congress Committee economic review. New Delhi
AICR	All India co-operative review. New Delhi. (formerly: Indian co-operative review. 1935-1953. Madras)
AIOCPT	All India Oriental Conference. Proceedings and transactions. Gauhati. (formerly: Oriental Conference, 1928-1930)
AJ	The Asiatic journal and monthly register for British and Foreign India, China and Australia. London
AJCP	American journal of clinical pathology. Baltimore, Md.
AJI	Agricultural journal of India. Calcutta
AJPA	American journal of physical anthropology. Philadelphia
AJS	American journal of sociology. Washington, D. C.
AL	Art and letters. London. (Indian Art and letters, v. 1-2 [1925-1926], n.s., v. 1-21 [1927-1947])
ALB	Adyar library bulletin (Brahmavidya). Madras
AM	Asiatick miscellany. Calcutta
AmerA	American anthropologist. Menasha, Wisconsin

List of Abbreviations of Periodicals Indexed

Anthropologist.	Delhi
Anthropos.	Posieux, Switzerland
Antiquity.	Newbury, Berks., England
AO	Acta orientalia. Copenhagen
AQ	Army quarterly and defense journal. London
AR	Asian review. (formerly: Asiatic quarterly review, 1886-90, 1913; Imperial and Asiatic quarterly review and Oriental and colonial record, 1891-1912; Asiatic review, 1914-1952)
Archaeologia.	London
ArchO	Archiv orientālnī. Prague
ArsO	Ars orientalis. Ann Arbor, Michigan
ArtAs	Artibus Asiae. Ascona, Switzerland
AS	Asian survey. Berkeley, California
ASBJ	Asiatic Society of Bombay. Journal. Bombay. (formerly: Royal Asiatic Society. Bombay Branch. Journal)
Asia.	New York
AsiaRes	Asiatick researches. Calcutta
AUJR	Agra University journal of research, letters. Agra
AV	Artha vijñana. Poona
BA	Books abroad. Norman, Oklahoma
BCQ	Bombay co-operative quarterly. Bombay
BDCRI	Bulletin of the Deccan College Research Institute. Poona
BEFEO	Bulletin de l'École Française d'Extrème-Orient. Hanoi
BGM	Bombay geographical magazine. Bombay
BIS	Bhāratīya itihāsa āṇi saskṛti. Bombay
BISMHM	Bhārata Itihāsa Sanshodhaka Mandaḷa historical miscellany. Poona
BITCM	Bulletin of the Institute of Traditional Cultures. Madras
BIVG	Bolletim do Instituto Vasco da Gama. Nova Goa
BM	Blackwood's magazine. Edinburgh. (formerly Blackwood's Edinburgh magazine)
BPP	Bengal: past and present. Calcutta
BPWMWI	Prince of Wales Museum of Western India. Bulletin. Bombay
BQR	Bombay quarterly review. Bombay
BRBI	Bulletin of the Reserve Bank of India. Bombay
BSOAS	Bulletin of the School of Oriental and African Studies. London
BV	Bharatiya Vidya. Bombay
CA	Civic affairs. Kanpur

List of Abbreviations of Periodicals Indexed

CHJ	Cambridge historical journal. London
CIEH	Contributions to Indian economic history. Calcutta
CIL	Contemporary Indian literature. New Delhi
CJ	Chamber's journal. Edinburgh
CM	Cornhill magazine. London
CNFI	Cultural news from India. New Delhi
CR	Calcutta review. Calcutta
CS	Current science. Bangalore
Demography.	Washington, D. C.
DG	Deccan geographer. Secunderabad, A. P.
DUS	Dacca University studies, arts and sciences. Dacca
EA	Eastern anthropologist. Lucknow
E&W	East and West: a monthly review. Bombay
EDCC	Economic development and cultural change. Chicago
EduI	Educational India. Masulipatam
EE	Eastern economist. New Delhi
EHR	English historical review. London
EI	Epigraphia Indica. Delhi
EIM	Epigraphia Indo-Moslemica. Calcutta
EMM	Evangelisches mission-magazin. Basel
Enquiry.	Delhi
EQ	Education quarterly. New Delhi
ER	Edinburgh review. Edinburgh
Ethnos.	Stockholm
FAR	Foreign affairs reports. New Delhi
FES	Far Eastern survey. New York
FJ	Folklore journal. London (formerly: Folk-lore record)
FL	Folk lore. Calcutta. (formerly: Indian folk lore, 1957)
Folklore.	London
FR	Fortnightly review. London
GBA	Gazette des beaux-arts. Paris
Geografia.	Karachi
GeoM	Geographical magazine. London
GJRIJ	Ganganatha Jha Research Institute journal. Allahabad
GM	Gandhi Marg. Bombay
GW	Goan world. Bombay
HB	Human biology. Baltimore, Md.
Hemisphere.	North Sydney
HJ	The Hibbert journal. London
HJE	Hitotsubashi journal of economics. Tokyo

HLS	Herald of library science. Varanasi
HR	Hindustan review. Patna. (formerly: Kayastha Samachar. Allahabad, 1899-1912; Hindustan review and Kayastha Samachar. Calcutta)
HT	History today. London
HumR	Humanist review. Bombay
IA	Indian antiquary. Bombay
IAC	Indo-Asian culture. New Delhi
IAR	Indian affaris record. New Delhi
IArch	India (Republic) Department of Archaeology. Indian archaeology, a review. New Delhi
IC	Islamic culture. Hyderabad
ICOP	International Congress of Orientalists. Proceedings
ICQ	India cultures quarterly. Jabalpur
ICR	Indian co-operative review. New Delhi. (Succeeds All India co-operative review)
IDAB	India (Republic) Department of Anthropology. Bulletin. Delhi
IEJ	Indian economic journal. Bombay
IER	Indian economic review. Delhi
IERJ	Institute of Economic Research. Journal. Dharwar
IESHR	Indian economic and social history review. Delhi
IF	Indian folklore. Calcutta
IFR	Indian and foreign review. New Delhi
IGJ	Indian geographical journal. Madras. (formerly: Madras Geographical Association. Journal. 1926-1941)
IHCP	Indian History Congress, Proceedings. Aligarh
IHQ	Indian historical quarterly. Calcutta
IHRCP	Indian Historical Records Commission. Proceedings. New Delhi
II	Indo-Iranica. Calcutta
IIJ	Indo-Iranian journal. The Hague
IJAE	Indian journal of agricultural economics. Bombay
IJAEd	Indian journal of adult education. New Delhi
IJAS	Indian journal of agricultural sciences. New Delhi
IJC	Indian journal of commerce. Lucknow
IJE	Indian journal of economics. Allahabad
IJHM	Indian journal of the history of medicine. Madras
IJLE	Indian journal of labour economics. Lucknow

List of Abbreviations of Periodicals Indexed

IJMR	Indian journal of medical research. New Delhi
IJP	Indian journal of psychology. New Delhi
IJPS	Indian journal of political science. Delhi
IJSW	Indian journal of social work. Bombay
IL	Indian linguistics. Poona
ILG	Indian labour gazette. Delhi
ILib	Indian librarian. Jullundur City
ILit	Indian literature. New Delhi
ILRR	Industrial and labor relations review. Ithaca, N. Y.
IMJ	Indian music journal. Delhi
INC	Indian numismatic chronicle. Patna
IndA	Indian archives. New Delhi
IndC	Indian culture. Calcutta
Indica.	Bombay
IP.E.N.	Indian P.E.N. Bangalore
IR	Indian review. Madras
Islamica.	Leipzig
ISMR	Indian state railways magazine. Delhi
IWT	Indian writing today. Bombay
IYBIA	Indian year book of international affairs. Madras
JA	Journal asiatique. Paris
JAAS	Journal of Asian and African studies. Leiden
JAF	Journal of American folklore. Austin, Texas
JAHRS	Journal of the Andhra Historical Research Society. Rajahmundry
JAOS	Journal of the American Oriental Society. New Haven, Conn.
JAS	Journal of Asian studies. Ann Arbor, Michigan
JASB	Journal of the Anthropological Society of Bombay. Bombay
JASBen	Journal of the Asiatic Society of Bengal. Calcutta
JASC	Journal of the Asiatic Society of Calcutta. Calcutta
JASP	Journal of the Asiatic Society of Pakistan. Dacca
JBHS	Journal of the Bombay Historical Society. Bombay
JBRS	Journal of Bihar Research Society. Patna
JEH	Journal of economic history. New York
JFW	Journal of family welfare. Bombay
JG	Journal of geography. Coral Gables, Fla.
JGRS	Journal of the Gujarat Research Society. Bombay

JHAS	Journal of the Hyderabad Archaeological Society. Bombay
JHR	Journal of historical research. Ranchi, India (City)
JIAI	Journal of Indian art and industry. London. (formerly: Journal of Indian art, 1886–1892)
JIH	Journal of Indian history. Madras
JIIB	Journal of the Indian Institute of Bankers. Bombay
JITH	Journal of Indian textile history. Ahmedabad
JJS	Jewish journal of sociology. London
JKU	Journal of Karnatak University. Dharwar
JMAM	Journal of the Music Academy of Madras. Madras
JMaU	Marathwada University Journal. Aurangabad
JMH	Journal of modern history. Chicago
JMU	Journal of Madras University. Madras
JMyU	Journal of Mysore University. Mysore
JNSI	Journal of the Numismatic Society of India. Bombay
JOG	Journal of obstetrics and gynaecology. New Delhi
JOIB	Journal of the Oriental Institute. Baroda
JOR	Journal of oriental research. Madras
JPUHS	Journal of the Panjab University Historical Society. Lahore
JRAIGB	Royal Anthropological Institute of Great Britain and Ireland. Journal. London
JSAHR	Journal of the Society for Army Historical Research. London
JSemS	Journal of Semitic studies. Oxford, England
JSR	Journal of social research. Ranchi
JSS	Journal of social studies. New York
JSWCI	Journal of soil and water conservation in India. Hazaribagh
JTSML	Journal of the Tanjore Sarasvati Mahal Library. Tanjore
JUB	Journal of the University of Bombay. Bombay
JUC	Journal of the University of Calcutta. Calcutta
JUP	Journal of the University of Poona. Poona
JWCI	Journal of the Warburg and Courtland Institutes. London
JWH	Journal of world history. Paris. (French title: Cahiers d'histoire mondiale)
KHR	Karnataka historical review. Dharwar
Language.	Baltimore, Md.

List of Abbreviations of Periodicals Indexed

Lingua.	Amsterdam
LH	Library herald. Delhi
LK	Lalit kala. New Delhi
LSBT	Literary Society of Bombay. Transactions. London
MA	Maharashtra archives. Bombay
Man.	London
MangR	The Mangalorean review. Bombay
Mankind.	Delhi
Marg.	Bombay
MarI	March of India. Delhi
MAS	Modern Asian studies. London, N.Y.
MB	Maha Bodhi. Calcutta. (formerly: The Maha-Bodhi and the United Buddhist world)
MCCM	Madras Christian College magazine. Madras
MCQ	Maharashtra co-operative quarterly. Bombay
MI	Man in India. Ranchi
MIGS	India. Geological survey. Memoirs. Delhi
MIQ	Medieval India quarterly. Aligarh
MJLS	Madras journal of literature and science. Madras
MMFQ	Milbank memorial fund quarterly. N. Y.
MP	Maharashtra Parichaya. New Delhi
MR	Modern review. Calcutta
MSUBJ	Maharaja Sayajirao University of Baroda. Journal. Baroda
MusR	Muslim review. Calcutta
MW	Muslim world. Hartford
NAA	Narody Azii i Afriki. Moskva. (formerly: Sovetskoe Vostokovedenie, 1953-1956; Problemi Vostokovedenija, 1959-1960)
Nature.	London
NC	Nineteenth century. London
NGJI	National geographical journal of India. Banaras
NIA	New Indian antiquary. Bombay
NO	New Orient. N. Y., 1923-1927; Praha, 1960-1968
NR	New review. Calcutta
NS	New society. London
NUJ	Nagpur University journal. Nagpur
NumCir	Numismatic circular. London
NYSPSAP	New York State Political Science Association. Proceedings. N. Y.
OR	Oriental repertory. London
PA	Public affairs. Bangalore
PacA	Pacific affairs. Vancouver

PB	Prabuddha Bharata (Awakened India). Calcutta
PE	Progress of education. Poona
PHSJ	Pakistan Historical Society. Journal. Karachi
PI	Poetry India. Bombay
PO	Poona orientalist. Poona
Population.	Paris
POQ	Public opinion quarterly. Princeton
PR	Population review. Madras
PS	Population studies. London
PSR	Political science review. Jaipur
PUJ	Patna University journal. Patna
Puranam.	Varanasi
QBES	Quarterly bulletin of economics and statistics. Bombay
QJISSS	Quarterly journal of Indian studies in social sciences. Bombay
QJLSGI	Quarterly journal of the Local Self Government Institute. Bombay
QJMS	Quarterly journal of the Mythic Society. Bangalore
QJPSS	Poona Sarvajanik Sabha, Poona, India. Quarterly journal. Poona
QRHS	Quarterly review of historical studies. Calcutta
Quest.	Bombay
RASGBIJ	Royal Asiatic Society of Great Britain and Ireland. Journal. London
RASGBIT	Royal Asiatic Society of Great Britain and Ireland. Transactions. London
RCASJ	Royal Central Asian Society journal. London
Réalités.	Paris. (English ed.)
RI	Rural India. Bombay
RP	Rational planning. Bombay
RPR	Review of philosophy and religion. Poona
RSAJ	Royal Society of Arts. Journal. London
RSPJ	Research Society of Pakistan. Journal. Lahore
RUSIIJ	Royal United Service Institution of India. Journal. New Delhi
SAISR	Johns Hopkins School of Advanced International Studies. Review. Washington
Sankhya.	Calcutta
SB	Sociological bulletin. Bombay
SC	Science and culture. Calcutta
SE	Secondary education. Delhi
Seminar.	New Delhi
SF	Social forces. Chapel Hill, N. C.

List of Abbreviations of Periodicals Indexed

SFQ	Southern folklore quarterly. Gainesville, Fla.
SikhR	Sikh review. Calcutta
SN	Sangeet Natak. New Delhi
SOA	Studies on Asia. Lincoln, Nebraska
SocA	Social action. Chicago
Spectator.	London
SR	Sociological review. Keele, Staffordshire, England
SSQ	Social service quarterly. Chicago
TdM	Le tour du monde. Paris
Teaching.	Bombay
TLCD	Linguistic circle of Delhi. Transactions. New Delhi
TQ	Tata quarterly. Bombay
Transfusion.	Philadelphia
Triveni	Madras
UA	United Asia. Bombay
UB	Uttar Bharati. Lucknow
UNESCOC	UNESCO courier. N. Y.
UNW	United Nations world. N. Y.
UPHSJ	Uttar Pradesh Historical Society. Journal. Allahabad
URPT	Urban and rural planning thought. New Delhi
USIIJ	United Service Institution of India and Pakistan. Journal. Simla
Vanyajati.	New Delhi
VBQ	Visva-Bharati quarterly. Santiniketan
VIJ	Vishveshvaranand Indological journal. Hoshiarpur
Vikram.	Ujjain
VS	Vox Sanguinis. Basel
VSW	Vierteljahrschrift für Sozial-und Wirtschaftsgeschichte. Wiesbaden
Word.	N. Y.
WR	Westminster review. London
ZDMG	Zeitschrift d. Deutschen morgenländischen Gessellschaft. Wiesbaden
ZE	Zeitschrift für Ethnologie. Braunschweig, W. Germany
ZMA	Zeitschrift für Morphologie und Anthropologie. Stuttgart
ZST	Zoological Society transactions. London
ZVR	Zeitschrift für Vergleichende Rechtswissenschaft. Stuttgart

BIBLIOGRAPHY

General | Bibliography & Reference

A-1

Adam, Margaret Isabella, comp.
Guide to the principal Parliamentary papers relating to the Dominions, prepared by Margaret I. Adam, John Ewing, and James Munro. Edinburg, Oliver and Boyde, 1913. 200p.

A-2

All-Indian Oriental Conference.
Proceedings and transactions. 1st- 1919- Gauhati. Indexes: vols.1-12, 1919-44. 1v. vols.13-17, 1945-54. 1v. vols.18-22, 1955-65. 1v.

A-3

Annual index to Indian periodicals in English, Gujarati, Hindi and Marathi. Surat. v.1- 1966-

U of R

A-4

Ansari, Muhammad Azhar.
A bibliography of materials from original sources on provinces, cities, towns and trade routes during 16th and 17th centuries. Allahabad, University of Allahabad, History section, 1965. 16p.

index islamicus 66-73, 1.257

A-5

Asian social science bibliography. Delhi, Vikas Publications. no.15- 1966- Continued Southern Asia social science bibliography.

U of R

A-6

Asiatic Society of Bombay. Library.
General catalogue of the library of the Bombay Branch of the Royal Asiatic Society. Rev. & brought up to the end of 1915-1917. Bombay, Society's Library, 1917-22. 2v.

A-7

Association for Asian Studies.
Reprints and microfilm materials in Asian studies. Comp. by the Foreign Area Materials Center, University of the State of New York. Ann Arbor, Michigan, 1968-

U of R

A-8

Balfour, Edward Green, 1813-1889.
The cyclopaedia of India and of eastern and southern Asia, commercial, industrial, and scientific; products of the mineral, vegetable, and animal kingdoms, useful arts and manufactures. By Surgeon General Edward Balfour ... Reprint of 3d ed. Graz, Austria, 1967-68. 3v.

U of R

A-9

Bhandarkar Oriental Research Institute, Poona, India.
Index to Annals, vol.22-33 (1941-1952), comp. by G.N. Shrigondekar, ABORI, v.34 (1953), pp.1-122.

A-10

Bhandarkar Oriental Research Institute, Poona, India. Post-graduate and Research Dept.
Index to papers in commemoration volumes. Poona, 1963. (Its Postgraduate and Research Dept. series, no.5) 655p.

U of R

A-11
Bhāratīya Sāskṛtikośa. Ed.by Mahadeoshastri
Joshi. Poona, Bhāratīya Sāskṛtikośa
Mandala, 1962-67. 4v.

A-12
Bibliography of Asian studies. Ann Arbor,
Mich., Pub.by Association for Asian Studies,
1948-

A-13
Bihar Research Society.
Journal. Index to articles published in the
Journal, vols.1-47 (1915-61). Comp.by Gopi
Raman Choudhari. Patna, 1915-61. 1v.

A-14
Birdwood, Sir George Christopher Molesworth,
1832-1917.
Report on the old records of the India
Office, with supplementary note and appendices,
by Sir George Birdwood ... 2d reprint. London, W.H.Allen & Co., Ltd., and at Calcutta,
1891. 329p.

A-15
Bloomfield, Barry Cambray.
Theses on Asia; accepted by universities in
the United Kingdom and Ireland, 1877-1961;
comp.by B.C.Bloomfield. London, Cass, 1967.
132p.

A-16
Books and articles on Oriental subjects
published in Japan. Tokyo, Tōhō Gakkai,
Institute of Eastern Culture. annual.

A-17
Boxer, Charles Ralph, 1904-
A tentative check-list of Indo-Portuguese
imprints, 1556-1674. Bastora, Goa, Tipo-
graphia Rangel, 1956.

A-18
Buist, George.
Index to books and papers on the physical
geography, antiquities and statistics of
India. Bombay, Education Society's Press,
1852. 103p.

A-19
Burgess, James, 1832-1916.
The chronology of modern India, for four
hundred years from the close of the 15th
century, A.D. 1494-1894. Edinburgh, J.
Grant, 1913. 491p.

A-20
Calcutta. National Library.
Author catalogue of printed books in
European languages. Calcutta, Printed by
Manager, Government of India Press, 1941-63.
9v.

A-21
Calcutta. National Library.
   A bibliography of Indology, enumerating basic publications on all aspects of Indian culture. Comp.by J.M.Kanitkar. Calcutta, 1960-   v.1, Indian anthropology.

A-22
Calcutta. National Library.
   Catalogue of periodicals, newspapers and gazettes. Calcutta, Government of India Press, 1956.

A-23
Campbell, Francis Bunbury Fitzgerald.
   An index catalogue of bibliographical works (chiefly in the English language) relating to India, a study in bibliography. London, Library Bureau Co., 1897. 99p.

A-24
Campbell, Francis Bunbury Fitzgerald.
   Index-catalogue of Indian offial publications in the Library, British Museum. London, Library Supply Co., 1900. 579p.

A-25
Central Provinces, India.
   Central Provinces district gazetteers. Allahabad, Printed at the Pioneer Press, 1906-10. 22v.

A-26
Central Provinces and Berar.
   Catalogue of publications; 1892-1923, 1931-1938. Zug, Switzerland, Interdocumentation Co., 196?

A-27
Chaudhuri, Sashi Bhusan, 1904-
   History of the gazetteers of India. New Delhi, Ministry of Education, Govt.of India, 1964. 237p.

A-28
Chaudhuri, Sibadas.
   Bibliography of Indological studies in 1958; a survey of periodical publications. Calcutta, Asiatic Society, 1958. 54p.

A-29
Chaudhuri, Sibadas.
   Bibliography of Indological studies in 1955; a survey of periodical publications. Calcutta, Asiatic Society, 1967. 134p.

A-30
Chaudhuri, Sibadas.
   Bibliography of Indological studies in 1954; a survey of periodical publications. Calcutta, Asiatic Society, 1958. 64p.

A-31
Chicago. University. College.
Introduction to the civilization of India;
South Asia, an introductory bibliography.
Prepared and ed.by Maureen L.P.Patterson
and Ronald B.Inden. Chicago, Syllabus
Division, Univ.of Chicago Press, 1962. 448p.

4 of R

A-32
Chicago. University. Far Eastern Library
The University of Chicago doctoral dissertations and masters' theses on Asia, 1894-
1962. Chicago, 1962.

A-33
Cumming, Sir John Ghest, 1868-
Bibliography relating to India (1900-1927)
London, The Gresham Press, 1927. (National
book council bibliography no.62, rev.ed.)
16p.

4 of R

A-34
Cumulative bibliography of Asian studies,
1941-1965; author bibliography. Boston,
Mass., G.K.Hall, 1969 [i.e.1970] 4v.

4 of R

A-35
Cumulative bibliography of Asian studies,
1941-1965: subject bibliography. Boston,
Mass., G.K.Hall, 1970. 4v.

4 of R

A-36
The Cyclopedia of India; bibliographical,
historical, administrative, commercial.
Calcutta, Cyclopedia Pub.Co., 1907-09?
3v.

4 of R

A-37
Datta, Rajeshwari.
Guide to South Asian material in the
libraries of London, Oxford & Cambridge.
2d ed. Cambridge, University (Centre of
South Asian Studies), 1966. 21p.

4 of R

A-38
Dictionary of national biography. Ed.by S.P.
Sen. Calcutta, Institute of Historical
Studies, 1972-

4 of R v 1 2

A-39
Diehl, Katharine Smith.
Early Indian imprints by Katharine Smith
Diehl, assisted in the oriental languages
by Hemendra Kumar Sircar. New York,
Scarecrow Press, 1964. 533p.

4 of R

A-40
Diehl, Katharine Smith.
Religions, mythologies, folklore, an anno-
tated bibliography. New Brunswick, N.Y.,
Scarecrow Press, 1956. 315p.

-BL

4 of R

A-41
Dodwell, Edward and Miles, James Samuel.
    Alphabetical list of the officers of the
Indian Army; with the dates of their respec-
tive promotion, retirement, resignation, or
death, whether in India or in Europe; from
the year 1760, to the year 1834 inclusive,
corrected to Sept. 30, 1837. Comp.and ed.
by Dodwell and Miles. London, Longman, Orme,
Brown, 1838. 1v.

A-42
East India Company (English) Library.
    A catalogue of the Library of the Hon.
East India Company. London, Printed by J.&
H.Cox, 1845. 332p.

A-43
Garde, P.K.
    Directory of reference works published in
Asia. Nijmegen, The Netherlands, Pub.by
UNESCO, 1956. 166p.

A-44
Garrett, John.
    A classical dictionary of India; illustra-
tive of the mythology, philosophy, literature,
antiquities, arts, manners, customs, etc. of
the Hindus. Delhi, Oriental Publishers, 1971.
803p.

A-45
The Gazetteer of India; Indian Union. Comp.by
the Central Gazetteers Unit, Govt.of India.
Pref.by Humayun Kabir. Delhi, Publications
Division, Ministry of Information and
Broadcasting, 1965-

A-46
Godabole, Raghunatha Bhaskara, d.1887.
    Bharatavarshiya pracina aitihasika kosa.
Bombay, 1876. 714p.

A-47
Great Britain, British Council.
    British books on India, a selection written
between the eighteenth century and the present,
showing something of the contribution made by
British scholars to Indian studies. An exhibi-
tion arranged by the British Council, India
1961. London, 1961. 142p.

A-48
Great Britain. India Office.
    East India (Parliamentary papers) Annual
lists and general index to the parliamentary
papers relating to the East Indies published
during years 1801 to 1907 inclusive. London.
Eyre and Spottiswoode, 1909. (Parliament,
House of Commons. Reports and papers. 1909,
no.89)

A-49
Great Britain. India Office.
    A guide to the India Office records, 1600-
1858. By William Foster, C.I.E., registrar and
superintendent of records. London, Printed
for the India Office by Eyre and Spottiswoode,
1919. 130p.

A-50
Great Britain. India Office.
    A list of the principal Indian government
publications, on sale in this country and at
the various government presses in India.
London, Eyre & Spottiswoode, 1891. 38p.

A-51
  Great Britain. India Office. Record Branch.
    Catalogue of the Home miscellaneous series
  of the India Office records, by Samuel Charles
  Hill. London, Printed by HMSO for the India
  Office Library, 1927. 689p.

U of R

A-52
  Great Britain. India Office. Record Branch.
    List of proceedings etc., Bombay 1702-
  1900, preserved in the Record Department
  of the India Office, London. London, 1899.

A-53
  Guide to Indian periodical literature. Gurgaon,
  Prabhu Book Services [etc.] v.1-
  Mar.1964-

U of R

A-54
  Gupta, Brijen Kishore, 1929-
    India in English fiction, 1800-1970: an
  annotated bibliography. Metuchen, N.J.,
  The Scarecrow Press, Inc., 1973. 310p.

U of R

A-55
  Hamilton, Walter.
    A geographical, statistical and historical
  description of Hindostan and the adjacent
  countries. London, John Murray, 1820. 2v.

A-56
  Harvard University. Library.
    Southern Asia: Afghanistan, Bhutan, Burma,
  Cambodia, Ceylon, India, Laos, Malaya, Nepal,
  Pakistan, Sikkim, Singapore, Thailand,
  Vietnam. Cambridge, Distributed by Harvard
  University Press, 1968. (Its Widener Library
  shelflist, 19) 547p.

U of R

A-57
  Hindustan year-book who's who. Calcutta,
  M.C.Sarkar. v.1-   1933-   annual.

U of R

A-58
  Hobbs, Cecil Carleston, 1907-
    Understanding the peoples of southern
  Asia: a bibliographical essay. Urbana,
  1967. 58p.

U of R

A-59
  Hunter, Sir William Wilson, 1840-1900.
    The imperial gazetteer of India. 2d ed.
  London, Trubner, 1885-87. 14v.

U of R

A-60
  Hyderabad, India (State) Department of
    Statistics and Census.
    List of uruses, melas, jatras, etc. in H.E.H
  the Nizam's dominions, 1349 F. (1940 A.D.) by
  Mazhar Husain, Director of Statistics. Hyderabad-Deccan, Government Central Press, 1940.
  271p.

U of R

A-61
    Impex reference catalogue of Indian books.
    New Delhi, Indian Book Export and Import
    Co., 1960-62. 2v.

U of R

A-66
    India. Survey Department.
    Historical records of the survey of India
    ...; comp.by R.H.Phillimore. Dehra Dun,
    1946-58. 4v.

A-62
    Index India, a quarterly documentation list
    of selected articles, editorials, notes &
    letters etc. from periodicals & newspapers
    published in English language all over the
    world. Jaipur, Rajasthan University Library.
    v.1-   Jan./Mar.1967-

U of R

A-67
    India (Republic) Government of India Publi-
    cation Branch.
    List of official publications not included
    in the general catalogue of Government of
    India publications, issued during the period
    1-1-1940 to 31-12-1960. Delhi, Manager of
    Publications, 1967. 95p.

U of R

A-63
    Index Indo-Asiaticus. Calcutta, G.Chaudhuri.
    v.1-   1968/69-

U of R

A-68
    India (Republic) Laws, statutes, etc. (Indexes)
    Index and chronological table of central
    acts and ordinances, repealed and un-repealed
    from 1834 to June 1951, by Jnanendra Nath
    Baksi. Calcutta, Bhowanipur Book Bureau
    [pref.1951] 289p.

4 of R

A-64
    Index to journals. (American Academy of
    Benares) Varanasi. 1969-   irregular.

A-69
    India (Republic) Office of the Registrar of
    Newspapers.
    Report. New Delhi. 1956-   annual.

U of R

A-65
    India. Imperial Record Dept.
    A hand-book to the records of the government
    of India in the Imperial Record Department
    1748-1859. Calcutta, 1925.

A-70
    India. (Republic) Parliament. House of the
    People.
    Catalogue of parliamentary publications
    (for sale). New Delhi, Lok Sabha Secretariat,
    1967. 54p.

U of R

A-71
India, a reference annual. Delhi, Ministry of
Information and Broadcasting. 1953-

U of R

A-72
India: Who's who. New Delhi, INFA Publications. 1969-

U of R

A-73
India Office Library.
Catalogue of European printed books. Boston,
G.K.Hall, 1964. 10v.

U of R

A-74
India Office Library.
Catalogue of the library of the India Office.
London, Eyre & Spottiswoode, 1908.

U of R

A-75
India Office Library.
A guide to the India Office Library, with a
note on the India Office Records, by S.C.Sutton,
Librarian, Keeper of the Records. 2d ed. Lon-
don, H.M.S.O., 1967. 129p.

U of R

A-76
India Office Library.
Index of post-1937 European manuscript
accessions. Boston, G.K.Hall, 1964. 156p.

U of R

A-77
Indian books. Varanasi, Indian Bibliographic
Centre. 1969-

U of R

A-78
Indian Council for Cultural Relations.
Aspects of Indian culture; select biblio-
graphies. Editors: H.S.Patil [and] R.N.Sar.
New Delhi, sole distributors: Bhatkal Books
International, Bombay, 1966-

A-79
Indian national bibliography. Calcutta.
v.1-   1958-   annual.

U of R

A-80
Indian news index. Ludhiana, India, Panjab
University, Extension Library. ("A quarterly
subject guide to selected English newspapers of India.") v.1-   Jan./Mar.1965-

U of R

A-81
International guide to Indic studies. Darien,
Conn., American Bibliographic Service.
v.1-   June 1963-

U /R

A-82
Inter-University Board, India.
Bibliography of doctorate theses in science
and arts accepted by Indian Universities.
Madras, 1930-41.

A-83
Inter-university Board of India and Ceylon.
A bibliography of Doctoral dissertations
accepted by Indian universities, 1857-1970.
New Delhi, 1972-

U of R v.1-6

A-84
Inter-University Board of India and Ceylon.
List of subjects in arts and sciences in
which research was carried out in the
universities and research institutions
during 1958-1966. New Delhi, 1968-

U /R

A-85
Inter-University Board of India and Ceylon.
Research in progress; a record of subjects
taken up for research by scholars registered
for doctoral degrees with the Indian universities during 1958-66. New Delhi, 1968-

U /R

A-86
Janert, Klaus Ludwig.
An annotated bibliography of the catalogues
of Indian manuscripts. Wiesbaden, F.Steiner,
1965-   (Verzeichnis der orientalischen
Handschriften in Deutschland. Supplementband
1)

U of R

A-87
Jayakar Library.
Catalogue of theses and dissertations (1950-
1969). Comp.by K.S.Hingwe. Poona, Univ.of
Poona, 1971. 261p.

U of R

A-88
Kothari, Hemraj, 1933-
Who's who in India. Calcutta, Kothari
Publications, 1973. 471p.

U of R

A-89
Kozicki, Richard J. and Ananda, Peter.
South and Southeast Asia: doctoral disser-
tations and masters' theses completed at
the University of California at Berkeley,
1906-1968. Berkeley, Center for South and
Southeast Asia studies, University of
California, 1969. (California. University.
Center for South and Southeast Asia Studies.
Occasional paper, no.1) 57p.

U /R

A-90
Krishnaswami, Meena, comp.
Abstracts of doctoral and post-doctoral
dissertations in the humanities and social
sciences in Mysore University. Madras,
American Institute of Indian Studies, 1972.
47p.

U /R

A-91
  London. University. School of Oriental and
    African Studies. Library.
    Index Islamicus. Comp.by J.D.Pearson, li-
  brarian, with the assistance of Julia F.Ashton.
  Cambridge, England, W.Heffer, 1958-

4 7R

A-92
  London. University. School of Oriental and
    African Studies. Library.
    Library catalogue. Boston, G.K.Hall, 1963.
  28v. First supp. Boston, G.K.Hall, 1968.
  16v.

4 7R

A-93
  Low, Donald Anthony, ed.
    Government archives in South Asia; a guide
  to national and state archives in Ceylon,
  India and Pakistan; ed.by D.A.Low, J.C.
  Iltis and M.D.Wainwright. London, Cambridge
  U.P., 1969. 362p.

A-94
  Luard, Charles Eckford, 1869-1927.
    A bibliography of the literature dealing
  with the Central India Agency, to which is
  added a series of chronological tables.
  London, Printed at Eyre and Spottiswoode,
  1908. 118p.

A-95
  Mahar, J.Michael.
    India; a critical bibliography. Tucson,
  Univ.of Arizona Press, 1964. 119p.

A-96
  Men of sciences and technology in India.
  New Delhi, Premier Publishers, 1964-

4 7R

A-97
  Moraes, George Mark.
    Bibliography of Indological studies, 1942.
  Bombay, Examiner Press, 1945.

A-98
  Mukerjee, A.K.
    Bibliography of periodicals. Delhi, Central
  Institute of Education, 1963.

A-99
  Nagaraja Rao, K.
    Bibliography of Indian culture and its
  preparations. Lahore, The Modern Librarian,
  Punjab Library Assoc., 1945. (Library in
  India, series no.2) 39p.

A-100
  The national bibliography of Indian litera-
  ture. General editors: B.S.Kesavan and
  V.Y.Kulkarni. 1st ed. New Delhi, Sahitya
  Akademi, 1962-70. 3v.

4 7R

A-101
Náry Xavier, Filippe, 1804-1874?
Serie chronologica dos vice-reis e gover-
nadores geraes do estado da India. Nova-Goa,
Imprensa nacional, 1852.

Zewellerg-Portuguese b

A-102
New York. Public Library. Reference Dept.
Dictionary catalogue of the Oriental
collection. Boston, G.K.Hall, 1960. 16v.

4 of R

A-103
Nifor guide to Indian periodicals. Poona,
National Information Service, 1955/56-

A-104
Nunn, Godfrey Raymond, 1918-
South and Southeast Asia; a bibliography
of bibliographies. Honolulu, East West
Center Library, 1966. (Occasional papers
of East-West Center Library, no.4) 65p.

4 of R

A-105
Oriental bibliography. Comp.by Lucian Scherman.
Berlin, H.Reuther. v.1-26,pt.1 1887-1926.

4 of R

A-106
Pareek, Udai Narain, 1925-   comp.
A guide to Indian behavioural science
periodicals. Comp.and ed.by Udai Pareek.
Research associate, V.K.Kumar. Delhi,
Behavioural Science Centre, 1966. 130p.

4 of R

A-107
Pearson, James Douglas, 1911-
Oriental and Asian bibliography: an introduction with some reference to Africa. London, Lockwood, 1966. 277p.

4 of R

A-108
Quarterly checklist of Oriental studies,
an international index of current books,
monographs, brochures and separates. Darien,
American Bibliographic Service, 1959-

4 of R

A-109
Risley, Sir Herbert Hope, 1851-1911.
The people of India. 2d ed., ed.by W.Crooke
... with 36 illustrations and ethnological
map of India. Delhi, Oriental Books Reprint
Co., 1969. 504p.

4 of R

A-110
Rose, Horace Arthur, 1867-
Index to Panjab notes and queries, Indian
and North Indian notes and queries. Calcutta,
Asiatic Society, 1908. (Royal Asiatic of
Bengal journal and proceedings, v.4) 127p.

A-111
Sahitya Akademi.
Who's who of Indian writers. New Delhi,
Sahitya Akademi, 1961. 410p.

4 of R

A-112
Scholberg, Henry.
The district gazetteers of British India.
A bibliography. Zug, Poststr. 4, Inter Docu-
mentation, 1970. 149p.

4 of R

A-113
Sengupta, Benoyendra, 1910-
Indiaana; a select list of reference and
representative books on all aspects of
Indian life and culture. Calcutta, World
Press, 1966. 139p.

4 of R

A-114
Serampore College, Serampore, India. William
Carey Historical Library.
Carey Library pamphlets (secular series);
a catalogue, prepared by Katharine Smith
Diehl. Serampore, India, Council of Seram-
pore Colleges, 1968. 114p.

4 of R

A-115
Sewell, Robert, 1845-1925.
Indian chronography; an extension of the
"Indian calendar" with working examples.
London, G.Allen & co., 1912. 199p.

LC

A-116
Sharma, Hari Dev, 1928-   and Mukherji,
Shasanka Prasad, 1937-
Indian reference sources; an annotated guide
to Indian reference books. Varanasi, Indian
Bibliographic Centre, 1972. 320p.

4 of R

A-117
Shulman, Frank J.
Doctoral dissertations on South Asia, 1966-
1970; an annotated bibliography covering
North America, Europe, and Australia. Ann
Arbor, Center for South and Southeast Asian
Studies, Univ.of Michigan, 1971. (Michigan
papers on South and Southeast Asia, 4) 250p.

4 of R

A-118
Singh, Sher, 1934-
Indian books in print, 1955-67; a select bib-
liography of English books published in India.
Comp.by Sher Singh and S.N.Sadhu, assisted by
Vimla Sadhu. Delhi, Indian Bureau of Biblio-
graphies, 1969. 1116p.

4 of R

A-119
Singh, Sher, 1934-   and Sadhu, S.N, 1922-
comps.
Indian books in print, 1972; a bibliography
of Indian books published up to December,
1971, in English language. 2d ed. Delhi,
Indian Bureau of Bibliographies, 1972. 3v.

4 of R

A-120
Single, Nirmal.
Bibliography of selected Indian books, 1970-
1971. New Delhi, Navrang, 1971. 179p.

4 of R

A-121
Shagen, Kiki.
Bibliographical resources about India; an
annotated list of English-language reference
works published in India, 1965-70. Washington, U.S. Dept.of Health, Education, and
Welfare; for sale by the Supt.of Docs., U.S.
Govt.Print.Off., 1972. (DHEW publication
no. (OE) 72-190) 33p.

A-122
South Asia: a bibliography for undergraduate
libraries by Louis A.Jacob and others.
Williamsport, Pa., Bro-Dart Pub.Co., 1970.
(University of the State of New York.
Foreign Area Materials Center. Occasional
publication no.11) 119p.

A-123
Southern Asia social science bibliography.
(United Nations Educational, Scientific,
and Cultural Organisation. Research center
on social and economic development in
Southern Asia) Delhi, no.1-   1952-

A-124
Spencer, Dorothy Mary, 1907-
Indian fiction in English; an annotated
bibliography. Philadelphia, Univ.of Pennsylvania Press, 1960. 98p.

A-125
Stewart, Charles, 1764-1837.
A descriptive catalogue of the oriental
library of the late Tipoo Sultan of Mysore.
To which are prefixed, memoirs of Hyder Aly
Khan, and his son Tipoo Sultan. Cambridge.
Printed at the Univ.Press, 1809. 372p.

A-126
Stucki, Curtis W.
American doctoral dissertations on Asia,
1933-June 1966; including appendix of master's
theses at Cornell University, 1933-June 1968.
Ithaca, N.Y., Southeast Asia Program, Cornell
Univ., 1968. (Cornell University. Southeast
Asia Program. Data paper no.71) 304p.

A-127
Taleyarkhan, Homi Jehangirji H.
Know your state and country, 1956.
Bombay, Bombay Legislature Congress Party,
1956. 252p.

A-128
Thornton, Edward, 1799-1875, comp.
A gazetteer of the territories under the
government of the East-India company, and
of the native states on the continent of
India. Comp.by the authority of the Hon.
Court of Directors, and chiefly from docu-
ments in their possession. New ed. London,
W.H.Allen, 1962. 1014p.

A-129
The times of India directory and year book,
including who's who. Bombay, 1914-

A-130
Union catalogue of Asian publications 1965-
1970. Ed.by David E.Hall. Comp.under the
auspices of the Orientalists' Group, Standing
Conference of National and University Libraries. Sponsored by and ed.at the School of
Oriental and African Studies, Univ.of London. London, Mansell, 1971. 4v.

A-131
United Nations. E.C.A.F.E. Library.
Asian bibliography. Bangkok, 1952-
semi-annual.

(

A-132
U.S. Dept.of the Army. Army Library.
South Asia and the strategic Indian Ocean;
a bibliographic survey of literature. Washington, D.C., Dept.of the Army, 1973. 388p.

4 7 R   (

A-133
U.S. Library of Congress. American Libraries
Book Procurement Center, Delhi.
Accession list, India. New Delhi, July
1962-

य 7 R   (

A-134
U.S. Library of Congress. Orientalia Division.
Southern Asia accessions list, 1952-60.
Washington, 1952-60.

(

A-135
An up-to-date encyclopaedia of all Indological
publications published in India and other
countries relating to ancient Indian learning.
Classified and arranged subjectwise in
alphabetical order. Delhi, Mehar Chand
Lachhman Das, 1962. 426p.

य 7 R   (

A-136
Varma, Om Prakash, comp.
333 great Indians, who is who and who was
who, from the remotest past to the nearest
present. New Delhi, Varma Brothers, 1963.
274p.

1. India - Biography.

LC   (

A-137
Wainwright, Mary Doreen and Matthews, Noel,
comps.
A guide to Western manuscripts and documents
in the British Isles relating to South and
South East Asia. Comp.under the general
supervision of J.D.Pearson. London, New
York, Oxford Univ.Press, 1965. 551p.

U 7 R   (

A-138
Who's who in India, Burma and Ceylon. Ed.by
Thomas Peters. 10th ed. Bombay, Sun Pub.
House, 1939.

U 7 R   (

A-139
Who's who in India, containing lives and
portraits of ruling chiefs, notables,
titled personages, and other eminent
Indians. Lucknow, Newal Kishore Press,
1911-14. 3v.

4 7 R   (

A-140
Who's who of Indian martyrs. Chief editor: P.N.
Chopra; advisory committee chairman: Y.B.Cha-
van. New Delhi, Ministry of Education and
Youth Services, Govt.of India, 1969. 3v.

य 7 R   (

A-141
Wilson, Horace Hayman, 1786-1860.
A glossary of judicial and revenue terms and of useful words occuring in official documents relating to the administration of the Govt.of British India. 2d ed. Delhi, Munshiram Manoharlal, 1968. 752p.

4 MR

A-142
Yule, Henry, 1820-1889 and Burnell, Arthur Coke, 1840-1882.
Hobson-Jobson: a glossary of colloquial Anglo-Indian words and phrases, and of kindred terms, etymological, historical, geographical and discursive. New ed. Ed.by William Crooke. Delhi, Munshiram Manoharlal, 1968. 1069p.

4 MR

A-143
Zenker, Julius Theodor, 1811-1884.
Bibliotheca orientalis. Manuel de bibliographie orientale ... Amsterdam, Oriental Press, 1966. 2v.in 1.

4 MR

Maharashtra

A-144
Asiatic Society of Bombay.
Index to the transactions of the Literary Society of Bombay, vols.I-III, and to the Journals of the Bombay Branch, Royal Asiatic Society, vols.I-XVII with a historical sketch of the society. By Ganpatrao Krishna Tivarekar. Bombay, Printed at the Education Society's Press, 1886. 196p.

A-145
A bibliography of the books and articles by the late Dr. A.S.Altekar compiled by Prof. V.D.Rao, Prof.C.M.Kulkarni and Mr. Bernard Anderson, IHCP, v.22 (1959), pp.34-42.

A-146
Bombay. Institute of Science.
List of periodicals in the Bombay Presidency. Comp.by M.B.Arte. Bombay, Govt.Central Press, 1931.

A-147
Bombay (Presidency)
Bombay civil list, etc. Bombay, 1855-

A-148
Bombay (Presidency)
Catalogue of books printed in the Bombay Presidency during the quarter ending 31st of March, 1894-December 31, 1950. Bombay, Government Central Press, 1894-1950.

4 MR

A-149
Bombay (Presidency)
Chronological tables containing corresponding dates of different eras used in the Bombay Presidency by Christians, Hindoos, Mahamedans, and Parsees; for the century from A.D.1752 to A.D.1852. Bombay, Published by order of the Government. 1850.

Calcutta Nat L.b

A-150
Bombay (Presidency)
Gazetteer. Bombay, Government Central Press, 1877-1904. 27v.in 35.

4 MR

A-151
Bombay (Presidency)
List of official publications printed in the Bombay Presidency, etc. (List of non-confidential publications exempted from registration, which were issued by the Department of the Government of Bombay, etc.) Bombay, 1892-1926. 60pts.

A-152
Bombay (Presidency) Army.
The Bombay army list. Also the Hyderabad Contingent list, the Indian Navy list, and the Bombay Civil list. Bombay, 1854-75. 3pts.

A-153
Bombay (Presidency) Bureau of Economics and Statistics.
Statistical atlas of Bombay State (provincial part) Rev.ed. Bombay, 1950. 228p.

A-154
Bombay (Presidency) Educational Department.
Catalogue of native publications in the Bombay Presidency for 1st January 1865 to 30th June 1867, and of some works omitted in the previous catalogue; prepared under orders of Government, by J.B.Peile. Bombay, Education Society's Press, 1869.

A-155
Bombay (Presidency) Educational Department.
Catalogue of native publications in the Bombay Presidency up to 31st December 1864. Prepared under orders of government by A. Grant. 2d ed., with numerous additions, and corrections. Bombay, Education Society's Press, Byculla, 1867.

A-156
Bombay (Presidency) General Dept.
A handbook of the Bombay government records. By A.F.Kindersley. Bombay, 1921.

A-157
Bombay (Presidency) Victoria and Albert Museum.
Catalogue of the collection of maps, prints, and photographs illustrating the history of the island and city of Bombay. Comp.by Cecil Laurence Burns. Bombay, 1918.

A-158
Bombay (State)
List showing newspapers published in the State of Bombay. Corrected up to 31st March 1957. Bombay, Printed at the Govt.Central Press, 1957 or 8. 21p.

A-159
Bombay (State)
Reference annual of the state. Bombay, 1954-1959.

A-160
Date, Shankar Ganesh, 1905-   comp.
Marāthī-grantha-suci. Poona, 1943-1961. 2v.

A-161
Dodwell, Edward and Miles, James Samuel.
Alphabetical list of the Hon'ble East
India Company's Bombay civil servants from
the year 1798 to the year 1839. London,
Woking, 1839. 213p.

A-166
India Office Library.
Catalogue of the Marathi manuscripts in the
India Office Library, by the late James Fuller
Blumhardt and Sadashiv Govind Kanhere. Oxford,
Pub.for the India Office Library at the Claren-
don Press, 1950. 133p.

A-162
Forrest, Sir George William, 1846-1926.
Index to the selections from the letters
despatches and other state papers preserved
in the Bombay Secretariat. Bombay, 1899.

A-167
Kulke, Eckehard.
Die Parsen; bibliographie über ein indische
Minorität. The Parsees: a bibliography on an
Indian minority. Freiburg I.Br., Bertelsmann
Universitätsverlag, 1968. (Materlallen des
Arnold-Bergstraesser-Instituts für Kultur-
wissenschaftliche Forschung, 17) 76p.

A-163
Gavaskar, Surendra Atmaram.
Marāthi dolamudritem. 2d rev.& enl.ed.
Mumbai, Marathi grantha sangrahalay, 1961.

A-168
Lyall, Sir Alfred Comyn, 1835-1911.
Gazetteer for the Haidarabad assigned
districts, commonly called Berar, 1870.
Bombay, Education Society's Press, 1870.

A-164
Gazetteer of Bombay city and island ... Comp.
by S.M.Edwardes. Bombay, Printed at the
Times Press, 1909-10. 3v.

A-169
Maharashtra, India (State)
Catalogue of books printed in the State of
Maharashtra. Bombay, 1961-

A-165
Gode, Parashuram Krishna, 1891-
Thirty years of historical research, or,
bibliography of the published writings of
P.K.Gode ... with a foreword by ... K.V.
Rangaswami Aiyangar. 3d ed. Poona, 1947.
90p.

A-170
Maharashtra, India (State)
Civil list. Bombay, Govt.Print.& Stationery,
1960-

A-171
  Maharashtra, India (State)
    Maharashtra State gazetteers: General series.
  Rev.ed. Bombay, Directorate of Govt.Print.,
  Stationery and Pubs., 1967-

A-176
  Rāshtrīya grantha sūci. Marāṭhi vibhāga. Ed.
    by B.S.Kesavan. Prepared by the staff of
    the Central Reference Library, Calcutta.
    1958/59-

47ρ

A-172
  Maharashtra, India (State)
    The state of Maharashtra. Bombay, 1962.

A-177
  Times of India, Bombay.
    Directory of Bombay (city and province)
    including Karachi and Hyderabad State. Bombay.

LC

LC

A-173
  Maharashtra, India (State) Directorate of
    Publicity.
    Handbook of Maharashtra State. Bombay,
  1960. 137p.

A-178
  Who's who in western India, ed.and comp.by
    Thos.Peters. Rev.,enl.,and illustrated.
    Poona, Sun Pub.House [pref.1934] 486p.

Lc

Bibliography & Reference   Anthropology & sociolo
Anthropology & sociology -
General

A-174
  Maharashtra, India (State) Examiner of Books
    and Publications.
    List showing newspapers published in the
  Maharashtra State, corrected up to 31st
  Dec., 1960. Bombay, Govt.Print.& Stationery,
  1963. 79p.

B-1
  Anthropological Society of Bombay.
    Index to the journal of the Anthropological
  Society of Bombay, 1886-1936. Bombay, 1937.

47ρ

A-175
  Murray, John, publisher, London.
    Handbook of the Bombay Presidency. 2d ed.
  London, J.Murray, 1881. 417p.

B-2
  Bacon, Elizabeth E.
    Selected and annotated bibliography of the
  sociology of India, by E.Bacon, M.E.Opler &
  E.LeClair, jr. New Haven, Human Relations
  Area Files, 1957.

B-3
Bhagwat, Durga Narayan, 1910-
A critical bibliography of folklore of Maharashtra (1806-1950), <u>ASBJ</u>, n.s.,v.39/40 (1964/65), pp.273-320; v.41/42 (1966/67), pp.203-40.

4 of R

B-4
Citalia, K.J., ed.
Directory of women's institutions, Bombay Presidency. Pt.I - Social section. A reference book on women's work and women's institutions in the Presidency of Bombay. Bombay, Servants of India Society, 1936. 86p.

B-5
Damle, Yashwant Bhaskar, 1923-
Caste: a review of the literature on caste. Cambridge, Massachusetts Institute of Technology, Center for International Studies, 1961. 125p.

LC. 6 3/8

B-6
Directory of social work in the city and island of Bombay. Ed.by D.S.Savardekar. Bombay, Social Service League, 1926. (Social work directories, no.3) 128p.

B-7
Encyclopaedia of social work in India. Foreword by S.Radhakrishnan. Delhi, Publications Div., Ministry of Information & Broadcasting, 1968. 3v.

4 of R

B-8
Field, Henry, 1902-   and Laird, Edith M.
Bibliography on the physical anthropology of the peoples of India, Coconut Grove, Fla., Field Research Projects, 1968. 88p.

4 of R

B-9
Fürer-Haimendorf, Elizabeth von, 1909-
An anthropological bibliography of South Asia, together with a directory of recent anthropological field work. With a foreword by Christoph von Fürer-Haimendorf. Paris, Mouton, 1958-70. 3v.

4 of R

B-10
Gilbert, William Harlen.
Caste in India, a bibliography. Pt.I. Washington, D.C., 1948.

B-11
Gokhale, Sharad W., 1942-
Directory of social welfare agencies in Greater Poona. Poona, Co-ordinating Council Publication, 1969. 286p.

4 of R

B-12
India (Republic) Office of the Registrar General.
Bibliography on scheduled castes, scheduled tribes, and selected marginal communities of India. Comp.by H.L.Harit; assistance: Charan Singh, K.R.Kapoor and Ram Gopal. Supervision and editing: B.K.Roy Burman. New Delhi, 1968.

4 of R

B-13
   Indian Conference of Social Work.
      Directory of social welfare agencies in
greater Bombay. 2d rev.ed. Bombay, Popular
Book Depot, 1957. 121p.

B-14
   Indian Council of Social Science Research.
      Doctorates in social science awarded by
Indian Universities. New Delhi, 1968-
annual. (Its Research information series)

B-15
   Indian folklore; select bibliography, CNFI,
      v.8 (1967), pp.53-64.

B-16
   Kirkland, Edwin Capers.
      A bibliography of South Asian folklore.
Bloomington, Indiana Univ.Research Center
in Anthropology, Folklore, and Linguistics,
1966. (Asian folklore monographs, no.4)
315p.

B-17
   Mandelbaum, David Goodman, 1911-
      Materials for a bibliography of the ethnology
of India. Berkeley, Dept.of Anthropology,
Univ.of California, 1949.

B-18
   Regamy, Constantin.
      Bibliographie analytique des travaux rela-
tifs aux elements anaryens dans la civilisation et les langues de l'Inde, BEFEO,
v.34 (1934), pp.429-566.

B-19
   Sen Gupta, Sankar and Parman, Shyam.
      A bibliography of Indian folklore and related
subjects. Calcutta, Indian Publications,
1967. (Indian folklore series, no.11) 196p.

B-20
   Siegling, W.
      A list of the more important works on Indian
ethnography. In: Ethnography; castes and
tribes. By Sir J.A.Baines, 1912. pp.173-
211.

B-21
   A survey of research in sociology and social
      anthropology. Bombay, Popular Prakashan,
1972-

B-22
   UNESCO. Research Centre on the Social Impli-
      cations of Industrialization in Southern
Asia.
      Bibliography on urbanization in Asia (ECAFE
region) Provisional ed. Prepared for the joint
UN-UNESCO seminar on urbanization in the ECAFE
region. Bangkok, 8-18 August 1956. Calcutta,
1956.

B-23
    Agarwal, Chhotelal Bhugwandas.
        The Harijans in rebellion. Case for the
removal of the untouchability. Bombay, D.B.
Taraporevala Sons & co., 1934. 127p.

11 NYPL

B-24
    Bopegamage, A. and Veeraraghavan, P.V.
        Status images in changing India, a study
based on two surveys. Bombay, Manaktalas,
1967. 222p.

4 of R

B-25
    Bragança Pereira, Antonio Bernardo de.
        Etnografia da India Portuguesa.
Bastora, 1940. 2v.

SOAS

B-26
    Damle, Yashwant Bhaskar, 1923-
        College youth in Poona: a study of elite
in the making. Poona, Deccan College (mimeo-
graphed) 1966. 735p.

B-27
    Damle, Yashwant Bhaskar, 1923-
        Social differentiation and differentiation
in emoluments. Poona, 1955. 186p.

Anthropology & Sociology
BDCR, p. 125

B-28
    D'Souza, Bento Graciano.
        Goan society in transition: a study in
social changes. Bombay, Univ.of Bombay,
1970. *

Sociology
BDD

B-29
    Enthoven, Reginald Edward, 1869-
        The results of the ethnographic survey of
Bombay. JASB, v.12 (1921-1924). pp.113-26.

Furer

B-30
    Enthoven, Reginald Edward, 1869-
        The study of ethnography in Bombay Presi-
dency. JASB, v.8 (1909). pp.433-35.

Sen Gupta

B-31
    Frere, Mary Eliza Isabella, d.1911.
        Fairy tales from India; edited by Katharine
Pyle. Philadelphia and London, Lippincott,
1926. 240p.

        1. Folk-lore - India.

LC

B-32
    Hooda, Sukhdev Singh.
        The Bombay collegian: a study in social
background. Bombay, Univ.of Bombay, 1969. *

Sociology Educational
group
BDD

B-33
Isaacs, Harold Robert, 1910-
India's ex-untouchables. New York, John
Day. Co., 1965. 188p.

1. Untouchables. 2. Social mobility.

N u R
LC

B-34
Karve, Irawati (Karmarkar) 1905-1970.
The Hindu society; an interpretation. Poona,
Deccan College, 1961. 171p.

sociology & anthropology - Gen.

1. Caste - India.   *General*

U of R

B-35
Karve, Irawati (Karmarkar), 1905-1970 and
Acharya, Hemalata.
The role of weekly markets in the tribal,
rural and urban setting. By Irawati Karve and
Hemalata Acharya. 1st ed. Poona, Published by
S.M.Katre for Deccan College Post-graduate and
Research Institute, 1970. (Deccan College
Building Centenary and Silver Jubilee Series,
no.70). 148p.

*Anthropology & Sociology
BDCRI*

B-36
Kulkarni, Vaman Balaji.
Through literature to society. AIOCPT, v.13
(1946), pp.216-23.

U of R

B-37
Kumar, Ravinder.
Western India in the nineteenth century: a
study in the social history of Maharashtra.
London, Routledge and K.Paul, Toronto, Univ.
of Toronto Press, 1968. (Studies in social
history) 359p.

U of R

B-38
Modi, Jivanji Jamshedji, 1854-1933.
Anthropological papers. Bombay, British
India Press, 1911-34. 5v.

U of R

B-39
Modi, Jivanji Jamshedji, 1854-1933.
Asiatic papers: papers read before the
Bombay Branch of the Royal Asiatic Society.
Pts.1-4, 1905,17,27,29. Bombay, Bombay
Education Society's Press, 1905-29.

B-40
Natarajan, Swaminath, 1918-
A century of social reform in India.
New York, Asia Pub.House, 1959. 228p.

1. India - soc. condit.

U of R

B-41
Professor Ghurye felicitation volume. Ed.by
K.M.Kapadia. Bombay, Popular Book Depot,
1954. 307p.

1. Sociology - Addresses, essays, lectures.

U of R

B-42
Sankalia, Hasmukhlal Dhirajlal, 1908-
Sir Rustom and research in anthropology,
JASB, v.10,no.1 (1966), pp.5-6.

U of R

B-43
Sovani, Nilkanth Vitthal and Dandekar,
Vinayak Mahadeo, 1920-
Changing India; essays in honour of
Prof.D.R.Gadgil. Bombay, Asia Pub.House,
1961. 360p.

1. India - Civilization - Addresses, essays, lectures.

Uy'R

Castes and tribes

B-44
The Adivasis of Maharashtra. Hyderabad,
Government Central Press, 1961.

BDD

B-45
Apte, Hari Moreshwar.
The Madhyandina Brahmins of Maharashtra.
Bombay, Univ.of Bombay, 1944. *

B-46
Betham, Robert Mitchell.
Marathas and Dekhani Musalmans. Calcutta,
Superintendent of Government Printing, 1908.
(Handbooks of the Indian Army). 196p.

BM

caste

B-47
Bhagat, Mahadeo Gopal.
The untouchable classes of Maharashtra.
Bombay, M.G.Bhagat, School of Sociology &
Economics, Univ.of Bombay, 1935. 45p.

BM

B-48
Bhagat, Mahadeo Gopal.
The untouchable classes of Maharashtra.
JUB. v.4 (1935), pp.160-74.

JUB

B-49
Bhagat, Mahadeo Gopal.
The untouchable classes of the Janjira
State, JUB, v.7 (1938-39), pp.131-54.

Furer

B-50
Bhagawat, Rajaram Ramkrishna, 1851-1908.
The Deccani Brahmin. Poona, Scottish Mis-
sion Industries Co., 1907. 23p.

JUB v.20

B-51
Bharatiya, L.K.
The influence of the co-working of adivasis
and non-adivasis in Ghoti, JASB, v.14,no.1
(1969), pp.26-35.

JASB '69 405R

NO ENTRY

B-52
Bhatt, Vamanrai A.
The harijans of Maharashtra. Delhi,
Harijan Sevak Sangh, 1941. 61p.

VVVLC

B-53
Bhide, Vidyadhar Vaman, 1861-1936.
Statistics of civil conditions among the
Deccan and Konkan Brahmins, QJPSS, v.17,no.4
(1894), pp.1-12.

B-54
Bhole, R.R.
An untouchable speaks. London, Brittain
Pub.Co., 1944. 20p.

VVCEJ 1943-48

B-55
Bidkar, D.H.
A note on the condition of the Kathodies,
Vanyajati, v.2 (1954), pp.132-34.

Furer

B-56
Bombay (Presidency)
Notes on criminal classes in the Bombay
Presidency, with appendices regarding
some foreign criminals who occasionally
visit the Presidency including hints on
the detection of counterfeit coin.
Bombay, Government Central Press.
1908. 363p.

Calcutta Ant Lib

B-57
Bombay (Presidency) Depressed Classes and
Aboriginal Tribes Committee.
Report. Bombay, Government Central
Press, 1930. 88p.

B-58
Briggs, John, 1785-1875.
Account of the origin, history and manners
of the race of men called Bunjaras, LSBT,
v.1 (1819), pp.159-82.

B-59
Carter, H.V.
The castes of the Bombay Presidency, IA,
v.2 (1873), pp.154,242,274,372; v.13 (1874),
p.208.

B-60
Chapekar, Laxman Narayan, 1906-
Thakurs of the Sahyadri. Bombay, N.Y.,
Indian Branch Oxford Univ.Press, 1960.
(Univ.of Bombay Publications, Sociology
series, no.5). 235p.

Oath

B-61
Conlon, Frank Fowler.
The emergence of the Saraswat Brahmans,
1830-1930: a study of caste and social change
in modern India. Minneapolis, University of
Minnesota, 1969. 359p.

B-62
Correia, Alberto Carlos Germano da Silva, 1888-
Les Mahrattes de l'Inde Portugaise,
memoire present au congres International
des Sciences anthropologiques et ethnolo-
giques de Londres, en Juillet-Aout, 1934.
Bastora, 1934.

Uof Rorder

B-63
Correia, Alberto Carlos Germano da Silva,
1888-
Les Ranes de Satary. Nova Goa, 1928.

Field

B-64
Damle, Yashwant Bhaskar, 1923-
Caste in Maharashtra, JUP, v.9 (1958),
pp.87-98.

*South Asia Social Science
Bibliography's Sociology, p.+*

B-65
Desai, Kirtidev D.
Non-Aryans on the western coast, JUB, v.28
(1959-1960), pp.10-31.

Snce

B-66
D'Souza, Victor S.
Measurement of rigidity - fluidity dimension
of social stratification in six Indian villages,
SB, v.18 (1969), pp.35-49.

*sociology & anthropology...
AAS Sept 19..*

B-67
DuBoulay, J.
On the Bari or Pamuli caste in Khandesh
district. JASB, v.4 (1895-1899), pp.444-49.

B-68
DuBoulay, J.
On the Koli caste in the Khandesh district,
JASB, v.5 (1895-1899), pp.58-62.

B-69
DuBoulay, J.
On the Pawra caste in Khandesh district,
JASB, v.4 (1895-1899), pp.437-43.

B-70
Dutt, K.Guru.
Chitrapur Saraswat retrospect; a historical
and sociological study. Bangalore, B.B.Power
Press, 1955. 295p.

1. Saraswats.

B-71
Edwardes, Stephen Meredyth, 1873-1927.
Note on the Bombay Kolis, JASB, v.7 (1905-
1907), pp.516-21.

B-72
 Enthoven, Reginald Edward, 1869-
  The tribes and castes of Bombay. Bombay,
 Govt.Central Press, 1920. 3v.

B-73
 Ferreira, John V.
  The Katharis: an evaluation of available
 material, JSR, v.5,no.2 (1962), pp.64-70.

Fürer

B-74
 Forsyth, James, 1838-1871.
  The highlands of central India; notes on
 their forests and wild tribes, natural history
 and sports. New ed. London, Chapman and
 Hall, 1919. 398p.

4 A R

B-75
 Frias, Antonio João de, 1664-1727.
  Avreola dos indios, e nobiliarchia
 bracmana: tratado historico, genealogico,
 panegyrico, politico, e moral...escrito
 pelo licenciado Antonio Joao de Frias...
 Lisboa, Na Officina de M.Deslandes, 1702.
 238p.

B-76
 Ghurye, Govind Sadashiv, 1893-
  The aboriginals "so-called" and the future.
 Poona, D.R.Gadgil, 1943. (Gokhale Institute
 of Politics and Economics, Pub.no.11) 246p.

4 A R

B-77
 Ghurye, Govind Sadashiv, 1893-
  Caste and race in India. London, Kegan,
 Paul, Trench, Trübner, 1932. (The history
 of civilization, prehistory and antiquary)
 216p.

  1. Caste - India. 2. Ethnology - India.
 3. Hindus.

4 A R

B-78
 Ghurye, Govind Sadashiv, 1893-
  Caste, class and occupation. 4th ed. Bom-
 bay, Popular Book Depot, 1961. 371p.

4 A R

B-79
 Ghurye, Govind Sadashiv, 1893-
  The Mahadev Kolis. Bombay, Popular Praka-
 shan, 1963. 272p.

  1. Kolis.

4 A R

B-80
 Ghurye, Govind Sadashiv, 1893-
  The scheduled tribes. 2d ed. Bombay,
 Popular Book Depot, 1959. 299p.

U A R

B-81
 Gibbs, T.E.
  Bhils in the Dangs, IA, v.5 (1876), p.83.

Fürer

B-82
Gorey, L.K.
The adivasis of Maharashtra, MR, v.111
(1962), pp.397-411.

MR

B-83
Graham, Douglas Cunningham.
Brief historical sketch of the Bheel Tribes
inhabiting the province of Khandesh. London,
under orders from the Court of Directors,
East India Company, 1845. 25p.

IOL

B-84
Griffin, Sir Lepal.
The Bhils and their country, AR, v.7 (1889),
pp.438-66.

AR

B-85
Grigson, Wilfred Vernon, 1896-
The Aboriginal problem in the Central
Provinces and Berar. Nagpur, Govt.Print.,
C.P.& Berar, 1944.

Lib. of Indology

B-86
Gulati, R.K.
An analysis of the inter-group differences
in an artisan caste (Kumbhar) of Maharashtra.
Poona, Univ.of Poona, 1968.   *

Anthropology & sociology.

BDCRI

B-87
Gulati, R.K.
An analysis of the intergroup differences
in an artisan caste of Maharashtra. Field
research projects. Miami, Florida, U.S.A.,
1970, 122p.

Anthropology & Sociology
BDCRI : 727

B-88
Gunthorpe, Edward James.
Note on the Bhonde Koomars, JASB, v.1
(1886-1889), pp.409-14.

Susor

B-89
Gunthorpe, Edward James.
Notes on criminal tribes residing in or
frequenting the Bombay Presidency. Berar,
and the Central Provinces. Bombay, Times
of India Steam Press, 1882. 114p.

B-90
Gupte, Balkrishna Atmaram, 1851-
The Kayastha Prabhus of Bombay, Baroda,
Central India, and Central Provinces. Cal-
cutta, Ramchandra B.Gupte, Bee Press, 1913.
82p.

BM

B-91
Gupte, Tryambak Vasudeva, d.1918, comp.
Ethnographical notes on Chandraseniya
Kayastha Prabhu. Poona, 1904.

Calcutta Nat'l Lib.

B-92
  Johnson, William.
    The oriental races and tribes, residents
  and visitors of Bombay; a series of photographs, with letterpress descriptions. London, W.J.Johnson, 1866. 2v.

B-93
  Joshi, Purushottam Balkrishna, 1856-1930.
    History of the Pathare Prabhus and their
  gurus or spiritual guides. Bombay, 1914.

B-94
  Joshi, Purushottam Balkrishna, 1856-1930.
    The Mangelas, a caste of Konkan mariners.
  JASB, v.8 (1907-1909), pp.574-77.

B-95
  Joshi, Purushottam Balkrishna, 1856-1930.
    On the Gondhalis, a class of Marathi bards.
  JASB, v.1 (1886-1888), pp.371-77.

B-96
  Jungblut, Leonhard.
    Die Missetäterstämme: ein Buch von
  Indiens ältestem volk...aus dem nieder-
  ländischen übertragen mit Vorwort von
  Prof. P.Dr.Wilhelm Koppers. Mödling,
  Missionsdruckerei St.Gabriel, 1945. 342p.

B-97
  Kale, Dattatraya Nagesh.
    Agris; a socio-economic survey. Bombay,
  Asia Pub.House, 1952. 418p.

B-98
  Kanara Saraswat Association. Census Working
  Committee.
    Portrait of a community: Chitrapur Saraswat
  census report. Comp.by Census Working Committee
  of Kanara Saraswat Association. General ed.:
  Brahmanand S.Mavinkurve. Bombay, Popular
  Prakashan, 1972. 166p.

B-99
  Kanara Saraswat Association, Bombay.
    The Chitrapur Saraswat 1956 census
  report and directory, compiled by the
  Census Working Committee of the Kanara
  Saraswat Association, Bombay. Bombay,
  G.S.Mavinkurve, 1956. (Chitrapur Sara-
  swat series, 10). 516p.

B-100
  Kane, Pandurang Vaman, 1880-
    A note on the Kayasthas, NIA, v.1 (1939),
  pp.740-43.

B-101
  Karve, Irawati (Karmarkar) 1905-1970.
    The Bhils of West Khandesh: a socio-economic
  survey. Bombay, 1961. 85p.

B-102
Karve, Irawati (Karmarkar) 1905-1970.
Ethnic affinities of the Chitpavans, JUB,
v.1 (1932-1933), pp.383-400; v.2 (1933-1934),
pp.132-158.

Furer

B-103
Karve, Irawati (Karmarkar) 1905-1970 and
Acharya, Hemalata.
Neo-Buddhism in Maharashtra, JUP, v.15
(1962), pp.130-33.

JuP

B-104
Khan, Ghulam Ahmed.
The Bhils of Khandesh, MI, v.15 (1935),
pp.133-43.

Furer

B-105
Kishori, Kalasinh F.
Dangs natives at a glance, Vanyajati, v.10
(1962), pp.120-23.

Furer

B-106
Kogekar, S.V.
The problem of caste in Maharashtra, JUP,
no.7 (1956), pp.102-103.

JuP

B-107
Koppers, Wilhelm, 1886-
Die Bhil in Zentralindien. Horn, F.Berger,
1948. (Wiener Beiträge zur Kulturgeschichte
und Linguistik, Jahrg, 7) 373p.

B-108
Kothurkar, Vasudeo Krishna.
A study of social prejudice in three villages:
the problem of Nav-Buddhas, JUP, v.15 (1962),
pp.123-29.

a BR

B-109
Kulkarni, Krishnaji Pandurang, 1893-
The Ahirs of Khandesh and their language,
JASB, v.2 (1948), pp.47-68.

Furer

B-110
Mackintosh, Alexander.
An account of the origin and present condition of the tribe of Ramoossies including the
life of the Chief Oomiah Naik. Bombay, American Mission Press, 1833. 253p.

B-111
Mackintosh, Alexander.
An account of the tribe of Mahadeo
Kolies, MJLS, v.4 (1837), pp.71-112.

MJLS

B-112
MacMunn, Sir George Fletcher, 1869-1952.
The martial races of India. London,
Sampson, Low, Marston & co.,ltd.,1933.
382p.

1. Untouchables. 2. Social mobility.
2. Ethnology-India. 3. Caste-India. 4. India-
Hist., Military
N.P.
U of R

B-113
Mahratta Education Fund. Madras.
South Indian Maharashtrians: cultural and
economic studies. Madras, 1937. (Silver
jubilee souvenir) 215p.

1. Caste - India.

RM

B-114
Malcolm, Sir John, 1769-1833.
Essay on the Bhils, RASGBIT, v.1 (1827),
pp.65-91.

Fürer

B-115
Mann, Harold Hart, 1872-
The "Mahars" of a Deccan village, SSQ, v.2
(1916), pp.1-8.

B-116
Mann, Harold Hart, 1872-
The untouchable classes of an Indian
city, HR, v.25 (1912), pp.233-40, 317-24.
Also in: SR, v.5 (1912), pp.42-55.

Mann

B-117
Marriott, McKim.
Caste ranking and community structure in
five regions of India and Pakistan. Poona,
Deccan college postgraduate and research
inst., 1965. (Building centenary and
silver jubilee series, 30). 111p.

1. Caste- India

U of R

B-118
Mazumdar, Bijay Chandra.
The aborigines of the highlands of Central
India. Calcutta, University of Calcutta,
1927. 84p.

U of R

B-119
Mehta, Behram Hormasji.
Social and economic conditions of the Megh-
wal untouchables of Bombay City, with special
reference to the community centre at Valpakha-
dy. Bombay, Univ.of Bombay, 1937. *

cit. of PhD thesis

B-120
Modi, Jivanji Jamshedji, 1854-1933.
The Dhangurs and the Chavars of Mahableshwar,
JASB, v.3 (1893-1894), pp.471-83.

Fürer

B-121
Modi, Jivanji Jamshedji, 1854-1933.
Note on the Kolis of Bassein, JASB, v.7
(1905-1907), pp.521-25.

Fürer

B-122
Modi, Jivanji Jamshedji, 1854-1933.
The Thakurs of Matheran, JASB, v.5 (1900-01),
pp.458-65.

Furer

B-123
Modi, Jivanji Jamshedji, 1854-1933.
The Vadaris of villages around Deolali Camp,
in the Nasik District, JASB, v.8 (1910-13),
pp.425-30.

Furer

B-124
Morab, S.G.
Caste council of the Bhandari of Dapoli,
MI, v.46 (1966), pp.154-63.

Inter Guide to Indы Studies

B-125
Moray, V.E.
The patterns of caste and family in Wai
Taluka. Bombay, Univ.of Bombay, 1959. *

Furer

B-126
Moray, V.E.
The patterns of caste and family in Wai
taluka, JUB, v.28 (1959), pp.74-75.

*Southern Asia Social
Science Bibliography,*

B-127
Mowat, Alexander G.
Mungki, what is it? A criticism and opinion
being a discussion as to the status of Mangs
in villages. Poona, Scottish Mission Industries Co., 1909. 23p.

Bom (Pris) cat

B-128
Mullins, Esther Molleson.
Brahman beliefs and practices in Maharashtra.
London, Univ.of London, 1962. 365p. *

SOAS Supp

B-129
Naik, Thakorlal Bhanabhai, 1922-
The Bhils; a study. Delhi, Bharatiya Adim-
jati Sevak Sangh, 1956. 381p.

47R

B-130
Orenstein, Henry.
Caste and the concept "Marātha" in Mahara-
shtra, EA, v.16 (1963), pp.1-9.

JAS L3

B-131
Orenstein, Henry.
Caste, leadership and social change in a
Bombay village. Berkeley, Univ.of California,
1957. *

Furer

B-132
    Orenstein, Henry.
    Leadership and caste in a Bombay village.
    In: Seminar on leadership and political
    institutions in India. Ed.by Richard L.Park
    and Irene Tinker. Princeton, New Jersey,
    Princeton University Press, 1959. pp.415-426.

B-133
    Orenstein, Henry.
    Village caste, and the welfare state.
    In: Contours of culture change in
    South Asia. Ed.by William L.Rowe.
    Kentucky, Society for Applied Anthro-
    pology, 1966. (Society for Applied
    Anthropology Monograph no.9). pp.83-89.

B-134
    Paranjape, Anand Chintaman.
    A psycho-social study of caste. Poona,
    Univ.of Poona, 1967. *

B-135
    Paranjpe, Anand Chintaman.
    Caste, prejudice, and the individual. Bom-
    bay, Lalvani Pub.House, 1970. 252p.

B-136
    Parulekar, S.V.
    Revolt of the Varlis. Bombay, People's Pub.
    House, 1947. 92p.

B-137
    Patrick, Clarence H.
    The criminal tribes of India with special
    emphasis on the Mang Garudi: a preliminary
    report, MI. v.48 (1968), pp.244-57.

B-138
    Patterson, Maureen L.P.
    Changing patterns of occupation among
    chitpavan brahmans, IESHR, v.7 (1970),
    pp.375-96.

B-139
    Patterson, Maureen L.P.
    Chitpavan Brahman family histories: sources
    for a study of social structure and social
    change in Maharashtra. In: Structure and
    change in Indian Society, ed.by Milton
    Singer and Bernard S.Cohn. Chicago, Aldine
    Pub.Co., 1968. pp.397-411.

B-140
    Patwardhan, Sunanda Padmakar.
    Social mobility and conversion of the
    Mahars, SB, v.17 (1967-68), pp.187-202.

B-141
    Patwardhan, Sunanda Padmakar.
    Study of the scheduled castes in an urban
    setting. Poona, Deccan College Postgraduate
    and Research Institute, 1965. *

B-142
  Pundalik, B.G. and Patwardhan, Sunanda Padmakar.
    A note on the behavior of the caste in a
  crisis-situation, <u>SB</u>, v.11 (1962), pp.68-72.

SB

B-143
  Punekar, Vijaya Bhaskar.
    Son Kolis. Bombay, Popular Book Depot,
  1959. 314p.

Sociology - racial groups
BDD

B-144
  Punekar, Vijaya Bhaskar.
    Son-kolis of Bombay, <u>JUB</u>, v.27 (1958),
  pp.87-88.

So Asia Soc. Sci. Lib

B-145
  Rajagopalachari, Chakravarti, 1879-
    Ambedkar refuted. Bombay, Hind Kitabs,
  1946. 38p.

UofR

B-146
  Ramachandra, H.R. and Sahasrubudhe, N.G.
    On the Chitpawan or Konkanasthas, <u>JASB</u>,
  v.4 (1895-1899), pp.368-373.

Fürer

B-147
  Rangarao, K.
    The wrongs of the Panchamas. Manglore,
  the author, 1908. 12p.

Bom (Pres) Inf

B-148
  Rao, Vasant Dinanath, 1913-
    The Pathare Prabhus of Bombay. Bombay,
  Univ.of Bombay, 1946. *

Sociology - racial groups
EDD

B-149
  Rao, Vasant Dinanath, 1913-
    The Pathare Prabhus, traditional origin
  and history. <u>JUB</u>, v.38 (1969), pp.235-59.

UofR

B-150
  Report on the sample survey of ex-criminal
  tribes in certain selected settlements in
  pre-reorganised Bombay State, <u>CBES</u>, v.3
  (1959), pp.1-45.

Southern Asia Social Science Field camping's Social Anthropology

B-151
  Robertson, Alexander, 1877-
    The Mahar folk: a study of untouchables in
  Maharashtra. London, New York, H.Milford,
  Oxford Univ.Press, 1938. 101p.

LC

B-152
Rothfeld, Otto.
Notes on the Son Kolis (Fisherman Kolis)
and on the Agri caste of Kolaba district.
JASB, v.9 (1910-1913), pp.179-88.

Furer

B-153
Sadashiv, R.B.R.
Pathare Prabhus of Bombay: their origin,
customs and manners. JASB, v.8 (1907-1909),
pp.29-46.

PS
472
A+355
Furer

B-154
Saldanha, Jerome Anthony.
Gosavis of western India, JASB, v.9 (1910-
1912), pp.126-37.

Furer

B-155
Saldanha, Jerome Anthony.
Kanarian-Konkani castes and communities
in Bombay; some remarkable features in their
ethnography. JASB, v.10 (1914), pp.508-15,
703-707.

Furer

B-156
Saldanha, Jerome Anthony.
Savantvadi castes and village communities.
JASB, v.8 (1909), pp.498-520.

Furer

B-157
Saletore, R.N.
The Bhils of Maharashtra, NIA, v.1 (1938),
pp.322-36.

NIA

B-158
Saletore, R.N.
The Kolis in the Marāthā empire, IHQ, v.15
(1939), pp.228-53.

B-159
Sangave, Vilas A.
Changing pattern of caste organization in
Kolhapur City. SB, v.11 (1962), pp.36-61.

JASB 62

B-160
Sangave, Vilas A.
Phanse-Paradhis of Kolhapur: a tribe in
transition. SB, v.16,no.1 (1967), pp.81-
87. Continued in: v.16,no.2 (1967), pp.67-
76.

SB

B-161
Sanjana, Jehangir Edalji, 1880-
Caste and outcaste. Bombay, Thacker, 1946.
249p.

LC

B-162
Save, Khanderao Jagannath.
The Warlis, with a foreword by B.G.Kher.
Bombay, Padma Pubs., 1945. 280p.

LC

B-163
Scott.
On the Kaikadis of Malsiras in the Sholapore
district, JASB, v.4 (1895-1899), pp.357-367.

*Anthropological Biol. of
South Asia - Fürer v.1*

B-164
Sedgwick, Leonard John.
A note on the Marathas Kunbis and Kanbis,
JASB, v.11 (1917-1921), pp.1066-71.

Fürer

B-165
Sinclair, William F.
Notes on castes in the Dekkan, IA, v.3
(1874), pp.44-46, 73-77, 126-32, 184-90,
337-39.

Fürer

B-166
Siraj-ul-Hasan, Syed.
The castes and tribes of H.E.H. the Nizam's
Dominions. Bombay, Times Press, 1920. 651p.

B-167
Socio-economic conditions of fishermen in
Bombay, ILG, v.13 (1956), pp.942-45.

B-168
Temple, Sir Richard, 1826-1902.
Personal traits of Mahratta Brahman princes.
JNSI, v.1 (1884), pp.289-308.

rose

B-169
Thakkar, Amritlal Vithaldas.
The problem of aborigines in India. Poona,
1941. (Gokhale School of Politics and Economics, R.R.Kale memorial lecture, 1941). 37p.

1, India - native race
LC

B-170
Thomas, C.
Tribal welfare in Maharashtra State, SocA,
v.14 (1964), pp.179-84.

SocA

B-171
Wagh, Madhav Chintaman.
Rigvedi Desastha Brahmins of Maharashtra.
Bombay, Univ.of Bombay, 1948. *

Sociology religion

B-172
Wagle, N.K.
The history and social organization of the Gauda Sāraswata Brāhmanas of the west coast of India, *JIH*, v.48 (1970), pp.7-25, 295-333.

JIH

B-173
Weling, A.N.
The Katkaris: a sociological study of a tribe of the Bombay Presidency. Bombay, Book Depot, 1934. 160p.

BM

B-174
Wilson, John, 1804-1875.
Aboriginal tribes of the Bombay Presidency; a fragment. Bombay, Govt.Central Press, 1876. 63p.

SOAS

B-175
Wilson, John, 1804-1875.
Account of the Waralis and Katodia - two of the forest tribes of the northern Konkan, *BASGBIJ*, v.7 (1942/43), pp.14-31.

B-176
Wilson, John, 1804-1875.
Tribes and languages of the Bombay Presidency, *IA*, v.3 (1874), pp.221-31.

B-177
Zimmerman, Robert.
The Khandalla Katkaris (a presidential address). Bombay, British India Press, 1921. 18p.

SOAS Supp

B-178
Zimmerman, Robert.
The Khandalla Katkaris, *JASB*, v.12 (1921-1924), pp.154-72.

Communities

B-179
Banaji, M.M.
Sublime though blind: a tale of Parsi life, men and manners. Bombay, 1922. 522p.

SOAS

B-180
Baptista, Elsie Wilhelmina, 1908-
The East Indians; Catholic community of Bombay, Salsette and Bassein. Bombay, Bombay East Indian Association, 1967. (Publications of the Anthropos Institute, Indian branch, 3). 255p.

B-181
Baptista, Elsie Wilhelmina, 1908-
Indian Christian community with particular reference to the East Indians, *JUB*, v.26 (1958), pp.113-17.

B-182
Baptista, Elsie Wilhelmina, 1908-
The Indian Christian community with particular reference to the East Indians of Bombay, Salsette and Bassein. Bombay, Univ.of Bombay, 1957. *

B-183
Barnouw, Victor.
The social structure of a Sindhi refugee community. SF, v.33 (1954), pp.142-52.

Furer

B-184
Briggs, Henry George, 1824-1872.
Parsis, or modern Zerdusthians: a sketch. Edinburgh, Oliver & Boyd; London, Andrew Dunlop, 1852. 158p.

BM

B-185
Dalal, Faredoon Manekji.
The social life and manners of the parsis in Iran and in India. Bombay, Univ.of Bombay, 1949. *

Sociology religious groups
BDD

B-186
Damishky, Paul J.E.
The Moslem population of Bombay. MM, v.1 (1911), pp.117-29.

Onio

B-187
Darukhanawala, Hormusji Dhunjishaw.
Parsi lustre on Indian soil; with a foreword by the Marquess of Wellington and an introduction by J.R.B.Jeejeebhoy. Bombay, G. Claridge, 1939-

B-188
Davar, Sehrab Rustamji, 1879-
The history of the Parsi punchayet of Bombay. Bombay, New book co., 1949. 80p.

SOAS

B-189
De Mello, John.
Some materials for a history of the Bombay East Indian Community. Bombay, John De Mello, 1938. 166p.

BM

B-190
Desai, Sapur Faredun.
A community at the cross-roads. Bombay, New Book Company, 1948. 217p.

LC

B-191
Desai, Sapur Faredun.
Survival value of the Parsi: a socio-anthropological approach, JASB, v.4 (1950), pp.40-48.

Furer

B-192
Diskalkar, Dattatraya Balkrishna, 1892-
Parsis in India, *IAC*, v.5 (1957), pp.445-51.

Social Science Bibliography —
India & Pakistan 1957 —
Sociology, p.3

B-193
Dobbin, Christine Elizabeth.
The Parsi Panchayat in Bombay city in the
nineteenth century, *MAS*, v.4,pt.2 (1970),
pp.149-64.

BAS 1975

B-194
D'Souza, Victor S.
The Kanadis of Maharashtra. *JKU*, v.1
(1957), pp.48-58.

JdS 58

B-195
Eastwick, Edward Backhouse, 1814-1883.
Translation from the Persian, of the
Kissehi-i-Sanjan; or, history of the
arrival and settlement of the Parsis in
India, *ASBJ*, v.1 (1884), pp.167-91.

ASBJ

B-196
Ezekiel, Moses.
History and culture of the Bene-Israel in
India. Nadiad, 1948. 116p.

1. Beni-Israel.

LC

B-197
Gaikwad, V.R., 1933-
Anglo-Indian; a study in the problems and
processes involved in emotional and cultural
integration. Bombay, Asia Pub.House, 1967.
317p.

1. Anglo-Indians.

U of R

B-198
Griffin, Nora.
European social life in Bombay: 1804 and
1929, *ASBJ*, n.s.,v.6 (1930), pp.322-26.

ASBJ

B-199
Hodivala, Shahpurshah Hormasji.
Parsi history; being a series of five
lectures delivered in 1925. Bombay,
British India Press, 1926. (K.R.Cama
Oriental Institute, Bombay, Pub.no.1).
126p.

1. Bombay (City)-Hist. 2. Parsees - Hist.

NYPL   *23208*
              K 3619

B-200
Hodivala, Shahpurshah Hormasji.
Studies in Parsi history. Junagadh, the
author, 1921. 350p.

NUR

B-201
Irani, Meherwanji Sheheriyarji, 1894-
The story of Sanjan; or, the supposed history
of Parsi migration to India from Khorasan.
Poona, M.S.Irani, 1943. 126p.

BM

B-202
Israel, Benjamin J.
Religious revolution among the Bene Israel of India since 1750. Bombay, 1963. 22p.

1. Jews in India. 2. Ben-Israel.

LC

B-203
Jeejeebhoy, Jeejeebhoy Rustomji Byramji, 1885-
Communal discipline among the Bombay Parsees in olden times. In: M.P.Khareghat Memorial Volume of the Parsi Punchayet Funds and Properties. Bombay, 1953. pp.295-323.

Bhandarkar Index
Orient & African Studies

B-204
Jhabvala, Shavakasha Hormusji, 1885-
A brief history of Parsees. Bombay, S.H.Jhabvala, 1952?. 36p.

B M

B-205
Jhabvala, Shavakasha Hormusji, 1885-
Giants of immortality, world's smallest minority; its past and present briefly told. Bombay, 1963. 80p.

1. Parsees - Hist.

LC

B-206
Joshi, Purushottam Balkrishna, 1856-1930.
Side lights on the past history of the Parsis, ASBJ, v.26 (1921-23), pp.177-94.

ASBJ

B-207
Karaka, Dosabhai Framjee, 1829-1902.
History of the Parsis, including their manners, customs, religion and present position. London, Macmillan and Co., 1884. 2 vols.

1. Parsees. 2. Zoroastrianism.

U of R

B-208
Karaka, Dosabhai Framjee, 1829-1902.
The Parsees: their history, manners, customs, and religion. London, Smith, Elder, 1858. 301p.

U of R

B-209
Karaka, Dosoo Framjee, 1911-
I go west. London, M.Joseph ltd., 1938. 288p.

1. India - Soc.condit.

LC

B-210
Kehimkar, Haeem Samuel, 1830-1909.
The history of the Bene Israel of India. Ed. by I.Olsvanger. Tel-Aviv, Dayag Press, ltd., London, G.Salby, 1937. 326p.

1. Beni-Israel.

N of R
LC

B-211
Khan, Nazir Mohmodkhan Gulabkhan.
A socio-economic survey of the Muslims of Poona. Bombay, Univ.of Bombay, 1952. *

Sociology Religions
BDD   groups

B-212
   Navalwala, Jamshed D.
      Some acculturation effects on the Parsees,
   Vanyajati, v.4 (1956), pp.41-43.

Fürer

B-213
   Menant, Delphine, 1850-
      Les Parsis. Histoire des communautés
   zoroastriennes de l'Inde. Paris, 1898.
   (Annales du Musée Guimet. Bibliothèque
   d'Etudes. t.7). 504p.

SAS

B-214
   Menant, Delphine, 1850-
      Les Parsis. Trans.in part by Ratanbai Arde-
   shir Vakil. London, Printed for private cir-
   culation, 1902. 123p.

   1. Parsees. 2. Zoroastrianism

4 of R

B-215
   Menant, Delphine, 1850-
      The Parsis in India. Bombay, 1917. 2v.

Ca. Nat'l Lib

B-216
   Mitra, Rajendralala, raja, 1824-1891.
      The Parsis of Bombay, a lecture delivered
   on Feb.26, 1880 at a meeting of the Bethune
   Society. Calcutta, Thacker, Spink and Co.,
   1880. 43p.

B-217
   Modi, Jivanji Jamshedji, 1854-1933.
      A few events in the early history of the
   Parsis and their dates. Bombay, 1905.

Harvard Univ Lib

B-218
   Mutatkar, R.K. and Ansari, A.
      Muslim caste in an Indian town: a case
   study, *BDCRI*, v.25 (1966), pp.163-90.

Anthropology & Sociology
BDCRI 1966

B-219
   Seth, Mesrovb Jacob.
      History of Armenians in India from the
   earliest times to the present day. Calcutta,
   the author, 1895. 214p.

LC

B-220
   Sternbach, Ludwik.
      Jews in the mediaeval India as mentioned
   by western travelers, *IHCP*, v.9 (1945),
   pp.169-95.

IHCP

B-221
   Strizower, Schifra.
      The Bene-Israil, *JASB*, v.9 (1955), pp.49-58.

B-222
Strizower, Schifra.
Jews as an Indian caste, JJS, v.1 (1959),
pp.43-57.

NR&
Fürer
○

B-223
Strizower, Schifra.
The Jews in India, NS, v.67 (1964), pp.16-
17.

Fürer
○

B-224
Strizower, Schifra.
The social structure of an Indian-Jewish
community. London, Univ.of London, 1967. *

Sociology & anthropology

BAS 1970
○

B-225
Syed, Mujtaba Ali, 1904-
The origin of the Khojans and their religious
life today. Bonn, L.Röhrscheid, 1936. 113p.

1. Khojans.

LC
○

B-226
Taraporewala, Irach Jehangir Sorabji, 1884-
1956.
The exact date of the arrival of Parsis in
India. In: A volume of studies in Indology
presented to Prof.P.V.Kane, ed.by S.M.Katre
and P.K.Gode. Poona, Oriental Book Agency,
1941. pp.506-14.

U of R
○

B-227
Temple, Sir Richard Carnac, 1850-1931.
Ignicoles, a name for the Parsees, IA,
v.57 (1928), p.73.

JBHs
○

B-228
Tyabji, F.B.
Social life in 1804 and 1929 amongst Muslims
in Bombay, ASBJ, v.6 (1930), pp.286-300.

Case
○

B-229
Wadia, Pestonji Ardesir, 1878-
Parsis ere the shadows thicken, with the
collaboration of four ex-members of the Central
Investigation Bureau, Sheroo Mehta and others.
Bombay, 1949. 165p.

1. Parsees. 2. Bombay - Soc.condit.

U of R
○

B-230
Wadia, Pestonji Ardesir, 1878-
The Parsis of Bombay and Parsi charities,
JUB, v.4 (1935), pp.88-104.

Case
☽

B-231
Wilson, John, 1804-1875.
The Bene-Israel of Bombay, IA, v.3 (1874),
pp.321-23.

S1
☽

Census

B-232
　　Raines, Sir Jervoise Athelstane, 1847-
　　Imperial census of 1881. Operations and
　　results in the Presidency of Bombay, including
　　Sind. Bombay, 1882. 2 vols.

B-237
　　Bombay State. Census, 1951.
　　　Language handbook; by J.B.Bowman.
　　pt.I: Dangs, Thana and Banaskantha Districts.
　　pt.II: Sholapur, Satara South, Bijapur and
　　Kolhapur Districts. Bombay, 1955. 2pts.

IOL P365 [V14614]

B-233
　　Bombay (Presidency)
　　　Census of the Bombay Presidency, taken on
　　the 21st February 1872. Bombay, Printed at
　　the Government Central Press, 1875. 2pts.

B-238
　　Buckland, A.W.
　　　Central provinces of India Census,
　　JRAIGB, v.25 (1896), pp.165-72.

LC

B-234
　　Bombay (Presidency)
　　　Census of the island of Bombay, taken
　　2nd February, 1864 by Andrew Harrison Leith.
　　Bombay, Printed for Government at the
　　Education Society Press, 1864. 1v.

B-239
　　The census report of 1891 of the Bombay
　　Presidency, QJPSS, v.15,no.4 (1892),
　　pp.1-17.

U of R

PSS

B-235
　　Bombay (Presidency) Public Health Department.
　　　Census of the City and Island of Bombay
　　taken on the 17th of February 1881. By T.S.
　　Weir. Bombay, 1883.

B-240
　　Central Provinces.
　　　Central Provinces census 1872. [Calcutta?
　　1874?] 398p.

BM

B-236
　　Bombay (State).
　　　Bombay Census 1951. Language Handbooks.
　　Bombay, Government Central Press, 1955.

B-241
　　Central Provinces.
　　　Report on the census of the Central Prov-
　　inces efected on the 5th November 1866.
　　Nagpoer, 1867. 19p.

Furer

Gubester Census

B-242
　　Great Britain. India Office.
　　　Memorandum on the Census of British India
　　of 1871-72. Presented to both Houses of Parl-
　　iament by Command of Her Majesty. London,
　　.H.M.Stationer Office, 1875. 65p.

Duboster, item 10

B-243
　　India. Census. 1881.
　　　Census of the Central Provinces, 1881.
　　T.Drysdale, Esq., Deputy Superintendent of
　　Census, Central Provinces. Bombay, Printed
　　at the Education Society's Press, Byculla,
　　1882-83. vol.9. 2pts.
　　　Pt.I. Tables, imperial and supplementary,
　　　　1882. 420p.
　　　Pt.II. Report, with appendices, 1883. 386p.

NRU

B-244
　　India. Census. 1881.
　　　Imperial census of 1881. Digest of the
　　results in the presidency of Bombay, including
　　Sind. By order of the Government. Bombay,
　　Printed at the Govt.Central Press, 1882.
　　v.6,pt.3. 283p.

Duboster Census

B-245
　　India. Census. 1881.
　　　Imperial census of 1881. Operations
　　and results in the Presidency of Bombay,
　　including Sind. By J.A.Baines. F.S.S.of
　　the Bombay Civil Service. Bombay,
　　Printed at the Government Central Press,
　　1882. vol.6. 2pts.
　　　Pt.I. Text. 273p.
　　　Pt.II.Tables. 259p.

NRU
Duboster census

B-246
　　India. Census. 1881.
　　　Report on the census of Berar 1881.
　　By Eustace J.Kitts, B.C.S., Deputy
　　Superintendent of Census Operations,
　　Berar. Bombay, Printed at the Education
　　Society's Press, Byculla, 1882. vol.5.
　　456p.

NRU
Duboster census

B-247
　　India. Census. 1891.
　　　Berar, or the Hyderabad assigned districts.
　　By Warren Hastings, Captain, Indian Staff
　　Corps, Deputy Commissioner, Hyderabad Assigned
　　Districts, and Provincial Superintendent of
　　Census Operations. To be obtained from the
　　Curator, Government Central Book Depot, Akola,
　　Berar. Calcutta, Office of the Superintendent
　　of Government Printing, India, 1892. vol.6.
　　641p.

NRU

B-248
　　India. Census. 1891.
　　　Bombay and its feudatories... By W.W.Drew, of
　　the India Civil Service, Provincial Superintendent
　　of Census operations. Bombay, Printed at the
　　Government Central Press, 1892. 2v.
　　　vol.VII. Report. 265p.
　　　vol.VIII. Imperial tables. 764p.

NRU
Duboster, Census

B-249
　　India. Census. 1891.
　　　The Central Provinces and feudatories...
　　By B.Robertson, of the Indian Civil Service,
　　Provincial Superintendent of Census
　　Operations. Calcutta, Office of the Super-
　　intendent of Government Printing, India,
　　1893. 2v.
　　　vol.XI. The report. 346p.
　　　vol.XII. Imperial tables and supplementary
　　　　returns. 404p.

NRU
Census-Duboster

B-250
　　India. Census. 1901.
　　　Berar... By Ardaseer Dinshawji Chinoy. Super-
　　intendent of Census Operations. Allahabad, Pioneer
　　Press, 1902. 3pts.
　　　vol.VIII. Report. 259p.
　　　vol.VIIIA. Imperial tables. 208p.
　　　vol.VIIIB. Provincial tables. 123p.

UgR
Census-Duboster

B-251
　　India. Census. 1901.
　　　Bombay... By R.E.Enthoven, of the Indian
　　Civil Service, in charge of census operations.
　　Bombay, Printed at the Government Central Press,
　　1902. 3vols.
　　　vol.IX. Report. 267p.
　　　vol.IXA. Imperial tables. 673p.
　　　vol.IXB. Provincial tables. 281p.

NRU
Census-Duboster

B-252
India. Census. 1901.
    Bombay (town & island)...By S.M.Edwardes,
I.C.S. Bombay, Printed at the Times of
India Press, 1901. 3v.
      Vol. X. History. 157p.
      Vol. XI. Report. 116p.
      Vol. XIA. Tables. 329p.

NRO
Census- Dubraer

B-253
India. Census. 1901.
    Central Provinces... By R.V.Russell, I.C.S.,
Superintendent of Census Operations. Nagpur,
Printed at the Secretariat Press, 1902. 3pts.
      vol.XIII. Report. 325p.
      vol.XIIIA. Imperial tables. 599p.
      pt.III. Provincial tables. 157p.

NRU
Census-Dubleton

B-254
India. Census. 1901.
    Hyderabad ... By Mirza Mehdy Khan, in charge
census operations. Hyderabad, Deccan, A.
Venoogopaul Pillai & Sons, Printers to H.H.
the Nizam's Government, 1902-03. 2pts.
      vol.XXII. Report. 1903. 503p.
      vol.XXIIA. Tables. 1902. 218p.

NRU

B-255
India. Census. 1911.
    Bombay... By P.J.Mead and G.Laird Macgregor of
the Indian Civil Service, in charge census
operations. Bombay, Printed at the Government
Central Press, 1912. vol.VII. 2pts.
      Pt.I. Report. 356p.
      Pt.II. Imperial tables. 577p.

NRU
Census. Dubonin

B-256
India. Census. 1911.
    Bombay (town & island). Parts I and II. Report
and tables. By P.J.Mead and G.Laird Macgregor of
the Indian Civil Service, in charge census operations. Bombay, Printed at the Government Central
Press, 1912. vol.VIII. 195p.

NRU
Census-Dubli-in

B-257
India. Census. 1911.
    Central Provinces and Berar... By J.T.Marten,
M.A., I.C.S., Superintendent of Census Operations,
Central Provinces and Berar. Calcutta, Super-
intendent Government Printing, India, 1912-13.
vol.X. 3pts.
      Pt.I. Report. 1912. 283p.
      Pt.II. Tables. 1912. 375p.
      Pt.III. Provincial tables. 1913. 109p.

NRU
Census. Nubester

B-258
India. Census. 1911.
    Hyderabad State... Mahomed Abdul Majid, H.C.S.,
Census Superintendent. Bombay, Printed at the
Times Press, 1913. vol.XIX. 2pts.
      Pt.I. Report. 168p.
      Pt.II. Imperial and provincial tables. 346p.

NRU
Census Dabeter

B-259
India. Census. 1921.
    Bombay Presidency... By L.J.Sedgwick of the
Indian Civil Service, Superintendent of Census
Operations. Bombay, Printed at the Government
Central Press, 1922. vol.VIII. 2pts.
      Pt.I. General report. 384p.
      Pt.II. Tables (imperial and provincial). 458p.

NRU
Census Dabeter

B-260
India. Census. 1921.
    Central Provinces and Berar... By N.J.Roughton,
B.A., I.C.S., Superintendent of Census Operations,
Central Provinces and Berar. Nagpur, Printed at
the Government Press, 1922-23. vol.XI. 3pts.
      Pt.I. Report. 1923. 213p.
      Pt.II. Tables. 1923. 437p.
      Pt.III. Administration report of the Census
         Department, Central Provinces and Berar.
         1922. 48p.

URU
Census Dabester

B-261
India. Census. 1921.
    Cities of the Bombay Presidency. By L.J.Sedgwick,
I.C.S., Superintendent of Census Operations,
Bombay. Poona, Printed at the Yeravda Prison
Press; and copies obtainable from the Superinten-
dant, Government Printing, Poona, 1922. vol.IX.
2pts.
      Pt.I. Report. 110p.
      Pt.II. Tables. 319p.

URU
Census Dabeter

B-262
India. Census. 1921.
    Hyderabad State... By Mohammed Rahmatulla,
Superintendent of Census Operations, Hyderabad
State. Hyderabad-Deccan, Printed at the Government
Central Press, 1922-23. vol.XXI. 2pts.
    Pt.I. Report. 1923. 338p.
    Pt.II. Imperial tables. 1922. 269p.

NRU
Censun. Dubester   O

B-263
India. Census. 1931.
    Bombay Presidency ... By A.H.Dracup, B.A.,
Bombay Provincial Civil Service, Superin-
tendent of Census Operations, Bombay Presi-
dency up to May 26th, 1932 and H.T.Sorley,
M.A., Indian Civil Service, Superintendent
of Census Operations, Bombay Presidency from
May 27th till October 31st, 1932. Bombay,
Printed at the Govt.Press, 1933. 2pts.

O

B-264
India. Census. 1931.
    Central Provinces and Berar... By W.H.Shoobert
of the Indian Civil Service, Superintendent of
Census Operations, Central Provinces and Berar.
Nagpur, Government Printing, C.P., 1932-33. vol.
XII. 2pts.
    Pt.I. Report. 452p.
    Pt.II. Tables. 523p.

NRU
Censun. Dubester   O

B-265
India. Census. 1931.
    The cities of the Bombay Presidency. In two
parts. Part I-Report. Part II-Statistical tables.
By H.T.Sorley, M.A., Indian Civil Service,
Provincial Superintendent of Census Operations,
Bombay Presidency. Bombay, Printed at the
Government Central Press, 1933. vol.IX. 362p.

NRU
Censun. Dubester   O

B-266
India. Census. 1941.
    Bombay. Tables, by A.H.Dracup, Superin-
tendent of Census Operations, Bombay, 1942.
vol.III. 154p.

NRU   O

B-267
India. Census. 1941.
    Central Provinces & Berar. Tables, by R.K.
Ramadhyani, I.C.S., Superintendent of Census
Operations, Central Provinces and Berar, 1942.
vol.VIII. 60p.

NRU
Censun. Dubester   O

B-268
India (Republic) Office of the Registrar
    General.
    Census of India, 1961; a guide to the census
publication programme. New Delhi, Ministry
of Home Affairs, Office of the Registrar
General, 1964.

U of R   O

B-269
India (Republic) Office of the Registrar
    General.
    Census of India, 1961. Vol.10 - Maharashtra.
Pt.1-C. Subsidiary tables. Delhi, Manager
of Publications, 1965. 639p.

O

B-270
India (Republic) Office of the Registrar
    General.
    Census of India, 1961. Vol.10 - Maharashtra.
Pt.2-A. General population tables. Delhi,
Manager of Publications, 1963. 377p.

U of R   )

B-271
India (Republic) Office of the Registrar
    General.
    Census of India, 1961. Vol.10 - Maharashtra.
Pt.2-B(i). General economic tables; indus-
trail classification. Delhi, Manager of
Publications, 1964. 603p.

U of R   )

B-272
India (Republic) Office of the Registrar
General.
Census of India, 1961. Vol.10 - Maharashtra.
Pt.2-B(ii). General economic tables; occu-
pational classification. Delhi, Manager of
Publications, 1964. 517p.

U of R

B-273
India (Republic) Office of the Registrar
General.
Census of India, 1961. Vol.10 - Maharashtra.
Pt.2-C(i). Social and cultural tables.
Delhi, Manager of Publications, 1965. 314p.

U of R

B-274
India (Republic) Office of the Registrar
General.
Census of India, 1961. Vol.10 - Maharashtra.
Pt.2-C(ii). Migration tables. Delhi, Mana-
ger of Publications, 1966. 564p.

U of R

B-275
India (Republic) Office of the Registrar
General.
Census of India, 1961. Vol.10 - Maharashtra.
Pt.3. Household economic tables. Delhi,
Manager of Publications, 1964. 525p.

U of R

B-276
India (Republic) Office of the Registrar
General.
Census of India, 1961. Vol.10 - Maharashtra.
Pt.4. Report on housing and establishments.
Delhi, Manager of Publications, 1964. 585p.

U of R

B-277
India (Republic) Office of the Registrar
General.
Census of India, 1961. Vol.10 - Maharashtra.
Pt.5-A. Scheduled castes and scheduled
tribes in Maharashtra. Delhi, Manager of
Publications, 1964. 440p.

U of R

B-278
India (Republic) Office of the Registrar
General.
Census of India, 1961. Vol.10 - Maharashtra.
Pt.6. Village survey monographs. Delhi,
Manager of Publications, 1966. 147p.
(i) Kunkeri village.
(ii) Agarsure village. Delhi, Manager of
Publications, 1966. 76p.
(iii) Shirvali village. Delhi, Manager of
Publications, 1967. 73p.

U of R

B-279
India (Republic) Office of the Registrar
General.
Census of India, 1961. Vol.10 - Maharashtra.
Pt.7-A.
(i)　Himroo works of Aurangabad. Delhi,
　　Manager of Publications, 1965. 55p.
(ii)　Handicrafts on clay images of Gana-
　　pati and images of plaster of paris.
　　Delhi, Manager of Publications, 1966.
　　48p.
(iii)　Handicrafts in Kosa silk weaving at

(Continued)

Ganeshpur. Delhi, Manager of Publications, 1966. 37p.
(iv&v) Wooden toys of Savantvadi, and Coir
ropes of Achare. Delhi, Manager of
Publications, 1968. 52p.

U of R

B-280
India (Republic) Office of the Registrar
General.
Census of India, 1961. Vol.10 - Maharashtra.
Pt.7-B. Fairs and festivals in Maharashtra.
Delhi, Manager of Publications, 1962-

LC accessions

B-281
India (Republic) Office of the Registrar
General.
Census of India, 1961. Vol.10 - Maharashtra.
Pt.8-A. Administration report on enumera-
tions. Delhi, Manager of Publications, 1965.
177p.

LC accessions

B-282
India (Republic) Office of the Registrar
General.
Census of India, 1961. Vol.10 - Maharashtra.
Pt.10(2-12). Cities of Maharashtra census
tables. Delhi, Manager of Publications, 1968.
747p.

U of R

B-283
India (Republic) Office of the Registrar
General.
Census of India, 1961. Vol.10 - Maharashtra.
Pt.10-B(1). Greater Bombay census tables.
Delhi, Manager of Publications, 1964. 259p.

U of R

B-284
India (Republic) Office of the Registrar
General.
Census of India, 1961. Vol.10 - Maharashtra.
Pt.10-C(1). Greater Bombay. Special migra-
tion tables. Delhi, Manager of Publications,
1966. 331p.

U of R

B-285
India (Republic) Superintent of Census
Operations.
Census of India, 1951. Vol.4-Bombay,
Saurashtra and Kutch.
Pt.I. Report and subsidiary tables. By J.B.
Bowman of the Indian Civil Service. Bombay,
Printed at the Govt.Central Press, 1953.

NRU

B-286
India (Republic) Superintendent of Census
Operations.
Census of India, 1951. Vol.4-Bombay,
Saurashtra and Kutch.
Pt.II-A. General population tables, social
and cultural tables and summary figures by
talukas and petas. By J.B.Bowman of the Indian
Civil Service. Bombay, Printed at the Govt.
Central Press, 1953.

NRU

B-287
India (Republic) Superintendent of Census
Operations.
Census of India, 1951. Vol.4-Bombay,
Saurashtra and Kutch.
Pt.II-B. Economic tables and household and
age (sample) tables. By J.B.Bowman of the
Indian Civil Service. Bombay, Printed at
the Govt.Central Press, 1953.

NRU

B-288
India (Republic) Superintendent of Census
Operations in Bombay.
District census handbook based on the 1951
census. 1952-53. 28v.

Union cat

B-289
India (Republic) Superintendent of Census
Operations, Maharashtra.
District census handbook [Maharashtra]
census of India, 1961. Comp.by the Maharashtra
census office. Bombay, Director, Govt.Print.
and Stationery, Maharashtra State, 1963-68.
25v.

U of R

B-290
Sykes, William Henry, 1790-1872.
On the census of the islands of Bombay and
Colaba, taken on the 1st of May, 1849, by
Capt.Baynes, Supit.of Police. London, 1852.
12p.

Cal Nat Lib

B-291
U.S. Library of Congress. Census Library
Project ...
Census and vital statistics of India and
Pakistan contained in official publications
and famine documents, an annotated bibliogra-
phy by Henry J.Dubester, chief. Washington,
1950.

U of R Customs

B-292
Abbott, John.
Totemism and Maratha 'Devak', RPR, v.2
(1931), pp.1-16.

Fürer

B-293
Birdwood, Sir George Christopher Molesworth,
1832-1917.
A sunset on Matheran, RSAJ, v.57 (1908),
pp.788-90.

B-294
Chapekar, Laxman Narayan, 1906-
Riddles, puzzles and cat's cradles of the
Thakur, JUB, (1954), pp.55-64.

Fürer

B-295
Coen, T.B.Creagh.
Witchcraft in the Dangs, MI, v.25 (1954),
pp.187-88.

Kirk

B-296
Crawford, C.E.G.
Corruptions of Portuguese names in Salsette
and Bassein, IA, v.19 (1890), pp.442-43.

√√DA

B-297
Da Cunha, Joseph Gerson, 1842-1900.
On amulets, JASB, v.1 (1886), p.378.

JaSB

B-298
De Cunha, John.
Omens among the Hindus, JASB, v.1 (1886-
1888), pp.295-99.

Kirk

B-299
D'Penha, George F.
Superstitions and customs in Salsette, IA,
v.28 (1899), pp.113-19.

Fürer

B-300
Ferreira, John V.
The problem of Maratha totemism, IJSW,
v.25 (1964), 135-51.

JaS 64

B-301
Godabole, Narayana Balakrishna.
Proper names in Thana district. *IA*, v.12 (1883), p.259.

NIA

B-302
Gupte, Balakrishna Atmaram, 1851-
A Prabhu marriage. Customary and religious ceremonies performed in the marriage of a member of the Chandraseni Kayasth Prabhus of Bombay. Calcutta, Superintendent, Govt.Print, 1911. 79p.

LC

B-303
Jagannathji, K.
Bombay social customs, pregnancy. *IA*, v.18 (1889), p.287.

Surer

B-304
Joshi, Purushottam Balkrishna, 1856-1930.
On the evil eye in the Konkan. *JASB*, v.1 (1886-1888), pp.120-28.

Surer

B-305
Khanapurkar, D.P.
The Dubala. *JUB*, v.14 (1945), pp.33-38.

Surer

B-306
Kirtikar, K.R.
Some forms of Bombay amulets. *JASB*, v.9 (1910-1912), pp.55-66.

Kirk

B-307
Knowles, J.Hinton.
Social customs; death. *IA*, v.18 (1889), p.287.

Kirk

B-308
Krishnanath Raghunathji.
On the pitar or tank. *JASB*, v.1 (1886), p.363.

JASB

B-309
MacClure, D.
Towers of silence: Parsee burial customs. *Spectator*, v.178 (1947), p.202.

Surer

B-310
Mehendale, Y.S.
Wadi-names of the Ratnagiri district, *BDCRI*, v.8 (1948), pp.404-21.

BDCRI

B-311
Modi, Jivanji Jamshedji, 1854-1933.
The kiss of peace among the Bene-Israels of
Bombay and the Hamazor among the Parsees. JASB,
v.8 (1907-1909), pp.84-95.

OB

B-312
Modi, Jivanji Jamshedji, 1854-1933.
Marriage customs amongst the Parsees and
their comparison with similar customs of
other nations. JASB, v.5 (1900-1901), pp.
242-82.

B-313
Modi, Jivanji Jamshedji, 1854-1933.
Omens among the Parsees. JASB, v.1 (1886-
1889), pp.269-95.

Furer

B-314
Modi, Jivanji Jamshedji, 1854-1933.
Some Parsee marriage customs. JASB, v.8
(1907-09), pp.425-30.

Furer

B-315
Patell, Bombanji Byramji.
A few dreams and their interpretations
among the natives of Bombay. JASB, v.7
(1905-1907), pp.135-47.

Furer

B-316
Rehatsek, E.
On superstitions of the Goa people from
Portuguese sources. JASB, v.2 (1890),
pp.22-35.

Keek

B-317
Sismonds, Roy.
Humours of India, being sketches of every-
day phases of life in India. 2d ed. Bombay,
Advocate of India Press, 1913. 96p.

Bom (Bee) cat

The family and
marriage

B-320
Aphale, Champa Anant.
Child in home and school: a study of up-
bringing of children in Maharashtrian Hindu
families in Poona. Poona, Univ.of Poona,
1962.

Anthropology & sociology

BDCRI p.124

B-321
Bhagwat, K.P.
Mate selection in the unmarried and married.
JUP, v.3 (1954), pp.113-17.

SSB 1954

B-322
Dasle, Yaswant Bhaskar, 1923-
Divorce in Poona district. In: Society
in India. Ed.by A.Aiyappan and L.K.Bala
Ratnam. Madras, Social sciences assoc-
iation, 1956. pp.186-193.

B-323
Dandekar, Vinayak Mahadeo, 1920-   and
Pethe, Vasant P.
Size and composition of rural families,
AV, v.2 (1960), pp.189-99.

Southern Asia Social Science
Bibliography: Sociology, p. 11

B-328
Hunebelle, Danielle.
A Hindu family tells its story, Réalités,
no.149 (1963), pp.62-69.

Finer

B-324
Deshpande, C.G.
A comparative study of caste and inter-
caste married couples in Maharashtra with
special reference to social, marital and
personal adjustment. Poona, Univ.of Poona,
1970.

Sociology
BDD

B-329
Jain, P.K.
Marriage age patterns in India, AV, v.11
(1969), pp.662-97.

BAS 1970

B-325
Fonseca, M.B.
Family disorganization and divorce in Indian
communities (Greater Bombay), SB, v.12 (1963),
pp.14-33; v.13 (1964), pp.47-60.

Soc. Rec.

B-330
Kannan, Chirayil Thumbayil, 1921-
Inter-caste and inter-community marriages
in India. Bombay, Allied Pubs., 1963. 246p.

Sociology
BDD #174

B-326
Ghosh, Jogendra Chandra.
Gotra and Pravaras of the Kadambas, NIA,
v.1 (1938), pp.144-46.

Finer

B-331
Kannan, Chirayil Thumbayil, 1921-
Intercaste marriage in Bombay, SB, v.10
(1961), pp.53-68.

99 S '61

B-327
Ghurye, Govind Sadashiv, 1893-
Family and kin in Indo-European culture.
Bombay, New York, Indian Branch, Oxford Univ.
Press, 1955. (University of Bombay pubs.,
sociology series, no.4) 254p.

1. Family. 2. Kinship.

u gR

B-332
Karve, Dinakar Dhondo, 1899-   ed.& tr.
The new Brahmans; five Maharashtrian
families. Berkeley, University of California
Press, 1963. 303p.

1. Maharashtra India (State) -
Biog.

u nR

B-333
Karve, Irawati (Karmarkar) 1905-1970.
A family through six generations. In:
Anthropology on the march; recent studies
of Indian beliefs, attitudes and social
institutions. (A commemorative volume in
honour of L.K.Anantha Krishna Iyer, 1861-
1937, notable anthropologist) Ed.by L.K.
Balla Ratnam. Madras, Book Centre, 1963.
pp.241-62.

Fürer

B-334
Karve, Irawati (Karmarkar) 1905-1970.
Kinship organization in India. 3d ed. New
York, Asia Pub.House, 1968. 454p.

1. Kinship. 2. Family - India. 3. India -
Soc.condit.

U of P

B-335
Karve, Irawati (Karmarkar) 1905-1970.
Kinship terminology and kinship usages of
the Maratha country, BDCRI, v.2,no.1 (1940),
pp.9-33; v.2,no.4 (1940), pp.327-89.

Anthropology
BDCRI

B-336
Khambata, K.J.
Divorce law reform amongst the Parsis, JUB,
v.1 (1932), pp.148-57.

JUB

B-337
Kulkarni, Anant Ramchandra, 1925-
Invitation of marriage to the dead - a
social custom, BDCRI, v.25 (1966), pp.191-94.

History

B-338
Kulkarni, Madhav Gururao, 1923-
Spatial distribution of migrants and
marriage-connections in Gokak Taluka,
AV, v.2 (1960), pp.287-306.

NRO
Fürer

B-339
Mādhavadāsa Raghunāthadāsa.
Story of a widow remarriage; being the experiences of Madhowdas Rugnathdas, merchant
of Bombay. Bombay, S.K.Khambata and co.,
1890. 118p.

LC

B-340
Mokashi, Pandharinath Ramchandra.
Some social aspects of marriages in Poona
district, 1955-56. Poona, Deccan College
Postgraduate and Research Institute, 1963. *

Graphasis #1530

B-341
Morrison, William A.
Family types in Badlapur: an analysis of
a changing institution in a Maharashtrian
village, SB, v.8 (1959), pp.45-67.

Southern Asia Social
Sciences Bibliography; Said
1949 p.15

B-342
Nikambe, Shevantibai M.
Ratanbai: a sketch of a Bombay high caste
Hindu young wife. London, Marshall Brothers,
1895. 96p.

1. India - Soc.life.

B-343
Oturkar, Rajaram Vinayak, 1898-
Matrimonial problems in 18th century Maharashtra. IHCP, v.10 (1947), pp.453-55.

IHCP

B-344
Pethe, Vasant P.
Life cycle of families in an urban community (Sholapur). SB, v.12 (1963). pp.39-46.

SB

B-345
Phipson, Pechey.
Address to the Hindoos of Bombay on the subject of child marriage. Bombay, Bombay Gazette Steam Press, 1890. 15p.

Cal nat hib

B-346
Ranadive, Jayant Sadashiv.
Family in urban and rural areas. Poona, Univ. of Poona, 1961. *

Sociology
GPS

B-347
Rowlatt, Mary.
An early Victorian family in Bombay. RCASJ, v.47 (1960), pp.171-74.

Ja S 60

B-348
Satthianadhan, Krupabai.
Kamala: a story of Hindu life. Madras, Srinivasa Varadachari and co., 1894. 245p.

BM

B-349
Shastri, B.V.
Notes on high class marriages among the Maratha Sudras. IA, v.25 (1896), pp.286-87.

✓✓✓ IA

B-350
Shastri, B.V.
Notes on Maratha marriages, marriage custom amongst Marathas. IA, v.28 (1899), pp.112, 162, 224.

flver

B-351
Shejwalkar, Trymbak Shankar.
A unique Maratha marriage invitation to the dead. BDCRI, v.4 (1942), p.80.

fwir

B-352
Velankar, Hari Damodar, 1893-
The family - hymns in the family - Mandalas, ASBJ, v.18 (1942), pp.1-22.

Eira

Family planning & fertility

B-353
Chandrasekaran, C., 1911- and Kuder, K.
Family planning through clinics; report of a survey of family planning clinics in greater Bombay. Bombay, Allied Pubs., 1965. (Demographic training and research center, Bombay. Research monograph, no.2). 300p.

B-354
Dandekar, Kumudini.
Promotion of family planning in rural areas; a field experiment, AV, v.3 (1961), pp.24-37.

B-355
Dandekar, Kumudini.
Sterilization programme: its size and effects on birth rate, AV, v.1 (1959), pp.220-31.

B-356
Dandekar, Kumudini.
Vasectomy camps in Maharashtra, PS, v.17 (1963), pp.147-54.

B-357
Dandekar, Kumudini and Bhate, Vaijayanti.
Family planning in the city of Poona, IERJ, v.3,no.1 (1968), pp.1-21.

B-358
Dandekar, Vinayak Mahadeo, 1920- and Dandekar, Kumudini.
Survey of fertility and mortality in Poona. Poona, D.R.Gadgil, 1953. (Gokhale Inst.of Politics and Economics, pub.no.27). 191p.

B-359
Maharashtra, India (State) Directorate of Publicity.
Family planning, achievements and prospects. Bombay, 1962. 75p.

B-360
Pethe, Vasant P.
Levels of fertility and reproduction and differential fertility in Sholapur city, IEJ, v.8 (1960), pp.70-80.

B-361
Singh, Amrit Wardev and Gunde, Sumar B.
Analysis of couples following family planning on advice of Regional Family Planning Training Centre, Poona, JFW, v.9 (1962), pp.7-19.

B-362
Sovani, Nilkanth Vitthal and Dandekar, Kumudini.
Fertility survey of Nasik, Kolaba, and Satara (North) districts. Poona, D.R.Gadgil, 1955. (Gokhale Inst.of Politics and Economics, no.31). 167p.

Festivals & ceremonies

B-363
Straus, Marray A. and Winkelmann, Dorothea.
Social class, fertility, and authority in
nuclear and joint households in Bombay, JAAS,
v.4 (1969), pp.61-74.

Sociology y Anthropology - O

B-364
Apte, Vasudeo Govind, 1871-1930.
Marriage ceremony among Maharashtra Brah-
mins, MR, v.37 (1925), pp.145-47.

MR O

B-365
Athalye, Yasvant Vasudev.
On betrothal among the Maharashtra Brahmanas,
JASB, v.1 (1886-1889), pp.61-75.

Furer O

B-366
Barnouw, Victor.
The changing character of a Hindu festival,
AmerA, v.56 (1954), pp.74-86.

Furer O

B-367
Bhagwat, Durga Narayan, 1910-
Kamar marriage song, MI, v.23 (1943),
p.27.

Kirk O

B-368
Bhagwat, Durga Narayan, 1910-
Premarital puberty-rites of girls in
western Maharashtra, MI, v.23 (1943),
pp.123-26.

Furer O

B-369
Birth ceremonies of the Prabhus, FJ, v.6
(1888), pp.75-77.

Kirk O

B-370
Caland, W.
Vaidik wedding song, AO, v.7 (1929),
pp.305-11.

Furer O

B-371
Codrington, Kenneth de Burgh.
Bara gari, the dragging of the twelve
carts, Man, v.38 (1938), pp.163-168.

Kirk O

NO ENTRY

B-372
   Codrington, Kenneth deBurgh.
     Possession rite in a Deccan village
(abstract), Nature, v.142 (1938), p.800.

Fures

B-373
   Crooke, C.William.
     Hut-burning in the ritual of India, Man,
v.19 (1919), pp.18-25.

Kirk

B-374
   Deshpande, Kamalabai, 1898-
     Some religious observances (vratas) and
festivals (utsawas) mentioned in the Desina-
mamala, ABORI, v.36 (1955), pp.340-51.

B-375
   Drower, E.S.
     The role of fire in Parsi ritual, JRAIGB,
v.74 (1944), pp.75-89.

Furer

B-376
   Enthoven, Reginald Edward, 1869-
     The Devaks of the Deccan and Konkan, JASB,
v.13 (1924), pp.1-14.

Furer

B-377
   Enthoven, Reginald Edward, 1869-
     Some further notes on the Devaks of the
Bombay Presidency, JASB, v.13 (1924), pp.
649-57.

Sen Gupta

B-378
   Fuller, Mary Lucia Bierce.
     Nagpanchami, MI, v.24 (1944), pp.75-81.

JASB

B-379
   Galatgekar, S.S.
     The sweet harvest in a southern Maharashtra
village, IGJ, v.8 (1933), pp.25-35.

Furer

B-380
   Grieve, Lucia C.G.
     The Desara festival at Satara, India, JAOS,
v.30 (1910), pp.72-76.

Kirk

B-381
   Gupte, Balkrishna Atmaram, 1851-
     Hindu holidays and ceremonials. 2d ed.
Calcutta, Thacker, Spink, 1919. 288p.

4 & R

B-382
Gupte, Balkrishna Atmaram, 1851-
   Note on the Dark Monday Somvati, ASBJ,
   n.s.,v.7 (1911), pp.631.

ASBJ

B-383
Kashikar, C.G.
   Report of the Vajapeya performance committee,
Poona, for 1955-56. Poona, Office of the Com-
mittee, 1957. 48p.

Surer

B-384
Kashikar, C.G.
   The Srauta ritual and the Vajapeya sacri-
fice. Poona, Vajapeya Performance Committee,
1955. 59p.

IOL

B-385
Khambata, Sorabji Kavasji.
   Parsi funeral and initiatory rites. IA,
v.7 (1878), pp.179-80.

Surer

B-386
Kikar, Dr.
   Birth ceremonies of Prabhus (of Bombay),
FJ, v.6 (1888), pp.75-77.

Sen Gupta

B-387
Kirtikar, K.R.
   On the ceremonies observed among Hindus
during pregnancy and parturition, JASB,
v.1 (1886), p.394.

JASB

B-388
Krishnanath Raghunathji.
   The ceremony of matrimonial separation in
Bombay. IA, v.13 (1900), p.393.

Surer

B-389
Krishnanath Raghunathji.
   The Gaur Feast. Bombay, Fort Print.Press,
1899. 12p.

Bom (Pres) Cat

B-390
Krishnanath Raghunathji.
   A housewarming custom in Bombay. IA, v.29
(1900), p.392.

Surer

B-391
Krishnanath Raghunathji.
   Marriage to a dagger in Bombay. IA, v.29
(1900), p.392.

Surer

B-392
Krishnanath Raghunathji.
The potter's obsequies or Kumbhar Kriya.
Bombay, Fort Print.Press, 1899. 15p.

1. Funeral rites - Potters.

Bom (Pres) Cat

B-393
Malcolm, Sir John, 1769-1833.
On the institution and ceremonies of the
Hindoo festival of the Dusrah, with a short
account of the Kurradee Brahmins, LSBT, v.3
(1823), pp.73-89.

B-394
Masani, Sir Rustom Pestonji, 1876-1966.
The Sinhast fair and the cult of nudity,
JASB, v.15 (1932-1940), pp.215-50.

Furer

B-395
Mehta, S.S.
Dagada-Chouth or vestiges of moon worship
in the Bombay Presidency, JASB, v.11 (1917-
1921), pp.290-96..

Furer

B-396
Mitra, Sarat Chandra.
On some Indian ceremonies for disease
transference, ASBJ, v.13 (1917), pp.13-21.

Furer

B-397
Modi, Jivanji Jamshedji, 1854-1933.
Birth customs and ceremonies of the Parsees,
JASB, v.9 (1910-1913), pp.568-78.

Furer

B-398
Modi, Jivanji Jamshedji, 1854-1933.
Consecration ceremonies among the Parsees,
JASB, v.11 (1917-1921), pp.496-545.

Furer

B-399
Modi, Jivanji Jamshedji, 1854-1933.
The funeral ceremonies of Parsees, their
origin and explanation. Bombay, Education
Society's Steam Press, 1923.

Kirk

B-400
Modi, Jivanji Jamshedji, 1854-1933.
The initiation ceremonies and customs of
the Parsees, JASB, v.11 (1917-1921), pp.454-
85.

Furer

B-401
Modi, Jivanji Jamshedji, 1854-1933.
The liturgical services of the Parsees, the
Yacha: its liturgical apparatus, JASB, v.11
(1917-1921), pp.996-1065.

Furer

B-402
Modi, Jivanji Jamshedji, 1854-1933.
   On the funeral ceremonies of the Parsees,
their origin and explantation, JASB, v.2
(1890-1892), pp.405-40.

Furer

B-403
Modi, Jivanji Jamshedji, 1854-1933.
   The outer liturgical services of the Parsees,
JASB, v.12 (1921-1924), pp.39-92.

Furer

B-404
Modi, Jivanji Jamshedji, 1854-1933.
   The Parsee purifactory ceremonies-
purifactory processes in daily life,
JASB, v.11 (1917-1921), pp.365-75.

Furer

B-405
Modi, Jivanji Jamshedji, 1854-1933.
   The Parsee purifactory ceremonies, the
Bareshnum and the Riman; a study, JASB,
v.11 (1917-1921), pp.224-89.

Furer

B-406
Modi, Jivanji Jamshedji, 1854-1933.
   The purifactory ceremonies of the Parsees -
The Padiyab, the Nan, JASB, v.11 (1917-1921),
pp.169-85.

Furer

B-407
Modi, Jivanji Jamshedji, 1854-1933.
   The religious ceremonies and customs of
the Parsees. 2d ed. Bombay, J.B.Karani's
sons, 1937. 455p.

LC

B-408
Modi, Jivanji Jamshedji, 1854-1933.
   Some prayer-gestures of the Babylonians
and Assyrians; their parallels among the
ancient Iranians and modern Parsees, ASBJ,
v.25 (1917-1921), pp.504-28.

Furer

B-409
Monier-Williams, Monier, 1819-1899.
   Parsi funeral and initiatory rites, and
the Parsi religion, IA, v.6 (1877), pp.311-
15.

Furer

B-410
Monier-Williams, Monier, 1819-1899.
   Parsi funeral and initiatory rites, IA,
v.7 (1878), pp.227-28.

Furer

B-411
Padhye, K.A.
   Annual festival near Kolhapur in honour
of the celebration of the marrige of God
Jotiba with his sister, JASB, v.15 (1932-
1934), pp.515-24.

Furer

B-412
Pertold, O.
    The liturgical use of Mahuda liquor by
Bhils, ArchO, v.3 (1931), pp.400-407.

Furer

B-413
Rajalakshmi, C.R.
    On ancestor worship among Son Kolis, IDAB,
v.11 (1962), pp.81-84.

Furer

B-414
Rodrigues, Lucio.
    St. John's day: a water festival in Goa,
FL, v.5 (1964), pp.401-405.

Sen Gupta

B-415
Shah, P.G.
    Origin of S'alagrama and Tulasi worship,
JASB, Jubilee Volume (1937), pp.207-35.

Furer

B-416
Sinclair, William F.
    Notes on the Muharram Festival. Thana
Collectorate, Kolhapur, IA, v.6 (1877),
pp.79, 230-31.

Furer

B-417
Stevenson, John, 1798-1858.
    On the anti-Brahmanical worship of the
Hindus in the Dekkan: Divali festival and
the worship of Vetal, RASGBIJ, v.1 (1843?),
pp.189, 195.

JASB

B-418
Thite, Ganesh Umakant.
    Caturmasya - sacrifices researched, JUP,
v.31 (1969), pp.57-79.

Folklore articles
BAS 1969

B-419
Townsend, Donald C.
    Colera's festival celebrated by the people
of Wai in South India, UNW, v.1 (1948), pp.
44-45.

Furer

B-420
West, Edward William, 1824-1905.
    The Bendur ceremonies at Sangli, IA, v.5
(1876), p.355.

Furer

B-421
Wiesinger, Rita.
    The woman's part in the religious life of
the Bhil, Anthropos, v.62 (1967), pp.497-508.

JAS

B-422
Wiley, A.L.
    Progress of the revival at Ratnagiri.
Ratnagiri, the author, 1906. 4p.

Bom.(Pres)cat

B-423
Wiley, A.L.
    Revival at Ratnagiri. Ratnagiri, the author,
1906. 8p.

Bom.(Pres) cat

B-424
Wrede, Francis.
    An account of the festival of Mamangom,
LSBI, v.1 (1819), pp.1-5.

Folk lore & arts

B-425
Agarkar, Achyut Jagannath.
    Rain-lore on the western coast, JUB, v.22
(1953), pp.65-69.

Siirer

B-426
Allchin, Frank Raymond, 1923-
    Poor men's Thalis: a Deccan potter's tech-
nique, BSOAS, v.22 (1959), pp.250-57.

Surer

B-427
Ansari, Zainuddin Dawood.
    A potter at Work, BDCRI, v.24 (1963-64),
pp.1-14.

NUA
Surer

B-427a
Babar, Sarojini Krishnarao, 1920-
    Folk literature of Maharashtra. New
Delhi, Maharashtra Information Centre,
1968. 39p.

PL 480 1/69

B-427b
Babar, Sarojini Krishnarao, 1920-
    Rainy season in Marathi folksongs, Folklore,
v.3 (1962), pp.15-18.

Dis Gupta

B-427c
Babar, Sarojini Krishnarao, 1920-
    Women in Marathi folklore, Folklore, v.9
(1968), pp.7-16.

JAS 68

B-428
Bachmann de Mello, Hedwig.
    On the soul of the Indian woman, as re-
flected in the folk-lore of the Konkan,
trans.by Shilavati Ketkar. Bastora Goa,
Tip Rangel, 1942-43. 2v.

    1. Women in India.

B-429
    Barreto, Floriano.
       The mando dance. _Marg_, v.8 (1954), pp.56-
    58.

Kirk

B-430
    Beames, John, 1837-1902.
       A lake legend of the Central Provinces. _IA_,
    v.1 (1872), p.143.

JASB

B-431
    Bhagwat, Durga Narayan, 1910-
       Folk-etymology with reference to Indian
    folklore, _JASB_, n.s.,v.10 (1956), pp.1-7.

Kirk

B-432
    Bhagwat, Durga Narayan, 1910-
       Folk-songs from the Satpura valleys, _JUB_,
    n.s.,v.8 (1940), pp.131-91.

Kirk

B-433
    Bhagwat, Durga Narayan, 1910-
       Introduction to Sava, _IF_, v.2 (1959),
    pp.216-17.

Kirk

B-434
    Bhagwat, Durga Narayan, 1910-
       The killer of thirty; a folk tale of
    Maharashtra, _FL_, v.3 (1961), pp.19-22.

Kirk

B-435
    Bhagwat, Durga Narayan, 1910-
       A Maharashtrian folktale: the stick fast,
    _FL_, v.5 (1964), pp.446-47.

JAS '64

B-436
    Bhagwat, Durga Narayan, 1910-
       The money-lender's daughter, _FL_, v.2
    (1961), pp.375-82.

Kirk

B-437
    Bhagwat, Durga Narayan, 1910-
       An outline of Indian folklore. Bombay,
    Popular Book Depot. 1958. 69p.

4 MR

B-438
    Bhagwat, Durga Narayan, 1910-
       Some folk tales of Maharashtra, _FL_, v.4
    (1963), pp.392-96.

JAS '63

B-439
    Bhagwat, Durga Narayan, 1910-
      Sonsakhali: Maharastrian folktale, FL,
    v.3 (1962), pp.225-26.

Fürer

B-440
    Bhagwat, Durga Narayan, 1910-
      The sparrow and the crow, a folktale from
Maharashtra, IF, v.2 (1959), pp.213-15.

Fürer

B-441
    Bødker, Laurits.
      Indian animal tales, a preliminary
survey. Helsinki, Suomalainen Tiedeakatemia,
1957. (F.F. communications, v.68, no.170).
143p.

LC

B-442
    Bolton, H.Carrington.
      The counting-out rhymes of children, JAF,
v.1 (1888), pp.31-37.

Kirk

B-443
    Borse, D.G.
      The special characteristics of Marathi
folk-literature, IF, v.2 (1959), pp.57-63.

Fürer

B-444
    Chavan, Viththal Pandurang.
      The Konkani folk-lore tales, JASB, v.13
(1924-1928), pp.438-64.

Fürer

B-445
    Chittanah, Hideran N.
      Versions of the legend of the clever
builder, IA, v.40 (1911), p.152.

Kirk

B-446
    Codrington, Kenneth deBurgh.
      The use of counter irritants in the Deccan,
JRAIGB, v.66 (1936), pp.369-77.

Fürer GN
         2.786

B-447
    Crawford, Arthur Travers, 1835-1911.
      Legends of the Konkan. Allahabad, Pioneer
Press, 1909. 305p.

          1. Legends - India - Konkan.

LC

B-448
    Damle, Yashwant Bhaskar, 1923-
      A note on harikatha, EDCRI, v.17 (1955-56),
pp.15-19.

Fürer

B-449
De Cunha, John.
On the evil eye among the Bunnias (Bombay),
JASB, v.1 (1886-1888), pp.128-32.

B-450
Dinshaw, V.
Deccan parallels to the Burj-Namah, JAOS,
v.35 (1915), pp.293-96.

B-451
D'Penha, George F.
A cumulative rhyme on the tiger, IA, v.23
(1894), p.167.

B-452
D'Penha, George F.
Folklore in Salsette, IA, v.16 (1887), pp.
327-34; v.17 (1888), pp.13-17, 50-54, 104-
112; v.19 (1890), pp.314-16; v.20 (1891),
pp.29-35, 80-83, 111-13, 142-47, 183-87,
332-36; v.21 (1892), pp.23-27, 45-47, 312-17,
345-47; v.22 (1893), pp.53-56, 243-50, 276-84,
306-15; v.23 (1894), pp.134-39; v.26 (1897),
pp.337-41; v.27 (1898), pp.54-56, 82, 304-306.

B-453
Dexter, Wilfred E.
Marathi folk tales; illustrated by Earnest
Aris. London, George G.Harrap & co., 1938.
190p.

B-454
Dutta, Ajit Kumar.
Special characteristics of Maratha folk-
literature, IF, v.2 (1959), pp.57-63.

B-455
Edwardes, Stephen Meredyth, 1873-1927.
A Koli ballad, IA, v.52 (1923), pp.41-56.

B-456
Enthoven, Reginald Edward, 1869-
The folklore of Bombay. Oxford, Clarendon
Press, 1924. 354p.

1. Folk-lore - India - Bombay (Presidency)

B-457
Enthoven, Reginald Edward, 1869-
Folklore of the Konkan, IA, v.43 (1914),
pp.1,13; v.44 (1915), pp.25,33,49,53,65,
73,85.

B-458
Enthoven, Reginald Edward, 1869-
Limes, rice straw and concolvulus in
Indian primitive practice, Folklore, v.48
(1932), pp.29-41.

B-459
Frere, Mary Eliza Isabella, d.1911.
Old Deccan days, or Hindoo fairy legends,
current in Southern India. London, J.Murray,
1929. 256p.

1. Folk-lore - India.

U q/R

B-460
Fuller, Mary Lucia Bierce.
Maher, MI, v.23 (1943), pp.112-22.

B-461
Fuller, Mary Lucia Bierce.
Marathi grinding songs, NR, v.11 (1940),
pp.382-92, 508-20.

Kirk

B-462
Fuller, Mary Lucia Bierce.
Sixteen Marathi grinding songs, MI, v.23
(1943), pp.19-20.

B-463
Gaur, G.D.
A study of the folk songs of the Marathi
dialect. London, London Univ., 1958-59. *

Bloomfield

B-464
Godabole, Narayana Balakrishna.
Folklore: the story of Chandrahasya, IA,
v.11 (1882), pp.84-86.

Kirk

B-465
Grieve, Lucia C.G.
Some folk stories of Ramdas, the last of
the sages, JAOS, v.25 (1904), pp.185-88.

Furer

B-466
Gupta, Joya Dutta.
The potters' craft in Poona City, IDAB,
v.11 (1962), pp.67-74.

B-467
Gupte, Balkrishna Atmaram, 1851-
Folklore in caste proverbs, ASBJ, n.s.,v.13
(1917), pp.1-12.

B-468
Gupte, Balkrishna Atmaram, 1851-
Folklore of the origin of the constellation
of Mrigashirsha, ASBJ, n.s.,v.7 (1911), p.93.

B-469
Jackson, Arthur Mason Tippetts, d.1909.
Folklore notes. Comp.by R.E.Enthoven. Bombay, British India Press, 1914-15. 2v.

1. Folk-lore - India.

Lc

B-470
Jacobi, Hermann Georg, 1850-1937.
Hindu tales. An English translation of Jacobi's Ausgewählte erzählingen in Maharastri. By J.J.Meyer. London, Luzac & co., 1909. 315p.

Lc   Meyer John Jacob 1870-

B-471
Joshi, Purushottam Balkrishna, 1856-1930.
The Phudgis, and the methods adopted for improving them, JASB, v.7 (1904-1906), pp. 350-55.

OB 1907

B-472
Karve, Irawati (Karmarkar) 1905-1970.
Brother and sister in Marathi folksong, SC, v.8 (1942), pp.214-17.

AEIHJ, 5

B-473
Karve, Irawati (Karmarkar) 1905-1970.
Folksongs of Maharashtra, BDCRI, v.1 (1939), p.79.

Sen. Gupta

B-474
Karve, Irawati (Karmarkar) 1905-1970.
A Marathi version of the Oedipus story, Man, v.50 (1950), pp.71-72.

Kirk

B-475
Karve, Irawati (Karmarkar) 1905-1970.
The Parashurama myth, JUB, n.s.,v.1 (1932-1933), p.115.

JASB

B-476
Karve, Irawati (Karmarkar) 1905-1970.
Some folk songs of the Maharashtra, BDCRI, v.1 (1939), pp.79-95.

Furer

B-477
Kavadi, Naresh Bhikaji, 1922-   and Tulpule, S.G.
Folk-songs from Dang, JUP, v.1 (1953), pp. 26-48.

Kirk

B-478
Khanapurkar, D.P.
Bombay villages through folk songs, JUB, n.s.,v.19 (1950), pp.27-31.

Kirk

B-479
    Khanapurkar, D.P.
      The folk-songs of Dangi Bhils. In: Snow
balls of Garhwal, folk-culture series.
Lucknow, 1946. pp.9-17.

Kirk   O

B-480
    Khanapurkar, D.P.
      Folk-songs of Dangi Bhils, MR, v.80
(1946), pp.144-45.

Kirk   O

B-481
    Khanapurkar, D.P.
      Rani Paraj proverbs, JUB, n.s.,v.17 (1949-
1950). p.9.

JASB   O

B-482
    Kincaid, Charles Augustus, 1870-
      Our Hindu friends. Bombay, The Times of
India Press, 1930. 72p.

1 Rites & ceremonies - India

U of R
Bib of Ind Lit   O

B-483
    Kincaid, Charles Augustus, 1870-
      Our Parsi friends. Bombay, The Times of
India Press, 1922. 64p.

1 Parsees

U of R   O

B-484
    Kincaid, Charles Augustus, 1870-   ed.& tr.
      Deccan nursery tales, or fairy tales from
the south. London, Macmillan & co., 1914.
142p.

U of R   O

B-485
    Knight, Arthur Lee.
      Told in the Indian twilight: Mahratta fairy
tales. London, 1913. 143p.

BM   O

B-486
    Macmillan, Michael, 1853-1925.
      Matheran folk songs, ASBJ, v.21 (1907-08),
p.517.

O

B-487
    Martins, Micael.
      The Mando, Marg, v.8 (1954), pp.62-63.

Kirk   )

B-488
    Masani, Sir Rustom Pestonji, 1876-1966.
      Folklore of Bombay wells, JASB, v.10
(1914-1917), pp.708-28. Also in ASBJ,
v.10 (1913), p.708.

Kirk   )

B-489
Masani, Sir Rustom Pestonji, 1876-1966.
Folklore of wells being a study of water
worship in East and West. Bombay, D.B.Tara-
porevala, 1918.

Sen Gupta

B-490
Menezes, Armando, 1902-
Some impression of Cunbi dance, Marg, v.8
(1958), pp.50-51.

Sen Gupta

B-491
Mitra, Sarat Chandra.
Three recent instances of beliefs in witch-
murders, JASB, v.15 (1932-1936), pp.675-76.

Kirk

B-492
Modi, Jivanji Jamshedji, 1854-1933.
A few marriage songs of the Parsees at
Nargol, JASB, v.13 (1926), pp.623-38; v.14
(1928), pp.244-56.

Kirk

B-493
Modi, Jivanji Jamshedji, 1854-1933.
A few Parsee Nirangs (incantations or
religious formulae), JASB, v.11 (1917-
1921), pp.843-63.

Sen

B-494
Modi, Jivanji Jamshedji, 1854-1933.
Nirang-i-Jashan-i-Burzigaran, JASB, v.5
(1901), pp.398-405.

Kirk

B-495
Modi, Jivanji Jamshedji, 1854-1933.
Parsee life in Parsee songs, JASB, v.5
(1901), pp.427-45.

Kirk

B-496
Moothiah, J.S.
Folk-tales from the Deccan, IA, v.53
(1924), pp.271-72.

Kirk

B-497
Munshi, Rustamji Nasarvanji.
A few Parsee riddles, JASB, v.10 (1913),
pp.94-100, 409-25.

Kirk

B-498
Nayak, D.G.
Rise and decline of Dashawatar. Bombay,
Konkan Marathi Dialects Research Institute,
1962. 28p.

Sen

B-499
Padhye, K.A.
    A few notes as regards the custom of
weaving garments peculiar to the Deccan
females, <u>JASB</u>, v.15 (1938), pp.396-400.

B-504
Pithawalla, Maneck Bejanji.
    Another Parsee cradle song, <u>JGRS</u>, v.8
(1946), pp.127-31.

kirk

B-500
Paranjpe, S.S.
    Folk dances of Maharashtra and Konkan,
<u>Marg</u>, v.13 (1959-1960), pp.45-48.

Surer

B-505
Raja, K. Ramavarma.
    Story of Vrishakapi and his transformation,
<u>QJMS</u>, v.21 (1930), pp.10-17.

subject : anthropology

QJMS

B-501
Parpia, Y.R.
    Marathi social ballads, <u>AL</u>, n.s.,v.2
(1928), pp.49-61.

J B HS

B-506
Rao, Vasant Dinanath, 1913-
    The Pathare Prabhu folk songs. Fourth in-
stallment, <u>JUB</u>, n.s.28 (1960), pp.54-60.

cumulative bib.
JAS

B-502
Patel, Jaya S. and Brewster, Paul G.
    The Indian game of Sagargote (Kooka), <u>ZE</u>,
v.82 (1957), pp.186-90.

Surer

B-507
Rao, Vasant Dinanath, 1913-
    The Pathare Prabhu folklore, <u>JUB</u>, v.15 (1947),
pp.47-62; v.24 (1955), pp.42-50; v.28 (1960),
pp.54-60.

Surer

B-503
Patil, Gajanan M.
    A Warli tale, <u>IL</u>, v.17 (1955-1956), pp.
259-65.

Surer

B-508
Rodrigues, Lucio.
    Folk-songs of Goa. Durpod: the song of joy.
In: Studies in Indian folk culture. By
Sankar Sen Gupta. Calcutta, Indian Pubs.,
1964. pp.18-49.

4 of R

B-509
Rodrigues, Lucio.
Konkani folksongs, JASB, n.s.,v.2 (1948),
pp.1-9.

Kirk

B-510
Rodrigues, Lucio.
Konkani folk-songs of Goa: 2 Dakni - the
song of the dancing girl, JUB, v.23 (1954),
pp.65-75.

Chaudhri

B-511
Rodrigues, Lucio.
The love song of Goa, Marg, v.8 (1954),
pp.53-55.

Kirk

B-512
Saldanha, Jerome Anthony.
Folklore of Savantvadi: gods and ghosts of
the village of Matond on the Savantvadi State,
JASB, v.10 (1914), pp.178-87.

Kirk

B-513
Shah, A.F.Byram.
Magical beliefs and practices of the
Parsees, MCCM, v.4 (1924), pp.217-27.

Kirk

B-514
Simcox, Arthur Henry Addenbrooke.
Gerlert in the East, Man, v.32 (1932),
pp.16-17.

H of R folk lore 2 end

B-515
Sinclair, William F.
Flint remains in the Kolaba district,
JASB, v.2 (1889-1892), pp.75-79.

Furer

B-516
Sinclair, William F.
Some songs of western India, IA, v.4
(1875), pp.350-52.

Kirk

B-517
Sisodia, V.N.R.
A note on the classification of the musical
instruments of the Varlis, Ethnos, v.31
(1966), pp.120-30.

JaS 9/68

B-518
Sisodia, V.N.R.
Three styles in the architecture of Varli
dwellings, Anthropos, v.59 (1964), pp.159-
64.

JaS 64

B-519
   Swynnerton, Fred.
      On some rude stone implements from back
   bay, middle Colaba, Bombay, <u>JASB</u>, v.3
   (1893-1895), pp.189-97.

Surer

B-524
   India (Republic) Directorate of National
      Sample Survey.
      Report on the sample survey of displaced
   persons in the urban areas of Bombay State,
   July-September 1953 by Satyabrata Sen. With
   a foreword by S.C.Mahalanobis. Issued by the
   Cabinet Secretariat, Govt.of India. Calcutta,
   Printed at the Eka Press, foreword 1957.
   (The national sample survey, no.9) 98p.

B-520
   Thompson, Stith, 1885- and Balys, Jonas, 1909-
      The oral tales of India. Bloomington,
   Indiana University Press, 1958. (Indiana
   University Publications. Folklore series,
   no.10). 474p.

1. Folklore - India - Indexes.

Vol R

B-525
   Karve, Irawati (Karmarkar), 1905-1970 and
      Nimbkar, Jai.
      A survey of the people displaced through
   the Koyna Dam. By Irawati Karve and Jai Nimb-
   kar. Poona, Deccan College Post-graduate
   and Research Institute, 1969. 8p.

Anthropology & Sociology
BDCRI, p.120

B-521
   Vavikar, Yadhav Shankar.
      Notes on Maratha folklore, <u>IA</u>, v.27 (1898),
   pp.306-308.

Kirkland

B-526
   Lakdawala, Dansukhlal Tulsidas.
      An enquiry into the conditions of the refu-
   gees in Bombay city, <u>JUB</u>, v.20 (1952), pp.62-
   69.

JUB

B-522
   Wadia, Putlibai D.H.
      Folklore in western India, <u>IA</u>, v.14 (1885),
   pp.311-31; v.15 (1886), pp.2-6,46-47,171-72,
   221-22,365-68; v.16 (1887), pp.28-31,188-94,
   210-14,322-27; v.17 (1888), pp.75-81,128-32;
   v.18 (1889), pp.21-26,146-51; v.19 (1890),
   pp.152-55; v.20 (1891), pp.107-10; v.21 (1892),
   pp.160-66; v.22 (1893), pp.213-19,315-21;
   v.23 (1894), pp.160-64.

Surer

B-527
   Lakshminarayanan, Mythili Krishnaswamy.
      A socio-ecological study of an immigrant
   community. Bombay, Univ.of Bombay, 1959. *

Sociology
BDD

B-523
   Wadia, Putlibai D.H.
      Parsi and Gujarati Hindu nuptial songs, <u>IA</u>,
   v.19 (1890), pp.374-78; v.21 (1892), pp.113-
   16.

IA

B-528
   Padki, M.B.
      Outmigration from a Konkan village to
   Bombay, <u>AV</u>, v.6 (1964), pp.27-35.

Ja 864

B-529
Sen, Satyabrata,
  Report on the sample survey of displaced
persons in the urban areas of Bombay State,
July-Sept.1953. Delhi, Cabinet Secretariat,
Govt.of India, 1958. (India. National Sample
survey. no.9) 106p.

IO L

B-53̆4
Vaswani, M.H.
  Some aspects of the rehabilitation of
displaced persons in Bombay State, JUB,
v.20 (1952), pp.1-4.

JUB

B-530
Singh, Ajit.
  Displacement and resettlement of Sindhi
displaced persons settled in Pimpri and
Poona. Poona, Gokhale Institute of Politics
and Economics, Poona University, 1965.*

Jayakar Lib #1965

B-535
Zachariah, Kunniparampil Curien, 1924-
  Bombay migration study: a pilot analysis
of migration to an Asian metropolis, Demography, v.3 (1966), pp.378-92.

JA 1 66

B-531
Vakil, Chandulal Nagindas, 1895-   and
  Cabinetmaker, Perin Hormasji.
  Government and the displaced persons; a
study in social tensions. Bombay, Vora &
co., 1956. 162p.

LC

B-536
Zachariah, Kunniparampil Curien, 1924-
  Juvenile working migrants in greater Bombay,
IJSW, v.27 (1966), pp.255-62.

g(! 9/6 8

B-532
Valunjkar, Trivikram Narayan.
  Social organization and the migration pattern
of a village community. Poona, University of
Poona, 1960. *

Anthropology-sociology

B-537
Zachariah, Kunniparampil Curien, 1924-
  The Maharashtrian and Gujarati migrants in
greater Bombay, SB, v.15 (1966), pp.68-87.

gai ..

B-533
Valunjkar, Trivikram Narayan.
  Social organization, migration, and
change in a village community. Poona,
Deccan College Postgraduate and Research
Inst., 1966. (Deccan College dissertation
series, 28). 78p.

i.Villages-Maharashtra, India - case studies
Uof 2

B-538
Zachariah, Kunniparampil Curien, 1924-
  Migrants in greater Bombay. New York,
Asia Pub.House, 1968. (Demographic Train-
ing and Research Centre, Bombay. Research
monograph no.5). 365p.

y.2 R

B-539
    Zachariah, Kunniparampil Curien, 1924-
      Migration to greater Bombay, 1941-1951,
    IJSW, v.20 (1959), pp.189-92.

Occupational groups

B-544
    Krishnanath Raghunathji.
      Bombay beggars and criers, IA, v.9 (1880),
    pp.247-50, 278-80; v.10 (1881), pp.71-75,
    145-47, 286-87; v.11 (1882), pp.22-24, 44-
    47, 141-46, 172-74.

Surv

B-540
    Athavale, K.K.
      The Madhukari, MR, v.10 (1911), pp.286-88.

M R

B-545
    Krishnanath Raghunathji.
      Bombay dancing girls, IA, v.13 (1884),
    pp.165-78.

Surv

B-541
    Bhaiji, M.Mohsin.
      The functional distribution of Muhammedan
    population in Bombay City, JUB, v.6 (1938),
    pp.163-74.

JUB

B-546
    Mehta, Aban B.
      The domestic servant class. Bombay,
    Popular Book Depot, 1960. 334p.

Sociology Occupational
と コ コ   groups

B-542
    Damle, Yashwant Bhaskar, 1923-
      Social structure of the intellectuals in
    Poona, a study of college and university
    professors. Poona, University of Poona
    (Deccan College), 1968.

Anthropology & Sociology
BDCRI, p. 125

B-547
    Ramaswamy, Y.
      Matunga labour camp: a sociological study
    of a workers' settlement, JUB, v.28, (1959),
    pp.76-82.

Southern Asia Social Science
Bibliography 1959 - Sociology

B-543
    Gadgil, Dhananjaya Ramchandra, 1901-
      Immigrant traders in Poona in the 18th
    century, AV, v.1 (1959), pp.8-16.

B-548
    UNESCO Research Centre on Social and Economic
      Development in Southern Asia.
      Social and cultural factors affecting pro-
    ductivity of industrial workers in India.
    Delhi, 1961. 181p.

So Asia Soc Sci B.

Physical anthropology

B-549
Athawale, M.C.
Estimation of height from lengths of forearm bones: a study of one hundred Maharashtrian male adults of ages between twenty-five and thirty years, AJPA, v.21 (1963), pp.105-12.

Fürer

B-550
Aust, C.H., et al.
A family of 'Bombay' blood type with suppression of blood group substance, A, AJCP, v.37 (1962), pp.579-83.

Fürer

B-551
Banker, D.D. and Vyas, G.N.
Determination of blood groups and other genetical characters in certain endogamous Gujarati groups in the city of Bombay, JGRS, v.17 (1955), pp.157-61.

4.fR

B-552
Bansal, Inderjit Singh.
Frequency of A-B ridge counting among the Maharashtrians of India, EA, v.19 (1966), pp.117-22.

JAS '66

B-553
Bansal, Inderjit Singh.
The pattern intensity index in the Lallacal area in plantar dermatoglyphics of the Maharashtrians of India, Anthropologist, v.13 (1966), pp.89-93.

JAS '68

B-554
Basu, Arabindu.
The frequency of colour blindness in some population groups of Maharashtra (India), AHG, v.28,no.2 (1964-65), pp.129-32.

Fürer

B-555
Bhatia, H.M. and Sanghvi, L.D.
Rare blood groups and consanguinity: 'Bombay' phenotype, VS, v.7 (1962), pp.245-48.

Fürer

B-556
Bird, G.W.G.
A-intermediates in Maharastrian blood donors, VS, v.9 (1964), pp.629-30.

Fürer

B-557
Desai, Sapur Faredun.
Parsis and eugenics. Bombay, 1940. 146p.

IOL

NO ENTRY

B-558
Gulati, R.K.
Morphological and biological differences in three endogamous groups of an artisan caste of Maharashtra, <u>BDCRI</u>, v.29 (1970), pp.16-36.

BDCRI, p. 124

B-559
Hakim, S.A., et al.
Eleven cases of 'Bombay' phenotype in six families: Suppression of ABO antigen demonstrated in two families, <u>Transfusion</u>, v.1 (1961), pp.218-22.

Surer

B-560
India. Ethnographic Survey.
Anthropometric data from Bombay. Calcutta, Office of the Supt.,Govt.Print., India, 1907. 344p.

1. Anthropometry-India - Bombay (Presidency)
1C

B-561
Jayant, K. and Mehta, A.
A study of congenital malformations in Bombay, <u>JOG</u>, v.11 (1961), pp.280-94.

Surer

B-562
Karve, Irawati (Karmarkar), 1905-1970.
Anthropometric investigation of the Madhyandina Brahmins of the Maratha country, <u>BDCRI</u>, v.3 (1941), pp.1-74.

Surer

B-563
Karve, Irawati (Karmarkar), 1905-1970.
Anthropometric measurements in Karnatak and Orissa and a comparison of these two regions with Maharashtra, <u>ASBJ</u>, n.s.,v.8 (1954), pp.45-75.

Studies in biology

B-564
Karve, Irawati (Karmarkar), 1905-1970.
Anthropometric measurements of the Marathas. 1st ed. Poona, Deccan College Postgraduate and Research Institute, 1948. (Deccan College Monograph series, 2). 71p.

1. Anthropometry-India 2. Marathas.
UofR

B-565
Karve, Irawati (Karmarkar) 1905-1970 and Dandekar, Vinayak Mahadeo, 1920-
Anthropometric measurements of Maharashtra. 1st ed. Poona, S.M.Katre for the Deccan College Post-graduate and Research Institute, 1951. (Deccan College monograph series, 8) 134p.

X &R

B-566
Malhotra, Kailash Chandra.
Anthropometric measurements and blood groups of Maharashtrian Brahmins. Poona, Univ.of Poona, 1966. *

Anthropology: ...
BDCRI

B-567
Mason, Eleanor D. and Jacob, Mary.
Racial group differences in the basal metabolism and body composition of Indian and European women in Bombay, <u>HB</u>, v.36 (1964), pp.374-96.

Surer

B-568
Mason, Eleanor D. and Mundkur, V.
   Basal energy metabolism and heights, weights,
arm skinfold and muscle of young Indian women
in Bombay with prediction standards for B.M.R.,
IJMR, v.51 (1963), pp.925-32.

Surer   (

B-569
Mavalwala, Jamshed D.
   Anthropometric survey of the Parsi community in India. Delhi, Univ.of Delhi,
1959. *

Srikk   (

B-570
Mavalwala, Jamshed D.
   Correlations between ridge-counts on all
digits of the Parsis of India, AHG, v.26
(1962-63), pp.137-38.

Surer   (

B-571
Mavalwala, Jamshed D.
   The dermatoglyphics of the Parsis of India,
ZMA, v.54 (1963-64), pp.173-89.

Surer   (

B-572
Mavalwala, Jamshed D.
   A note on the inheritance and distribution
of mid-digital hair among the Parsi community
in India, Anthropologist, v.4 (1957), pp.7-13.

u of R   (

B-573
Mavalwala, Jamshed D.
   Quantitative analysis of finger ridge counts
of the Parsi community in India, AHG, v.26
(1962-63), pp.305-13.

Surer   (

B-574
Mavalwala, Jamshed D.
   The utility of the angle 'atd' in dermato-
glyphics, AJPA, v.21 (1963), pp.77-80.

Surer   (

B-575
Mehrotra, Kailash Chandra.
   Anthropometric measurements and blood groups
of Maharashtrian Brahmins. Poona, Deccan
College Postgraduate and Research Institute,
1966. *

Jaykar Lib.-LL1542   (

B-576
Mital, M.S., et al.
   A focus of sickle cell gene near Bombay.
Preliminary communication, ActaH, v.27
(1962), pp.257-67.

Surer   (

B-577
Rakshit, Hirendra K.
   The Mahars of Maharashtra: an anthropometric appraisal, IDAB, v.9,no.1 (1960),
pp.61-78.

Surer   (

B-578
Report of the survey on heights and weights of school children in Bombay suburbs undertaken by the Gujarat Research Society and comparison of the results with municipal data, JGRS, v.19 (1957), pp.158-217.

U of R

B-583
Dandekar, Kumudini,
Demographic survey of six rural communities. Bombay, Asia Pub.House, 1959. 187p.

Southern Asia Social Science Bibliography Sociology, P.5

B-579
Rife, D.C. and Malhotra, Kailash Chandra.
An investigation of the incidence of light eyes within a Brahman population, AGMG, v.12 (1963), pp.158-61.

Fürer

B-584
De Souza, J.P.
The population of Bombay at the beginning of British rule, IHCP, v.28 (1966), pp.404-16.

U of R

B-580
Sanghvi, L.D.
Diversité génétique des populations de langue Mahrathi dans l'Inde de l'ouest, Population, v.10,no.3 (1955), pp.443-54.

Fürer

Population

B-585
East India Company (English)
Area and population of each division of each Presidency of India. London, 1857. 16p.

BM

B-581
Borkar, Vishnu Vinayak and Kate, P.V.
Some characteristics of the population of Marathwada, JMaU, v.6,no.1 (1966), pp.24-53.

JMcV

B-586
Mahaley, K.L., 1922-
The estimated population of Shivaji's kingdom in Maharashtra, QRHS, v.7 (1967-1968), pp.250-54.

QRHS

B-582
Choudhari, R.E. and Ramachandran, K.V.
Population projections for Maharashtra State 1951-1981, QBES, c.2, no.3 (1961), pp.1-26.

B-587
Mukerji, V.
Application of some simple multiregional growth and migration models to district level census data in Maharashtra, AV, v.6 (1964), pp.187-205.

U of P

B-588
Orr, James Peter.
Density of Population in Bombay. Bombay,
1914. 26p.

BM

B-593
Raghava Rao, G.
A population policy for the Bombay Presidency, JUB, v.8 (1939), pp.71-87.

JUB

B-589
Pethe, Vasant P.
Demographic profiles of an urban population.
Bombay, Popular Prakashan, 1964. 160p.

1. Sholapur, India (City) - Population.

USYR

B-594
Strip, Percival and Strip, Olivia.
The peoples of Bombay. Bombay, Thacker and
co., 1944. 50p.

Caste - India - Bombay
LC

B-590
Pethe, Vasant P.
Population and fertility in Sholapur City:
a survey. Poona, Univ.of Poona, 1957-58. *

Gupta

B-595
Strizower, Schifra.
Bombay and its people, Hemisphere, v.14,
no.8 (1970), pp.19-24.

Rural society

B-591
Pithawalla, Maneck Bejanji and Rustomji,
B.S.H.J.
Population trends of Parsi settlements on
the west coast of India, JUB, v.13 (1945),
pp.30-44.

JUB

B-596
Aitihasika.
A history of village communities in western
India, a reply, IHQ, v.11 (1935), pp.155-61.

IHQ

B-592
Raghava Rao, G.
The nature of the growth of population in
the British districts of the Bombay Presidency,
JUB, v.6 (1938), pp.125-62.

JUB

B-597
Altekar, Anant Sadashiv, 1898-
A history of the village communities of
western India, IHQ, v.11 (1935), pp.153-54,
162-66.

Index to IHQ

B-598
Altekar, Anant Sadashiv, 1898-
A history of village communities in western India. Bombay, H.Milford, Oxford University Press, 1927. (University of Bombay. Economic series, no.5). 160p.

Uc+R

B-599
Coats, Thomas.
Account of the present state of the township of Lony; in illustration of the Marratta cultivators. LSBT, v.3 (1823), pp.172-264.

f urer

B-600
Costa, Constancio Roque da.
Les communautés des villages à Goa; mémoire présenté à la 10e session du Congrès international des orientalistes par C.R.da Costa, M.S.G.L. Lisbonne, Imprimerie nationale, 1892. 34p.

B-601
Deb, Prafulla Chandra.
Social life of an Indian rural community: Waddhama, a village in Vidarbha, Maharashtra. Nagpur, Nagpur Univ., 1965. *

Sociology
c D D

B-602
Desai, M.N.
Rural Karnatak. Detailed study of the rural conditions in the Bombay and Karnatak with reference to Gokak Taluka. Poona, Anand N. Desai, 1945. 422p.

Rein (Prosar

B-603
Edwardes, Stephen Meredyth, 1873-1927.
Side-lights on Dekkan village life in the 18th century, IA, v.5 (1926), pp.108-13.

furer

B-604
Ghurye, Govind Sadashiv, 1893-
After a century and a quarter; Lonikand then and now. Bombay, Popular Book Depot, 1960. 166p.

U xfR

B-605
Ghurye, Govind Sadashiv, 1893-
Anatomy of a rururban community. Bombay, Popular Prakashan, 1963. 238p.

1. India - Rural conditions.

U xR

B-606
Jagalpure, L.B., and Kale, K.D.
Sarola Kasar; a study of a Deccan village in the famine zone. Ahmednagar, L.B.Jagalpure, 1938. 480p.

BM

B-607
Karve, Irawati (Karmarkar) 1905-1970.
The Indian village, BDCRI, v.18 (1957), pp.73-106.

BDCRI

B-608
    Karve, Irawati (Karmarkar), 1905-1970 and
      Damle, Yashwant Bhaskar, 1923-
      Group relations in village community.
    Poona, Pub.by S.M.Katre for the Deccan
    College Postgraduate and Research Institute,
    1963. (Deccan College monograph series,
    24). 491p.

. villages—India—case studies. 2 India-Rural
conditions.
UofR

B-609
    Karve, Irawati (Karmarkar) 1905-1970 and
      Ranadive, Jayant Sadashiv.
      Social dynamics of a growing town and its
    surrounding area. Poona, Univ.of Poona,
    1965. 324p.

Sociology & anthropology

BDCEI

B-610
    Kosambi, Damodar Dharmanand, 1907-1968.
      The village community in the 'old conquests'
    of Goa, JUB, v.15 (1947), pp.63-78.

ICL

B-611
    Kulkarni, Madhav Gururao, 1923-
      Socio-ecological study of Gokak Taluka.
    Bombay, Univ.of Bombay, 1958. *

B-612
    Kumar, Ravinder.
      The rise of the rich peasants in western
    India. In: Soundings in modern South
    Asian history. Ed.by D.A.Low. Berkeley,
    Univ.of California Press, 1968. pp.25-58.

B-613
    Kumar, Ravinder.
      Rural life in western India on the eve of
    British conquest, IESHR, v.2 (1965), pp.201-
    20.

IESHR

B-614
    Mandlik, Vishvanath Narayan, 1833-1889.
      Preliminary observations on a document
    giving an account of the establishment of
    a new village named Muruda, in Southern
    Konkana, ASBJ, v.8,no.23 (1865), pp.1-48.

ASBJ

B-615
    Mann, Harold Hart, 1872-
      A Deccan village under the Peshwas, IJE,
    v.4 (1923), pp.30-46.

Fircer

B-616
    Marriott, McKim, ed.
      Village India; studies in the little com-
    munities. Menasha, Wis., American Anthro-
    pological Association, 1955. (Comparative
    studies of cultures and civilizations, no.6)
    288p.

    1. Villages - India - Case studies.
    2.India - Soc.condi
UofI

B-617
    Morrison, William A.
      Knowledge of political personages held by
    the male villagers of Badlapur: an intro-
    ductory delineation, SB, v.10 (1961), pp.1-
    26. Continued in v.12 (1963), pp.1-17.

B-618
Orenstein, Henry.
Gaon: conflict and cohesion in an Indian
Village. Princeton, New Jersey, Princeton
Univ.Press, 1965. 341p.

1. Poona, India (District)

u of R

B-623
Acharya, Hemalata N.
A note on social welfare in Nasik district,
AICCER, v.11 (1959), pp.17-23.

Southern Asia Social Science

B-619
Patel, Kunj M.
Effects of Bombay cotton mill industry on
Ratnagiri's rural population, JUB, v.30,n.s.
(1961-62), pp 131-32.

U q R

B-624
Aiyar, S.P. and Rao, Malathi K.
Medical social work in Bombay, IJSW, v.25
(1964), pp.249-60.

Guide to Indian periodicals
JAS '64

B-620
Pedder, W.G.
Village communities in western India, AR.
v.5 (1888), pp.128-43.

AR

B-625
Alvares, Leela.
A study of problem children in the city of
Bombay. Bombay, Univ.of Bombay, 1961. *

Sociology Children
13 DD

B-621
Punit, A.E.
The Goacarias of Goa, MI, v.46 (1966),
pp.207-14.

Internat'l Guide to
India Studies

B-626
Balakrishna, Kulamarva.
A portrait of Bombay's underworld. Bombay,
Manaktalas, 1966. 183p.

1. Crime & criminals - Bombay.

u q R

B-622
Sundaram, M.J.
A Deccan Village in India, JG, v.30 (1931),
pp.49-60.

Furer

B-627
Bhansali, Mansen Damodar.
Prohibition inquiry report in Bombay State.
Bombay, Printed at the Govt.Central Press,
1952. 58p.

LC Accessions 1959 p 124

B-628
Bhatt, Madhav Dattatray.
Some social problems of technological devel-
opment as studied in Tarapur area. Bombay,
Univ.of Bombay, 1969. *

Sociology
BDD

B-629
Bhatt, Usha Ghanshyam.
The physically handicapped in India.
Bombay, Popular Book Depot, 1963. 392p.

Sociology handicapped
BDD persons

B-630
Bombay (Presidency)
Repression of female infanticide in the
Bombay Presidency; a compilation report
setting out briefly all the measures taken
to repress the crime in Gujarat and some
of the neighbouring native states, and
the result of those measures. By Henry Reade
Cooke. Bombay, 1875. (Bombay Presidency.
Selections from the records, n.s.,no.147).
107p.

Brit Mus

B-631
Cabinetmaker, Perin Hormasji.
Social services in India with special
reference to city of Bombay. Bombay, Univ.
of Bombay, 1950. *

Social Welfare
BDD

B-632
Desai, Maganlal Bhagwanji, 1918- and Rao,
V.M.
Survey of drink habit and socio-economic
conditions in Vidarbha and Marathwada. Bom-
bay, Univ.of Bombay, 1960. 95p.

LC

B-633
Driver, Edwin D.
Interaction and criminal homicide in India,
SF, v.40 (1961-62), pp.153-58.

Fuser

B-634
Godbole, N.D.
Sir Dorabji Tata Trust--Rural Welfare Board,
IJSW, v.17 (1956), pp.94-101.

LC 2000-sem, 1958

B-635
Gokhale, S.D.
Rehabilitation of beggars in Bombay State,
IJSW, v.19 (1959), pp.325-330.

Southern Asia Social Sciens
Bibliography; Sociology, p.41

B-636
Jahangir, Rustam Pestanji.
A short history of the lives of Bombay opium
smokers. Bombay, J.B.Marzban and co., 1893.
139p.

BM

B-637
Jayakar, Ramchandra Bhowanji.
Prostitution in the city of Bombay. Bombay,
Univ.of Bombay, 1950. *

Sociology
BDD

B-638
Jeejeebhoy, Jeejeebhoy Rustomji Byramji, 1885-
Bribery and corruption in Bombay; being an
historical account from the earliest to very
recent times ... Bombay, 1952. 324p.

NYPL

B-639
Kerawalla, Perin Kawas.
Study of Indian crime. Bombay, Popular
Book Depot, 1959. 228p.

Social welfare
Criminology
BDD

B-640
Krishnan, O.M.
The night side of Bombay. Bombay, Tatva-
Vivechaka Press, 1923. 84p.

Bom (P.) Cat

B-641
Letters to government on the Deccan dacoities,
QJPSS, v.2,no.1 (1879), pp.68-74; v.2,no.2
(1879), pp.120-26.

B-642
Lorenzo, A.M.
The drink problem in urban Bombay; an inquiry
into the social and economic aspects of drinking
in urban centres of Bombay State; report.
Bombay, Printed at the Government Central Press,
1953. 139p.

LC accessions 1958

B-643
Manshardt, Clifford, 1897-   ed.
Some social services of the Government of
Bombay; a symposium. Bombay, D.B.Taraporevala
vala sons & co., 1938. 145p.

LC

B-644
Moorthy, M.Vasudeva.
Beggar problem in greater Bombay; a research
study. Bombay, Indian Conference of Social
Work, 1959. 111p.

NUC 58/62

B-645
Motivala, Bhavanidas Narandas.
The beggar problem in Bombay. Bombay, Social
Service League Pub., 1920. 46p.

IOL

B-646
Naik, V.P.
Maharashtra and prohibition, IR, v.63
(1964), pp.131-32.

JAS 64

B-647
The native poor of Bombay, BQR, v.4 (1856),
pp.235-72.

4 of c

B-648
Patell, Bombanji Byramji.
Suicides among the Parsees of Bombay
during the last twelve years, JASB, v.4
(1895-1899), pp.14-22.

Case

B-649
Punekar, S.D. and Rao, Kamala.
A study of prostitutes in Bombay, with
reference to family background. 2d ed.
Bombay, Lalvani Pub.House, 1967. 260p.

4 of R

B-650
Raval, Indubhai B.
A study of crime among the Bhils, MI.
v.44 (1964), pp.221-32.

g a 165

B-651
Rehatsek, E.
Statistics of suicides committed in the
city of Bombay during the year 1886 [1887,
1888, 1889, 1890], JASB, v.1 (1886-1888),
pp.330-40, 442-48; v.2 (1889-1892), pp.65-
71, 255-60, 294-300.

Case

B-652
Ross, Allen V.
Vice in Bombay. London, Tallis Pubs.,
1969. (Orig.pub.as Bombay after dark,
1968) 192p.

Sociology & anthropology.

BAS Sept 1970

B-653
Ruttonsha, Goshasp N. (Satarawala)
Juvenile delinquency and destitution in
Poona. Poona, S.M.Katre for the Deccan
College Post-graduate and Research Inst.,
1947. (Deccan College Dissertation series,
no.4) 180p.

Social pathology
U of R

B-654
Sheppard, Samuel Townsend, 1880-
Underground in Bombay, IHCP, v.10 (1947),
pp.478-80.

IHCP

B-655
Sheth, Hansa Bhudherbhai.
Juvenile delinquency in an Indian setting.
Bombay, Popular Book Depot, 1961. 320p.

Social welfare - juvenile delinquency
BDD   IOL

B-656
Tata Institute of Social Sciences, Bombay.
Socio-economic survey of drink problem
in urban Vidarbha and Marathwada. By
S.D.Punekar and P.Ramachandran. Bombay,
Director, Government Printing and Station-
ery, 1962.

1. 1157 et ly

Tiss Bom (.ra 166)

B-657
Tata Institute of Social Sciences. Bureau of
Research and Publications.
Living planes of drinkers' families in
urban Bombay, by A.M.Lorenzo ... and A.E.
Antony ... Bombay, Printed at Govt.Central
Press, 1953. 141p.

B-658
Varshney, N.K.
Criminality among the Bhils, <u>Vanyajati</u>,
v.15 (1967), pp.81-86.

ga s 9/68   O

B-659
Venkataraman, S.R., 1899-
Thakkar Bapa, <u>MR</u>, v.89 (1951), pp.224-25.

Case   O

B-660
Vyas, Rajendra Tansukhram.
Visually handicapped in Bombay State:
their social background and present status.
Bombay, Univ.of Bombay, 1958. *

*Sociology-handicapped
persons*
BDD   O Social psychology

B-661
Barnouw, Victor.
An experiment to gauge the psychological
effects of sterilization in a rural community in India, <u>AV</u>, v.8 (1966), pp.53-65.

NYPL   O

B-662
Bhagwatwar, P.A.
A comparative psycho-social study of the
impact of community development programme
on personality dynamics, attitudes and social
change in rural community in Maharashtra
with special reference to social, marital
and personal adjustment. Poona, Univ.of
Poona, 1970. *

*Sociology
BDD*   O

B-663
Durrett, Mary Allen.
Normative data on the children's manifest
anxiety scale for Marathi speaking Indian
children of different income levels, <u>IJP</u>,
v.40 (1965), pp.1-6.

ga2 65   O

B-664
Murphy, Gardner, 1895-
In the minds of men; the study of human
behaviour and social tensions in India; based
on the UNESCO studies by social scientists
conducted at the request of the Govt.of India.
New York, Basic Books, Inc.Pub., 1953. 320p.

1. India - Soc.condit.

u of R   O

B-665
Ramanathan, Gopalakrishna, 1905-
Indian Babu: a study in social psychology.
New Delhi, Sudha Pubs., 1965. 284p.

1. Clerks - Bombay - Case studies. 2.
Social psychology. 3. Railway clerks -
Bombay city.

k of R   )

B-666
Ramanathan, Gopalakrishna, 1905-
Social attitudes of clerks in Bombay city,
<u>JUB</u>, v.24 (1956), pp.27-39.

*SSB 1956 - Sociology
Social Science Bibliography*   )

B-667
Sirsikar, V.M.
Social and political attitudes of post-
graduate students of the University of Poona,
1960-61, <u>JUP</u>, v.17 (1963), pp.1-66.

ga s 63   )

B-668
Vakil, Chandulal Nagindas, 1895- and Mehta, Usha.
Government and the governed: a study in social tensions. Bombay, Vora & co., 1956. 114p.

1. Social survey - Bombay.

/Social reform & social change

B-669
Acharya, Hemalata N.
Nasik through a century: a study in social change. Poona, Deccan College, 1966. *

Jayakar Lib.

B-670
Agarwala, B.R.
Nature and extent of social change in a mobile-commercial community (Marwadis of Rajasthan in Bombay City), SB, v.11 (1962), pp.141-45.

5B

B-671
Ambedkar, Bhimrao Ramji, 1892-1952.
Thus spoke Ambedkar. Ed.by Bhagwan Das. Jullundur, Bheem Patrika Prakashan, 1969. 2v.

Indian Books Register

B-672
Anantram Iyer, Indira.
Agencies of rural development with special reference to village panchayats, village cooperatives and village schools in the Kalyan and Navsari development blocks. Bombay, Univ.of Bombay, 1964. *

Sociology BDD

B-673
Apte, Mahadeo Laxman.
Lokahitavadi and V.K.Chiplunkar: spokesmen for change in nineteenth-century Maharashtra, MAS, v.7 (1973), pp.193-208.

B-674
Ballhatchet, Kenneth.
Social policy and social change in western India, 1817-1830. London and New York, Oxford University Press, 1957. (London oriental series, v.5). 442p.

UofR

B-675
Bedekar, Dinkar Keshav, 1910-
Social thought in Maharashtra, JUP, v.15 (1962), pp.135-37.

JaS '68

B-676
Cabinetmaker, Perin Hormasji.
Some observations of social changes in camps for displaced persons, JASB, v.10 (1958), pp.27-44.

B-677
Chandavarkar, Ganesh L.
Maharshi Karve. Bombay, Popular Book Depot, 1958. 228p.

1. Karve, Dhondo Keshav, 1858-1962. 2. Women in India.

UofR MQ

B-678
Chapekar, Narayan Govind.
Social change in rural Maharashtra. In:
Professor Ghurye felicitation volume.
Ed.by K.M.Kapadia. Bombay, Popular
book depot, 1954. pp.169-82.

U of R

B-679
Devadhar, Gopal Krishna, 1871-1935.
A paper and discussion of Mr. Gokhale's
Servants of India Society and its work.
Guilford imprint, 1919. 24p.

IOL

B-680
Ghurye, Govind Sadashiv, 1893-
Social change in Maharashtra, SB, v.1
(1952), pp.71-86; v.3 (1954), pp.42-60.

Surer

B-681
Gune, Vithal Trimbak.
The social development in Maharashtra,
A.D.1400 to 1800. In: Professor P.K.Gode
commemoration volume. Ed.by H.L.Hariyappa
and M.M.Patkar. Poona, Oriental Book
Agency, 1960. pp.147-50.

U of R

B-682
Harper, Edward B.
Social consequences of an "unsuccessful"
low caste movement. In: Social mobility
in the caste system in India. Ed.by James
Silverbert. The Hague, 1968. pp.36-65.

Caste + Communalism
BAS Apr 1970

B-683
Jagirdar, Prabhakar Janardan, 1904-
Studies in the social thought of M.G.Ranade.
Bombay, N.Y., Asia Pub.House, 1963. 154p.

U of R

B-684
Jagirdar, Prabhakar Janardan, 1904-
Western elements in the social thought of
Mahadeo Govind Ranade. IJPS, v.23 (1962),
pp.179-84.

Jaipur

B-685
Jatava, Daya Ram, 1933-
The social philosophy of B.R.Ambedkar.
Agra, Agra University, 1965. 277p.

JAS '65

B-686
Joshi, Laxmanshastri.
Jyotirao fule, 1827-1890, rationalists of
Maharashtra. Calcutta, Indian Renaissance
Institute, 1962.

x Pc

B-687
Karkaria, Rustomji Pestonji, 1869-1919.
India: forty years of progress and
reform. Being a sketch of the life and
times of Behramji M.Malabari. London,
M.Frowde, 1896. 151p.

U of R

B-688
Karve, Irawati (Karmarkar) 1905-1970.
The social dynamics of a growing town and
its surrounding area. Poona, Deccan College,
1965. (Deccan College building centenary
and silver jubilee series, 29) 324p.

4 of R

B-689
Karve, Irawati (Karmarkar), 1905-1970.
Some studies in the making of a culture
pattern. In: Essays in anthropology
presented to Rai Bahadur Sarat Chandra
Roy. Ed.by J.P.Mills, et al., 1941. pp.
206-14.

B-690
Keer, Dhananjay, 1913-
Mahatma Jotirao Phooley, father of our social
revolution. Bombay, Popular Prakashan, 1964.
298p.

U of R

B-691
Kumar, Ravinder.
The new Brahmans of Maharashtra. In: Sound-
ings in modern South Asian history. Ed.by
D.A.Low. Berkeley, Univ.of Californin Press,
1968. pp.95-130.

B-692
McDonald, Ellen E.
English education and social change in
late nineteenth century Bombay, 1858-1958.
Berkeley, Univ.of California, 1965. *

B-693
McDonald, Ellen E.
English education and social reform in
late nineteenth century Bombay: a case study
in the transmission of a cultural ideal,
JAS, v.25 (1966), pp.453-70.

JAS

B-694
Menant, Delphine, 1850-
Un réformateur parsi dans l'histoire con-
temporaine de l'Inde: Behramji M.Malabari;
trad.de l'anglais d'après M.Dayaram Gidumal...
préface de J.Menant. Paris, Ernest Flammarion,
1898. 406p.

Bibliothèque Nationale
(XII E I 64,700)

B-695
Orr, James Peter.
Social reform and slum reform. Bombay,
1917. 2 pts.
Pt.1 - General.
Pt.2 - Bombay Past and Present.

BM

B-696
Patwardhan, Sunanda Padmakar.
Changing religious behaviour and traditions
of scheduled castes. In: Deccan College
Research Institute. Bulletin. v.28, (1967/68),
pp.54-65.

Literature-articles
R DC 1970

B-697
Pethe, Vasant P.
Spatial-occupational mobility between three
generations in rural households, AV, v.4
(1962), pp.253-62.

NYPL

B-698
    Sahiar, Gooloo H.
        Social change with particular reference to
        the Parsi community. Bombay, Univ.of Bombay,
        1956. *

Siner

*Social science bibliography-
India 1956-Sociology, p.13*

B-699
    Sahiar, Gooloo H.
        Social change with particular reference
        to the Parsi community, JUB, v.24 (1956),
        pp.47-49.

*Social Science Bibliography-
India 1956-Sociology p.14*

B-700
    Sovani, Nilkanth Vitthal and Pradhan, Kusum.
        Occupational mobility in Poona City
        between three generations, IER, v.2 (1955),
        pp.23-26.

Furer

B-701
    Tope, Trimbak Krishna.
        Dr.B.R.Ambedkar, a symbol of social revolt.
        New Delhi, Maharashtra Information Centre,
        1964.

Urban life & Urbanization

B-702
    Acharya, Hemalata N.
        Nasik: a socio-cultural study, JASB, v.14,
        no.1 (1969), pp.51-65.

B-703
    Acharya, Hemalata N.
        Urbanizing role of a one-lakh city, SB,
        v.5 (1956), pp.89-101.

*Social science bibliography-
India 1956-Sociology, p.13*

B-704
    Arunachalam, B., 1933-
        Bombay City: stages of development, BGM,
        v.3 (1955), pp.34-39.

ease

B-705
    Barve, Sadashiv Govind, 1914-1967.
        Urbanization in Maharashtra state:
        problems and a plan of action. In:
        Seminar on urbanization in India.
        Berkeley, University of California
        Press, 1962. pp.347-60.

B-706
    Bulsara, Jal Feerose, 1899-
        Bombay's unplanned growth. CA, v.13
        (1966), pp.23-31.

gas'66

B-707
    Bulsara, Jal Feerose, 1899-
        Patterns of social life in metropolitan
        areas: with particular reference to
        Greater Bombay. Bombay, 1970. (New
        Delhi, Research Programmes Committee,
        Planning Commission, Govt.of India; dis-
        tributors: Bhatkal Books International).
        456p.

B-708
Desai, Akshayakumar Ramanlal.
    A profile of an Indian slum. Bombay,
University of Bombay, 1972. 282p.

B-709
Desai, K.G. and Naik, R.D.
    Problems of retired people in Greater Bombay.
Bombay, Tata Institute of Social Sciences,
1974. 195p.

B-710
Dharmarajan, S.
    Bombay's shanty towns, CA, v.16,no.8 (1969),
pp.13-14,25.

B-711
Dikshit, Kamal.
    City of Bombay: a study in urban geography.
Poona, Univ.of Poona, 1961. 2v. *

B-712
Dixit, K.R.
    The city of Sholapur; a brief study of some
aspects of its urban geography, MSUBJ, v.8
(1959), pp.51-66.

B-713
D'Souza, J.B.
    Urban development in Marathwada, JMaU, v.5,
no.2 (1965), pp.37-45.

B-714
Edwardes, Stephen Meredyth, 1873-1927.
    By-ways of Bombay. 2d ed. Bombay, D.B.
Taraporevala sons & co., 1912. 139p.

B-715
Ellefsen, Richard A.
    City-hinterland relationships in India.
With special reference to the hinterlands
of Bombay, Delhi, Madras, Hyderabad, and
Baroda. In: Seminar on Urbanization in
India. Berkeley, University of California
Press, 1962. pp.94-116.

U.F.R.
Seminar ✓

B-716
Ezekiel, Nissim, comp.
    Cultural profiles - Poona. Bombay, Inter-
national Cultural Centre, 1961. 99p.

J.BP

B-717
Fielder, Edward J.
    Saving Bombay from ugliness, CA, v.13
(1966), pp.31-35.

JAS 46

B-718

Gandhi, N.K.
A brief study of the Bombay Town Planning
Act of 1954, QJLSGI, v.30 (1960), pp.459-78.

qal '60 O

B-719

Ghurye, Govind Sadashiv, 1893-
Bombay: a brief review of the unofficial
metropolis. In: Cities and civilisation.
By Govind Sadashiv Ghurye. Bombay,
Popular Prakashan, 1962. pp.265-82.

uofR O

B-720

Ghurye, Govind Sadashiv, 1893-
Bombay: a century of metropolitan endeavour
I.& II. In: Cities and civilisation. By
Govind Sadashiv Ghurye. Bombay, Popular
Prakashan, 1962. pp.222-64.

u 3R O

B-721

Ghurye, Govind Sadashiv, 1893-
Bombay suburbanites: some aspects of their
working life, SB, v.13 (1964), pp.73-83.
Continued in v.14 (1965), pp.1-8.

qal 64-65 O

B-722

Gore, M.S.
Immigrants and neighborhoods: two
aspects of life in a metropolitan city.
Bombay, Tata Institute of Social Sciences,
1970. (Tata Institute of Social Sciences
series, 21). 303p.

Urbanization + ...
BAS 1970

B-723

Gouri, Gangadhar Shrishailappa.
Impact of urbanisation on rural economy
with special reference to Bombay State.
Bombay, Univ.of Bombay, 1952. *

Sociology
BDD O

B-724

Jain, N.G.
The emergence of urban centres in the
eastern districts of Vidarbha (Maharashtra),
NGJI, v.10 (1964), pp.146-63.

qal 66 O

B-725

Kaldate, Sudha.
Urbanization and disintegration of rural
joint family (Bombay State), SB, v.11 (1962),
pp.103-11.

Soc Bul O

B-726

Kashyap, A.
Nagpur: a study in city morphology. Nagpur,
Nagpur Univ., 1966. *

Law
BDD

B-727

Lewis, Reba.
Three faces has Bombay. Sketches by
K.K.Hebbir. Bombay, Popular Book Depot,
1957. 234p.

1. India Soc life + cust

U 7R

B-728
Life in Bombay. CR, v.17 (1852), pp.97-113.

Case

(

B-729
Life in Bombay and the neighbouring outstations. London, R.Bentley, 1852. 368p.

42 R

(

B-730
Maharashtra, India (State) Urban Development, Public Health and Housing Dept.
Urban development in Maharashtra: progress and prospect. Bombay, 1967. 177p.

1. Cities & towns - Planning - Maharashtra, India (State)

LC

(

B-731
Malshe, Prabhakar T.
Kolhapur: study in urban geography. Poona, Poona Univ., 1967. 2v. *

(

B-732
Mathure, R.R.
Thana (a study in urban landscape), BGM, v.14 (1966), pp.65-74.

Jas 9/68

(

B-733
Mehta, Surinder K.
Patterns of residency in Poona, India, by caste and religion: 1822-1965, Demography, v.6 (1969), pp.473-91.

Demography-articles
BAS 1969

(

B-734
Modak, S.K.
Nagpur-today and tomorrow - Is restraint on growth necessary, CA, v.15 (1967), pp.13, 15, 17, 19-20.

Jas 9/68

(

B-735
Mody, Maki Shafurji H.
Worli in evolution: a study in city development. Bombay, Univ.of Bombay, 1951. *

Sociology
3 DD

(

B-736
Nagpur Improvement Trust.
Master plan of Nagpur 1953. Nagpur, Madhya Pradesh, Govt.Print., 1954. 39p.

LC accessions 1965 p19

(

B-737
Nayar, Sushila.
Fifty years of town planning in Maharashtra, CA, v.12 (1965), pp.2-5.

Jas '65

(

B-738
Pai, Nagesh Vishvanath.
  Stray sketches in Chakmakpore from the note-
book of an idle citizen. Bombay, Caxton Print.
Works, 1894. 180p.

  1. Bombay - City.

Bom (Pros) cat

B-739
Patel, Freny K.
  Poona: a sociological study. Poona, Univ.
of Poona, 1955. *

Sociology
BDD

B-740
Perspective plan for Bombay metropolitan
region, CA, v.17, no.7 (1970), pp.9-11,
13.

Urbanization + innovation
BAS 1970

B-741
Plan for Poona metropolitan region: some
broad features of draft plan, CA, v.17,
no.12 (1970), pp.9-14, 17.

urbanization +
  modernization
BAS 1970

B-742
Rajagopalan, C.
  Bombay: a study in urban demography and
ecology, SB, v.9 (1960), pp.16-38.

sociology

B-743
Rajagopalan, C.
  An ecological analysis of the growth of
Bombay City, Geografia, v.2 (1963), pp.99-
105.

JAS '64

B-744
Rajagopalan, C.
  The Greater Bombay: a study in suburban
ecology. Bombay, Popular Book Depot, 1962.
233p.

  1. Bombay metropolitan area.

U of R

B-745
Ramachandran, P.
  Kherwadi in transition, IJSW, v.18 (1957),
pp.29-34.

Social Science Bibliography-
India & Pakistan 1957 - 360-361
p. 2

B-746
Rao, Vatsala.
  Rural reactions to urbanization. Bombay,
Univ.of Bombay, 1957. *

Sociology

B-747
Sovani, Nilkanth Vitthal.
  The social survey of Kolhapur City. Poona,
Gokhale Institute of Politics and Economics,
1948-1952. (Pub.of the Gokhale Institute of
Politics and Economics, no.23 & 24). 3v.

U of R

B-748
    Valavalkar, Pandharinath Hari.
    The social effects of urbanisation on
    industrial workers. In: Society in India.
    Ed.by A.Aiyappan and L.K.Bala Ratnam.
    Madras, Social sciences association, 1956.
    pp.149-60.

v√x

B-749
    Valavalkar, Pandharinath Hari.
    Social effects of urbanization on the
    industrial workers in Bombay, SB, v.5
    (1956), pp.29-50,127-43; v.6 (1957), pp.
    14-33.

Vital statistics

B-750
    Bombay (Presidency) Office of the Surgeon
    General.
    Deaths in Bombay during 1851(1865). 18th
    Mortuary Report. 1855-(67). 12parts.

BM

B-751
    El-Badry, M.A.
    An evaluation of the parity data collected
    on birth certificates in Bombay City. HAFQ,
    v.40 (1962), pp.328-55.

JaS 42

B-752
    Gandotra, M.M.
    Standardised birth rate of greater Bombay,
    JFW, v.13 (1967), pp.1-5.

JaS 9/48

B-753
    Pai, D.N.
    Natality and mortality patterns of Bombay
    City. JGRS, v.26 (1964), pp.204-51.

JaS

B-754
    Ranganathan, H.N.
    Recent trends in birth order statistics of
    Poona City. PR, v.9 (1965), pp.82-85.

JaS 44   Women

B-755
    Bachmann de Mello, Hedwig.
    Von der Seele der indischen Frau, im
    Spiegel der Bolkssprüche des Konkan. Trans.
    by Shilavati Ketkar, on the soul of the
    Indian woman. Bastora, India Portuguesa,
    Tip.Rangel, 1941. 467p.

LC

B-756
    Gisbert, P.
    The Warli woman, JASB, v.9 (1955), pp.1-
    24.

Furer

B-757
    Hate, Chandrakala Anandrao, 1903-
    Changing status of women in post-independence
    India. Bombay, Allied Publishers, 1969. 248p.

Sociology & Anthropology — books 37
IAS 1969

Art & architecture

B-758
James, Ralph C.
Discrimination against women in Bombay
textiles. ILRR, v.15 (1962), pp.209-20.

ga s 62

C-1
Boston, Museum of Fine Arts.
Bibliographies of Indian art, by A.K.
Coomaraswamy. Boston, Mass., 1925. 59p.

B-759
Karve, Dhondo Keshav, 1858-
Professor Karve's work in the cause of
Indian women as described by himself. MR,
v.18 (1915), pp.537-46.

Case

C-2
Boston, Museum of Fine Arts.
Catalogue of the Indian collections in the
Museum of Fine Arts, 1923-   3v.

U of R

B-760
Rakshit, Sipra.
Reproductive life of some Maharashtrian
Brahman women, MI, v.42 (1962), pp.139-59.

ga s 62

C-3
Cousens, Henry, 1854-1934, comp.
List of antiquarian remains in the Central
Provinces and Berar. Calcutta, Office of
the Superintendent of Government Printing,
1897. (Archaeological survey of India.
Reports. Imperial series, v.19) 110p.

N Y PL

B-761
Ramabai Sarasvati, pundita, 1858-
The high-caste Hindu woman. 2d ed. Philadelphia, Press of the J.B.Rodgers Print.Co.,
1887. 159p.

u of f   *MR v*

C-4
India (Republic) Office of the Registrar
General.
Bibliography of Indian arts and crafts.
New Delhi, Office of the Registrar General,
India. Ministry of Home Affairs, 1968.
(Census of India, 1961. v.1,pt.11(2).)

B-762
Ramanamma, A.
Position of women in India with special
reference to Poona. Poona, Univ.of Poona,
1969. *

BDD

C-5
Mitra, Haridas.
Contribution to a bibliography of Indian
art and aesthetics. Santiniketan, Visva-
Bharati, 1951. 240p.

N Y R

General

C-6
Aall, Ingrid.
The Ajanta murals: a modern perspective on form and content, ICOP, v.26,pt.3 (1964), pp. 525-28.

C-7
Abbott, Justin Edwards, 1853-1932.
Recently discovered Buddhist caves at Madsur and Nenavali in the Bhor state, Bombay Presidency, IA, v.20 (1891), pp. 121-23.

IA

C-8
Acharya, G.V.
Memorial stones in the Bombay Presidency, AIOCPT, v.3 (1924), pp.237-41.

4 4 R

C-9
Architectural and archaeological remains in Khandesh in 1877. Bombay, 1877.

vv Calcutta Nat'l Lib

C-10
Azevedo, Carlos de.
Arte cristã na India portuguesa. Lisboa, Junta de Investigações do Ultramar, 1959. 156p.

C-11
Banerjee, Jitendra Nath, 1895-
The so-called Trimurti of Elephanta, AA, v.2 (1955), pp.120-26.

C-12
Barrett, Douglas Eric.
A guide to the Buddhist caves of Aurangabad. Bombay, Bhulabhai Memorial Institute, 1957. (Ancient monuments of India, no.3). 46p.

1. Sculpture - Aurangabad, India (Haidurabad)
2. Art, Buddhist   3. Cave temples
NUR
LC

C-13
Barrett, Douglas Eric.
A guide to the Karla caves. Bombay, Bhulabhai Memorial Institute, 1957. (Ancient monuments of India. Karla, no.1). 13p.

NUR
SOAS

C-14
Barrett, Douglas Eric.
A group of bronzes from the Deccan, LK, v.3/4 (1965), pp.39-45.

C-15
Barrett, Douglas Eric.
Painting of the Deccan, XVI-XVII century; with an introd.&notes. London, Faber & Faber, 1958. (Faber gallery of oriental art). 24p.

1. Painting - Deccan, India. 2. Paintings, India.
lot 2

C-16
Barrett, Douglas Eric.
  Some unpublished Deccan miniatures. LK.
  v.7 (1960), pp.9-13.

9865

C-17
Bhagawat, N.K.
  Two symbols from Karad Caves, JUB, v.6
  (1937), pp.41-48.

√√√ JUB

C-18
Birdwood, Sir George Christopher Molesworth,
  1832-1917.
  The inlaid work of Bombay, ASBJ, v.7 (1861-62),
  appendix pp.18 & 21.

India

C-19
Birdwood, Sir George Christopher Molesworth,
  1832-1917.
  Rock-cut elephant from Gharapuri: A
  letter from Sir George Birdwood, ASBJ, v.25,
  no.71 (1917), pp.201-03.

NRU
JRASBom

C-20
Blennerhasset, Arthur.
  The cotton fabrics of the Central Province,
  JIAI, v.17,no.131 (1916), pp.41-44.

India

C-21
Bombay (Presidency)
  Report on the Government Central Museum,
  and on the Agricultural and Horticultural
  Society of Western India for 1863...; being
  the history of the establishment of the Vic-
  toria and Albert Museum and of the Victoria
  Gardens. By George Christopher Molesworth
  Birdwood, 1832-1917. Bombay, 1864. (Bombay
  Presidency. selections from the records, n.s.
  no.83). 175p.

Brit Mus

C-22
Bombay (Presidency)
  Reports on the work of Copying the paintings
  in the caves of Ajanta. By John Griffiths.
  Bombay, 1872-86.

IOL

C-23
Bradley, W.H.
  Buddhist cave temples in the circars of
  Baitalbari and Dowlatabad, in H.H.the Nizam's
  Dominions, ASBJ, v.5 (1953), pp.117-24.

ASBJ

C-24
A brief account of the minor Bauddha caves
  of Beira and Bajah, in the neighbourhood
  of Karli. Communicated in a letter,
  from Mr.Westergaard, to James Bird, Esq.,
  with translations, by the latter, of
  inscriptions found at both, ASBJ, v.1,
  no.7 (1844), pp.439-43.

C-25
Burgess, James, 1832-1916.
  A guide to Elura Cave temples. Hyderabad,
  Archaeological Dept., 194? 70p.

C-26
    Burgess, James, 1832-1916.
      Memorandum on the Buddhist caves at
Junnar, by J.Burgess...and translations
of three inscriptions from Badami,
Pattadkai, and Aiholli, by J.F.Fleet.
Bombay, Govt.Central Press, 1874.
(Archaeological survey of western India.
Old series,no.1). 15p.

u+c+c+
c+c+l+t+s

C-27
    Burgess, James, 1832-1916.
      Provisional lists of architectural and
other archaiological remains in western
India, including the Bombay Presidency,
Sindh, Berar, Central Provinces and
Haidarabad. Bombay, 1875. (Archaeo-
logical survey of western India. Reports.
Old series,no.4). 60p.

f+ 56 imprints

C-28
    Burgess, James, 1832-1916.
      Report on the cave temples and their in-
scriptions. Being part of the 4th, 5th and
6th seasons operations of the Archaeological
Survey of western India, (1876-77, 1877-79).
In: Archaeological Survey of Western India,
vol.4, Varanasi, Indological Book House,
1964.

4 H R

C-29
    Burgess, James, 1832-1916.
      Report on the Elura cave temples and the
Brahmanical and Jaina caves in western India:
completing the results of the fifth, sixth,
and seventh seasons' operations of the
Archaeological Survey, 1877-78, 1878-79,
1879-80. Varanasi, Indological Book House,
1970. (Archaeological survey of western
India, 5). 89p.

BAS 1970

C-30
    Burgess, James, 1832-1916.
      Revised lists of antiquarian remains in
the Bombay Presidency and the native state
of Baroda, Palanpur, Radhanpur, Kathiawad,
Kachh, Kolhapur, and the Southern Maratha
minor states. Rev.by Henry Cousens.
Bombay, 1897. (Archaeological survey of
India. Reports. New imperial series, vol.
XVI). 401p.

C-31
    Chandra, Moti.
      Jain miniature paintings from western
India. Ahmedabad, Sarabhai Manilal Nawab,
1949. (Jain art publication series, no.1).
202p.

U+f 2

C-32
    Chandra, Moti.
      Three Deccani paintings on canvas from the
Right Hon'ble Sir Akbar Hydari collection in
the Prince of Wales Museum of Western India,
JUB, v.7 (1938), pp.108-19.

JuB

C-33
    Chandra, Pramod.
      Elephanta caves, Gharapuri: a pictorial
guide. [rev.ed. Bombay, Bhulabhai Memorial
Instutute; distributors: Madhliso, 1970]
(Ancient monuments of India series, 2).
10p.

Arts architecture - books
BAS 1970

C-34
    Chandra, Pramod.
      A guide to the Elephanta caves. Bombay,
Bhulabhai Memorial Institute, 1957. (Ancient monuments of India, no.2). 15p.

NUR
Le

C-35
    Codrington, Kenneth deBurgh.
      The culture of medieval India as illustrated
by the Ajanta frescoes, IA, v.59 (1930), pp.
159-62, 169-72.

C-36
Couldrey, Oswald Jennings.
   Masterpieces of Deccan rock-sculpture,
GeoM. (1948), pp.337-44.

1. Ellora caves.

IoL

C-37
Cousens, Henry, 1854-1934.
   The architectural antiquities of western
India. London, India Society. 1926.

VV/SO AS

C-38
Cousens, Henry, 1854-1934.
   Conservation of ancient monuments in the
Bombay Presidency, ASBJ, v.21 (1900-05),
pp.149-62.

ASBJ

C-39
Cousens, Henry, 1854-1934.
   Medieval temples of the Dakhan. Calcutta,
Govt.of India central publication branch,
1931. (Archaeological survey of India,
New Imperial series, vol.48). 93p.

UofR

C-40
Czuma, Stanislaw Jerzy.
   The Brahmanical Rashtrakuta monuments of
Ellora. Ann Arbor, Univ.of Michigan, 1968.
711p. *

Shulman

C-41
D'Costa, Anthony.
   The Deccan and Elephanta Island, Indica,
v.2 (1965), pp.47-58.

998 46

C-42
D'Costa, Anthony.
   The Kanheri caves as seen by Dom Joao
De Castro, Indica, v.3 (1966), pp.51-59.

Indica

C-43
Deb, R.
   Pilgrimage to Ajanta and Ellnora, PB,
v.70 (1965), pp.342-50.

JAS '65

C-44
DeBrugh, W.T.
   History of the Elephanta caves, Gharapuri
... Bombay, "Advocate of India" Steam Press,
1901. 19p.

C-45
Dehejia, Vidya.
   The chronology and the development of the
cave architecture of western India (c.200 B.C.
to c.A.D.200). Cambridge, Cambridge Univ.,
1966-67. *

Shulman

C-46
Dehejia, Vidya.
    Early Buddhist caves at Junnar, AA, v.31, no.2/3 (1969), pp.147-66.

Art & architecture—articles
BAS 1969

C-47
Delhi. Lalit Kala Akadami.
    Ajanta painting, 20 plates in colour. New Delhi, Lalit Kala Akadami, 1956. 4p.

LC

C-48
Deo, Shantaram Bhalchandra, 1923-
    A pancanmukha piece from Poona, BDCRI, v.18 (1957), pp.107-109.

BDCRI

C-49
Description of the caves or excavation, on the mountain, about a mile to the eastward of the town of Ellora ..., AsiaRes, v.6 (1809), pp.389-424.

Asiatic +

C-50
Deshpande, M.N.
    Places of Buddhist pilgrimage: rock-cut sanctuaries around Bombay, IAC, v.3 (1954), pp.67-76.

LC accessions

C-51
Deshpande, M.N.
    The rock-cut caves of Pitalkhora in the Deccan, AI, v.15 (1959), pp.66-93.

AI

DS
416
A54

C-52
Deshpande, Yeshwant Khushal, 1884-
    Buddhistic remains in Berar and in ancient Vidarbha, AIOCPT, v.7 (1933), pp.729-30.

U of R

C-53
Dewar, F.
    Silk fabrics of the Central Provinces, JIAI, v.10 (1904), pp.7-12.

India

C-54
Dey, Mukul Chandra.
    My pilgrimage to Ajanta and Bagh. 2d ed. London, 1950. 207p.

IOL

C-55
Dhavalikar, Madhukar Keshav.
    Kailāsa: a jyotirlinga at Ellora, IHQ, v.36 (1960), pp.80-82.

C-56
Dhavalikar, Madhukar Keshav.
    Life in the Deccan as depicted in the Ajanta
paintings. Poona, Univ.of Poona, 1963-64. *

BDRI

C-57
Dhavalikar, Madhukar Keshav.
    New inscriptions from Ajanta, ArsO, v.7
(1968), pp.147-153.

Epigraphy-articles
BAS 1967

C-58
Dhavalikar, Madhukar Keshav.
    A prehistoric deity of western India, Man,
v.5 (1970), pp.131-32.

Archaeology
Man
?.Cx . v.

C-59
Dhavalikar, Madhukar Keshav.
    Sri Yugadhara - a master-artist of
Ajanta, AA, v.31,no.4 (1969), pp.301-
308.

Art and architecture -articles
BAS 1969

C-60
Dikshit, Moreshwar Gangadhar, 1915-
    Fresh light in the Pitalkora Caves, JBHS,
v.6 (1941), pp.112-21.

vvv JBHS

C-61
Dikshit, Moreshwar Gangadhar, 1915-
    Some medieval sculptures from the Konkan,
BPWMWI, v.9 (1964-1965), pp.34-42.

JAS 1/68

C-62
Erskine, William
    Account of the cave-temple of Elephanta,
with a plan and drawings of the principal
figures, LSBT, v.1 (1819), pp.198-250.

C-63
Fabri, Charles.
    Frescoes of Ajanta, Marg, v.8 (1955), pp.
61-76.

Choudhary

C-64
Fergusson, James, 1808-1886.
    History of Indian and eastern architecture.
Rev.& ed.by James Burgess and P.Phene Spiers.
Delhi, Munshiram Manoharlal, 1967. 2v.

U of R

C-65
Fergusson, James, 1808-1886.
    Illustrations of the rock-cut temples of
India: selected from the best examples of the
different series of caves at Ellora, Ajanta,
Cuttack, Salsette, Karli and Mahavellipore.
From sketches made in the years 1838-1839.
London, J.Weale, 1845. 78p.

    1. Temples - India. 2. Caves.

LC

C-66
Fergusson, James, 1808-1886.
Tree and serpent worship: or, illustrations
of mythology and art in India in the first and
fourth centuries after Christ. London, India
Museum, W.H.Allen & co., 1868. 260p.

1. Tree-worship. 2. Serpent-worship. 3.
Art - India. 4. Architecture - India. 5.
Art & mythology.

LC

C-67
Fletcher, W.K.
Of the famous island of Salsette at
Bassein, and of its wonderful pagoda
called Canari; and of the great labyrinth
which this island contains (Coutto's
Decade VII-Book III-Chap.X), ASBJ, v.1,no.1
(1841), pp.34-40.

NA
ASBJ

C-68
Fletcher, W.K.
Of the very remarkable and stupendous
Pagoda of Elephanta (Coutto's decade VII-
Book II-Chapter XI), ASBJ, v.1 (1841), pp.
40-49.

ASBJ

C-69
Gadre, Anant Shankar, 1901-
A rare image of Hanuman, NIA, v.2 (1939),
pp.113-14.

NIA

C-70
Gai, Govind Swamirao, 1917-
On the date of the Ellora plates of
Dantidurga, AIOCPT, v.16 (1951), pp.205-
208. Also in IHQ, v.28,pt.1 (1952), pp.
79-82.

U of R

C-71
Gangoly, Ordhendra Coomar, 1881-
Art of the Rashtrakutas; text and descrip-
tive notes. Comp.and ed.by A.Goswami. New
York, G.Wittenborn, 1958. (Indian sculpture
series, v.3) 31p.

Sculpture - India.

LC

C-72
Ghosh, Manoranjana.
Rock paintings and other antiquities of
prehistoric and later times. Calcutta,
1932. (India. Archaeological Survey.
Memoirs no.24) 28p.

U of R

C-73
Goetz, Hermann, 1898-
Ajanta; portfolio. New Delhi, National
Book Trust, 1964. 5p.

1. Mural painting & decoration - Ajanta.
2. Art, Buddhist. 3. Cave temples.

C-74
Goetz, Hermann, 1898-
The art of the Marathas and its problems.
In: B.C.Law Volume. Ed.by D.R.Bhandarkar
and others.Pt.II. Poona, Bhandarkar
Oriental Research Institute, 1945-46.
pp.433-44.

U of R

C-75
Goetz, Hermann, 1898-
The fall of Vijayanagar and the nationali-
sation of Muslim art in Dakhan, JIH, v.19
(1940), pp.249-55.

JIH

C-76
Goldingham, J.
Some accounts of the cave in the island of Elephanta, AsiaRes, v.4 (1807), pp.407-15.

Asiatic Researches

C-77
Goloubew, Victor.
Documents pour servir à l'étude d'Ajanta, les peintures de la première grotte. Paris et Bruxelles, G.Vanoest, 1927. (Ars asiatica: études et documents pub.par Victor Goloubew...10). 48p.

Paintings - Ajanta = Mural paintings decorate.
3. Cave temples 7. Art, Buddhist = Temple, Buddhist
UofR

C-78
Gough, Richard, 1735-1809.
Comparative view of the ancient monuments of India near Bombay, chiefly those in the Island of Salset described by different writers. London, 1785. 101p.

BM

C-79
Griffiths, John.
The brass and copper wares of the Bombay Presidency. JIAI, v.7 (1897), pp.13-22.

furer

C-80
Griffiths, John.
The paintings in the Buddhist cave-temples of Ajanta, Khandesh, India. London, 1896-1897. 2v.

Paintings - India - Ajanta.
LC

C-81
Gupta, Samarendra Nath.
Classic art of Ajanta, MR, v.16 (1914), pp.63-70.

MR

C-82
Gupta, Balkrishna Atmaram, 1851-
Thana silks, JIAI, v.1 (1884), pp.34-36.

furer

C-83
Gupte, Ramesh Shankar.
The iconography of the Buddhist sculptures (caves) of Ellora. Aurangabad, M.E.Chitnis, Registrar, Marathwada Univ., 1964. 176p.

1. Sculpture - Ellora, India. 2. Art, Buddhist. 3. Cave temples.

LC

C-84
Gupte, Ramesh Shankar.
An interesting panel from Aurangabad, JMaU, v.3,no.2 (1963), pp.59-63.

JMaU

C-85
Gupte, Ramesh Shankar.
A note on the first Brahmanical cave of the Aurangabad group, JMaU, v.1,no.1 (1961), pp.173-76.

JMaU

C-86
Gupte, Ramesh Shankar.
Some Buddhist sculptures of Ellora, JMaU,
v.1,no.1 (1961), pp.119-34.

JMaU

C-87
Gupte, Ramesh Shankar.
Some interesting forms of Avalokitesvara
at Ellora, JMaU, v.2,no.1 (1961), pp.145-
58.

JMaU

C-88
Gupte, Ramesh Shankar and Mahajan, B.D.
Ajanta, Ellora and Aurangabad caves. With
15 illus.in colour, 334 in monochrome half-
tone and 58 line drawings. 1st ed. Bombay,
D.B.Taraporevala, 1962. 308p.

1. Art - Ajanta. 2. Art - Ellora, India.
3. Art - Aurangabad, India (Haidarabad) 4.
Cave temples. 5. Art, Buddhist.

u & R

C-89
Gupte, Y.R., 1881-
Inscriptional, architectural and sculptural
value of the Pandava-Lene caves at
Nasik. In: Mahamahopadhyaya Prof.
D.V.Potdar sixty-first birthday commem-
oration volume. Ed.by Surendra Nath
Sen. Poona, 1950. pp.284-92.

C-90
Gupte, Y.R., 1881-
The marriage of Siva and Parvati as
depicted in the main cave at Elephanta,
BISMHM, (1928), pp.27-28.

C-91
Gupte, Y.R., 1881-
The peculiarities of the art of Ajanta.
In: Professor P.K.Gode commemoration volume.
Ed.by H.L.Hariyappa and M.M.Patkar. Poona,
Oriental Book Agency, 1960. pp.151-54.

U of R

C-92
Hyderabad, India (State) Archaeological Depart-
ment. Committee for the Preservation and
Maintenance of Ajanta and Ellora Caves.
Report... Secunderabad, 1949. 2v.in 1.

U & R

C-93
India. Curator of Ancient Monuments.
Preservation of national monuments, Bombay
Presidency. Ahmedabad. Poona. Karli. Am-
barnath. Elephanta. 5th July 1881. Pre-
liminary report by Captain H.H.Cole...
Curator of ancient monuments in India...
Simla, Government central branch press,
1881. (Preservation of National Monuments,
Bombay Presidency).

C-94
India (Republic) Ministry of Transport, Tour-
ist Division.
Cave temples of western India. New Delhi,
Tourist Division, Ministry of Transport, 1956.
32p.

SOAS

C-95
India Society.
Ajanta frescoes; being reproductions in colour
and monochrome of frescoes in some of the caves
at Ajanta after copies taken in the years 1909-
1911 by Lady Herringham and her assistants.
London, New York [etc.] H.Milford, Oxford Univ.
Press, 1915. 28p.

C-96
Indian art. Bruxelles, Galerie Veranneman,
1970. 68p.

Bom (Pres) cat

C-97
Kanade, S.G.
Wonders of the Bor Ghat; or, cave temples
at Kârlâ and Bhâjâ. Poona, 1937. 16p.

IOL

C-98
Katare, Sant Lal.
An inscribed sculpture inspired by Hala's
Gathasaptaśati. IHQ, v.28 (1952), pp.379-85.

Index to IHQ

C-99
Kramrisch, Stella, 1898-
The image of Mahadeva in the cave-temple
on Elephanta Island, AI, v.2 (1946), pp.1-3.

AI

C-100
Kramrisch, Stella, 1898-
A survey of painting in the Deccan. Hydera-
bad, Archaeological Dept., H.E.H.The Nizam's
Govt., 1937. 247p.

1. Painting - Deccan, India.

C-101
Krishnanath Raghunathji.
The Hindu temples of Bombay (containing
descriptions of temples from nos.73-92).
Bombay, Fort Print.Press, 1899. 44p.

Bom (Pres) cat

C-102
Krishnanath Raghunathji.
The Hindu temples of Bombay (from nos.94-
156). Bombay, Fort Print.Press, 1899. 50p.

Bom (Pres) Cat

C-103
Krishnanath Raghunathji.
The Hindu temples of Bombay (from nos.157-
224). Bombay, Fort Print.Press, 1899. 50p.

C-104
Krishnanath Raghunathji.
The Hindu temples of Bombay (from nos.225-
270). Bombay, Fort Print.Press, 1899. 50p.

Bom (Pres) cat

C-105
Krishnanath Raghunathji.
The Hindu temples of Bombay (from nos.271-
297). Bombay, Fort Print.Press, 1900. 51p.

Bom (Pres) Cat

C-106
Krishnanath Raghunathji.
    The Hindu temples of Bombay (from nos.298-325). Bombay, Fort Print.Press, 1900. 48p.

Bom (Pres) cat

C-107
Krishnanath Raghunathji.
    The Hindu temples of Bombay (from nos.326-363). Bombay, Fort Print.Press, 1900. 35p.

Bom (Pres) cat

C-108
Krishnanath Raghunathji.
    The Hindu temples of Bombay (from nos.364-403). Bombay, Fort Print.Press, 1900. 146p.

Bom (Pres) cat

C-109
Krishnanath Raghunathji.
    The Hindu temples of Bombay, Bhuleshwar and Mahalakshumi groups (containing descriptions of temples, from nos.56-73). Bombay, Fort Print.Press, 1899. 33p.

Bom (Pres) cat

C-110
Krishnasvami Aiyangar, Sakkottai, 1871-
    The great Siva image at elephanta, NIA, Extra series 1 (1939) - A Volume of Eastern and Indian Studies presented to Professor F.W. Thomas...on his 72 birthday. Ed.by S.M.Katre and P.K.Gode, pp.215-25.

School of Oriental & African Studies

C-111
Kundangar, K.G.
    Notes on Shri Maha-Lakshmi temple of Kolhapur. Kolhapur, 19-   44p.

JBHS v 4,no.2

C-112
Lal, B.B.
    Studies in early and mediaeval Indian ceramics, some glass and glass-like artifacts from Bellary, Kolhapur, Maski, Nasik and Maheshwar. BDCRI, v.14 (1952), pp.48-58.

BDCRI

C-113
Levine, Deborah Brown.
    Aurangabad: a stylistic analysis, ArtAs, v.28 (1966), pp.175-204.

Qas 66

C-114
Macneil, Hector.
    An account of the caves of Cannara, Ambola, and Elephanta, in the East Indies, Archaeologia, v.8 (1786), pp.251-89.

Archaeologia

C-115
Majumdar, Manjulal Ranchhodlal, 1897-
    Specimens of arts allied to painting from Western India, NIA, v.1 (1938), pp.377-82.

NIA

C-116
Mandlik, Vishvanath Narayan, 1833-1889.
Notes on the shrine of Mahabales'vara,
ASBJ, v.10 (1871-74), pp.1-18.

ASBJ

C-117
Mate, Madhukar Shripad.
Deccan woodwork. Poona, Deccan College
Postgraduate Research Institute, 1967.
(Deccan College building centenary and
silver jubilee series, 49)

on order

C-118
Mate, Madhukar Shripad.
Islamic architecture of the Deccan, BDCRI,
v.22 (1961/62), pp.1-91.

JAS 64

C-119
Mate, Madhukar Shripad.
Maratha architecture, 1650 A.D. to 1850
A.D. Poona, Univ.of Poona, 1959. 140p. *

C-120
Mate, Madhukar Shripad.
A note on some wall patterns, BDCRI, v.21
(1962-63), pp.23-30.

NRU

C-121
Mate, Madhukar Shripad.
Revisited and revised, ASBJ, n.s.,v.36/37
(1961/62), pp.63-66.

On Ajanta - Ellora caves.

JAS '64

C-122
Mate, Madhukar Shripad.
Temples and legends of Maharashtra.
Bombay, Bharatiya Vidya Bhavan, 1962.
(Bhavan's book university, 97). 240p.

UofR

C-123
Mishra, V.
Unique painting in Tulja caves at Padali
(Junnar), JIH, v.18 (1960), pp.189-92.

JIH

C-124
Mitra, Asok.
The Ajanta and Bagh styles, IFR, v.3
(1966), pp.10-13, 15.

JAS '66

C-125
Mitterwallner, Gritti von.
Chaul: eine unerforschte stadt an der
Westküste Indiens. Berlin, De Gruyter,
1964. (Neue Münchner Beiträge zur Kunst-
geschichte, Bd.6). 282p.

NRU

C-126
Moeller, M.E.
An Indo-Portuguese embroidery from Goa, <u>GBA</u>,
v.34 (1948), pp.117-32.

u f R (GBA)

C-127
Mukherjee, D.P.
The Mahar handprints. A preliminary report,
<u>CS</u>, v.31 (1962), pp.66-67.

NRU
Fürer

C-128
Naik, A.V.
Structural architecture of the Deccan,
<u>NIA</u>, v.9 (1947), pp.188-329.

NIA

C-129
Neff, M.H.
The place of the Elephanta cave temples in
Indian art. London, Oxford Univ., 1956-57. *

C-130
Nilsson, Sten Ake, 1936-
European architecture in India, 1750-1850.
New York, Taplinger Pub.Co., 1968. 214p.

4 f R

C-131
Pal, Ahil Chandra.
A study of the pottery of the Jorwe culture
of Maharashtra. London, Univ.of London, 1969. *

Shulman # 457

C-132
Pal, Anjali.
Jatak tales from the Ajanta mural. Bombay,
Indian Book House, 1969.

IB '69

C-133
Pingree, David.
The Indian iconography of the Deccan and
Hōras, <u>JWCI</u>, v.26 (1963), pp.223-54.

JAS 1.3

C-134
Pratinidhi, Bhavanarao.
The art of Ajanta. In: Har Bilas Sarda
commemoration volume; presented on the
occasion of his completing seventy
years. Ed.by P.Seshadri. Ajmer, Vedic
Yantralaya, 1937. pp.350-52.

C-135
Pyke, Captain.
Account of a curious pagoda near Bombay,
<u>Archaeologia</u>, v.7 (1785), pp.323-32.

Archaeologia

C-136
Raikar, Y.A.
   The so-called hemadpanti temples in Maharashtra. In: Studies in Indian history, Dr.A.G. Pawar felicitation volume. Ed.by V.D.Rao. Kolhapur, Y.P.Pawar, 1968. pp.258-65.

C-137
Ravenshaw, C.W.
   Bombay pottery (glazed), JIAI, v.2 (1888), pp.2-3.

C-138
Ray, Amita.
   Aurangabad sculptures. Calcutta, Firma K.L.Mukhopadhyay, 1966. 49p.

   1. Sculpture - Aurangabad, India.

C-139
Salt, Henry
   Account of the cave in Salsette, illustrated with drawings of the principal figures and caves, LSBT, v.1 (1819), pp.41-52.

C-140
Sama Rao, P.
   The Ajanta tradition, PB, v.69 (1964), pp.393-95.

C-141
Sama Rao, P.
   Painting at Ajanta, PB, v.69 (1964), pp.115-22.

C-142
Sankalia, Hasmukhlal Dhirajlal, 1908-
   A unique VI century inscribed sati stele from Sangsi, Kolhapur State, BDCRI, v.9 (1948), pp.161-66.

C-143
Sareen, Tilak Raj.
   Conservation of Ajanta caves, MR, v.112 (1962), pp.226-29.

C-144
Sastri, Hirananda.
   A guide to Elephanta. Delhi, Manager of Publications, Govt.of India, 1934. 81p.

C-145
Seely, John Benjamin.
   The wonders of Elora; or, the narrative of a journey to the temples and dwellings excavated at Elora, in the East Indies. London, Printed for G.& W.B.Whittaker, 1824. 575p.

C-146
Sengupta, R.
A guide to the Buddhist caves of Elura.
Bombay, Bhulabhai Memorial Institute, 1958.
(Ancient Monuments of India, no.4) 32p.

C-151
Sengupta, R.
The Yajñaśālā of Kailāsa at Ellora and identification of some of its sculptures, IHQ, v.36
(1960), pp.58-67.

Index to IHQ

C-147
Sengupta, R.
Icongraphic notes on some Buddhist sculptures
at Ellora, IHQ, v.34 (1958), pp.187-92.

IHQ

C-152
Sinclair, William F
Notes on the cave of Panchalesvara in
Mouje Bhamburde, Taluka Haveli, Zilla Poona,
IA, v.6 (1877), pp.98-99.

IA

C-148
Sengupta, R.
An interesting representation of Avalokitesvara from Ellora, JMaU, v.1,no.1 (1961),
pp.135-39.

JMaU

C-153
Singh, Madanjeet.
Ajanta; Ajanta painting of the sacred and
the secular. New York, Macmillan, 1965. 189p.

LJR

C-149
Sengupta, R.
The panels of Kalyanasundaramurti at Ellora,
LK, v.7 (1960), pp.14-18.

Ja S 65

C-154
Singh, Madanjeet.
The cave paintings of Ajanta. London,
Thames and Hudson, 1965. 189p.

LC

C-150
Sengupta, R.
Repairs to the Ellora caves, AI, v.17
(1961), pp.46-67.

AI

C-155
Singh, Madanjeet.
India; paintings from Ajanta caves. New
York, New York Graphic Society, 1954. 10p.

U of R

C-156
Sinha, Sri Krishna, 1920-
Deccani architecture in the history of
India, NO, v.5 (1966), pp.73-75.

ga8 66   O

C-157
Sircar, Dineschandra, 1907-
Inscription in cave IV at Ajanta, EI,
v.33 (1960), pp.259-62.

ga8 61   O

C-158
Sohoni, Shridhar V.
The great temple at Elephanta, JUB, v.5
(1936), pp.30-35.

JU B   O

C-159
Solomon, William Ewart Gladstone, 1880-
Bombay and revival of Indian art, AL,
v.1 (1925), pp.11-22.

Clase   O

C-160
Solomon, William Ewart Gladstone, 1880-
Mural paintings of the Bombay school. Bombay,
The Times of India Press, 1930. 125p.

1. Mural painting and decoration.

LC   O

C-161
Soundara Rajan, K.V.
On the chronology of Ellora caves, JMaU,
v.2,no.1 (1961), pp.138-44.

JMaU   O

C-162
Spink, Walter.
Ajanta to Ellora. Bombay, Pub.by Marg Pubs.
for the Center for South and Southeast Asian
Studies, Univ.of Michigan, 1967. 67p.

1. Cave temples. 2. Art, Buddhist - Ajanta.

LC   O

C-163
Spink, Walter.
Ajanta's chronology: the problem of cave
eleven, ArsO, v.7 (1968), pp.155-68.

Art & architecture—articles
EAS 1969

C-164
Spink, Walter.
History from art history: monuments of the
Deccan, ICOP, v.26,pt.3 (1964), pp.789-91.

U of R   )

C-165
Stevenson, John, 1798-1858.
Parting visit to the Sahyadri caves,
ASBJ, v.5 (1853), pp.426-29.

ASB   )

C-166
    Stevenson, John, 1798-1858.
        The theory of the great Elephanta caves,
    ASBJ, v.4, no.16 (1852), pp.261-75.

ASBJ

C-167
    Sykes, William Henry, 1790-1872.
        An account of the caves of Ellora, LSBT,
    v.3 (1823), pp.265-323.

C-168
    Sykes, William Henry, 1790-1872.
        On the three-faced busts of Siva in the
    cave-temples of Elephanta, near Bombay; and
    Ellora, near Dowlatabad, RASGBIJ, v.5 (1838),
    pp.81-90.

VRU
(Markham (microfilm))

C-169
    Tarr, Gary.
        The architecture of the early Western
    Chalukyas. Los Angeles, Univ.of California,
    1969. 548p. *

    Architecture

BAS 1970

C-170
    Taylor, Meadows, 1808-1876.
        Sketches in the Deccan...Drawn on stone
    by Weld Taylor, E.Morton and G.Childs.
    London, Charles Tilt, 1837.

F.M.

C-171
    Tiwari, R.G.
        The Dasavatara cave (no.XV) of Ellora:
    its time, PO, v.26 (1961), pp.24-40.

JAS '62

C-172
    Traditional arts and crafts: Maharashtra,
    BITCM, v.1 (1957), pp.206-08.

Furer

C-173
    United Nations Educational, Scientific and
    Cultural Organization.
        The Ajanta caves; early Buddhist paintings
    from India. New York, New American Library
    of World Literature, 1963. 29p.

    1. Mural painting and decoration - Ajanta.

LC

C-174
    Vakil, Kanaiyalal Hardevram.
        At Ajanta. Bombay, D.B.Taraporevala, 1929.
    82p.

JBHS

C-175
    Vakil, Kanailal Hardevram.
        Rock-cut temples around Bombay; at Elephanta
    and Jogeshwari, Mandapeshwar and Kanheri.
    Bombay, D.B.Taraporevala sons & co., 1932.
    180p.

U of R

C-176
Vakil, Kanaiyalal Hardevram, ed.
Modern art in western India. Bombay. New
Book Co., 1935. 52p.

NYPL

C-177
Welch, Stuart C., Jr.
Mughal and Deccani miniature paintings
from a private collection, ArsO, v.5
(1963), pp.221-33.

C & 65

C-178
West, Edward William, 1824-1905.
Copies of inscriptions from the Buddhist
cave temples of Kanheri etc., in the island
of Salsette, with a plan of the Kanheri caves,
ASBJ, v.6,no.21 (1861), pp.1-14.

ASBJ

C-179
West, Edward William, 1824-1905.
Descriptions of some of the Kanheri topes,
ASBJ, v.6 (1862), pp.116-21.

ASBJ

C-180
West, Edward William, 1824-1905.
Result of excavations in cave 13 at Kanheri,
ASBJ, v.6 (1862), pp.157-61.

ASBJ

C-181
West, Edward William, 1824-1905 and
West, Arthur J.
Nasik cave inscriptions, ASBJ, v.7 (1861-64),
pp.37-53.

ASBJ

C-182
Wilson, John, 1804-1875.
Memoir on the cave temples and monasteries,
and other ancient Buddhist, Brahmanical, and
Jaina remains of western India, ASBJ, Pt.2,
v.3,no.13 (1850), pp.36-107.

ASBJ

C-183
Wilson, John, 1804-1875.
Second memoir on the cave temples and
monasteries, and other ancient Buddhist,
Brahmanical and Jaina remains of western
India, ASBJ, v.4,no.17 (1853), pp.340-79.

ASBJ

C-184
Yazdani, Ghulam, 1885-
Ajanta; the colour and monochrome reproduc-
tions of the Ajanta frescoes based on photo-
graphy. London, Humphrey Milford, Oxford
Univ.Press, 1930-33. 3v.

Painting - Ajanta.

C-185
Yazdani, Ghulam, 1885-
The wall-paintings of Ajanta, JBRS, v.27
(1941), pp.6-33.

Earth Science and Life Sciences Bibliography & Reference General

D-1
Barnes, H. Edwin.
Handbook to the birds of the Bombay Presidency. Calcutta, 1885. 486p.

D-6
Aitken, Edward Hamilton, 1851-1909.
The common birds of Bombay. 2d ed. Bombay, 1919. 209p.

D-2
Bombay (State)
Gazetteer (rev.series) General - A. Botany: pt.1. Medicinal plants [by S.P.Agharkar] Bombay, 1953-

I OL

D-7
Bombay (Presidency) Prince of Wales Museum of West Indies. Natural History Section. Birds of Bombay and Salsette. By Salim 'Ali and Humayun 'Abd Ul-'Ali. Bombay, 1941.

BM

D-3
Graham, John, 1805-1839.
A catalogue of the plants growing in Bombay and its vicinity. Published under the auspices and for the use of the Agrihorticultural society of western India. Bombay, Printed at the Govt. Press, 1839. 269p.

1. India - Bombay. Botany.

LC

D-8
Carter, H.J.
Geology of the island of Bombay. ASBJ, v.4, no.15 (1852), pp.161-215.

ASBJ

D-4
La Touche, Thomas Henry Digges, 1855-
A bibliography of Indian geology and physical geography. Calcutta, Geological Survey of India, 1917-26.

D-9
Carter, H.J.
On contributions to the geology of central and western India, ASBJ, v.5, no.20 (1855), pp.614-38.

NEU
JRAS Bom

D-5
Mantri, Pandurang Gopal, 1842-1898.
A catalogue of drugs indigenous to the Bombay Presidency, arranged according to Drury's useful plants of India. Bombay, Byculla, Education Society's Press, 1874. 42p.

Cal Nat Lib

D-10
Carter, H.J.
On contributions to the geology of western India, including Sind and Beloochistan, ASBJ, v.6, no.21 (1861), pp.161-206.

ASBJ

D-11
Chitaley, S.D.
Contributions to the knowledge of the Deccan Intertrappean flora of India. Berkshire, Eng., Reading Univ., 1954-55. *

Bloomfield

O

D-12
Cooke, Thedore
The flora of the Presidency of Bombay. London, Taylor and Francis, 1803-1807. 5v.

y of R.

O

D-13
Dalgado, Daniel Gelanio, 1850-1923.
Flora de Goa e Savantvadi. Catalogo methodico das plantas medicinaes, alimentares e industriaes, pelo D.G.Dalgado... (Quarto centenario do descobrimento da India. Contribuiçoes da Sociedade de geographia de Lisboa). Lisboa, Imprensa nacional, 1898. 308p.

LC

O

D-14
Dalzell, Niclo Alexander, 1817-1878 and Gibson, Alexander, 1800-1867.
The Bombay flora; or, short descriptions of all the indigenous plants hitherto discovered in or near the Bombay presidency: together with a supplement of introduced and naturalized species. Bombay, Printed at the Education Society's Press, 1861. 336p.

1. Botany - India - Bombay Presidency
LC

O

D-15
Foote, R. Bruce.
The geological features of the South Mahratta country and adjacent districts, MGSI, no.12 (1876), pp.1-268.

Furer

O

D-16
Galvao da Silva, Manoel.
Observações sobre a historia natural de Goa, feitas no anno de 1784...Publicadas por J.H.da Cunha Rivara. Nova Goa, 1862.

NRC

O

D-17
Graham, John, 1805-1839.
Catalogue of plants collected at Bombay, MJLS, v.4 (1837), pp.178-83.

MJLC

O

D-18
Great Britain. India Office.
The meteorology of the Bombay Presidency. By Charles Chambers. London, 1878.

BM

O

D-19
Karakare, S.G.
Geochemical studies of the Deccan traps. Varanasi, Banaras Hindu University, 1965. 128p.

PL480 '66

)

D-20
Lisboa, José Camillo, 1822?-1897.
A list of some plants undescribed in the "Bombay flora" by Dr.Gibson and Mr.Dalzell, found by A.K.Nairne, Esq.,C.S., ASBJ, v.14, no.37 (1878-80), pp.264-66.

ASBJ

)

D-21
Lisboa, José Camillo, 1822?-1897.
Notes on some plants undescribed in the
"Bombay flora" by Dr.Gibson and Mr.Dalzell,
ASBJ, v.14,no.36 (1878-80), pp.117-46.

ASBJ

D-22
Lisboa, José Camillo, 1822?-1897.
Some plants undescribed in the "Bombay
flora" by Dr.Gibson and Mr.Dalzell, ASBJ,
v.13 (1877), pp.131-51.

ASBJ

D-23
Maharashtra, India (State) Directorate of
Geology and Mining.
Geology and mineral resources of Maha-
rashtra. Nagpur, 1968. 129p.

D-24
Maharashtra, India (State) Directorate of
Publicity.
Minerals in Maharashtra: exploitation pro-
spects. Bombay, 1961. 61p.

1. Mines & mineral resources - India -
Maharashtra (State)

LC

D-25
Mann, Harold Hart, 1872-   and Paranjpe, S.R.
The hot springs of the Ratnagiri District,
ASBJ, v.24 (1915-1917), pp.185-212.

D-26
Mann, Harold Hart, 1872-   and Paranjpe, S.R.
Intermittent springs at Rajapur in the
Bombay Presidency, ASBJ, v.24 (1915-1917),
pp.14-32.

NRO
ASBJ

D-27
Nairne, Alexander Kyd.
The flowering plants of western India.
London, W.H.Allen & co., ltd., 1894. 458p.

LC

D-28
Nichols, Jasper
Remarks upon the temperature of the Island
of Bombay during the years 1803 and 1804,
LSBT, v.1 (1819), pp.4-9.

D-29
Ray, Joges Chandra.
Venkatesh B.Ketkar, MR, v.48 (1930), pp.
497-500.

astronomy

MR

D-30
Roy, Bhabesh Chandra, 1907-
Mineral resources of Bombay, with a
mineral map of Bombay. Bombay, Printed
at the Govt.Central Press, 1951. 146p.

D-31
Santapau, H.
The flora of Khandala on the Western
Ghats of India. Delhi, Manager of Pub-
lications, 1953. (India (Republic)
Botanical Survey. Records, v.16,no.1).
423p.

(series)

LC

E-2
Birdwood, Sir George Christopher Molesworth,
1832-1917.
Catalogue of the economic products of the
Presidency of Bombay; being a catalogue of
the Govt.Central Museum. Division I. Raw
produce (vegetable) Bombay, Printed at the
Education Society's Press, 1962. 377p.

D-32
Talbot, William Alexander.
Forest flora of the Bombay Presidency and
Sind. Poona, 1909. 2 vols.

BM

E-3
Dawson, William Albert, 1924-
An introductory guide to central labour
legislation. Bombay, New York, Asia Pub.
House, 1967. 246p.

U of R

D-33
Talbot, William Alexander.
Trees, shrubs and woody climbers of the
Bombay Presidency. 2d ed. Bombay, Govt.
Central Press, 1902. 410p.

BM

E-4
De Benko, Eugene and Krishnan, Vadakkencherry
Narayan.
Research sources for South Asian studies in
economic development; a select bibliography
of serial publications. East Lansing, Asian
Studies Center, Michigan State University,
1966. (Asian Studies Center occasional paper,
no.4) 108p.

U of R

D-34
Thomson, Robert D.
Sketch of the geology of the Bombay Islands.
MJLS, v.4 (1837), pp.159-77.

Economics | Bibliography & Reference

E-5
Guha, Partha Subir.
Directory of economic research centres in
India. Calcutta, Information Research Aca-
demy, 1972. 426p.

U of R

E-1
Bala-Krishna, 1882-
The economic history of India, materials
for research at Bombay. JBHS, v.1 (1928),
pp.43-64.

Economic history

E-6
Gupta, Giriraj Prasad.
Economic investigations in India; a bibliography of researches in commerce and economics
approved by Indian universities, with supplement, 1966. Agra, Ram Prasad, 1966.

U of R

E-7
    Index to Indian economic journals. (Information Research Academy) Calcutta. v.1, no.1/2, Jan./Jund 1966-

E-8
    India (Republic) Directorate of Economics and Statistics.
    Agricultural economics in India, a bibliography. Delhi, Government of India Press, 1960.

E-9
    India (Republic) Labour Bureau.
    Annotated bibliography of labour research in India, 1955-62. Simla, 1963. (Its Labor Bureau pamphlet series 4) 146p.

E-10
    India (Republic) Ministry of Labour.
    Bibliography on wages. Ed.by P.N.Kaula. New Delhi, 1959. (Its Bibliographical series 5) 76p.

E-11
    India (Republic) Ministry of Labour.
    Bibliography on workers' education. Ed.by P.M.Kaula. New Delhi, Ministry of Labour and Employment, Library, Govt.of India, 1959. (Its Bibliographical series 7) 57p.

E-12
    India (Republic) Ministry of Labour.
    Labour literature; a bibliography, 1951-57. New Delhi, 1957. 327p.

E-13
    India (Republic) Ministry of Labour.
    A select bibliography on labour problems, 1951-57. New Delhi, 195? 30p.

E-14
    India (Republic) Ministry of Labour.
    Trade unionism, a bibliography. New Delhi, 1959. (Its Bibliographical series 8) 71p.

E-15
    Irdian Agricultural Research Institute, Delhi.
    Bibliography of IARI publications, 1905 to 1963; scientific contributions from IARI. New Delhi, 1965. 204p.

E-16
    Kannappan, Subbiah.
    A preliminary bibliography on the labour problems in Indian economic development. Cambridge, Industrial Relations Section, Dept.of Economics and Social Science. Massachusetts Institute of Technology, 1955.

E-17
Keddie, Nikki Reichard, ed.
Annotated bibliography on the economy of India. Annotations by Ravi S. Sharma [and others] Arrangement and editing by Nikki R. Keddie and Elizabeth K. Bauer. Berkeley, Calif., Human Relations Area Files, South Asia Project, University of Calif., 1956. 37p.

U of R

E-18
Maharashtra, India (State) Bureau of Economics and Statistics.
Handbook of basic statistics. Bombay, Govt. of Bombay, 1960-

U of R

E-19
Maharashtra, India (State) Bureau of Economics and Statistics.
Statistical abstract of Maharashtra State. Bombay, 1960/61-

U of R

E-20
Maharashtra, India (State) Directorate of Industries.
Commercial directory of industries in Maharashtra. Bombay, 1962-63. 3v.

NUC

E-21
Men of agriculture and veterinary sciences in India. 1st ed. New Delhi, Premier Publishers, 1965/66-

U of R

E-22
Morris, Morris David and Stein, Burton.
The economic history of India: a bibliographic essay, *JEH*, v.21 (1961), pp.179-207.

E-23
Pathak, H.N.
Select bibliography of articles on India's five year plans. Ahmedabad, New Order Book Co., 1962. 53p.

U of R

E-24
Prasad, Jagdish.
Bibliography of economic books relating to India. Calcutta, Printed at the Banerjee Press, 1923. 64p.

E-25
Rath, Vimal, 1929-
Index of Indian economic journals, 1916-1965. Poona, Gokhale Institute of Politics and Economics; Orient Longman, 1971. 356p.

U of R

E-26
Raychaudhuri, Tapan Kumar.
Some recent writing on the economic history of British India: an essay in bibliography, *CIEH*, v.1 (1960), pp.115-49.

U of R

E-27
A selected bibliography of books and articles
on banking, JIIB, v.38 (1967), pp.64-69,161-
66,264-68,370-74.

E-28
Sethi, Narendra Kumar.
A bibliography of Indian management with
reference to the economic, industrial,
international, labour, marketing, organiza-
tional, productivity and the public administration perspectives. Bombay, Popular
Prakashan, 1967. 132p.

E-29
Sharma, Jagdish Saran, 1924-
Vinoba and Bhoodan: a selected descriptive
bibliography of Bhoodan in Hindi, English
and other Indian languages. New Delhi,
Indian National Congress, 1956. 92p.

E-30
Singhvi, M.L. and Schrimali, D.S.
Reference sources in agriculture; an anno-
tated bibliography. Udaipur, Rajasthan
College of Agriculture, Consumers' Co-Opera-
tive Society, 1962. (R.C.A.Consumers' Co-
Operative Society. Pub.no.1) 428p.

E-31
Sparks, Stanley V. and Shourie, Arun.
Bibliography on development administration,
India and Pakistan. Syracuse, Center for
Overseas Operations and Research, Maxwell
Graduate School of Citizenship and Public
Affairs, Syracuse Univ., 1964. (Maxwell
Graduate School of Citizenship and Public
Affairs, Syracuse University. Pub.no.11)
51p.

U of R   ZHC

E-32
United Nations. E.C.A.F.E.
A selected bibliography of economic planning
in Asia and the Far East, 1952-58. Bangkok,
1959.

E-33
Watt, Sir George, 1851-1930.
A dictionary of the economic products of
India. Calcutta, Superintendent of Govt.
Print, 1889-96. 7v.in 10.

U of R   Agriculture, irrigation
& forestry

E-34
Adhikari, Gopala Govinda.
Food in Bombay Province. Bombay, People's
Pub.House, 1944. 48p.

Bom(Pres) cat

E-35
Agrawal, Ganga Dhar and Khudanpur, G.J.
Methods and practice of farm accounts:
report on the pilot project, Bombay, 1955-
56 and Uttar Pradesh 1956-57. Poona, Gokhale
Institute of Politics and Economics, N.Y.,
Asia Pub.House, 1961. (Gokhale Institute
studies, no.40) 86p.

Agriculture -
accounting
LC

E-36
Amrite, V.G.
Land utilisation in coastal Thana district
(N.Konkan), EGM, v.13 (1965), pp.149-60.

JAS 9/68

E-37
  Apte, D.P. and Mulla, Ghulamdastgir Rahman.
    Comparative costs of lifting water from
  wells; a case study of banana cultivation,
  AV, v.5 (1963), pp.282-95.

E-42
  Bhat, Shridhar Bhaskar.
    Letter of national importance about 80
  years old. IHRCP, v.35 (1960), pp.44-48.

E-38
  Arunachalam, B., 1933-
    Kelye-Mazagaon Valley (Lat.17 5'N.; Long.
  73 18'E.). A study in land-use with reference
  to planning in a part of South Konkan, BGM,
  v.14 (1966), pp.1-20.

JAC 9/68

E-43
  Birdwood, Sir George Christopher Molesworth,
    1832-1917.
    Catalogue of vegetable productions of the
  Presidency of Bombay; including a list of
  drugs sold in the bazars of western India.
  Bombay, Education Society's Press, 1865.
  503p.

E-39
  Badari, V.S.
    Crop constellations in Maharashtra, AV,
  v.8 (1966), pp.382-410.

gas '68

E-44
  Birdwood, Sir George Christopher Molesworth.
    1832-1917.
    The Mahratta plough, AR, series 1, v.6
  (1888), pp.417-72.

E-40
  Barve, Sadashiv Govind, 1914-1967.
    Before the commission of inquiry; Panshet
  and Khadakwasla dams. Poona, Venus Book
  Stall, 1962. 48p.

Ord. not l Bd. '62

E-45
  Birdwood, Sir George Christopher Molesworth,
    1832-1917.
    The Mahratta plough, RSAJ, v.57 (1908),
  pp.897-911, 919-31.

SVA

E-41
  Best, James William, 1882-
    Forest life in India. London, John Murray,
  1935.

    1. Forests & forestry - India - Central
  Provinces. 2. Hunting - India - Central
  Provinces. 3. Central Provinces, India -
  Descr.& trav.

Lc

E-46
  Bombay (Presidency)
    Papers and proceedings connected with the
  passing of the Deccan Agriculturists' Relief
  Act, XVII of 1879, from 6th April, 1877 to
  24th March, 1880. Bombay, 1882. (Bombay
  Presidency, selections from the records, n.s.
  no.157)

IOL

E-47
  Bombay (Presidency)
    Report on project for reclaiming the land
  between Bombay and Trombay. By Walter Mardon
  Ducat. Bombay, 1863. (Selections from the
  records of the Bombay Govt., n.s.,no.68).
  12p.

Brit Mus

E-48
  Bombay (Presidency)
    Selections from the records of the
  Bombay Government. Irrigation series.
  Bombay, 1866-67. No.1-8.

Brit Mus

E-49
  Bombay (Presidency)
    Summary of proceedings connected with
  the Government cotton experiments in the
  Southern Mahratta County, under the Bombay
  Presidency, from 1830 to 1848. Bombay,
  1849.

Brit Mus

E-50
  Bombay (Presidency) Department of Agriculture.
    The crops of the Bombay Presidency: their
  geography and statistics. Bombay, 1922.
  2pts. (Bombay. Department of Agriculture.
  Bulletins, no.109,146).
  Part I by P.C.Patil.
  Part II by G.R.Ambedkar.

IOL

E-51
  Bombay (Presidency) Department of Agriculture.
    Economic value of fruit farming in western
  India. By G.S.Cheema and P.G.Dani. Bombay,
  1928. (Bombay Presidency. Department of
  Agriculture. Bulletins. no.153).

IOL

E-52
  Bombay (Presidency) Department of Agriculture.
    Grape culture in western India. By
  S.R.Gandhi. Bombay, 1930. (Bombay Presidency. Department of Agriculture Bulletin
  no.156).

IOL

E-53
  Bombay (Presidency) Department of Agriculture.
    Grassland problems of western India. By
  W.Burns, L.B.Kulkarni and S.R.Godbole. Bombay,
  1933. (Bombay Presidency. Department of
  Agriculture. Bulletins. no.171).

IOL

E-54
  Bombay (Presidency) Department of Agriculture.
    Groundnuts in the Bombay Deccan. By G.K.
  Kelkar. Bombay, 1911. (Bombay Presidency.
  Department of Agriculture, Bulletin no.41)
  17p.

IOL

E-55
  Bombay (Presidency) Department of Agriculture.
    Improvement of the indigenous plough of
  western India. By S.S.Godbole. Bombay, 1914.
  (Bombay Presidency. Department of Agriculture,
  Bulletin no.57) 19p.

IOL

E-56
  Bombay (Presidency) Department of Agriculture.
    Indigenous implements of the Bombay Presi-
  dency. By G.K.Kelkar. (Bombay Presidency.
  Department of Agriculture, Bulletin no.66)
  106p.

IOL

E-57
Bombay (Presidency) Department of Agriculture.
Irrigation projects for the Bombay Presi-
dency; land in the Paihra (sic) and Godavery
valleys, near Nowassa, in the Ahmednuggur
Collectorate, the Lakh project. By J.F.Fife.
Bombay, 1866. (Bombay Presidency. Selections
from the records, Irrigation series no.3)

IOL

E-58
Bombay (Presidency) Department of Agriculture.
Note on cattle in the Bombay Presidency.
By Gerald Francis Keatinge. Poona, 1917.
(Bombay Presidency. Department of Agriculture,
Bulletin no.85).

Brit Mus
Ind OAP Lib

E-59
Bombay (Presidency) Department of Agriculture.
Note on cattle of the Bombay Presidency.
By G.K.Kelkar. Poona, 1915. (Bombay Presi-
dency. Department of Agriculture, Bulletin,
no.75) 49p.

I OL

E-60
Bombay (Presidency) Department of Agriculture.
Palm gul manufacture in the Bombay Presi-
dency, principally date palm. By V.G.Gokhale.
Poona, 1920. (Bombay Presidency. Department
of Agriculture, Bulletin no.93)

IOL

E-61
Bombay (Presidency) Department of Agriculture.
A paper on irrigation in the Deccan and
southern Maratha country. By J.W.Playfair.
Bombay, 1866. 19p.

IOL

E-62
Bombay (Presidency) Department of Agriculture.
Papers relating to the system of periodical measurements of irrigated lands and
the distribution and economy of water.
Bombay, 1865. (Bombay Presidency. Selections
from the records, n.s.,no.89). 67p.

Ind OAP Lib

E-63
Bombay (Presidency) Department of Agriculture.
Preliminary note on Bombay cottons. By F.
Fletcher. Bombay, 1907. (Bombay Presidence.
Department of Agriculture. Bulletins. no.29)

IOL

E-64
Bombay (Presidency) Department of Agriculture.
Preliminary studies of important crops
in the Bombay Deccan in the post-war
period. By Rao Bahadur, P.C.Patil and
others. Bombay, 1932. (Bombay Presidency.
Department of Agriculture, Bulletin no.
168). 206p.

BM v.171

E-65
Bombay (Presidency) Department of Agriculture.
Sugarcane varieties of Bombay Presidency,
India. By J.B.Knight. Poona, 1925. (Bombay
Presidency. Department of Agriculture. Bul-
letin no.122)

E-66
Bombay (Presidency) Department of Agriculture.
Summary of the work done on a Jalgaon farm.
By P.C.Patil. Poona, 1921. (Bombay Presi-
dency. Department of Agriculture. Bulletin
no.108)

IOL

E-67
    Bombay (Presidency) Department of Agriculture.
    Tobacco cultivation in the southern Maratha
    country. By G.S.Salimath. Poona, 1927. (Bom-
    bay Presidency. Department of Agriculture,
    Bulletin no.140) 13p.

IOL

E-72
    Carroll, G.R.
    Resevoirs on the Dekkan rivers, Bombay,
    1867. 7p.

IOL

E-68
    Bombay (Presidency) Department of Agriculture.
    Well waters from the trap area of western
    India. By H.H.Mann, Poona, 1915. (Bombay
    Presidency. Department of Agriculture. Bul-
    letin no.74).

E-73
    Correspondence with the Bombay government in
    regard to the forest grievances of Thana
    and Kolaba, QJPSS, v.13,no.2 (1890), pp.63-
    69.

E-69
    Bombay (Presidency) Forest Department.
    The Bombay forests. By W.E.Copleston.
    Bombay, 1925.

BM

E-74
    The dams and rivers of Khandesh, BQR, v.5
    (1857), pp.48-73.

E-70
    Bombay (Presidency) Forest Department.
    Report of the Bombay Forest Commission.
    Bombay, 1887. 4v.
    1849-50
    1855-56
    1857-

BM

E-75
    Date, Y.G.
    Geography of foodgrains of Maharashtra,
    BGM, v.14 (1966), pp.21-32.

JAS 9/68

E-71
    Brown, Michael H.
    India need not starve! Bombay, A.W.Barker,
    1944. 199p.

E-76
    Faridunji Jamshedji.
    Notes on the agriculture of the district of
    Aurangabad, H.H.Nizam's dominions. Bombay,
    1879. 120p.

BM

E-77
Forest conservancy in the Bombay Presidency.
QJPSS, v.5,no.3 (1882), pp.1-18.

PSS

E-78
Gadgil, Dhananjaya Ramchandra, 1901-
A brief account of the Deccan Agricultural
Association. Poona, Deccan Agricultural
Association, 1962.

Dhananjaya ...

E-79
Gadgil, Dhananjaya Ramchandra, 1901-
Economic effects of irrigation: report of
a survey of the direct and indirect benefit
of the Godavari and Pravara Canals. Poona,
1948. (Gokhale Institute of Politics and
Economics. Pub.no.17) 130p.

LC

E-80
Gadgil, Madhukar Vasudeo.
Study of water use under some irrigation
tanks in the Bombay Deccan. Poona, Gokhale
Institute of Politics and Economics, 1961. *

Jayakar Lib. #1955

E-81
Gadgil, Madhukar Vasudeo and Kanetkar, B.D.
Some problems of management and pricing
on the irrigation works in Bombay, AV, v.2
(1960), pp.220-29.

JAS '60

E-82
Gibson, Alexander, 1800-67.
Notes on Indian agriculture, as practised
in the Western or Bombay Province of India,
RASGBIJ, v.8 (1846), pp.93-103.

Furer

E-83
Godambe, V.P.
A preliminary report on the sample survey
for assessment of benefits from major irrigation projects in Bombay State, QBES, v.8
(1955), pp.1-79.

*Economic irrigation
social service Bib. 1955*

E-84
Gokhale, V.K.
Land reclamation and prevention of damage
in the canal irrigated tracts of the Bombay
Deccan. Bombay, Univ.of Bombay, 1940. *

E-85
Humfrey, John.
Horse-breeding in the Bombay Presidency.
Bombay, Reprinted from the Times of India,
1885.

E-86
India (Republic) Directorate of Economics &
Statistics.
Maharashtra and Gujarat agricultural statis-
tics. Delhi, Manager of Publications, 1962.
442p.

E-87
  Indian National Congress. Maharashtra Pro-
    vincial Congress Committee.
    Report of the Peasant Enquiry Committee.
  Poona, S.D.Deo, 1936. 107p.

Patterson

E-88
  Joglekar, N.M. and Shingarey, M.K.
    Economics of fertilizer use on the Nagpur
    farm, IJAE, v.20 (1965), pp.61-64.

JaS '65

E-89
  Joshi, Ganesa Venkatesa, rao bahadur, 1851-
    1911.
    Note on agriculture in Bombay, QJPSS, v.17,
    no.2 (1894), pp.1-49.

QJPSS

E-90
  Joshi, Lemuel Lucas.
    The milk problem in Indian cities, with
    special reference to Bombay. Bombay, 1916.
    245p.

BM

E-91
  Kadam, D.B.
    Utilisation of long-term finance for new
    wells. Poona, Univ.of Poona, 1969. *

agricultural credit
BDD

E-92
  Kanetkar, B.D.
    The problem of irrigation use in Maharashtra,
    JUP, v.15 (1962), pp.157-62.

JaS 63

E-93
  Kaul, Satyender Nath.
    A study on dynamics of cotton acreage
    response in Maharashtra Region. Delhi,
    Univ.of Delhi, 1969. *

Industrial economics
agriculture
BDD

E-94
  Keatinge, Gerald Francis, 1872-
    Agricultural progress in western India.
    London, Longmans, Green, 1921. 253p.

    1. Agriculture - India - Bombay (Presidency)

Lc

E-95
  Khandewale, Shrinivas Vishnupant.
    Cotton industry of Vidarbha: an analytical
    study of cultivation, processing and marketing.
    Nagpur, Nagpur Univ., 1970. *

Industrial economics
Secondary industries
BDD

E-96
  Khudanpur, Govind Jivaji.
    Entrepreneurial behavior under conditions
    of scarcity and famine. Case studies of pro-
    duction, marketing and investment decisions
    of farmers in a Deccan village (India).
    Lexington, University of Kentucky, 1967.*
    418p.

Shulman
agriculture & forestry — books
BAS Sept 1970

E-97
Kibe, M.M. and Purank, N.V.
Note on soil conservation survey for land-use planning in Koyna project, Satara, Bombay State, JSWCI, v.6 (1958), pp.176-83.

South Asia Social Science
Bibliography; Economics, p.47

E-102
Lisboa, José Camillo, 1822?-1897.
List of Bombay grasses and their uses.
Bombay, Printed at the Govt.Central Press,
1896. 152p.

1. Gramineae. 2. India - Bombay Presidency - Botany.

LC

E-98
Laud, D.S.
Food supplies of Bombay, QJLSGI, v.7
(1937), pp.89-100.

Case

E-103
Logan, Frenise A.
The American Civil War: an incentive to western India's experiments with foreign cotton seeds. AH, v.30 (1956), pp.35-40.

Case

E-99
Leshnik, Lawrence S.
Early settled farmers in Central India and the Deccan. In: Heidelberg. Universität. Südasien-Institut. Jahrbuch, 1966. Wiesbaden, 1967. pp.43-55.

JAS 9/68

E-104
Maharashtra, India (State). Department of Agriculture.
Ghod river project. 1st ed. Poona, 1970. 57p.

irrigation works,
BAS 1970

E-100
Letter to the government of Bombay on the apprehended deficiency of rainfall, QJPSS, v.14,no.1 (1891), pp.6-8.

QJPSS

E-105
Maharashtra, India (State) Directorate of Publicity.
Power from Koyna; story of a unique project. 4th rev.ed. Bombay, 1962. 20p.

LC

E-101
A letter to the government of Bombay on the Bombay irrigation bill, QJPSS, v.1,no.4 (1878), pp.49-60.

QJPSS

E-106
Maharashtra, India (State) Finance Department. Planning Division.
Report of the evaluation enquiry into the working of intensive cultivation of food crops and pulses in the State of Maharashtra. Bombay, 1968. 93p.

Agriculture & forestry

BAS

E-107
Mann, Harold Hart, 1872-
Rainfall and famine; a study of rainfall in the Bombay Deccan, 1865-1938. Bombay, Pub.by M.B.Desai for the Indian Society of Agricultural Economics, 1955. (Publications of the Indian Society of Agricultural Economics, 16). 47p.

1. Rain & rainfall—India 2. Crop yields. 3. India—famines

E-108
Mann, Harold Hart, 1872-
The social framework of agriculture, India, Middle East, England. Ed.by Daniel Thorner. N.Y., Kelley, 1967. 531p.

1. Villages - India - Addresses, essays, lectures. 2. India - Rural conditions - Addresses, essays, lectures. 3. Agriculture - Economic aspects

E-109
Mann, Harold Hart, 1872-
The sources of the milk supply of Poona City, AJI, v.14 (1919), pp.628-38.

E-110
Mathur, P.N.
Cropping pattern in Vidarbha, IJAE, v.18 (1963), pp.38-43.

E-111
Mohan Rao, Vidyananda.
Changing agrarian pattern in Deccan. Bombay, Univ.of Bombay, 1963. *

E-112
Mohile, V.G.
Agricultural holdings in India with special reference to the Bombay Presidency, JUB, v.1 (1932), pp.65-82.

E-113
Nadkarni, Anand S.
A study of the agricultural income of Maharashtra, 1951-52 to 1958-59. Poona, Univ.of Poona, 1968. *

E-114
Naik, V.P.
Green revolution. MCQ, v.53 (1969), pp.4-6.

E-115
Neill, J.W.
The ryots of the Dekhan, and the legislation for their relief, AR, v.7 (1894), pp.396-419.

E-116
Orenstein, Henry.
Irrigation, settlement pattern and social organisation. In: Men and Cultures. Selected papers of the fifth international congress of anthropological and ethnological sciences, Philadelphia, 1956. Ed.by Antony F.C.Wallace. Philadelphia, University of Pennsylvania Press, 1960. pp.318-323.

E-117
Padhye, M.D.
Size of 'owned' and 'cultivated' holdings in Marathwada, *JMaU*, v.4,no.1 (1963), pp.48-54.

Jmau

E-118
Padhye, S.S.
Climate of the Deccan trap region of Vidarbha. *IGJ*, v.38 (1963), pp.79-98.

gq8'43

E-119
Patil, S.M.
A case study of repayment of crop loans and causes of their non-repayment in Maharashtra State, *IJAE*, v.22 (1967), pp.87-91.

gaß 9/68

E-120
Patvardhan, V.S.
Food control in Bombay Province, 1939-49. Poona, D.R.Gadgil, 1958. (Gokhale Institute of Politics and Economics. Pub.no.36) 226p.

LC

E-121
People's United Food Committee, Bombay & Maharashtra.
For a people's food policy. Issued by the sub-committee, People's United Food Committee, Bombay & Maharashtra, pref.1952.

Wilson

E-122
Raghava Rao, G.
The growth of agricultural production in the Bombay Presidency, *JUB*, v.7 (1939), pp.98-117.

Case

E-123
Ranadive, Bhalchandra Trimbak.
Food in Bombay Province. Bombay, People's Pub.House, 1944. 48p.

BM

E-124
Sabade, B.R.
Tractor-operating costs and performances, on three farms in Kopergaon Taluka, *AV*, v.2 (1960), pp.70-82.

South Asia Social Science Bibliography Economics, P. 93

E-125
Sapre, Sharad Ganesh.
Changes in land utilization and in cropping pattern in an irrigated village over the two decades ending in 1960, *AV*, v.6 (1964), pp.106-16.

UoR

E-126
Sapre, Sharad Ganesh.
A note on the cost of production of milk in Poona, *AV*, v.1 (1959), pp.307-18.

47ß

E-127
Sapre, Sharad Ganesh.
  Study of the dairy industry in Poona.
Poona, Gokhale Institute of Politics and
Economics, 1960. *

Jayakar Lib #1497 (

E-128
Savale, Raghunath S.
  Farm planning and possibilities of capital
accumulation on selected farms in Nasik
District of Maharashtra state, India; an
application of multi-period programming
procedures. Manhattan, Kansas State Univ.,
1964.

Stucki (

E-129
Savale, Raghunath S.
  A multi-period programming model showing
the possibilities of capital formation in
farming in Maharashtra area, IJAE, v.20
(1965), pp.29-38.

IAS '65 (

E-130
Singh, Govind Saran, 1930-
  Agricultural patterns of Maharashtra,
JKU, v.8 (1964), pp.323-35.

JaS 64 (

E-131
Sykes, William Henry, 1790-1872.
  The fishes of the Deekhun, ZST, v.2 (1841),
pp.343-78.

IOL (

E-132
Taylor, Philip Meadows, 1808-1876.
  A statement and remarks relating to the
expenses of irrigation from wells in the
Deccan, Khandesh, etc. Bombay, Printed at
the Bombay Education Press, 1856. 38p.

(

E-133
Telang, M.A. and Chavan, B.W.
  Role of bovine population in Maharashtra's
economy with special reference to milk production, IJAE, v.20 (1965), pp.83-91.

JaS (

E-134
Thorat, Sudhakar Shankar.
  Certain social factors associated with the
adoption of recommended agricultural practices
by rural local leaders and ordinary farmers in
India. East Lansing, Michigan State Univ.,
1966. 133p. *

Shulman #993 (

E-135
Umarji, B.B.
  Farms and holdings in Bombay-Karnatak,
JUB, v.18 (1950), p.107.

JUB (

E-136
Varma, K.N.
  Orange cultivation in Vidarbha, DG, v.2
(1963), pp.63-70.

JaS 64 (

E-137
Vartak, H.G.
Progress in procurement of food grains
in Maharashtra, MCQ, v.53 (1969), pp.107-10.

Food policy-articles
BAS Sept 1970

Cooperative movement

E-138
Acharya, Hemalata N.
Experience of co-operative farming in
Nasik District; a study of four co-operative
farming societies, IJAE, v.13 (1958), pp.
58-65.

LC Accessions 1957
p. 126

E-139
Anekar, R.B.
An economic survey of the co-operative
sugar factories in Maharashtra (1963-64).
Gwalior, Jiwaji Univ., 1970. *

E-140
Apte, J.S.
Cooperative movement among the tribals of
district Thana, Bombay State, Vanyajati, v.8
(1960), pp.102-104.

E-141
Bapat, N.V.
Cooperative finance in Berar with particu-
lar reference to agriculture. Nagpur, Nagpur
Univ., 1959. *

Credit cooperatives
BDD

E-142
Bapat, V.S.
Co-operative publicity in Maharashtra,
AICR, v.28 (1963), pp.667-69.

JAB 63

E-143
Baviskar, Baburao Shravan.
Co-operatives and castes in Maharashtra;
a case study, SB, v.18,no.2 (1969), pp.148-
66.

SB

E-144
Baviskar, Baburao Shravan.
A sociological study of a cooperative
sugar factory in rural Maharashtra. Delhi,
Univ.of Delhi, 1970. *

Sociology - Industrial
BDD

E-145
Belge, Madhukar Wamanrao.
Cooperative farming in Maharashtra. Nagpur,
Nagpur Univ., 1969. *

Industrial cooperatives
BDD

E-146
Bhalerao, Madhukar Mahadeo.
Economics of service cooperatives in
Jalgaon District. Maharashtra. Varanasi,
Banaras Hindu Univ., 1967. *

Cooperation
BDD

E-147
  Bombay (State)
    Fifty years of cooperation in the Bombay
  State. Bombay, Printed at the Govt.Central
  Press, 1957. 361p.

LC แผนงาน 1959 ที่ 9

E-148
  Candidus, pseud.
    The Maharashtra Co-operative Societies Act:
  an objective study, MCQ, v.47 (1963), pp.92-
  100.

JaS 63

E-149
  Candidus, pseud.
    Some thoughts on consumers' co-operation
  in Maharashtra State, MCQ, v.47 (1963),
  pp.3-13.

E-150
  Chinmulgund, P.J.
    Cooperative farming in Bombay, AICR, v.20
  (1954), pp.151-54.

E-151
  Co-op Industries Commission in Maharashtra:
  a review of its work, AICR, v.28 (1963),
  pp.647-80.

JaS 63

E-152
  Co-operative Maharashtra. Bombay, Service
  Pubs. annual.

    1. Cooperation - Maharashtra, India (State) -
  Period. 2. Copperative societies - Maharashtra,
  India (State) - Period.

LC

E-153
  Deshpande, Shridhar Atmaram.
    Co-operative rice mills in Vidarbha, AV,
  v.7 (1965), pp.232-47.

JaS '65

E-154
  Driver, Pesy N.
    Co-operation in the canal tracts of the
  Deccan, JUB, v.2 (1933), pp.101-31.

JUB

E-155
  Gadgil, Dhananjaya Ramchandra, 1901-
    Sugar co-operatives in Mah-rashtra. New
  Delhi, National Federation of Co-operative
  Sugar Factories Ltd., 1965.

Dhananjaya

E-156
  Ghorpade, Jaisingh Vishwasrao.
    A study of relative effectiveness of joint
  stock and cooperative sugar factories located
  in Maharashtra, India. Los Angeles, Univ.of
  California, 1968. 304p. *

Shulman

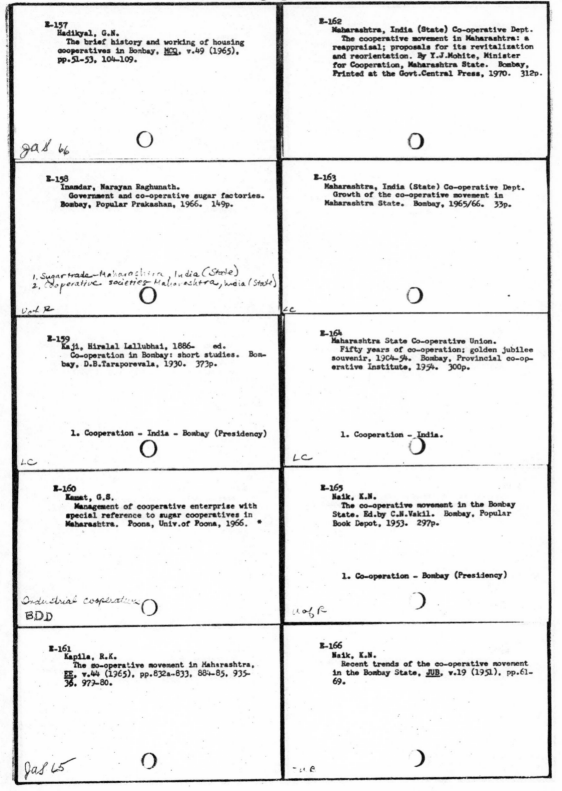

E-157
Hadikyal, G.N.
The brief history and working of housing cooperatives in Bombay. MCQ. v.49 (1965). pp.51-53, 104-109.

Jas 66

E-162
Maharashtra, India (State) Co-operative Dept.
The cooperative movement in Maharashtra: a reappraisal; proposals for its revitalization and reorientation. By Y.J.Mohite, Minister for Cooperation, Maharashtra State. Bombay, Printed at the Govt.Central Press, 1970. 312p.

E-158
Inamdar, Narayan Raghunath.
Government and co-operative sugar factories. Bombay, Popular Prakashan, 1966. 149p.

1. Sugar trade—Maharashtra, India (State)
2. Cooperative societies—Maharashtra, India (State)

Vol R

E-163
Maharashtra, India (State) Co-operative Dept.
Growth of the co-operative movement in Maharashtra State. Bombay, 1965/66. 33p.

LC

E-159
Kaji, Hiralal Lallubhai, 1886-   ed.
Co-operation in Bombay: short studies. Bombay, D.B.Taraporevala, 1930. 373p.

1. Cooperation - India - Bombay (Presidency)

LC

E-164
Maharashtra State Co-operative Union.
Fifty years of co-operation; golden jubilee souvenir, 1904-54. Bombay, Provincial co-operative Institute, 1954. 300p.

1. Cooperation - India.

LC

E-160
Kamat, G.S.
Management of cooperative enterprise with special reference to sugar cooperatives in Maharashtra. Poona, Univ.of Poona, 1966. *

Industrial cooperation
BDD

E-165
Naik, K.N.
The co-operative movement in the Bombay State. Ed.by C.N.Vakil. Bombay, Popular Book Depot, 1953. 297p.

1. Co-operation - Bombay (Presidency)

U of R

E-161
Kapila, R.K.
The co-operative movement in Maharashtra, EE, v.44 (1965), pp.832a-833, 884-85, 935-36, 977-80.

Jas 65

E-166
Naik, K.N.
Recent trends of the co-operative movement in the Bombay State, JUB, v.19 (1951), pp.61-69.

E-167
Nayak, N.V.
Fifty years of co-operation in the Bombay
State. Bombay, Central Press, 1957. 373p.

IOL

E-168
Patil, Bhaskar Hari.
Management of cooperative sugar factories:
a case study of Pravara Sahakari Sakhar
Karkhana, Ltd. Nagpur, Nagpur Univ., 1969. *

Industrials cooperatives,
BDD

E-169
Patil, M.B.
The performance and problems of cooperative
fair price shops in Poona district, MCQ, v.54
(1970), pp.17-22.

BAS 1970

E-170
Problems in the co-operative development in
Maharashtra, MCQ, v.52 (1969), pp.339-424.

BAS Sept 1998

E-171
Ranbhise, N.P.
A review of co-operative movement in Marath-
wada:1950-55. Bombay, Bombay State Co-operative
Union, June 1959. 74p.

Southern Asia Social Science
Bibliography; Economics

E-172
Shah, D.D.
Co-operative housing movement in Bombay
State, BCQ, v.43 (1959), pp.8-13.

Southern Asia Social Science
Bibliography; Economics,

E-173
Shirodkar, Satchidanand Laxman.
Co-operative movement in Kolhapur District:
a study. Poona, Gokhale Institute of Politics
and economics, 1967. *

Jayakarful # 501

E-174
Shrishrimal, Walchand Chunilal.
Amendment to the co-operative law in
Maharashtra and the future of the co-
operative movement, MCQ, v.53 (1969),
pp.131-36.

E-175
Shrishrimal, Walchand Chunilal.
Maharashtra Co-operative Industries Com-
mission, ICR, v.3 (1966), pp.836-43.

E-176
Srivastava, R.N.
The functioning of the co-operative society
in Dhanaura, JSS, v.1 (1958), pp.33-46.

JAS 58

E-177
Subramanian, V.
Co-operatives and decentralised economic development, MCQ, v.51 (1968), pp.257-66.

Economic History | Economic History - India

E-178
Adhya, Govinda Lal, 1924-
Early Indian economics; studies in the economic life of northern and western India, c.200 B.C.-300 A.D. London, Univ.of London, 1961-62. 231p. *

Bloomfield

E-179
Bhatia, B.M.
Famines in India; a study in some aspects of the economic history of India, 1860-1965. 2d ed. Bombay, N.Y., Asia Pub.House, 1967.

PL 480

E-180
Buchanan, Daniel Houston.
The development of capitalistic enterprise in India. New York, Macmillan, 1934. 497p.

U of R

E-181
Chablani, Hashmatrai Lekhraj, 1890-1934.
The economic condition of India during the sixteenth century. Delhi, Oxford Book and Stationery Co., 1929. 113p.

1 Economic history - India

NYPL

E-182
Dar, Usha.
The significance of revenue deficit in state budgets: a case study, AICCER, v.11 (1960), pp.43-48.

Jas'60

E-183
Das, Manmath Nath.
Studies in the economic and social development of modern India, 1848-56. Calcutta, Mukhopadhyay, 1959. 471p.

1. India - Econ.condit. 2. India - Soc. condit. 3. Dalhousie, James Andrew Brown Ramsay, 1st marquess of, 1812-1860.

NUR
LC

E-184
Gadgil, Dhananjaya Ramchandra, 1901-
The industrial evolution of India in recent times. 4th ed. London, Oxford Univ.Press, 1950. 340p.

1. India - Econ.condit. - 1918-1945. 2. India - Indus. 3. Agriculture - India.

U of R

E-185
Ghate, Bhalchandra G.
The problem of rural indebtedness in Indian foreign exchanges since 1927. London, London Univ., 1937. *

Bloomfield

E-186
Gokhale, Gopal Krishna, 1866-1915.
Statement before the Royal Commission on Indian expenditure. Poona, Dnyan Prakash Press, 1897. 75p.

BM

E-187
    Gopalkrishnan, Panikkanparambil Kesavan.
        Development of economic ideas in India (1880-
    1950). New Delhi, People's Pub.House, 1959.
    216p.

        1. Economics - Hist - India. 2. India -
        Economic policy.

NUR
LC

E-188
    Joshi, Ramchandra Mahadeo, 1888-1933.
        Prof.R.M.Joshi's papers and writings;
    (on Indian economic and educational
    problems). Collected and ed.by A.R.Bhat.
    Poona City, N.K.Publishing House, 1944.
    132p.

1 India-Econ conditi-1918   2. Education -India

LC

E-189
    Kale, Vaman Govind, 1876-
        Gokhale and economic reforms: a brief account
    of the ... agitation for economic reforms
    carried on by ... G.K.Gokhale, etc. Poona,
    1916. 246p.

E-190
    Komarov, E.N.
        Colonial exploitation and economic develop-
    ment (Some problems of the economic history
    of India under colonial rule). In: Deuxième
    conférence internationale d'histoire écono-
    mique (Aix-en-Provence). Paris, Mouton,
    1952. pp.731-49.

Cash

E-191
    Mehta, S.D.
        The cotton mills of India, 1854 to 1954.
    Bombay, Textile association of India, 1954.
    322p.

U of R

E-192
    Moreland, William Harrison, 1868-1938.
        From Akbar to Aurangzeb; a study in Indian
    economic history. London, Macmillan & co.,
    ltd., 1923. 372p.

        1. India - Econ.condit. 2. India - Comm. -
        Hist. 3. India - Hist. - European settlements,
        1500-1765.

LC

E-193
    Moreland, William Harrison, 1868-1938.
        India at the death of Akbar; an economic
    study. Delhi, Atma Ram, 1962. 306p.

1 India-Econ condit. 2 India - Hist. 1500
1765

4 of R

E-194
    Morris, Morris David.
        Toward a reinterpretation of nineteenth
    century Indian economic history, JEH, v.23
    (1963), pp.606-18.

Cap

E-195
    Naoroji, Dadabhai, 1825-1917.
        Poverty and un-British rule in India. Lon-
    don, S.Sonnenschein & co., 1901. 689p.

IOL

E-196
    Pavlov, V.I.
        The Indian capitalist class. New Delhi,
    People's Publishing House, 1964. 420p.

NUR
Cap Class

E-197
Ranade, Mahadev Govind, 1842-1901.
Essays in Indian economics: a collection of
essays and speeches. Bombay, Thacker & Co.,
1899. 332p.

NUR
Bom. (Pres) cat

Economic History -
Maharashtra

E-198
Altekar, Anant Sadashiv, 1898-
Economic conditions of western India during
200 B.C. to 500 A.D., IHCP, v.14 (1951), pp.
27-32.

Economic history
U of R

E-199
Bombay (Presidency)
The economic progress of the rural areas
of the Bombay Presidency, 1911-22. By
Harold Hart Mann. Bombay, Government Cen-
tral Press, 1924.

Mann

E-200
Bombay (Presidency)
Reports on the working of the Indian
Factories Act in Bombay. By W.E.Meade-King.
Bombay, 1882.

IOL

E-201
Catanach, I.J.
Agrarian disturbances in nineteenth century
India, IESHR, v.3 (1966), pp.65-84.

J & S+R

E-202
Choksey, Rustom Dinshaw, 1914-
Economic history of the Bombay Deccan and
Karnatak (1818-1868). Poona, R.D.Choksey,
1945. 376p.

1. Bombay (Presidency) - Econ.condit. 2.
Deccan, India & Econ.condit. 3. Carnatic -
Econ.condit.

U of R

E-203
Choksey, Rustom Dinshaw, 1914-
Economic life in the Bombay Deccan, 1818-
1939. Bombay, Asia Pub.House, 1955. 227p.

U of R

E-204
Choksey, Rustom Dinshaw, 1914-
Economic life in the Bombay-Gujarat (1800-
1939). Bombay, Asia Pub.House, 1968. 299p.

U of R

E-205
Choksey, Rustom Dinshaw, 1914-
Economic life in the Bombay Karnatak, 1818-
1939. Bombay, N.Y., Asia Pub.House, 1963.
212p.

1. Karnatic - Econ.condit.

U of R

E-206
Choksey, Rustom Dinshaw, 1914-
Economic life in the Bombay Konkan
1818-1939. Bombay, N.Y., Asia Publishing
House, 1960. 215p.

NRU
Euro

E-207
Croome, H.
    Economics and the State of Bombay. Bombay,
Casement Publishers, 1954. 33p.

Economic study
SSB 1954

E-208
Das, Dipakranjan, 1939-
    Economic history of the Deccan, from the
first to the sixth century A.D. Delhi, Munshiram Manoharlal, 1969. 358p.

PL 480. '69

E-209
Deshpande, S.H.
    Economy of Maharashtra. Shri C.V.Joag
felicitation volume.

E-210
Digby, William, 1849-1904.
    The "Indian Phantom" no phantom, but a
grievous reality, AR, ser.3,v.15 (1903),
pp.339-66.

Economic condition
Case

E-211
Gokhale, Balkrishna Govind, 1919-
    Capital accumulation in 17th century
western India, ASBJ, n.s.,v.39-40 (1964/65),
pp.51-60.

Indic Studies

E-212
    The internal economy of Bombay a century ago,
BQR, v.3 (1856), pp.324-52.

NR4

E-213
Kerur, D.B.
    Economic development of Maharashtra: some
aspects of the problem, JUP, v.9 (1958), pp.
117-23.

South Asia Social Science
Bibliography; Economics; p.45

E-214
Kunte, Bhagwan Ganesh.
    The economic prosperity of Bombay Province
and Sind 1919-1939. Bombay, Univ.of Bombay,
1959. *

Economics Hist &
conditions
BDD

E-215
Kunte, Bhagwan Ganesh.
    Economic prosperity of Bombay province
and Sind 1919-1939, JUB, v.28 (1959), pp.
60-64.

Southern Asia Social
Science Bib. Economics

E-216
    A letter to the Hon. Sir David Wedderburn,
bart. M.P. containing a proposal for a royal
commission of inquiry into the condition of
the Deccan, QJPSS, v.4,no.1 (1881), pp.6-16.

QJPSS

E-217
  Maharashtra, India (State) Bureau of Economics
  and Statistics.
    Maharashtra, an economic review. Bombay,
  n.d. annual.

NRC

E-218
  Narayan, B.K.
    The economic development of the Hyderabad
  State. Mysore, Mysore Univ., 1958. 433p. *

Mysore Univ.
Dissertations

E-219
  National Council of Applied Economic Research.
    Demand for energy in Western India. New
  Delhi, 1965. 232p.

    1. Power resources - India.

U of R

E-220
  National Council of Applied Economic Research.
    Techno-economic survey of Maharashtra. New
  Delhi, 1963. 311p.

    1. Maharashtra, India (State) - Econ.pol.

U of R

E-221
  Pandit, Yeshwant Sakharam, 1910-
    Economic conditions of Maharashtra and
  Karnatak. Poona, Tilak Swarajya Sangh, 1936.
  215p.

    1. India - Econ.condit. - 1918-1947.

U of R

E-222
  Pavlov, V.I.
    Economic changes in Maharashtra towns in the
  second half of 19th century. In: Tilak and
  the struggle for Indian freedom. Ed.by I.M.
  Reisner and N.M.Goldberg. New Delhi,
  People's Pub.House, 1966. pp.171-212.

E-223
    Problems of Maharashtra; report of a seminar
  held under the auspices of the Indian Committee for Cultural Freedom, the Asian
  Office, Congress for Cultural Freedom, and
  the Sadhana weekly. Bombay, Indian Committee for Cultural Freedom, 1960. 208p.

    1. Maharashtra, India (State) - Econ.condit.
    2. Maharashtra, India (State) - Pol.& govt.

LC

E-224
  Ranbhise, N.P.
    Regional economic disparities in Bombay
  state; study based on 1951 census reports.
  Aurangabad, 1960. 79p.

    1. Bombay (Province) Econ.condit.

LC

E-225
  Ranbhise, N.P.
    Regional economic disparities in Maharashtra,
  JMaU, v.2,no.1 (1961), pp.74-102.

JMaU

E-226
  Sovani, Nilkanth Vitthal.
    Economic conditions in Maharashtra, JUP,
  no.9 (1958). pp.105-16.

JUP

E-227
  Telang, M.A. and Chavan, B.W.
    Report on the state income of Maharashtra,
    1955-56 to 1958-59. QBES, v.2,no.2 (1961),
    pp.1-87.

So Asia Lib. Science | Economic policy & planning |

E-228
  Bombay (Presidency)
    The Greater Bombay scheme-reports of the
    Industries and Communications panel. 1946.

E-229
  Bombay (Presidency)
    Post-war reconstruction proposals for
    Satara taluka. Bombay, 1945.

NYPL

E-230
  Bombay (Presidency)
    Preliminary report of the Post-war Develop-
    ment Committee for the Bombay City. 1939.

E-231
  Bombay (State).
    Plans of the state. Bombay, 1952-1960.

E-232
  Bombay (State) Directorate of Publicity.
    Multipurpose development projects for
    schedules tribes in Bombay state.
    Bombay, Directorate of Publicity, 1957.
    38p.

E-233
  Bombay (State) Political and Services Depart-
    ment.
    Second five year plan - 1956-57 to
    1960-61, Bombay state. Bombay, Political
    and Services Department, 1958. i + 543p.

E-234
  The Bombay plan and other essays. Bombay,
    Lalvani Pub.House, 1968. (A.D.Shroff
    memorial lectures, 2) 85p.

BAS Sept 1973

E-235
  Bombay - Poona metropolitan planning, CA,
    v.16,no.7 (1969), pp.17-19.

Municipal govt & urban development - articles
BAS 1969

E-236
  Borkar, Vishnu Vinayak.
    Planning for balanced regional development:
    the case study of Marathwada, QJISSS, v.2,
    no.3/4 (1968), pp.42-48.

BAS 1970

E-237
Desai, Thakorlal Maganlal.
The development programme of the Bombay
government, JUB, v.19 (1951), pp.48-60.

y u B

E-238
India (Republic) Planning Commission.
Third five year plan; progress report, 1961-
62. Delhi, Manager of Publications, 1963.
220p.

u of R

E-239
Kolhapur, India (State) Planning and Develop-
ment Dept.
A development plan for the Kolhapur State.
Kolhapur, 1946. 184p.

Asie Book Rul 2/71

E-240
Maharashtra, India (State).
Detailed estimates of the five-year plan
schemes, presented to the Legislature under
Article 202 (1) of the Constitution of
India. v.1. 1969-70. Bombay, Printed at
the Govt.Central Press, 1969. 1v.

*Economic planning - India
PAS Sept 770*

E-241
Maharashtra, India (State) Directorate of
Publicity.
Maharashtra; pattern of plenty. Bombay,
1962.

LC

E-242
Maharashtra, India (State) Finance Department.
Detailed estimates of the third five-
year plan schemes, for the year 1963-64.
Bombay, 1963. 348p.

*YNB 1963 p59
U of R*

E-243
Maharashtra, India (State) Finance Dept.
Schemes in the third five-year plan, Mahara-
shtra State. Bombay, Printed by the Manager,
Govt.Central Press, 1961. 538p.

1. Maharashtra, India (State) - Economic
policy.

LC

E-244
Maharashtra, India (State) Finance Dept.
The third five-year plan, Maharashtra State.
Bombay, Govt.Central Press, 1961. 265p.

NUC

E-245
Modak, N.V. and Mayer, Albert.
An outline of the master plan for Greater
Bombay; a report. Bombay, Printed at the
Bombay Municipality Print.Press, 1948. 73p.

Cities - Plans - India - Bombay (City)

NYPL

E-246
Mukerjee, Radhakamal, 1890-
Planning the countryside; first report.
2d ed. Bombay, 1950. 200p.

IOL

E-247
    Naik, J.P.
      The problem of rural planning in Kolhapur
    state. Kolhapur, Govt.Press, 1947. 16p.

NYPL

E-248
    National Council of Applied Economic Research.
      Industrial programmes for the fourth plan,
    Maharashtra. New Delhi, 1966. 189p.

4 7R

E-249
    Planning at state level-Maharashtra's
    experience. TQ, v.18 (1963), pp.35-55.

JaS 63

E-250
    Rajwade, L.G.
      Regional planning in Maharashtra, CA,
    v.17,no.1 (1969), pp.13-15.

BAS 1970

E-251
    Wadia, Pestonji Ardesir, 1878-   and Merchant,
    Kanchanlal Tribhovandar.
      The Bombay plan: a criticism. 2d ed. Bombay,
    Popular Book Depot. 1946. 64p.

    1. India - Econ.pol.

LC

E-252
    Wanmali, Sudhir Vyandatesh.
      The hierarchy of towns in Vidarbha, India,
    and its significance for regional planning.
    London, Univ.of London, 1968. *

Economics

Economic theory

E-253
    Gadgil, Dhananjaya Ramchandra, 1901-
      Gokhale as an economist. In: Gokhale: the
    man and his mission. Ed.by C.P.Ramaswamy
    Aiyar and others. New York, Asia Pub.
    House, 1966. pp.41-68.

Unt R
Dhanajaya

E-254
    Ganguli, Birendranath.
      Dadabhai Naoroji and the mechanism of
    'external drain'. IESHR, v.2 (1965), pp.
    85-102.

Case

E-255
    Ganguli, Birendranath.
      Dadabhai Naoroji and the drain theory.
    Bombay, Asia Pub.House, 1965. (Dadabhai
    Naoroji Memorial Prize Fund lectures, 1964).
    161p.

(series)
disregard

.LC

E-256
    Ganguli, Birendranath.
      Dadabhai Naoroji, Gokhale and Gandhi as
    exponents of national economic thought,
    IJSW, v.31 (1970), pp.243-62.

Economics
BAS 1969

E-257
Ganguli, Birendranath.
Gopal Krishna Gokhale: his economic thinking.
In: Gokhale, the man and his mission. Ed.by
C.P.Ramaswamy Aiyer, et al. Bombay, Asia
Pub.House, 1966. pp.69-128.

U-R

E-258
Jagirdar, Prabhakar Janardan, 1904-
Ranade and the historical school of economics,
IJE, v.34 (1954), pp.195-201.

SSB 1954

E-259
Kale, Vaman Govind, 1876-
The economic creed of the late Mr.Ranade,
HR, v.26 (1912), pp.9-14.

Case

E-260
Namjoshi, M.V.
The economic thought of Gopal Krishna
Gokhale. In: Gopal Krishna Gokhale, a
centenary tribute. Bombay, Printed at
the government central press, 1966. pp.
109-124.

U+R

E-261
Naoroji, Dadabhai, 1825-1917.
Speeches and writings of Dadabhai Naoroji.
Madras, G.A.Natesan, 1906. 882p.

U-R

E-262
Saxena, Oudh Kishore.
Economic thought in India from Dada Bhai
Naoroji to Tilak, 1856-1919. Agra, Agra
Univ., 1962. *

Economics
BDD

E-263
Sovani, Nilkanth Vitthal.
Ranade's model of the Indian economy, AV,
v.4 (1962), pp.10-20.

India

E-264
Archibald, E.D.
The Cycle of drought and famine in southern
India, CR, v.66 (1878), pp.125-51.

Case

E-265
Lambert, George.
India, the horror-stricken empire. Contain-
ing a full account of the famine, plague and
earthquake of 1896-97. Including a complete
narration of the relief work through the
Home and Foreign Relief Commission. Elkhart,
Ind., Mennonite Pub.Co., 1898. 480p.

1. India - Famines. 2. Plague - Bombay.

U-R

E-266
Loveday, Alexander.
The history and economics of Indian famines.
London, G.Bell & sons, ltd., 1914. 174p.

LC

E-267
    Nash, Vaughn.
    The great famine and its causes. London,
New York, etc., Longmans, Green & co., 1900.
271p.

    1. India - Famines.

LC

E-268
    Srivastava, Hari Shanker.
    The history of Indian famines and develop-
ment of famine policy, 1858-1918. Agra, Sri
Ram Mehra, 1968. 436p.

4th R   Maharashtra

E-269
    Bombay (Presidency)
    Famine relief code. Bombay presidency,
1912. Bombay, Govt.central press, 1912.
225p.

E-270
    Bombay (Presidency)
    Report on past famines in the Bombay
Presidency;...by A.T.Etheridge, with the
resolution of Government thereon. Bombay,
1868. 156p.

E-271
    Bombay (Presidency)
    Report on the famine in the Bombay Presi-
dency, 1899-1902. Vol.I, Report; Vol.II,
Appendices. Bombay, 1903. 2v.

E-272
    Bombay (Presidency)
    Report on the famine in the Bombay Presi-
dency, 1905-1906. Bombay, 1907.

BM

E-273
    Bombay (Presidency)
    Report on the famine in the Bombay Presi-
dency, 1911-12. Bombay, 1913.

BM

E-274
    Bombay (Presidency)
    Report on famine relief in the southern
division of the Bombay Presidency. Bombay,
1893.

Brt Mus

E-275
    Correspondence with government in regard to
    the special officer's report on the working
    of the Deccan Agriculturists' Relief Act,
    QJPSS, v.13, no.4 (1890), pp.89-93; v.14,
    no.1 (1891), pp.1-6.

E-276
    Correspondence with the Bombay government on
    the famine in the Deccan, QJPSS, v.14,no.4
    (1891), pp.35-46.

E-277
Correspondence with the Bombay government regarding the impending famine, QJPSS, v.14,no.3 (1891), pp.22-29.

PSS

E-278
Devadhar, Gopal Krishna, 1871-1935.
The famine of 1908 in India and the work done by non-official agencies, MR, v.6 (1909), pp.250-64.

case

E-279
Digby, William, 1849-1904.
The famine campaign in southern India; Madras and Bombay Presidencies and province of Mysore, 1876-1878. London, Longmans, Green, 1878. 2 vols.

u n p

E-280
Etheridge, Alfred Thomas, 1825-
Report on past famines in the Bombay Presidency ... with the resolution of Government thereon. Bombay, Printed for the Govt. at the Education Society's Press, Byculla, 1868. 216p.

Bombay (Presidency) - Famines

LC

E-281
Famine administration in the Bombay Presidency, QJPSS, v.1,no.3 (1878), pp.1-31.

PSS

E-282
Famine narratives, QJPSS, v.1,no.4 (1878), pp.52-73.

PSS

E-283
India. Home Department.
Papers relating to the Deccan Agriculturists' Relief Act during the years 1875-94. Calcutta, 1897. (Selections from the Records of the Government of India, Home Department. no.342. Home Department. Serial no.20) 2v.

SOAS

E-284
A letter to the government of India making some suggestions regarding the Famine Commission, QJPSS, v.1,no.1 (1878), pp.1-28.

QJPSS

E-285
A letter to the secretary of the Famine Commission on the subject of remissions of the land assessment, QJPSS, v.2,no.1 (1879), pp.61-67.

QJPSS

E-286
Padhye, S.S.
Desertion of villages in the Deccan trap region of Vidarbha, BGM, v.13 (1965), pp. 137-48.

QAS 9/68

E-287
Scott, J.E.
The famine land; observations and experiences in India during the great drought of 1899-1900. New York and London, Harper and Brothers, 1904. 205p.

BM

E-288
Stephens, W.H.
The Poona district in famine days: a backward look from better days. Poona, 1919. 16p.

√√IOL

Housing

E-289
Batley, Claude, 1879-
Bombay's houses and homes. Bombay, 1949. (Bombay Citizenship Series). 47p.

IOL

E-290
Bhaiji, M.Mohsin.
Housing and rent among the Muhammedan working classes of Bombay. JUB, v.6 (1937), pp. 113-20.

JUB

E-291
Bombay (Presidency)
The Greater Bombay scheme report of the housing panel. 1946.

E-292
Bombay (Presidency)
Report on the possibilities of development of Salsette as a residential area. By M.J. Meade. Bombay, Govt.Central Press, 1909.

E-293
Dandekar, Vinayak Mahadeo, 1920-
A survey of rural housing in a Deccan village (Sholapur district), BDCRI, v.14 (1952), pp. 132-50.

BDCRI

E-294
Mann, Harold Hart, 1872-
The housing of the untouchable classes in an Indian city, SSQ, v.1 (1916), pp.1-10.

Mann

E-295
More, S.S.
The urban housing problem. Bombay, C.D. Barfivala, 1956. (All-India Institute of Local Self-Government. Series no.1, pub.no. 18) 46p.

PL480 1958

E-296
Ramachandran, P.
Social and economic rents and subsidies for low-income groups in Greater Bombay, by P.Ramachandran and A.Padmanabha. Bombay, Lalvani Pub.House, 1967. (Tata Institute of Social Sciences series, no.18). 79p.

1. Housing - Bombay metropolitan area. 2. Rent control - Economic aspects (low income)

UTR

E-297
Report on the survey of building activity:
Bombay, Calcutta, and Madras, <u>BRBI</u>, v.14
(1960), pp.495-511.

Industry

E-302
Bhatt, A.R.
Industrial development of Maharashtra,
<u>JUP</u>, no.15 (1962), p.163.

JUP

E-298
Agaskar, M.S.
Early history of the Bombay docks and
ship-building. In: Mahamahopadyaya Prof.
D.V.Potdar. Ed.by Surendra Nath Sen.
Poona, 1950. pp.323-36.

*Industry —
Bhandarkar index
Comm vols.*

E-303
Bhattacharya, Ardhendu.
Industries in Poona region: an analysis of
inter-industry linkage, <u>JUB</u>, n.s.,v.39 (1970),
pp.163-204.

BAS 1970

E-299
Basu, Satishchandra.
Crisis in the Bombay cotton mill
industry, <u>MR</u>, v.9 (1911), pp.283-84.

MR

E-304
Bombay (Presidency)
Iron and steel work in the Bombay Presidency. By W.V.Scudamore. Bombay, 1907.
14p.

Ind Off Lib

E-300
Basu, Satishchandra.
The present situation in the Bombay cotton
mill industry and its problems, <u>MR</u>, v.11
(1912), pp.243-47.

Case

E-305
Bombay (Presidency)
The marine fisheries of the Bombay Presi-
dency. By Herbert Tower Sorley. Bombay,
Printed at the Government Central Press,
1933.

LC

E-301
Bharucha, K.B.
The history of the cotton mill industry
in western India. London, Univ.of London,
1927. *

Bloomfield

E-306
Bombay (Presidency)
A monograph of wire and tinsel in the
Bombay Presidency. By Joseph Nissim. Bom-
bay, Printed at the Govt.Central Press,
1909.

LC

E-307
　Bombay (Presidency).
　　A monograph on dyes and dyeing in the
Bombay Presidency. By C.G.H.Fawcett.
Bombay, 1896.

　Brit.Mus.

E-308
　Bombay (Presidency)
　　A monograph on gold and silver work in the
Bombay Presidency with 39 illustrations.
By Cecil Laurence Burns, 1863-1929. Bombay,
Govt.Central Press, 1904. 25p.

UMR

E-309
　Bombay (Presidency)
　　Monograph on ivory carving. By Cecil
Laurence Burns. Bombay, 1900.

Brit Mus.

E-310
　Bombay (Presidency)
　　A monograph on paper-making in the Bombay
Presidency. By R.T.F.Kirk. Bombay, 1908.
9p.

Brit. MUS.

E-311
　Bombay (Presidency)
　　A monograph on tanning and working in
leather in the Bombay Presidency. By
J.R.Martin. Bombay, 1903. 39p.

BritMus.

E-312
　Bombay (Presidency)
　　A monograph on the art and practice of
carpet-making in the Bombay Presidency; by
H.J.R.Twigg. Bombay, Government Central
Press, 1907.

IOL xxx

E-313
　Bombay (Presidency)
　　A monograph on the pottery and glassware
of the Bombay Presidency. By Evan Maconochie,
1868- . Bombay, 1895.

Brit Mus.

E-314
　Bombay (Presidency)
　　A monograph on stone carving and inlaying
in the Bombay Presidency. By J.H.E.Tupper.
Bombay, 1906.

India

E-315
　Bombay (Presidency)
　　A monograph on the woollen fabrics of the
Bombay Presidency. By Benjamin Adams
Brendon. Bombay, 1899. 13p.

Brit Mus.

E-316
　Bombay (Presidency)
　　A monograph on wood carving in the
Bombay Presidency. By John Wales and
Adolphus Gatgens. Bombay, 1871. 11p.

E-317
Bombay (Presidency)
A monograph upon the silk fabrics of the
Bombay Presidency. By Stephen Meredyth
Edwardes. Bombay, Printed at the Govt.
Central Press, 1900.

U & R

E-318
Bombay (Presidency).
Report on leather industries of the
Bombay Presidency. By Allan Guthrie.
Bombay, 1910. 35p.

Brit. Mus.

E-319
Bombay (Presidency)
Report on the hand loom industry of the
Bombay Presidency. By P.N.Mehta. Bombay,
1909. 19p.

IOL
Brit. Mus.

E-320
Bombay (Presidency) Department of Agriculture.
Notes on the Indian textile industry with
special reference to hand weaving. By R.D.
Bell. Bombay, 1926.

IOL

E-321
Bombay (Presidency) Department of Agriculture.
Sugar industry in western India and methods
of sugar manufacture. By R.G.Padhye. Poona,
1924. (Bombay Presidency, Department of
Agriculture, Bulletin no.116). 223p.

nd Ctl Lib

E-322
Bombay (Presidency) Department of Industries.
Possibilities of the development of fibre
industry. By J.K.Sircar. Bombay, 1940.

E-323
Bombay (Presidency) Factory Commission.
Report and proceedings of the commission
appointed to consider the working of the
factories in the Bombay Presidency. Bombay,
1885.

Brit. Mus

E-324
Bombay (State) Village Industries Committee.
Village industries in Bombay State, 31st
March 1951. Bombay, 1952.

IOL

E-325
Bopegamage, A.
Ecology of business in Poona City, PR, v.7
(1963), pp.57-68.

E-326
Brendon, Benjamin Adams.
Woollen fabrics of Bombay Presidency,
JIAI, v.10 (1903), pp.17-18.

India

E-327
Chandrakantham, M.N.
Structure and organisation of the cotton textile industry in India. Nagpur, Nagpur Univ., 1962. *

Industrial economics
Secondary industries
BDD

E-332
Davar, Rustom Sohrab.
Management process in marketing management with special reference to cotton textile industry in Bombay. Delhi, Univ.of Delhi, 1970. *

Management
Marketing
BDD

E-328
Chinoy, Sir Sultan, 1885-
Pioneering in Indian business. 2d ed. N.Y., Asia Pub.House, 1962.

4 of R

E-333
Desai, Maganlal Bhagwanji, 1918-   and
Baichwal, P.R.
Economic survey of fishing industry in Thana District, Bombay State, India. In: The economic role of middlemen and co-operatives in Indo-Pacific fisheries. Ed.by E.F. Szezepanik. Rome, United Nations Food and Agriculture Organization, v.1, 1960. pp.1-76.

E-329
Chirmade, S.R.
Industrial development of Jalgaon District. Poona, Univ.of Poona, 1969. *

Industrial economics
BDD

E-334
Deshpande, Shridhar Atmaram.
Rice milling industry in Vidarbha. Nagpur, Nagpur Univ., 1965. *

Industrial Economics
Secondary industries
BDD

E-330
Cotton manufacture in the Bombay Presidency. QJPSS, v.14,no.3 (1891), pp.1-18.

PSS

E-335
Doshi, Ravindra Rajaram.
Processing and marketing of bidi tobacco in Nipani tract. Poona, Gokhale Institute of Politics and Economics, 1965. *

Jayakar Lib # 14/71

E-331
Das Gupta, Ashin.
A note of the out-station factories (Bombay), BPP, v.76 (1957), pp.162-65.

gqd

E-336
Edwardes, Stephen Meredyth, 1873-1927.
Silk fabrics of Bombay Presidency, JIAI, v.10 (1904), pp.1-5.

India

E-337
Enthoven, Reginald Edward, 1869-
The cotton fabrics of the Bombay Presidency.
Bombay, 1897. 51p.

BM

E-342
Gothoskar, S.P.
Report on the survey of cottage metal
industry in Maharashtra State, QBES, v.1,
no.4 (1961), pp.1-20.

So Asia Sec Sci Lib.

E-338
Enthoven, Reginald Edward, 1869-
Cotton fabrics of Bombay Presidency. JIAI,
v.10 (1904), pp.19-20.

India

E-343
Harris, Frank Reginald.
Jamsetji Nusserwanji Tata, a chronicle of
his life. 2d ed. Bombay, Blackie, 1958.
362p.

1. Jamshedji Nasarvanji Tata, 1839-1904.
2. Tata Iron & Steel Company, ltd.

V of R

E-339
Fukazawa, Hiroshi.
A history of the cotton mill industry of
India with special reference to protection
and development, 1851-1956. Lucknow, Univ.
of Lucknow, 1959. *

Industrial economics-
Secondary industries
BDD

E-344
India (Republic) Khadi and Village Industries
Commission.
A village plan. Bombay, 1958-59. 164p.

1. India - Economic development. 2. Villages -
India.

LC

E-340
Gadgil, Dhananjaya Ranchandra, 1901-
Origins of the modern Indian business class;
an interim report. New York, International
Secretariat, Institute of Pacific Relations,
1959. 50p.

1. India - Comm. - Hist.

V of R

E-345
India (Republic) Tariff Commission.
Report on the review of the antimony industry,
Bombay 1962. Delhi, Manager of Publications,
1962. 14p.

1. Antimony - India.

LC

E-341
Gananathan, V.S. and Iyer, Bhanumathi V.
Manufacturing industries in and around
Poona, IGJ, v.38 (1963), pp.65-74.

ga & 63

E-346
Jagtap, M.B.
'Ghongdi' (woolen hand-woven blanket)
industry in a village during 1943-58, AV,
v.2 (1960), pp.15-27.

Case

E-347
Jain, Sagar C.
Social origins and careers of industrial
managers in India. Ithaca, Cornell Univ.,
1965. *

E-348
Jain, Sukumal Kumar.
Organisation and financing of newspaper
industry of Bombay. Jabalpur, Univ.of
Jabalpur, 1970. *

E-349
Joshi, Nilkanth Maheshwar.
Urban handicrafts of the Bombay Deccan.
Poona, D.R.Gadgil, 1936. (Gokhale Institute
of Politics and Economics, Pub.no.5).
217p.

E-350
Kalele, J.C.
Some aspects of small-scale soap industry
in Poona, AV, v.2 (1960), pp.327-338.

E-351
Kerur, D.B.
Principles of industrial policy for the
State of Maharashtra: some aspects of the
problem, JUP, v.15 (1962), pp.167-76.

E-352
Khanolkar, G.D.
Walchand Hirachand: man, his times, and
achievements. Bombay, Walchand, 1969.
719p.

E-353
Kulkarni, G.S.
Industrial landscape of greater Poona, BGM,
v.8-9 (1961), pp.85-94.

E-354
Kulkarni, M.R.
Small industry in two big cities, Delhi
and Bombay: a study in comparison of
some important findings, IEJ, v.12 (1965),
pp.452-59.

E-355
Kulkarni, Narhar Kalyan.
Economic survey of the weaving industry of
Ichalkaranji 1954. Poona, Univ.of Poona,
1959. *

E-356
Kulkarni, Narhar Kalyan.
The weaving industry of Ichalkaranji, AV,
v.3 (1961), pp.1-10.

E-357
Kulkarni, Pandurang Vinayak.
   Industrial development of Konkan: Thana,
Kolaba and Ratnagiri Districts. Bombay,
Univ.of Bombay, 1961. *

Industrial economics
ROD

E-362
Manviker, K.S.
   Cottage and village industries in the
Bombay, AICR, v.22 (1957), pp.653-57.

Social Science Bibliography-
India & Pakistan 1957 - Economics,
p. 48

E-358
Lakdawala, Dansukhlal Tulsidas and Mehta, B.V.
   Small and medium scale engineering factories
in Bombay city, JUB, v.26 (1958), pp.50-103.
Continued in: v.28 (1959), pp.32-59.

JAS '59

E-363
Mehta, S.D.
   The Indian cotton textile industry, an
economic analysis. Bombay, Pub.by G.K.Ved
for the Textile Assoc., India, 1952. 232p.

U & R

E-359
Lakdawala, Dansukhlal Tulsidas and
Sandesara, J.C.
   Shops and establishments in Greater Bombay,
JUB, v.25 (1957), pp.56-103.

Social Science Bibliography-
India & Pakistan 1957 - Economics,
p. 46

E-364
Money, William Taylor.
   Observations on the expediency of
shipbuilding at Bombay, etc. London,
1811.

BM

E-360
Lakdawala, Dansukhlal Tulsidas and Sandesara,
J.C.
   Small industry in a big city: a survey in
Bombay. Bombay, 1960. (University of Bom-
bay. Series in economics, no.10) 403p.

Bombay - Indus
4 1 R

E-365
Mudholkar, Gauri-Vrinda Govind.
   The entrepreneurial and technical cadres of
the Bombay cotton textile industry between 1854
and 1914: a study in the international transmission and diffusion of techniques. Chapel
Hill, Univ.of North Carolina, 1969. 389p. *

Shulman - 51

E-361
Mali, H.B.
   Analysis of 1961 census data of household
industry and employment in Maharashtra state,
QJISSS, v.2,no.3/4 (1968), pp.50-54.

Industry + Commerce
1970

E-366
Nag, S.P.
   Under-utilization of installed capacity
in the cotton textile industry in India,
1948-58, IER, v.5 (1961), pp.274-84.

E-367
  Mandedkar, Durganath Janardan.
    Evaluation of labour management in the
  Bombay film industry. Baroda, The Maharaja
  Sayajirao Univ.of Baroda, 1969. *

Personnel management
BDD

E-372
  Pruthi, S.P.S.
    A study of productivity problems in the
  cotton industries of the U.K.(Lancashire)
  and India (Bombay and Ahmedabad) since the
  Second World War. London, London University,
  1961-62.*

QJISS

E-368
  National Council of Applied Economic Research.
    Survey of the handloom industry in Karnataka
  and Sholapur. New York, Asia Pub.House, 1959.
  285p.

    1. Hand weaving.

UMR

E-373
  Report on cottage carpentry industry in
    Maharashtra and Gujarat regions of Bombay
  State, QBES, v.2 (1958), pp.50-103.

South Asia Social Science
Bibliography, Economics, p.51

E-369
  Palsapure, Prabhakar Zangoba.
    Industrial development of Vidarbha. Nagpur,
  Nagpur Univ., 1969. *

Industrial economics
BDD

E-374
  Report on the census of cottage and small
    scale dyeing and printing and coir making
  industries in selected centres of pre-
  reorganised Bombay State, QBES, v.1 (1957),
  pp.1-56.

Social Science Bibliography-
India Pakistan 1954-Economics,
p. 48

E-370
  Pandit, Y.G.
    Report on the oil-pressing industry of the
  Bombay Presidency. Bombay, Printed at the
  Govt.Central Press, 1914. 87p.

    1. India - Bombay (Presidency) - Statistics.
    2. Seeds. 3. Oils & fats.

Lc

E-375
  Report on the sample survey of cottage coir
    industry in reorganised Bombay State, QBES,
  v.2 (1958), pp.1-49.

South Asia Social Science
Bibliography; Economics: 57

E-371
  Papola, Trilok Singh.
    Criteria determination: a study of cotton
  textile industry of India. Lucknow, Univ.of
  Lucknow, 1967. *

Industrial economics
Secondary industries
BDD

E-376
  Report on the sample survey of the cottage
    weaving industry in the old Bombay State,
  QBES, v.1 (1957), pp.1-52.

Soc Sci Bib

E-377
Rutnagar, Sorabji M., ed.
   Bombay industries: the cotton mills. A
review of the progress of the textile industry in Bombay from 1850 to 1926 and the
present constitution, management and financial position of the spinning and weaving
factories. Bombay, The Indian Textile
Journal, ltd., 1927. 760p.

1. Cotton growing & manufacture. 2. Bombay (Pres.) - Econ.
condit. 3. Bombay (Pres) - Industries & resources

NUR
LC

E-378
Sandesara, J.C.
   Small-scale industries in India with special
reference to Bombay City. Bombay, Univ.of
Bombay, 1959. *

Gupta

E-379
Scudamore, Walter Victor.
   Iron and steel work in the Bombay Presidency:
a monograph. Bombay, Govt.Central Press, 1907.
14p.

I OL

E-380
Sen, Sunil K.
   The Tatas during the war, 1914-1918. IHCP,
v.26, pt.2 (1964), pp.222-24.

IHCP

E-381
Shende, K.K.
   Salt industry of Bombay Province. Bombay,
the author: Mangalwadi, Girgaum, 1947. 128p.

SOAS supp

E-382
Shroff, Aloo Dinshaw.
   The conciliation and arbitration of industrial disputes in India with special reference
to Bombay Province. Bombay, Univ.of Bombay,
1949. *

Economics - Industrial
relations
BDP

E-383
Sundararama Sastri, N.
   Localisation of cotton textile industry
in India, JMU, v.10 (1938), pp.226-37.

Case:

E-384
Venkataraman, K.S.
   The handloom industry: its economics in
the light of the study of the industry in
certain centres of the Madras Presidency and
the Bombay Deccan. Madras, University of
Madras, 1937. *

Bb Ph.D. thesis

E-385
Wacha, Dinsha Edulji, 1844-1936.
   The life and life work of J.N.Tata. 3d ed.
Madras, Ganesh and co., 1918. 202p.

U of R

E-386
Wadia, Ardeshir Ruttonji, 1888-
   The Bombay dockyard and the Wadia master
builders. Bombay, the author, 1957. 454p.

1. Bombay (City) - Docks. 2. Ship-building -
Bombay (City)

LC

E-387
   Wadia, Ardeshir Ruttonji, 1888-
      Scions of Lowjee Wadia. [A Parsi family,
   master builders to the East India Company.]
   Bombay, the author, 1964. 344p.

SOAS curr

E-388
   Zacharia, Kalathil Abraham.
      Industrial relations with special reference
   to post-war conditions in Bombay. Bombay,
   Univ.of Bombay, 1951. *

Economic - Industrial
   relations
BDD   Labor & employment

E-389
   Ahmad, Zainul Abidin.
      Woman and child industrial labour in the
   Bombay Presidency. London, London Univ.,
   1935. 296p. *

Bloomfield

E-390
   Bhatt, Bhalchandra Jeyshanker.
      A case study in the emerging industrial
   labor force in four factories in Bombay.
   Madison, Univ.of Wisconsin, 1966. 252p. *

Shulman #369   23185
                    558

E-391
   Bombay (Presidency)
      Report of the commissioners appointed ...
   to inquire into the condition of the opera-
   tives in the Bombay factories and the
   necessity or otherwise for the passing of
   a Factory Act. Bombay, 1875.

BM

E-392
   Bombay (State) Labour Department.
      Report on an inquiry into the conditions
   of labour in the cinema industry in Bombay
   State. Bombay, Government Printer and Publisher, 1960. 94p.

Southern Asia Social Science
Bibliography; Economics, p.83

E-393
   A brief sketch of the work of the Kamgar Hit-
      wardhak Sabha, Bombay, 1908-19. Bombay, H.
   A.Talcherkar, 1919. 32p.

Bom (Pres) Cat

E-394
   Burnett-Hurst, Alexander Robert.
      Labour and housing in Bombay; a study in
   the economic conditions of the wage-earning
   classes in Bombay. London, P.S.King & son,
   ltd., 1925. 166p.

      1. Labor & laboring classes - Bombay. 2.
   Housing - Bombay. 3. Labor & laboring
   classes - Dwellings.

LC

E-395
   Chirde, Shridhar Bapurao.
      Industrial labour in Bombay: a socio-econo-
   mic analysis with special reference to industrial workers residing in Bombay. Bombay,
   Univ.of Bombay, 1949. *

Economics - Labour
   force
BDD

E-396
   Cholia, Rasiklal P.
      Dock labourers in Bombay. Calcutta,
   Longmans & Co., 1941. (Studies in Indian
   economics, no.14) 181p.

BM

E-397
Cholia, Rasiklal P.
Dock labourers in Bombay. <u>JUB</u>, v.6 (1937-38), pp.121-34,175-89.

furer

E-402
Deodhar, Laxman Dattatraya.
Labour in the sugar industry of Bombay Deccan. Bombay, Univ.of Bombay, 1951. *

Economics - Sugar industry
BDD

E-398
Conditions of labour in cinema industry in Bombay, <u>ILG</u>, v.15 (1958), pp.1009-14.

LC accessions n58

E-403
Desai, Maganlal Bhagwanji, 1918-
A survey of the nature and extent of non-farm employment in Thana District, <u>IJAE</u>, v.13 (1958), pp.59-78.

LC Accessions 1957, p. 336

E-399
Dabholkar, Venu Achyut.
Life and labour of employed women in Poona, Poona, Gokhale Institute of Politics and Economics, 1960.*

Jayakar Lib # 1470

E-404
Desai, Maganlal Bhagwanji, 1918-   and Baichwal, P.R.
Survey of the nature and extent of non-farm employment of Thana District. New Delhi, I.C.A.R., 1969. 224p.

E-400
Dabholkar, Venu Achyut.
Life and labour of employed women in Poona, <u>AV</u>, v.3 (1961), pp.181-93.

JAS '61

E-405
Deshmukh, Prabhakar Janardhanpant.
A study of the employment exchanges in Maharashtra. Nagpur, Nagpur Univ., 1969. *

Economic - Employment sources
BDD

E-401
Dawson, William Albert, 1924-
Trade union development in western Indian textiles. Madison, Univ.of Wisconsin, 1971. 306p. *

Schulman # 373

E-406
Dhavle, Shalini.
Hired labour and wage rates for farm operations in eleven selected rural centers of Maharashtra, <u>AV</u>, v.6 (1964), pp.127-41.

JAS '64

E-407
Donde, Vishnu Balkrishna.
Rural labour in Konkan. Bombay, Univ.of
Bombay, 1951. *

Economics Labour force
BDD (

E-408
Gharpurey, Prabha Madhav.
Life and labour of the full-time domestic
servants in Poona City. Poona, Gokhale
Institute of Politics and Economics, 1959. *

Jayakar Lib # 1474 (

E-409
Gokhale, R.G.
The Bombay cotton mill worker. Bombay,
The Millowners' Association, 1957. 126p.

Social Science Bibliography India & Pakistan 195?-Ec... (

E-410
Gokhale, R.G.
Principles and practice of productivity;
special reference to Bombay textile industry.
Bombay, Millowners Assoc., 1959. 97p.

1. Labor productivity, Textile industry.
2. Textile trade & statistics - India - Bombay.

Lc (

E-411
Gordon, Leonid Abramovich.
Iz istorii rabochego klassa Indii; polozhenie
bombeiskogo proletariata v noveishee vremia.
Moskva, Izd-vo vostochnoi lit-ry, 1961. (Akad-
emia nauk SSSR. Institut narodov Azii). 252p.

1. Labor & laboring classes - India
Lc (

E-412
Huddar, Arunkumar.
Labour welfare activities in cotton textile
mills in Vidarbha region. Indore, Univ.of
Indore, 1970. *

Economics Labour welfare (
BDD

E-413
Hurst, Alexander Robert Burnett.
Labour and housing in Bombay. London, P.S.
King and Son, 1925. (Studies in Economics
and Political Science, no.75) 166p.

BM (

E-414
Indapurkar, C.D.
Workers in Ahmednagar sugar factories: a
study of their educational problems, IJAEd,
v.18 (1957), pp.20-26.

Social Science Bibliography India & Pakistan 1957 (

E-415
India. Royal Commission on Labour.
Evidence. London, 1930. Vol.I - Bombay
Presidency, including Sind. Written evidence,
oral evidence.

SOAS supp (

E-416
India (Republic) Dept.of Labour.
Report on an enquiry into family budgets of
industrial workers in various localities. By
S.R.Deshpande. Delhi, 1946. 70p.

BM (

E-417
India (Republic) Ministry of Labour.
Agricultural labour enquiry; report on intensive survey of agricultural labour: employment, underemployment, wages and levels of
living. Delhi, 1955. 7 vols.in 3.

1. Agricultural laborers - India. 2.
Peasantry - India. 3. India - Rural conditions.

U of R

E-418
James, Ralph C.
Labor and technical change: the Bombay
cotton textile industry. Ithaca, Cornell
Univ., 1957. *

Stuckie

E-419
Joshi, L.G.
Industrial labour in C.P.& Berar. Nagpur,
Nagpur Univ., 1953. *

E-420
Joshi, Vidyapati Pralhad.
Strikes in the Bombay cotton textile indus-
try, AV, v.11 (1969), pp.431-91.

*Industry
BAS 1970*

E-421
Joshi, Vidyapati Pralhad.
Study of strikes in the Bombay cotton textile
industry. Poona, Gokhale Institute of Politics
and Economics, 1966. *

Jayakar Lib.

E-422
Lambert, Richard D.
Factory workers and the non-factory population in Poona, JAS, v.18 (1958-1959),
pp.21-42.

Suren

E-423
Lambert, Richard D.
Workers, factories, and social change in
India. Princeton, N.J., Princeton University,
Press, 1963. 260p.

1. Poona, India (City) - Indus. 2. Poona,
India (City) - Soc.condit. 3. Labor & laboring
classes - Poona, India (City). 4. Industrial-
isation - Case studies.

U of R

E-424
Madhya Pradesh, India. Directorate of Economics
and Statistics.
Survey of educated unemployment in Nagpur
City; being the results of a sample investigation among persons who had passed their
matriculation from various examination centres
in Nagpur City during the years 1950-54.
Nagpur, Govt.Print., Madhya Pradesh, 1956.
21p.

LC

E-425
Majumdar, N.A.
Some problems of under-employment; a study
in rural employment, with reference to Bombay-Karnatak. Bombay, Univ.of Bombay, 1957. *

Gupta

E-426
Makharia, Mohanlal Piramal.
Social conditions of textile labour in
Bombay with special reference to produc-
tivity. Bombay, Univ.of Bombay, 1959. *

*Sociology- Occupational
groups
BDD*

E-427
Mann, Harold Hart, 1872-
Land and labor in a Deccan village. By
H.H.Mann, in collaboration with D.L.Sahas-
rabuddhe, N.V.Kanitkar, V.A.Tamhane, and
others. London and Bombay, H.Milford,
Oxford Univ.Press, 1917. (Univ.of Bombay,
Economic series, no.1). 189p.

LC

E-428
Mehta, M.M., 1921-
Survey of educated un-employment in
Nagpur City, AICCER, v.7 (1956), pp.15-16.

JAS 9.

E-429
Morris, Morris David.
The emergence of an industrial labor force
in India; a study of the Bombay cotton mills,
1854-1947. Berkeley, Univ.of California
Press, 1965. 263p.

1. Labor & laboring classes - India - Hist.
2. Textile workers - Bombay.

U of R

E-430
Morris, Morris David.
A history of the creation of a disciplined
labor force in the cotton textile industry
of Bombay City, 1851-1951. Berkeley, Univ.
of California, 1954. *

Case

E-431
Mukherjee, K.
Factory employment in the state of Mahara-
shtra, JUP, v.15 (1962), pp.151-56.

JUP

E-432
Nair, P.A.
Employment market in an industrial metro-
polis; a survey of educated unemployment in
Bombay. Bombay, Lalvani Pub.House, 1968.
110p.

Employment & labor force - Books
JAS Sept 1920

E-433
Newman, R.K.
Labour organisation in the Bombay textile
industry, 1918-1929. Sussex, Univ.of Sussex,
1970. *

Shulman - # 518

E-434
A note on the 1954 census of staff employed
under the Government of Bombay, QBES, v.9
(1956), pp.61-85.

E-435
Pandhe, Madhukar Kashinath.
Labour organizations in Sholapur City.
Poona, Gokhale Institute of Politics and
Economics, 1960. *

Gupta Bib. # 1

E-436
Patel, Kunj M.
Rural labour in industrial Bombay. Bombay,
Popular Prakashan, 1963. 191p.

LC

E-437
Pethe, Vasant P.
Occupational pattern and dispersion of earnings in Sholapur, IJLE, v.4,no.2 (1961), pp.109-19.

So. Asia Soc. Sci. Bib

E-438
Phadke, J.K.
Industrial labour in Khandesh. Bombay, Univ.of Bombay, 1953. *

Gupta

E-439
Pradhan, Gopinath Ramchandra.
Bombay workers of untouchable classes, JUB, v.4 (1936), pp.134-61.

Case

E-440
Pradhan, Gopinath Ramchandra.
Untouchable workers of Bombay city, with a foreword by B.R.Ambedkar. Bombay, Karnatak Pub.House, 1938. 170p.

LC

E-441
Rairikar, Balkrishna Rangnath.
Development of the trade union movement in Bombay State, IJLE, v.1 (1958), pp.124-28.

So. Asia Social Science Bib; Economics

E-442
Ridgel, Gus T.
A study of the labor movement and industrial relations in the cotton textile industry in Bombay, India. Madison, Univ.of Wisconsin, 1957. *

Stachi

E-443
Shah, Maneklal Maganlal.
Labour recruitment and turnover in the textile industry of Bombay Province. Bombay, Univ.of Bombay, 1941. *

Economics - Employment records
BSD

E-444
Sharma, B.D.
Labour problems in cotton textile industry in India. Nagpur, Nagpur Univ., 1958. *

Economics - Welfare
BSD

E-445
Sharma, Dwarka Prasad.
Economic condition of landless agricultural labour in Vidarbha. Nagpur, Nagpur Univ., 1968. *

Economics - Agriculture
BSD

E-446
Talcherkar, Vinayak A.
Our mill hands and the factory labour agitation. Bombay, the author, 1909. 45p.

Econ (Prosp) cat.

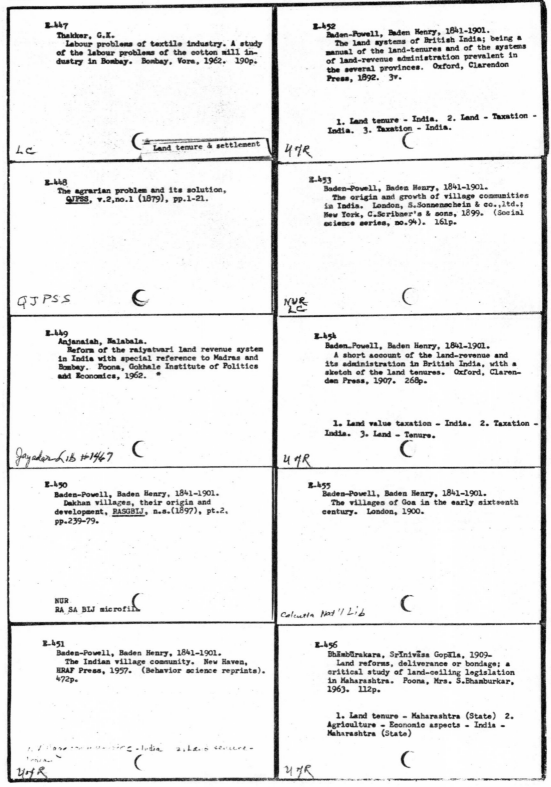

E-447
Thakker, G.K.
Labour problems of textile industry. A study of the labour problems of the cotton mill industry in Bombay. Bombay, Vora, 1962. 190p.

Land tenure & settlement

LC

E-448
The agrarian problem and its solution, QJPSS, v.2,no.1 (1879), pp.1-21.

QJPSS

E-449
Anjanaiah, Malabala.
Reform of the raiyatwari land revenue system in India with special reference to Madras and Bombay. Poona, Gokhale Institute of Politics and Economics, 1962. *

Jayakar Lib #1467

E-450
Baden-Powell, Baden Henry, 1841-1901.
Dakhan villages, their origin and development, RASGBIJ, n.s.(1897), pt.2, pp.239-79.

NUR
RA SA BIJ microfilm

E-451
Baden-Powell, Baden Henry, 1841-1901.
The Indian village community. New Haven, HRAF Press, 1957. (Behavior science reprints). 472p.

1. Land tenure - India. 2. Land tenure - India.

U J R

E-452
Baden-Powell, Baden Henry, 1841-1901.
The land systems of British India; being a manual of the land-tenures and of the systems of land-revenue administration prevalent in the several provinces. Oxford, Clarendon Press, 1892. 3v.

1. Land tenure - India. 2. Land - Taxation - India. 3. Taxation - India.

47R

E-453
Baden-Powell, Baden Henry, 1841-1901.
The origin and growth of village communities in India. London, S.Sonnenschein & co.,ltd.; New York, C.Scribner's & sons, 1899. (Social science series, no.94). 161p.

NUR
LC

E-454
Baden-Powell, Baden Henry, 1841-1901.
A short account of the land-revenue and its administration in British India, with a sketch of the land tenures. Oxford, Clarendon Press, 1907. 268p.

1. Land value taxation - India. 2. Taxation - India. 3. Land - Tenure.

U J R

E-455
Baden-Powell, Baden Henry, 1841-1901.
The villages of Goa in the early sixteenth century. London, 1900.

Calcutta Nat'l Lib

E-456
Bhāmbūrakara, Srīnivāsa Gopāla, 1909-
Land reforms, deliverance or bondage; a critical study of land-ceiling legislation in Maharashtra. Poona, Mrs. S.Bhamburkar, 1963. 112p.

1. Land tenure - Maharashtra (State) 2. Agriculture - Economic aspects - India - Maharashtra (State)

U J R

E-457
  Bhat, Parsharam Abaji.
  Kolaba Khoti question, QJPSS, v.20,no.3
  (1917), pp.190-208.

PSS

E-458
  Bhave, Vinoba, 1895-
  Bhoodan Yajna (land gifts missions). Ahme-
  dabad, Navajivan Pub.House, 1953.

  1. Land tenure - India.

U of R

E-459
  Blair, George Mackenzie.
  Report to the Government of Bombay on the
  revenue system in the Poona Collectorate.
  Dated Poona, 7 Dec.1828. Bombay, 1828?

BM

E-460
  Bombay (Presidency)
  Calendar of Land Revenue Settlements for the
  districts comprised in the Bombay Presidency,
  including Sind. Bombay, 1899, 1906. 2pts.

BM

E-461
  Bombay (Presidency)
  Correspondence regarding the concealment by
  the hereditary officers and others of the
  revenue records of the former Government and
  the remedial measures in progress. Bombay,
  1856. (Bombay Presidency. Selections from
  the records, n.s.,no.29) 57p.

IOL

E-462
  Bombay (Presidency)
  Official correspondence relating to the
  system of revenue survey and assessment and
  its administration in the Bombay Presidency.
  With the proceedings of the Bombay Legislative Council and the debates on the introduction of Act I of 1865. Containing also
  the revised "Survey Rules"...and selections
  from the official correspondence connected
  with the "Joint Report." Bombay, Educational
  Society's Press, 1869.

pre 56 imprints
Bri-Mus

E-463
  Bombay (Presidency)
  Papers relating to the revision of the
  rates of assessment on the expiration of
  the first settlement into the villages
  of the old Parasgad Taluka of the
  Belgaum Collectorate. Bombay, Printed at
  the Government Central Press, 1886. 91p.

UofR

E-464
  Bombay (Presidency)
  Selections with notes from the records
  of the Government, regarding the Khoti
  tenure. Compiled by E.T.Candy. Bombay,
  Reprinted at the Government Central Press,
  1895. 77p.

UofR

E-465
  Bombay (Presidency)
  The survey and settlement manual, etc.
  (vol.2 compiled by F.B.Young, J.C.Whitcombe
  and H.V.Sathe. vol.3 compiled by H.V.Sathe).
  Bombay, 1882, 1902. 3v.

Bri-Mus

E-466
  Bombay (Presidency) Department of Land Records
  and Agriculture.
  Jamabandi reports of northern, central and
  southern divisions and annual report of the
  Dept.of Land Records & Agriculture. Bombay,
  1874-1904. 6 vols.
  Continued as: Land Revenue Administration
  reports, 1903/04-1930/31.

pre 56 imprints

E-467
Bombay (Presidency) Inam Commission.
Correspondence exhibiting the results
of the scrutiny by the Inam Commission
of the lists of Deccan surinjams prepared
in 1844 by the agent for sirdars, Mr.Warden,
and revised...in 1847 by...Mr.Brown:...
also, the proceedings which have taken place
regarding these holdings from the introduction of British rule to the present
period, etc. Bombay, 1856. (Bombay Presidency. Selections from the records, n.s.
no.31).

Ind Off Lib

E-468
Bombay (Presidency) Inam Commission.
Narrative of the Bombay Inam Commission
and Supplementary settlements. By Alfred
Thomas Etheridge. Poona, 1873. (Bombay
Presidency. Selections from the records,
n.s.,no.132).

E-469
Bombay (Presidency) Inam Commission.
Proceedings relative to the resumption
of certain villages and lands held by the
late Anajee Nursew; and claimed as hereditary
inams by his son, Konher Row Anajee. Bombay,
Selections from the records of the Bombay
Government, old series, no.15, 1855.

Ind Off Lib
Brit Mus

E-470
Bombay (Presidency) Revenue Department.
Land revenue in Bombay and Central Provinces.
Bombay, 1870. (Reprint from Times of India
with notes)

E-471
Bombay (Presidency) Revenue Survey Department.
Correspondence relating to the conditions
on which certain estates are held in the
Salsette Taluka of the Thana collectorate.
By Pestanji Jehangir. Bombay, 1886.
(Bombay Presidency. Selections from the
records, n.s.,no.180). 157p.

I.O. Brit Mus

E-472
Bombay (Presidency) Revenue Survey Department.
Correspondence relating to the tenure of
the possessions in the Deccan held by
H.H.Jayajee Rao Sindia under the treaty of
Surje Anjungaum. Bombay, 1856. (Bombay
Presidency. Selections from the records,
n.s.,no.38). 83p.

IOL p 322

E-473
Bombay (Presidency) Revenue Survey Department.
Letters relating to assessment of Lohara
and Wurrungaum pergunnas and nine villages
in Challisgaum talooka. Bombay, Education
Society's Press, 1866. (Bombay Presidency.
Selections from the records, n.s.,no.97).
108p.

pre-Jl imprints

E-474
Bombay (Presidency) Revenue Survey Department.
Manual of revenue accounts of the villages,
talukas and districts of the Bombay Presidency.
By F.G.Hartwell Anderson. Bombay, 1931.

BM

E-475
Bombay (Presidency) Revenue Survey Department.
Official correspondence on the system
of revenue survey and assessment best
adapted for, and more or less completely
carried into effect in the collectorate
of Poona, Sholapoor, Ahmednuggur, Belgaon
and Dharwar in the Bombay Presidency.
Bombay, 1850.

Ind Off Lo

E-476
Bombay (Presidency) Revenue Survey Department.
Official correspondence on the system
of revenue survey and assessment in the
Bombay Presidency. rev.ed. Bombay, 1859.

IOL

E-477
Bombay (Presidency) Revenue Survey Department.
Papers relating to the first revision
settlement in 7 Government villages, second
revision settlement in 56 Government villages and
first revision settlement in 1 and second revision
in 13 inam villages of the Sirur taluka of the
Poona collectorate. By R.D.Bell and others.
Bombay, 1919. (Bombay Presidency. Selections
from the records, n.s.,no.558) 174p.

10L

E-482
Bombay (Presidency) Revenue Survey Department.
Papers relating to the original survey
settlement of the Devgad taluka of the
Ratnagiri collectorate. Bombay, Govt.
Central Press, 1892. (Bombay Presidency.
Selections from the records, n.s.,no.253)
49p.

pre '56 imprints

E-478
Bombay (Presidency) Revenue Survey Department.
Papers relating to the introduction of a
survey settlement into the Mokha 'da Maha'l
in the Shahapur taluka of the Thana collectorate. By C.W.Godfrey and others. Bombay,
1890. (Bombay Presidency. Selections from
the records, n.s.,no.237) 60p.

10L

E-483
Bombay (Presidency) Revenue Survey Department.
Papers relating to the original survey
settlement of the Khed petha of the old
Suvarndurg taluka of the Ratnagiri
collectorate. Bombay, Govt.Central Press,
1892. (Bombay Presidency. Selections from
the records, n.s.,no.254).

pre 56 imprints

E-479
Bombay (Presidency). Revenue Survey Department.
Papers relating to the introduction of
the first survey settlement into the 3
villages forming the Pal Tappa colony in the
Savda taluka of the Khandesh collectorate.
Bombay, Govt.Central Press, 1887. (Bombay Presidency. Selections from the records, n.s.,no.207).

pre 56 imprints

E-484
Bombay (Presidency) Revenue Survey Department.
Papers relating to the original survey
settlement of the village Ghatyacha Khota
in the Panvel taluka of the Kolaba
collectorate. Bombay, Govt.Central Press,
1893. (Bombay Presidency. Selections from
the records, n.s.,no.276). 38p.

pre 56 imprints

E-480
Bombay (Presidency) Revenue Survey Department.
Papers relating to the introduction of the
original survey settlement into 144 villages
of the Sangameshvar taluka of the Ratnagiri
collectorate. Bombay, Govt.Central Press,
1885. (Bombay Presidency. Selections from
the records, n.s.,no.171)

pre '56 imprints

E-485
Bombay (Presidency) Revenue Survey Department.
Papers relating to the original survey
settlement of the village Maldeo in the
Javli taluka of the Satara collectorate.
Bombay, Govt.Central Press, 1912. (Bombay
Presidency. Selections from the records,
n.s.,no.512)

pre '56 imprints

E-481
Bombay (Presidency) Revenue Survey Department.
Papers relating to the original survey
settlement of 124 villages of the Rajapur
taluka of the Ratnagiri collectorate. Bombay, Govt.Central Press, 1888. (Bombay
Presidency. Selections from the records, n.s.,
no.222)

pre '56 imprints

E-486
Bombay (Presidency) Revenue Survey Department.
Papers relating to the original survey
settlement of Vaijapur, a village of the
Chopda taluka of the Khandesh District.
Bombay, Govt.Central Press, 1893. (Bombay
Presidency. Selections from the records,
n.s.,no.271).

pre '56 imprints

E-487
Bombay (Presidency) Revenue Survey Department.
Papers relating to revised rates of
assessment for thirteen different talukas
of the Tanna collectorate. Bombay,
Education Society's Press, 1866. (Bombay
Presidency. Selections from the records,
n.s.,no.96). 444p.

ple 56 imprints

E-488
Bombay (Presidency) Revenue Survey Department.
Papers relating to the second revision settlement of Jaoli taluka and Mahableshwar mahal of
the Satara District. By T.Kothavala and others.
Bombay, 1929. (Bombay Presidency. Selections from
the records, n.s.,no.628) 116p.

10L

E-489
Bombay (Presidency) Revenue Survey Department.
Report on the village communities of the
Deccan, with special reference to the claims
of the village officers in the Ahmednuggur
collectorate to "purbhara Huks," or remuner-
ation from their villages, independent of
what they receive from government. By
R.N.Gooddine. Bombay, 1852. (Bombay
Presidency. Selections from the records,
no.4).

✓✓ BM
✓✓✓ 102

E-490
Bombay (Presidency) Revenue Survey Department.
Revision settlement report on the villages
of talukas Chandor, Nandgaon, Yeola, Niphad
and Kopergaon comprised in the old Patoda
District. By E.L.Taverner. And Supplement:
report on the settlement of the Patoda
District, 1846; by D.Davidson. Bombay, 1876.

10L

E-491
Bombay (Presidency) Settlement Department.
Captain Dowell's notes on the survey of
old Ratnagiri taluka. Bombay, 1912. (Bombay Presidency. Selections from the records,
n.s.,no.197) 468p.

IOL

E-492
Bombay (Presidency) Settlement Department.
Character of land tenure and system of
survey and settlement in the Bombay Presi-
dency. Bombay, 1908. (Bombay Presidency.
Selections from the records, n.s.,no.278)

IOL

E-493
Bombay (Presidency) Settlement Department.
Papers relating to the introduction of the
survey settlement into the village of Rumbhodi
of the Akola taluka of the Ahmednagar collectorate. By W.M.Fletcher and others. Bombay, 1887. (Bombay Presidency. Selections
from the records, n.s.,no.208) 10p.

IOL

E-494
Bombay (Presidency) Settlement Department.
Papers relating to the Joint Report of
1847, with the measurement and classification
rules of the Deccan, Gujarat, Konkan and
Kanara surveys. By H.E.Goldsmid, G.Wingate
and D.Davidson. Bombay, 1917. (Bombay
Presidency, Selections from the records,
n.s.,no.532).

Ind Off Lib

E-495
Bombay (Presidency) Settlement Department.
Papers relating to the modification of
second revision settlement rates in the
Indapur taluka of the Poona collectorate.
By J.P.Brander and others. Bombay, 1912.
(Bombay Presidency. Selections from the
records, n.s.,no.516)

IOL

E-496
Bombay (Presidency) Settlement Department.
Papers relating to the original settlement
of the Akrani mahal of the West Khandesh
District. By T.T.Kothavala and others.
Bombay, 1930. (Bombay Presidency. Selections
form the records, n.s.,no.645)

E-497
Bombay (Presidency). Settlement Department.
Papers relating to the original survey
settlement of the village of Gaonkhadi
in the Rajapur taluka of the Ratnagiri
collectorate. By A.W.W.Mackie. Bombay,
1910. (Bombay Presidency, Selections
from the records, n.s.,no.502). 6p.

Ind Off Lib

E-498
Bombay (Presidency) Settlement Department.
Papers relating to the original survey
settlement of the village of Kotimbe in
the Karjat taluka of the Kolaba collectorate.
By J.L.Lushington and others. Bombay,
1910. (Bombay Presidency, Selections
from the records, n.s.,no.503). 5p.

Ind Off Lib

E-499
Bombay (Presidency) Settlement Department.
Papers relating to the original survey
settlement of the village of Moula in
the Chopda taluka of the East Khandesh
collectorate. By R.G.Gordon and others.
Bombay, 1912. (Bombay Presidency,
Selections from the records, n.s.,no.514).
3p.

Ind Off Lib

E-500
Bombay (Presidency) Settlement Department.
Papers relating to the original survey
settlement of the village of Padale Khurd
in the Raver taluka of the East Khandesh
collectorate. By H.V.Sathe and others.
Bombay, 1911. (Bombay Presidency, Selections
from the records, n.s.,no.508). 7p.

Ind Off Lib

E-501
Bombay (Presidency) Settlement Department.
Papers relating to the original survey
settlement of the village of Ringangaon of
the Erandol taluka of the Khandesh collectorate. By R.B.Pitt and others. Bombay, 1890.
8p.

Ind Off Lib

E-502
Bombay (Presidency) Settlement Department.
Papers relating to the revision and
original settlements of 133 villages
pertaining to the Karvir taluka of the
Kolhapur State. By P.Young. Bombay,
1907. (Bombay Presidency, Selections
from the records, n.s.,no.471).

Ind Off Lib

E-503
Bombay (Presidency) Settlement Department.
Papers relating to the revision of the
rates of assessment on the expiration of
the first settlement in the old Indapur,
Bhimthari, Pabal and Haveli talukas of the
Poona collectorate. Bombay, 1877. (Bombay
Presidency, Selections from the records,
n.s.,no.151).

Ind Off Lib

E-504
Bombay (Presidency) Settlement Department.
Papers relating to the revision of the
rates of assessment on the expiration of
the first settlement in the old Madham,
Sholapur, Mohol, Barsi and Karmala talukas
of the Sholapur Collectorate. Bombay, 1877.
(Bombay Presidency. Selections from the
records, n.s.,no.150).

Ind Off Lib

E-505
Bombay (Presidency) Settlement Department.
Papers relating to the revision of the rates
of assessment on the expiration of the first
settlement in the Shevgaon taluka of the
Ahmednagar collectorate. By J.C.Whitcombe
and others. Bombay, 1885. (Bombay Presidency. Selections form the records, n.s.,
no.167)

I OL

E-506
Bombay (Presidency) Settlement Department.
Papers relating to the revision of the rates
of assessment on the expiration of the first
settlement into 156 villages of the Junnar
taluka of the Pooan collectorate. By G.A.
Laughton and others. Bombay, 1887. (Bombay
Presidency. Selections from the records, n.s.,
no.205)

I OL

E-507
Bombay (Presidency) Settlement Department.
Papers relating to the revision of the rates
of assessment on the expiration of the first
settlement of 114 Government and 6 Inam
villages of the Rahuri taluka of the Ahmednagar
collectorate. By G.A.Laughton and others.
Bombay, 1887. (Bombay Presidency. Selections
from the records, n.s.,no.206)

IOL

E-508
Bombay (Presidency) Settlement Department.
Papers relating to the revision of the rates
of assessment on the expiration of the first
settlement on the Igatpuri taluka of the Nasik
collectorate. By G.A.Laughton and others.
Bombay, 1885.

IOL

E-509
Bombay (Presidency) Settlement Department.
Papers relating to the revision settlement
of 1 saranjam village of the Sangli State.
By F.B.Young and others. Bombay, 1908.
(Bombay Presidency. Selections from the
records, n.s.,no.475). 13p.

Ind Off Lib

E-510
Bombay (Presidency) Settlement Department.
Papers relating to the revision settlement
of 17 villages and second revision settlement
of 103 villages of the Shirpur taluka of the
West Khandesh District. By J.Abbott and
others. Bombay, 1920. (Bombay Presidency.
Selections from the records, n.s.,no.568)

IOL

E-511
Bombay (Presidency) Settlement Department.
Papers relating to the revision settlement
of the Deogad taluka of the Ratnagiri District.
By S.B.Vaidya and others. Bombay, 1929.
(Bombay Presidency. Selections from the
records, n.s.,no.636).

Ind Off Lib

E-512
Bombay (Presidency) Settlement Department.
Papers relating to the revision settlement
of the Nandurbar taluka of the West Khandesh
collectorate. By H.B.Clayton and others.
Bombay, 1912. (Bombay Presidency. Selections
from the records, n.s.,no.510).

Ind Off Lib

E-513
Bombay (Presidency) Settlement Department.
Papers relating to the revision settlement
of the Rajapur taluka of the Ratnagiri
District. By S.B.Vaidya and others. Bombay,
1929. (Bombay Presidency. Selections from
the records, n.s.,no.630)

IOL

E-514
Bombay (Presidency) Settlement Department.
Papers relating to the revision settlement
of the Sangameshwar taluka of the Ratnagiri
collectorate. By J.A.Madan and others. Bombay, 1919. (Bombay Presidency. Selections
from the records, n.s.,no.559)

IOL

E-515
Bombay (Presidency) Settlement Department.
Papers relating to the revision settlement
of the Taloda taluka of the West Khandesh
District. By J.Abbott and others. Bombay,
1921. (Bombay Presidency. Selections from
the records, n.s.,no.582)

IOL

E-516
Bombay (Presidency) Settlement Department.
Papers relating to the revision settlement
report of the three villages of the Barsi
taluka of the Sholapur collectorate. By R.B.
Pitt and others. Bombay, 1892. (Bombay
Presidency. Selections from the records,
n.s.,no.257)

IOL

E-517
    Bombay (Presidency) Settlement Department.
    Papers relating to the revision survey
    settlement of 55 Government villages of the
    Khatav taluka of the Satara collectorate. By
    T.M.Ward and others. Bombay, 1890. (Bombay
    Presidency. Selections from the records,
    n.s.,no.241)

IOL

E-518
    Bombay (Presidency) Settlement Department.
    Papers relating to the revision survey
    settlement of 57 Government villages of
    the Malsiras taluka of the Sholapur col-
    lectorate. By W.M.Fletcher and others.
    Bombay, 1891. (Bombay Presidency. Selec-
    tions from the records, n.s.,no. 247).

Ind Off Lib

E-519
    Bombay (Presidency) Settlement Department.
    Papers relating to the revision survey
    settlement of 5 villages of the Bhimthadi
    taluka of the Poona collectorate. By
    W.M.Fletcher and others. Bombay, 1889.
    (Bombay Presidency. Selections from the
    records, n.s.,no.230). 19p.

Ind Off Lib

E-520
    Bombay (Presidency) Settlement Department.
    Papers relating to the revision survey
    settlement of 14 villages of the Peint taluka
    of the Nasik collectorate. By W.M.Fletcher and
    others. Bombay, 1891. (Bombay Presidency.
    Selections from the records, n.s.,no.248)

IOL

E-521
    Bombay (Presidency) Settlement Department.
    Papers relating to the revision survey
    settlement of 19 Government villages of
    the Kopargaon and Sangamner talukas of the
    Ahmednagar collectorate. By W.M.Fletcher
    and others. Bombay, 1889. (Bombay Presi-
    dency. Selections from the records, n.s.,
    no.234)

IOL

E-522
    Bombay (Presidency) Settlement Department.
    Papers relating to the revision survey
    settlement of one Government village
    (Ardhnari) of the Sholapur collectorate.
    By R.B.Pitt and others. Bombay, 1892.
    (Bombay Presidency. Selections from the
    records, n.s.,no.265).

Ind Off Lib

E-523
    Bombay (Presidency) Settlement Department.
    Papers relating to the revision survey
    settlement of one government village, Yelavi,
    of the Tasgaon taluka of the Satara collector-
    ate. By R.B.Pitt and others. Bombay, 1892.
    (Bombay Presidency. Selections from the records
    n.s.,no.256) 12p.

IOL

E-524
    Bombay (Presidency) Settlement Department.
    Papers relating to the revision survey
    settlement of 118 villages of the Chopda
    taluka of the Khandesh collectorate. By
    W.M.Fletcher and others. Bombay, 1888.
    (Bombay Presidency. Selections from the
    records, n.s.,no.221).

Ind Off Lib

E-525
    Bombay (Presidency) Settlement Department.
    Papers relating to the revision survey
    settlement of 147 darbari and 6 inam villages
    of the Bhudargad taluka of the Kolhapur
    State. By F.Young and others. Bombay, 1908.
    (Bombay Presidency, Selections from the
    records, n.s.,no.474).

Ind Off Lib

E-526
    Bombay (Presidency) Settlement Department.
    Papers relating to the revision survey
    settlement of 142 villages of the Maval
    taluka of the Poona collectorate. By W.M.
    Fletcher and others. Bombay, 1837. (Bom-
    bay Presidency. Selections from the records,
    n.s.,no.211)

IOL

E-527
Bombay (Presidency) Settlement Department.
Papers relating to the revision survey
settlement of 193 villages of the Khed
taluka of the Poona collectorate. By
W.M.Fletcher and others. Bombay, 1889.
(Bombay Presidency. Selections from the
records, n.s.,no.225).

Ind Off Lib

E-528
Bombay (Presidency) Settlement Department.
Papers relating to the revision survey
settlement of 171 Government villages of
the Jamner taluka of the Khandesh collectorate. By W.S.Turnbull and others. Bombay,
1891. (Bombay Presidency. Selections from
the records, n.s.,no.250)

IOL

E-529
Bombay (Presidency) Settlement Department.
Papers relating to the revision survey
settlement of 116 villages of the old
Khalapur Peta of the Karjat taluka of the
Thana collectorate. By C.W.Godfrey and
others. Bombay, 1888. (Bombay Presidency.
Selections from the records, n.s.,no.223)

IOL

E-530
Bombay (Presidency) Settlement Department.
Papers relating to the revision survey
settlement of 165 villages of the old
Nasrapur, now Karjat taluka of the Thana
collectorate. By C.W.Godfrey and others.
Bombay, 1889. (Bombay Presidency. Selections
from the records, n.s.,no.224)

IOL

E-531
Bombay (Presidency) Settlement Department.
Papers relating to the revision survey
settlement of 102 Dangi villages of the
Akola taluka of the Ahmednagar collectorate.
By W.M.Fletcher and others. Bombay, 1889.
(Bombay Presidency. Selections from the
records, n.s.,no.216)

IOL

E-532
Bombay (Presidency) Settlement Department.
Papers relating to the revision survey
settlement of 78 1/2 Government villages
of the Shrigonda taluka of the Ahmednagar
collectorate. By W.M.Fletcher and T.H.
Stewart. Bombay, 1889. (Bombay Presidency.
Selections from the records, n.s.,no.233)

IOL

E-533
Bombay (Presidency) Settlement Department.
Papers relating to the revision survey
settlement of 72 Government villages of the
Karjat taluka of the Ahmednagar collectorate.
By T.M.Ward and others. Bombay, 1890.
(Bombay Presidency. Selections from the
records, n.s.,no.246).

Ind Off Lib

E-534
Bombay (Presidency) Settlement Department.
Papers relating to the revision survey
settlement of 72 Government villages of the
Man taluka of the Satara collectorate. By
T.M.Ward and others. Bombay, 1890. (Bom-
bay Presidency. Selections from the records,
n.s.,no.240)

IOL

E-535
Bombay (Presidency) Settlement Department.
Papers relating to the revision survey
settlement of 16 villages of the Karmala
taluka of the Sholapur collectorate. By
R.B.Pitt and others. Bombay, 1892. (Bombay Presidency. Selections from the records,
n.s.,no.258)

IOL

E-536
Bombay (Presidency) Settlement Department.
Papers relating to the revision survey
settlement of 69 Government villages of
the Khanapur taluka of the Satara collectorate. By W.M.Fletcher and others. Bombay,
1892. (Bombay Presidency. Selections from
the records, n.s.,no.259)

IOL

E-537
Bombay (Presidency) Settlement Department.
Papers relating to the revision survey
settlement of the Jalgaon taluka of the
Khandesh collectorate. By W.M.Fletcher and
others. Bombay, 1892. (Bombay Presidency.
Selections from the records, n.s.,no.262)

IOL

E-538
Bombay (Presidency) Settlement Department.
Papers relating to the revision survey
settlement of the Koregaon taluka of the
Satara collectorate. By W.M.Fletcher and
others. Bombay, 1893. (Bombay Presidency.
Selections from the records, n.s.,no.267)

IOL

E-539
Bombay (Presidency) Settlement Department.
Papers relating to the revision survey
settlement of the Malwan taluka of the
Ratnagiri collectorate. By G.S.Hardy and
others. Bombay, 1915. (Bombay Presidency.
Selections from the records, n.s.,no.528)

IOL

E-540
Bombay (Presidency) Settlement Department.
Papers relating to the revision survey
settlement of the Mulshi petha of the
Haveli taluka of the Poona collectorate.
By R.B.Pitt and others. Bombay, 1893.
(Bombay Presidency. Selections from the
records, n.s.,no.274)

IOL

E-541
Bombay (Presidency) Settlement Department.
Papers relating to the revision survey
settlement of the Navasa taluka of the
Ahmednagar collectorate. By G.A.Laughton
and others. Bombay, 1892. (Bombay Presidency. Selections from the records, n.s.,
no.260)

IOL

E-542
Bombay (Presidency) Settlement Department.
Papers relating to the revision survey
settlement of the Pachora taluka of the
Khandesh collectorate. By R.B.Pitt and others.
Bombay, 1893. (Bombay Presidency. Selections
from the records, n.s.,no.266)

IOL

E-543
Bombay (Presidency) Settlement Department.
Papers relating to the revision survey
settlement of the Pandharpur taluka of the
Sholapur collectorate. By R.B.Pitt and
others. Bombay, 1893. (Bombay Presidency.
Selections from the records, n.s.,no.275)

IOL

E-544
Bombay (Presidency) Settlement Department.
Papers relating to the revision survey
settlement of the Panvel taluka of the
Kolaba collectorate. By W.S.Turnbull and
others. Bombay, 1892. (Bombay Presidency.
Selections from the records, n.s.,no.264).

Ind Off Lib

E-545
Bombay (Presidency) Settlement Department.
Papers relating to the revision survey
settlement of the Sangola taluka of the
Sholapur collectorate. By R.B.Pitt and
others. Bombay, 1893. (Bombay Presidency.
Selections from the records, n.s.,no.268).

Ind Off Lib

E-546
Bombay (Presidency) Settlement Department.
Papers relating to the revision survey
settlement of the Sindkhed taluka of the
Khandesh collectorate. By R.B.Pitt and
others. Bombay, 1893. (Bombay Presidency.
Selections from the records, n.s.,no.273).

Ind Off Lib

E-547
Bombay (Presidency) Settlement Department.
Papers relating to the revision survey
settlement of the villages of Hingangaon
in the Khanapur taluka of the Satara
collectorate. By H.V.Sathe. Bombay,
1912. (Bombay Presidency, Selections from
the records, n.s.,no.513).

Ind Off Lib

E-552
Bombay (Presidency) Settlement Department.
Papers relating to the revision survey
settlement of the 22 darbari and 1 inam
villages of the Atpadi thana of the Aundh
State. By Fred Young and others. Bombay,
1914. (Bombay Presidency. Selections from
the records, n.s. ,no.526).

Ind Off Lib

E-548
Bombay (Presidency) Settlement Department.
Papers relating to the revision survey
settlement of 237 Government villages of
the Bhusaval taluka of the Khandesh collectorate. By W.S.Turnbull and others. Bombay,
1891. (Bombay Presidency. Selections from
the records, n.s.,no.249)

IOL

E-553
Bombay (Presidency) Settlement Department.
Papers relating to the revision survey
settlement of 275 1/2 Government villages
of the Amalner taluka of the Khandesh
collectorate. By W.Turnbull and others.
Bombay, 1889. (Bombay Presidency. Selections from the records, n.s.,no.229)

IOL

E-549
Bombay (Presidency) Settlement Department.
Papers relating to the revision survey
settlement of 38 villages of the Peint
taluka of the Naaik collectorate. By W.M.
Fletcher and others. Bombay, 1889. (Bombay Presidency. Selections from the records,
n.s.,no.232)

IOL

E-554
Bombay (Presidency) Settlement Department.
Papers relating to the revision survey
settlement of 227 villages of the Erandol
taluka of the Khandesh collectorate. By
R.B.Pitt and others. Bombay, 1890. (Bombay Presidency. Selections from the records,
n.s.,no.239)

IOL

E-550
Bombay (Presidency) Settlement Department.
Papers relating to the revision survey
settlement of 36 villages of the Tasgaon
taluka of the Satara collectorate. By H.K.
Disney and others. Bombay, 1888. (Bombay
Presidency. Selections from the records,
n.s.,no.204)

IOL

E-555
Bombay (Presidency) Settlement Department.
Papers relating to the second revision of
the Wai taluka and Khandala mahal of the
Satara District. By M.Webb and others.
Bombay, 1929. (Bombay Presidency, Sel-
ections from the records, n.s.,no.626).

Ind Off Lib

E-551
Bombay (Presidency) Settlement Department.
Papers relating to the revision survey
settlement of 25 Government villages of the
Haveli taluka of the Poona collectorate. By
J.C.Whitcombe and others. Bombay, 1890.
(Bombay Presidency. Selections from the
records, n.s.,no.238)

IOL

E-556
Bombay (Presidency) Settlement Department.
Papers relating to the second revision
settlement of Mulshi peta of the Poona
collectorate. By Rao Bahadur, B.R.Dikshit
and others. Bombay, 1929. (Bombay Presidency, Selections from the records, n.s.,
no.637).

Ind Off Lib

E-557
Bombay (Presidency) Settlement Department.
Papers relating to the second revision
settlement of Pandharpur taluka of the
Sholapur District. By J.H.Garrett and
others. Bombay, 1924. (Bombay Presidency.
Selections from the records, n.s.,no.601)

IOL

E-558
Bombay (Presidency) Settlement Department.
Papers relating to the second revision
settlement of Satara taluka of the Satara
District. By H.D.Baskerville and others.
Bombay, 1929. (Bombay Presidency. Selections
from the records, n.s.,no.635).

Ind Off Lib

E-559
Bombay (Presidency) Settlement Department.
Papers relating to the second revision
settlement of the Alibag taluka of the
Kolaba District. By J.R.Hood and others.
Bombay, 1929. (Bombay Presidency. Selec-
tions from the records, n.s.,no.632).

Ind Off Lib

E-560
Bombay (Presidency) Settlement Department.
Papers relating to the second revision
settlement of the Akola taluka of the
Ahmednagar District. By N.H.Hey and others.
Bombay, 1920. (Bombay Presidency. Selections
from the records, n.s.,no.573).

Ind Off Lib

E-561
Bombay (Presidency) Settlement Department.
Papers relating to the second revision
settlement of the Ambernath taluka of the
Bombay Suburban District. By M.J.Dikshit
and others. Bombay, 1930. (Bombay
Presidency. Selections from the records,
n.s.,no.644).

Ind Off Lib

E-562
Bombay (Presidency) Settlement Department.
Papers relating to the second revision
settlement of the Bassein taluka of the
Thana District. By M.J.Dikshit and others.
Bombay, 1930-33. (Bombay Presidency.
Selections from the records, n.s.,no.643).
2pts.

Ind Off Lib

E-563
Bombay (Presidency) Settlement Department.
Papers relating to the second revision
settlement of the Bhimthadi taluka of the
Poona collectorate. By J.P.Brander and
others. Bombay, 1912. (Bombay Presidency.
Selections from the records, n.s.,no.520).

Ind Off Lib

E-564
Bombay (Presidency) Settlement Department.
Papers relating to the second revision
settlement of the Bhiwndi taluka of the
Thana District. By M.J.Dikshit and others.
Bombay, 1929. (Bombay Presidency. Seclections
from the records, n.s.,no.638)

E-565
Bombay (Presidency) Settlement Department.
Papers relating to the second revision
settlement of the Chalisgaon taluka of the
East Khandesh District. By C.H.Bristow and
others. Bombay, 1927. (Bombay Presidency.
Selections from the records, n.s.,no.614)

IOL

E-566
Bombay (Presidency) Settlement Department.
Papers relating to the second revision
settlement of the Chopda taluka of the East
Khandesh District. By J.Abbott and others.
Bombay, 1920. (Bombay Presidency. Selections
from the records, n.s.,no.576)

IOL

E-567
Bombay (Presidency) Settlement Department.
Papers relating to the second revision
settlement of the Dhulai taluka of the West
Khandesh District. By J.Abbott and others.
Bombay, 1921. (Bombay Presidency. Selections
from the records, n.s.,no.583)

IOL

E-568
Bombay (Presidency) Settlement Department.
Papers relating to the second revision
settlement of the Haveli taluka of the
Poona District. By R.D.Bell and others.
Bombay, 1920. (Bombay Presidency. Selections
from the records, n.s.,no.577)

IOL

E-569
Bombay (Presidency) Settlement Department.
Papers relating to the second revision
settlement of the Igatpuri, Dindori, Nasik,
Niphad, Sinnar, Chandor, Yeola and Nangaon
talukas of the Nasik District, with reports
on inam villages. By J.H.Garrett and others.
Bombay, 1916-1920. (Bombay Presidency.
Selections from the records, n.s.,no.531)
3v.

IoL

E-570
Bombay (Presidency) Settlement Department.
Papers relating to the second revision
settlement of the Jamkhed mahal of the
Ahmednagar District. By A.H.Draoup and
others. Bombay, 1925. (Bombay Presidency.
Selections from the records, n.s.,no.604)

IOL

E-571
Bombay (Presidency) Settlement Department.
Papers relating to the second revision
settlement of the Junnar taluka of the Poona
collectorate. By R.D.Bell and others. Bombay, 1919. (Bombay Presidency. Selections
from the records, n.s.,no.561)

IOL

E-572
Bombay (Presidency) Settlement Department.
Papers relating to the second revision
settlement of the Kalyan taluka of the
Thana District. By M.J.Dikshit and others.
Bombay, 1927. (Bombay Presidency. Selections
from the records, n.s.,no.613)

IOL

E-573
Bombay (Presidency) Settlement Department.
Papers relating to the second revision
settlement of the Karad taluka of the Satara
District. By C.H.Bristow and others.
Bombay, 1929. (Bombay Presidency, Selections
from the records, n.s.,no.631).

Ind Off Lib

E-574
Bombay (Presidency) Settlement Department.
Papers relating to the second revision
settlement of the Karjat taluka of the
Ahmednagar District. By A.H.Draoup and
others. Bombay, 1925. (Bombay Presidency.
Selections from the records, n.s.,no.605)

E-575
Bombay (Presidency) Settlement Department.
Papers relating to the second revision
settlement of the Khanapur taluka of the
Satara District. By M.Webb and others. Bombay, 1928. (Bombay Presidency. Selections
from the records, n.s.,no.620)

IOL

E-576
Bombay (Presidency) Settlement Department.
Papers relating to the second revision
settlement of the Khatav taluka of the
Satara District. By M.Webb and others.
Bombay, 1928. (Bombay Presidency. Selections
from the records, n.s.,no.682).

Ind Off Lib

E-577
Bombay (Presidency) Settlement Department.
Papers relating to the second revision
settlement of the Khed taluka of the Ratnagiri District. By R.G.Gordon and others.
Bombay, 1929. (Bombay Presidency. Selections
from the records, n.s.,no.627)

IOL

E-578
Bombay (Presidency) Settlement Department.
Papers relating to the second revision
settlement of the Koregaon taluka of the
Satara District. By M.Webb and others.
Bombay, 1930. (Bombay Presidency. Selec-
tions from the records, n.s.,no.642)

IOL

E-579
Bombay (Presidency) Settlement Department.
Papers relating to the second revision
settlement of the Man taluka of the Satara
District. By M.Webb and others. Bombay,
1929. (Bombay Presidency. Selections from
the records, n.s.,no.634).

Ind Off Lib

E-580
Bombay (Presidency) Settlement Department.
Papers relating to the second revision
settlement of the Mandangad petha of the
Ratnagiri District. By R.G.Gordon and
others. Bombay, 1928. (Bombay Presidency.
Selections from the records, n.s.,no.619)

IOL

E-581
Bombay (Presidency) Settlement Department.
Papers relating to the second revision
settlement of the Maval taluka of the Poona
collectorate. By R.D.Bell and others. Bombay, 1919. (Bombay Presidency. Selections
from the records, n.s.,no.565)

IOL

E-582
Bombay (Presidency) Settlement Department.
Papers relating to the second revision
settlement of the Murbad taluka of the Thana
District. By M.J.Dikshit and others. Bombay,
1928. (Bombay Presidency. Selections from
the records, n.s.,no.618)

IOL

E-583
Bombay (Presidency) Settlement Department.
Papers relating to the second revision
settlement of the Nagar taluka of the
Ahmednagar collectorate. By J.H.Garrett
and others. Bombay, 1920. (Bombay Presidency. Selections from the records, n.s.,
no.575).

Ind Off Lib

E-584
Bombay (Presidency) Settlement Department.
Papers relating to the second revision
settlement of the Panvel taluka including
Uran mahal of the Kolaba District. By J.R.
Hood and others. Bombay, 1925. (Bombay
Presidency. Selections from the records,
n.s.,no.609)

IOL

E-585
Bombay (Presidency) Settlement Department.
Papers relating to the second revision
settlement of the Parner taluka of the
Ahmednagar collectorate. By J.H.Garrett
and others. Bombay, 1920. (Bombay Presidency. Selections from the records, n.s.,
no.567)

IOL

E-586
Bombay (Presidency) Settlement Department.
Papers relating to the second revision
settlement of the Patan taluka of the Satara
District. By C.H.Bristow and others. Bombay,
1928. (Bombay Presidency. Selections from
the records, n.s.,no.623)

IOL

E-587
Bombay (Presidency) Settlement Department.
Papers relating to the second revision
settlement of the Pen taluka including
Nagothna mahal and 32 villages of Roha
taluka of the Kolaba District. By J.R.Hood
and others. Bombay, 1928. (Bombay Presidency. Selections from the records, n.s.,
no.624).

Ind Off Lib

E-588
Bombay (Presidency) Settlement Department.
Papers relating to the second revision
settlement of the Purandhar taluka of the
Poona collectorate. By R.D.Bell and others.
Bombay, 1920. (Bombay Presidency. Selections
from the records, n.s.,no.571).

Ind Off Lib

E-589
Bombay (Presidency) Settlement Department.
Papers relating to the second revision
settlement of the Ratnagiri taluka of the
Ratnagiri collectorate. By J.A.Madan and
others. Bombay, 1920. (Bombay Presidency.
Selections from the records, n.s.,no.574).

Ind Off Lib

E-590
Bombay (Presidency) Settlement Department.
Papers relating to the second revision
settlement of the Raver taluka of the East
Khandesh District. By E.H.P.Jolly and others.
Bombay, 1920. (Bombay Presidency. Selections
from the records, n.s.,no.570)

E-591
Bombay (Presidency) Settlement Department.
Papers relating to the second revision
settlement of the Roha taluka of the Kolaba
District. By R.P.Pandit and others. Bombay,
1929. (Bombay Presidency. Selections from
the records, n.s.,no.640)

E-592
Bombay (Presidency) Settlement Department.
Papers relating to the second revision
settlement of the Sangola taluka of the
Sholapur District. By J.H.Garrett and
others. Bombay, 1924. (Bombay Presidency.
Selections from the records, n.s.,no.602).

Ind Off Lib

E-593
Bombay (Presidency) Settlement Department.
Papers relating to the second revision
settlement of the Shahada taluka of the West
Khandesh District. By J.Abbott and others.
Bombay, 1920. (Bombay Presidency. Selections
from the records, n.s.,no.578)

IOL

E-594
Bombay (Presidency) Settlement Department.
Papers relating to the second revision
settlement of the Shevgaon taluka including
the Pathardi mahal of the Ahmednagar collectorate. By J.P.Brander and others. Bombay, 1920. (Bombay Presidency. Selections
from the records, n.s.,no.569)

IOL

E-595
Bombay (Presidency) Settlement Department.
Papers relating to the second revision
settlement of the Sindkheda taluka of the
West Khandesh District. By J.H.Garrett and
others. Bombay, 1925. (Bombay Presidency.
Selections from the records, n.s.,no.610)

IOL

E-596
Bombay (Presidency) Settlement Department.
Papers relating to the second revision
settlement of the South Salsette taluka of
the Bombay Suburban District. By M.J.Dikshit
and others. Bombay, 1929. (Bombay Presidency. Selections from the records, n.s.,
no.641)

IOL

E-597
Bombay (Presidency) Settlement Department.
Papers relating to the second revision
settlement of the Tasgaon taluka of the
Satara District. By A.Master and others.
Bombay, 1910. (Bombay Presidency. Selections
from the records, n.s.,no.572)

IOL

E-598
Bombay (Presidency) Settlement Department.
Papers relating to the second revision
settlement of the Thana mahal of the Thana
District. By M.J.Dikshit and others. Bombay, 1929. (Bombay Presidency. Selections
from the records, n.s.,no.639)

IOL

E-599
Bombay (Presidency) Settlement Department.
Papers relating to the second revision
settlement of the Valva taluka and Shirala
petha of the Satara District. By C.H.Bristow
and others. Bombay, 1929. (Bombay Presidency. Selections from the records, n.s.,no.
625)

IOL

E-600
Bombay (Presidency) Settlement Department.
Papers relating to the second revision
settlement of the Yawal taluka of the
East Khandesh District. By E.H.P.Jolly
and others. Bombay, 1919. (Bombay Presidency. Selections from the records, n.s.,
no.562)

IOL

E-601
Bombay (Presidency) Settlement Department.
Papers relating to the settlement of the
hereditary district officers' watans in the
Deccan and Gujarat. By H.Hart and others.
Bombay, 1895. (Bombay Presidency. Selections
from the records, n.s.,no.174)

IOL

E-602
Bombay (Presidency) Settlement Department.
Papers relating to the survey settlement of
21 villages: revision settlement of 1 darbari
village original ... of 20 (18 darbari and 2
inam) villages of the Aundh State. By J.C.
Whitcombe and others. Bombay, 1894. (Bombay
Presidency. Selections from the records,
n.s.,no.341)

E-603
Bombay (Presidency) Settlement Department.
Papers relating to the third revision
settlement of the Kopergaon taluka of the
Ahmednagar District. By A.H.Dracup and
others. Bombay, 1925. (Bombay Presidency.
Selections from the records, n.s.,no.608).

Ind Off Lib

E-604
Bombay (Presidency) Settlement Department.
Papers relating to the third revision
settlement of the Sangamner taluka of the
Ahmednagar. By A.H.Dracup and others. Bombay, 1925. (Bombay Presidency. Selections
from the records, n.s.,no.606)

IOL

E-605
Bombay (Presidency) Settlement Department.
Papers relative to the introduction
of revised rates of assessment into
eight talukas and two pettas of the
Khandesh collectorate. Bombay, 1856.
(Bombay Presidency, Selections from the
records, n.s.,no.93).

Ind Off Lib

E-606
Bombay (Presidency) Settlement Department.
Papers relative to the introduction of
revised rates of assessment into part of
the Niphar and Chandur talukas in the Nasik
collectorate, with an appendix showing
progress of the survey in 1840-43. Bombay,
1872. (Bombay Presidency. Selections from
the records, n.s.,no.130)

E-607
Bombay (Presidency) Settlement Department.
Papers relative to the introduction of
revised rates of assessment into the Dhoolia
and Chaliagaum talookas of the Khandesh collectorate. By P.A.Elphinstone. Bombay, 1863.
(Bombay Presidency. Selections from the
records, n.s.,no.72)

IOL

E-608
Bombay (Presidency) Settlement Department.
Papers relative to the introduction of
revised rates of assessment into the Mahim
talooka of the Tanna collectorate. By
W.Waddington and others. Bombay, 1863.
(Bombay Presidency. Selections from the
records, n.s.,no.73).

Ind Off Lil

E-609
Bombay (Presidency) Settlement Department.
Papers relative to the introduction of
revised rates of assessment into the
Mamlutdar's and Tulleh Mahalkurree's
divisions of the Rajpooree talooka of
the Colaba sub-collectorate. By J.T.Francis
and others. Bombay, 1863. (Bombay Presidency. Selections from the records, n.s.,
no.74).

Ind Off Lib

E-610
Bombay (Presidency) Settlement Department.
Papers relative to the introduction of
revised rates of assessment into the Mawul
talook of the Poona collectorate. By J.T.
Francis and others. Bombay, 1863. (Bombay Presidency. Selections from the records,
n.s.,no.70)

IOL

E-611
Bombay (Presidency) Settlement Department.
Papers relative to the introduction of
revised rates of assessment into the Moorbar
talook of the Tanna collectorate. By J.
Francis and J.R.Morgan. Bombay, 1861.
(Bombay Presidency. Selections from the
records, n.s.,no.62)

IOL

E-612
Bombay (Presidency) Settlement Department.
Papers relative to the introduction of
revised rates of assessment into the Walwa
talooka of the Satara collectorate. By W.C.
Anderson and others. Bombay, 1863. (Bombay Presidency. Selections from the records,
n.s.,no.75) 15p.

IOL

E-613
Bombay (Presidency) Settlement Department.
Papers relative to the revision of assess-
ment of certain villages in the talukas of
Chandore, Dindori, Niphar and Nasik, in the
Nasik collectorate. By W.Waddington and
others. Bombay, 1875. (Bombay Presidency.
Selections from the records, n.s.,no.145).

Ind Off Lib

E-614
Bombay (Presidency) Settlement Department.
Papers relative to the revision of the
assessment of the Indapoor talooka in the
Poona collectorate. By J.Francis and others.
Bombay, 1868. (Bombay Presidency. Selections
from the records, n.s.,no.107).

Ind Off Lib

E-615
Bombay (Presidency) Settlement Department.
Papers relative to the revision of the
rates of assessment of the Kharapat lands
of the Alibagh taluka. By J.Gibson and
others. Bombay, 1874. (Bombay Presidency.
Selections from the records, n.s.,no.144).

ad Off Lib

E-616
Bombay (Presidency) Settlement Department.
Report by Capt.Wingate ... on the plan of
survey and assessment most suitable to the
Province of Khandesh, and also the instruc-
tions issued on the subject by Government.
Bombay, 1852. (Bombay Presidency. Selections
from the records, no.1)

IOL

E-617
Bombay (Presidency) Settlement Department.
Report by Capt.Wingate ... on the subject
of introducing a survey and revision of
assessment in the Rutngherry collectorate,
also a letter from the Revenue Commissioner,
S.D., submitting the above report and the
instructions issued by the Government.
Bombay, 1852. (Bombay Presidency. Selections
from the records, no.2)

IOL

E-618
Bombay (Presidency) Settlement Department.
Report on revision of assessment of 118
Government and 19 inam villages of the Navasa
taluka, Nagar Collectorate. By G.A.Laughton.
Bombay, 1882.

IOL

E-619
Bombay (Presidency) Settlement Department.
Report on revision of assessment of 142
Government villages of the Junnar taluka,
Poona Collectorate. By G.A.Laughton. Bom-
bay, 1883.

IOL

E-620
Bombay (Presidency) Settlement Department.
Report on revision of assessment of 37
Government villages of the Sirur taluka,
Poona Collectorate, and survey rates to be
introduced for the first time into one
Government village. By G.A.Laughton. Bom-
bay, 1883.

IOL

E-621
Bombay (Presidency) Settlement Department.
Report on the experimental revenue settlement of certain villages in the broken and
hilly country forming the Kownaee talooka
of the Nassick sub-collectorate; by C.E.Fraser
Tytler...and letters on the subject from
H.E.Goldsmid...and J.Vibart, etc. Bombay,
1853. (Bombay Presidency. Selections from
the records, no.6).

Ind Off Lib

E-622
Bombay (Presidency) Settlement Department.
Report on the revised settlement of 14
villages of the old Pabal taluka, transferred
to Junnar. By G.A.Laughton. Bombay, 1883.

Ind Off Lib

E-623
Bombay (Presidency) Settlement Department.
Report on the revision of land assessment
in the Oomergaum peita of the Sunjaun
taluka, Tanna collectorate. By J.T.Francis
and others. Bombay, 1865. (Bombay
Presidency, Selections from the records,n.s.,
no.88). 16p.

Ind Off Lib

E-624
Bombay (Presidency) Settlement Department.
Report on the revision of assessment of
the Nagar taluka, Ahmednagar collectorate.
By G.A.Laughton. Bombay, 1884.

IOL

E-625
Bombay (Presidency) Settlement Department.
Reports on the assessment of the Rahooree
talooka in the Ahmednagar collectorate. By
G.S.A.Anderson. Bombay, 1870. (Bombay
Presidency. Selections from the records,
n.s.,no.117)

IOL

E-626
Bombay (Presidency) Settlement Department.
Revenue survey and settlement atlas of the
Khandesh collectorate. Bombay, 1876.

Markham

E-627
 Boyd, William Sprott.
  A report dated 26th Nov.1828 on the revenue
 system of the Ahmednuggur Collectorate. Bombay, 1830?

B.M.

E-628
 Central Provinces, India. Settlement Dept.
  Report of the land revenue settlement of
 the Bhandara district in Central Provinces,
 effected during the years 1894-1899, by A.B.
 Napier. Nagpur, 1902.

vp IOL

E-629
 Central Provinces and Berar, India.
  The Berar revenue manual. vol.2. Nagpur,
 Govt.Press and Book Depot., 1968.

E-630
 Dandekar, Gopal Krishna.
  The law of land tenures in the Bombay Presi-
 dency. Bombay, 1912. 2v.

E-631
 Dandekar, Vinayak Mahadeo, 1920-
  Crucial considerations in a land policy for
 Maharashtra, JUP, v.15 (1962), pp.164-65.

E-632
 Dandekar, Vinayak Mahadeo, 1920-   and
  Khudanpur, G.J.
  Impact of tenancy act in Maharashtra. In:
 Rural sociology in India. By A.R.Desai.
 3d ed. Bombay, Indian Society of Agri-
 cultural Economics, 1961. pp.479-504.

E-633
 Dandekar, Vinayak Mahadeo, 1920- and
  Khudanpur, G.J.
  Working of Bombay tenancy act, 1948;
 report of investigation. Poona, D.R.Gadgil,
 1957. (Gokhale Institute of Politics and
 Economics, pub.no.35). 194p.

1.Farm tenancy - Bombay (state)
UofR

E-634
  The Deccan Agriculturists' Bill, QJPSS, v.2,
 no.2 (1879), pp.43-67.

PSS

E-635
 Deshpande, V.D.
  History of tenancy relations in the State
 of Maharashtra since 1900, AV, v.12 (1970),
 pp.193-236.

BAS 1970

E-636
 Dutt, Romesh Chunder, 1848-1909.
  The peasant proprietors of India, AR,
 ser.3 (1903), pp.231-44.

E-637
Elliot, Sir Walter.
Ancient tenures of land in the Maharashtra country, IA, v.15 (1886), pp.268-72.

N IA*

E-638
Etheridge, Alfred Thomas, 1825-
An epitome of the Inam Commission. n.p., 1875? 104p.

U of R

E-639
Feudal oppression in Hyderabad (Deccan). Being a survey of the conditions in the Paigha Jagirs of H.E.H. the Nizam. Poona, Yashvant Krishna Vaswani, 1939. 42p.

Bom (Pres) cat

E-640
Gadgil, Dhananjaya Ramchandra, 1901-
Bombay land revenue system. A booklet criticising the Bombay land revenue system. Surat, the author, 1928. 34p.

Bom (Pres) cat

E-641
Gharat, Ramji Lakshman.
Alibag revision settlement: being a series of letters indicating a departure in the land revenue policy of the Bombay government as applied to the Konkan districts. Bombay, Subodh Prakash Press, 1896. 240p.

BM

E-642
Giberne, George and Simpson, James B.
Reports on the system of revenue management within the Collectorate of Candeish and the Northern Concan. Bombay? 1830?

LM

E-643
Gordon, R.G.
The Bombay survey and settlement manual. 2d ed. Nagpur, Govt.Press, 1959-60. 2v.

U of R

E-644
Gordon, R.G.
Some notes on the village system of the Bombay Presidency, JASB, v.12 (1921-1924), pp.92-101.

fiver

E-645
Green, Henry.
The Deccan ryots and their land tenure. Bombay, Bombay Gazette Press, 1852. 136p.

BM

E-646
Gupte, Kashinath Shrikrishna.
The Bombay tenancy problem. Bombay, 1938. 43p.

E-647
Hate, Manohar Vinayakrao.
   Farm ownership and tenancy with particular
reference to the effect of tenancy in Thana
District. Bombay, Univ.of Bombay, 1950. *

*Tenancy + land
& reform*
BDD

E-648
Hyderabad, India (State) Royal Commission on
   Jagir Adimination and Reforms.
   Report. Bangalore City, Printed at the
Bangalore Press, 1947. 150p.

UofR

E-649
Inam; and what's in a name, BQR, v.3 (1856),
pp.153-90.

E-650
India. Dept.of Revenue and Agriculture.
   Papers connected with the Bombay revenue and
settlement system. Comp.by order of the secre-
tary, Revenue and Agricultural Dept., Govt.of
India. Calcutta, Office of the Supt.of the
Govt.Print., India, 1883. 225p.

LC

E-651
Indian Society of Agricultural Economics.
   Land tenures in India. 1st ed. Bombay,
Vora, 1946. "Reprinted from the Indian
Famine Commissioners Report, v.II,pt.4."
90p.

   Land tenure - India.

LC

E-652
Jhirad, J.F.M.
   The Khandesh survey riots of 1852: government
policy and rural society in western India,
RASGBIJ, no.3/4 (1968), pp.151-65.

BAS 1970

E-653
Joshi, Tryambak Mahadeo.
   Agricultural land revenue in the Bombay
State. Philadelphia, Univ.of Pennsylvania,
1959. *

Stucki

E-654
Kamerkar, M.P.
   The use of the Bhandari (guarantee) system
by the British in Baroda State, IHCP, v.27
(1965), pp.358-66.

IHcP

E-655
Knight, Robert.
   The Inam Commission unmasked. London,
Effingham Wilson, 1859.

BM

E-656
Kotovsky, G.G.
   Agrarian relations in Maharashtra in late
19th and early 20th centuries. In: Tilak
and the struggle for Indian freedom. Ed.by
I.M.Reisner and N.M.Goldberg. New Delhi,
People's Pub.House, 1966. pp.95-170.

UofR

E-657
Kshirsagar, Devadatta Bhalchandra.
Law of land tenures, containing a full statement of ryotwari tenure, inams, saranjams and watans ... as prevalent in the Bombay Presidency. Poona, 1929. 201p.

IOL

E-658
Land revenue in Bombay and Central Provinces, etc. Reprint from 'Times of India' with notes. Bombay, 1870.

Cal Nat l Lib

E-659
Lobo, Sylvester.
A document with the early revenue of Bombay, QJMS, v.18 (1927), pp.100-14.

QJMS

E-660
Maharashtra, India (State) Laws, statutes, etc.
The Bombay land revenue code, 1879, Bombay Act no.V of 1879, as amended up-to-date. With explanatory and critical notes, exhaustive commentary, summary of land revenue rules, government resolutions, orders, High Court rulings, B.R.T. decisions, etc., by K.S.Gupte. 5th rev.& enl.ed. Poona, K.S.Gupte, 1962. 1084p.

1. Land - Taxation - Maharashtra, India (State)
2. Land tenure - Maharashtra, India (State)

LC

E-661
Maharashtra, India (State) Laws, statutes, etc.
The Bombay tenancy and agricultural lands act with rules (Bombay act no.LXVII of 1948) as amended by Maharashtra act VII of 1963 and Gujarat act XXVII of 1961. By K.S.Gupte. 8th rev.& enl.ed. Poona, K.S.Gupte, 1963. 712p.

N U C

E-662
Maharashtra, India (State) Revenue and Foreign Dept.
Unification of land revenue laws; scrutiny of the report of the Unification Committee. Nagpur, Govt.Press, 1965. 440p.

1. Land tenure - Maharashtra, India (State) - Law. 2. Landlord & tenant - Maharashtra, India (State). 3. Land value taxation - Maharashtra, India (State)

LC

E-663
Marchant, Pierre.
Vinoba Bhave: the silent voice all India listens to, Réalités, v.182 (1966), pp.32-37.

Ja S '66

E-664
Memorial to the government of Bombay regarding the bill to amend the Deccan Agriculturists' Relief Acts (1879-86), QJPSS, v.17, no.2 (1894), pp.16-22.

QJPSS

E-665
Minocha, V.S.
Ranade on the Agrarian problem, IESHR, v.2 (1965), pp.357-66.

Case

E-666
Mr. Wedderburn and his critics on a permanent settlement for the Deccan, QJPSS, v.3,no.3 (1880), pp.17-36.

QJPSS

E-667
Modak, D.S.
The Bombay land system and village administration. Poona, Pub.by the author, 1934.
537p.

Modak R

E-668
Mody, Ramniklal R.
Inami lands in Bombay City. JUB, v.2 (1934),
pp.213-35.

JuB

E-669
Mulla, Ghulamdastgir Rabman.
Factors influencing patterns on individual
holdings. (Jalgaon District, Maharashtra
State) Poona, Gokhale Institute of Politics
and Economics, 1968. 2v. *

Gokhale Inst Econ

E-670
Murdeshwar, Ganesh Padmanabh.
A synopsis of the law of Inam, Sarajam and
Watan. Bombay, the author, 1911. 80p.

BM (Priv Cat

E-671
Nanekar, K.R.
Land reforms in Vidarbha; an enquiry into
the implementation of land reforms in the
Vidarbha region. Calcutta, Oxford and IBH
Pub.Co., 1968. 334p.

Land reform & reorganisation ...
IAS Sept 1970

E-672
The new settlement of the Khoti dispute.
QJPSS, v.2,no.2 (1879), pp.18-44.

QJPSS

E-673
Nisbet, Josiah, and Reid, Lestock R.
Reports on the system of revenue management
in the Collectorates of Dharwar and the Southern Concan. Bombay, 1830.

BM

E-674
Patel, Govindlal Dalsukhbhai, 1908-
Agrarian reforms in Bombay; the legal and
economic consequences of the abolition of
land tenures. Bombay, G.D.Patel, 1950. 241p.

LC

E-675
Patel, Govindlal Dalsukhbhai, 1908-
Land problem of reorganised Bombay State.
Bombay, N.M.Tripathi, 1957. 466p.

Social Science Bibliography - India
Publication 1957 - Economics, p.57

E-676
Representation on the Deccan Agriculturists'
relief bill, QJPSS, v.2,no.3 (1879), pp.
103-119.

QJPSS

E-677
A representation on the introduction of revised land revenue rates in the Mawal taluka
of the Poona district, QJPSS, v.11,no.1
(1888), pp.1-5.

QJPSS

E-678
A representation on the report of the Deccan
Agriculturists' Relief Act Commission,
QJPSS, v.15,no.3 (1892), pp.46-51.

QJPSS

E-679
The revenue system of Bombay, CR, v.44
(1867), pp.355-68.

E-680
Rogers, Alexander.
The land revenue administration of Poona,
AR, v.7 (1889), pp.134-89.

E-681
Rogers, Alexander.
The land revenue of Bombay; a history of
its administration, rise and progress. London, W.H.Allen and co., 1892. 2v.

E-682
Settlement of land revenue, and the future
of the agricultural classes, BQR, v.4
(1856), pp.386-418.

UofR

E-683
Shingarey, M.K.
Effects of recent tenancy legislation in
Berar; a case study, IJAE, v.12 (1957), pp.
126-34.

E-684
Shivamangi, H.B.
Agrarian reforms in Bombay State. Bombay,
Univ.of Bombay, 1955. *

E-685
Shivamangi, H.B.
Working of farm tenancy legislation in
Bombay, IEJ, v.3(2) (1955), pp.192-210.

E-686
Siddiqi, A.
Land revenue administration in the ceded
and conquered provinces and its economic
background, 1819-33. Oxford, Oxford Univ.,
1962-63. *

E-687
Sinha, Ram Mohan.
Revenue administration of Nagpur State
under the British management (1818-1830).
JIH, v.43 (1965), pp.633-45.

JaS66

E-688
Sykes, William Henry, 1790-1872.
Land tenures of Dukkun. London, Printed by
James Moyes, 1836. 29p.

cal nat Lib

E-689
Venkataramana, Varanasi.
Land reforms in India with special reference
to Hyderabad since 1947. Hyderabad, Osmania
Univ., 1958. *

Tenancy: land
reform
BDD

E-690
A vindication of the Khoti settlement of 1880.
QJPSS, v.5,no.3 (1882), pp.19-31.

GJPSS

E-691
Wedderburn, William, 1838-
Mr. Wedderburn and his critics on a permanent settlement for the Deccan. QJPSS, v.3
(1880), pp.17-36.

Case

E-692
Wunderlich, Gene L.
The Bombay Tenancy and Agricultural Lands
Act as a means of Agrarian Reform. Cedar
Falls, Iowa State Univ., 1955. *

Stucki

Local economic conditions
& community development

E-693
Bapat, Nilkanth Gangadhar.
Economic development of Ahmednagar District.
Poona, Brihan Maharashtra College of Commerce,
Univ.of Poona, 1968. *

Jayaker Lib # 1525

E-694
Bhagat, Mahadeo Gopal.
The farmer, his welfare and wealth.
Bombay, Co-operators' Book Depot, 1943.
(Studies in agricultural economics. Study
no.1). 319p.

Bhiwandi, India (Taluka) - Soc. condit. 2. Peasantry-
India - Bhiwandi (Taluka)
u

E-695
Bombay (City) Rotary Club. Community Services
Committee.
Dharavi; an economic and social survey of
a village in the suburbs of Bombay. By A.K.
Nagaraj and others. Bombay, 1945. 49p.

IOL

E-696
Bombay (Presidency) Labour Office.
Report on an enquiry into family budgets of
cotton mill workers in Sholapur City, etc.
Bombay, 1928.

E-697
Bombay (Presidency) Labour Office.
Report on an enquiry into middle class
family budgets in Bombay City, etc. Bombay,
1928.

E-702
Borkar, Vishnu Vinayak and Padhye, M.D.
Purna River-Valley project; a study of the
socio-economic benefits. Aurangabad, Marathwada Univ., 1971?

PL 480 72

E-698
Bombay (Presidency) Labour Office.
Report on an enquiry into middle class
unemployment in the Bombay Presidency, etc.
Bombay, 1927.

BM

E-703
Chapekar, Laxman Narayan, 1906-
Community development project blocks in
Badlapur, SB. v.7 (1958), pp.111-22.

South Asia Social Science
Bibliography; Economics, n.71

E-699
Bombay (Presidency) Labour Office.
Report on an enquiry into working class
family budgets in Bombay City, etc. (1932-
33) Bombay, 1935. 45p.

E-704
Crawfurd, John, 1783-1868.
Letters from British settlers in the interior
of India, descriptive of their own condition,
and that of the native inhabitants under the
Government of the East India Co. London,
J.Ridgway, 1831. 105p.

1. British in India. 2. East India Co.
(English) 3. India - Econ.condit.

LC

E-700
Bombay (Province) Labour Office.
Report on an enquiry into working class
budgets in Bombay, by G.Findlay Shirras.
Bombay, Printed at the Govt.Central Press,
1923. 303p.

U of R

E-705
Dandekar, Vinayak Mahadeo, 1920-
Report on the Poona schedules of the
National Sample Survey, 1950-51. Poona,
D.R.Gadgil, 1953. (Gokhale Institute of
Politics and Economics, pub.no.26) 231p.

N of R

E-701
Bombay (State) Labour and Social Welfare
Department.
Report on an enquiry into the socio-economic
conditions of fishermen in selected centres in
Bombay area. Bombay, Director, Printing and
Stationery, 1959. 40p.

E-706
Dandekar, Vinayak Mahadeo, 1920-
Second report of the Poona Schedules of
the National Sample Survey (1950-55).
Poona, Gokhale Institute of Politics and
Economics, 1954. 171p.

E-707
Datar, B.N.
Middle class cost of living index, Bombay
City, IEJ, v.1 (1954), pp.365-79.

ll autumn, 1955

E-708
Deshpande, U.G. and Savale, R.S.
Nhavari: a socio-economic study. 1st ed.
Poona, Department of Agriculture, Maharashtra
State, 1967. (Socio-economic studies, 3).
(Maharashtra, India (State). Department of
Agriculture, Research Bulletin 6).

PL 480, 772 p.914

E-709
Diskalkar, P.D.
Pimple-Saudagar after four decades: a
resurvey, IJAE, v.13 (1958), pp.46-56.

*South Asia Social Science
Bibliography, Economics*

E-710
Diskalkar, P.D.
Resurvey of a Deccan village:Pimple Saudagar.
Bombay, Indian Society of Agricultural Econ-
omics, 1960. 174p.

*South Asia Social Science
Bibliography, economics, p.*

E-711
Gadgil, Dhananjaya Ramchandra, 1901-
Poona: a socio-economic survey. Poona,
D.R.Gadgil, 1945-52. (Gokhale Institute
of Politics and Economics. Pub.no.12).
2v.

*1. Poona (India City) Economic cond. 2. Poona,
India City) Soc. cond.*

E-712
Gadgil, Dhananjaya Ramchandra, 1901-
Sholapur city; socio-economic studies.
Bombay, N.Y., Asia Pub.House, 1965.
(Gokhale Institute studies, no.46). 349p.

*1. Sholapur, India (City) Econ. condit. 2. Sholapur,
India (City) Soc. condit.*

Cat 2

E-713
Ghodke, N.B.
Socio-economic survey of Lohgaon and
Jigla, Nanded, Shri Sharda Bhuvan. Education
Society's Yeshwant Mahavidyalaya, 1965? 59p.

PL 480, 1968 p.422

E-714
Godbole, S.H.
Kelshi village survey, RP, v.1,no.3 (1954),
pp.22-34.

E-715
Gordon, Leonid Abramovich.
Social and economic conditions of Bombay
workers on the eve of the 1908 strike.
In: Tilak and the struggle for Indian
freedom. Ed.by I.M.Reisner and N.M.Goldberg.
New Delhi, People's publishing house, 1966.
pp.471-544.

Vol 2

E-716
Gracias, João Baptista Amancio.
Regimen economico-financeiro da Índia
Portuguesa. Nova Goa, 1909.

E-717
Hate, Chandrakala Anandarao, 1903-
The economic conditions of educated women in
Bombay City. JUB. v.3 (1935). pp.1-43.

Case

E-718
Hulbe, Sindha Kashinath.
Economic development through persuasion:
case studies of community development in
Ahmednagar Block (India). Austin, Univ.of
Texas, 1966. 466p. *

Shulman #1033

E-719
Inamdar, Narayan Raghunath.
Report of the survey of the administration
of the community development block Haveli.
Poona, Univ.of Poona, 1962. 141p.

U of R

E-720
India (Republic) Planning Commission.
Programme Evaluation Organisation.
Bench mark survey report. Kolhapur
project, Bombay. Delhi, Planning Commission,
Programme Evaluation Organisation, 1956.
(Planning Commission, Programme Evaluation
Organisation Pub.no.16). 179p.

Furer

E-721
India (Republic) Planning Commission.
Programme Evaluation Organisation.
Bench mark survey report on Morsi block,
Bombay. Delhi, Planning Commission,
Programme Evaluation Organization, 1956.
(Planning Commission, Programme Evaluation
Organisation Pub.no.17). 218p.

Furer

E-722
India (Republic) Planning Commission. Programme
Evaluation Organization.
Report on the bench mark survey of the
Kolhapur Community Development Project -
Block 1, Bombay, July 1956. Delhi, Manager
of Publication, 1957. (Its P.E.O.Publication
no.16). 182p.

LC Accessions 1957, p.82

E-723
Indian Merchants Chamber.
Techno-economic survey of Konkan region; an
underdeveloped area of Maharashtra. Bombay,
1964? 146p.

1. Konkan - Econ.condit.

U of R

E-724
Indian Statistical Institute. Bombay Branch.
Report on the survey into the economic
conditions of middle class families in
Bombay City. Bombay, Indian Statistical
Inst., 1955. 73p.

LC

E-725
Israel, Sarah.
A follow-up study of 4401 households in an
industrial area in Bombay over a four year
period, PUJ, v.20 (1965), pp.110-25.

JAS '66

E-726
Jakhade, V.M. and Joshi, D.A.
An ad-hoc survey report on the working of
pilot integrated area development (PIAD)
scheme in Sangli district, BRBI, v.24
(1970), pp.28-55.

E-727
Jervis, Thomas Best.
　　A report on the weight and measures of the
Konkan Province and the territories subject
to the Government of Bombay. Bombay, 1829.
178p.

IOL

E-728
Joshi, C.B.
　　Indapur village: a study in economic history.
IHRCP, v.15 (1938), pp.175-81.

Case

E-729
Joshi, Vishnushankar Hargovind.
　　Dongargaon; a socio-economic study. Poona,
Dept.of Agricutlure, Maharashtra State, 1967.
(Socio-economic studies, 4. Maharashtra, India
(State) Dept.of Agriculture. Research bulletin
8) 131p.

PL 480 12/72

E-730
Junghare, Y.N.
　　Community development block, Risod, RI, v.22
(1959), pp.315-18.

Southeast Asia Social Science

E-731
Kadri, S.K.
　　An inquiry into the socio-economic condition
of employees in the hair cutting establishments
in the city of Bombay, JUB, v.21 (1953), pp.
91-93.

E-732
Kakade, Raghunath Govind.
　　A socio-economic survey of weaving communities
in Sholapur. Poona, D.R.Gadgil, 1947. (Gokhale
Institute of Politics and Economics, no.14)
231p.

E-733
Keatinge, Gerald Francis, 1872-
　　Rural economy in the Bombay Deccan.
London, N.Y., Bombay and Calcutta, Long-
mans, Green and Co., 1912. 234p.

1. Agriculture - India - Bombay Presidency
2. Agriculture - Economic aspects.

4 of R

E-734
Kulkarni, Jyoti S.
　　The economic activities of the Katkaris of
Veti, JASB, v.13,no.2 (1968), pp.27-39.

E-735
Kulkarni, Madhav Gururao, 1923-
　　Problem of tribal development; a case study,
Harsul Block, Nasik District, Maharashtra.
Poona, Gokhale Institute of Politics and
Economics, 1968. (Gokhale Institute mimeo-
graph series, no.3) 245p.

E-736
Lakdawala, Dansukhlal Tulsidas.
　　Work, wages and well-being in an Indian
metropolis; economic survey of Bombay
City. Bombay, University of Bombay, 1963.
(University of Bombay series in economics,
no.11). 889p.

E-737
Maharashtra, India (State) Dept.of Agriculture.
　　Natambi; a socio-economic study. 1st ed.
Poona, 1966. (Its socio-economic studies, 1)
114p.

PL 480 1972

E-738
Maharashtra, India (State) Fact-Finding Committee for Survey of Scarcity Areas in Bombay State.
Report. Bombay, Director, Govt.Print & Stationery, Maharashtra State, 1960-

NUC

E-739
Mann, Harold Hart, 1872-
Economic conditions in some Deccan areas, AJI, v.14 (1919), pp.804-10.

Mann

E-740
Mann, Harold Hart, 1872-
The economics of a Deccan village, IJE, v.1 (1916), pp.409-33.

Mann

E-741
Pande, Vinayak Krishnarao.
Economic problems of Marathwada, JMaU, v.5,no.2 (1965), pp.9-17.

JMaU

E-742
Parikh, Natvarlal Sevaklal and Thirumalai, S
Bhadkad: social and economic survey of a village; a comparative study, 1915 and 1955. Bombay, 1957. (Indian Society of Agricultural Economics. Bombay). 82p.

IOL

E-743
Patil, Chandrakant S.
A socio-economic survey of the middle class in Bombay, JUB, v.15 (1956), pp. 20-24.

Social Science Bibliography India 1956 - Economics, p. 39

E-744
Patil, Pandurang Chimnaji.
Regional survey of economic resources. India, Kolhapur; a typical study of the resources and utility services of a region of the Indian Dominion. Bombay, 1950. 425p.

E-745
Pethe, Vasant P.
Changes in economic conditions of an urban community, AV, v.3 (1961), pp.169-76.

QaS '61

E-746
Pethe, Vasant P.
Poverty and destitution in an industrial city, AICCER, v.15,no.11 (1963), pp.27-31.

So. Asia Soc Sci

E-747
Poona, India (City) Municipal Corporation.
An outline of a master plan for greater Poona. Poona, 1952. 49p.

IOL

E-748
Poona, India (City) University. Evaluation
Committee to Examine the Community Develop-
ment Project, Kolhapur.
Evaluation of community project work in
Kolhapur, from the report of the Evaluation
Committee, AV, v.2 (1960), pp.263-70.

AV

E-749
Ranade, Vinayak Govind.
A social and economic survey of Konkan
village. Bombay, S.S.Talmaki, 1927.
(Provincial Co-operative Institute, Bombay.
Rural economics series, no.3). 113p.

UofR.

E-750
Rao, V.M.
A note on government expenditure and
physical achievements in the community
projects of Bombay Deccan, JUB, n.s.,
v.29 (1960), pp.379-401.

JAS '61

E-751
Report on the study of analysis of development
expenditure, block Sirur, district Poona,
QEES, v.3,no.4 (1963), pp.1-48.

E-752
Samaj Prabodhan Sanstha.
Agro-industrial balance; an expository
survey of Sirur Taluka. Bombay, Popular
Prakashan, 1964. 111p.

1. Community development - Sirur Taluka,
India. 2. Sirur Taluka, India - Rural Conditions.

LC

E-753
Sangave, Vilas A.
Community development programme in Kolhapur
project, SB, v.7 (1958), pp.97-111.

fürer

E-754
Sathe, Madhusudan Dattatraya.
Economic study of a region with special
reference to the consumption pattern - a
tribal region in Ahmednagar District,
Maharashtra State. Poona, Poona Univ., 1967.[2]

Jayakar Lib. #1498

E-755
Sathe, Madhusudan Dattatraya.
Research of unpublished records throwing
light on political, social and mainly on
the economic history of Vidarbha during the
Mahomedan period, IHRCP, v.11 (1928), pp.
88-91.

IHRCP

E-756
Shah, C.H.
Conditions of economic progress of farmers:
an analysis of thirty-six case studies. Bombay, Indian Society of Agricultural Economics,
1960. 135p.

fürer

E-757
Shah, C.H. and Shukla, Tara.
Impact of a community development project,
JUB, v.26 (1957-1958), pp.18-31.

E-758
Sinnarkar, N.P. and Diskalkar, P.D.
Koke: a socio-economic study. 1st ed. Poona,
Department of Agriculture, Maharashtra State,
1967. 92p.

PL 450 2/73

E-759
Sovani, Nilkanth Vitthal.
Poona, a survey: the changing pattern of
employment and earnings. Poona, Gokhale
Institute of Politics and Economics, 1956.
575p.

Social Science Bibliography—
India-1956- Economics, p.44

E-760
Sykes, William Henry, 1790-1872.
Special report on the statistics of the
four collectorates of Dukhan under the
British govt. London, 1838. (Reprinted
from the 7th report of the British Association for the Advancement of Science).
20p.

SOAS

E-761
Udeshi, Jayant Jivanlal.
An evaluation of community development
project in the Purandhar Taluka of Poona
District of Maharashtra State. Bombay,
Univ.of Bombay, 1965. *

Industrial Economics—
Planning & growth

E-762
Udeshi, Jayant Jivanlal.
An evaluation of community development
project in the Purandhar Taluka of Poona
District of Maharashtra State, JUB, v.38
(1969), pp.146-47.

E-763
Valsan, Easwaramangalath Hariharan.
A comparative study of four cases of com-
munity development programs and rural local
government in India and the Philippines.
Bloomington, Indiana Univ., 1967. 556p. *

Shulman #716

E-764
Walker, A.
Statistics of the city of Aurangabad,
MJLS, v.16 (1850?), pp.1-33.

E-765
Wanmali, Sudhir Vyandatesh.
Regional planning for social facilities:
an examination of central concepts and their
application: a case study of eastern Maharashtra. Hyderabad [India] National Institute
of Community Development, 1970. 94p.

Community Development & Cooperatives -books
Economic planning & development - books
Innovation & social change - books
BAS 1970

E-766
Wardha, India (District) Zilla Parishad.
A preliminary report on the survey of
Hinganghat Mandi area... Wardha?, 1966?

PL 480   Prices, Wages, Banking
                  & Finance

E-767
Acharya, Indradeo.
Critical review of the work of minimum wage
committees in Bombay State, JUB, v.21 (1953),
pp.23-38.

E-768
Rapat, L.G.
    Cooperative credit in Maharashtra, AICCER,
    v.21,no.4 (1969), pp.23-24,31.

Banking & finance.

BAS Sept 1970 (

E-769
Bhatwadekar, M.V.
    A history of Indian currency. Bombay,
Popular Book Depot, 1944. 199p.

NUR
LC (

E-770
Bombay (Presidency)
    Memorandum by the Commission appointed
to collect information on the subject of
prices as affecting all classes of Government servants. Bombay, 1865?

Brit Mus (

E-771
Bombay (Presidency) Labour Office.
    General wage census. Part I: Perennial
factories, May 1934. Part II: Seasonal
factories, 1936. Bombay, Government Central
Press, 1935-1939. 4v.

IOL (

E-772
Bombay (Presidency) Labour Office.
    Report on an enquiry into the wages and
hours of labour in the cotton mill industry.
By G.Findlay Shirras. Bombay, 1923. 123p.

IOL (

E-773
Bombay (Presidency) Labour Office
    Report on an enquiry into wages, hours
of work and conditions of employment in
the retail trade of some towns of the
Bombay Presidency. Bombay, 1936. 106p.

BM (

E-774
Bombay (Presidency) Provincial Banking Enquiry
Committee.
    Bombay Provincial Banking Enquiry Committee,
1929-30. Bombay, Central Govt.Press, 1930.
4 vols.

    1. Banks and banking - India. 2. Bombay -
Econ.condit.

Pre '56 imprints (

E-775
Catanach, I.J.
    Rural credit in western India, 1875-1930.
Berkeley, University of California Press,
1970. 280p.

UYR (

E-776
Chakrabarti. B.
    Wages, grades and scale of pay, dearness
allowance, leave and holidays, amenities in
the engineering industry in the State of
Maharashtra. Calcutta, Indian Industrial
and Commercial Service, 1963. 139p.

Ind nat'l Bib (

E-777
Chudgar, Popatlal.
    Share and cotton gambling in Bombay. An
appeal and a warning to banks and other finan-
ciers. Bombay, Praja Mitra Press, 1922. 4p.

Bom (Pres) Cat (

E-778
Correspondence with the Bombay government regarding the personnel of the Land Indebtedness Commission. QJPSS, v.14,no.3 (1891), pp.17-21.

PSS

E-779
Desai, Thakorlal Maganlal.
The finance of Bombay Government 1935-36 to 1950-51. Bombay, Univ.of Bombay, 1951. *

Public finance, Hist + conditions
BDD

E-780
Deshpande, Lalit Khanderao.
Evolution of wage structure in Bombay City, Bombay, Univ.of Bombay, 1965. *

Economics - Wages
BDD

E-781
Dhekney, Bhalchandra Ramchandra.
Studies in municipal finance in Bombay Presidency. Bombay, Univ.of Bombay, 1943. *

Public finance - Hist + Conditions
BDD

E-782
Ghoshal, Upendra Nath.
Contributions to the history of the Hindu revenue system. Calcutta, University of Calcutta, 1929. 331p.

1. Finance - India - Hist. 2. Revenue- India.

4 MR

E-783
Ghurye, Govind Sadashiv, 1893-
Salary and other conditions of work of clerks in Bombay City, JUB, v.9 (1941), pp.106-36.

case

E-784
India. Bombay Provincial Banking Enquiry Committee.
Report of the Bombay Provincial Banking Enquiry Committee, 1929-30. Bombay, Govt. Central Press, 1930. 4 vols.

4 MR

E-785
Joshi, Tryambak Mahadeo.
Bombay finance (1921-1946). Poona, 1947. (Gokhale Institute of Politics and Economics, Pub.no.16). 220p.

UMR

E-786
Joshi, Tryambak Mahadeo.
Fiscal planning for the state of Maharashtra, JUP, no.15 (1962), p.166.

SUP

E-787
Kulkarni, Anant Ramchandra, 1925-
Banking in Maharashtra in the 17th century, IHCP, v.27 (1965), pp.222-28.

E-788
    Kulkarni, Arun Prabhakar.
        Behaviour of prices of groundnut pods in
    some regulated markets in Maharashtra.
    Poona, Univ.of Poona, 1962. *

E-789
    Kulkarni, Arun Prabhakar.
        Nature of data on prices and arrivals in
    regulated markets, AV, v.6 (1964), pp.206-13.

E-790
    Kulkarni, N.S.
        Co-operative credit in Vidarbha, MCQ,
    v.46 (1963), pp.184-87.

E-791
    Mahajan, M.P.
        Consumers' stores and the priceline, MCQ,
    v.46 (1963), pp.279-82.

E-792
    Mahajan, M.P.
        Difficulties of land development banks in
    Maharashtra, AICR, v.28 (1963), pp.662-66.

E-793
    Mann, Harold Hart, 1872-
        Interest payable by Deccan cultivators,
    BCQ, v.7 (1923), pp.1-6.

E-794
    Mann, Harold Hart, 1872-
        Note on the increase in the cost of living
    in the Deccan, IJE, v.2 (1919), pp.1-5.

E-795
    Mukerji, Kshitimohan.
        Trend in real wages in cotton textile
    mills in Bombay City and Island, from 1900
    to 1951. AV, v.1 (1959), pp.82-96.

E-796
    Mutalik Desai, Sadashiv Shrinivas.
        Review of the finances of the Bombay prov-
    ince/state from 1946-47 to 1960-61. Poona,
    Gokhale Institute of Politics and Economics,
    1966. *

E-797
    Naik, K.K.
        Municipal finance in the Bombay State 1939-
    1955. Dharwar, Karnatak Univ., 1966. *

E-798
Padhye, M.D.
Growth of central co-operative financing
agencies in Marathawada, MCQ, v.52 (1968),
pp.139-52.

comm Dev. & cooperative
EA= 1970

E-799
Paisa Fund-utterjak Mandali.
The Paisa fund movement. Bombay, Vijaya
Printing Press, 1904. 16p.

Bombay (Pres) cat

E-800
Pande, Vinayak Krishnarao.
Municipal finance in Marathwada. Aurangabad,
Marathwada Univ., 1969. 415p.

U of R

E-801
Parekh, Hasmukhlal Thakordas.
The Bombay money market. Bombay, New
York, Oxford Univ.Press, 1953. 226p.

U of R

E-802
Patwardhan, Moreshwar Vaman.
Growth of Bank of Maharashtra Limited in its
area of operation: a case study in monetary
economics and banking theories. Poona, Gokhale
Institute of Politics and Economics, 1966. *

guptas Lit. +? 1-71

E-803
Rairikar, Balkrishna Rangnath.
Wages and earnings in engineering indus-
try in Bombay City and suburbs. Bombay,
Univ.of Bombay, 1967. *

Economics. Wages
BDD

E-804
Ramachandra Rau, B.
The early history of the Presidency
Bank of Bombay (based on manuscript
records of the Government of Bombay),
CR, v.42 (1932), pp.89-107, 177-200.

cole

E-805
Ramachandra Rau, B.
Some specific services of the indigenous
bankers of Bombay, IHRCP, v.12 (1929), pp.
54-58.

I HRCP

E-806
Ramachandra Rau, B.
Early banking institutions in Bombay and
their lesson 1720-1857. Calcutta, Calcutta
Univ., 1931. *

financial economics
BDD

E-807
Rath, N. and Satyapriya, V.S.
Seasonal movement of price of jowar in
Maharashtra and Mysore, AV, v.7 (1965),
pp.54-65.

JaS 65

E-808
Reserve Bank of India. Committee of Direction of the All India Rural Credit Survey.
District monograph: Akola. Bombay, 1959. 174p.

E-809
Reserve Bank of India. Committee of Direction of the All India Rural Credit Survey.
District monograph: Osmanabad, by V.M. Dandekar. Bombay, 1957. 82p.

E-810
Reserve Bank of India. Committee of Direction of the All India Rural Credit Survey.
District monograph: West Khandesh. Bombay, 1957. 87p.

E-811
Savkar, Dattatraya Sitaram.
Banking and finance in Bombay. Bombay, 1948.

E-812
Sharma, Jagdish Saran, 1924–
Effects of price on marketable surplus of wheat in Maharashtra, India. Urbana, Illinois Univ., 1962. *

assoc for Asian Studies

E-813
Shirras, George Findlay, 1885–
Report on an enquiry into agricultural wages in the Bombay Presidency. Bombay, Govt.Central Press, 1924. 155p.

BM

E-814
Trivedi, Vishnu Ratilal.
Profits and wages in the cotton industry of the Bombay Province. Bombay, Univ.of Bombay, 1950. *

Industrial economics
secondary industries
BDD

E-815
Wacha, Dinsha Edulji, 1844–1936.
A financial chapter in the history of Bombay city. 2d ed. Bombay, A.J.Cambridge, 1910. 230p.

1. Finance – Bombay. 2. Banks and banking – Bombay.

NUR
Revenue and taxation

E-816
Banerjee, Tara Sankar, 1898–
Transit and town duties in Bombay and Madras in the first half of the nineteenth century. EPP, v.82 (1963), pp.21-43.

Case

E-817
Bombay (Presidency) Customs Dept.
A short review of George Plowden's report on the salt revenue of Bombay, by Nicholas Alexander Dalzell. Bombay, 1858. (Bombay Presidency. Selections from the records, n.s.,no.48)

BM

R-818
Bombay (Presidency) Financial Department.
A handbook for revenue officers in the
Presidency of Bombay. By A.K.Nairne. 3rd
ed., rev.up to the end of 1882. By Harry
Arbuthnot Acworth. Bombay, 1884.

IOL

R-819
Fresh taxation of native states in the Bombay
Presidency, QJPSS, v.3,no.1 (1880), pp.1-29.

PSS

R-820
Godha, Javerchand Khushalchand.
Working and administration of sales tax
in Bombay, Maharashtra State (1946-1964).
Poona, Brihan Maharashtra College of Commerce,
1969. *

Jeegakar Lib. #1508

R-821
Lethbridge, Roper, 1840-1917.
The late Mr. Justice Ranade as a tariff
reformer, AR, ser.3,v.27 (1909), pp.252-57.

Case

Trade, Commerce &
Marketing

R-822
Ahirwadkar, Laxmikant Jankirampant.
Agricultural marketing in Marathwada with
a special reference to cotton and groundnut.
Aurangabad, Marathwada Univ., 1970. *

*Internal trade -
Marketing*
BDD

R-823
Avalaskar, Shantaram Vishnu, 1907-
and Apte, M.D.
The toll and trade in Poona, AV, v.6
(1964), p.126. (Summary of preceding
article in Marathi).

Jhs'64

R-824
Bliss, Don Carrol, 1897-
The Bombay bullion market. Washington,
Government Printing Office, 1927. (U.S.
Bureau of Foreign and Domestic Commerce
[Department of Commerce] trade information
bulletin, no.457) 81p.

4 of R

R-825
Bokhare, M.G.
Marketing of agricultural produce in Madhya
Pradesh. Nagpur, Nagpur Univ., 1961. *

Gupta

R-826
Bombay (Presidency)
Report of the Commerce (External Commerce)
of Bombay (Annual Statement of the Trade and
Navigation of the Presidency of Bombay) for
the year 1849-50. Bombay, 1851.

Brit Mus

R-827
Bombay (Presidency) Department of Agriculture.
Marketing of some agricultural products
exported from Bombay to the United Kingdom.
By T.G.Shirname. Bombay, 1933. (Bombay
Presidency. Department of Agriculture.
Bulletins. no.173).

IOL

E-828
Brahme, Sulabha, 1932-
Distribution and consumption of cloth in
Poona. Bombay, N.Y., Asia Pub.House, 1962.
(Gokhale Institute studies, no.42) 115p.

u c/r

E-829
Commercial crisis in Bombay. QJPSS, v.1,no.4
(1878), pp.24-41.

PSS

E-830
Das, Harihar.
Rustamji Manak: a notable Parsi broker, IA,
v.59 (1930), pp.106-108, 136-41.

E-831
Das Gupta, Biman Kumar [et al]
A note on the weekly market at Gokulpeth
(Nagpur), EA, v.16 (1963), pp.148-49.

E-832
Furber, Holden, 1903-
The country trade of Bombay and Surat in
the 1730's, Indica, v.1 (1964), pp.39-46.

JAS '66

E-833
Gadgil, Dhananjaya Ramchandra, 1901-
A survey of the marketing of fruit in
Poona. Poona, Gokhale Institute of Politics
and Economics, 1933. (Gokhale Institute of
Politics and Economics. Pub.no.3). 192p.

'. Fruit trade - Poona, india (Bombay) 2. Fruit-
Marketing

LC

E-834
Gadgil, Dhananjaya Ramchandra, 1901-
and Gadgil, Vaman Ramchandra.
A survey of farm business in Wai taluka.
Poona, Gokhale Institute of Politics and
Economics, 1940. (Gokhale Institute of
Politics and Economics. Pub.no.7) 152p.

1. Agriculture - Econ.aspects - India -
Bombay (Presidency)

LC

E-835
Irwin, John.
Indian textile trades in the seventeenth
century-Western India, JITH, no.1 (1955),
pp.5-24.

India

E-836
Joshi, M.G.
The problem of livestock in Poona district
with special reference to marketing. Poona,
Univ.of Poona, 1950-51. *

Gupta

E-837
Kulkarni, Arun Prabhakar.
Marketing of ground nut in some regulated
markets in Maharashtra, AV, v.5 (1963),
pp.337-64.

E-838
Lele, Uma J.
Efficiency of Jowar marketing; a study of
regulated markets in Western India. Ithaca,
Cornell Univ., 1966. *

Stacks

E-839
Madalgi, Shivaling Shivayogi.
A note on the marketing of tobacco in the
Nipani market, JUB, n.s., v.26 (1957), pp.
33-43.

Jal '57

E-840
Madalgi, Shivaling Shivayogi.
The problems of marketing of farm products
in Maharashtra with special reference to
cash crops in Kolhapur District. Bombay,
Univ.of Bombay, 1957. *

Management-marketing
BDD

E-841
Madalgi, Shivaling Shivayogi.
Some problems of marketing of cash crops
in Kolhapur district, LJAS, v.28 (1958),
pp.613-21.

LC accessions

E-842
Oturkar, Rajaram Vinayak, 1898-
Marketing organization and price control
under the Marathas in the 18th century,
IHCP, v.6 (1943), pp.305-306.

IHCP

E-843
Pearson, Michael Naylor.
Commerce and compulsion: Gujarati merchants
and the Portuguese system in western India,
1500-1600. Ann Arbor, Univ.of Michigan, 1971.
401p. *

Shulman #492

E-844
Pointon, A.C.
The Bombay Burmah Trading Corporation Ltd.,
1863-1963. Southampton, England, Milbrook
Press, 1964. 151p.

LC

E-845
Ranjan, K.Som.
Seasonality in the incidence of strikes
in the Bombay textile industry, Sankhyā,
v.13 (1954), pp.423-28.

SSB 1954

E-846
Robertson, William, 1721-1793.
An historical disquisition concerning the
knowledge which the ancients had of India;
and the progress and trade with that country prior to the discovery of the passage
to it by the cape of Good Hope. London,
Printed for Whitmore & Fenn, etc., 1824.
(His Works, v.9). 341p.

India – Comm – Hist
UofP

E-847
Saletore, G.N.
Aspects of Maratha trade in the 18th cent.,
JUB, v.24 (1955), pp.1-8.

E-848
Salvi, Parasharam Ganapatarao.
    Commodity exchanges, with special reference
to India in general and Bombay in particular.
Bombay, Co-operators' Book Depot, 1947. 249p.

4 of R

E-853
Bhandarkar, Devadatta Ramakrishna, 1875-
    Shipping in Bombay in 1795-96, IHRCP, v.13
(1930), pp.73-84. Also in: BPP, v.41 (1931),
pp.129-33.

Case

E-849
Seminar on Exports of Cotton Textiles, Bombay,
1965.
    Conclusions and recommendations. New Delhi,
Institute of Foreign Trade, 1965. 36p.

LC

E-854
Bombay (Presidency)
    Bombay, Baroda and Central India Railway.
By J.P.Kennedy. Bombay, 1855.

IOL

E-850
Shrishrimal, Walchand Chunilal.
    Trade of Kolhapur City; a survey. Bombay,
Univ.of Bombay, 1952. *

Internal trade
   marketing
BDD

E-855
Bombay cotton, and Indian railways, CR, v.13
(1850), pp.328-44.

case

E-851
Sulivan, Raymond J.F.
    One hundred years of Bombay; history of the
Bombay Chamber of Commerce, 1836-1936. Bombay,
Times of India Press, 1938. 319p.

LC
                    Transportation &
                    Communication

E-856
Chandrasekaran, C., 1911-   and Bebarta, P.C.
    The relative role of information sources
in the dissemination of knowledge of
family planning methods in Bombay City,
JFW, v.9 (1963), pp.5-14.

JFW '63

E-852
Athavale, M.V.
    Employee communication and consultation in
private sector industry with special reference
to industrial units in Poona. Poona, Univ.
of Poona, 1968. *

Personnel management
BDD

E-857
Chavan, B.W.
    Preference indexes for goods traffic by
different modes of transport in Maharashtra,
AV, v.11 (1969), pp.88-96. tables.

Trans & Communication
articles
BAS Sept 1970

R-858
Clunes, John.
   Itinerary and directory for western India,
being a collection of routes through the
provinces subject to the Presidency of
Bombay. Calcutta, H.Townsend, 1826. 2v.

CM

R-859
Damle, Yashwant Bhaskar, 1923-
   Communication of modern ideas in Indian
villages, POQ, v.20 (1956), pp.257-70.

Surer

R-860
Damle, Yashwant Bhaskar, 1923-
   Harikatha: a study in communication, BDCRI,
v.20 (1960), pp.63-107.

Surer

R-861
Damle, Yashwant Bhaskar, 1923-
   The problem of cultural communication of
modern ideas in Indian villages, AUJR, v.3
(1955), pp.109-14.

Surer

R-862
Dandekar, Kumudini.
   Communication in family planning;
report on an experiment. Poona, Gokhale
Institute of Politics and Economics;
Bombay, N.Y., Asia Pub.House, 1967.
(Gokhale Institute series, no.49). 121p.

U of R

R-863
Delhi. Central Road Research Institute.
   History of road development in India; a
brief account of the genesis and development
of the Indian road system. New Delhi,
Council of Scientific and Industrial Research,
1963. 161p.

LC

R-864
Desai, S.V.
   Restructuring Bombay: an enduring solution
for the city's traffic and other problems,
URPT, v.13 (1970), pp.152-62.

BAS 1970

R-865
Deshmukh, V.M.
   Communication and public transport services
in Buldana District, DG, v.7 (1969), pp.93-
108.

journalism + ...
BAS

R-866
Ezekiel, Hannan and Koach, Neville.
   The debt of the Bombay Port Trust, 1914-
1957, JUB, v.27 (1958), pp.25-60.

g4 B

R-867
Gadgil Dhananjaya Ramchandra, 1901-
   and Gogate, L.V.
   Survey of motor-bus transportation in
six districts of the Bombay Presidency.
Poona, Gokhale Institute of Politics and
Economics, Printed at the Ayrabhushan Press,
1935. (Gokhale Institute of Politics and
Economics, Pub.no.4). 182p.

LC

E-868
Gananathan, V.S.
    The distribution of railway communication in western India, IGJ, v.30 (1955), pp.95-98.

E-873
Logan, Frenise A.
    The American Civil War: a major factor in the improvement of the transportation system of western India, JIH, v.33 (1954), pp.91-102.

E-869
Gananathan, V.S.
    Roads in western India, BGM, v.3 (1955), pp.27-33.

E-874
Modak, Shanker Keshav.
    Some aspects of road transport in eastern districts of Vidarbha. Nagpur, Nagpur Univ., 1970. *

E-870
Ghorpade, S.R.
    Organizational setup, administrative problems and working of the Bombay State Road Transport Corporation: a study of a public undertaking. Poona, Univ.of Poona, 1963. *

E-875
Nayeem, M.A.
    Evolution of postal communications and administration in the Deccan, from 1294 A.D. to the formation of Hyderabad State in 1724 A.D. Bombay, Jal Cooper, 1968. 10p.

E-871
Grant, Charles William.
    Bombay cotton and Indian railways. London, 1850. 151p.

E-876
Padhye, S.S.
    History of road and rail in the Deccan trap region of Vidarbha, BGM, v.12 (1964), pp.31-37.

E-872
Indian Institute of Foreign Trade.
    Shipowners' problems at the Port of Bombay; analysis and recommendations. New Delhi, 1968. v.5. 131p.

E-877
Patankar, Vyankatesh S.
    Passenger and goods transport business in Poona. Poona, Univ.of Poona, 1961. *

E-876
Patwardhan, S.G.
Local passenger transport in Bombay. Bombay, Univ. of Bombay, 1941. *

Gupta

E-879
Projects for improved shipping accomodation in Bombay harbour, BQR, v.5 (1857), pp. 385-97.

u z R

E-880
Rahudkar, Wasudeo B.
Communication of farm information in an Indian Community. IJSW, v.23 (1962-63), pp. 99-103.

NAU
fires

E-881
Shejwalkar, P.C.
Transport in Maharashtra, JUP, v.15 (1962), pp. 144-50.

JUX '63

E-882
Vaidya, Keshav Balkrishna, 1896-
The sailing vessel traffic on the west coast of India and its future. Bombay, Popular Book Depot. 1945. 332p.

u + A

E-883
Williamson, Thomas.
Two letters on the advantages of railway communication in western India, addressed to the Rt.Hon.Lord Wharncliffe. London, John E. Taylor, 1846. 38p.

| Education | Bibliography & Reference |

F-1
Bombay (Presidency) Educational Department.
Directory of the Bombay Educational Department for 1894-95 (-1919-20) Bombay, 1895-1920.

F-2
Brembeck, Cole Speicher and Weidner, Edward W.
Education and development in India and Pakistan; a select and annotated bibliography.
East Lansing, Michigan State University College of Education & International Programs, 1963. (Michigan State Univ. Education in Asia series 1)

u il

F-3
Delhi. National Institute of Basic Education.
Basic education bibliography. Delhi, Manager of Publications, 1960. 52p.

u oz t

F-4
Directory of vernacular teachers employed in Local Board and Municipal Schools in the Marathi districts of the southern division, viz, Ratnagiri and Kolaba. Ratnagiri, Bakul Press, 1911. 48p.

F-5
Distinguished teachers in India. New Delhi, Premier Publishers, 1965-

4 of R

F-6
Greaves, Monica Alice.
Education in British India 1698-1947. A bibliography and guide to the sources of information in London. London, University of London, Education libraries bulletin, Supplement 13, 1966.

4 of R

F-7
India (Republic) Central Bureau of Health Intelligence.
Directory of medical colleges in India. New Delhi. 1964-

4 of R

F-8
Indian Law Institute.
Directory of law colleges and law teachers in India. Bombay, N.M.Tripathi, 1962. 162p.

F-9
Indian year book of education. New Delhi, National Council of Educational Research and Training. 1961-

F-10
National Council of Educational Research and Training.
Educational investigations in Indian Universities (1939-1961) A list of theses and dissertations approved for Doctorate and Master's degrees in education. New Delhi, Chief Publication Officer, National Council of Educational Research and Training, 1966. 286p.

4 of R

F-11
Singh, Mohinder, M.A.
Learned institutions in India, activities & publications, comp.& ed.by Mohinder Singh. [Assisted by J.F.Pandya; indexes comp.by G.J.Tripathi & H.D.Sanghvi; secretarial work by R.V.Patel] with a foreword by Laurence J. Kipp. Ahmedabad, Balgovind Prakashan, 1969. 281p.

4 of R

F-12
Universities handbook; India. New Delhi, Inter-University Board of India. 17th-1973-

4 of R

F-13
Universities handbook, India & Ceylon. New Delhi, Inter University Board of India & Ceylon, 1927-

Education - General

F-14
The Annals of native education, BQR, v.2 (1855), pp.122-66.

NUR
B2 R microfiche

F-15
    Basu, Baman Das, 1867-1930.
      History of education in India under the rule of the East India Company. Calcutta, Modern Review Office, 1922. 229p.

NUR
LC

F-16
    Bhatt, B.D., comp.
      Educational documents in India, 1813-1968; survey of Indian education. Ed.by B.D.Bhatt and J.C.Aggarwal. New Delhi, Arya Book Depot, 1969. 335p.

      1. Education - India. 2. Schools - Records & correspondence.

U of R

F-17
    Bombay (Presidency) Education League.
      Correspondence relating to the system of education in the Bombay Presidency. Bombay, 1860.

greaves M A

F-18
    Bombay (Presidency) Educational Department.
      The problem of Urdu teaching in the Bombay Presidency. Bombay, Govt.Pub., 1914.

greaves M A

F-19
    Bombay (Presidency) Educational Department.
      Report of the Director of Public Instruction. Bombay, Govt.Central Press, 1859-99.

U of R

F-20
    Bombay (Province) Committee on Primary and Secondary Education, 1929.
      Report ... Bombay, Govt.Central Press, 1930. 85p.

pre 56 imprints

F-21
    Bombay (State) Department of Education.
      A Review of Education in Bombay State, 1885-1955. A volume in commemoration of the centenary of the Dept.of Educ.,Bombay. Poona (1958),ii,542p.ill., diagrs.,tables.

F-22
    Bombay Native Education Society.
      Annual reports of 1823-24 to 1839-40. Bombay, 1824-41.

F-23
    Central Provinces and Berar, India. Education Dept.
      Report[s] on the state and progress of education in the Central Provinces and Berar ... 1903-04 (to 1920-21, 1924-25, 1925-26; and for the quinquennium ending 31st March, 1927. and for ... 1927-28, 1934-35) Nagpur, Govt. Pub., 1904-1940.

NYPL

F-24
    Chavan, B.W.
      Education in Maharashtra, QBES, v.1,no.4 (1961), pp.21-57.

F-25
Choudhari R.E. and Ramachandran, K.V.
Projection of primary and secondary school
populations for Maharashtra State, 1951-1981,
AV, v.4 (1962), pp.98-116.

F-30
Kamat, A.R., 1912-
Progress of education in rural Maharashtra,
post-independence period. Poona, Gok-
hale Inst.of Politics and Economics, 1968.
(Gokhale Inst.studies no.56). 359p.

F-26
Chowdhury, Jogindra Nath.
Condition of education and architecture in
the Bahmani kingdom, IHQ, v.5 (1929), pp.124-
28.

F-31
Kantawala, S.T.
Report on the survey of school children in
Bombay suburbs, JGRS, v.19 (1957), pp.226-31.

F-27
Dongerkery, Kamala Sunderrao Kulkarni, 1909-
On the wings of time; an autobiography.
Bombay, Bharatiya Vidya Bhavan. 1968.
253p.

F-32
Maharashtra, India (State) Directorate of
Education.
Education in Maharashtra. Poona, 1961 -
annual.

F-28
Government education in the Bombay Presidency,
BQR, v.4 (1856), pp.321-86.

F-33
Maharashtra, India (State) Education and
Social Welfare Department.
Education in Maharashtra; annual admin-
istration report. Bombay, 1959/60-

F-29
India. Bureau of Education.
Selections from educational records, pt.I
1781-1839. Calcutta Govt.of India, Bureau
of Education, 1920. 2 vols.

F-34
Maharashtra, India (State) Education and
Social Welfare Department.
Educational development in Maharashtra
State, 1950-51 to 1965-66. Bombay, 1968.
101p.

F-35
Miller, Ernest E.
    The problem of literacy in Central Provinces
and Berar, India. New York, New York University. 1940. *

Stucki

F-36
Muranjan, S.K., 1900–
    Education and educational finance in Bombay
Presidency. IJE, v.11 (1930), pp.1-40.

Cru

F-37
Nabar, Rajaram Atmaram.
    The history of education in the city of
Bombay from 1820 to 1920. Bombay, Univ.
of Bombay, 1964. *

Education – History
BDD   & conditions

F-38
Naik, Chitra.
    Educational change: concern for quality in
Maharashtra. PE, v.41 (1967), pp.285-89, 293.

JaS 9/68

F-39
Naik, J.P.
    History of the Local Fund Cess, appropri-
ated to education in the Province of Bombay.
Bombay, Local Self-Govt.Inst., 1942. 148p.

BM

F-40
Panse, Keshav Vithal.
    Effect of supplementary diet on the
physique of school children. Poona, Univ.
of Poona, 1959. *

Education – student
                     health
BDD

F-41
Parasnis, Narhar Ramchandra, 1908–
    The history and survey of education in Thana
District, former Bombay State, now Maharashtra
State. Bombay, University of Bombay,1967.
489p.

PL480 '69

F-42
Parulekar, Ramchandra Vithal, ed.
    The educational writings; selected and with
an introductory essay on his life and work
by J.P.Naik. Bombay, Asia Pub.House, 1957.
307p.

    1. Education – India. 2. Illiteracy – India.

NU R
LC

F-43
Parulekar, Ramchandra Vithal.
    Mass education in India with special refer-
ence to Bombay Presidency. Bombay, Local
Self-Government Inst., 1934. 48p.

IOL

F-44
Parulekar, Ramchandra Vithal, ed.
    Selections from the records of the Govt.of
Bombay. Education. Bombay, Asia Pub.House,
1953-57. (Narayanrao Topiwala memorial
education research series, v.3-5) 3v.

U of R

F-45
Patwardhan, Chintamani Nilkant.
Education in the state of Maharashtra, India.
Bombay, Dept.of Services to Schools, St.Xaviers
Institute of Education, 1964. 50p.

LC

F-46
Patwardhan, Chintamani Nilkant.
History of education in medieval India.
Rise, growth and decay of the Aryan system
of education, 600-1200 A.D. Bombay, C.N.
Patwardhan, 1939. 153p.

BM

F-47
Pithawalla, Maneck Bejanji.
Five fingers of Parsee education. Bombay,
Sanj Vartaman Press, 1931.
(Reprint from 'Sanj Vartaman Annual', 1931)

Greaves ma.

F-48
Rao, L.N.
Educational efforts in Satara, MR, v.68
(1940), pp.218-21.

MP

F-49
Rege, Moreswar Shivram.
The history and survey of education in the
Ratnagiri District. Bombay, Univ.of Bombay,
1962. *

F-50
Shahu Chhatrapati, Maharaja of Kolhapur, 1874-
1922.
Maratha Educational Conference, 21st sitting.
Khamgaon, 1917. 10p.

BM

F-51
Shukla, Devendra Nath.
History of Indian educational policy 1854-
1904. Allahabad, Univ.of Allahabad, 1943. *

Case

F-52
Singham, B.S.
Multipurpose schools in Vidarbha -
a retrospect, SE, v.8 (1964), pp.22-25.

Ja864

F-53
A survey of school children in Bombay City,
with special reference to their physical,
physical efficiency, mental and nutritional
status. By K.V.Ramachandran and others.
Bombay, New York, Asia Pub.House, 1968.
(Bombay. Demographic Training and Research
Centre. Research monograph, no.4). 232p.

BAS Sept 1970

F-54
Vaidya, Manubhai Pranjivan, 1905-
Trends in education: Maharashtra State,
JGRS, v.24 (1962), pp.15-17.

4 oR.

F-55
Vakil, K.S.
Education in Bombay City (1804-1929), ASBJ,
v.6 (1930), pp.310-12.

Theory and practice of
Education

F-56
Acharya, Shridhar Ramkrishna.
Contributions of eminent Indian education-
ists to the theory and practice of Indian
education during the 19th and 20th centuries
with special reference to Maharashtra. Poona,
Tilak College of Education, 1966. *

Jayakar Lib #

F-57
Boman-Behram, B.K.
Educational controversies in India; the
cultural conquest of India under British
imperialism. Bombay, D.B.Taraporevala sons
& co., 1943. 649p.

1. Education - India - Hist. 2. Languages -
Political aspects. 3. English language in
India.

LC

F-58
Bombay (Province) Committee on the Training
of Primary Teachers.
Report. Bombay, Govt.Central Press, 1938.
114p.

1. Teachers, Training of - India - Bombay
(Presidency)

pre '56 imprints

F-59
Bruce, C.H.
Pioneers of secondary education in the Bom-
bay Presidency: American Mission Girls' High
School, founded in 1838, PE, v.15 (1938), pp.
13-26.

Golden Jubilee Comm Vol

F-60
Coelho, Elias Philip.
Four centuries of christian education in
Bassein with a special reference to the
educational contribution made by the
Archbishop T.Roberts. Bombay, Univ.of
Bombay, 1959. *

Education - philosophy
BDD   + theory

F-61
Coverton, A.L.
The educational policy of Mountstuart
Elphinstone, ASBJ, n.s.,v.2 (1926), pp.
53-73.

F-62
Dhar, G.S.
School education and teacher training in
Maharashtra during the second plan, EQ, v.14
(1962), pp.123-29.

Ja 864

F-63
The educational policy of the Bombay government,
QJPSS, v.11,no.2 (1888), pp.21-69.

P55

NO ENTRY

F-64
Ezekiel, Nancy.
Teacher participation in school administration in Greater Bombay. Bombay, Univ.
of Bombay, 1967. *

Education administration
BDD

F-65
Goel, B.S.
G.K.Gokhale: his role in the development
of primary education, EQ, v.22 (1971), pp.
13-19.

F-66
Gothivrekar, Shankar Ramkrishna.
The secondary school curriculum in the
Province of Bombay: a critical analysis and
examination of its basis, present structure
and future reconstruction. Bombay, Univ.of
Bombay, 1947. *

Secondary education

F-67
Hampton, Henry Verner, 1890-
Biographical studies in modern Indian
education. Madras, Indian Branch, Oxford
Univ.Press, 1947. 264p.

1. Educators, East Indian.

F-68
Jhabvala, Shavakasha Hormusji, 1885-
E.D.Talati, an eminent Parsee educationist
and pioneer of Parsi public school movement.
Khar, 1938. 90p.

F-69
Kale, B.M.
A social and economic study of the municipal
primary teachers in Bombay, JUB, v.4 (1936),
pp.162-86.

JUB

F-70
Kamat, A.R., 1912-
Gokhale as an educationist. In: Gopal
Krishna Gokhale, a centenary tribute.
Bombay, Printed at the government central
press, 1966. pp.90-108.

v of 2

F-71
Kamat, V.V.
Educational research in the Bombay Presidency,
JGRS, v.4 (1942), pp.30-37.

F-72
Karve, Dhondo Keshav, 1858-
Looking back. Poona, Hindu Widow's Home
Association, 1936. 211p.

1. Education - India. 2. Women in India.

F-73
Karve, Dhondo Keshav, 1858-
My twenty years in the cause of Indian women;
or, a short history of the origin and growth of
the Hindu widow's home and cognate institutions;
a paper read ... before a public meeting in
Poona ... on 28th Aug., 1913 and the President's
remarks. 2d ed. Poona, 1916. 54p.

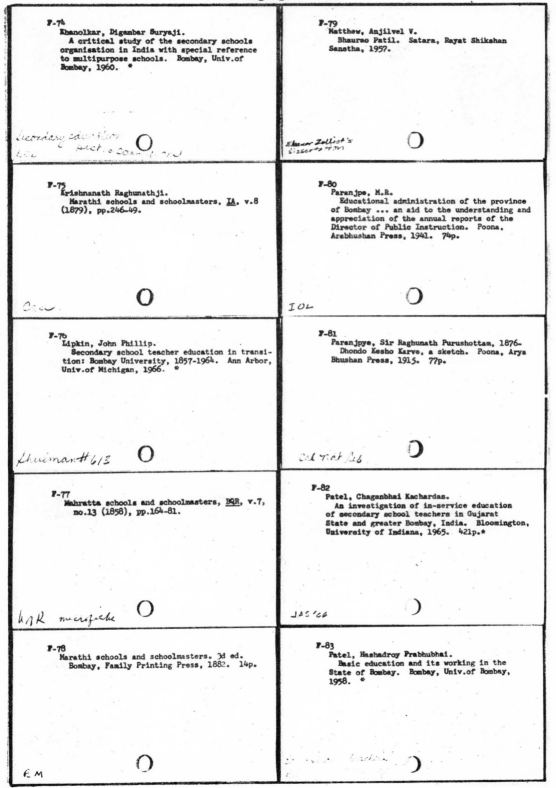

F-74
Khanolkar, Digambar Suryaji.
   A critical study of the secondary schools
organisation in India with special reference
to multipurpose schools. Bombay, Univ.of
Bombay, 1960. *

Secondary education
Hist. o coll.

F-75
Krishnanath Raghunathji.
   Marathi schools and schoolmasters, _IA_, v.8
(1879), pp.246-49.

Craw.

F-76
Lipkin, John Phillip.
   Secondary school teacher education in transi-
tion: Bombay University, 1857-1964. Ann Arbor,
Univ.of Michigan, 1966. *

Khueman # 613

F-77
   Mahratta schools and schoolmasters, _BQR_, v.7,
no.13 (1858), pp.164-81.

BQR microfiche

F-78
   Marathi schools and schoolmasters. 3d ed.
Bombay, Family Printing Press, 1882. 14p.

EM

F-79
Matthew, Anjilvel V.
   Bhaurao Patil. Satara, Rayat Shikshan
Sanstha, 1957.

Eleanor Zelliot's
Dissertation

F-80
Paranjpe, M.R.
   Educational administration of the province
of Bombay ... an aid to the understanding and
appreciation of the annual reports of the
Director of Public Instruction. Poona,
Arabhushan Press, 1941. 74p.

IOL

F-81
Paranjpye, Sir Raghunath Purushottam, 1876-
   Dhondo Kesho Karve, a sketch. Poona, Arya
Bhushan Press, 1915. 77p.

Cal Tict Lib

F-82
Patel, Chaganbhai Kachardas.
   An investigation of in-service education
of secondary school teachers in Gujarat
State and greater Bombay, India. Bloomington,
University of Indiana, 1965. 421p.*

JAS '66

F-83
Patel, Hashadroy Prabhubhai.
   Basic education and its working in the
State of Bombay. Bombay, Univ.of Bombay,
1958. *

F-84
Pethe, Vasant P.
Living and working conditions of primary
school teachers, a Sholapur survey. Bombay,
Popular Book Depot, 1962. 70p.

LC

F-85
Shah, Madhuri R.
The administration of education in the
province of Bombay, CJLSGI, v.20 (1949),
pp.196-279.

cic

F-86
Shreemati Nathibai Damodar Thackersey Women's
University, Bombay.
The founder's centenary, Dr.D.K.Karve, the
founder completes his birth centenary on 18.4.
1958. Bombay, The University, 1958.

Greaves, M.A.

F-87
Sorabji, Cornelia, 1866-
Susie Sorabji, Christian Parsee educational-
ist of western India, a memoir by her sister.
London, Oxford University Press, 1932. 84p.

1. Sorabji, Susie, 1861-1931.

LC

F-88
Spear, Thomas George Percival.
Bentinck and education, CHJ, v.6 (1938),
pp.78-101.

CHJ

F-89
Upasani, Narayan Keshav.
An evaluation of the existing teacher
training programme for primary teachers
in the State of Maharashtra with special
reference to rural areas. Poona, Univ.
of Poona, 1966. *

Education - teachers

History of Education   Primary

F-90
Bapat, Bhalchandra Gopal.
An investigation into the condition of pre-
primary education in the Poona University
area with a view to finding out its problems
and suggesting solutions of some of them.
Poona, Univ.of Poona, 1956. *

Elementary education
BDD   Hist & conditions

F-91
Bombay (Presidency) Committee on Free and
Compulsory Primary Education.
Report of the committee appointed by
the Government to consider and report on
the question of the introduction of free
and compulsory primary education in the
Bombay Presidency. Poona, Govt.Pub., 1922.

Greaves, M.A.

F-92
Bombay (State) Integration Committee for
Primary Education.
Primary education in the State of Bombay;
a report on integration and development.
Bombay, 1959. 108p.

IOL

F-93
Desai, Dhanwant M.
Comparative primary education in the
province of Bombay (1813-1947), CJLSGI,
v.19 (1949), pp.262-314; v.20 (1949),
pp.49-80.

F-94
Desai, Dhanwant M.
Compulsory primary education in the Province of Bombay; foreword by R.V.Parulekar. Bombay, Local Self-Government Institute, 1950. 88p.

Lc acessions, 1958

F-95
Gadgil, Dhananjaya Ramchandra, 1901- and Dandekar, Vinayak Mahadeo, 1920-
Primary education in Satara District; reports of two investigations. Poona, 1955. (Gokhale Institute of Politics and Economics. Pub.no.32). 172p.

vol R

F-96
Ghurye, Govind Sadashiv, 1893-
The financing of primary education in Bombay City, JUB, v.5 (1936), pp.71-90.

Case

F-97
Kale, B.M.
A brief history of the growth of primary education in the city of Bombay, QJLSGI, v.7 (1937), pp.18a-18k.

Case

F-98
Kale, B.M.
The financing of primary education in Bombay City, JUB, v.5 (1936), pp.71-86.

JUB

F-99
Kale, B.M.
Some suggestions for the financial and constitutional improvements in the system of primary education in Bombay City, JUB, v.6 (1937), pp.92-112.

JUB

F-100
Khanolkar, Vaman Pandurang, ed.
Indigenous elementary education in the Bombay Presidency in 1855 and thereabouts (being a departmental survey of indigenous education). Bombay, Indian Institute of Education; sole distributors: Orient Longmans, Calcutta, 1965.

1. Education - Bombay (Presidency)

4 of R

F-101
Mangudkar, Manik Padmanna.
Public instruction by the Poona municipality (1884-1952), JUP, v.3 (1954), pp.139-50.

case

F-102
Naik, J.P.
Administration and finance of primary education in the province of Bombay, 1870-1902, QJLSGI, v.19 (1948), pp.56-135.

Case

F-103
Naik, J.P.
The finance of primary education in municipal areas of the province of Bombay, QJLSGI, v.13 (1943), pp.563-78.

Case

F-104
Natarajan, S.
Finance and school administration in
Maharashtra, Teaching, v.36 (1963), pp.54-55.

F-105
Patole, Sarayan Khanderav.
Study of teaching of science in rural
primary schools standards I to VII. Poona,
Univ.of Poona, 1966. *

F-106
Sane, Sarala P.
Investigation into the condition of primary
education in the educationally backward parts
of the Poona Municipal Corporation area etc.,
with special reference to (a) non-attendance
of pupils coming under the provisions of the
Bombay Primary Education Act 1947, and (b)
irregular attendance of pupils actually
under instruction. Poona, Univ.of Poona,
1960. *

F-107
Shah, Madhuri R.
The organisation and administration of
primary education in Bombay and London: a
comparative study. London, London Univ.,
1953-54. *

F-108
Tannu, Jankiran Balwantrao.
The place of the shift system in the
primary schools in the State of Bombay.
Bombay, Univ.of Bombay, 1959. *

F-109
Thakkar, Amritlal Vithaldas.
Primary education in the city of Bombay, a
paper read before the members of the District
Congress Committees on 29th, August 1916.
Bombay, M.Joshi, 1916. 13p.

F-110
Vaidya, B.N.
History of primary education in the province
of Bombay for 1815-1940. Bombay, Local Self-
Govt.Institute, 1947. 138p.

Secondary

F-111
Bombay (State) Education Department.
List of recognised secondary schools in
the State of Bombay. Bombay, Director,
Govt.Print,Publications and Stationery,
1958.

F-112
Bombay (State) Integration Committee for
Secondary Education.
Integration of secondary education in the
reorganized Bombay state: report of a study
by the ... Committee ... appointed by the
Bombay State Government. 443p.

F-113
Desai, Ishwarlal Pragji.
High school students in Poona, BDCRI, v.12
(1953), pp.271-393.

F-114
Fraser, James Nelson, 1869-1918.
Training of secondary teachers in Bombay.
Calcutta, Govt.Pub., 1909. (India. Education Dept. Occasional reports, no.5,pt.III)

LC main

F-115
Joshi, N.G.
A year of social service in a secondary school (Bombay). PE, v.38 (1964), pp.240-45.

ja s 64

F-116
Kothurkar, Vasudeo Krishna.
Psychological survey of the secondary school children of Poona. Poona, University of Poona, 1962. 117p.

LC

F-117
Manohar, Priyanwada Mukund.
Reading interests of Marathi speaking boys and girls at the secondary school stage. Bombay, Univ.of Bombay, 1953. *

Secondary education
BDD

F-118
A memorial to the government of Bombay against the proposed abolition of the Poona High School and the connected correspondence. QJPSS, v.11,no.2 (1888), pp.7-30.

QJPSS

F-119
Mone, Surendra S.
Reorganization of secondary education in Bombay Province, India. New York, Columbia Univ., 1950. *

Stucki

F-120
Patwardhan, Chintamani Nilkant.
New code for recognition of an aid to secondary schools. PE, v.38 (1963-1364), pp.199-202, 218-20.

ja s64

F-121
Pendse, Vinayak Vishwanath.
Experimental study of the processes of leadership among secondary school children of Greater Poona. Poona, Univ.of Poona, 1961. *

Educational psychology
BDD

F-122
Poona, India (City)
Proceedings of a meeting held at the town hall, Poona ... 1884, to consider the desirability of establishing a High School for native girls. Poona, Gazette Press, 1884.

Graves MA.

F-123
Sharma, V.P.
Evaluation of attainment in Federal Hindi at secondary school level in West Maharashtra. Poona, Univ.of Poona, 1967. *

Secondary education

F-124
  Working of the Maharashtra S.S.C. Examination
    Board. *PK*, v.37 (1962), pp.114-20.

QaS63   Higher

F-125
  Altbach, Philip Geoffrey, 1941-
    Student politics in Bombay. New York, Asia
  Pub.House, 1968. (Indian education series,
  no.3) 226p.

4 of R

F-126
  Altbach, Philip Geoffrey, 1941-
    Students, politics, and higher education
  in a developing area: the case of Bombay,
  India. Chicago, Univ.of Chicago, 1966.
  305p. *

Shulman #391

F-127
  Bapat, Nilkanth Gangadhar.
    Commerce education in universities in
  Maharashtra, *IJC*, v.22,no.4 (1969), pp.
  196-206.

BAS 1969

F-128
  Dhamankar, V.K.
    Development of universities in Maharashtra,
  JMaU, v.4,no.1 (1963), pp.63-86.

JMaU.

F-129
  Dongerkery, Sunderrao Ramrao, 1898-
    Bombay University and colleges. Bombay,
  1948.

Pusalkar

F-130
  Dongerkery, Sunderrao Ramrao, 1898-
    Memories of two universities. Bombay,
  Manktalas, 1966. 288p.

4 of R

F-131
  Dongerkery, Sunderrao Ramrao, 1898-
    Problems of universities in Maharashtra,
  JMaU, v.1, no.1 (1961), pp.163-72.

in JMaU

F-132
  Gense, James H.
    The Bandra riddle and the Bassein answer,
  Indica, v.2 (1965), pp.121-29.

  (John Fryer's account of Bandra confused
  with Bassein)

F-133
  Jubilee souvenir of St. Xavier's College and
    High School. Comp.by E.Blatter. Bombay,
  the Times Press, 1921. 275p.

Bom (Pres) cat

F-134
Kamat, A.R., 1912-
   The internal and external assessments: a
study based on the pre-degree examination,
1962, of the University of Poona, AV, v.5
(1963), pp.171-88, 301-25.

gab 63

F-135
Kamat, A.R., 1912-
   Two studies in education. Poona,
Gokhale Institute of Politics and Economics.
London, Asia Publishing House, 1968. (Gok-
hale Institute of Politics and Economics.
Gokhale Institute studies, no.55). 137p.

Education- books
BAS 1969

F-136
Kamat, A.R., 1912-   and Deshmukh, A.G.,
   1932-
   Wastage in college education; two studies
about students of the University of Poona.
Poona, Gokhale Institute of Politics and
Economics; N.Y., Asia Pub.House, 1963.
(Gokhale Institute of Politics and Economics,
Studies no.43) 202p.

LC

F-137
Poona, India (City) University. Dept.of Mathematics and Statistics.
   A socio-economic sample survey of college
students in Poona City, 1955-56. Poona,
1960. 102p.

NUR
SOAS NUFF

F-138
Reddy, P.H.
   Family position and higher education,
BDCRI, v.24 (1963-64), pp.36-43.

NRU
Tiree

F-139
Representation on the proposed abolition of
   the Deccan College, QJPSS, v.9,no.2 (1886),
   pp.1-49.

OJPSS

F-140
Sharma, Ramesh Chandra.
   To investigate the professional needs of
teacher educators of undergraduate training
institutions of Madhya Pradesh and Maharashtra. Ujjain, Vikram Univ., 1970. *

Individual Institutions

F-141
Ahmednagar College.
   Profile of a college; a self-study of
Ahmednagar College, Ahmednagar, Maharashtra.
Ed.by Thomas Barnabas and others. 2d rev.ed.
Bombay, Machiketa Pubs., 1972. 257p.

4 NR

F-142
Correspondence with the Finance Committee
regarding the proposed abolition of the
Deccan College, QJPSS, v.9,no.4 (1886),
pp.51-55.

PSS

F-143
Dīvān, Śārdā.
   S.N.D.T.Women's University - Dr. Karve's
experiment, EduI, v.27 (1961), pp.389-90.

Golden Jubilee Comm
Vol. #672

F-144
Dongerkery, Sunderrao Ramrao, 1898-
A history of the University of Bombay,
1857-1957. Bombay, University of Bombay,
1957. 313p.

F-145
Driver, Pesy N.
National Cooperative College and Research
Institute, Poona; a descriptive account, ICR,
v.4 (1967). pp.409-20.

Ja.S 9/68

F-146
Elphinstone College, Bombay.
Centenary commemoration lectures, by M.P.
Desai ,and others;. Bombay, Centenary Cele-
bration Comn., 1958. 160p.

F-147
Golden jubilee commemoration volume, 1916-1966.
Editors: G.B.Sardar, Shakuntala Mehta and
Neera Desai. Bombay, Shreemati Nathibai
Damodar Thackersey Women's Univ., 1968. 1vol.

1. Education of women.

U of R

F-148
Javoronkov, Vadim A.
Bombay Institute of Technology: engineers
in the new India, UNESCOC, v.18 (1965),
pp.14-17, 33.

F-149
Karve, Dinakar Dhondo, 1899-
The Deccan education society. JAS, v.20
(1961), pp.205-22.

Ra S61

F-150
Karwa, J.P. and Gaikwad, N.V.
Psycho-educational study of the students
of Yeshwant Mahavidyalaya, Nanded. Nanded,
Yeshwant Mahavidyalaya, 1968? (Yeshwant
Mahavidyalaya. Survey series no.2). 99p.

PL 480, s/s

F-151
Limaye, Parashuram Mahadev.
History of the Deccan Education Society,
1880-1935. Poona, M.K.Joshi, Secretary,
Deccan Education Society, 1935. 722p.

U of R

F-152
Mackichan, Dugald, 1851-1932.
Forty five years in India; memoir and reminis-
cances of Principal Mackichan of Wilson College,
Bombay. Ed.by David Williamson. London, I.
Nicholson & Watson, 1td., 1934. 127p.

LC

F-153
Naik, M.B.
Fifty fruitful years (Golden jubilee year
of Maharashtra vidyalaya), PE, v.45 (1970),
pp.139-40, 143.

Education study + teaching
BAS 1970

F-154
Nowrosjee Wadia College. Poona, India. Joag
Commemoration Committee.
Joag: commemoration volume. Poona, P.R.
Damle, 1965. 207p.

LC

F-159
Bapat, Vinayak Dhundiraj.
A psychological study of the methods of
measurement and prediction of athletic
ability in Kabaddi and Kho-Kho. Bombay,
Univ.of Bombay, 1966. *

Psychology - aptitude tests
BDD

F-155
Nowrosjee Wadia College. Poona, India. Silver
Jubilee Publicity Committee.
Silver jubilee commemoration volume. Ed.by
P.R.Damle. Poona, the college, 1958. 201p.

IOL

F-160
Bombay (Presidency) Educational Department.
Compilation of opinions on the subject of
the education of girls and women called for
by Govt.order no.1268 dated May 15th, 1916.
Bombay, Govt.Central Press, 1916. 473p.

Golden Jubilee Comm Vol

F-156
Sharma, Shripad Rama, 1897-
Fergusson College through sixty years.
Bombay, Karnatak Pub.House, 1945. 80p.

NUR 102

F-161
Bombay (Presidency) Educational Department.
Mahomedan education; recent developments in
the Bombay Presidency. Bombay, Govt.Pub.,
1914.

Greaves M.A.

F-157
Taraporewala, Irach Jehangir Sorabji, 1884-1956.
The Deccan College: its past history and
its future hopes, BDCRI, v.2 (1940), pp.1-8.

Case

Special aspects of
education

F-162
Bombay (Province) Educational Dept.
Report of the Adult Education Committee,
1938. Bombay, Govt.Central Press, 1938.
90p.

1. Education of adults. 2. Education -
India - Bombay (Presidency)

pre '56 imprints

F-158
Advani, Kanhayalal Ramchand.
Problems - educational and psychological -
of the blind children in the age group 7
to 21 years. Bombay, Univ.of Bombay,
1966. *

Education handicapped children
BDD

F-163
Chonkar, Ramkrishna M.
Twenty years of technical education in
Bombay, being a record of twenty years progress
of the Victoria Jubilee Technical Inst.
Bombay, 1907. (Supplement 1907/08-
1912/13). Bombay, Times Press, 1908,1913).
168p.

SeAS Supp

F-164
Council on World Tensions.
Report on a survey of the attitudes, opinions and personality traits of a sample of 1706 students of the University of Bombay, sponsored by World Brotherhood, Bombay. Bombay, Orient Longmans Priv.Ltd., 1960. 77p.

1. Bombay - University - Students. 2. Attitude (Psychology)

Lc

F-165
Daji, J.K.
Parsi education. Bombay J.K.Daji, 1925. 129p.

BM

F-166
Deshpande, V.D. and Sapre, S.G.
Extent of literacy in the rural Maharashtra, LJAE, v.18 (1963), pp.294-301.

JAS '64

F-167
The exclusion of religious instruction from government schools in India. Resolution of the Bombay government, no.1725, dated the 6th of July 1857, BQR, v.6 (1857), pp. 355-90.

U of R microfiche

F-168
Female education in western India, BQR, v.3 (1856), pp.388-405.

F-169
Haidari, M.Z.
Muslim education in the Presidency of Bombay. Poona, 1927. 6p.

IOL

F-170
India (Republic) Education Commission.
Report on Gram shikshan mohim of Maharashtra. New Delhi, 1965. 37p.

1. Illiteracy - India - Maharashtra (State)

Lc

F-171
Jasbhai Manibhai.
A memorandum on Hindu female education in the Bombay Presidency. Bombay, 1896. 165p.

F-172
Josephine, Sala.
Catholic education in the Province of Bombay. Bombay, Univ.of Bombay, 1952.

Education - philosophy + theory
B D D

F-173
Kale, S.V. and Phadke, K.M.
Report of an attitude survey (attitude of students of the University of Bombay towards shramdan-voluntary manual labour scheme), JUB, v.39 (1970), pp.205-17.

Children & adolescents
BAs 1970

F-174
Khanapurkar, H.K. and Khanapurkar, U.H.
Science education in Marathwada, PE, v.44
(Apr.1970), pp.335-41; v.44 (May/June 1970),
pp.373-76, 385.

education study + teaching
BAS 1970

F-175
Koppiker, G.K.
The education of the Adivasis in Thana
District. New Delhi, Manager of Publica-
tions, 1956. (India (Republic) Ministry
of Education. Pub.no.223). 34p.

1, Education - India - Thana (District) 2. Adivasis.
LC

F-176
Manibhai Jasbhai.
A memorandum on Hindu female education in
the Bombay presidency. Bombay, Bombay Gazette
Steam Printing Works, 1896. 167p.

Bom. (Pres.) col

F-177
Mascarenhas, Juliet.
An investigation into the suitability of
students for admission to the medical
college of Bombay University. Bombay, Univ.
of Bombay, 1964. *

Higher education
BDD

F-178
Merchant, Shakkarkhanoo Jooma.
The language development of Gujarati speak-
ing Bohra girls of Standard IV of a typical
Bohra girls' school. Bombay, Univ.of Bombay,
1961. *

Elementary education
Curricu
BDD

F-179
Naik, Chitra.
The education of women in the province of
Bombay: a retrospect and a prospect. Bombay,
Univ.of Bombay, 1949. *

Women's education
BDD

F-180
Naik, Chitra.
Women's education in the state of Bombay.
In: Bombay year book of education 1951;
ed.by Indra Kumar. Bombay, Education Year
Book Co., 1951. pp.93-99.

Golden Jubilee Comm Vol #374

F-181
Paranjape, Lata S.
Problems of women primary teachers in the
Poona Revenue region. Poona, Univ.of Poona,
1970. *

Education Organization
+ administration
BDD

F-182
Pathak, A.K.
Construction and standardization of group
intelligence tests in Marathi for ages 9 to
13. Bombay, Univ.of Bombay, 1961. *

natl council of
Ed Research

F-183
Samant, Bhagwant Bhikaji, 1906-
A survey of teaching of mathematics in
secondary schools with special reference
to Bombay Province. Bombay, Univ.of Bombay,
1945. *

Secondary education
BDD

F-184
Sayani, I.M.
An enquiry into the condition of Mahomedan education in the Bombay Presidency in the official year, 1878-79. Surat, Mission Press, 1884.

Cal Nat Lib

G-1
Chaudhuri, Sibadas, comp.
Bibliography of studies in Indian epigraphy, 1926-50. Baroda, Oriental Institute, 1966. (M.S.University oriental series, no.6) 123p.

F-185
Tamhankar, Vasant Sitaram.
A study of achievement motivation among the young adolescent boys in the Poona city. Poona, Univ.of Poona, 1968. *

Educational psychology
BDD

G-2
Epigraphia Indica. v.1-34, 1888-1962, Index, by A.N.Lahiri. Ootacamund, South India, Issued by Dr.G.S.Gai, Government Epigraphist for India, 196- 204p.

General

F-186
Tarachand, D.E.
A study of the intelligence of Gujarati-speaking children in suburban Bombay. JGRS, v.19 (1957), pp.21-29.

U of R

G-3
Bakhle, Vidyasagar Sadashiv.
Setagiri of the Nasik inscription, IHQ, v.2 (1926), pp.351-52.

U of R
Index to I.H.Q.

F-187
Vaidya, Manubhai Pranjivan, 1905-
Bilingualism in education (descriptive and experimental) with special reference to greater Bombay. Bombay, University of Bombay, 1954.*

Nat Council Ed. Research

G-4
Bendrey, Vasudeo Sitaram, 1896-
A study of Muslim inscriptions. Bombay, Karnatak Pub.House, 1944. 208p.

U of R

F-188
Vakil, Vidya Vanraj.
Girls' education in modern India with special reference to its expansion in the State of Bombay. Bombay, Univ.of Bombay, 1967. *

Womens Education

G-5
Bhandarkar, Ramkrishna Gopal, 1837-1925.
Deoli plates of Krishna III, saka samvat 862, EI, v.5 (1989-99), pp.188-97.

EI

G-6

Bhandarkar, Ramkrishna Gopal, 1837-1925.
On Dr. Hoernle's version of a Nasik
Inscription and the Gatha dialect, IA,
v.12 (1883), pp.133-47.

JWIA

G-7

Bhandarkar, Ramkrishna Gopal, 1837-1925.
A revised transcript and translation of
a Chalukya copper plate grant first published
in the Journal of the Royal Asiatic Society,
Bombay Branch, vol.2, with remarks on the
genealogy and chronology of the early
kings of the Chalukya dynasty, ASBJ, v.14
(1878-80), pp.16-28.

JRASBom

G-8

Bhandarkar, Ramkrishna Gopal, 1837-1925.
Transcripts and translations with remarks
of Rashtrakuta and Kalachuri copper-plate
grants, ASBJ, v.18 (1890-94), pp.239-81.

NRU

G-9

Bühler, G.
The Ilichpur grant of Pravarasena II of
Vākāṭaka, IA, v.12 (1883), pp.239-47.

G-10

Central Provinces and Berar, India.
Inscriptions in the Central Provinces and
Berar; by Hira Lal. 2d ed. Nagpur, 1932.
311p.

Scholberg

G-11

Chaghtai, M.A.
Adil Shahi grants to Shaikh Muhammad Abu
Turab Mudarria, IHRCP, v.21 (1944), pp.7-9.

EI

G-12

Das Gupta, Charu Chandra, 1908-
Shelarwadi cave inscription, EI, v.28
(1949), pp.76-77.

E.I.

G-13

Derozario, M
The complete monumental register: containing
all the epitaphs, inscriptions, etc., in the
different churches & burial grounds, in &
about Calcutta ... Together with inscriptions
from the presidencies of Madras, Bombay, Isle
of France, etc. Calcutta, Printed by P.Ferris,
1815. 237p.

1. Epitaphs - India.

LC

G-14

Desai, P.B.
Methi inscription of Yadava Krishna: s-ka
1176, EI, v.28 (1950), pp.312-20.

EI

G-15

Deshpande, Yeshwant Khushal, 1884-   and
Mahajan, D.B.
The earliest copper grant of the Vākāṭaka
dynasty, IHCP, v.3 (1939), pp.449-60.

AMR

G-16
Dikshit, Moreshwar Gangadhar, 1915-
Dive Agar Marathi copper charter, saka 982,
EI, v.28 (1949), pp.121-24.

EI

G-17
Dikshit, Moreshwar Gangadhar, 1915-
Kolhapur inscription of Silahara Bhoja II,
Saka 1104, EI, v.29 (1951), pp.13-18.

EI

G-18
Dikshit, Moreshwar Gangadhar, 1915-
Nahul (Trombay) inscription of Hari-
paladeva, Saka 1075, EI, v.37 (1967),
pp.165-66.

BAS 1967

G-19
Dikshit, Moreshwar Gangadhar, 1915-
Sivapura (Goa) plates of Candravarman, NIA,
v.4 (1941), pp.181-84.

G-20
Dikshit, Moreshwar Gangadhar, 1915-
Thana plates on Silahara Nagarjuna, Saka
961, EI, v.37 (1968), pp.247-56.

BAS

G-21
Dikshit, Moreshwar Gangadhar, 1915-   ed.
Selected inscriptions from Maharashtra,
5th to 12th century, A.D. [summaries only
in English] Poona, Bharata Itihasa Samsodha-
ka Mandala, 1947. (Sviya Grantha Mala, no.
67) 131p.

SoAS

G-22
Diskalkar, Dattatraya Balkrishna, 1892-
A copper-plate grant of Rana Arisimha to
Ahilyabai Holkar, IHQ, v.24 (1948), pp.141-
42.

Index to IHQ

G-23
Doderet, W.
A fourteenth century Marathi inscription,
BSOAS, v.5 (1930), pp.37-42.

JBHS

G-24
Fernandes, Braz A.
Armas e inscrições do forte de Baçaim...;
prefacio, notas e tradução do Antonio Machado
de Faria. Lisboa, 1957. (Academia Portuguesa
da Historia) 308p.

IOL

G-25
Fleet, John Faithfull, 1847-1917.
A copper-plate grant of the Devagiri-
Yadava king Singhana II, ASBJ, v.15,
no.40 (1882), pp.383-90.

NRU

G-26
Fleet, John Faithfull, 1847-1917.
Inscriptions relating to the Ratta Chieftains of Saundatti and Belgaum, with remarks. ASBJ, v.9 (1871-74), pp.167-298.

ASBJ

G-27
Fleet, John Faithfull, 1847-1917.
On some Sanskrit copper-plates found in the Belgaum collectorate, ASBJ, v.9 (1867-68), pp.229-49.

ASBJ

G-28
Fleet, John Faithfull, 1847-1917.
Sanskrit and old Canarese inscriptions, relating to the Yādava kings of Dēvagiri, ed. from the originals, with translations, ASBJ, v.12, no.33 (1876), pp.1-50.

ASBJ

G-29
Fleet, John Faithfull, 1847-1917.
Translations of inscriptions from Belgaum and Kaladgi Districts in the report of the first season's operation of the Archaeological Survey of Western India. Bombay, 1876. (Archaeological Survey of Western India, miscellaneous publications, no.5). 45p.

M

G-30
Gokhale, Shobhana.
The Pandharpur stone inscription of the Yadava king Mahadeva, saka 1192, IA, v.4 (1970), pp.42-49.

Ep graphy
BAS 1970

G-31
Gore, Narayan Anant.
The Beed grant of Govinda III, JMaU, v.3, no.1 (1962), pp.76-85.

JMaU

G-32
Gupte, Y.R., 1881-
A newly discovered grant of Govinda III, JIH, v.4 (1925), pp.100-102.

JiH v.4

G-33
Gupte, Y.R., 1881-
A supplementary note on the 'newly discovered grant of Govind III of the saka year 732', JIH, v.5 (1925), pp.98-100.

JIH

G-34
Haig, Sir Wolseley, 1865-1938.
Some inscriptions in Berar, EIM, (1907-1908), pp.10-21.

OB

G-35
Indraji, Bhagvanlal.
Copper-plate of the Silahara Dynasty, ASBJ, v.13, no.35 (1877), pp.1-17.

NRL

G-36
    Indraji, Bhagvānlāl.
        A new copper-plate grant of the Chālukya Dynasty, found at Navsāri, ASBJ, v.16, no.42 (1883-85), pp.1-7.

NRD
JRASB...

G-37
    Kadiri, A.A.
        Inscriptions of the Sidi chiefs of Janjira, EI, Arabic and Persian Supp. (1966), pp.55-76.

JAS 9/68

G-38
    Kasinatha Tryambaka Telanga, 1840-1893.
        Three Kadamba copperplates: with remarks, ASBJ, v.12,no.33 (1876), pp.300-24.

NRD
...

G-39
    Katare, Sant Lal.
        Sirpur Gandheśvara Temple inscription (of the time of Somavamsi Mahaśivagupta), IHQ, v.33 (1957), pp.229-34.

Index to IHQ

G-40
    Kern, H.
        The inscriptions in Junnar, IA, v.6 (1877), pp.39-41.

✓✓IA

G-41
    Khan, M.K.
        Inscriptions of the Qutb Shahi kings, EI, Arabic and Persian supplement, (1966), pp.27-34.

PS417 E66
EI

G-42
    Khare, Ganesh Hari, 1901-
        The Kolhapur plates of Śilahara Gandaraditya, Śaka 1037, EI, v.27 (1947), pp.176-82.

EI

G-43
    Khare, Ganesh Hari, 1901-
        A note on the Yadava copper-plate grant of Saka 974, AIOCPT, 18th session (1955), pp.344-46.

U of R

G-44
    Khare, Ganesh Hari, 1901-
        A note on three gun inscriptions from Poona, IHRCP, v.34,pt.2 (1958), pp.158-59.

U of R

G-45
    Khare, Ganesh Hari, 1901-
        Tasgaon plates of Yadava Krsna, Saka 1173, EI, v.27 (1947), pp.208-16.

EI

G-46
Kielhorn, Franz, 1840-1908.
    The date of one of the Kanheri inscriptions
of Amoghavarasha 1. IA, v.20 (1891), pp.421-22.

✓ // IA

G-47
Kielhorn, Franz, 1840-1908.
    Vakkaleri plates of Kirtivarman II, saka
samvat 679. EI, v.5 (1989-99), pp.200-205.

EI

G-48
Kolte, Vishnu Bhikaji, 1908-
    Kasar-Sirsi copperplates of Vijayaditya, NUJ,
v.17 (1967), pp. 143-49.

NuJ

G-49
Kolte, Vishnu Bhikaji, 1908-
    Pauni plates of Pravarasena II, NUJ, v.18
(1967), pp.73-7.

NuJ

G-50
Kolte, Vishnu Bhikaji, 1908-
    Two Vajirkheda copperplate grants of Indra III,
NUJ, v.17 (1967), pp.117-42.

NuJ

G-51
Master, Alfred, 1883-
    Some Marathi inscriptions, A.D.1060-1300,
BSOAS, v.20 (1957), pp.417-36.

BSOAS

G-52
Mirashi, Vasudev Vishnu, 1893-
    An odd copper-plate grant of the Yadava King
Ramachandra, IHCP, v.22 (1959), pp.196-200.

IHCP

G-53
Mirashi, Vasudev Vishnu, 1893-
    Dongargaon stone inscription of the time of
Jagaddeva: saka 1034. EI, v.26 (1941), pp.
177-84.

EI

G-54
Mirashi, Vasudev Vishnu, 1893-
    The Indragaah stone inscription of Rastrakuta
Nanna. IHQ, v.31 (1955), pp.99-104.

Chandeur

G-55
Mirashi, Vasudev Vishnu, 1893-
    Jambgaon plates of Indra III, Saka 836,
EI, v.36 (1966), pp.223-38.

JaS '66

G-56
Mirashi, Vasudev Vishnu, 1893-
　　Khanapur plates of Madhavarman, EI, v.27
(1948), pp.312-18.

E-I

G-57
Mirashi, Vasudev Vishnu, 1893-
　　Minor plates of Rashtrakuta Dantidurga,
IHCP, v.21 (1958), pp.49-53.

IHCP

G-58
Mirashi, Vasudev Vishnu, 1893-
　　Minor plates of Rāṣṭrakūṭa Dantidurga, Śaka
year 671, IHQ, v.35 (1959), pp.183-88.

Index to IHQ

G-59
Mirashi, Vasudev Vishnu, 1893-
　　Pandarangapalli grant of Rashtrakuta avidheya.
In: Studies in Indian history, Dr.A.G.Pawar
felicitation volume. Ed.by V.D.Rao. Kol-
hapur, Y.P.Pawar, 1968. pp.190-200.

U J R

G-60
Mirashi, Vasudev Vishnu, 1893-
　　Two inscriptions from Berar, EI, v.21 (1931),
pp.127-32.

U J R

G-61
Mukherjee, B.N.
　　On the interpretation of a word in a Kanheri
inscription, IHCP, v.23 (1960), pp.55-57.

U J R

G-62
Naik, A.V.
　　Inscriptions of the Deccan, an epigraphical
survey, BDCRI, v.9 (1947), pp.71-100.

BDCRI p 148

G-63
Prasanna, Kumud.
　　Chalukya inscription - a study, JUB, n.s.,
v.39 (1970), pp.343-61.

BAS 1970

G-64
Ritti, Shrinivas, 1929-   and Shelke, G.C.
　　Inscriptions from Nanded District. Nanded,
Yeshwant Mahavidyalaya, 1968. 329p.

PL 480 4/70

G-65
Sankalia, Hasmukhlal Dhirajlal, 1908-
　　Cultural significance of the personal names
in the early inscriptions of the Deccan,
BDCRI, v.3 (1941), pp.349-91.

Annual Bibs of Ind History + Indology

G-66
    Sarma, M.Somasekhara.
       Three grants of Chalukya Jayasimha I, EI,
    v.31 (1955), pp.129-38.

Chaudhuri ◯

G-67
    Senart, E.
       The inscriptions in the caves at Nasik,
    EI, v.8 (1905-1906), pp.59-96.

Epigraphia India ◯

G-68
    Shaikh, C.H.
       The original places of some Indo-Muslim inscrip-
    tions of Ahmadnagar. In: A Volume of Studies in
    Indology presented to Professor P.V.Kane on
    his sixty-first birthday. Ed.by S.M.Katre and
    P.K.Gode. Poona, Oriental book agency, 1941.
    pp.423-27.

UজR
Bhandarkar Indus
comm vol. ◯

G-69
    Sharma, B.C.S.
       The Prince of Wales Museum inscription of
    Jayakesi III, the Kadamba King of Goa, JIH,
    v.10 (1931), pp.2-9.

JJH ◯

G-70
    Sircar, Dineshandra, 1907-
       Some technical expressions in inscriptions,
    QJMS, v.51 (1960), pp.1-4.

GJMS ◯

G-71
    Stevenson, John, 1798-1858.
       Historical names and facts contained in
    the Kānheri (Kenery) inscriptions; with
    translations appended, ASBJ, v.5,no.18 (1853),
    pp.1-34.

NRU
ASBJ ◯

G-72
    Stevenson, John, 1798-1858.
       Note on the rock inscriptions in the
    island of Salsette, ASBJ, v.4 (1852),
    pp.132-35.

ASBJ ◯

G-73
    Stevenson, John, 1798-1858.
       On the Nasik cave inscriptions, ASBJ,
    v.5,no.18 (1853), pp.35-57.

ASBJ ◯

G-74
    Stevenson, John, 1798-1858.
       Sahyādri inscriptions, ASBJ, v.5 (1853),
    pp.151-79.

ASBJ ◯

G-75
    Tripathi, Narayan.
       An incomplete charter of a Somavamsi king,
    found at Ratnagiri, JBRS, v.16 (1930), pp.
    206-10.

JBHS ◯

G-76
    Verma, B.D.
        'Ādil Shāhī epigraphy in the Deccan, <u>JUB</u>,
        v.8 (1939), pp.13-51.

JUB

G-77
    West, Arthur A.
        Copies of inscriptions from the caves near
        Bedsa, with a plan, <u>ASBJ</u>, v.8 (1863-66), pp.
        222-25.

Geography   Bibliography & Reference

H-1
    Apte, Narhar Gangadhar, 1900-
        Mahārāshtra grāmakośa. Poona, Maharashtra
        Gramakosa Mandala, Tilak Maharashtra Vidya-
        pitha, 1967. 2v.

4 ʸR

H-2
    Baness, J.Frederick.
        Index geographicus indicus: being a list,
        alphabetically arranged, of the principal
        places in Her Imperial Majesty's Indian
        Empire ... London, Edward Stanford, 1881.
        318p.

4 ʸR

H-3
    Dey, Nundo Lal.
        Geographical dictionary of ancient and
        medieval India, with an appendix on modern
        names of ancient Indian geography. Calcutta,
        W.Lewman & co., 1899. 271p.

4 ʸR

H-4
    The Geographical encyclopaedia of ancient and
        medieval India; based on Vedic, Puranic,
        Tantric, Jain, Buddhistic literature and
        historical records. Chief editor: K.D.Bajpai.
        Varanasi, Indic Academy, 1967-

4 ʸR

H-5
    Gosling, Lee Anthony Peter, 1927-
        Maps, atlases, and gazetteers for Asian
        studies: a critical guide. New York, State
        Education Dept., 1965. (Foreign Area Mate-
        rials Center. University of the State of New
        York. Occasional publication no.2) 33p.

4 ʸR

H-6
    Sharma, Jagdish Saran, 1924-
        The national geographical dictionary of
        India. New Delhi, Sterling Publishers, 1972.
        223p.

General

H-7
    Abbott, Justin Edwards, 1853-1932.
        Identification of Nagapura in the Konkan,
        <u>IA</u>, v.24 (1895), p.83.

V V VIA

H-8
    Arunachalam, B., 1933-
        Coastal features in the vicinity of
        Ratnagiri Town, <u>BUM</u>, v.12 (1964), pp.39-
        47.

IAS '66

H-9
    Arunachalam, B., 1933-
      Maharashtra; a study in physical and
    regional setting and resource development.
    Bombay, A.R.Sheth, 1967. 308p.

/// PL4 80, '69

H-10
    Bellasis, Augustus Fortunatus.
      An account of the Hill Station of Matheran,
    near Bombay. Bombay, 1869.

Calcutta Nat'l Lib

H-11
    Bhatt, Harsa J., ed.
      Ports of India; reference manual. Vol.1 -
    Port of Bombay. Bombay, 1959. 60p.

1. Harbors — India

LC
IBP

H-12
    Bombay (State).
      List of districts, talukas, towns,
    railway stations and post offices in
    the State of Bombay. Bombay, Printed
    at the Govt.Central Press, 1951. 46p.

LC Accessions ... p.200

H-13
    Bombay (State) Bureau of Economics and
      Statistics.
      Bombay State in maps. Bombay, Bureau
    of Economics and Statistics, 1956. 99p.

Furer

H-14
    Chaturvedi, B.N.
      The Godavari Krishna water dispute -
    a geographical appraisal, DG, v.5,nos.1/2
    (1969), pp.30-58.

Geography - Descr & travel - articles
PAS Sep 1970

H-15
    Cunningham, Sir Alexander, 1814-1893.
      The ancient geography of India. Part I:
    the Buddhist period, including the campaigns
    of Alexander, and the travels of Hwen Thsang.
    Varanasi, Indological Book House, 1963.
    556p.

4 of R

H-16
    Deoras, V.R.
      The rivers and mountains of Maharashtra,
    IHCP, v.21 (1958), pp.202-209.

IHCP

H-17
    Deshpande, C.D.
      Settlement types of Bombay Karnatak, IGJ,
    v.17 (1942), pp.115-31.

H-18
    Deshpande, C.D.
      Western India: a regional geography. Dhar-
    war, Students' Own Book Depot, 1948. 293p.

SOAS

N-19
Dikshit, K.R. and Sawant, S.B.
Hinterland as a region: its type, hierarchy, demarcation and characteristics, illustrated in a case study of the hinterland of Poona, NGJI, v.14 (1968), pp.1-22. figs.

BAS Sept 1970

N-20
Fernandes, Braz A.
Sopara: the ancient port of the Konkan, JBHS, v.1 (1928), pp.65-77.

JBHS

N-21
Fleet, John Faithful, 1847-1917.
Hiuen Tsiang's capital of Maharashtra, IA, v.22 (1893), pp.113-16.

N-22
Freire de Andrade, Jacinto, 1597-1675.
Vida de Dom Joao de Castro, quarto viscrey da India. Lisboa, 1786. 356p.

NUR
BM

N-23
Gananathan, V.S.
Western districts of upland Maharashtra, IGJ, v.37 (1962), pp.121-32.

Jas 43

N-24
India. Survey Department.
Catalogue of maps and plans of India. Calcutta, Printed by the Superintendent of government printing, 1885-1899.
Issued as separate pamphlets, each with own cover and title page.
Item 4 - Bombay Presidency, 1889.

N-25
International Publications, Delhi.
The State of Maharashtra: Political. Delhi, 196-?

1. Maharashtra, India (State) - Maps.
LC

N-26
Joppen, Charles.
Historical atlas of India, for use of high schools, colleges and private students. London, N.Y., Longmans, Green, & Co., 1914. 20p.

1. India - Historical geography. 2. Atlases.
LC

N-27
Joshi, C.B.
The historical geography of the islands of Bombay, BGM, v.4 (1956), pp.5-13.

Case

N-28
Kane, Pandurang Vaman, 1880-
Ancient geography and civilisation of Maharashtra, ASBJ, v.24 (1923), p.616.

JAS Bom

H-29
Kane, Pandurang Vaman, 1880–
Ancient geography of Konkan, AIOCPT, v.2
(1928-30), pp.365-92.

vi vol of studies in Indology

H-30
Kane, Pandurang Vaman, 1880–
Ancient geography of Maharashtra, ASBJ,
v.26 (1925), pp.613-57.

Vol of Studies in Indology

H-31
Kane, Pandurang Vaman, 1880–
Notes on the ancient history and geography
of the Konkan, AIOCPT, v.1 (1919), pp.264-92.

Moraes

H-32
Karmarkar, Anant Parashurampant, 1906–
Boundaries of ancient Maharashtra and Karna-
taka, IHQ, v.14 (1938), pp.773-86.

IHQ

H-33
Kniazhinskaia, Larisa Aleksandrovaa.
Zapadnaia Indiia: ekonomiko-geograficheskaia
kharaktistika. Moskva, Gos.izd-vo geogr.Lit-ry,
1959. (Akademiia nauk SSSR. Institut geografii)
308p.

LC

H-34
Law, Bimala Churn, 1892–
Historical geography of ancient India.
Paris, Société Asiatique de Paris, 1954.
354p.

LC

H-35
Lewis, J.P.
The rugby guide to Matheran. Poona, Fram-
roze S.Chenai, 1908. 100p.

Room - Free Cat

H-36
Mulay, Sumati Dattatray.
Studies in the historical and cultural
geography and enthnography of the Deccan
(based entirely on the inscriptions of the
Deccan from 5th-13th century A.D.). Poona,
Deccan College Postgraduate and Research
Institute, 1954.

Jayakar Dil #1 1434

H-37
Nainar, Muhammad Husain.
Arab geographers' knowledge of southern
India. Madras, Univ.of Madras, 1942. 205p.

1. India - Historical geography.

LC

H-38
Padhye, S.S.
The geographic co-relations of Vaidarbhian
toponyms. NGJI, v.13 (1967), pp.14-2..

JAS 9/68

H-39
Padhye, S.S.
    Physical setting of the Deccan trap region of Vidarbha, NGJI, v.7 (1961), pp.165-70.

ga S 62

H-40
Phatak, G.N.
    A detailed geographic study of the Deccan. Poona, G.N.Phatak, 1938. 28p.

e M

H-41
Ramamurthy, K.
    Geographical aspects of dykes in Dhulia district of Maharashtra, BGM, v.13 (1965), pp. 81-84.

ga S 9/68

H-42
Rennell, James, 1742-1830.
    Memoir of a map of Hindoostan; or, the Mogul empire. London, Printed by M.Brown for the author, 1788. 335p.

4.7 R

H-43
Shende, Shankar Ramachandra.
    Extent of Maharashtra as described by the Mahanubhavas, IHCP, v.10 (1947), pp.273-75.

I HC P

H-44
Shende, Shankar Ramachandra.
    The extent of Maharastra as found in the Aihole inscription, ABORI, v.23 (1942), pp. 494-509.

ABORI

H-45
Shende, Shankar Ramachandra.
    How, whence and when Maharastra came into being, IHCP, v.10 (1947), pp.200-201.

IHCP

H-46
Simkins, Ethel.
    The agricultural geography of the Deccan plateau of India. London, G.Philip and son, 1926. 92p.

LC

H-47
Sinclair, William F.
    Notes on the central Talukas of the Thana Collectorate, IA, v.4 (1875), pp.65-69.

VW IA

H-48
Singh, Ujagir.
    Bombay: a study in historical geography 1667-1900 A.D., NGJI, v.6 (1960), pp.19-29.

case

H-49
The southern Ghats, CR, v.38 (1863),
pp.286-320.

Case

H-50
Spate, Oskar Hermann Khristian and Learmonth,
A.T.A..
India and Pakistan: a general and regional
geography, by O.H.K.Spate and A.T.A.Learmonth
and a chapter on Ceylon by B.J.Farmer. 3rd
ed. London, Methuen, 1967. 910p.

1. India
U of R

H-51
Tirtha, Ranjit.
Geographical reorganization of Indian States,
1947-1960. Chapel Hill, Univ.of North Carolina,
1962. *

Bibliography & Reference   History

I-1
Annual bibliography of Indian history and
Indology, 1938-42. Comp.by B.A.Fernandes.
Bombay, Bombay Historical Society, 1938-
49. 5v.

U of R

I-2
Beale, Thomas William, d.1875.
An oriental biographical dictionary, founded
on materials collected by Thomas William
Beale. A new ed., rev.and enl., by Henry
George Keene. London, 1894. New York,
Kraus Reprint Corp., 1965. 438p.

U of R

I-3
Bhattacharya, Sachchidananda.
Dictionary of Indian history. Calcutta,
Univ.of Calcutta, 1967. 900p.

U of R

I-4
Higham, Charles Clive.
The Viceroys and Governors-General of India,
1757-1947. London, John Murray, 1949. 190p.

U of R

I-5
Bombay (Presidency) Alienation Office.
Handbook to the records of the Alienation
Office, Poona. Comp.by Govind Sakharam
Sardesai. Bombay, Government Central Press,
1933. 2v.

I-6
Bose, Birendranath.
Bibliography of Jadunath's works, research
papers and articles, etc. (English) In:
Life and letters of Sir Jadunath Sarkar.
Ed.by Hari Ram Gupta. Hoshiarpur (India),
Panjab Univ., 1957. pp.108-13.

U of R

I-7
Buckland, Charles Edward, 1847-1941.
Dictionary of Indian biography. London,
Swan Sonnenschein & co., 1906. 506p.

U of R

I-8
Burnell, Arthur Coke, 1840-1882.
A tentative list of books and some mss.
relating to the history of the Portuguese
in India. Mangalore, Printed at Basel Mission
Press, 1880. 139p.

I-13
Das-Gupta, H.D.
Bibliography of prehistoric Indian antiqui-
ties, JASBen, v.27 (1931), pp.1-96.

I-9
Case, Margaret H.
South Asian history, 1750-1950; a guide to
periodicals, dissertations, and newspapers.
Princeton, N.J., Princeton Univ.Press, 1968.
574p.

I-14
Elliot, Henry Miers, 1808-1853.
Bibliographical index to the historians of
Muhammedan India. Calcutta, 1849. v.1 -
General histories.

I-10
Chanda, Ramaprasad.
Annual bibliography of Indian archaeology,
MR, v.51 (1932), pp.51-60.

I-15
Ferreira Martins, José Frederico, 1874-
Os vice-reis da India, 1505-1917 ...
Lisboa, Imprensa nacional da Lisboa, 1935.
337p.

I-11
Cockle, Maurice James Draffen.
A catalogue of books relating to the mili-
tary history of India. Simla, Govt.Central
Press, 1901. 105p.

I-16
Grant, Sir Charles, 1836-1903, ed.
The Gazetteer of the Central Provinces of
India. 2d ed. Bombay, Printed at the Edu-
cation Society's Press, 1870. 629p.

I-12
Cohn, Bernard S.
The development and impact of British
administration in India, a bibliographic
essay. New Delhi, Indian Institute of
Public Administration, 1961. 38p.

I-17
Kern Institute, Leyden.
Annual bibliography of Indian archaeology.
Leyden, E.J.Brill, 1926-

I-18
Ladendorf, Janice M.
The revolt in India 1857-58. An annotated
bibliography of English language materials.
Zug, Inter Documentation Co., 1966. (Biblio-
theca Indica, no.1) 197p.

ひぅR   O

I-19
Lethbridge, Roper, 1840-1919.
The golden book of India: a genealogical and
biographical dictionary of the ruling princes,
chiefs, nobles and other personages, titled or
decorated, of the Indian empire, with an appendix for Ceylon. London, S.Low, Marston and Co.,
1900. 388p.

1. India - Biog. 2. Ceylon - Biog.

LC   O

I-20
McCully, Bruce Tiebout, 1904-
Bibliographical article: The origins of
Indian nationalism according to native
writers, JMH, v.7 (1935), pp.295-314.

O

I-21
Marshall, D.N.
Mughals in India; a bibliographical survey.
Bombay, New York, Asia Pub.House, 1967-
v.1 - Manuscripts.

ひぅR   O

I-22
Raghubir Library, Sitamau, India.
A hand-list of important historical manuscripts in the Raghubir Library, Sitamau, India,
by Raghubir Sinh. Sitamau (Malwa), 1949. 72p.

ひぅR   O

I-23
Ram, Sadhu, 1901-
Index to the Indian historical quarterly,
1925-1963. New Delhi, Vijay Mohan, 1970.
187p.

ひぅR   )

I-24
Rickmers, Christian Mabel (Duff) 1866-
The chronology of Indian history, from the
earliest times to the beginning of the sixteenth century. Delhi, Cosmo Publications,
1972. (Studies in Indian history, no.2)
420p.

ひぅR   O

I-25
Sardesai, Govind Sakharam, 1865-1959.
Indexes to the Selections from the Peshwas'
daftar, nos.1-25. Bombay, Printed at the
Govt.Central Press, 1933. 1v.

ひぅR   )

I-26
Sarkar, Sir Jadunath, 1870-1958.
A guide to Indian historical literature,
MR, v.2 (1907), pp.392-99.

MR   )

I-27
Sarma, M.Somasekhara.
The chronology of the Sultans of Gulbarga,
JBRS, v.27 (1941), pp.455-72.

II   )

I-28
Sharma, Jagdish Saran, 1924-
India since the advent of the British; a
descriptive chronology from 1600 to Oct.2,
1969. 1st ed. Delhi, S.Chand, 1970. 847p.

4 9R

I-29
Sharma, Jagdish Saran, 1924-
Indian National Congress: a descriptive
bibliography of India's struggle for freedom.
Foreword by U.N.Dhebar. Pref.by Shriman
Narayan. Delhi, S.Chand, 1959. (National
bibliographies, no.3) 854p.

I-30
Sharma, Jagdish Saran, 1924-
The national biographical dictionary of
India. New Delhi, Sterling Publishers, 1972.
302p.

4 9R

I-31
Sharma, Sri Ram, 1900-
A bibliography of Mughal India, 1526-1707 A.D.
Bombay, Karnatak Pub.House, 1938? 226p.

4 9R

I-32
Spring, Frederick William MacKenzie, comp.
The Bombay artillery. List of the officers
of the Bombay artillery from its formation
in 1749 to the amalgamation with the Royal
artillery. London, W.Clowes, 1902. 147p.

4 9R

I-33
Taraporevala, Vicaji Dinshah B. and Marshall,
D.N.
Mughal bibliography; select Persian sources
for the study of Mughals in India. Bombay,
New Book Co., 1962. 164p.

4 9R
Descr.& trav.

I-34
"A.B.C."
A French traveller in India in the last
century, MR, v.12 (1912), pp.28-41.

Case

I-35
An account of a voyage to India, China, etc.
in His Majesty's ship Caroline; performed
in the years 1803-4-5, etc. By an officer
of the Caroline. London, R.Phillips, 1806.
138p.

NUPL

I-36
Aubrey, D.
Letters from Bombay. London, Remington &
co., 1884. 316p.

1005?cc 3
des. ytrav.
IVBM NUC pr-11-6
Bombay, City

I-37
Bagchi, Prabodh Chandra, 1898-1955.
Victor Jacquemont in India, CR, v.56
(1936), pp.51-60.

Case   Desc. ytrav.

I-38
Barbosa, Duarte, d.1521, supposed author.
The book of Duarte Barbosa. An account of
the countries bordering on the Indian Ocean
and their inhabitants ... completed about
the year 1518 A.D., tr.from the Portuguese
text ... and ed.and annotated by Mansel
Longworth Dames. London, Hakluyt Society,
1918. 2v.

U of R

I-39
Barncastle, Julius, d.1870.
A voyage to China; including a visit to the
Bombay Presidency; the Mahratta country; the
cave temples of western India; Singapore; the
straits of Malacca and Sunda; and the Cape of
Good Hope. London, W.Shoberl, 1850. 2v.

I-40
Bernier, François, 1620-1688.
Travels in the Mogul empire, A.D.1656-1668.
A rev.and improved 2d ed.based upon Irving
Brock's trans.,by Archibald Constable.
Delhi, S.Chand, 1968. 524p.

U of R

I-41
Bevan, Henry.
Thirty years in India: or a soldier's
reminiscences of native and European life
in the presidencies, from 1808-1838. London, P.Richardson, 1839. 2v.

India - Descr.& trav.

U of R

I-42
"Bibliophile."
Bishop Heber's journal (1824-25), MR, v.32
(1922), pp.155-63.

Case

I-43
Birdwood, Sir George Christopher Molesworth,
1832-1917.
SVA; ed.by F.H.Brown. London, Philip Lee
Warner, 1915. 397p.

India.- Descr trav

4 of R

I-44
Bissoondoyal, B.
India as seen by French travellers, IAC,
v.11 (1962), pp.434-43.

Case

I-45
Buchanan, Francis Hamilton, 1762-1829.
A journey from Madras through the countries
of Mysore, Canara, & Malabar, performed under
the orders of the ... Marquis Wellesley, ...
for the express purpose of investigating the
state of agriculture, arts, and commerce; the
religion, manners & customs; the history,
natural & civil, & antiquities of the dominions of the Rajah of Mysore; & the countries
acquired by the Hon.East India Co., in the
late & former wars, from Tipoo Sultan; with
(Continued on next card)

LC

Buchanan, Francis Hamilton, 1762-1829.
(Card 2)
a memoir of the author, 2d ed. Madras,
Higginbotham, 1870. 2v.

I-46
Burford, Robert, 1791-1861.
Description of a view of the island and
harbour of Bombay. London, Printed by T.
Brettell, 1831. 12p.

1. Bombay - Descr. 2. Panoramas.

LC

I-47
Caine, William Spreston, 1842-1903.
Picturesque India; a hand-book for European
travellers. London, N.Y., George Routledge &
sons, 1898. 707p.

1. India - Descr.& trav.

4 ŋ R

I-48
Carré,   17th cent.
The travels of Abbé Carré in India and the
Near-East, 1672-1674. Tr.by Lady Fawcett
and ed.by Sir Charles Fawcett. London,
Hakluyt society, 1947-

1. India - Descr.& trav. 2. Asia - Descr.&
trav.

4 ŋ R V.1-3

I-49
Carré,   17th cent.
Voyage des Indes Orientales, Mêlé de
plusieurs histoires curieuses. Par
Mr.Carré... Paris, La veuve de C.Barbin,
1699. 2v.

1. India - Descr. & travel.   2. Asia - Descr, & trav.
LC

I-50
Castro, João de, 1500-1548.
Cartas. Coligidas e anotadas por
Elaine Sanceau. Lisboa, Agência Geral
do Ultramar, Divasao de Publiçaões e
Biblioteca, 1954. i.3. 1955. 433p.

LC

I-51
Castro, João de, 1500-1548.
Cosmographia e descripção do Reino
da Daquem. 1843.

I-52
Castro, Joao de, 1500-1548.
Primeiro roteiro da Costa da India; desde
Goa até Dio: narrando a viagem que fez o vice-
rei, D.Garcia de Noronha ... Porto, Typ.
Commercial Portuense, 1843. 340p.

1. India, Portuguese - Descr.& trav. 2.
Portuguese in India - Hist.

4 ŋ R

I-53
Castro, João de, 1500-1548.
Roteiro em que se contem a viagem que
fizeram os Portuguezes no anno 1541,
partindo do nobre cidade de Goa atee Soez,
que he no fim, e stremidade do mar Roxo.
[ed.] pelo doutor Antonio Nunes de
Carvalho...Paris, Baudry, 1833. 400p.

Egypt - Descr. & hi

LC

I-54
Cawasji, Temulji.
The Poona guide for 1902. Poona, Observer
Press, 1902. 60p.

Bm (Bria) Cat

I-55
Churchill, Awnsham, d.1728, comp.
Collection of voyages and travels, some
now first printed from original manuscripts
others now first pub.in English ... London,
J.Walthoe [etc] 1732. 6 vols.

4 ŋ R

I-56
Closson, Henry.
Guide to Khandala - the Borghat sanitarium.
Bombay, M.E.Pub.House, 1898. 39p.

BM

I-57
Codrington, Kenneth deBurgh.
A Bombay diary of 1838, AR, n.s.,v.35 (1939), pp.112-22.

Case

I-58
Commissariat, Manekshah Sorabshah, 1881-
Mandelslo's travels in western India. London, Oxford Univ.Press, 1931. 135p.

U of R

I-59
Commissariat, Manekshah Sorabshah, 1881-
Ovington's account of life on Bombay Island 240 years ago (A.D.1690), JUB, v.1 (1932), pp.5-12.

II

I-60
Coverte, Robert.
The travels of Captain Robert Coverte. Ed. by Boies Penrose. Philadelphia, 1931. 115p.

1. India - Descr.& trav. 2. Mogul empire. 3. Persia - Descr.& trav. 4. Levant - Descr.& trav.

LC

I-61
Coverte, Robert.
A true and almost incredible report of an Englishman, that (being cast away in the good ship called the Ascension, in Cambaya, the farthest part of the East Indies) travelled by land through many unknown kingdoms, and great cities. London, 1612. 72p.

LC

I-62
Crane, Walter, 1845-1915.
India impressions, with some notes of Ceylon during a winter tour, 1906-7. London, Methuen, 1907. 340p.

India - Descr. + trav.
U of R

I-63
Croft-Cooke, Rupert, 1903-
The gorgeous east; one man's India. London, W.H.Allen, 1965. 195p.

1. India - Soc.life & cust. 2. India - Descr.& trav. - 1947-

U of R

I-64
Descriptive guide to the City of Bombay and the surrounding districts, with a map of Bombay. Bombay, Times of India, 1891. 57p.

BM

I-65
Divanji, Prahlad Chandrashekar, rao bahadur, 1885-
Guide to the Bombay Presidency excluding Sind, with a map of that territory. Tasgaon, District Satara, 1920. 231p.

U of R

I-66
Early European travellers in the Nagpur territories, reprinted from old records. Nagpur, 1930.

NLC

I-67
Fah-hsien, fl.399-414 A.D.
The travels of Fah-Hian and Sung-Yun, Buddhist pilgrims, from China to India. Translated from the Chinese by Samuel Beal. London, Trübner, 1869. 281p.

BM

I-68
Fitzclarence, George.
Journal of a route across India through Egypt to England, in the latter end of the year 1817, and the beginning of 1818. London, 1819. 526p.

BM

I-69
Forbes, James, 1749-1819.
Oriental memoirs: selected and abridged from a series of familiar letters written during 17 years residence in India: including observations on parts of Africa and South America; and a narrative of occurences in four Indian voyages. London, White Cochrane & co., 1813. 4 vols.

1. India - Descr.& trav.

LC

I-70
Forrest, Sir George William, 1846-1926.
Cities of India. Westminster, Archibald Constable & co., ltd., 1903. 372p.

1. India - Descr.& trav.

U of R

I-71
Forrest, Sir George William, 1846-1926, ed.
Selections from the travels and journals preserved in the Bombay secretariat. Bombay, Govt.Central Press, 1906. 361p.

U of R

I-72
Forrest, W.G.
A descriptive guide to the city of Bombay and the surrounding districts with a map of Bombay. Bombay, Times of India Press, 1891. 57p.

Bom(Pres)Cat

I-73
Foster, Sir William, 1863-   ed.
Early travels in India, 1583-1619. Delhi, S.Chand, 1968. 365p.

India - Desc & travel

U of R

I-74
Fraser, Sir Andrew Henderson Leith, 1848-
Among Indian Rajahs and ryots; a civil servant's recollections and impressions of 37 years of work and sport in the Central Provinces & Bengal. London, Seeley, 1911. 383p.

1. Central Provinces, India. 2. Bengal. 3. India - Pol.& govt. - 1765-1947.

U of R

I-75
Frederici, Cesare.
The voyage and travaile of M.C.Frederici, merchant of Venys into the Easte India and Indyes and beyond the Indyes...Trans. by T.Hickok from the Italian original of 1587. London, 1588. 4v.

I-76
Fryer, John, d.1733.
A new account of East India and Persia. Ed.by William Crooke. London, Hakluyt Society, 1909-15. 3v.

U of R

I-77
Garbe, Richard von, 1857-1927.
Indische Reiseskizzen. München-Neubiberg.
O.Schloss, 1925. 226p.

desc. of travel

4 of R

I-78
Glasfurd, Alexander Inglis R.
Leaves from an Indian gathered during
thirteen years of a jungle life in the
Central Provinces, the Deccan and Berar.
Bombay, 1903. 247p.

IOL.

I-79
Grose, John Henry, fl.1750-1783.
Voyage to the East Indies; containing
authentic accounts of the Mogul govt.in
general, the viceroyalties of the Deccan &
Bengal ... London, S.Hooper. 1772. 2 vols.

1. India - Descr. & trav.

LC

I-80
Guide to Panchgani. 1913.

I-81
Guthrie, Katherine Blanche.
Life in Western India. London, Hurst &
Blackett, 1881. 2 vols.

Del. v trav

4 of R

I-82
Hamilton, Alexander, d.1732.
A new account of the East Indies; being
observations and remarks of Capt.Alexander
Hamilton, who resided in those parts from the
year 1688 to 1723. Trading and travelling, by
sea and land ... between the Cape of Good-
Hope and the Island of Japan. 2d ed. London.
A.Bettesworth & C.Hitch, 1739. 2 vols.

1. East Indies - Descr.& trav. 2. Asia -
Descr.& trav.

LC

I-83
Hamilton, Alexander, d.1732.
A new account of the East Indies, by Alexander
Hamilton, with numerous maps and illustrations;
now edited, with introduction and notes, by
Sir William Foster... London, The Argonaut
Press, 1930. 2v.

4 of R

I-84
Hodges, William, 1744-1797.
Travels in India. During the years 1780,
1781, 1782, and 1783. London, 1783. 156p.

1. India - Descr.& trav.

4 of R

I-85
Ibn Batuta, 1304-1377.
Travels in Asia and Africa, 1325-54. Ed.by
Hamilton Alexander Rosskeen Gibb. New York,
R.M.McBride & Co., 1929.

4 of R

I-86
Illustrated guide to Goa. A book containing
the past history and detailed description
of Goa, the capital of Portugal India.
Bombay, Times of India Press, 1931. 153p.

Bom.(Pres) Cat

I-87
India (Republic) Ministry of Transport. Tourist Division.
Guide to Bombay. New Delhi, 1957. 40p.

IOL

I-92
Kumthekar, K.M.
Poona and its suburbs. A description of Poona and adjoining country. Poona, Shri Shetkari Press, 1910. 68p.

OB 1909/10

I-88
Kamthekar, K.M.
Poona and its suburbs: a description of Poona and adjoining country. Poona, the author, 1910. 68p.

Bom (Pres) cat

I-93
Lambert, Mascarenhas.
The first city. A humorous description of Bombay. Baroda, Padmaja Pubs., 1948. 120p.

Bom (Pres) cat

I-89
Karkaria, Rustomji Pestonji, 1869-1919, ed.
The charm of Bombay; an anthology of writings in praise of the first city in India. Bombay, D.B.Taraporevala sons & co., 1915. 654p.

1. Bombay - Descr.& trav.

44R

I-94
Land of the Rupee; a comprehensive description of British India and Burma, copiously illustrated from photographs of views and buildings in the principal cities, scenes of natural beauty and ruins of sacred and historical interest. Bombay, Bennett, Coleman, 1912. 500p.

1 India — descr + trav

44R
LC

I-90
Kemp, Phyllis Mary, trans. and ed.
Russian travelers to India and Persia: 1624-1798: Kotov, Yefremov and Danibegov. Delhi, Jiwan Prakashan, 1959. 137p.

44R
LC

I-95
Landon, Perceval, 1869-1927.
Under the sun; impressions of Indian cities: with a chapter dealing with the later life of Nana Sahib. New York, Doubleday, Page & Co., 1907. 300p.

44R

I-91
Kerr, Robert, 1755-1813, ed.
A general history and collection of voyages and travels. Edinburgh, W.Blackwood, 1824. 18v.

LC

I-96
Leckie, Daniel Robinson.
Journal of a route to Nagpore by the way of Cuttac, Burrosumber, and the southern Bunjare Ghaut, in the year 1790. With an account of Nagpore and a journal from that place to Benares by Soohagee Pass. London, 1800. 102p.

SOAS

I-97
Linschoten, Jan Huyghen van, 1563-1611.
The voyage of John Huyghen van Linschoten to the East Indies. From the old English translation of 1598. Ed.by Arthur Coke Burnell and P.A.Tiele. London, Hakluyt Society, 1885. (Works issued by the Hakluyt Society, no. 70-71) 2v.

O

I-98
Locke, John Courtenay, 1880-   ed.
The first Englishmen in India; letters and narratives of sundry Elizabethans written by themselves & ed.by J.Courtenay Locke. London, George Routledge & sons, ltd., 1930. 245p.

1. Voyages & travels. 2. India - Descr.& trav. 3. Asia, Western - Descr.& trav.

U of R

O

I-99
Lowther, Alice (Blight) Lady.
Land of the gold mohur. London, Philip Allan, 1932. 238p.

1. India - Descr. & Trav.

U of R

O

I-100
Lynn, Whitney V.
Guide to Panchgani. Panchgani? pref.1913. 34p.

Panchgani, India - Descr. - Guide-books.

U of R

O

I-101
Maclean, James Mackenzie, 1835-1906.
A guide to Bombay: historical, statistical, and descriptive. 27th ed., rev.to date and enl. Bombay, "Bombay Gazette" Steam Press, 1902. 715p.

1. Bombay - Description - Guidebooks. 2. Bombay - Directories.

U of R

O

I-102
Maharashtra, India (State) Directorate of Publicity.
Maharashtra State is launched; an artist's review of events that marked the formation of the State, April 27-May 1, 1960. Bombay, Director of Publicity, Govt.of Maharashtra, 1960. 87p.

LC

O

I-103
Maharashtra, India (State) Directorate of Tourism.
A panorama of Maharashtra. Bombay, Printed at the Govt.Central Press, 1962. 171p.

1. Maharashtra, India - Guidebooks, 1962.

NUC

O

I-104
Markham, Clements Robert, 1830-1916.
A memoir on the Indian surveys. 2d ed. Amsterdam, Meridean Pub.Co., 1968. 521p.

Descr. & Travel.

U of R

)

I-105
Merewether, Francis Henry Shafton.
A tour through the famine districts of India. London, A.D.Innes, 1898. 350p.

1. India - Descr.& trav.

U of R

)

I-106
Minaev, Ivan Pavlovich, 1840-1890.
Travels in and diaries of India and Burma (1880-1886). Calcutta, D.P.Mukhopadhyaya, 1956.

Low

)

I-107
　　Minturn, Robert Bowne, 1836-1889.
　　　From New York to Delhi, by way of Rio
　　de Janeiro, Australia, and China.
　　London, Longman, Brown, Green, Longmans,
　　and Roberts, 1858. 480p.

1. India - Descr. & travel   2. Voyages & travels.

I-112
　　Muehl, John Frederick.
　　　Interview with India. New York, John Day,
　　1950. 310p.

　　　1. India - Descr.& trav. 2. India - Soc.
　　life & cust.

I-108
　　Modi, Jivanji Jamshedji, 1854-1933.
　　　Anquetil du Perron of Paris-India as
　　seen by him (1755-60), ASBJ, v.24 (1915-17),
　　pp.313-81.

I-113
　　Mukerji, Dhan Gopal, 1840-1936.
　　　Visit India with me. New York, E.P.Dutton
　　and co., 1929. 313p.

　　　1. India - Descr.& trav. 2. Art - India.
　　3. India - Soc.life & cust.

I-109
　　Modi, Jivanji Jamshedji, 1854-1933.
　　　Bombay as seen by Dr.Edward Ives in the
　　year 1754 A.D., ASBJ, v.22 (1905-1908),
　　pp.273-97.

I-114
　　Murray, Hugh, 1779-1846.
　　　Historical account of discoveries and travels
　　in Asia, from the earliest ages to the present
　　time. Edinburgh, Printed for A.Constable &
　　co., 1820. 3v.

I-110
　　Moreland, William Harrison, 1868-1938.
　　　From Gujarat to Golconda in the reign of
　　Jahangir, JIH, v.17 (1938), pp.135-50.

I-115
　　Narain, Brij, ed.and tr.
　　　A contemporary Dutch chronicle of Mughal
　　India. Translated and edited by Brij Narain
　　and Sri Ram Sharma. Calcutta, Susil Gupta,
　　1957. (European travellers in India. Sec-
　　ond series). 104p.

I-111
　　Moses, Henry.
　　　Sketches in India: with notes on the seasons,
　　scenery and society of Bombay, Elephanta and
　　Salsette. London, S.Marshall & co., 1750.
　　300p.

　　　1. India - Descr.& trav.

I-116
　　Newell, Herbert Andrews, 1896-1934.
　　　Bombay, the gate of India, a guide to places
　　of interest with maps. 2d ed. Bombay, 1920.
　　148p.

　　　1. Bombay - Descr. - Guide-books.

I-117
Oaten, Edward Farley.
European travelers in India during the
15th, 16th and 17th centuries; the
evidence afforded by them with respect to
Indian social institutions and the nature
and influence of Indian governments.
London, Kegan Paul, Trench, Trübner, and
co.,ltd., 1909. 296p.

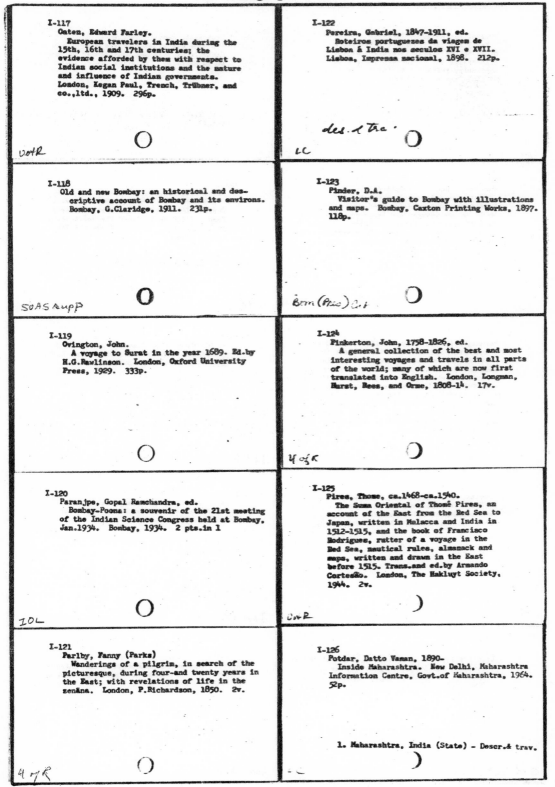

UofR

I-118
Old and new Bombay: an historical and des-
criptive account of Bombay and its environs.
Bombay, G.Claridge, 1911. 231p.

SOAS &UPP

I-119
Ovington, John.
A voyage to Surat in the year 1689. Ed.by
H.G.Rawlinson. London, Oxford University
Press, 1929. 333p.

I-120
Paranjpe, Gopal Ramchandra, ed.
Bombay-Poona: a souvenir of the 21st meeting
of the Indian Science Congress held at Bombay.
Jan.1934. Bombay, 1934. 2 pts.in 1

IOL

I-121
Parlby, Fanny (Parks)
Wanderings of a pilgrim, in search of the
picturesque, during four-and twenty years in
the East; with revelations of life in the
zenāna. London, P.Richardson, 1850. 2v.

4 ⁊R

I-122
Pereira, Gabriel, 1847-1911, ed.
Roteiros portuguezes da viagem de
Lisboa á India nos seculos XVI e XVII.
Lisboa, Imprensa nacional, 1898. 212p.

des.&tra.

LC

I-123
Pinder, D.A.
Visitor's guide to Bombay with illustrations
and maps. Bombay, Caxton Printing Works, 1897.
118p.

Bom (Phis) C.t

I-124
Pinkerton, John, 1758-1826, ed.
A general collection of the best and most
interesting voyages and travels in all parts
of the world; many of which are now first
translated into English. London, Longman,
Hurst, Rees, and Orme, 1808-14. 17v.

4 ojK

I-125
Pires, Thomé, ca.1468-ca.1540.
The Suma Oriental of Thomé Pires, an
account of the East from the Red Sea to
Japan, written in Malacca and India in
1512-1515, and the book of Francisco
Rodrigues, rutter of a voyage in the
Red Sea, nautical rules, almanack and
maps, written and drawn in the East
before 1515. Trans.and ed.by Armando
Cortesão. London, The Hakluyt Society,
1944. 2v.

UofR

I-126
Potdar, Datto Vaman, 1890-
Inside Maharashtra. New Delhi, Maharashtra
Information Centre, Govt.of Maharashtra, 1964.
52p.

1. Maharashtra, India (State) - Descr.& trav.

I-127
　　Prasad, Ram Chandra, 1922-
　　　Early English travelers in India; a
　　study in the travel literature of the
　　Elizabethan and Jacobean periods with
　　particular reference to India.　Delhi,
　　Motilal Banarsidas, 1965.　414p.

U of R

I-128
　　Purchas, Samuel, 1577?-1626.
　　　Hakluytus posthumus, of Purchas his
　　Pilgrimes: contayning a history of the
　　world in sea voyages and lande travells
　　by Englishmen and others.　Glasgow,
　　J.MacLehose and sons, 1905-07. (Hakluyt
　　Society. Extra series, no.14-33).　20v.

U of R

I-129
　　Raynal, Guillaume Thomas François, 1713-1796.
　　　Histoire philosophique et politique des
　　établissemens et du commerce des Européens
　　dans les deux Indes...Nouv.ed., cor.et augm.
　　d'après les manuscrits autographes de l'aut-
　　eur. Précédée d'une notice biographique et
　　de considérations sur les écrits de Raynal,
　　par M.A.Jay; et terminée par un volume sup-
　　plémentaire contenant la situation actuelle
　　des colonies, par M.Peuchet.　Paris, A.Costes
　　et cie, 1820-21.　12v.

I-130
　　Raynal, Guillaume Thomas François, 1713-1796.
　　　Histoire philosophique et politique des
　　establissemens et du commerce des Europeans
　　dans les deux Indes.　Genève, 1780.　10v.

BM

I-131
　　Recollections of the Deccan with miscellaneous
　　sketches and letters. By an officer of
　　cavalry.　Calcutta, Bengal Military Orphan
　　Press, 1838.　124p.

Cal natl Lib

I-132
　　Rousselet, Louis, 1845-1929.
　　　L'Inde des rajahs; voyage dans l'Inde
　　Centrale et dans les présidences de Bombay
　　et du Bengale.　Paris, Hachette, 1875.　811p.

　　　1. India - Descr.& trav.　2. India - Kings &
　　rulers.

LC

I-133
　　Rousselet, Louis, 1845-1929.
　　　India and its native princes; travels in
　　Central India and in the Presidencies of
　　Bombay and Bengal. Carefully rev.& ed.by
　　Lt.-Col.Buckle.　London, Chapman & Hall,
　　1876.　599p.

　　　1. India - Descr.& trav.

U of R

I-134
　　Saletore, Bhasker Anand.
　　　Kosmos Indikopleustus and western India.
　　JIH. v.41 (1963), pp.1-12.

JIH 63

I-135
　　Saletore, Bhasker Anand.
　　　Ptolemy and western India. JIH. v.40
　　(1962), pp.41-84.

JIH 62

I-136
　　Sathaye, D.D.
　　　A short guide to Bombay. A book intended to
　　serve as a guide to new-comers to the city of
　　Bombay.　Bombay, the author, 1933.　84p.

Bom (Pres) cat

I-137
Scavenius, Peer.
Indiske Dage, fra Bombay til Madras,
samt Rejser-i det sydlige Dekan. Koben-
havn, Gyldendalske, Boghandel, 1898. 372p.

Cal Nat Lib

I-138
Schaeffer, E.N.
Pictorial Bombay. An illustrated and descrip-
tive book on the city of Bombay. Bombay, Kitab
Mahal, 1936. 80p.

Bom (Press) cat

I-139
Selle, Götz von.
Martin Haug in Poona (in German). In:
Oriental Studies in honour of Cursetji
Erachji Pavry. Ed.by Jal Dastur Cur-
setji Pavry, with a forward by A.V.Wil-
liams Jackson. London, Oxford Univ.Press,
1933. pp.450-56.

I-140
Sen, Surendra Nath, 1890-   ed.
Indian travels of Thevenot and Careri;
being the third part of the travels of M.de
Thevenot into the Levant and the third part
of a voyage round the world by Dr. John
Francis Gemelli Careri. New Delhi, Nat'l
Archives of India, 1949. 500p.

LC

I-141
Shalom, A.
The illustrated guide to Poona, Mahabalesh-
var, Panchgani, Lanowli, Khandala, Purandhar,
Singhur. Poona, Israelit Press, 1902. 107p.

Bom (Press) cat

I-142
Sleeman, William Henry, 1788-1856.
Rambles and recollections of an Indian
official. London, J.Hatchard, 1844. 2v.

1. India - Descr & travel.

I-143
Smith, John Young.
Matheran Hill; its people, plants and ani-
mals. 2d ed. Bombay, Thacker, 1881. 184p.

1. Matheran - Descr.

I-144
Sorabji Jehangir and sons.
The Poona guide and directory, 1902. Poona,
Deccan Herald Press, 1902. 70p.

Bom (Press) cat

I-145
Taylor, Meadows, 1808-1876.
The story of my life. Ed.by his daughter,
with a preface by Henry Reeve. Edinburgh,
William Blackwood, 1878. 2v.

I-146
Temple, Sir Richard, 1st bart., 1826-1902.
Journals kept in Hyderabad, Kashmir,
Sikkim, and Nepal. By Sir Richard Temple...
Edited, with introductions, by his son,
R.C.Temple... London, W.H.Allen & co.,
1887. 2v.

I-147
  The Times of India, Bombay.
    Guide to Poona, June, 1902. Bombay, 1902.

Harvard, Yew Lib.

I-152
  The world desplayed, or a curious collection
  of voyages and travels, selected from the
  writers of all nations. London, T.Carman
  and F.Newberry, 1762-1790. 20v.

LC

I-148
  Travernier, Jean Baptiste, baron d'Aubonne,
  1605-1689.
    Travels in India. Trans.from the original
  French edition of 1676, with a biographical
  sketch of the author, by V.Ball. London,
  N.Y., Macmillan, 1889. 2v.

4 of R

I-153
  Young, Marianne.
    The Moslem noble; his land and people. With
  some notices of the Parsees, or ancient Per-
  sians. London, Saunders and Otley, 1857.
  192p.

    1. Bombay - Descr. 2. Mohammedens in Bombay.

4 of R

Historiography

I-149
  Valentijn, François, 1656-1727.
    Oud en nieuw Oost-Indiën, vervattende een
  naaukeurige en uitvoerige verhandelinge van
  Nederlands mogentheydin die gewestenk, benevens
  eene wydluftige beschryvinge der Moluccos...
  en alle de eylanden onder dezelve landbestier-
  ingen behoorende; het Nederlands comptoir op
  Suratte, en de levens der Groote Mogols...
  door François Valentyn. Dordrecht, J.van
  Braam, 1724-1726. 5v.in 9.

LC   des'. Travel

I-154
  Ahluwalia, M.L.
    Jadunath's contributions to the Indian
  historical records commission. In: Life
  and letters of Sir Jadunath Sarkar. Ed.by
  Hari Ram Gupta. Hoshiarpur (India)
  Panjab Univ., 1957. pp.94-100.

4 of R

I-150
  Valle, Pietro della.
    The travels of della Valle in India. From
  the old English trans.of 1664 by G.Havers,
  ed.by E.Grey. London, Hakluyt Society, 1882.
  (Hakluyt Society, v.84 & 85). 2v.

I-155
  Correia-Afonso, John.
    Jesuit letters and Indian history; a
  study of the nature and development of the
  Jesuit letters from India (1542-1773) and
  their value for Indian historiography.
  Bombay, Indian Historical Research Inst.,
  1955. (Studies in Indian history of the
  Indian Historical Research Inst.,no.20).
  227p.

U of R

I-151
  Varthema, Lodovico de, 15th cent.
    The nauigation and vyages of Lewis Werto-
  mannus, in the yeere of Our Lorde 1503 ...
  Edinburgh, Priv.print.for the Aungervyle
  society, 1884. 280p.

4 of R

I-156
  Datta, Kalikinkar, 1905-
    A survey of recent studies on modern Indian
  history. 2d ed. Calcutta, Firma K.L.Mukho-
  padhyay, 1963. 115p.

4 of R

I-157
De, Barun.
A preliminary note on the writing of the
history of modern India, QRHS, v.3 (1963-
1964), pp.39-46.

Case

I-158
Dighe, Vishvanath Govind.
Modern historical writing in Marathi. In:
Historians of India, Pakistan and Ceylon.
E.by C.H.Philips. London, Oxford Univer-
sity Press, 1961. pp.473-80.

U of R

I-159
Grewal, J.S.
James Grant and the Marathas, IHCP, v.29,
pt.I (1967). pp.395-401.

U of R

I-160
Gupta, Hari Ram, 1902-   ed.
Life and letters of Sir Jadunath Sarkar.
Hoshiarpur, Punjab University, 1957.
(Sir Jadunath Sarkar commemoration
volume,1). 383p.

U of R

I-161
Gupta, Hari Ram, 1902-
Sir Jadunath Sarkar Commemoration volume.
Hoshiarpur, Panjab Univ., 1957-58. 2v.

LC

I-162
Hardy, Peter.
Historians of medieval India; studies in
Indo-Muslim historical writing. London,
Luzac, 1960. 151p.

U of R

I-163
Hasan, Mohibbul, comp.
Historians of medieval India. With a
foreword by Muhammad Mujeeb. Meerut, Meenakshi Prakashan, 1968. 307p.

U of R

I-164
Ithape, Usha.
Dr.A.G.Pawar – A biographical sketch.
In: Studies in Indian history; Dr.A.G.Pawar
f-licitation volume. Ed.by V.D.Rao.
Kolhapur, Y.P.Pawar, 1968. pp.xi-xvi.

U of R

I-165
Kibe, Madhav Vinayak, 1877-
Reminiscences. In: Life and letters of
Sir Jadunath Sarkar. Ed.by Hari Ram Gupta.
Hoshiarpur (India), Panjab University,
1957. pp.80-81.

U of R

I-166
Kulkarnee, N.H.
A brief survey of recent Marathi historical
writings. QRHS, v.8 (1968-1969), pp.232-236.

History – articles
BAS Sept 1970

I-167
Kulkarni, Anant Ramchandra, 1925-
Mountstuart Elphinstone and Maratha history,
MPP, v.89 (1970), pp.199-210.

modern history
BAS 1970

I-168
Luniya, Bhanwarlal Nathuram, 1917-
Some historians of medieval India. Agra,
Lakshmi Narain Agarwal, 1969. 207p.

U y R

I-169
Maas, Walther.
Sammel Bericht. Zur Indischen wirtschafts-
geschichte; summary report, on Indian economic
history, VSW, v.43 (1956), pp.368-72.

Case

I-170
Majumdar, Ramesh Chandra, 1888-
Historiography in modern India. Bombay, New
York, Asia Pub.House, 1970. (Heras memorial
lectures, 1967) 61p.

I-171
Moraes, George Mark.
Panegyric upon the life and work of the late
Dr. A.S.Altekar, IHCP, v.22 (1959), pp.6-7.

IHCP

I-172
Oturkar, Rajaram Vinayak, 1898-
Lacunae in the study of Maratha history,
IHCP, v.23 (1960), pp.178-80.

U y R

I-173
Phatak, Narahara Raghunatha, 1894-
Research and writing of history in Maharashtra. In: Historiography in Indian
languages, ed.by J.P.DeSousa and C.M.
Kulkarni. Delhi, Oriental Pubs., 1972.
pp.148-56.

U y R

I-174
Philips, Cyril Henry, 1912-
James.Mill, Mountstuart Elphinstone, and the
history of India. In: Historians of India,
Pakistan and Ceylon. Ed.by Cyril Henry Philips.
London, Oxford University Press, 1961. pp.217-
29.

I-175
Qanungo, Kalikarajan, 1895-
Jadunath Sarkar (a biographical sketch)
In: Life and letters of Sir Jadunath Sarkar.
Ed.by Hari Ram Gupta. Hoshiarpur (India)
Panjab Univ., 1957. pp.35-54.

I-176
Qanungo, Kalikarajan, 1895-
Jadunath Sarkar as a historian. In: Life
and letters of Sir Jadunath Sarkar. Ed.by
Hari Ram Gupta. Hoshiarpur (India),
Panjab Univ., 1957. pp.55-73.

I-177
    Sardesai, Govind Sakharam, 1865-1959.
        Jadunath Sarkar as I know him. In:
        Life and letters of Sir Jadunath Sarkar.
        Ed.by Hari Ram Gupta. Hoshiarpur (India),
        Panjab University, 1957. pp.18-34.

UofR

I-178
    Sardesai, Govind Sakharam, 1865-1959.
        Present needs of Maratha history. IHRCP,
        v.12 (1929), pp.20-26.

IHRCP

I-179
    Sardesai commemoration volume. Ed.by Shripad
        R.Tikekar. Bombay, Keshav Bhikaji Dhawale,
        1938. 314p.

LC

I-180
    Sarkar, Sir Jadunath, 1870-1958.
        The historian Rajwade. MR, v.41 (1927),
        pp.184-87.

Case

I-181
    Sarkar, Sir Jadunath, 1870-1958.
        V.Khare. MR, v.42 (1927), pp.65-67.

VVMR
Case

I-182
    Sarkar, Jagadish Narayan.
        Survey of Indian historiography (Mediaeval
        period): history and historians of mediaeval
        India. [n.p., n.d.]

U JR

I-183
    Selections from Sarkar-Sardesai corres-
        pondence, 1907-56: G.S.Sardesai's letters
        to Jadunath Sarkar. In: Life and letters
        of Sir Jadunath Sarkar. Ed.by Hari Ram Gupta.
        Hoshiarpur (India), Panjab University, 1957.
        pp.275-357.

UofR

I-184
    Selections from Sarkar-Sardesai corres-
        pondence, 1907-56: Jadunath Sarkar's
        letters to G.S.Sardesai. In: Life and
        letters of Sir Jadunath Sarkar. Ed.by
        Hari Ram Gupta. Hoshiarpur (India),
        Panjab University, 1957. pp.127-274.

UofR

I-185
    Sen, Siba Pada, 1914-   comp.
        Studies in modern Indian history; a regional
        survey. Calcutta, Institute of Historical
        Studies, 1969. 241p.

PL 480 69

I-186
    Srivastava, Ashirbadi Lal.
        The historian Sir Jadunath Sarkar. UB,
        v.5 (1958), pp.1-7.

Case

I-187
Studies in Indian history; Dr. A.G.Pawar
felicitation volume. Ed.by V.D.Rao. Kolhapur, Appasaheb Pawar Satkar Samiti, 1968.
460p.

NUR
PL480, '68

I-192
Academia das sciencias de Lisboa.
Subsidios para a historia da India portugueza. O tombo do estado da India, por Simão
Botelho. Lisboa, Typ.do Academia real das
sciencias, 1868. (Collecção de monumentos
ineditos para a historia das conquistas dos
Portuguezes em Africa, Asia e America.
v.5. 1ª serie-historia da Asia) 483p.

I-188
Taylor, James.
Note on a letter from Mr.Grant Duff to
the late Mr.H.E.Goldsmid, Bombay Civil Service,
recounting the circumstances under which the
former wrote his History of the Marathas, ASBJ,
v.10,no.28 (1871-74), pp.120-25.

NRD
ASBJ

I-193
Ahluwalia, M.M.
Freedom struggle in India, 1858-1909.
Delhi, Ranjit Printers and Publishers, 1965.
(Modern historical series, no.3). 468p.

UofR

I-189
Tikekar, Shripad Ramachandra, 1900-
On historiography; a study of methods of
historical research and narration of J.N.
Sarkar, G.S.Sardesai and P.K.Gode. Bombay,
Popular Prakashan, 1964. 90p.

NUR
LC

I-194
'Ali Muhammad Khan, b.1700?
Mirat-i-Ahmadi; a history of Gujarat in
Persian of Ali Muhammad Khan. Ed.by Syed
Nawab Ali ... Baroda, Oriental Institute,
1928, '27. (Gaekwad's Oriental series,no.
33-34) 2v. (vol.1: English translation by
Syed Nawab Ali and Charles Norman Seddon)

U of R   18th century

I-190
Wilson, John, 1804-1875.
Review of the present state of oriental,
antiquarian, and geographical research
connected with the west of India and the
adjoining countries, ASBJ, v.5,no.20 (1855),
pp.497-520.

ASBJ

I-195
Allan, John and Haig, Sir Wolseley, 1865-
The Cambridge shorter history of India.
N.Y., Macmillan Co.; Cambridge, Eng., The
Univ.Press, 1934. 991p.

U of R

I-191
Wilson, John, 1804-1875.
Short memorial of the Hon.Mountstuart Elphinstone, and of his contributions to the oriental
geography and history, ASBJ, v.6,no.21 (1861),
pp.97-111.

ASBJ

I-196
Anderson, Bernard.
Diplomatic history of the East India Company
from 1798 to 1814 A.D. Bombay, Univ.of Bombay, 1970. *

I-197
Andrews, Charles Freer, 1871-1940 and Mooker-
jee, Girija K.
The rise and growth of the Congress in
India, 1832-1920. 2d ed. Meerut, Meenakshi
Prakashan, 1967. 222p.

4 of R

I-198
Archivo portugues-oriental. Edited by Joaquim
Heliodora da Cunha Rivera. Nova-Goa, Impren-
sa nacional, 1857-76. 6 vols.

NYPL

I-199
The armies of the native states of India.
Reprint from the "Times". London, 1884.

✓ ✓✓ Calcutta Nat'l Lib

I-200
Askari, Syed Hasan.
The Nizam and Cornwallis, IHCP, v.14 (1953),
pp.217-24.

4 of R

I-201
Barros, João de, 1496-1570.
Da Asia de João de Barros e de Diogo de
Couto. Nova ed. Lisbon, Na Regia officina
Typografico, 1777-88. 13pts.in 24vols.

1.Portugal - Hist. - Period of discoveries,
1385-1580. 2. Portuguese in India. 3. India -
Hist. - European settlements, 1500-1765. 4.
East (Far East) - Hist. 5. Discoveries (in
geography) - Portuguese.

4 of R

I-202
Basu, Baman Das, 1867-1930.
Rise of the Christian power in India.
Calcutta, R.Chatterji. 1931. 1018p.

1. India - Hist. - European settlements,
1500-1765. 2. India.- hist. British occupation, 1765-

4 of R

I-203
Basu, Kamal Krishna.
The memoirs of two Bijapuri nobles, IndC,
v.6 (1939-40), pp.61-66.

Adil Shahs of Bijapur.

II

I-204
Beaulieu, Augustin.
A compleat history of the rise and
progress of the Portuguese empire in
the East-Indias, their discoveries set
forth in their natural order, the
form of their govt. in those parts
explained; the causes of the declension
of their power examined, and the present
posture of their affairs, in those parts
of the world, truly stated. In:Navigan-
tium atque itinerantium bibliotheca:

(Continued on next card)

IN

or, a compleat collection of voyages and
travels, Consisting of above four hundred
of the most authentic writers by
John Harris, London, 1705. 2vols. pp.662-
700.

I-205
Beveridge, Henry, 1799-1863.
A comprehensive history of India, civil,
military and social, from the first landing
of the English, to the suppression of the
Sepoy revolt; including an outline of the
early history of Hindoostan. London, 1865.
3v.

R of R

I-206
Biddulph, John.
   The pirates of Malabar. London, Smith,
Elder and co., 1907. 347p.

4 of R

I-207
Bilgrami, Saiyid Husain, 1844-   comp.
   Historical and descriptive sketch of His
Highness the Nizam's dominions. Bombay,
Times of India, 1883-84. 2v.

Haidarabad, India (State)

LC

I-208
Bocarro, Antonio.
   Decada 13 da historia da India, publicada
da Academia real das sciencias de Lisboa...
Lisboa, 1876. 2pt. (Collecção de monumentos
ineditos para a Historia das Conquistas dos
Portuguezes em Africa, Asia e America.
tom 6).

BM

I-209
Bondurant, Joan Valérie, 1819-
   Regionalism versus provincialism; a
study in problems of Indian national unity.
Berkeley, Univ.of California, 1958. (Indian
press digests. Monograph series, no.4). 169p.

U of R

I-210
Bouvier, René, 1883-   and Maynial, Edouard.
   Le dernier des grands Mogols; vie d'Aureng
Zeb. Paris, A.Michel, 1947. 312p.

4 of R

I-211
Boxer, Charles Ralph, 1904-
   Four centuries of Portuguese expansion,
1415-1825; a succinct survey. Johannesburg,
Witwatersrand Univ.Press, 1961. (Publications
of the Ernest Oppenheimer Institute of Portuguese Studies of the Univ.of the Witwatersrand, Johannesburg, 3). 102p.

1. Portugal - Colonies - Hist.

U of R

I-212
Boxer, Charles Ralph, 1904-
   The Portuguese seaborne empire, 1415-1825.
New York, A.A.Knopf, 1969. 465p.

4 of R

I-213
Boxer, Charles Ralph, 1904-
   Portuguese society in the tropics; the
municipal councils of Goa, Macao, Bahia
and Luanda, 1510-1800. Madison, Univ.of
Wisconsin Press, 1965. (Paul Knaplund
lectures, 1964). 256p.

U of R

I-214
Boxer, Charles Ralph, 1904-
   Race relations in the Portuguese Colonial
Empire, 1415-1825. Oxford, Clarendon Press,
1963. 143p.

   1. Portugal - Colonies - Native races.

LC

I-215
Briggs, Henry George, 1824-1872.
   The Nizam, his history and relations with
the British government. London, Bernard
Quaritch, 1861. 2v.

4 of R

I-216
Briggs, John, 1785-1875.
Letters addressed to a young person in
India: calculated to afford instruction for
his conduct in general, and more especially
in his intercourse with the natives. London,
John Murray, 1828. 249p.

BM

I-217
Bruce, John, 1745-1826.
Annals of the Hon.East India Company from
their establishment by the charter of Queen
Elizabeth, 1600, to the union of the London
and English East-India companies, 1707-1708.
London, Black, Parry & Kingsbury, 1810.
3 vols.

NUR
LC

DS
465
B88a
1810

I-218
Buch, Maganlal Amritlal.
Rise and growth of Indian liberalism, from
Ram Mohun Roy to Gokhale. Baroda, 1938.
340p.

1. India - Civilization - Hist.

NUR
LC

I-219
Calcutta Gazette and Oriental Advertiser.
Selections from Calcutta Gazettes of ...
1784, 1785, 1786, 1787, and 1788-1885 [vols.
1-3 by W.S.Seton-Karr; Calcutta, O.T.Cutter,
1864-   5 vols.

1. India - Hist., 18th cent-19th cent. 2.
India - Soc.life, 18th-19th cent.

NYPL

I-220
Capper, John.
The three presidencies of India: a history
of the rise and progress of the British
Indian possessions, from the earliest records
to the present time. London, Ingram, Cooke
and co., 1853. 504p.

4 yR

I-221
Castro, Joao de, 1500-1548.
Roteiros. 2.ed prefaciada e anotada
por A.Fontoura da Costa. Lisboa, Agência
Geral das Colónias, 1939. 3v. in 5.

LC

I-222
Chand, Tara.
History of the freedom movement in India.
Delhi, Publications Division, Ministry of
Information and Broadcasting, 1961-1967.
2v.

4 yR

I-223
Chandra, Bipan.
The problem of poverty and Indian national
leadership, 1880-1905, Enquiry, n.s.,v.1
(1964), pp.54-106.

Case

I-224
Chandra, Bipan.
Two notes on the agrarian policy of Indian
nationalists, 1880-1905, IESHR, v.1 (1964),
pp.143-74.

Ja 8 '64

I-225
Chandra, Sudhir.
The loyalty of educated Indians to the
British rule, 1858-1885, JIH, v.54 (1966),
pp.417-28.

I-226
Chaves, Balthasar Manuel de.
Annal Indico historico do governo do illus-
trissimo excellentissimo Senhor Marquez de
Tavora. Lisbon, 1754. 3 parts.

I-227
Closets d'Errey, H. de.
Précis chronologique de l'histoire de
l'Inde française, 1664-1816, suivi d'un
relevé des faits marquants de l'Inde française
au XIX° siècle. Pondichérry, 1934.
(Société de l'Histoire de l'Inde Française.
Pondicherry, Publications). 102p.

I-228
Clunes, John.
An historical sketch of the princes of
India, stipendiary, subsidiary, protected,
tributary and feudatory, with a sketch of
the origin and progress of British power
in India; by an officer in the service
of the Hon'ble East India Company.
Edinburgh, 1833. 221p.

I-229
Colebrooke, Sir Thomas Edward, 4th bart., 1813-
1890.
Memoir of the Hon'ble Mountstuart Elphinstone,
RASGBIJ, v.18 (1861), pp.221-344.

I-230
Colebrooke, Sir Thomas Edward, 4th bart.,
1813-1890.
Memoir of the Honourable Mountstuart
Elphinstone. London, Bernard Quaritch,
1861. 124p.

I-231
Contzen, Leopold.
Goa im wandel der Lahrhunderte,
Beiträge zur portugiesischen Kolonial-
geschichte. Berlin, 1902. 89p.

I-232
Corrêa, Gaspar, 16th cent.
Lendas da India, por Gaspar Corrêa, publicadas de ordem da Classe de sciencias moraes,
politicas e bellas lettras da Academia real
das sciencias de Lisboa e sob a dirrecção de
Rodrigo José de Lima Felner... Lisboa, Typ.
da Academia real das sciencias, 1858-66.
(Collecção de monumentos ineditos, para a
historia das conquistas dos Portuguezes, em
Africa, Asia e America publicada da Academia
real das sciencias de Lisboa, v.1-4). 4v.

I-233
Couto, Diogo do, 1542-1616.
Decada quinta da "Àsia". Texte inédit
publié d'après un manuscrit de la Bibliothèque de l'Université de Leyde par
Marcus de Jong ... Coimbra, Biblioteca
da Universidade, 1937. 767p.

I-234
Couto, Diogo do, 1542-1616.
Observations sobre as Principaes Causas da
Decadencia dos Portuguezes na Asia, publicadas
... por Antonio Caetano do Amaral ... Lisboa,
Academia das scienceas de Lisbon, 1790. 295p.

I-235
Crowther, K.J.
Portuguese society in India in the sixteenth
and seventeenth centuries. London, Oxford
University. 1959-60.

I-236
Curtis, William Eleroy, 1850-
Modern India. Chicago, Fleming H.Revell
Co., 1905. 513p.

1. India.

4 of R

I-237
Da Cunha, Joseph Gerson, 1842-1900.
The English and their monuments at Goa,
ASBJ, v.13 (1877), pp.109-30.

ASBJ

I-238
Danvers, Frederick Charles, 1833-1906.
The Portuguese in India; being a history
of the rise and decline of their Eastern
empire. N.Y., Octagon Books, 1966. 2v.

1. India - Hist. 2. India - Descr.& explor.
3. Portuguese in India.

R of R

I-239
Davies, Alfred Mervyn.
Strange destiny; a biography of Warren
Hastings, maker of British India. N.Y.,
G.P.Putnam's sons, 1935. 481p.
London ed., 1935, has title: Warren
Hastings.

4 of R

I-240
Dickinson, John.
Last counsels of an unknown counsellor. Ed.
by Major Evans Bell. London, Macmillan and
Co., 1877. 188p.

BM

I-241
Digby, William, 1849-1904.
The native newspapers of India and Ceylon,
CR, v.65 (1877), pp.356-94.

Case

I-242
D'Orsey, Alexander James Donald, comp.
Portuguese discoveries, dependencies
and missions in Asia and Africa. London,
W.H.Allen, 1893. 458p.

Scholberg - Portuguese

I-243
Downing, Clement.
A history of the Indian wars. Ed.by William
Foster. Oxford, H.Milford, Oxford Univ.Press,
1924. 238p.

1. India - Hist. - European settlements,
1500-1765. 2. Mogul empire. 3. Kanhoji
Angria, d.1731. 4. Plantain, John, pirate.
5. Pirates.

Earlier ed.: London, T.Cooper, 1737.

4 of R

I-244
East India Company (English)
An appeal to British Justice and Honour.
The treatment of the protected native states
of India by the Govt.of the East India Company. London, Smith, Elder & Co., 1841.
42p.

BM

I-245
East India Company (English)
Letters received from the East India Company
from its servants in the East. Transcribed
from the "Original Correspondence" series of
India Office Records. Ed.by W.Foster. London, S.Low, Marston, 1896-1902.

1. Gt.Brit. - Colonies - Hist. 2. Gt.Brit. -
Comm. - Hist. 3. India - Hist.

4 of R multifische

I-246
East India Company (English)
Treaties and grants from the country to the
East India Company, respecting their Presidency of Fort St.George, on the coast of
Choromandel; Fort William, in Bengal; and
Bombay, on the coast of Malabar; from the
year 1756 to 1772. London, 1774.

BM

I-247
Egerton, Wilbraham Egerton, Earl, 1832-1909.
A description of Indian and oriental
armour, new ed. London, W.H.Allen & co.,ltd.,
1896. 196p.

1. Arms & armor. 2. Arms & armor, Oriental.

LC

I-248
Elliot, Henry Miers, 1808-1853.
A history of India as told by its own
historians: the Muhammadan period; the posthumous papers of Sir H.M.Elliot. Ed.by John
Dowson. Calcutta, Susil Gupta (India) Private
₍1952-60₎ 30 vols.

1. India - Hist.

4 MR

I-249
Elphinstone, Mounstuart, 1779-1859.
The history of India; the Hindu and Mahomtan
periods. 8th ed. London, John Murray, 1905.
799p.

11. India - History.

4 MR

I-250
Elphinstone, Hon.Mountstuart, 1779-1859.
The rise of the British power in the East;
being a continuation of his "History of India
in the Hindú and Mahomedan periods"; ed.by
Sir Edward Colebrooke. London, J.Murray,
1887. 573p.

1. India - Hist. - European settlements,
1500-1765.

LC

I-251
Faria e Sousa, Manuel de, 1590-1649.
Asia portvgvesa. Lisboa, H.Valente de
Oliveira, 1666-75. 3v.

I-252
Faria e Sousa, Manuel de, 1590-1649.
The Portuguese Asia: or, the history of the
discovery and conquest of India by the Portuguese. Trans.into English by Capt.J.Stevens.
London, C.Brome, 1695. 3v.

LC

I-253
Ferguson, Charles Albert, 1921- and
Gumperz, John Joseph, 1922- eds.
Linguistic diversity in South Asia:
studies in regional, social and functional
variation. Bloomington, Indiana, 1960.
(Pub.of the Indiana University Research
Center in Anthropology, Folklore, and
Linguistics, 13). 125p.

4 MR

I-254
Ferreira Martins, José Frederico, 1874-
Cronica dos vice-reis e governadores da
India. Nova Goa, Imprensa nacional, 1919.
699p.

1. Portuguese in India. 2. Portugal - Biog.

4 MR

I-255
Firishtah, Muhammad Kāsim-ibn Hindū Shāh,
Astarābādī.
Firishta's history of the Dekkan from the
first Mahummedan conquests, with a continuation
to the present day: and the history of Bengal
from the Accession of Aliverdee Khan to the
year 1780. Trans.by J.Scott. Shrewsbury,
Printed for the editor by J.& W.Eddowes, 1794.
2 vols.

4 MR

I-256
Firishtah, Muhammad Qasim Hindu Shah Astarabadi.
The history of Hindostan. Trans.from Persian
by Alexander Dow. 2d ed. New Delhi, Today
and Tomorrow's Printers and Pubs., 1973.
3v.

I-261
Fraser, Hastings.
Memoir and correspondence of General James
Stuart Fraser. London, Whiting and co., 1885.
536p.

GM

I-257
Firishtah, Muhammad Kasim-ibn Hindu Shah,
Astarabadi.
History of the rise of the Mahomedan power
in India till the year A.D.1612. Tr.by John
Briggs. Calcutta, Editions Indian, 1966.
3v.

UZA

I-262
Fraser, James Baillie, 1783-1856.
Military memoirs of Lt.Col.James Skinner,
C.B. ... London, 1851. 2 vols.

G M

I-258
Fonseca, Felix Feliciano da.
Relação dos felicissimos sucessos obrados
na India Oriental em o Vice-Reinado do Marquez
do Tavora. Lisboa, 1753.

I-263
Fraser, Sir William, 1816-1898.
The Elphinstone family book of the lords
Elphinstone, Balmerino and Coupar. Edinburgh,
Printed by T.&A.Constable at the Edinburgh
Univ.Press, 1897. 2v.

1. Elphinstone fam...

LC

I-259
Foster, Sir William, 1863-   ed.
English factories in India, 1651-1654;
a calendar of documents in the India
Office, Westminster. Oxford, Clarendon
Press, 1915. 363p.

UofR

I-264
Freire de Andrade, Jacinto, 1597-1657.
The life of Dom John do Castro, the 4th
Viceroy of India. Wherein are seen the
Portuguese voyages to the East Indies;
their discoveries and conquests there, the
form of government, etc., in the East, and
the topography of all India and China.
London, Printed for H.Herringman, 1664.
272p.

NY PL

I-260
Francklin, william, 1763-1839.
The history of the reign of Shah Aulum,
the present emperor of Hindostaun. Containing
the transactions of the Court of Delhi, and
the neighboring states, during a period of
thirty-six years. London, Printed for the
author, by Cooper & Graham, 1798.   278p.

1. Shāh 'Alam, emperor of Hindustan, 1728-
1806. 2. Delhi, India (City) - Descr.&-trav
3. mogul empire.

NUR
LC

I-265
Furber, Holden, 1903-
John Company at work; a study of European
expansion in India in the late eighteenth
century. Cambridge, Harvard Univ.Press, 1948.
418p.

U of R

I-266
Gaitonde, Pundlik.
The Goa problem, FAR, v.4 (1955), pp.152-60.

gas 56

I-267
Gaspar, Rodriguez de San Bernardino.
Itinerário da India por terra até à
Ilha de Chipre...Introdução e notas por
Augusto Reis Machado. Lisboa, 1953.
270p.

I-268
Ghauri, Iftikhar Ahmad.
Muslims in the Deccan: an historical
survey, RSPJ, v.2 (1965), pp.1-19.

JAS '66

I-269
Ghauri, Iftikhar Ahmad.
Organization of the army under the Sultanates of the Deccan. PHSJ, v.14 (1966),
pp.147-71.

J.a d '66

I-270
Ghose, Loke Nath.
The modern history of the Indian Chiefs,
Rajas, Zamindars, etc. Calcutta, J.N.Ghose,
1879-1881. 2v.

4 of R

I-271
Ghosh, Biswanath.
British policy towards the Pathans and the
Pindaris in central India, 1805-18. 1st ed.
Calcutta, Punthi Pustak, 1966. 364p.

4 of R

I-272
Gill, Conrad, 1883-
Merchants and mariners of the eighteenth
century. London, E.Arnold, 1961. 176p.

History - General

LC

I-273
Gleig, George Robert, 1796-1888.
The life of Major-General Sir Thomas Munro,
bart. and K.C.B., late governor of Madras,
with extracts from his correspondence and
private papers. New ed. London, H.Colburn &
R.Bentley, 1831. 2v.

1. Munro, Sir Thomas, bart., 1761-1827. 2.
India - Hist. - Brittish occupation, 1765-1947.

4 of R

I-274
Gleig, George Robert, 1796-1888.
Memoirs of the life of the Right Hon.
Warren Hastings, first governor-general
of Bengal. London, R.Bentley, 1841. 3v.

4 of R

I-275
Glover, Elizabeth Rosetta (Scott) lady, d.1927.
Great queens; famous women rulers of the
East. London, Hutchinson & co., ltd., 1928.
283p.

1. Chand Bibi & Rani of Jhansi.

I-276
Gode, Parashuram Krishna, 1891-
The history of the sling (Gophanas) in India and other countries (between B.C.300 and A.D. 1900). JTSML, v.10 (1955), pp.13-22.

Chaudhuri

O

I-277
Gode, Parashuram Krishna, 1891-
The manufacture and use of fire-arms in India between A.D. 1450 and 1850. BV, v.9 (1948), pp.202-28.

Case

O

I-278
Golwalkar, Madhav Sadashiv.
Thoughts on some current problems. Bombay, the author, 1958. 40p.

Ind nat'l Ref '58

O

I-279
Gopal, Sarvepalli.
British policy in India, 1858-1905. Cambridge (England) University Press, 1965. (Cambridge South Asian studies, no.1). 434p.

1. India - Hist. - British occupation, 1765-1947.
notR

O

I-280
Gopalakrishna, S.
Allan Octavian Hume and the foundation of the Congress. MR, v.117 (1965), pp.120-21.

Ja S 65

O

I-281
Gracias, Amancio.
Ingleses em Goa, HIVG, v.4 (1928), pp.41-52.

JB+15

O

I-282
Gracias, José Antonio Ismael, 1857-1919.
O imposto eo regimen tributario da India Portugueza. Nova Goa, 1898.

NLC

O

I-283
Great Britain. Parliament. House of Commons.
Appendix to the fifth report from the Committee of Secrecy, appointed to enquire into the cause of the war in the Carnatic, and of the condition of the British possessions in those parts. First Maratta war. London, 1782? 2 vols.

O

I-284
Great Britain. Parliament. House of Commons.
Appendix to the sixth report from the Committee of secrecy, appointed to enquire into the causes of the war in the Carnatic, and of the condition of the British possessions in those parts. Second Maratta war. London, 1782? 200p.

SOAS

)

I-285
Great Britain. Parliament. House of Commons.
Fifth report from the Committee of secrecy, appointed to enquire into the causes of the war in the Carnatic, and of the condition of the British possessions in those parts. London, 1782? 170p.

SOAS

)

I-286
Great Britain. Parliament. House of Commons.
First and second report from the Committee
of secrecy, appointed to enquire into the
causes of the war in the Carnatic, and of the
condition of the British possessions in those
parts. London, 1782. 2 vols.

SOAS

I-291
Handa, Rajendra Lal, 1912-
History of freedom struggle in princely
states. New Delhi, Central News Agency,
1968. 414p.

1. India - Pol.& govt. - 1919-1947.

U of R

I-287
Great Britain. Parliament. House of Commons.
Fourth report from the Committee of Secrecy,
appointed to enquire into the causes of the
war in the Carnatic, and of the condition of
the British possessions in those parts. London,
1782. 192p.

SOAS

I-292
Hastings, Warren, 1732-1818.
Letters to Sir John Macpherson, ed.by Henry
Dodwell. London, Faber & Gwyer, 1927. 252p.

1. India - Hist. - British occupation, 1765-
1947.

U of R

I-288
Grover, B.L.
A new look on modern Indian history: from
1707 to the present day. By B.L.Grover and
R.R.Sethi. 2d ed. Delhi, S.Chand, 1970.
495p.

BAS 1970

I-293
The history and culture of the Indian people.
Ed.by R.C.Majumdar and A.D.Pusalker. London,
G.Allen & Unwin, 1952-

U of R (v. 1-6, 9-10)

I-289
Guyon, Claude Marie, 1699-1771.
Histoire des Indes Orientales, anciennes
et modernes; par Mr.l'Abbé Guyon. Paris,
1744. 3v.

SOAS

I-294
Holdich, Sir Thomas Hungerford, 1843-1929.
India. N.Y.,D.Appleton and Co., 1905.
387p.

1. India
LC

I-290
Habib, Irfan, 1931-
The agrarian system of Mughal India, 1556-
1707. Bombay, Asia Pub.House, 1963. 462p.

1. Peasantry - India - Hist. 2. Land
tenure - India - History.

LC

I-295
Hunter, Sir William Wilson, 1840-1900.
A history of British India. Reprint. New
York, AMS Press, 1966. 2v.

U of R

I-296
Hunter, Sir William Wilson, 1840-1900.
Marquess of Dalhousie. Oxford, Clarendon
Press, 1895. (The Rulers of India, v.11).
232p.

1.Dalhousie, James Andrew Brown Ramsay,
1st marquess of, 1812-1860.

NUC
LC

I-297
Hunter, Sir William Wilson, 1840-1900.
The ruin of Aurangzeb; or the history of
a reaction. NC. v.21 (1887), pp.702-18.

NC

I-298
Husain, Agha Mahdi.
The Hindus of medieval India, IHCP, v.3
(1939), pp.712-24.

IHCP

I-299
Hyderabad, India (State) Dept.of Information
and Public Relations.
History and legend in Hyderabad. Hyderabad,
Osmania University Press, 1953. 124p.

1. Hyderabad, India (State) - Hist. 2.
Hyderabad, India (State) - Descr.& trav.

U of R

I-300
India. Committee on disturbances in Bombay,
Delhi and the Punjab.
Report of the committee appointed by the
Govt.of India to investigate the disturbances
in the Punjab, etc. London, H.M.S., 1920.
6 vols.

U of R

I-301
India. Foreign and Political Dept.
A collection of treaties, engagements and
sanads relating to India and neighbouring
countries, comp.by C.U.Aitchison. Calcutta,
Printed by G.A.Savielle and P.M.Cranenburg,
Bengal Print.Co., etc., 1862-1866. 7v.

U of R

I-302
India, Portuguese. Official documents.
Collecção de tratados e concertos de pazes
que o Estado da India Portugueza fez com os
Reis e Senhores com quem teve relações nas
partes da Asia e Africa Oriental desde o
principio da conquista até ao fim do
secula XVIII, por Julio Firmino Judice
Biker. Lisboa, 1881-87. 14 vols.

BM

I-303
Irvine, William, 1840-1911.
The army of the Indian Moghuls: its organi-
zation and administration. London, Leyden
Printed, 1903. 331p.

BM

I-304
Irvine, William, 1840-1911.
The later Moghuls (1707-1803) Ed.by Jadunath
Sarkar. Calcutta, M.C.Sarkar & sons, 1922.
2v.

1. Mogul empire. 2. India - Hist. - European
settlements, 1500-1765.

LC

I-305
Jones, Sir William, et al.
Dissertations and miscellaneous pieces relating to the history and antiquities, arts,
sciences, and literature of Asia. London,
1792-96. 3v.

IOL

I-306
   Joshi, Purushottam Mahadeo, 1906-
      The Raichur Doab in Deccan history; re-inter-
   pretation of a struggle, JIH, v.36 (1958), pp.
   379-96.

JIH

I-307
   Karkaria, Rustomji Pestonji, 1869-1919.
      Akbar and the Parsees, ASBJ, v.19
   (1895-1897), pp.289-305.

NYPL

I-308
   Keene, Henry George, 1825-1915.
      Fall of the Moghul empire; an historical
   essay. London, W.H.Allen, 1876. 323p.

      1. India - Hist. 2. Moghul Empire.

4 7R

I-309
   Kennedy, Pringle, 1885-1925.
      A history of the Great Moghuls; or, a history
   of the badshahate of Delhi from 1398 A.D. to
   1739, with an introd.concerning the Mongols and
   Moghuls of Central Asia. Calcutta, Thacker,
   Spink & co., 1905-11. 2 vols.

      1. India - Hist. 2. Mogul empire. 3. Mongols-
   Hist.

4 7R

I-310
   Khan, Saqi Must'ad.
      Masir-i-Alamgiri; a history of the
   Emperor Aurangzib-Alamgir (reign 1658-
   1707A.D.). Translated into English and
   annotated by Sir Jadunath Sarkar. Calcutta, Royal Asiatic Society of Bengal,
   1947. (Bibliotheca India; a collection
   of Oriental works. Work no.269, issue
   no.1556). 357p.

Vol R

I-311
   Khan, Yusuf Husain.
      The Deccan policy and campaigns of the
   Mughals, IC, v.18 (1944), pp.301-12.

II

I-312
   Kosambi, Damodar Dharmanand, 1907-1968.
      Myth and reality; studies in the
   formation of Indian culture. Bombay,
   Popular Prakashan, 1962. 187p.

      man - civilisation
VolR

I-313
   Kulkarni, Vaman Balaji.
      British statesmen in India. Bombay,
   Orient Longmans, 1961. 550p.

   1 India - Governors   2. British in India
VolR

I-314
   Laet, Joannes de, 1593-1649.
      The topography of the Mogul empire as known
   to the Dutch in 1681. Trans.from the Latin by
   E.Lethbridge. Calcutta, 1871.

Cal nat Lib

I-315
   Lee-Warner, Sir William, 1846-1914.
      The protected princes of India. London,
   New York, Macmillan & co., 1894. 408p.

      1. India - Hist.-British occupation, 1765-
   2. India Pol.& govt.

4 7R

I-316
Lopes de Castanheda, Fernão, d.1559.
The first booke of the historie of the
discoverie and conquest of the East Indias.
Trans.by Nicholas Lichefild. London,
T.East, 1582. 173p.

IOL

I-317
Lopes de Castanheda, Fernão, d.1559.
História do descobrimento & conquista da
India pelos portugueses. 3.ed.conforme a
ed. princeps, rev.e anotada por Pedro de
Azevedo. Coimbra, Impr.da Universidade,
1924-33. 4v. (Scriptores rerum lusitanarum,
série A).

U of R

I-318
Lovett, Sir Harrington Verney, 1964-
A history of the Indian nationalism move-
ment. New York, Stilkes, 1920. 302p.

1. India - Pol.& govt. - 1765-

U of R

I-319
Low, Charles Rathbone, 1837-
History of the Indian Navy (1613-1863)
London, R.Bentley and son, 1877. 2v.

LC

I-320
Luard, Charles Eckford, 1869-1927.
Gazetteer gleanings in Central India, IA,
v.37 (1908), pp.178-79,225-35,245-46; v.39
(1910), pp.107-10,329-31.

IA

I-321
Luthera, Ved Prakash.
Goa and the Portuguese republic, IJPS,
v.19 (1956), pp.261-80.

JAS 56

I-322
Lyall, Sir Alfred Comyn, 1835-1911.
The rise and expansion of the British
dominion in India. 5th ed. London, John
Murray, 1914. 417p.

1 India - Hist - British occupations
1765-

U of R

I-323
McCully, Bruce Tiebout, 1904-
English education and the origins of
Indian nationalism. New York, Columbia
university press; London, P.S.King and
son, ltd., 1940. (Studies in history,
economics and public law, Ed.by the Faculty of political science of Columbia
university, no.473). 422p.

U of R

I-324
Mackintosh, Sir James, 1765-1832.
Memoirs of the life of the Right Hon.Sir
James Mackintosh. Boston, Little, Brown &
co., 1853. 2v.

U of R

I-325
McLane, John R.
The development of Nationalist ideas and
tactics and the policies of the Govt.of
India, 1897-1905. London, London Univ.,
1961. *

JAS

I-326
    MacMunn, Sir George Fletcher, 1869-1952.
        The Indian States and princes. London,
    Jarrolds, ltd., 1936. 287p.

Le

I-327
    MacMunn, Sir George Fletcher, 1869-1952.
        Vignettes from Indian wars. London, S.Low,
    Marston & Co., ltd., 1932. 224p.

U M R

I-328
    Mahajan, Vidya Dhar.
        The nationalist movement in India and its
    leaders. Delhi, S.Chand, 1962. 133p.

U M R

I-329
    Major, Richard Henry, 1818-1891, ed.
        India in the fifteenth century. London,
    Hakluyt society, 1857. 220p.

N.U.C.
IOL

I-330
    Majumdar, Bimanbehari, 1900-
        Indian political associations and reform of
    legislature, 1818-1917. 1st ed. Calcutta,
    Firma K.L.Mukhopadhyay, 1965. 485p.

        1. Political parties - India - Hist. 2.
    India - Pol.& govt. - 1765-1947.

4 M R

I-331
    Majumdar, Ramesh Chandra, 1888-
        British paramountcy and Indian renaissance.
    Bombay, Bharatiya Vidya Bhavan, 1963-
    (Bharatiya Vidya Bhavan's history and culture
    of the Indian people, 9)

N U C

I-332
    Majumdar, Ramesh Chandra, 1888-
        The growth of nationalism in India. IAC,
    v.10 (1961), pp.95-113.

Ja S 61

I-333
    Majumdar, Ramesh Chandra, 1888-
        History of the freedom movement in India.
    Calcutta, Mukhopadhyay, 1962-63. 3v.

U M R

I-334
    Malcolm, Sir John, 1769-1833.
        The Government of India. London, 1833.
    543p.

IOL

I-335
    Malhotra, Pairea Lal.
        The internal administration of Lord Elgin
    in India, 1894-1898. London, London Univ.,
    1966. *

Case

I-336
Malleson, George Bruce, 1825-1898.
The decisive battles of India from 1746-
1849 inclusive. London, W.H.Allen & co.,
1885. 490p.

1. India - Hist., Military. 2. Battles - India

NUR
LC

I-337
Malleson, George Bruce, 1825-1898.
The founders of the Indian Empire: Clive,
Warren Hasting, and Wellesley. London, W.H.
Allen & Co., 1882. 556p.

UQ'R

I-338
Malleson, George Bruce, 1825-1898.
History of the French in India, from the
founding of Pondichery in 1674 to the capture
of that place in 1761. London, W.H.Allen,&
co.,ltd.,1893. 627p.

1 India - Hist - European settlements
1506 - 1765. French in India

4 4R

I-339
Malleson, George Bruce, 1825-1898.
Life of Warren Hastings, first governor-
general of India. London, Chapman & Hall,
1894. 575p.

4 4R

I-340
Malleson, George Bruce, 1825-1898.
Life of the Marquess Wellesley. London,
1895. (Statesmen series) 254p.

IOL

I-341
Manucci, Niccolò, 17th cent.
History of the Mogul dynasty in India, from
its foundation by Tamerlane, in the year 1399,
to the accession of Aurengzebe in the year
1657. Trans.from the Franch of Father François
Catrou ... London, J.M.Richardson, 1826.
345p.

LC

I-342
Manucci, Niccolo, 17th cent.
Storia do Mogor; or, Mogul India, 1653-
1708, translated with introduction and
notes by William Irvine. London, J.Murray,
1907-08. (The Indian texts series, 1).
4v.

1 ote

I-343
Marjay, Frederico Pedro.
Portuguese India, a historic study. Lisbon,
Livraria Bertrand, 1959.

Scholarly to support

I-344
Martin, Briton, Jr.
New India, 1885; a study of British official
policy and the emergence of the Indian National
Congress. Philadelphia, Univ.of Pennsylvania,
1964. 772p. *

JAS '66

I-345
Martin, François, 1634-1706.
Mémoires de François Martin, fondateur
de Pondichéry, 1665-1696. Paris, pub.
par A.Martineau, 1931-34. 3v.

IOL

I-346
Martin, Robert Montgomery, 1803?-1868.
  The Indian empire: history, topography,
geology, climate, population, chief cities
and provinces... London, N.Y., London Print.
and Pub.Co., ltd., 1858-61. 3 vols.

4 of R

I-347
Martin, Robert Montgomery, 1803?-1868.
  Statistics of the colonies of the British
empire. From the official records of the
colonial office. London, W.H.Allen, 1839.
914p.

LC

I-348
Martineau, Alfred Albert, 1859-
  Bussy in the Deccan being extracts from
"Bussy and French India." Trans.by A.Cam-
miade. Pondichery, Society for the
History of French India, 1941. 312p.

SOAS

I-349
Martineau, Alfred Albert, 1859-   ed.
  Lettres et conventions des Gouverneurs de
Pondichéry avec différents princes hindous,
1666 à 1793. Pondichéry, 1911-14. (Société
de l'Histoire de l'Inde Française, Pondicherry.
Publications) 402p.

I-350
Mehta, Mohan Sinha.
  Lord Hastings and the Indian States; being
a study of the relations of the British govt.
in India with the Indian states, 1813-1823.
Bombay, D.B.Taraporevala, 1930. 291p.

  1. India - Pol.& govt - 1765-   2. India -
Hist - British occupation, 1765-

4 of R

I-351
Menon, Vapal Pangunni.
  The story of the integration of the Indian
states. New York, Macmillan, 1956. 511p.

  1. State governments - India. 2. India -
Constitutional history.

U of R

I-352
Mitra, S.M.
  India in 1813 and 1913. FR, v.101 (1914),
pp.705-17.

Case

I-353
Moinul Haq, S., tr.
  Khafi Khan's history of Alamgir (English
translation), PHSJ, v.12,pt.4 (1964), pp.
255-90; v.13 (1965), pp.44-86, 168-99.

4 of R

I-354
Monaranjak Grantha Prasarak Mandali.
  Indian worthies. Bombay, Karnatak Print.
Press, 1906. v.1 194p.

Bom (Pres) cat

I-355
Moon, Penderel, 1905-
  Warren Hastings and British India. London,
Pub.by Hodder & Stoughton for the English
Universities Press, 1947. (Teach your-
self history library). 370p.

U of R

I-356
   Moraes, George Mark.
      The Kadamba Kula; a history of ancient
   and mediaeval Karnataka. Bombay, B.X.Fur-
   tado and sons, 1931. (Studies in Indian
   history of the Indian historical research
   institute, St.Xavier's College, Bombay,
   no.5). 527p.

1. Kadambas. 2. India - Hist - Early.

LC

I-357
   Muir, Ramsay, 1872-1941.
      The making of British India, 1756-1858,
   described in a series of despatches, treat-
   ies, statutes, and other documents. New
   York, Longmans, Green & Co., 1915.
   (Publications of the Univ.of Manchester
   Historical series, no.28). 412p.

1. India - Hist - European settlements, 1500-1765.
2. India - Hist - British occupation, 1765 -

MUR
LC

I-358
   Munshi, Kanaiyalal Maneklal, 1887-
      End of an era; Hyderabad memories. Bombay,
   B.V.Bhavan, 1957. 314p.

U of R

I-359
   Muttalib, M.A.
      The administration of justice under the
   Nizam, 1724-1947. Hyderabad, Osmania Univ.,
   1958. *

Justice
BDD

I-360
   Nambiar, Odayamadath Kunjappa, 1910-
      The Kunjalis; admirals of Calicut. London,
   Asia Pub.House, 1963. 167p.

1. Portuguese in India - Hist. 2. India -
Hist., Naval.

U of R

I-361
   Nambiar, Odayamadath Kunjappa, 1910-
      Portuguese pirates and Indian seamen. Ban-
   galore, M.Bhaktavatsalam, 1955. 218p.

LC

I-362
   Natarajan, L.
      Peasant uprisings in India, 1850-1900.
   Bombay, People's Pub.House, 1953. 80p.

1. Peasantry - India. 2. Revolutions -
India.

LC

I-363
   Orme, Robert, 1728-1801.
      Historical fragments. Ré-printed from the
   original edition of 1782. Calcutta, "Banga-
   basi" Office, 1905. 376p.

U of R

I-364
   Orme, Robert, 1728-1801.
      A history of the military transactions of
   the British nation in Indostan, from the year
   1745. Madras, Pharoah, 1861-62. 2v.

U of R

I-365
   Owen, Sidney James, 1827-1912.
      The fall of the Mogul Empire. 2d ed.
   Varanasi, Chowkhamba Sanskrit Series Office,
   1960. (Chowkhamba Sanskrit series. Studies,
   v.7). 218p.

1. Mogul Empire. 2. India Hist - Early
settlement, 1500 -

U of R

I-366
Owen, Sidney James, 1827-1912.
India on the eve of the British conquest;
an analytical history of India, 1627-1761.
2d ed. Calcutta, S.Gupta, 1954. 207p.

1. India - Hist. - European settlements,
1500-1765. 2. Mogul Empire. 3. Mahrattas.

4 M R

I-367
Panikkar, Kavalam Madhava, 1896-
A survey of Indian history. Bombay, Asia
Pub.House, 1960. 284p.

U of R

I-368
Parel, Anthony.
Hume, Dufferin and the origins of the
Indian National Congress, *JIH*, v.42 (1964),
pp.707-26.

J I H '64

I-369
Pearce, Robert Rouiere.
Memoirs and correspondence of the most
noble Marquess Wellesley. Comprising numerous letters and documents, now first published
from original mss. London, R.Bentley, 1846.
3 vols.

U of R

I-370
Pedroso, Sebastião José, 1810-
Resumo historico ácerca da antiga India
portugueza, acompanhado de algumas re-
flexões concernentes ao que ainda possuimos
na Asia, Oceania, China e Africa;com
um appendice por Sebastião José Pedroso.
Lisboa, Typographia Castro irmão, 1884.
482p.

4 M R

I-371
Philips, Cyril Henry, 1912-
The East India Company, 1784-1834.
Manchester, Manchester university press,
1940. (Publications of the University
of Manchester, no.270. Historical series,
no.77). 381p.

r R

I-372
Piggott, Stuart.
Some ancient cities of India. Bombay,
Oxford University Press, 1945. 108p.

N J R
J O L

I-373
Pillay, K.K.
Schwartz and the Maratha kings of Tanjavur.
In: Studies in Indian history; Dr.A.G.Pawar
felicitation volume. Ed.by V.D.Rao. Kolhapur,
Y.P.Pawar, 1968. pp.253-57.

U 3 R

I-374
Pina de Mello, Francisco de, b.1695.
A conquista de Goa, por Affonso de
Albuquerque,....poema epico. Coimbra,
1759. 367p.

B M

I-375
Pinto Pereira, Antonio, fl.1575.
Historia da India no tempo em que a
governovo visorey Dom Lvis de Ataide,
composta por Antonio Pinto Pereyra, Ord-
enada, e impressa per ordem de frey Miguel
da Cruz, frade da Ordem de Nosso Senhor
Iesu Christo theologo pregador. Le va dovs
indices, hvm no remate decada liuro em que
se apontão as pessoas de q nesta obra se
trata. Coimbra, N.Carulho, 1616. 2pts.
in 1v.

I-376

Pissurlencar, Panduronga S.S.
Portuguese records on Rustamji Manockji,
the Parsi broker of Surat. With an English
translation by S.B.D'Silva. Nova-Goa, 1933-
36. 2 vols.

u of R

I-377

Playne, Somerset.
The Bombay Presidency, the United Provinces,
the Punjab, etc., their history, people, commerce and natural resources. London, Foreign
and Colonial Compiling and Pub.Co., 1917-20.

History - General
Ris of Ind Lit

I-378

Pogson, Wredenhall Robert.
A history of the Boondelas. Calcutta, 1828.
184p.

BM History - General

I-379

Pondicherry.
Lettres et conventions des Gouverneurs de
Pondichéry avec differents princes hindous
1666 à 1793. Pondichéry, 1911-1914.
(Archives de l'Inde Française) 405p.

I-380

Prinsep, James, 1799-1840.
Essays on Indian antiquities, historic, nu-
mismatic and palaeographic, of the late James
Prinsep ... to which are added his useful
tables, illustrative of Indian history, chronology, modern coinages, weights, measures,
etc. Ed.by Edward Thomas. London, John Murray,
1858. 2v.

NRU

I-381

Purohit, B.R.
Hindu revivalism and Indian nationalism.
Sagar, Sathi Prakashan, 1965. 292p.

LC

I-382

Radcliffe, Cyril John Radcliffe, baron, 1899-
Mountstuart Elphinstone. Oxford, Clarendon
Press, 1962. (The Romanes lecture, 1962) 32p.

IOL

I-383

Rahim, A.
The Mogul diplomacy from Akbar to Aurangzeb.
London, London Univ., 1931-32. *

Bloomfield

I-384

Rahim, Muhammad Abdur.
Lord Dalhousie's administration of the conquered and annexed states. Delhi, S.Chand,
1963. 401p.

1. India - Pol.& govt. - 1765-1947.

NUR
LC

I-385

Rahman, Khalilur A.F.M.
Rise and fall of the Rohilla power in
Hindustan, 1707-74 A.D. London, London
Univ., 1936. *

Bloomfield

I-386
Ramananda Tirtha, Swami.
Memoirs of Hyderabad freedom struggle.
Bombay, Popular Prakashan, 1967. 247p.

History
Modern-books
BAS Sept 1970

I-387
Rawlinson, Hugh George, 1880-
British beginnings in western India, 1579-
1657; an account of the early days of the
British factory of Surat. Oxford, Clarendon
Press, 1920. 163p.

4 of R

I-388
Ray, Aniruddha.
Anarchiew, révoltes, et émeutes dans l'Inde
Mogole (1658-1739). Paris, Université de
Paris, 1967. 478p. *

Shulman # 495

I-389
Regani, Sarojini.
Nizam-British relations, 1724-1857. Hyderabad, India, distributed by Booklovers, 1963.
342p.

4 y R

I-390
Rego, Antonio da Silva, 1905-
Portuguese colonization in the sixteenth
century: a study of the royal ordinances.
Johannesburg, Witwatersrand University Press,
1959. (Pubs.of the Ernest Oppenheimer Inst.
of Portuguese Studies of the Univ.of Witwatersrand, Johannesburg, 1). 124p.

4 of R

I-391
Reid, C.Lestock.
Commerce and conquest, the story of the
Hon'ble East India Company. London, C.J.
Temple, 1947. 256p.

NUR
LC

I-392
Rennell, James, 1742-1830.
The marches of the British armies in the
Peninsula of India, during the campaigns of
1790-91. London, G.Nicol, 1792. 114p.

B M

I-393
Richmond, Sir Herbert William, 1871-1946.
The navy in India, 1763-1783. London, E.
Benn, ltd., 1931. 432p.

LC

I-394
Rivett-Carnac, Edward Stirling.
The presidential armies of India. London,
W.H.Allen and Co., 1890. 465p.

BM

I-395
Roberts, Paul Ernest, 1873-
A history of British India under the company
and the crown. Oxford, Clarendon Press, 1923.
633p.

History - General

4 y R

I-396
Roberts, Paul Ernest, 1873-
    India under Wellesley. London, G.Bell &
sons, ltd., 1929. 335p.

4개R

I-397
Ross-of-Bladensburg, John Foster George.
    The Marquess of Hastings. Oxford, Clar-
endon Press, 1893. (Rulers of India series).
226p.

NUR
IOL

I-398
Roy, M.P.
    Pindaris - their origin, growth and sup-
pression. Rajasthan, Rajasthan, Univ.,
1964. *

Rajasthan Univ Lib.

I-399
Roy, Nirod Bhushan.
    Lord Cornwallis's diplomacy. IHRCP, v.16
(1937), pp.113-21.

IARC

I-400
Roychoudhury, M. L.
    Hindu-Muslim relation during the Mughal per-
iod 1526-1707, A. D. , IHCP, v. 9 (1946), pp.
282-96.

JI

I-401
Saletore, Bhaskar Anand.
    The Sthanikas and their historical impor-
tance, JUB, v.7 (1938), pp.23-93.

fürer

I-402
Sanceau, Elaine.
    Indies adventure; the amazing career of
Afonso de Albuquerque, captain-general and
governor of India (1509-1515). London and
Glasgow, Blackie and son, ltd., 1936. 320p.

LC

I-403
Sanceau, Elaine.
    Knight of the Renaissance, D.João de Castro,
soldier, sailor, scientist, and Viceroy of
India, 1500-1548. London, Hutchinson, 1949.
235p.

4개R

I-404
Sareen, Tilak Raj.
    The Indian National Congress and the
Indian states, 1885-1890, BPP, v.83 (1964),
pp.115-17.

AS'6:

I-405
Sarkar, Sir Jadunath, 1870-1958.
    Fall of the Mughal empire. 3rd ed.
Calcutta, M.C.Sarkar and sons, 1964-66.
2v.

U개R

I-406
Sarkar, Sir Jadunath, 1870-1958.
History of Aurangzib based on original
sources. 2d ed. London, Longmans, Green,
1930-52. 5v.

U of R

I-407
Sarkar, Sir Jadunath, 1870-1958.
India's military decline in the 18th cent.,
MR, v.74 (1943), pp.97-100, 417-20.

Case

I-408
Sarkar, Sir Jadunath, 1870-1958.
Military history of India. 1st ed. Calcutta,
M.C.Sarkar, 1960. 179p.

U of R

I-409
Sarkar, Sir Jadunath, 1870-1958.
A short history of Aurangzib, 1618-1707.
3d ed. Calcutta, M.C.Sarkar, 1962. 478p.

U of R

I-410
Sarkar, Sir Jadunath, 1870-1958.
Studies in Aurangzib's reign (being
studies in Mughal India, first series).
Calcutta, M.C.Sarkar and sons, 1933. 305p.

Lc

I-411
Seal, Anil.
The emergence of Indian nationalism:
competition and collaboration in the later
nineteenth century. London, Cambridge
Univ.Press, 1968. (Political change in
modern South Asia). 432p.

(series)

U of R

I-412
Sen, Siba Pada, 1914-
The French in India 1763-1816. Calcutta,
K.L.Mukhopadhyay, 1958. 638p.

1. French in India - Hist.

U of R

I-413
Sen, Surendra Nath, 1890-
Studies in Indian history. Calcutta,
University of Calcutta, 1930. 276p.

1. India - History - Addresses, essays,
lectures.

Lc

I-414
Seton-Karr, Walter Scott, 1822-1910.
The Marquess Cornwallis and the consolidation
of British rule. Oxford, Clarendon Press, 1890.
(Rulers of India, v.10). 202p.

NUC
LC

I-415
Sewell, Robert, 1845-1925.
A forgotten empire, Vijayanagar; a contri-
bution to the history of India. Delhi, Pub.
Division, Ministry of Information and Broad-
casting, Govt.of India, 1962. 425p.

U of R

I-416
Sharadamma, M.
Akbar, Shivaji and Haidar Ali in a single perspective, IHCP, v.9 (1945), p.303.

IHCP

I-417
Sharma, Shripad Rama, 1897-
The crescent in India; a study in medieval history. Rev.3d ed. Bombay, Hind Kitabs, 1966. 755p.

1. India - Hist. 2. Mugul Empire. 3. Muslims in India.

U of A

I-418
Sharma, Shripad Rama, 1897-
The making of modern India from A.D.1526 to the present day. Bombay, Orient Longmans, 1951. 611p.

Lc

I-419
Shejwalkar, Trymbak Shankar.
Native supporters of the British dominion in India, BDCRI, v.2 (1940), pp.424-32.

BDCRI, p.

I-420
Sherwani, Haroon Khan, 1891-
Muhammad-Quli Qutb Shah, founder of Haidara-bad. London, Asia Publishing House, 1967. (Asia monographs, no.11). 163p.

(series)
History-General

U of A

I-421
Singh, Gulcharan.
The battles of Panipat. New Delhi, Army Educational Stores, 1966. 116p.

U of R

I-422
Sinha, Har Narain, 1900-
The newly discovered autograph letters of Wellington, BPP, v.39 (1930), pp.91-99.

Cose

I-423
Sinha, Har Narain, 1900-
The main currents of the 18th century Indian history, JIH, v.9 (1930), pp.37-48.

JBHS

I-424
Sinha, Narendra Krishna, 1903-
Haider Ali. 3d ed. Calcutta, A.Mukherjee and co., 1959. 309p.

U of R

I-425
Sir Richard Temple, QJPSS, v.2,no.2 (1879), pp.42-54.

QJPSS

I-426
Soares, Joaquim Pedro Celestino.
　Bosquejo das possessões portuguezas no
Oriente; ou, Resumo de algumas derrotas da
India e da China, por Joaquim Pedro Celestino
Soares... Lisboa, Imprensa nacional, 1851-53.
2v.

LC

I-427
Sousa Pinto, Manoel de.
　Dom João de Castro (1500-1548). Lisboa,
Baptista, Torres & co., 1912. 129p.

1. Castro, João de, 1500-1546.

LC

I-428
Spear, Thomas George Percival.
　Twilight of the Mughals; studies in late
Mughal Delhi. Oxford, Cambridge University
Press, 1951. 279p.

1. Mogul empire. 2. Delhi - Hist.

NUR
LC

I-429
Srikantaya, S.
　Foundation of the Vijayanagara empire and
Vidyaranya's part therein. QJMS, v.26 (1936),
pp.187-226.

(several paragraphs devoted to early conflicts
between Marathas and Muhammadans)

QJMS

I-430
Srinivasachari, Chidambaram S., 1890-1951.
　Histoire de Gingi. Pondicherry, Societe de
l'Histoire l'Inde Français, 1940.

4 of R

I-431
Srivastava, Ashirbadi Lal.
　The first two Nawabs of Oudh. 2d rev.ed.
Agra, Shiva Lal Agarwala, 1954. 326p.

1. Safdar Jang, Nawab Wazur of Oudh, 1708-
1754. 2. Saadat Khan Burhan-ul-Mulk, Nawab
of Oudh, 1680- 1739.

U of R

I-432
Stokes, E.T.
　Utilitarian influence and the formation of
Indian policy, 1820-1840. Oxford, Cambridge
University, 1952. *

QJISS

I-433
Sullivan, Richard Joseph, bart. 1752-1806.
　Analysis of the political history of India.
In which is considered the present situation
of the East and the connection of its several
powers with the Empire of Great Britain. 2d ed.
London, Printed for T.Becket, 1784. 337p.

1. India - Hist. - European settlements -
1500-1765.

LC

I-434
Sutherland, Lucy Stuart, 1903-
　The East India Company in eighteenth century
politics. Oxford, Clarendon Press, 1952.
430p.

1. East India Company (English)

U of R

I-435
Taleyarkhan, Dinshah Ardeshir.
　Selections from my recent notes on the
Indian empire. Bombay, Times of India Steam
Press, 1886. 465p.

4 of R

I-436
Temple, Sir Richard, 1st bart., 1826-1902.
Men and events of my time in India. London,
J.Murray, 1882. 544p.

UofR

I-437
Temple, Richard, 1st bart., 1826-1902.
The story of my life. London, Cassell and
co., ltd., 1896. 2v.

LC.

I-438
Thompson, Edward John, 1886-   and Garrett,
Geoffrey Theodore, 1888-
Rise and fulfillment of British rule in
India. London, Macmillan, 1934. 701p.

1. India - Hist. - European settlements,
1500-1765.

U of R

I-439
Thorat, S.P.P.
The regimental history of the Mahar MG
Regiment. Dehra Dun, The Army Press, 1954.

Eleanor Zelliot's
dissertation

I-440
Thornton, Edward, 1799-1875.
History of the British empire in India.
London, W.H.Allen, 1841-45. 6 vols.

1. India - Hist. - European settlements,
1500-1765.

U of R

I-441
Tirtha, Ramananda, Swami.
Memoirs of Hyderabad freedom struggle.
Bombay, Popular Prakashan, 1967. 255p.

1. Hyderabad, India (State) - Pol.& govt.

U of R

I-442
Tripathi, Amales.
Extremist challenge; India between 1890
and 1910. New Delhi, Orient Longmans, 1967.
261p.

1. India - pol & govt - 1765 - 1947.

LC

I-443
Useem, John and Useem, Ruth.
The western educated man in India; a study
of his social roles and influences. New York,
Dryden Press, 1955. 250p.

1. Students - Foreign. 2. Youth - India. 3. India -
Intellectual life.

U of R

I-444
Varma, Ramesh Chandra.
Foreign policy of the great Mughals, 1526-
1727 A.D. Agra, Shiva Lal Agarwala, 1967.
246p.

1. Moghul Empire - For.rel.

U of R

I-445
Varma, Vishwanath Prasad.
The genesis of extremism in Indian politics,
1897-98, PUJ, v.17 (1962), pp.1-24.

Case

I-446
Vasa, Raman C.
   Le protectorat français aux Indes sous
le marquis de Busay. Avec une préface de
M.Pagès...et avec une introduction de
M.Martineau... Paris, Librairie Picart,
1935. 244p. ●

History-General (

LC

I-447
Wellesley, Richard Colley Wellesley, marquis,
   1760-1842.
   A selection from the despatches, treaties
and other papers of the Marquess of Wellesley
during his government of India. Oxford, Clarendon Press, 1877. 924p.

U of R   (

I-448
Wellesley, Richard Colley Wellesley, marquis,
   1760-1842.
   The Wellesley papers. London, Herbert
Jenkins, 1914. 2v.

BM   (

I-449
Wellington, Arthur Wellesley, first duke of,
   1769-1852.
   Wellington at war, 1794-1815; a selection of
his wartime letters. Ed.by Antony Brett-James.
London, Macmillan; New York, St.Martin's Press,
1961. 427p.

U of R   (

I-450
Wellington in India, CR, v.27 (1856), pp.
376-430.

Case   (

I-451
Wheeler, James Talboys, 1824-1897.
   Early records of British India: a history of
the English settlements in India, told in the
Government records, the works of old travellers,
and other contemporary documents, from the
earliest period down to the rise of British
power in India. New ed. Calcutta, W.Newman &
Thacker, Spink, 1879. 422p.

   1. British in India.

U of R   (

I-452
Whiteway, Richard Stephen.
   The rise of Portuguese power in India, 1497-
1550. 2d ed. London, S.Gupta, 1967. 373p.

   1. Portuguese in India.

U of R   (

I-453
Wilks, Mark, 1789-1872.
   Historical sketches to the south of India,
in an attempt to trace the history of Mysoor:
from the origin of the Hindoo Government of
that state, to the extinction of the Mohammedan
dynasty in 1799. Ed.with notes by Murray Ham-
mick. Mysore, Printed at the Govt.Branch Press,
1930-32. 2 vols.

Maharashtra   (

I-454
Wilson, John, 1804-1875.
   The British sovereignty in India: a sermon
preached in behalf of the Bombay Scottish
Missionary Society. Bombay, 1836. 28p.

BM   (

I-455
'Ali Ibrahim Khan.
   Alee Ibraheem Khan's history of the Mah-
rattas translated from the Persian. (A some-
what abridged translation by E.J.Frissell of
Ali Ibrahim Khan's history of the Maratha
Wars [A.H. 1171-1199]) Poona, 1804. 97p.

SOAS   (

I-456
   Apte, B.K.
      The contents of Maratha nationalism, IHCP,
   v.16 (1953), pp.285-87.

U of R

I-457
   Apte, B.K.
      A history of the Maratha Navy. Poona,
   Univ.of Poona, 1944-45. *

maratha history
BDCRI

I-458
   Apte, B.K.
      The Maratha weapons of war, BDCRI, v.19
   (1958), pp.106-24.

Susex

I-459
   Apte, B.K.
      Sovereignty of the sea as practised in the
   Maratha period, IHCP, v.29,pt.I (1967), pp.
   255-61.

U of K

I-460
   Athavale, Sadashiv.
      Ideological background of Maratha history,
   HumR, v.2 (1970), pp.49-59.

History
BAS 1970

I-461
   Baker, Bernard Granville.
      11 articles on the Bombay army. London,
   1938-39. (various pagings).

IOL

I-462
   Belsare, R.D.
      Maharashtrians in East Africa and Nyasaland.
   Nairobi, Printed by W.Boyd, 1946. 122p.

U of R

I-463
   Birje, Vasudeva Lingoji.
      Who are the Marathas? Bombay, Nirnaya
   Sagar Press, 1899. 132p.

Bom. (Pres.) Int

I-464
   Chaghtai, M.A.
      The Deccan's contribution to Indian culture,
   IC. v.10 (1936), pp.40-62;428-50.

II

I-465
   Chintamani, T.R.
      Mahratha Hill fortresses, JUR, v.13 (1939),
   pp.143-46.

I-466
    Cox, Edmund Charles, bart., 1856-
        The police of the Bombay Presidency, AR,
    series 1, v.5 (1888), pp.144-53.

9 R

I-467
    Cox, Edmund Charles, bart., 1856-
        A short history of Bombay Presidency.
    Bombay, Thacker, 1887. 444p.

~u2
LC

I-468
    D'Costa, Anthony.
        The East India Company and the common folk
    of Bombay, BIS, v.6 (April 1969), pp.37-49.

VoTR

I-469
    Deopujari, M.B.
        A synoptical critique of the Maratha art
    of war, IHCP, v.25 (1963), pp.123-29.

4 R

I-470
    Desai, Walter Sadgun, 1892-
        Bombay and the Marathas up to 1774. New
    Delhi, Munshiram Manoharlal, 1970. 260p.

PL480 '70

I-471
    Duff, James Grant, 1789-1858.
        History of the Mahrattas. Calcutta, R.
    Cambray, 1912. 3v.

4 of R

I-472
    Ellis, R.R.W.
        Queries: Chakan, Balgam, and Chakabu, IA,
    v.4 (1875), p.352.

IA

I-473
    Fleet, John Faithfull, 1847-1917.
        Salivahana and the Saka era, RASGBIJ, ser.3
    (1916), pp.809-20.

Jaina Bib

I-474
    Furber, Holden, 1903-
        Bombay Presidency in the mid-eighteenth
    century. London, Asia Pub.House, 1965.
    (Heras Memorial Lectures, 1962). 81p.

Bombay (Presidency)-His

4 R

I-475
    Gorman, James Thomas.
        2nd Battalion 4th Bombay Grenadiers, King
    Edward's own formerly the 102nd King Edward's
    own Grenadiers. Weston-super-Mare, Lawrence
    Brothers, 1933. 173p.

CM

I-476
Gribble, James Dunning Baker, d.1906.
    A history of the Deccan. London, Luzac &
Co., 1896-1924. 2v.

1. Deccan, India - Hist.

LC

I-477
Gune, Vithal Trimbak.
    A critical analysis of Mahzars (A.D.1400-
1800), BDCRI, v.8 (1947), pp.260-380.

BDCRI

I-478
Gune, Vithal Trimbak.
    The indigenous tenures and the unification
of Maharashtra during the medieval period.
In: Mahamahopadhyaya Prof.D.V.Potdar
sixty-first birthday commemoration volume.
Ed.by Surendra Nath Sen. Poona, 1950.
pp.233-37.

Bhandarkar Index
Comm vol.

I-479
Gupte, Balkrishna Atmaram, 1851-
    The Modi character and its origin. Bombay,
the author, 1906. 50p.

Bom (Pres) cat

I-480
Haig, Sir Wolseley, 1865-1938.
    Historic landmarks of the Deccan.
Allahabad, Pioneer Press, 1907. 240p.

BM

I-481
Joshi, G.K.
    Maratha modes and weapons of warfare. Poona,
Deccan College Post-graduate and Research Inst.*

Datta

I-482
Joshi, S.B.
    Etymology of place names Patti-Hatti: some
observations on the history of Maharashtra
and Karnataka. ABORI, v.33 (1953). pp.41-56.

Bhard O.R.I

I-483
Joshi, Shankar Narayan, 1890-
    Masala. In: Professor P.K.Gode commemoration
volume. Ed.by H.L.Hariyappa and M.M.Patkar.
Poona, Oriental Book Agency, 1960. pp.186-
88.

UofR

I-484
Kale, D.V.
    The "national" character of the "historical"
Marathas, IHCP, v.2 (1938), pp.587-95.

IHCP

I-485
Kamalapur, J.N.
    The Deccan forts; a study in the art of
fortification in mediaeval India. Bombay,
Popular Book Depot, 1961. 140p.

1. Military architecture - India - Deccan.
2. Fortification - India - Deccan.

I-486
Kanetkar, Y.G.
Some political aphorisms and views of the
Marathas, IHQ, v.15 (1939), pp.254-64.

N YPL

I-487
Karkaria, Rustomji Pestonji, 1869-1919.
Scientific study of Maratha history. Bombay, 1907. 22p.

IOL

I-488
Karve, Irawati (Karmarkar) 1905-1970.
Maharashtra as a cultural region, JUP, v.9
(1958), pp.65-71.

Se Asia   Soc. Sci
B.b

I-489
Kelkar, Narsinha Chintaman, 1872-1947.
Pleasure and privileges of the pen. Ed.
by Kashinath N.Kelkar. Poona, K.N.Kelkar,
pref., 1929. 375p.

UofR

I-490
Kelkar, Narsinha Chintaman, 1872-1947.
Speeches and addresses. Popular ed. Ed.
by Kashinath N.Kelkar. Poona, 1929. 556p.

1. India-Pol & govt-20th cent.

I-491
Kerr, James, trans.
A short historical narrative of the rise
and rapid advancement of the Mahrattah state,
to the present strength and consequence it
has acquired in the East. Written originally
in Persian and translated into English by an
officer in the East India company's service,
i.e. James Kerr. London, T.Cadell, 1782.
170p.

BM

I-492
Khare, Ganesh Hari, 1901-
An interesting Adilshahi farman, IC, v.21
(1948), pp.48-51.

Khare

I-493
Khare, Ganesh Hari, 1901-
Select articles. Poona, 1966. (Bharata
Itihasa Samshodhaka Mandala Puraskrta
Granthamala no.56). 236p.

1. India-Antiq. 2. India-Hist. 3. India-Civil zation

UofR

I-494
Kincaid, Charles Augustus, 1870-
The tale of the Tulasi plant and other
studies. Poona, the author, 1908. 193p.

Bom (Pres) Cat

I-495
Kincaid, Charles Augustus, 1870- and
Parasnis, Dattatraya Balwant.
History of the Maratha people. London,
H.Milford, Oxford University Press, 1918-25.
3v.

1. Marathas. 2. India-Hist.-European settlements,
1500-1765.

U of R

I-496
Kulkarni, Anant Ramchandra, 1925-
Origin of Deshmukh and Deshpande institutions,
IHCP, v.31 (1969), pp.266-71.

History
BDCR I, p. 135

I-497
Kulkarni, Anant Ramchandra, 1925-
Social relations in the Maratha country:
presidential address of section II of the
Jabalpur Session, IHCP, v.32 (1970), pp.1-
34.

History
BDuR   p 135

I-498
Kulkarni, B.R.
Notes on some obscure taxes of the Maratha
regime, JUB, v.22 (1953), pp.1-3.

que

I-499
Leslie, J.H.
Materials for a history of the Bombay Army,
JSAHR, v.10 (1931), pp.155-61, 218-22.

Case

I-500
McDonald, Ellen E.
The growth of regional consciousness in
Maharashtra, IESHR, v.5 (1968), pp.223-43.

JAS aug. 1974

I-501
Machwe, Prabhakar Balvant, 1917-
Maharashtra and its tradition, IFR, v.4
(1967), pp.11, 14.

JAS 9/68   hulai

I-502
Mahajan, D.B.
The Atoles of Shelgaon in Berar. A summary,
IHCP, v.16 (1953), pp.272-73.

4 ofR

I-503
Mahajan, D.B.
Deocates of Sendursana, IHCP, v.15 (1952),
pp.284-88.

uofR

I-504
Mahajan, D.B.
The Deshmukh family of Parwa in Vidarbha,
IHCP, v.21 (1958), pp.343-50.

IHCP

I-505
Mahajan, D.B.
A warrior family of Berar, IHRCP, v.25
(1948), pp.125-30.

IHRC

I-506
   Maratha Bakhars or chronicles and Grant Duff's
   history of the Marathas, QJPSS, v.1,no.2
   (1878), pp.13-23.

GJPSS

I-511
   Nitsure, Keshav Gopal.
      Critical study of the provision for welfare
   activities in the Maratha empire. Poona,
   Univ.of Poona, 1964. *

Jayakar Lis #1458

I-507
   Master, Alfred, 1883-
      Maharastra and Kannada, IA, v.57 (1928),
   pp.174-76.

I-512
   Oturkar, Rajaram Vinayak, 1898-
      Dynamic contents of Chauth and Sardeshmukhi,
   IHCP, v.22 (1959), pp.288-92.

I HCP

I-508
   Merchant, K.D.
      British relations with Surat - 1600 A.D.
   to 1802 A.D. (foundation of the British
   empire in Western India). Bombay, St.Xavier
   College, 1948. *

Case

I-513
   Oturkar, Rajaram Vinayak, 1898-
      Rajput-Maratha cultural relationship, IHCP,
   v.14 (1951), pp.190-92.

4 of R

I-509
   Mukherjee, Jatindra Nath.
      The Maratha empire: rise and fall, MR, v.121
   (1967), pp.421-25.

MP

I-514
   Pagdi, Setumadhava Rao, 1910-
      A Persian chronicle of Maratha history, IHCP,
   v.21 (1958), pp.365-69.

Maratha - history - General

I HCP

I-510
   Nadkarni, Rajaram Vyankatesh.
      The rise and fall of the Maratha Empire.
   Bombay, Popular Prakashan, 1966. 428p.

4 MR

I-515
   Panikkar, Kavalam Madhava, 1896-
      The ring fence system and the Marathas,
   JIH, v.8 (1929), pp.336-45.

NYPL

I-516
  Panse, Murlidhar Gajanan, 1918-
    Regional individuality of Maharashtra,
    QRHS, v.9 (1969/70), pp.219-28.

History - articles
BAS 1970 O

I-517
  Parulekar, S.V.
    Bombay Presidency. Bombay, Social Reform
  Association, 1938.

Singh O

I-518
  Puntambekar, Shrikrishna Venkatesh.
    The Ajnapatra or royal edict, JIH, v.8
  (1929), pp.207-33.

✓✓✓ O

I-519
  Puntambekar, Shrikrishna Venkatesh.
    Maratha polity. Lahore, The Minerva
  Book Shop, 1942. (Minerva Series on
  Government. Pamphlet no.2). 43p.

U of R O

I-520
  Puntambekar, Shrikrishna Venkatesh.
    Old feudal nobility of Maharashtra, IHCP,
  v.5 (1941), pp.47-49.

U of R O

I-521
  Rama Rao, Maremanda, 1906-
    Glimpses of Dakkan history. Bombay, Orient
  Longmans, 1951. 159p.

    1. Deccan, India - Hist.

LC O

I-522
  Ramadas, G.
    Kingdoms of the Deccan, IHQ, v.1 (1925),
  pp.679-89.

IHQ O

I-523
  Ramamurti, Pratapgiri.
    Interstate relations in the Deccan (1294-
  1707). IHCP, v.8 (1944), pp.162-69,306-13.

II O

I-524
  Ranade, Mahadev Govind, 1842-1901.
    Rise of the Maratha power and other essays;
  and Gleanings from Maratha chronicles by K.T.
  Telang. Bombay, University of Bombay, 1961.
  253p.

U of R)

I-525
  Rao, Vasant Dinanath, 1913-
    Bardic literature as source of light on
  the social life of the Marathas, MR, v.71
  (1941), pp.466-87.

I-526
The rise of the navy and army at Bombay,
1742-1760, BQR, v.5 (1857), pp.265-300.

NRU

I-527
Robertson, H.D.
The early history of the Mahratta country,
AJ, v.23 (1827), pp.353-55.

I-528
Saletore, Bhasker Anand.
The antiquity and justification of Chauth,
JUB, v.30,n.s. (1961-62), pp.1-65.

UoR

I-529
Saletore, Bhasker Anand.
A note on Chauthai, its meaning and legality,
NIA, v.1 (1939), p.748.

I-530
Saletore, R.N.
Significance of Chauthai in Maratha history,
JUB, v.7 (1938), pp.94-107.

JUB

I-531
Sardesai, Govind Sakharam, 1865-1959.
The achievements and failures of the
Marathas, MR, v.65 (1939), pp.288-94.

MR

I-532
Sardesai, Govind Sakharam, 1865-1959.
Genealogy of the Bhosle families. Bombay,
India Press, 1941. 11p.

Cal nat Lib

I-533
Sardesai, Govind Sakharam, rao badahur,
1865-1959.
The main currents of Maratha history.
Patna, Patna Univ., 1926. 198p.

UoR

I-534
Sardesai, Govind Sakharam, rao bahadur,
1865-1959.
New history of the Marathas. Bombay,
Phoenix Pubs., 1948-56. 3v.

UoR

I-535
Sardesai, Govind Sakharam, 1865-1959.
The role of the Ghorpades in Maratha
history, MR, v.67 (1940), pp.523-26.

MR

I-536
Sarkar, Sir Jadunath, 1870-1958.
Maratha history newly presented, MR, v.80
(1946), pp.461-62.

Case

I-537
Sarkar, Upendra Nath.
A note on the genealogy of the Angrias,
IHQ, v.27 (1951), pp.161-65.

IHQ

I-538
Savarkar, Vinayak Damodar, 1883-1966.
Hindu-pad-padashahi; or, a review of the
Hindu empire of Maharashtra. Poona,
N.N.Kelkar, 1942. (Manohar Granth Mala
Publications, no.27). 292p.

IOL

I-539
Sen, Surendra Nath, 1890-
Administrative system of the Marathas, from
original sources. Calcutta, University of
Calcutta, 1923. 633p.

SOAS

I-540
Sen, Surendra Nath, 1890-
The Maratha maritime power - a review. In:
Bharata Kaumudi: Studies in Indology in
honour of Dr. Radha Kumud Mookerji. Alla-
habad, 1945-1947. pp.769-78.

Bhandarkar I n.t.y
Comm. vols.

I-541
Sen, Surendra Nath, 1890-
Military system of the Marathas. New ed.
Bombay, Orient Longmans, 1958. 248p.

1. Mahrattas. 2. India - Hist., Military.
3. India - Hist., Naval.

U of R

I-542
Sen, Surendra Nath, 1890-
The theory of the Maratha constitution,
MR, v.27 (1920), pp.640-46.

Case

I-543
Sen, Surendra Nath, 1890-
The survival of old Hindu institutions in
Maharashtra. In: Sir Asutosh Mukherji
Silver Jubilee Vol.I. Calcutta, Calcutta
Univ., 1921. pp.49-68.

U of R
Bhandarkar Inst.-Comm V
Orient & Afr Series

I-544
Sharma, Shripad Rama, 1897-
Maratha history re-examined, 1295-1707.
Bombay, Karnatak Pub.House, 1944. 348p.

LC

I-545
Shejwalkar, Trymbak Shankar.
The geographic factor in the history of
Maharashtra, BICRI, v.1 (1939), pp.112-13.

BICRI, p 137

I-546
 Shejwalkar, Trymbak Shankar.
  Is the Ajña-patra of Ramchandrapant spurious?
  In: A volume of studies in Indology presented
  to Prof.P.V.Kane, ed.by S.M.Katre and P.K.
  Gode. Poona, Oriental Book Agency, 1941.
  pp.447-55.

4 7 R

I-547
 Shejwalkar, Trymbak Shankar.
  What Shivaji and the Maratha state owed to
  Vijayanagar. In: Vijayanagara sexcentenary
  commemorative volume. Ed.by Vijayanagara
  Empire Sexcentenary Association. Dharwar,
  1936. pp.125-38.

4 7 R

I-548
 Shende, Shankar Ramachandra.
  Avanti deśa, birthplace of Maharashtra.
  In: Vikrama volume. Ed.by Radha Kumud Moo-
  kerji. Ujjain, Vikram bimillennium cele-
  bration committee, 1948. pp.547-56.

I O L P J . 5 8 7

I-549
 A short account of the Marratta State. Written
 in Persian, by a Munshy that accompanied
 Colonel Upton on his embassy to Poonah, tr.
 by William Chambers, AM, v.1 (1785), pp.
 213-49.

AM

I-550
 Shrivastavya, Vidayanand Swami.
  Angreys of Kolaba in British records, 1719
  A.D. to 1884 A.D. Poona, B.K.Shrivastavya,
  1950. 296p.

4 7 R

I-551
 Shrivastavya, Vidayanand Swami.
  Are Rajput-Maratha marriages morganatic?
  Ed.by Birendra Kumar Vidyanand Shrivastavya.
  Poona, Pub.by D.K.Shrivastavya for Aitihasik
  Gaurav Grantha Mala, 1952. 277p.

4 7 R

I-552
 Shrivastavya, Vidayanand Swami.
  Elements amongst the Marathas. Ed.by
  Birendra Kumar Vidyanand Shrivastavya.
  Poona, D.K.Shrivastavya for Aitihasik
  Gaurav Grantha Mala, 1952. 263p.

4 7 R

I-553
 Singh, Govind Saran, 1930-
  An evaluation of the State of Maharashtra,
  its historical development and factors of
  unity and disunity. Worcester, Mass., Clark
  University, 1961-62. *

case

I-554
 Singh, Govind Saran, 1930-
  Maratha geopolitics and the Indian nation.
  Bombay Manaktalas, 1966. 220p.

4 7 R

I-555
 Sprengel, Matthias Christian, 1746-1803.
  Geschichte der Maratten, bis auf den
  lezeten Frieden mit England, 1782. Nebst
  einer charte. Halle, Johann Jacob Gebaner,
  1786. 256p.

Cal Nat Lib

I-556
  Telang, Kasinath Trimbak, 1840-1893.
     Gleanings from Maratha chronicles, ICOP,
     v.9,pt.1 (1892), pp.252-81.

U ɤ R

I-561
  Translation of an account of the Morattas
     from the reign of Shaw Jehan to the begin-
     ning of that of Shaw Allum, from a Persian
     Ms.obtained at Allahabad, January 1769, OR,
     v.1 (1793), pp.403-418.

UɤR
inter library loan
Harvard (photocopy)

I-557
  Tikekar, Shripad Ramachandra, 1900-
     Indexing of books on Maratha history. In:
     Studies in Indian history; Dr.A.G.Pawar
     felicitation volume. Ed.by V.D.Rao. Kol-
     hapur, Y.P.Pawar, 1968. pp.322-33.

UɤR

I-562
  Vinchoorkar, S.R.
     A brief history of the Vinchoorkar family.
     Poona, the author, 1910. 128p.

Bom (Pres)cat

I-558
  Tikekar, Shripad Ramachandra, 1900-
     Maharashtra; the land, its people and their
     culture. New Delhi, Maharashtra Information
     Centre, 1966. 62p.

IBP

I-563
  Wagh, Dinkar Mukund.
     Geographical factors in the rise and fall
     of the Marathas. Poona, Poona Univ., 1966.
     2v. *

Jayakar Lib. # 1411

I-559
  Tone, William Henry, d.1802.
     Illustrations of some institutions of the
     Mahratta people. Calcutta, Printed by
     D.Lankheet, 1818. 77p.

Nat'l Lib Calcutta

I-564
  Waring, Edward Scott.
     A history of the Mahrattas; to which is
     prefixed, an historical sketch of the Deccan:
     containing a short account of the rise and
     fall of the Mooslim sovereignties prior to the
     era of Mahratta independence. London, Printed
     for John Richardson, 1810. 291p.

U ɤ R

I-560
  Tone, William Henry, d.1802.
     A letter to an officer on the Madras estab-
     lishment: being an attempt to illustrate some
     particular institutions of the Maratta people;
     principally relative to their system of war
     and finance. Also an account of the political
     changes of the empire, in the year 1796 as
     published in the Bombay Courier. Bombay,
     Printed at the Courier press, 1796. 118p.

NYPL

I-565
  Wheeler, James Talboys, 1824-1897.
     Summary of affairs of the Mahratta States,
     1627-1856. Bombay, Office of the Supit.of
     Govt.Print., 1878. 386p.

SOAS supp

I-566
Wilson, John, 1804-1875.
History of the suppression of Infanticide in western India under the government of Bombay, including notices of the provinces and tribes in which the practice prevailed. London, Smith, Elder & co., 1855. 457p.

Maharashtra - Hist. - Fiction

I-567
Abbott, Anstice.
Indian idylls. London, Elliot Stock, 1911. 160p.

Gupta #59

I-568
Bharucha, Perin.
The fire worshippers; a novel about the Parsis of India. Bombay, Strand Book Club, 1968. 219p.

PL 480
LC 1968

I-569
Bray, Claude Arthur.
Randall Davenant: a tale of the Mahrattas. London, F.Warne & co., 1892. 389p.

BM

I-570
Brereton, Frederick Sadlier, 1872-
Jones of the 64th: a tale of the battles of Assaye and Laswarie. London, Blackie & son, 1907. 349p.

BM
Gupta #319

I-571
Bruce, Henry.
The wonder mist; a sea story. London, John Long, 1917.

Gupta # 344

I-572
Chitale, Venu.
In transit. Bombay, Hind Kitabs, 1950. 514p.

U AR

I-573
Cox, Phillip.
Rani of Jhansi; a historical play in four acts. London, George Allen & Unwin, 1953. 119p.

1. Fiction.

I-574
Dutt, Romesh Chunder, 1848-1909.
Sivaji, a historical tale of the great Mahratta hero and patriot, tr.by Ajoy Chandra Dutt from the original Bengali. Allahabad, Kitabistan, 1944. 274p.

1. Sivaji, raja, 1627-1680 - Fiction.

U AR

I-575
Ennis, John.
The great Bombay explosion. New York, Duell, Sloan, and Pearce, 1959. 182p.

I-576
Fraser, William Alexander, 1859-1933.
Caste. Toronto, Hodder and Stoughton, 1922.
274p.

pre 56 imprints   Anglo-Marathe hostilities
Gupta # 768

I-581
Kincaid, Dennis, 1905-1937.
Their ways divide. London, Chatto and
Windus, 1936. 308p.

IOL   Anglo-marathe relations.
Gupta # 1142

I-577
Hockley, William Browne, 1792-1860.
Pandurang Hari, or, Memoirs of a Hindoo.
London, Printed for Geo.B.Whittaker, 1826.
3v.

pre '56 imprints   story of a marathe warlord.
Gupta #999

I-582
King, Dorothy Amelia, 1892-
In the days of Shivaji; from In wild Maratha
battle by Michael MacMillan. Bombay, Blackie,
19--. 128p.

4 of R

I-578
Home, Dhirendra Chandra, 1914-
So many! So gallant! Bombay, Current Book
House, 1951. 106p.

married group in Bombay in the thirties

I-583
Kotewal, Bejanji Ruttonji.
Matheran. Bombay, the author, 1906. 69p.

1. Matheran - Poetry.

Bom (Pres) cat

I-579
Judah, Aaron, 1923-
Clown of Bombay, a novel. London,
Faber and Faber, 1963. 252p.

LC.

I-584
Krishnanath Raghunathji.
Excess, or the first twenty-four years of
my neighbour's life. Bombay, Family Print.
Press, 1895. 116p.

Bom (Pres) cat

I-580
Kincaid, Dennis, 1905-1937.
The final image. London, Routlage, 1939.
246p.

BM
Gupta # 1139

I-585
Macmillan, Michael, 1853-1925.
In wild Maratha battle: a tale of the days
of Shivaji. London, Blackie & son, 1905.
239p.

BM
Gupta # 1227

I-586
  Macmillan, Michael, 1853-1925.
    The last of the Peshwas; a tale of
  the third Maratha War. London, Blackie,
  1919. (The Star of India series). 274p.

1, Maratha War, 1816-1818.—Fiction.

UofR

I-587
  Madhaviah, Appaviyar.
    Clarida: a historical novel. Madras,
  Authors Press, 1915. 266p.

IOL
Gupta #1238

I-588
  Mather, Berkely, pseud.
    The road and the star. London, Collins,
  1965. 306p.

LC 63/47

I-589
  Murad Ali Beg, Mirza.
    Lalun the beragun; or, the battle of Pani-
  pat. Bombay, Ranina's Union Press, 1884.
  217p.

Calcutta Nat'l Lib
Gupta #1368

I-590
  Phadke, Narayan Sitaram.
    Leaves in the August wind; a novel with the
  Indian upheaval of August 1942 for its back-
  ground. Bombay, Hind Kitabs, 1947. 174p.

            1. India - Hist., 1919-

NYPL

I-591
  Sellon, Edward.
    Herbert Breakspear: a legend of the Mahratta
  war. London, Whittaker, 1848. 148p.

IOL
Gupta # 1862

I-592
  Sorabji, Cornelia, 1866-
    The purdahnashin, etc. Calcutta, Thacker,
  Spink & co., 1917. 98p.

BM

I-593
  Spencer, Francis Angus.
    The four horned altar. London, Heath
  Cranton, 1913. 303p.

IOL
Gupta #1959

I-594
  Taylor, Meadows, 1808-1876.
    Tara, a Mahratta tale. Edinburgh, W.Black-
  wood, 1863. 3 vols.

UofR

I-595
  Verne, Jules, 1828-1905.
    The steam house. Trans. by Agnes D.Kingston.
  New ed. London, S.Low, Marston, Searle and
  Rivington, 1883. 142p.

NRO

I-596
White, Michael.
    Lachmi Bai Rani of Jhansi, the Jeanne d'Arc
of India. New York, J.F.Taylor, 1901. 297p.

    1. India - Hist. - Sepoy Rebellion - Fiction.

LC

I-597
White, Stanley.
    Brave Captain Kelso. London, Hutchinson,
1959. 224p.

Sources & documents

I-598
Albuquerque, Affonso de, 1453-1515.
    Cartas para el-rei d. Manuel I. Selecção,
prefácio e notas de António Baião. Lisboa,
Livraria Sá da Costa, 1942. (Colecçao de
classicos Sá da Costa). 279p.

LC

I-599
Avalikar, Dattatreya Narhar, 1931-
    Marathi manuscripts in Karnatak, *JKU*, v.2
(1958), pp.104-12.

I-600
Bokhari, S.A.R.
    Persian sources of the history of the
Carnatic, *JMU*, v.33,no.2 (1962), pp.137-
43.

JAS '62

I-601
Bombay (Presidency)
    Correspondence exhibiting the nature and use
of the Poona Duftur, and the measures adopted
for its preservation and arrangement since the
introduction of British rule. Also a selection
of papers explanatory of the origin of the
Inam Commission and of its progress from 1843...
until...1852... Bombay, Education Society's
Press, 1856. (Selections from the records,
n.s.,no.30).

I-602
Bombay (Presidency).
    Selections from the records of the
Bombay government... Bombay, Govt.Central
Press, 18- . v.

I-603
Bombay (Presidency) Record Office.
    Press list of ancient documents preserved
in the Bombay Record Office, 1646-1700
(-1740-1760) Bombay, 1904?-23.

I-604
Bombay (State).
    Source material for a history of the
freedom movement in India. Collected
from Bombay government records. Bombay,
Government Publications, 1957-1958. 2vols.
Part 1, 1818-1885; part 2, 1885-1920.

I-605
Bombay (State) Directorate of Archives.
    Descriptive catalogue of the Secret and
Political Department series, 1755-1820.
Comp.by V.G.Dighe. Bombay, Printed at the
Govt.Central Press, 1954. (Bombay records
series. Descriptive catalogue, v.1) 713p.

I-606
Bombay (State) Directorate of Archives.
Persian records of Maratha history.
General ed.P.M.Joshi. Bombay, 1953-
in progress.

SOAS

I-607
Cox, Edmund Charles, bart., 1856-
Bombay State papers. CR, v.87 (1888),
pp.1-19.

CR

I-608
Danvers, Frederick Charles, 1833-1906.
Dutch activities in the East, 17th century;
being a "Report on the records relating to
the state archives in the Hague", ed.by
Nihar-ranjan Ray. 1st ed. Calcutta, Book
Emporium, 1945. 101p.

4 of R

I-609
Das Gupta, Ashin.
Dutch materials and modern Indian history.
RHS, v.3 (1963-64), pp.47-50.

Case

I-610
D'Costa, Anthony.
Garcia de Orta: as a source of Indian
history, Indica, v.7 (1970), pp.121-32.

modern history — books
BAS

I-611
Diehl, Katharine Smith, comp.
Primary sources for 16th-19th century
studies in Bengal, Orissa, and Bihar librar-
ies; seminar papers. Calcutta, American
Institute of Indian Studies, Calcutta
Center, 1971. 280p.

4 of R

I-612
Dighe, Vishwanath Govind.
Jamav Daftar: an important source for the
social history of the Marathas, BV, v.9
(1948), pp.143-47.

Case

I-613
Douglas, James, 1826-1904.
Bombay and western India, a series of state
papers. London, S.Low, Marston, 1893. 2v.

U of R

I-614
East India Company (English)
An authentic copy of the correspondence in
India between the country powers and the ...
East India Company's Servants, ... together
with the minutes of the Supreme Council at
Calcutta. London, Printed for J.Debrett,
1787. 6 vols.

LC

I-615
East India Company (English)
Bengal, also Fort George and Bombay papers,
presented to the House of Commons, pursuant
to their orders of the 7th of May last, from
the East India Company, relative to the Marhatta War in 1803. London, 1804. 606p.

SOAS

I-616
  East India Company (English)
    Selection of papers from the records at
the East-India House, relating to the revenue,
police, and civil and criminal justice under
the company's governments in India. London,
1820-26. 4 vols.

BAS

I-617
  Extracts and documents relating to Maratha
history. Ed. by Surendra Nath Sen.
Calcutta, Univ.of Calcutta. 1920-
(Series)

U of R have, v 1-2

I-618
  Forrest, Sir George William, 1846-1926.
    Alphabetical catalogue of the contents of
the Bombay Secretariat Records, 1630-1780.
Bombay, 1887. 175p.

I-619
  Forrest, Sir George William, 1846-1926, ed.
    Selections from letters, despatches, and
other state papers preserved in the Bombay
Secretariat, Home series. Bombay, 1887. 2v.

I-620
  Forrest, Sir George William, 1846-1926, ed.
    Selections from the letters, despatches,
and other state papers preserved in the
Bombay Secretariat, Maratha series, vol.1.
Bombay, Printed at the Government Central
Press, 1885. 729p.

pv 1955 NUC

I-621
  Forrest, Sir George William, 1846-1926, ed.
    Selections from the letters, despatches,
and other state papers preserved in the
Foreign department of the Government of
India 1772-1785. Calcutta, Printed by the
Superintendent of Government Print., India,
1890. 3v.

U of R

I-622
  Forrest, Sir George William, 1846-1926, ed.
    Selections from the state papers of the
governors-general of India. Oxford, B.H.
Blackwell; London, Constable & co., ltd.,
1910-26. 4v.

U of R

I-623
  Great Britain. India Office.
    Report to the Secretary of State for India
by F.C.Danvers. Amsterdam, N.Israel, 1922.
(Original t.p. read: Report to the Secretary
of State for India in council on the Portu-
guese records relating to the East Indies ...
By F.C.Danvers, Superintendent of records
India Office, London. London, 1892) 221p.

U of R

I-624
  Gune, Vithal Trimbak.
    An outline of the administrative institutions
of the Portuguese territories in India and
the growth of their central archives at
Goa-16th to 19th century A.D. In: Studies
in Indian history, Dr. A.G.Pawar felicitation
volume. Ed.by V.D.Rao. Kolhapur, Y.P.Pawar,
1968. pp.47-92.

UofR

I-625
  Gupte, Balkrishna Atmaram, 1851- comp.
    Selections from the historical records of
the hereditary minister of Baroda. Consisting
of letters from Bombay, Baroda, Poona and
Satara governments. Collected by B.A.Gupte.
Calcutta, The Univ.of Calcutta, 1922. 135p.

    1. Baroda (State) - Hist. - Sources.

U of R

I-626
    Hague. International Court of Justice.
       Case concerning right of passage over
    Indian territory (Portugal v. India) ...
    Hague, 1960. (It's pleadings, oral
    arguments, documents) 5v.

4 of R

I-627
    India, Portuguese. Arquivo Historico do
       Estado da India.
       Agentes da diplomacia portuguesa na
    India (hindus, muçulmanos, judeus e
    parses) Documentos coordenados, anotados
    e prefaciados por Panduronga S.S.Pissur-
    lencar, director do Arquivo Historico do
    Estado da India. Bastora, Goa, Tip.
    Rangel, 1952. 715p.

1 India, Portuguese — Hist.-Sources.

LC

I-628
    India, Portuguese. Arquivo Historico do
       Estado da India.
       Roteiro dos Arquivos da India Portuguesa.
    Introdução e notas por Ponduronga S.S.Pissur-
    lencar. Bastora, Tip.Rangel, 1955. 282p.

1. Archives — India, Portuguese

LC

I-629
    India, Portuguese. Conselho do Estado.
       Assentos. Documentos coordenados e
    anotados por Panduronga S.S.Pissurlencar,
    director do Arquivo Historico do Estado da
    India. Bastora, Goa, Tip.Rangel, 1953-57.
    5 vols. (Publicações do Arquivo Histórico
    do Estado da India, 3-6,8).

(series)
1. India, Portuguese — Hist. — Sources.

U of R

I-630
    Khan, Sir Shafa'at Ahmad, 1893-
       Sources for the history of British India in
    the 17th century. London, N.Y., H.Milford,
    Oxford Univ.Press, 1926. (Allahabad Univer-
    sity studies in history, v.4) 406p.

    India - Hist. - Sources - Bibl.

LC

I-631
    Khare, Ganesh Hari, 1901-
       Archives from the Deshmukh and Deshpande
    families of Kasegaon, Sholapur, Bombay, IHRCP,
    v.31 (1955), pp.77-80.

IHRC

I-632
    Khare, Ganesh Hari, 1901-
       The archives of the Deshmukh family of
    Sholapur, IHCP, v.16 (1953), pp.273-75.

4 of R

I-633
    Khare, Ganesh Hari, 1901-
       A document on the influence of Shahaji in
    the South, JIH, v.30 (1952), pp.17-20.

JIH

I-634
    Khare, Ganesh Hari, 1901-
       Documents from the Ghatapande family of Junnar
    (Poona), IHRCP, v.29 (1953), pp.69-72.

II

I-635
    Khare, Ganesh Hari, 1901-
       Records from a Deshmukh family of Naldurg,
    IHRCP, v.32 (1956), pp.46-49.

IHRCP

I-636
Khare, Ganesh Hari, 1901-
  Records from the Mane family of Mhaswad,
North Satara, CR, v.135 (1955), pp.168-72.

Siver   O

I-637
Khare, Ganesh Hari, 1901-
  Records of a Ghatpande family of Junnar
(Poona), IHRCP, v.29 (1953), pp.69-72.

I H R C P   O

I-638
Khare, Ganesh Hari, 1901-
  Records of the Rajajna family of Wai,
IHRCP, v.27 (1950), pp.115-20.

UoqR   O

I-639
Khare, Ganesh Hari, 1901-
  Scraps from a scrap dealer, IHRCP, v.35
(1960), pp.134-39.

IHRC   O

I-640
Khare, Ganesh Hari, 1901-
  Some new records of the Peshwa Period,
IHRCP, v.23 (1946), pp.3-5.

U qR   O

I-641
Khare, Ganesh Hari, 1901-
  Some Persian records from a Sardar Natu
family of Poona, IHRCP, v.26 (1951), pp.12-
15.

IH RCP   O

I-642
Khare, Ganesh Hari, 1901-
  Some records of the Peshwa period, IHRCP,
v.23 (1946), pp.3-5.

I HRCP   O

I-643
Khare, Ganesh Hari, 1901-
  Two new documents on the battle of Sakhar-
khedle, 1724 A.D., IHRCP, v.25 (1950), pp.48-
51.

I HRC P   O

I-644
Kibe, Madhav Vinayak, 1877-
  Glimpses from the records of Diwan Palshikar
family, Indore, IHRCP, v.31 (1955), pp.157-
60.

4 qR   )

I-645
Kibe, Madhav Vinayak, 1877-
  A note on the Athalye collection at Shiposhi,
district Ratnagiri, Bombay Province, IHRCP,
v.17 (1940), pp.50-73.

IHRC   )

I-646
  Kibe, Madhav Vinayak, 1877-
    Some original Marathi documents, IHRCP,
    v.18 (1942), pp.323-27.

IHRC

I-647
  Maharashtra, India (State) Dept.of Archives.
  Marāthyāñcyā itihāsācī sādhane; Portugija
  daptara. Bombay, Dept.of Archives,

maharashtra Lasr...
Prakāsna 1971

I-648
  Monumenta Historiae Indiae.
    Extracts from the Dutch diaries of the
    castle of Batavia. VI. JBHS, v.2 (1929), pp.
    240-68.

JBHS

I-649
  Mostyn, Thomas.
    The third English embassy to Poona, com-
    prising Mostyn's diary, Sept.1772 to Feb.
    1774. Ed.by James H.Cense and D.R.Banaji.
    Bombay, D.B.Taraporevala and sons, 1934.
    446p.

    1. Bombay - Hist. - Sources.

4 of R

I-650
  Mundi, B.N.
    Some sources of Maratha history in Madhya
    Bharat. IHCP, v.15 (1952), pp.387-88.

4 of R

I-651
  Nilakanta Sastri, Kallidaikurichi Aiyah
  Aiyar, 1892-
    Some Dutch documents on the siege of Jinji
    and the capitulation of Pondicherry (1692-
    93 A.D.), IHRCP, v.17 (1940), pp.34-38.

U of R

I-652
  Nilakanta Sastri, Kallidaikurichi Aiyah
  Aiyar, 1892-
    Sources of Indian history with special
    reference to South India. London, Asia Pub.
    House, c.1964. (Heras memorial lectures,
    1961) 113p.

U of R

I-653
  Pagdi, Setumadhava Rao, 1910-
    Imshae Madhoram, a Persian source of Mughal-
    Maratha conflict (1690-1700). JIH, v.44 (1966),
    pp.269-88.

JIH 66

I-654
  Parasnis, Dattatraya Balwant, 1870-1926.
    Maratha historical literature, ASBJ, v.22
    (1905-1908), pp.168-78.

ASBJ

I-655
  Parasnis, Dattatraya Balwant, 1870-1926.
    A note on Marathi historical records and
    their publication, IHRCP, v.3 (1921), pp.51-
    63.

IHRCP

I-656
Parasnis, Dattatraya Balwant, 1870-1926.
A note on the Maratha records relating to
the history of South India, <u>IHRCP</u>, v.6 (1924),
pp.57-62.

IHRCP

I-657
Parasnis, Dattatraya Balwant, 1870-1926.
Note on the Peshwas' records and their
historical value with a few extracts from
Chitnishi letters, <u>IHRCP</u>, v.7 (1925), pp.
35-43.

IHRCP

I-658
Pissurlencar, Panduronga S.S.,ed.
Regimentos das fortalezas da India;
estudo e notas. Bastora, Tip.Rangel,
1951. 557p.

1.Gra-Polegovt   2. Gen-Hist.-Source
NUR
LC

I-659
Ranade, Mahadev Govind, 1842-1901.
Introduction to the Satara Raja's and
the Peshwa's diaries. Poona, D.B.Parasnis.
Deccan, Vernacular Translation Society,
1902. 30p.

Cop Nat'l Lib

I-660
Ranadive, R.K.
Maratha historical records, <u>IHRCP</u>, v.6
(1924), pp.63-73.

IHRCP

I-661
Rawlinson, Hugh George, 1880-
A visit to the Parasnis museum, <u>IHRCP</u>, v.11
(1928), pp.20-21.

IHRCP

I-662
Rawlinson, Hugh George, 1880- and
Patwardhan, R.P.
Source book of Maratha history. Bombay,
Govt.Central Press, 1929- 1v.

NYPL

I-663
Saletore, Bhasker Anand.
The value of Kannada sources for the
history of the Marathas, the Bijapur
and Mughal Sultans. In: Sardesai Commemorative Volume. Ed.by Shripad R.Tike-
kar. Bombay, 1938. pp.187-96.

Bhandarkar Index
to Current Vol's

I-664
Sardesai, Govind Sakharam, 1865-1959.
The historical records in Kotah, <u>MR</u>, v.94
(1953), p.451.

Case

I-665
Sardesai, Govind Sakharam, 1865-1959.
The Marathi records of Kotah, <u>IHRCP</u>, v.30
(1954), pp.120-26.

IHRCP

I-666
　　Sarkar, Sir Jadunath, 1870-1958.
　　　Maratha family records of the 17th century.
　　IHRCP, v.9 (1926), pp.22-24.

IHRCP

I-667
　　Sarkar, Sir Jadunath, 1870-1958.
　　　A new source of Maratha history, MR, v.77
　　(1945), pp.13-15.

Case

I-668
　　Sarkar, Sir Jadunath, 1870-1958.
　　　Sources of Maratha history ˌsources in the
　　Persian languageˌ. JUB, v.10 (1941), pp.1-22.

Case

I-669
　　Sarkar, Sir Jadunath, 1970-1958.
　　　Sources of the history of Shivaji critically
　　examined, JBRS, v.10 (1924), pp.70-87.

NYPL

I-670
　　Sarkar, Sir Jadunath, 1870-1958.
　　　True sources of Maratha history. MR, v.47
　　(1930), pp.305-309.

U of R

I-671
　　Sen, Surendra Nath, 1890-
　　　A brief survey of Portuguese sources of
　　Maratha history, BISMHM, (1928), pp.31-35.

NUR
JBHS (1929)

I-672
　　Sen, Surendra Nath, 1890-
　　　A preliminary report on the historical
　　records at Goa. Calcutta, Univ.Press, 1925.
　　90p.

NYPL

I-673
　　Sharma, Sri Ram, 1900-
　　　Newspapers as a source of modern Indian
　　history, IHRCP, v.29 (1953), pp.130-32.

Case

I-674
　　Singh, Ganda.
　　　The Persian Akhbars in the Alienation Office,
　　Poona, IHRCP, v.16 (1939), pp.123-28.

IHRCP

I-675
　　Srinivasachari, Chidambaram S., 1890-1951.
　　　Selections from Orme manuscripts. Annama-
　　lainagar, Annamalai University, 1952. 409p.

　　　1. India - Hist. - 18th cent. - Sources.

U of R

I-676
Srinivasachari, Chidambaram S., 1890-1951.
Sources of Maratha history, IR, v.43 (1943),
pp.467-69.

Maharashtrian areas | Local history

I-677
An age of progress in Bombay, 1740-1762, BQR,
v.5 (1857), pp.158-96.

NRU

I-678
Anderson, Philip, d.1857.
The English in western India; being the
early history of the factory at Surat, of
Bombay, and the subordinate factories on the
western coast. From the earliest period until
the commencement of the 18th cent. London,
Smith, Elder & co., 1864. 203p.

1. Surat, India - Hist. 2. Bombay - Hist.
3. India - History - European settlements, 1500-
1765. 4. East India Co. (English) 5. British
in India.

LC

I-679
An appeal to British justice and honour. The
treatment of the protected native states
of India by the government of the East India
Company, illustrated in the case of the
principality of Colaba. London, Smith,
Elder & co., 1841. 43p.

pre '56 imprints

I-680
Askari, Syed Hasan.
Mughal naval weakness and Aurangzeb's
attitude towards the traders and pirates
on the western coast, JBRS, v.45 (1960),
pp.1-15. Also in: IHCP, v.24 (1961),
pp.162-70.

II

I-681
Banaji, Dady Rustomji, 1903-
Bombay and the Sidis. London, Pub.for
the Univ.of Bombay, Macmillan, 1932. 505p.

I-682
Banerji, Adris.
Sivaneri; the birthplace of Sivaji, MR,
v.62 (1937), pp.267-71.

I-683
Basu, Baman Das, 1867-1930.
The story of Satara; ed.by Ramananda
Chatterjee. Calcutta, Modern Review office,
1922. 574p.

1. Satara, India (Principality)

I-684
Beckingham, C.F.
Amba Gesen and Asirgarh, JSemS, v.2 (1957),
pp.182-88.

1. Kings of Khandesh.

II

I-685
Bhave, Vasudeo Krishna, 1885-
Puri the capital of Konkan, IHCP, v.4 (1940),
pp.86-88.

I-686
Bhedwar, P.S.
Development of Bombay, 1797-1827.
Bombay, Bombay University, 195-*

I-687
Bombay (Presidency)
An historical account of the Belgaum
District in the Bombay Presidency. By
Henry John Stokes. Bombay, 1870. (Bombay
Presidency. selections from the records,
n.s.,no.115). 95p.

BM

I-688
Bombay (Presidency)
Memoir on the Satara territory. By Thomas
Robert Hughes. Bombay, Bombay Education
Society Press, 1857. (Bombay Presidency.
Selections from the records, n.s.,no.41)

IOL

I-689
Bombay (Presidency)
Rough notes containing historical, statistical and other information connected with ...
Junjeera and Jowar, in the Tanna collectorate;
Sucheen, Dhurumpoor and Bansda, in the Surat
collectorate; Cambay, in the Kaira collectorate;
Penth, in the Nasik sub-collectorate; and the
... states under the control of the Collector
of Khandesh. Historical narative of ... Cambay
from Sanskrit and Persian books ... Observations on the "bore" ... in ... the Gulf of
(Continued on next card)

Bombay (Presidency)   (Card 2)

Cambay ... Procedings connected with the ...
succession to the Penth estate ... 1837 ...
Historical sketch of the Bheel Tribes. Ed.by R.
Hughes Thomas. Bombay, 1856. (Bombay Presidency. Selections from the records, n.s.,
no.26) 268p.

I-690
Bombay (Presidency) Appendix.
A description of the Port and Island of
Bombay and an historical account of the
transactions between the English and Portu-
gueze concerning it, from the year 1661,
to this present time. London, 1724.

I-691
Bombay (Presidency) Political Department.
A memoir of the states of the southern
Maratha country. By Edward William West.
Bombay, 1869. (Bombay Presidency. Selections
from the records, n.s.,no.113).

LSR
BM

I-692
Bombay (Presidency) Political Department.
Memoir on the Sawunt Waree State by
W.Courtney and J.W.Auld, and statistical
report on the Portuguese settlements in
India...;by Captain Kol...;edited by
R.H.Thomas. Bombay, 1885. (Bombay Pres-
idency. Selections from the records, n.s.,
no.10).

IOL

I-693
Bombay (Presidency) Political Department.
Minute by John Malcolm on the territories
of Sattara, the Dooab and Colapore. Dated
Bombay, February 22, 1829. Bombay, 1829.

BM

I-694
Bombay (Presidency) Political Department.
Statistical report of the Colaba agency.
By W.M.Hearn. Bombay, 1854. (Bombay
Presidency. Selections from the records,
n.s.,no.7).

Ind Off Lib

I-695
Bombay (Presidency) Political Department.
Statistical report on the principality of
Kolhapoor, comp.by D.C.Graham, to which are
appended extracts from brief notes relative
to Kolhapoor and its dependent Jageerdars;
by G.Malcolm; ed.by R.H.Thomas. Bombay, 1854.
(Bombay Presidency. Selections from the
records. n.s.,no.8)

IOL

I-696
Bombay, as it was, 1668 and as it is 1878.
An appeal for labourers. London, 1879.

Calcutta Nat'l Lib.

I-697
Bombay Port Trust.
Bombay, the gateway of India. Compiled by
W.R.S.Sharpe, deputy chairman. Bombay, 1931.
91p.

u of R

I-698
Bombay through a camera. 6th ed. Bombay, D.B.
Taraporevala and sons, 1919. 24p.

I-699
Brydges, Sir Harford Jones, 1764-1847.
Case of the Rajah of Satara. Letter to the
Hoh.the Court of Directors of the East India
Company. London, J.Wilson, 1843. 15p.

I-700
Bulsara, Jal Feerose, 1899-
Bombay; a city in the making. Bombay,
1948. (Bombay citizenship series, no.1)
147p.

IOL

I-701
Burke, R.C., ed.
Notes on the Sangli State. Kolhapur Mission
Press, 1909? 477p.

1. Sangli, India (State) - Pol.& govt.

4 of R

I-702
Burnell, John, fl.1712.
Bombay in the days of Queen Anne, being
an account of the settlement, written by
John Burnell. London, Printed for the
Hakluyt Society, 1933. 122p.

U of R

I-703
Burton, R.W.
Poona and Ahmednagar: some former military
events. ISRM, v.1 (1928), pp.553-56.

I-704
Cadell, Sir Patrick Robert, 1871-
The acquisition and rise of Bombay, RASGBIJ,
series 3,pt.3&4 (1958), pp.113-21.

NRU

I-705
    Case of the deposed Rajah of Sattarat (sic)
    refusal of the Bombay government to inquire
    into charges against Lieut.Col.Ovans and
    Ballajee Punt Nathoo; preferred by Krushnajee
    Sudasew Bhidey. London, 1845.

NLC

I-710
    Chaghtai, M.A.
        Sixteenth century Persian documents concern-
    ing Nazarbas (Nandurbar) in Khandesh, IHRCP,
    v.19 (1943), pp.15-20.

II

I-706
    Castilho, Antonio de.
        Commentario de cerco de Goa e Chaul no anno
    de 1570. Lisboa Occidental, 1736. 32p.

I-711
    Chaghtai, M.A.
        Three Persian documents concerning Baglana
    (Baglan) in Khandesh, IHRCP, v.24 (1948),
    pp.14-17.

II

I-707
    Chaghtai, M.A.
        More about Poona in the Muslim period,
    NIA, v.5 (1942), pp.274-75.

Annual Bib of Hist &
Industry

I-712
    A chapter in the history of Bombay, BQR, v.3
    (1856), pp.56-77.

NRU

I-708
    Chaghatai, M.A.
        Nagpur - a forgotten kingdom, BDCRI, v.2,
    (1940-41), pp.166-83.

history

I-713
    Comes, Henry.
        Kalyan the ancient gateway of India,
    Indica. v.5 (1968), pp.1-23.

I-709
    Chaghtai, M.A.
        Poona in the Muslim period, BDCRI, v.2
    (1941), pp.406-10.

I-714
    Cowley, Cecil, 1884-
        Tales of Ahmednagar. Bombay, Thacker and
    Company, 1919. 75p.

1. Ahmednagar - Hist

I-715
Cox, Edmund Charles, bart., 1856-
My thirty years in India. London, Mills &
Boon, 1909. 317p.

Bombay - local history

NUR

I-716
Da Cunha, Joseph Gerson, 1842-1900.
Notes on the history and antiquities
of Chaul, ASBJ, v.12 (1876), pp.51-162.

ASBJ

I-717
Da Cunha, Joseph Gerson, 1842-1900.
Notes on the history and antiquities of
Chaul and Bassein. Bombay, 1876. 278p.

SOAS

I-718
Da Cunha, Joseph Gerson, 1842-1900.
Notes on the history and antiquities of
the island of Bassein, ASBJ, v.10 (1871-74),
pp.316-47.

ASBJ

I-719
Da Cunha, Joseph Gerson, 1842-1900.
The origin of Bombay, ASBJ, v.20 (1900),
pp.1-368.

I-720
Da Cunha, Joseph Gerson, 1842-1900.
Words and places in and about Bombay. IA,
v.3 (1874), pp.247-49, 292-95; v.4 (1875),
pp.358-61.

v.4 IA   DS
                         416
                         I 41

I-721
D'Costa, Anthony.
The history of the Bombay region, Indica,
v.5 (1968), pp.97-113.

I-722
D'Costa, Anthony.
The rendition of Chaul, Indica, v.5
(1968), pp.53-64.

I-723
D'Costa, Anthony.
Tombo de Baçaim 1610-1730, Indica, v.6
(1969), pp.105-118.

I-724
De Souza, J.P.
Edwin Montagu's visits to India and his
impressions of Bombay. In: Studies in
Indian history; Dr.A.G.Pawar felicitation
volume. Ed.by V.D.Rao. Kolhapur, Y.P.Pawar,
1968. pp.304-21.

I-725
De Souza, J.P.
    Gerald Aungier and his project of planting
an English colony at Bombay, IHCP , v.30 (1968),
pp.325-30.

vvuqR

I-726
De Souza, J.P.
    Why Bombay was transferred by the Crown to
the East India Company, IHCP, v.29,pt.II
(1967), p.73.

U of R

I-727
Dikshit, Moreshwar Gangadhar, 1915-
    Notes on political and cultural history
of Konkan, BDCRI, v.4 (1942), pp.379-86.

History
BDCRI , 13+

I-728
Diskalkar, Dattatraya Balkrishna, 1872-
    James Grant Duff's private correspondence
with Maharaja Pratapsimha of Satara, JIH,
v.15 (1936), pp.221-36,368-86.

JIH

I-729
Dobbin, Christine Elizabeth
    The growth of urban leadership in western
India, with special reference to Bombay City,
1840-1885. Oxford, Univ.of Oxford, 1967.

Shulman #551

I-730
Douglas, James, 1826-1904.
    A book of Bombay [from A.D.1661] Bombay,
Bombay Gazette Steam Press, 1883-86. 2v.

4 qR v2

I-731
Douglas, James, 1826-1904.
    Glimpses of old Bombay and Western India.
London, Sampson Low, Marston & co., ltd.,
1900. 342p.

BM

I-732
Drewitt, Frederic George Dawtrey, 1848-
    Bombay in the days of George IV; memoirs
of Sir Edward West, chief justice of the
King's court during its conflict with the
East India Company, with hitherto unpublished
documents ... 2d ed., rev.& enl. London,
Longmans, Green, 1907. 386p.

4 qR

I-733
East India Company (English)
    Debates at the India House: August 22 & 23,
and Sept.22, 1845, on the case of the deposed
Rajah of Satara & impeachment of Col.C.Ovans,
London, E.Wilson, 1845. 368p.

    1. Pratapa Simha, raja of Satara. 2. Satara,
India (Principality) - Pol.& govt.

LC

I-734
East India Company (English)
    Proceedings at a special general court of
proprietors of East India Stock ... 25 March
1847, relative to the production of certain
secret papers ... in the case of ... the
deposed Raja of Satara. London, 1847. 111p.

BM

I-735
East India Company (English)
    Report of proceedings [relative to the
dethronement of the Rajah of Sattara] at
a special general court of proprietors of
the...Company...25th April, 1849. Taken
in short-hand by Messrs. W.B.Gurney & sons.
London, 1849. 144p.

BM

I-736
East India Company (English)
    Report of proceedings at a special general
court of proprietors [concerning the annexation of the Sattara Territories] London,
1849. 36p.

BM

I-737
Edwardes, Stephen Meredyth, 1873-1927.
    Bombay, A.D. 1660-1667. IA, v.52 (1923),
pp.211-15.

II

I-738
Edwardes, Stephen Meredyth, 1873-1927.
    The Bombay city police, 1672-1916. London,
Oxford University Press, 1923. 223p.

U MR

I-739
Edwardes, Stephen Meredyth, 1873-1927.
    The rise of Bombay, a retrospect. Bombay,
Printed at the "Times of India" Press, 1902.
348p.

U MR

I-740
Franks, Horace George, 1895-
    The story of Ichalkaranji. Poona, Scottish
Mission Industries, 1929.
    138p.

NUC pre1956

I-741
Gense, James H.
    How Bombay was ceded. Bombay, D.B.Tara-
porevala Sons & Co., 1939. 111p.

LC

I-742
Gopal, B.R.
    Kalyana, the Chalukyan capital, JIH, v.37
(1959), pp.267-76.

JIH

I-743
Gupta, Chandrawali.
    A glimpse into the annexation of the Nagpur
state by the British, IHCP, v.23 (1960),
pp.118-19.

U MR

I-744
Haig, Sir Wolseley, 1865-1938.
    The Fārūqī dynasty of Khandesh, IA, v.47
(1918), pp.113-24;141-49;178-86.

    1. Kings of Khandesh.

II

I-745
Haig, Sir Wolseley, 1865-1938.
The history of the Nizam Shahi Kings of
Ahmadnagar. IA, v.49 (1920), pp.66-84,84-91,
102-108,123-28,157-67,177-88,197-204,217-24;
v.50 (1921), pp.1-8,25-31,73-80,101-106,141-
46,193-98,205-10,229-34,261-68,277-83,321-28;
v.51 (1922), pp.29-36,66-73,125-31,198-203,
235-42; v.52 (1923), pp.29-39,159-62,250-62,
287-300,331-46.

II

I-746
History of the Bhonsla family of Nagpore.
MJLS, v.22 (1854?), pp.213-25.

I-747
Hosten, H.
Father A.Monserrate, S.J., on Salsete
Chorao, Divar, and the Molucas, JASBen,
v.18 (1922), pp.349-69.

I-748
Husain, Agha Mahdi.
Khandesh in new light. Bangalore, India,
Mythic Society, 1963. 41p.

1. Khandesh, India (Bombay)

I-749
Husain, Agha Mahdi.
A short history of Khandesh (1382-1601),
QJMS, v.51 (1960), pp.120-28; v.51 (1961),
pp.180-86; v.52,(1961), pp.6-20; v.53
(1962), pp.30-40.

I-750
Hussain, Mahdi.
Arberry's legacy of Persia and new lights on
Khandesh. II, v.8 (1955), pp.15-19.

II

I-751
Ingram, Alexander Robertson, 1882-
The gateway to India; the story of Methwold
and Bombay. London, Oxford University Press,
1938. 220p.

1. East India Company (English). 2. Bombay -
Hist. 3. Surat, India.

LC

I-752
Jayram, Ramlingam.
Administration of the districts of Marath-
wada under the Nizams, 1853-1935. Aurangabad,
Marathwada Univ., 1969. *

I-753
Jenkins, Sir Richard, 1785-1853.
Report on the territories of the Raja of
Nagpur submitted to the Supreme Govt.of
India. Calcutta, G.H.Huttmann, 1827. 357p.

I-754
Jervis, Thomas Best.
Geographical and statistical memoir of the
Konkun. The revenue and land tenures of the
western part of India, considered with reference to their first institution and present
working. Calcutta, 1840.

I-755
    Joshi, Purushottam Balkrishna, 1856-1930.
      On the derivation of the word "Bombay",
    E&W, v.1 (1901), pp.1514-18.

Oriental Bib

I-756
    Joshi, Purushottam Balkrishna, 1856-1930.
      Short sketch of the early history of the
    town and island of Bombay. Bombay, Times of
    India Press, 1902.

      1. Hindu period.

Oriental Bib

I-757
    Kale, Yadav Madhava, 1881-
      History of Central Provinces and Berar. Lec-
    tures delivered by Y.M.Kale. Nagpur, Published
    by U.Misra, registrar, Nagpur University, 1938.
    23p.

UgR

I-758
    Karaka, Dosoo Framjee, 1911-
      There lay the city. Bombay, Thacker & co.
    ltd., 1944. 274p.

LC

I-759
    Khan, Ghulam Ahmed.
      History of the city of Aurangabad, IHCP,
    v.5 (1941), pp.105-107.

U of R

I-760
    Khan, Sir Shafa'at Ahmad, 1893-
      Anglo-Portuguese negotiations relating to
    Bombay, 1660-1677. London, H.Milford,
    1922. (Allahabad univ.studies in history,
    1). 544p.

U of R

I-761
    Khan, Sir Shafa'at Ahmad, 1893-
      Bombay in the reign of Aurangzeb, IC, v.5
    (1931), pp.251-81,372-406,422-61; v.6 (1932),
    pp.90-130,261-89,409-26.

II

I-762
    Khare, Ganesh Hari, 1901-
      Dr. Chaghatai and Poona in the Muslim period.
    NIA, v.5 (1943), pp.273-74.

K+NC

I-763
    Kies, George.
      Geographical and historical description
    of the southern Maratha country and North
    Kanara, comprising the four collectorates
    of Kaladgi, Belgaum, Dharwar and North
    Kanara. Bombay, 1876.

SAS

I-764
    Kulkarni, Anant Ramchandra, 1925-
      Grant Duff and the Satara case, IHCP, v.30
    (1968), pp.246-51.

I-765
Lal, Krishnan.
    Poona from 1817 to 1857, a summary. IHCP,
v.25 (1964), p.281.

U of R

I-766
Marshall, Thomas.
    Statistical reports on the Pergunnahs of
Padshapoor, Belgam, Kalaniddee and Chandgurh,
Khanapoor, Bagulkot and Badamy, and Hoond-
goond in the Southern Mahratta country. Bombay, Printed for the Govt.at the Gazette Press
by M.D.Cruz, 1822. 193p.

U of R

I-767
Mathur, B.S.
    Side lights on the medieval history of
Nagpur, IHCP, v.28 (1966), pp.139-44.

U of R
I HC P

I-768
Mehta, Ramakant Javerilal.
    Bombay today. Contains short history of
Bombay city. Bombay, D.B.Taraporevala sons,
and co., 1949. 150p.

Bom (Pres) cat

I-769
Mehta, Ramakant Javerilal.
    You will find it in Bombay. Bombay, D.B.
Taraporevala sons & co., 1937. 192p.

BM

I-770
Mishra, P.L.
    The annexation of the Nagpur State, IHCP,
v.30 (1968), pp.252-67.

of U of R

I-771
Modern Bombay and her patriotic citizens.
1st ed. Bombay, Who's Who Publishers,
1941. 340p.

          1. Bombay - Biog.

U of R

I-772
Moledina, Muhammed Hashim, khan bahadur,
1906-   comp.
    History of Poona Cantonment, 1818-1953.
Poona, M.N.Merchant, pref.1953. 125p.

U of R

I-773
Moor, Edward, 1771-1848.
    Bombay and western India, AJ, v.9 (1820),
pp.603-10.

Jaina Bib.

I-774
Moraes, George Mark.
    A forgotten chapter in the history of the
Konkan. In: Bharata Kaumudi; Studies
in Indology in honour of Dr.Radha Kumud
Mookerji. Allahabad, Indian press, 1945-
1947. pp.441-75.

I-775
  Moraes, George Mark.
    Sindabur of the Arab writers, JIH, v.10
  (1931), pp.191-95.

JIH

I-776
  Mulla, F.Dadabhai.
    Etymology of names of Khandesh, JASB, v.4
  (1895-1899), p.449.

Sen Gupta

I-777
  Nagpur.
    Administration of the Nagpore Province by
  Mr. G.Plowden, Commissioner from 1855 to 1859.
  Nagpur, 1920. 76p.

U of R

I-778
  Nagpur.
    The escheat of the Nagpore State, the
  arrangements for the administration of the
  new province and the settlement of the
  affairs of the Bhonsla family, 1853-54.
  Nagpur, 1918. 131p.

BM

I-779
  Nagpur.
    Report on the Nagpore State down to 1845
  by Captain G.Ramsay, Asst.Resident, written
  in January 1845. Nagpur, 1918. 45p.

SOAS

I-780
  Nagpur.
    Settlement of the affairs of the Ranees of
  Nagpore and the course of events after the
  escheat of the State, 1854-60. Nagpur, 1920.
  71p.

U of R

I-781
  Nairne, Alexander Kyd.
    History of the Konkan. Land between Western
  Ghats and Indian Ocean. Bombay, Govt.Central
  Press, 1894. 144p.

    1. Konkan - Hist.

U of R

I-782
  Nicholson, William Norris, 1815-1889.
    A statement of the case of the deposed Raja
  of Sattara, taken from the official papers
  printed by Parliament, and by the Court of
  Directors of the East India Company, with
  remarks upon the evidence adduced against him.
  London, Printed by G.Norman, 1845. 208p.

    1. Pratapa Simha, raja of Satara. 2. Satara,
  India - Hist.

LC

I-783
  Observations on the causes of the present dis-
    contents of the merchants and other inhabi-
    tants of the Island of Bombay ... with a few
    remarks, interesting to the owners of ship-
    ping employed by the Honourable company.
    London, W.Innes, 1794. 43p.

Cal nat L. 6

I-784
  Official papers appertaining to the case of
    the dethroned Raja of Sattara with a brief
    statement of the case. London, G.Norman
    Printers, 1843. 363p.

I-785
    Oliver, Elyne E.
        The hill station of Matheran. Bombay,
Times of India Office, 1905. 238p.

4 M R

I-786
    Parasnis, Dattatraya Balwant, 1870-1926.
        Mahabaleshwar ... Bombay, Lakshmi art
printing works, 1916. 265p.

4 M R

I-787
    Parasnis, Dattatraya Balwant, 1870-1926.
        Panhala. Bombay, Lakshmi Art Print.Works,
1923. 66p.

BM

I-788
    Parasnis, Dattatraya Balwant, 1870-1926.
        Poona in bygone days. Bombay, Times Press,
1921. 142p.

4 M R

I-789
    Parasnis, Dattatraya Balwant, 1870-1926.
        The Sangli state. Bombay, Lakshmi Art
Print.Works, 1917. 83p.

4 M R

I-790
    Parasnis, Dattatraya Balwant, 1870-1926.
        Satara; brief notes. Bombay, Tukaram
Javaji, 1909. 64p.

4 M R

I-791
    Pechel, Samuel.
        An historical account of the settlement and
possession of Bombay, by the English East
India Company, and of the rise and progress
of the war with the Mahratta nation. London,
Printed by W.Richardson, for J.Robson, 1781.
345p.

        1. Bombay - Hist. 2. East India Co. 3.
Mahratta war, 1775-1782.

LC

I-792
    Pereira, A.B.de Bragança.
        Os Portugueses em Baçaim. Bastorá,
Tip.Rangel, 1935.

I-793
    Petition, on behalf of Pratap Singh, Raja of
    Sattara, presented to both Houses of Par-
    lament; to the House of Lords by the Right
    Hon'ble Lord Beaumont, June 24, 1844; to
    the House of Commons by Joseph Hume, Esq.
    M.P.August 10, 1843. London, 1885. 16p.

Cal nat Lib

I-794
    Poona, India(City)
        Poona: look and outlook, 1951. Editor-in-
chief, R.V.Oturkar. Poona City, Poona
Municipal Corp., 1951. 144p.

LC accession 1957 / 103

I-795
 Potdar, Datto Vaman, 1890–
   A few glimpses of ancient Paithan.
   In: Commemorative essays presented to
   Professor Kashinath Bapuji Pathak.
   Poona, Bhandarkar Oriental Research
   Institute, 1934. pp.304–08.

VofR

I-796
 Pusalker, Achut Dattatraya, 1905– and
   Dighe, Vishwanath Govind.
   Bombay, story of the island city. Bombay,
   All India Oriental Conference, 1949. 125p.

VofR

I-797
 Ranade, Vinayak Govind and Joshi, V.N.
   A short history of the Bhor state. Poona,
   R.K.Deshpande, 1930. 96p.

EM

I-798
 Rao, Vasant Dinanath, 1913–
   The Chhatrapatis of Kolhapur. In: Studies
   in Indian history, Dr.A.G.Pawar felicitation
   volume. Ed.by V.D.Rao. Kolhapur, Y.P.Pawar,
   1968. pp.334–70.

Studies

I-799
 Refai, G.Z.
   Anglo-Mughal relations in western India
   and the development of Bombay, 1662-1690.
   Cambridge, Cambridge Univ., 1968. *

Shulman #497

I-800
 Richardson, A.
   Description of the Fort of Galna, in
   Khandesh, ASBJ, v.6,no.21 (1861), pp.143-45.

ASBJ

I-801
 Sabnis, Sir Ramchandra V.
   Notes on Kolhapur, by Rao Bahadur
   Sir R.V.Sabnis. Bombay, Times Press,
   1928. 98p.

I-802
 Saldanha, Jerome Anthony.
   Survival of Portuguese institutions in
   British western India, ASBJ, v.25,no.71
   (1917-1921), pp.153-60.

Case

I-803
 Sankalia, Hasmukhlal Dhirajlal, 1908–
   Origin of Bombay, JUB, v.15 (1947), pp.1-4.

JUB

I-804
 Sardesai, D.R.
   How the Portuguese ceded Bombay, IHCP, v.21
   (1958), p.566.

INCP

I-805
Saswadkar, Prabhakar Laxman.
Nagpur in the eighteenth century, IHCP,
v.31 (1969), pp.399-413.

History, IHCP
BPCRI, p.136

I-806
Satara - and British connexion therewith,
CR, v.10 (1848), pp.437-95.

Case

I-807
Shaikh, C.H.
Some literary personages of Ahmadnagar,
BDCRI, v.3 (1941), pp.212-18.

Annual Bibliog Ind Hist

I-808
Shakespear, Leslie Waterfield, 1860-
Local history of Poona and its battlefields.
London, Macmillan & co., ltd., 1916. 108p.

1. Poona, India (Bombay) - Hist.

U of R

I-809
Shastri, Haraprasad.
Bombay in the eleventh century. In: Commemorative Essays presented to Sir Ramkrishna
Gopal Bhandarkar. Poona, 1917. pp.249-54.

Orient & afr Studies

I-810
Sheppard, Samuel Townsend, 1880-
Bombay. Bombay, Times of India Press,
1932. 166p.

1. Bombay - Hist.

Dot 2

I-811
Sheppard, Samuel Townsend, 1880-
Bombay place-names and street-names; an
excursion into the history of Bombay City.
Bombay, Times Press, 1917. 148p.

U of R

I-812
Sheppard, Samuel Townsend, 1880-
The Bombay Volunteer Rifles: a history.
Bombay, The Times Press, 1919. 217p.

NuR
IOL

I-813
Sheppard, Samuel Townsend, 1880-
History of Bombay. A book containing the
history of the development of Bombay. Bombay,
Times of India Press, 1932. 195p.

Com (Prei)Cat

I-814
Sheppard, Samuel Townsend, 1880-
Some lucky escapes: episodes in the history
of Bombay, ISRM, v.1 (1928), pp.693-96.

JBHS

I-815
Shyam, Radhey.
The kingdom of Ahmadnagar. Delhi, Motilal
Banarsidass, 1966. 457p.

U of R

I-820
Talekar, Shrikrishna Raghunathshastri, 1826-
1880.
The legendary account of old Newasa, IA,
v.4 (1875), pp.353-55.

I-816
Sinha, Ram Mohan.
Bhonslas of Nagpur; the last phase, 1818-
1854. Delhi, S.Chand, 1967. 262p.

U of R

I-821
Taleyarkhan, Homi Jehangirji H.
Roads to beauty around Bombay. Bombay,
Popular Book Depot. 1953. 191p.

U of R

I-817
Soares, Anthony X.
Garcia d'Orta, a little known owner of
Bombay, ASBJ, v.28 (1921-23), pp.195-229.

ASBJ

I-822
Tatas' contribution to Bombay, EE, v.56,no.5
(1971), pp.58-60.

I-818
Soltykoff, Alexis.
Bombay and Calcutta in 1841, JPUHS, v.2
(1933), pp.72-84.

Case

I-823
Thompson, George, 1804-1878.
Case of...Pertaub Shean, the Raja of
Satara...dethroned by the East India Company
on the testimony of false witnesses, etc.
London, 1846.

BM

I-819
Suguna Bai, Rani of Satara.
Memorial to Her Majesty the Queen from the
late H.H.Suguna Bai Saheb Rani of Satara,
widow of the late H.H.Chhatrapati Appa Saheb
Maharaj, Raja of Sattara in the Deccan-East
Indies, dated March 14, 1874. Bombay, Printed
at the Union Press, 1874. 487p.

BM
Cal Nat Lib

I-824
Tugwell, W.B.P., Lt.-Col.
History of the Bombay pioneers. London,
Sidney Press, 1938. 453p.

BM

I-825
Upadhye, A.N.
References to Sindhu Durga and Vijaya Durga in
some Prakrit works. In: Studies in Indian
history; Dr.A.G.Pawar felicitation volume.
Ed.by V.D.Rao. Kolhapur, Y.P.Pawar, 1968.
pp.377-82.

I-826
Wacha, Dinsha Edulji, 1844-1936.
Shells from the sands of Bombay: being my
recollections and reminiscences, 1860-1875.
Bombay, K.T.Anklesaria, 1920. 809p.

1. Bombay - Hist.

I-827
Wadekar, D.D. and Kale, D.V.
A hand-book of Poona. Poona, Pub.by D.V.
Kale on behalf of the Kesari-Mahratta Trust,
1934. 80p.

I-828
West, Edward William, 1824-1905.
The fort of Panāla, ASBJ, v.9 (1867-68),
pp.201-08.

I-829
West, Edward William, 1824-1905.
Historical sketch of the Southern Maratha
country. Mussalman period 1347-1818. Bombay, Govt.Printing Office, 1878. 31p.

I-830
West, Edward William, 1824-1905.
A memoir of the states of the Southern
Maratha country. Bombay, 1869. (Selections
from the records, n.s.,no.113). 271p.

I-831
Wills, Cecil Upton.
A note on the paper entitled 'The grand
dynasty in Chanda' read by the Lord Bishop
of Nagpur at the eleventh session of the
Indian Historical Records Commission in 1928,
IHRCP, v.13 (1930), pp.144-45.

IHRCP

I-832
Wood, Rev.Alex.
The Gond Dynasty in Chanda, IHRCP, v.11
(1928), pp.47-54.

Predominately non-Maharashtrian
Areas

I-833
Ayalla, Frederico Diniz d'
Goa antiga e moderna. Lisboa, Typ.
do Jornal do Commercio, 1888. 286p.

LC

I-834
Bandodkar, D.B.
Goa's cultural heritage, AICCER, v.17
(1965), pp.15-16.

I-835
The Baroda blunder. WR, v.104 (1875), pp.391-414.

I-836
Basu, Kamal Krishna.
The Adil Shahs of Bijapur. Calcutta, Univ. of Calcutta, 1940. *

I-837
Bhatye, V.N., ed.
Indore affairs. Being in brief an exposition of the acts of wanton cruelty and waywardness of the Maharajah of Indore (Sivajirava Holkar). Abridged from the "Vikshipta". Bombay, Bombay New Press, 1896. 50p.

Sivaji Rao Holkar, 1886-1903

BM

I-838
Bombay (State) Directorate of Archives.
Historical selections from Baroda records. Baroda, Govt.Press [etc.] New ser. 2v.
v.1 - Sayaji Rao II 1826-35. Comp.by V.G. Joshi. Baroda, Govt.Press, 1955.
v.2 - Disturbances in Gujarat. Ed.by V.G. Khobrekar. Baroda, Record Office, 1962.

I-839
Copland, I.F.S.
The Baroda crisis of 1873-77: a study in government rivalry, MAS, v.2 (1968), pp.97-123.

I-840
Correia, Alberto Carlos Germano da Silva, 1888-
La Vieille-Goa. Aperçu historique, récits de voyageurs, Saint-François Xavier, chronique sanitaire, esquisse archéologique. Bastora, J.Rangel, 1931. 321p.

I-841
Cottineau de Kloguen, Dennis L., d.1830.
Bosquejo historico de Goa, escripto em inglez pelo reverendo Diniz L.Cottineau de Kloguen; vertido em portuguez, e accrescentado com algumas notas, e rectificações por Miguel Vicente d'Abreu. Nova-Goa, Imprensa nacional, 1858. 209p.

1. Goa - Hist.
2C

I-842
Cottineau de Kloguen, Dennis L., d.1830.
An historical sketch of Goa, the metropolis of the Portuguese settlements in India. Madras, 1831.

I-843
Cunha, Tristao de Bragança, 1891-1958.
Goa's freedom struggle. Bombay, Dr. T.B. Cunha Memorial Committee, 1961. 562p.

1. Goa - Hist.

I-844
Da Cunha, Joseph Gerson, 1842-1900.
An historical and archaeological sketch of the Island of Angediva, ASB, v.11 (1875), pp.288-310.

I-845
Da Cunha, Joseph Gerson, 1842-1900.
   The Island of Angediva; an account. Bombay,
1870.

NLC

I-846
Desai, Govindbhai Hathibhai and Clarke,
   Arthur Beaumarice.
   Gazetteer of the Baroda State. Bombay,
1923. 2v.

BM

I-847
Dhar, S.N.
   A glimpse of Indore ... a century ago,
IHRCP, v.23 (1946), pp.63-65.

4 of R

I-848
Dickinson, John.
   Dhar not restored, in spite of the House of
Commons and of public opinion. London, P.S.
King. 1864. 119p.

BM

I-849
East India Company (English)
   The restoration of the King of Tanjore
considered, by George Rous. London, 1777.
3v.

BM

I-850
Fonseca, José Nicolau da.
   An historical and archaeological sketch
of the city of Goa. Bombay, Thacker and
co.,ltd., 1878. 346p.

U of R

I-851
Furtado, Joseph.
   Golden Goa. Being an account of Goa based
chiefly on the manuscript diary of a Spanish
Dominican who had been a chaplain to the
Viceroys of Goa from 1538 to 1548. Poona,
the author, 1939. 233p.

U of R

I-852
Ghauri, Iftikhar Ahmad.
   The political institutions of Bijapur,
1536-1686, and Golconda, 1418-1636. London,
London Univ., 1960-61. *

Bloomfield

I-853
Gupta, Hira Lal.
   Dhar succession, 1834, IHRCP, v.34,pt.2
(1958), pp.134-39.

U of R

I-854
Gupta, Hira Lal
   Gwalior succession 1836-1843, JIH, v.34
(1956), pp.59-65.

JAS 56

I-855
Gupta, Hira Lal.
Gwalior succession, 1826-1827, JIH, v.34
(1956), pp.249-62.

JIH

I-856
Gupta, Hira Lal.
Holkar Succession, 1844, IHRCP, v.33
(1958), pp.85-93.

U of R

I-857
Gupta, Hira Lal.
Indore successions, 1833-34, IHCP, v.18
(1955), pp.243-51.

Chaudhuri

I-858
Hanumantha Rao, D.S.
A page from the Mahratta history, QJMS,
v.8 (1918), pp.310-13.

QJMS

I-859
Hurst, John F.
A dead Portuguese city in India, HNMM, v.75
(1887), pp.730-37.

1. Bassein.

IOL

I-860
Hyderabad, India (State) Central Records
Office.
The chronology of modern Hyderabad, 1720-
1890. Hyderabad, 1954. 415p.

Hyderabad, India (State) - Hist. - Chronology.

U of R

I-861
Hyderabad, India (State) Committee Appointed
for the Compilation of a History of the
Freedom Movement in Hyderabad.
The freedom struggle in Hyderabad; a con-
nected account. Hyderabad, Hyderabad State
Committee Appointed for the Compilation of a
History of the Freedom Movement in Hyderabad,
1956-66. 4v.

U of R

I-862
Joshi, Purushottam Mahadeo, 1906-
The kingdom of Bijapur. London, London
University, 1935.

Bloomfield

I-863
Kamerkar, M.P.
The role of the Bhils in the British-
Baroda conflict between 1820 and 1840,
IHCP, v.25 (1964), pp.245-50.

U of R

I-864
Kamerkar, M.P.
A study in British paramountcy: Baroda
(1870-75), IHCP, v.24 (1961), pp.225-37.

U of R

I-865
Kibe, Madhav Vinayak, 1877-
Fragments from the records of Devi Shri
Ahilya Bai Holkar, IHRCP, v.13 (1930), pp.
132-39.

I-866
Malet, Arthur, 1806-1888.
Narrative of the Baroda State. Calcutta,
Foreign Department Press, 1865. 107p.

I-867
Mankekar, D.R.
Goa action. Bombay, Popular Book Depot,
1962. 51p.

1. Goa - Hist.

I-868
Menezes, Juliao.
Goa's freedom struggle. A brief history.
Bombay, J.Menezes, 1947. 126p.

I-869
Muhammad 'Ali Khan, Nawab of Arcot.
Letter ... to the Court of Directors. To
which is annexed a state of facts relative
to Tanjore. With an appendix of original
papers. Few MS notes. London, 1777.

I-870
Néry Xavier, Filippe, 1804-1874?
Esboço de hum Diccionario historico-
administrativo, contendo os principios
geraes da administração civil, ecclesiastica,
e militar, baseado sobre a legislação antiga,
e moderna; e especialmente applicado ao estado da India portugueza; ... Nova-Goa,
Imprensa nacional, 1850.

I-871
Original papers relative to Tanjore: containing
all the letters which passed, and the conferences which were held between his highness
the Nabob of Arcot and Lord Pigot, on the
subject of the restoration of Tanjore. Together with the material part of Lord Pigot's
last dispatch to the East India Company. The
whole connected by a narrative and illustrated
with notes and observations. London, Printed
for T.Cadell, 1777. 322p.

I-872
A peep into Goa's history, IR, v.64 (1965),
pp.405-406.

I-873
Pereira, A.B.de Bragança.
...História das novas conquistas.
Bastorá, Tip.Rangel, 1939.

I-874
Phatak, D.M.
Indore-Shivaji Rao, A.D.1886-1903, an
unusual half anna coin, JNSI, v.24 (1962),
pp.152-63.

I-875
Qanungo, Kalikaranjan, 1895-
Some side-lights on the history of Benares, political and social, thrown by the selections from the Peshwa's Daftar, Poona, IHRCP, v.14 (1937), pp.65-68.

U of R
Case

I-876
Rajayyan, K., 1929-
A history of British diplomacy in Tanjore. Mysore, Rao & Raghavan, 1969. 124p.

U of R

I-877
Ramalingam, John A.
British policy in the context of Bhonsla-Bhopal relations, 1810-1914. IC, v.36 (1962), pp.129-42. Also in: IHQ, v.38 (1962), pp. 8-28.

Case

I-878
Ramanujam, Chidambaram Srinivasachari.
British relations with Tanjore (1748-1799). London, Univ.of London, 1968. *

Shulman, T'494

I-879
Renault-Roulier, Gilbert, 1904-
Goa, Rome of the Orient, by Rémy, pseud. Trans.from the French by Lancelot C.Sheppard. London, A.Baker, 1957. 238p.

I-880
Saldanha, Claudio F.
A short history of Goa. Goa, Imprensa nacional, 1957. 158p.

NUR
LC

I-881
Saldanha, Gabriel de.
História de Goa (política e arqueológica) por padre M.J.Gabriel de Saldanha...cum uma carta-prefacio por J.A.Ismael Gracias... 2d ed. Nova-Goa, Livraria Coelho, 1925. 2v.

LC

I-882
Shah, Manilal Hiralal.
Baroda by decades, 1871-1941. Baroda, Sudharak Press, 1942. 210p.

1. Baroda - Hist.

LC

I-883
Soares, A.
The political situation in Goa. SocA, v.16 (1966), pp.580-88.

I-884
Srivastava, Satya Prakash.
The Jhansi State and its annexation, IHCP, v.7 (1944), pp.457-65.

Case

I-885
Subramanian, K.R.
    The Mahratta Rajas of Tanjore. Mylapore,
Madras, the author, 1928. 107p.

    1. Tanjore, India (District) - Hist. 2.
Mahrattas.

U of R

I-886
Taleyarkhan, Dinshah Ardeshir.
    The revolution of Baroda, 1874-75. Bombay,
Hormusjee Sorabjee and co.; Atmaram Sagoon &
co., 1875. 93p.

BM

I-887
An unwritten chapter of Maratha history,
QJPSS, v.17,no.3 (1894), pp.1-12.

Tanjore history - 1675-1855

QJPSS

I-888
Yazdani, Ghulam, 1885-
    Bidar: its history and monuments. London,
Oxford University Press, 1947. 255p.

    1. Bidar, India (Dist.) - Hist.

U of R

Pre-hist.& archeol.

I-889
Allchin, Bridget and Allchin, Frank
    Raymond, 1923-
    The birth of Indian civilization; India
and Pakistan before 500 B.C. Baltimore,
Penguin Books, 1968. 365p.

U of R

I-890
Allchin, Frank Raymond, 1923-
    Neolithic cattle-keepers of South India;
a study of the Deccan ashmounds. Cambridge,
England, University Press, 1963. (University of Cambridge oriental pub.,9). 203p.

U of R

I-891
Allchin, Frank Raymond, 1923-   and Joshi,
J.P.
    Malvan - further light on the southern
extension of the Indus civilization, RASGBIJ,
ser.3,no.1 (1970), pp.20-28.

General Works
BAS 1970

I-892
Ansari, Zainuddin Dawood.
    Spiral-horned antelope motif in the Chalco-
lithic pottery of Nevasa and western Asia,
BDCRI, v.18 (1957), pp.110-16.

U of R

I-893
Banerjee, Krishna Das.
    Middle paleolithic cultures of the Deccan.
Poona, University of Poona, 1957-58. *

Archaeology
BDCRI

I-894
Bhandarkar, Devadatta Ramakrishna, 1875-
    The antiquity of the Poona district,
ASBJ, n.s.,v.6 (1930), pp.231-38.

ASBJ

I-895
    Bhandarkar, Ramkrishna Gopal, 1836-1925.
      Memorandum on some antiquarian remains
found in a mound and in the Brahmapuri
Hill near Kolhapur, ASBJ, v.14,no.36
(1878-80), pp.147-54.

ASBJ

I-896
    Bombay (Presidency)
      Report on the Collectorate of Sholapore.
By J.D.Inverarity. Bombay, 1854. (Bombay
Presidency. Selections from the records,
n.s.,no.4). 36p.

Ind Off Lib

I-897
    Bombay (Presidency)
      Report on the southern districts of the
Surat collectorate. By Augustus Fortunatus
Bellasis. Bombay, 1854. (Bombay Presidency, Selections from the records, n.s.,
no.2). 19p.

Ind Off Lic

I-898
    Bombay (Presidency)
      Revised list of tombs and monuments of
historical or archaeological interest in
Bombay and other parts of the Presidency.
Bombay, 1912.

Brit Mus

I-899
    Burgess, James, 1832-1916.
      Lists of the antiquarian remains in the
Bombay Presidency, with an appendix of
inscriptions from Gujarat; compiled from
information supplied by the revenue, ed-
ucational, and other government officers.
Bombay, Govt.Central Press, 1885.
(Archaeological survey of western India
[Reports] Old series, no.11).

1. Bombay (Presidency)-Antiq. 2. Indian and assigned
district. Gov R anti-fel

I-900
    Burgess, James, 1832-1916.
      Report on the first season's operations
in the Belgam and Kaladgi districts, Jan.
to May 1874. London, Indian Museum, 1874.
(Archeological survey of western India,
n.s.,vol.1). 53p.

LC

I-901
    Codrington, Kenneth deBurgh.
      Ancient sites near Ellora, Deccan. IA.
v.59 (1930), pp.211-18, 222-30.

JBHS

I-902
    Deo, Shantaram Bhalchandra, 1923-
      The personality of Vidharbha megaliths,
IA, v.4 (1970), pp.23-31.

General works
BAS 1970

I-903
    Deo, Shantaram Bhalchandra, 1923-
      Terracotta figurines and toys from Maheshwar
excavation, JASB, v.31 & 32 (1956-1957), pp.
38-44.

Surer

I-904
    Deo, Shantaram Bhalchandra, 1923-
      and Ansari, Zainuddin Dawood.
      Chalcolithic Chandoli. Poona. Deccan
College Postgraduate and Research Institute,
1965. (Deccan College building centenary
and silver jubilee series,39). 221p.

Gc R

I-905
Deo, Shantaram Bhalchandra, 1923-   and
Dhavalikar, Madhukar Keshav.
Report of Paunar excavation (1967), NUJ,
v.18 (1968), pp.201-334.

I-906
Deshpande, M.N.
A brief account of recent archaeological
exploration in Maharashtra, AIOCPT, v.17
(1953), pp.337-41.

I-907
Deshpande, Yeshwant Khushal 1884-
Jain antiquities in Vidarbha, the ancient
Berar, AIOCPT, v.9 (1937), pp.816-22.

I-908
Dhavalikar, Madhukar Keshav.
Genesis of the Jorwe culture, IA, v.4
(1970), pp.32-40.

I-909
Dikshit, D.P.
Two Pauranic sites of Vidarbha, Puranam,
v.9 (1967), pp.277-83.

I-910
Frere, H.B.E.
Memorandum on some Buddhist excavations
near Karadh, ASBJ, v.3,pt.2,no.13 (1850),
pp.108-18.

I-911
Gadre, P.B.
Cultural archaeology of Ahmednagar during
Nizam Shah period. Poona, University of
Poona, 1969. *

I-912
Ghosh, A.
Explorations and excavations: Bombay; Maharashtra, IArch, v.5 (1957-58), pp.11-24; v.6
(1958-59), pp.13-25; v.7 (1959-60), pp.25-37;
v.8 (1960-61), pp.19-27; v.9 (1961-62), pp.
28-34.

I-913
Goetz, hermann, 1898-
Archaeological observations on Satara Fort.
In:A volume of studies in Indology presented
to Prof.P.V.Kane, ed.by S.M.Katre and P.K.
Gode. Poona, Oriental Book Agency (Poona
Oriental Series no.75), 1941. pp.200-205.

I-914
Gokhale, Shobhana.
Recent Godavari flood and its relevance
to prehistoric archaeology, BDCRI, v.29
(1970), pp.118-34.

I-915
    Gupta, S.P.
      Is there a neolithic burial custom in the
Deccan?, JAHRS, v.29 (1964), pp.55-61.

Ja 8 65

I-916
    Gupte, Y.R., 1881-
      Archaeological and historical research,
its scope in the Satara district, ASBJ, n.s.,
v.4 (1928), pp.81-94.

JBHS

I-917
    Gupte, Y.R., 1881-
      Archaeological remains in Sanivara Peth,
Poona City, NIA, v.6 (1943), pp.57-60.

NIA

I-918
    Hunter, William, 1755-1812.
      An account of some artificial caverns in
the neighbourhood of Bombay, Archaeologia,
v.7 (1785), pp.286-302.

Archaeologia

I-919
    India. Archaeology Survey.
      Archaeological Survey of Western India.
Misc.reports in connection with the operation
of the Archaeological Survey, nos.1-11. Bombay,
1874-1885. 11 vols.in 3.

SOAS

I-920
    Indraji, Bhagvanlal.
      Antiquarian remains at Sopara and Padana,
ASBJ, v.15,no.40 (1882), pp.273-328.

ASBJ

I-921
    Joshi, Ramachandra Vinayak.and Sali, S.A.
      Middle Stone Age factory sites in western
India, Anthropos, v.63/64 (1968/69), pp.
818-827

I-922
    Joshi, Ramachandra Vinayak.
      Pleistocene studies in the Malaprabha
Basin. Poona, 1955. (Poona. Deccan
College Research Inst.and Dharwar.
Karnatak Univ.Joint Pubs.,no.1). 125p.

IOL

I-923
    Kapre, K.R.
      Archaeology of the ancient place-names in the
Deccan. Poona, Deccan College Postgraduate
and Research Institute, 1961. *

I-924
    Katare, Sant Lal.
      Excavations at Sirpur, IHQ, v.35 (1959).
pp.1-8.

I-925
    Kennedy, Kenneth A.R. and Malhotra, Kailash
      Chandra.
      Human skeletal remains from chalcolithic
    and Indo-Roman levels from Nevassa: an
    anthropometric and comparative analysis.
    Poona, Deccan College Postgraduate and
    Research Inst., 1966. (Deccan College
    Building Centenary and Silver Jubilee series,
    55). 145p.

1. Anthropometry—India—Nevassa.

UnR

I-926
    Khatri, A.Prakash.
      Koregaon - the mid-paleeolithic cum Chalco-
    lithic site on river Bhima (Maharashtra),
    Anthropologist, v.4 (1957), pp.14-19.

furer

I-927
    Kosambi, Damodar Dharmanand, 1907-1968.
      Megaliths in the Poona district, *Man*,
    v.62,no.108 (1962), pp.65-67.

JAS '62

I-928
    Kosambi, Damodar Dharmanand, 1907-1968.
      Pierced microliths from the Deccan Plateau,
    Man, v.62,no.5 (1962).

Furer

I-929
    Kosambi, Damodar Dharmanand, 1907-68.
      Prehistoric rock engravings near Poona,
    Man, v.63,article no.60 (1963), pp.57-58.

I-930
    Kosambi, Damodar Dharmanand, 1907-1968.
      Staple 'grains' in the western Deccan, *Man*,
    v.63 (1963), pp.130-31. Also in: *JASB*, n.s.
    v.36/37 (1961/62), pp.60-62.

JAS '63 '64

I-931
    Kumar, L.S.S.
      Identification of charred rafi and rice
    grains from the excavations at Kolhapur,
    1945-46, *BDCRI*, v.14 (1952), pp.79-80.

BDCRI

I-932
    Kundangar, K.G.
      Archaeological finds in Brahmapuri excava-
    tions, Kolhapur, *AIOCPT*, v.12 (1943/44), pp.
    599-601.

UnR

I-933
    Landge, D.G., 1891-
      Paoni, a centre of culture, *IHCP*, v.21 (1958),
    p.218.

IHCP

I-934
    Leshnik, Lawrence S.
      Early burials from the Nagpur district,
    Central India, *Man*, v.5,no.3 (1970), pp.498-
    511.

Sociology + Anthropology
BAS 1970

I-935
MacDonald, Archibald.
Historical narrative of the Dhar State.
Calcutta, J.L. Kingham, 1863. 141p.

NLC

I-936
Malcolm, Sir John, 1769-1833.
Report on the province of Malwa, and
adjoining districts. Submitted to the
supreme Government of British India.
Calcutta, 1822.

BM

I-937
Malet, Arthur, 1806-1888.
Historical narrative of the district of
Cambay from 1630 to 1847, compiled from the
records of the Bombay Government. Calcutta,
Foreign Department Press, 1865. 161p.

vvv Calcutta Nat'l Lib

I-938
Malik, S.C.
Stone age industries of the Bombay and
Satara districts. Baroda, Faculty of
Arts, Maharaja Sayajirao University of
Baroda, 1959. (Baroda. Maharaja Saya-
jirao University. Archaeology series
no.4). 76p.

1. Stone age — India.
Doth

I-939
Mate, Madhukar Shripad and Dhavalikar,
Madhukar Keshav.
Pandharpur excavation: 1968-a report.
ABORI, v.29 (1968-69), pp.76-117.

vvv U+R

I-940
Mitra, Sarat Chandra.
Biographical sketches of Indian antiquarians:
Professor Ramkrishna Gopal Bhandarkar. CR, v.129
(1909), pp.354-79.

Case

I-941
Nagaraja Rao, M.S.
Archaeological remains of the Dharwar
district; a review, ASBJ, n.s.,v.38 (1963),
pp.154-64.

JaS '65

I-942
Naik, A.V.
Archaeology of the Deccan. Poona, University
of Bombay, 1947-48. *

Archaeology
BDCRI, p.34

I-943
Rajaram, S.N. and Kennedy, Kenneth A.R.
The skeletal evidence for Pleistocene
man in India (Poona district), BDCRI, v.24
(1963-1964), pp.71-76.

BDC RI

I-944
Roy, Sourindranath.
The story of Indian archaeology, 1784-1947.
New Delhi, Archaeological Survey of India,
1961. 134p.

check JAS comm.
LC

I-945
    Saletore, Bhasker Anand.
      The antiquity of Pandharpur, IHQ, v.11
    (1935), pp.771-78.

I H Q

I-946
    Saletore, Bhasker Anand.
      The origin of Bombay, JUB, v.13 (1944), pp.
    1-9.

JUB

I-947
    Sali, S.A.
      A new ceramic of the Chalcolithic from
    Dhulia destrict, Maharashtra State, ASBJ,
    n.s.,v.38 (1963), pp.207-210.

JAS '65

I-948
    Sankalia, Hasmukhlal Dhirajlal, 1908-
      Ancient and prehistoric Maharashtra,
    ASBJ, v.27 (1952), pp.99-106.

I-949
    Sankalia, Hasmukhlal Dhirajlal, 1908-
      Animal-fossils and palaeolithic industries
    from the Pravara basin at Nevasa, district
    Ahmadnagar, AI, v.12 (1956), pp.35-52.

Suses

I-950
    Sankalia, Hasmukhlal Dhirajlal, 1908-
      Archaeology of Poona and its surroundings.
    38th All India Medical Conference Souvenir.
    Poona, 1962. pp.6-12.

Archaeology
BDCRI 280

I-951
    Sankalia, Hasmukhlal Dhirajlal, 1908-
      The excavations at Nasik and Jorwe, 1950-
    1951. By Hasmuklal Dhirajlal Sankalia and
    Shantaram Balchandra Deo. Poona, Deccan
    College Post-graduate and Research Institute,
    1955. 198p.

Archaeology
BDCRI 280

I-952
    Sankalia, Hasmukhlal Dhirajlal, 1908-
      Flat bronze axes from Jorwe, Ahmadnagar
    district, Deccan, Man, v.55 (1955), p.1.

man

I-953
    Sankalia, Hasmukhlal Dhirajlal, 1908-
      From history to pre-history at Nevasa, 1954-
    1956. Poona, Deccan College Post-graduate
    and Research Institute, 1960. (Deccan
    College dissertation series no.1). 584p.

Archaeology

I-954
    Sankalia, Hasmukhlal Dhirajlal, 1908-
      The Godavari palaeolithic industry.
    Poona, Deccan College Post-graduate and
    Research Inst., 1952. (Deccan College
    Monograph series, no.10). 61p.

I-955
Sankalia, Hasmukhlal Dhirajlal, 1908-
The history of man in Maharashtra: work
done and plan of work ahead. Bombay, Mumbai
Marathi Grantha Samgrahalaya, 1966. 32p.

I-960
Sankalia, Hasmukhlal Dhirajlal, 1908-
Prehistoric men and primitives in South
Gujarat and Konkan, JASB, v.12,no.1 (1966),
pp.34-38.

I-956
Sankalia, Hasmukhlal Dhirajlal, 1908-
Mahismati and Maheshwar, JIH, v.41 (1963),
pp.347-48.

I-961
Sankalia, Hasmukhlal Dhirajlal, 1908-
Rotary querns from India, Antiquity, v.33
(1959), pp.128-30.

I-957
Sankalia, Hasmukhlal Dhirajlal, 1908-
Megalithic monuments near Poona College,
BDCRI, v.1 (1940), pp.178-84.

I-962
Sankalia, Hasmukhlal Dhirajlal, 1908-
Stone age cultures of Bombay. A reapprai-
sal, JASB, v.34-35 (1959-60), pp.120-131.

I-958
Sankalia, Hasmukhlal Dhirajlal, 1908-
A note on the blade industry from excavations
at Nevasa (1954-1955), BDCRI, v.17 (1955-1956),
pp.150-51.

I-963
Sankalia, Hasmukhlal Dhirajlal, 1908-
Studies in prehistory of the Deccan
(Maharashtra): a survey of the Godavari
and the Kadva near Niphad, BDCRI, v.6,
no.3 (1944), pp.1-16; v.6,no.4 (1944),
pp.131-37.

I-959
Sankalia, Hasmukhlal Dhirajlal, 1908-
Prehistoric Ahmednagar. In: Studies in
Indian Culture Dr.Ghulam Yazdani Commem-
oration Volume. Ed.by Prof.H.K.Sherwani.
Hyderabad, A.P., 1966. pp.39-42.

I-964
Sankalia, Hasmukhlal Dhirajlal, 1908-
A unique realistic painting of the Chalco-
lithic period in the Deccan. In: Felici-
tation volume presented to Professor
Sripad Krishna Belvalkar. Ed.by S.Radha-
krishnan and A.S.Altekar. Banaras,
Motilal Banarassi Dass, 1957. pp.243-44.

I-965
Sankalia, Hasmukhlal Dhirajlal, 1908- and
Deo, Shantaram Bhalchandra.
Report of the excavations at Nasik and
Jorwe, 1950-51. Poona, Deccan College Post-
graduate and Research Inst., 1955. (Deccan
College Monograph Series, no.13). 198p.

U of R.

I-966
Sankalia, Hasmukhlal Dhirajlal, 1908-
and Dikshit, Moreshwar Gangadhar.
Excavations at Brahmapuri (Kolhapur) 1945-
46. Poona, Deccan College Postgraduate and
Research Institute, 1952. (Deccan College
Monograph series, 5) 169p.

I-967
Sinclair, William F.
Notes on the antiquities of the Talukas
of Parner, Sangamner, Ankole, and Kopargaum,
forming the charge of the Second Assistant
Collector, Ahmadnagar, by W.R.Sinclair; with
revised lists of remains in the Ahmadnagar,
Nasik, Puna, Thana, and Kaladgi Zillas, by
J.Burgess. Bombay, Government Central Press,
1874.

8 M

I-968
Sinclair, William F.
Rough notes on Khandesh, IA, v.4 (1875),
pp.108-10; 335-40.

I-969
Soundara Rajan, K.V. and Sengupta, R.
Flake and blade tool industries of the stone
age from Ellora, an investigation, JMaU, v.2,
no.2 (1962), pp.67-76.

JMaU

I-970
Taylor, Meadows, 1808-1876.
Megalithic tombs and other ancient remains in
the Deccan. Hyderabad, Archaeological Dept. of
Hyderabad, 1941. 122p.

I-971
Thapar, B.K.
A chalcolithic site of the southern Deccan,
AI, v.13 (1957), pp.114-15.

India

I-972
Todd, K.R.U.
The micolithic industries of Bombay, AI,
v.6 (1950), pp.4-16.

f user

I-973
Vaufrey, R.
Paleolithique et Mésolithique de Bombay,
Anthropos, v.52 (1948), p.182.

furv

I-974
Yazdani, Ghulam, 1885-
The antiquities of Bidar. Calcutta, Baptist
Mission Press, 1917. 30p.

LC

History - Earliest to 1600

I-975
Abdul Aziz, Mohammad.
The Deccan in the 15th century, _JASBen_,
v.21 (1925), pp.549-91.

I-976
Altekar, Anant Sadashiv, 1898-
The Deccan money-market during c.7-c.100A.D.
In: Commemorative Essays presented to Prof.
Kashinath Bapuji Pathnak. Poona, Bhandarkar
Oriental Research Institute, 1934. pp.
462-65.

Bhandarkar Orient
Research Inst.
U of R

I-977
Altekar, Anant Sadashiv, 1898-
The home and nationality of the Rastrakutas
of Malkhed, _AIOCPT_, v.6 (1930), pp.65-73.

U of R

I-978
Altekar, Anant Sadashiv, 1898-
Presidential address, read by Mahamahopadhyay
Prof.Datto Vaman Potdar Interim President, _IHCP_,
v.22 (1959), pp.13-33.

IHCP

I-979
Altekar, Anant Sadashiv, 1898-
The Rashtrakutas and their times. 2d rev.
ed. Poona, Oriental Book Agency, 1967.
(Poona Oriental series, no.36) 449p.

NR
LC

I-980
Altekar, Anant Sadashiv, 1898-
The Silaharas of western India, _IndC_, v.2
(1935). pp.393-434.

I-981
Altekar, Anant Sadashiv, 1898-
Society in the Deccan during 200 B.C. to
500 A.D., _JIH_, v.30 (1952), pp.57-66.

JIH

I-982
Altekar, Anant Sadashiv, 1898-
State and government in ancient India.
3d ed. Delhi, Motilal Banarsidass, 1958.
407p.

UofR

I-983
Banerjee, Anil Chandra, 1910-
'Alā-ud-Dīn Khaljī's Deccan expeditions,
IndC, v.2 (1935), pp.349-51.

1 Khalji's A.H. 689-720/AD 1290-1320

IndC

I-984
Banhatti, Shrinivas Narayan, 1901-
Material throwing light on the history
of the Yadavas of Devagiri, gleaned from
the Mahanubhava literature, _IHCP_, v.5
(1941), pp.91-93.

U of R

I-985
Basu, Kamal Krishna.
　　An account of Ibrahim 'Adil Shah of Bijapur
(1534-1557), JBRS, v.25 (1940), pp.60-81.

I-986
Basu, Kamal Krishna
　　Career of Yusuf 'Adil Shah of Bijapur, IndC,
v. 3 (1936-37), pp. 109-19.

I-987
Basu, Kamal Krishna.
　　A chapter from Golkonda history, JBRS,
v.27 (1941), pp.176-89.

I-988
Basu, Kamal Krishna.
　　A chapter on the reign of 'Ali 'Adil Shah
of Bijapur, NIA, v.2 (1939), pp.143-55.
Also in E.D.Ross Presentation Volume, (1939),
pp.1-13.

I-989
Basu, Kamal Krishna.
　　The Dasturu'l-amal of the Bijapur Court,
IHRCP, v.17 (1941), pp.123-29.

I-990
Basu, Kamal Krishna.
　　The early career of Quli Qutb Shah of Golconda,
IHQ, v.16 (1940), pp.711-18.

I-991
Basu, Kamal Krishna.
　　The early life of 'Ali Adil Shah of Bijapur,
KHR, v.4 (1937), pp.33-38.

1. Adil Shahs of Bijapur.

I-992
Basu, Kamal Krishna.
　　History of Ibrahim 'Adil Shah of Bijapur,
JBRS, v.24 (1938), pp.189-204.

I-993
Basu, Kamal Krishna.
　　The history of 'Isma'el 'Adil Shah of Bija-
pur, IndC, v.4 (1937-38), pp.1-17.

I-994
Basu, Kamal Krishna.
　　The reign of 'Ali Adil Shah of Bijapur,
part I, (1557-1564 A.D.), IndC, v.5 (1938-
39), pp.49-55.

Adil Shahs of Bijapur

I-995
Basu, Kamal Krishna.
Two traditions about ancestry of Yusuf 'Ādil
Shāh of Bijapur, IHQ, v.12 (1936), pp.345-54.

1. Adil Shahs of Bijapur

before 1600

II

I-996
Bendrey, Vasudeo Sitaram, 1896-
Death of Ahmad Nizam Shah I, Bahri, NIA,
v.4 (1941), pp.242-44.

NIA

I-997
Bhandarkar, Ramkrishna Gopal, 1837-1925.
Early history of the Dekkan down to the
Mahomedan conquest. Bombay. Printed at the
Govt.Central Press, 1884. 117p.

1. India - Histo. - Early to 324 B.C.

NUR
pre '56 imprints

I-998
Bhave, Vasudeo Krishna, 1885-
A peep into the ancient civilisation of
Maharashtra, IHCP, v.3 (1939), pp.147-49.

I.HCP

I-999
Burn, Sir Richard.
A note on the genealogy and chronology of
the Vakatakas, JIH, v.15 (1936), pp.260-65.

JIH

I-1000
Chand Bibi, sultana, d.1600.
Memoirs of Chand Bibi, the Princess of
Ahmednagar. By Sayyid Ahmadullah Qadri.
Hyderabad, 1930. (Historical society of
Hyderabad series, 2). 87p.

SHS

I-1001
Chowdhury, Jogindra Nath.
Administration of the Bahmani kingdom,
IHQ, v.2 (1926), pp.690-97.

IHQ

I-1002
Chowdhury, Jogindra Nath.
Life of Mahmud Gawan, IHQ, v.4 (1928), pp.
417-24.

IHQ

I-1003
Chowdhury, Jogindra Nath.
Observations on the cognomen Bahmani, IHQ,
v.3 (1927), pp.451-56.

II

I-1004
Chowdhury, Jogindra Nath.
Social and economic conditions of the people
under the Bahmani Sultanate, IHQ, v.4 (1928),
pp.721-24.

IHQ

I-1005
Correia, Alberto Carlos Germano da Silva, 1888-
Historia da colonizacao Portuguesa na India. Lisbon, Agencia geral das Colonias, 1948-58. 6v.

UYR

I-1006
Da Cunha, Antonio Maria.
Congresso Provincial da India Portuguesa. Subsidios para sua historia. Nova Goa, 1924-33. 6 vols.in 2.

SOAS

I-1007
Dalvi, D.A.
The early years of Portuguese dominance over the western coast of India, IHCP, v.26, pt.2 (1964), p.124.

IHCP

I-1008
Dar, M.I.
Riyād al-Insha: its literary and historical value, IC, v.24 (1950), pp.231-48.

1. Bahmanids, Kings of Kulbarga.

Index Islam

I-1009
Das Gupta, Nalini Nath.
On the reign of Krsna II, the Rastrakuta, IA, v.62 (1933), pp.134-36.

VIVIA

I-1010
D'Costa, Anthony.
Administrative, social and religious conditions in the Goa Islands 1510-1550, Indica, v.1 (1964), pp.19-38.

I-1011
D'Costa, Anthony.
The battles of Thana in local tradition, Indica, v.2 (1965), pp.141-50.

Internat'l Guide to India Studies

I-1012
D'Costa, Anthony.
Historical value of Mahim traditions, BIS, v.2 (Jan.1966), pp.48-53.

History - Mahim or Konkan
R

I-1013
Deoras, V.R.
The political history of Maharashtra from the earliest times to circa 1000 A.D. London School of Oriental and African Studies, 1940. *

Bloomfield

I-1014
Deoras, V.R.
Side-lights on the early history of the Yadavas of Devagiri. In: Indica (The Indian Historical Research Institute Silver Jubilee Commemoration Volume). Bombay, 1953. pp.84-88.

Bhandarkar Insti- comm. vol.

I-1015
Dikshit, D.P.
Adasa an ancient site of Vidarbha, NUJ, v.17 (1966), pp.26-38.

I-1016
Dutt, Sublimalchandra.
Some light on the history of western India in the 11th century A.D., IHCP, v.3 (1939), pp.826-31.

I HCP

I-1017
Fernandes, Braz A.
Ancient Goa; its origin and vicissitudes, GW, v.7 (1930), pp.9-10.

JBHS

I-1018
Fleet, John Faithfull, 1847-1917, ed.
The dynasties of the Kanarese districts of Bombay Presidency from earliest historical times to the Muhammadan conquest of A.D.1318. Bombay, 1882. (Gazetteer of the Bombay Presidency, v.1,pt.2).

BM

I-1019
Foulkes, T.
The civilisation of the Dakhan down to the sixth century B.C., IA, v.8 (1879), p.1.

Ec. Hist of the Decca

I-1020
Foulkes, T.
Dakhan in the time of Gautama Buddha, IA, v.16 (1887), pp.1,48.

Ec. Hist of the Decca

I-1021
Gairola, C.Krishna.
Administrative structure of the Satavahana empire, AL, v.20 (1955). pp.41-47.

Chaudhuri

I-1022
Gairola, C.Krishna.
Cultural history of the Satavahana Dynasty. London, Univ.of London, 1949. *

Bloomfield

I-1023
Gopalachari, K.
Legacy of Satavahana rule, IHCP, v.10 (1947), pp.103-13.

I HCP

I-1024
Gupte, Y.R., 1881-
Dr. Aiyangar on the Vakatakas, JIH, v.5 (1925), pp.399-408.

JIH

I-1025
Gupte, Y.R., 1881-
Yadavas mentioned in the religious books of the Mahanubhavas, *JIH*, v.5 (1925), pp. 198-203.

JIH

I-1026
Gurav, R.N.
Permadideva and Vijayaditya of the Kadambas of Goa, *QJMS*, v.55 (1964), pp.19-35.

Q JMS

I-1027
Gurty Rao, Venket.
The Bahmani-Vijayangar relations, *IHCP*, v.2 (1938), pp.264-77.

India In

I-1028
Gurty Rao, Venket.
Tribal affiliation and the home of the Satavahanas, *JIH*, v.29 (1951), pp.53-62.

JIH

I-1029
Haig, Sir Wolseley, 1865-1938.
The religion of Ahmad Shah Bahmani, *RASGBIJ*, Series 3 (1924), pp.73-80.

NRU

I-1030
The History of the Rashtrakutas, *JIH*, v.13 (1933), pp.99-102.

I-1031
Hosain, M.Hidayat.
Conquest of Sholapur by Burhan Nizam Shah I (914-961 A.D./1508-1553 A.D.), *JASBen*, v.5 (1939), pp.133-53.

II

I-1032
Hosain, M.Hidayat.
Shah Tahir of the Deccan, *NIA*, v.2 (1939), pp.460-73. Also in: E.D.Ross Presentation Volume (1939), pp.147-60.

NIA

I-1033
Houpert, Joseph C.
The martyrs of Salcette (1583). Trichinopoly, 1930. 32p.

I OL

I-1034
Husaini, Saiyid Abdul Quadir.
Bahman Shah, the founder of the Bahmani Kingdom. 1st ed. Calcutta, Firma K.L. Mudhopadhyay, 1960. 207p.

I-1035
Husaini, Saiyid Abdul Quadir.
Career of Hasan (Bahman Shah) before he became the Sultan of the Deccan, IC, v.33 (1959), pp.112-23.

I-1036
Husaini, Saiyid Abdul Quadir.
The cognomen, Gangui, attached to the name of the founder of the Bahmani kingdom, JASP, v.1 (1956), pp.65-77.

I-1037
Indraji, Bhagvanlal.
A new Yadava dynasty, IA, v.12 (1883), pp.119-129.

I-1038
Joglekar, S.A.
The home of the Satavahanas, ABORI, v.23 (1942), pp.196-205.

I-1039
Joshi, Purushottam Mahadeo, 1906-
Adilshahi administration, IHCP, v.4 (1940), pp.235-47.

I-1040
Joshi, Purushottam Mahadeo, 1906-
Ala-ud-Din Khal'i's first campaign against Devagiri. In: Studies in Indian culture. Dr.Ghulam Yazdani commemoration volume. Ed.by H.K.Sherwani. Hyderabad, 1966. pp.203-11.

I-1041
Joshi, Purushottam Mahadeo, 1906-
Party strife in the Bahmani Empire, IHCP, v.6 (1943), pp.212-18.

I-1042
Joshi, Purushottam Mahadeo, 1906-
The reign of Ibrahim Adil Shah II of Bijapur, BV, v.9 (1948), pp.284-309.

I-1043
Joshi, Purushottam Mahadeo, 1906-
Relations between the Adilshahi kingdom of Bijapur and the Portuguese at Goa during the 16th cnetury, NIA, v.2 (1939), pp.359-68. Also in E.D.Ross Presentation Volume (1939), pp.161-70.

I-1044
Jouveau-Dubreuil, Gabriel.
Ancient history of the Deccan. Trans. from the French by V.Swaminadha Dikshitar. Pondicherry, 1920.

I-1045
    Kale, Yadav Madhava, 1881-
      An examination of some theories about the
    Vakatakas. IHCP, v.2 (1938), pp.236-38.

IHCP

I-1046
    Katare, Sant Lal.
      The beginnings of the Calukyas of Kalyani.
    IHQ, v.13 (1937), pp.244-54.

Index to IHQ

I-1047
    Katare, Sant Lal.
      Early history of the Yadavas of Devagiri.
    JIH, v.30 (1952), pp.109-32.

JIH

I-1048
    Katare, Sant Lal.
      On the Satavahana, Sata, Sati and Sati. IHQ,
    v.34 (1958), pp.281-85.

Index to IHQ

I-1049
    Katare, Sant Lal.
      Struggle for supremacy in the Deccan, IHC,
    v.14 (1938), pp.613-32.

Index to IHQ

I-1050
    Kazimi, Masoom Raza.
      The Genesis of Iranian diplomacy in the
    Deccan, IHCP, v.29 (1967), pp.152-58.

DS
401
I425P v.29

UofP

I-1051
    Khare, Ganesh Hari, 1901-
      Dr. Saletore and the authenticity of the
    Mughol farmans, NIA, v.3 (1940), pp.186-90.

DS
401
N53 v.3

Khare

I-1052
    Khare, Ganesh Hari, 1901-
      A letter of assurance of Ali Adilshah I.
    A.D. 974/A.D. 1566, IHRCP, v.22 (1945), pp.
    10-11.

       1. Adil Shahs of Bijapur.

II

I-1053
    Krishna, M.H.
      The early Rashtrakutas of the Maharashtra.
    In: Professor K.V.Rangaswami Aiyangar
    Commemoration Volume. Essays and papers written
    by his friends, pupils and admirers...presented
    ...on his 61st birthday. Ed.by Shashtiabdapurti
    Commemoration Committee. Madras, Benares
    printed, 1940. pp.55-63.

Oriental + Afr Studies

I-1054
    Krishnamoorthy, A.Vaidehi.
      Social and economic conditions in Eastern
    Deccan from A.D.1000 to A.D.1250. Hyderabad,
    Osmania Univ., 1965. 487p. *

SOAS supp

I-1055
    Krishnarao, B.V.
        The origin and the original home of the
    Calukyas, IHCP, v.3 (1939), pp.386-410.

I HCP

I-1056
    Krishnasvami Aiyangar, Śakkoṭṭai, 1871-
        Abul Hasan Qutub Shah and his ministers,
    Madanna and Akkanna, JIH, v.10 (1931),
    pp.91-142.

J865
w:evo tiche
JIH

I-1057
    Krishnasvami Aiyangar, Sakkottai, 1871-
        A glimpse into the early history of Konkan,
    HISMHM. (1928), pp.1-6.

I-1058
    Krishnasvami Aiyangār, Śakkoṭṭai, 1871-
        The Vakatakas and their place in the history
    of India, JIH, v.6 (1926), supplement.

JIH

I-1059
    Krishnasvami Aiyangār, Sakkoṭṭai, 1871-
        The Vakatakas in Gupta history, JIH, v.6
    (1926), supplement.

JIH

I-1060
    Mandlik, Vishvanath Narayan, 1833-1889.
        Salivahana and the Salivahana Saptasati,
    ASBJ, v.9 (1871-74), pp.127-38.

ASBJ

I-1061
    Mirashi, Vasudev Vishnu, 1893-
        Identification of King Jaitugi, NUJ, v.17
    (1966), pp.1-3.

I-1062
    Mirashi, Vasudev Vishnu, 1893-
        Lacunae in the study of the ancient history
    of Vidarbha, IHCP, v.23,pt.2 (1960), pp.188-
    90.

4 of R

I-1063
    Mirashi, Vasudev Vishnu, 1893-
        Vākāṭaka chronology, IHCP, v.10 (1947),
    pp.84-90. Also in IHQ, v.24 (1948), pp.
    148-55.

IHCP

I-1064
    Mirashi, Vasudev Vishnu, 1893-
        The Vatsagulma branch of the Vakataka
    dynasty, IHCP, v.4 (1940), pp.79-85.

IHCP

I-1065
Mirashi, Vasudev Vishnu, 1893-
Were the Mahārējas of Khāndesh feudatories
of the Guptas?, IHQ, v.23 (1947), pp.156-59.

Order to IHQ

I-1066
Mirashi, Vasudev Vishnu, 1893-
Were the Vakatakas the rulers of Asmaka?
IHQ, v.22 (1946), pp.309-15.

I HQ

I-1067
Mukerjee, Bratindra Nath.
Kanishka I and the Deccan; an examination
of Levi's theory, JASC, 4th ser.,v.5 (1965-
1966), pp.130-41.

I-1068
Nagabhusanam, A.
Trade and commerce in Western Deccan (1000-
1300 A.D.), IHCP, v.24 (1961), pp.83-84.

I-1069
Nandi, Ramendra Nath.
Social life in the Agraharas of the Deccan
(c.A.D.600-1000), IHCP, v.28 (1966), pp.97-
106.

I-1070
Nandimath, Shivalingayya Chennabasavagya, 1903-
The relation between the Chalukyas of
Badami and Kalyana, QJMS, v.48 (1957-1958),
pp.16-27.

QJMS

I-1071
Newton, Justice.
On recent additions to our knowledge of
the ancient dynasties of western India, ASBJ,
v.9 (1867-68), pp.1-19.

ASBJ

I-1072
Nunes, Leonardo, fl.1550.
Cronica de dom João de Castro, ed.by J.D.M.
Ford. Cambridge, Mass., Harvard Univ.Press,
1936. 269p.

I-1073
Pai, M.Govind.
Genealogy and chronology of the Vakatakas,
JIH, v.14 (1935), pp.1-26.

JIH

I-1074
Pai, M.Govind.
The genealogy and early chronology of the
early Kadambas of Banavasi, JIH, v.13 (1933),
pp.18-34,132-173.

I-1075
Puri, Baij Nath.
The dates of the Kadphises kings and their relations with the Saka Ksatraps of Western India, JIH, v.17 (1938), pp.275-87.

JIH

I-1080
Raghavachari, K.
Singhana II the Yadava King of Devgiri, IHCP, v.15 (1952), pp.191-96.

U of R

I-1076
Purohit, B.S.
The Vākatākas, IHQ, v.26 (1950), pp.301-308.

Order to IHQ

I-1081
Raikar, Y.A.
Yadava of Seunadesa, MSUBJ, v.14 (1965), pp.93-104.

I-1077
Pusalker, Achut Dattatraya, 1905-
Early history of Maharastra, ALB, v.25 (1961), pp.381-96.

I-1082
Ramacandraiya, O.
The death of Yusuf Adil Shah - the date?, IHCP, v.2 (1938), pp.319-23.

II

I-1078
Qanungo, Kalikaranjan, 1895-
Origin of the Bahmani Sultans of the Deccan, DUS, v.1 (1936), pp.137-44.

II

I-1083
Ramacandraiya, O.
Salivahana-hala, JIH, v.38 (1960), pp.365-68.

JIH

I-1079
Radhey Shyam.
Shah Tahir, influence and role in the politics of Deccan, JHR, v.12,no.2 (1970), pp.20-29.

I-1084
Ranade, P.V.
The origin of the Satavahanas - a new interpretation, IHCP, v.26,pt.1 (1964), pp.60-68. Also in: JMaU, v.5,no.1 (1964), pp.61-70.

I-1085
Rao, Rama.
The Kakatūjal and the Yādavas, AIOCPT,
v.10 (1940), pp.423-28.

vvvUofR

I-1086
Rao, Vasant Dinanath, 1913-
Identity of Raja Bimb with whom the Pāthāre
Prabhus migrated to Bombay in the 13th
century A.D., IHCP, v.10 (1947), pp.516-20.

IHCP

I-1087
Raychaudhuri, G.
History of the Western Chalukyas (political
and administrative) London, Univ.of London,
1948. *

Bloomfield

I-1088
Reddy, Y.G.
Kakatiya Ganapati Deva and the Yadavas of
Devagiri, JAHRS, v.30 (1964-1965), pp.63-70.

JaS '66

I-1089
Reu, Bisheshwar Nath, 1890-
The early Rāṣṭrakūtas of the Deccan and
Nizam's dominions, AIOCPT, v.10 (1940),
pp.411-18.

U of R

I-1090
Reu, Bisheshwar Nath, 1890-
The early Rashtrakutas of the Deccan and the
present Mysore State, JIH, v.12 (1933), pp.253-
58.

JIH

I-1091
Reu, Bisheshwar Nath, 1890-
History of the Rashtrakutas and Prof.Majum-
dar, JIH, v.16 (1937), pp.19-23.

JIH

I-1092
Roy, Nirod Bhushan.
The transfer of capital from Delhi to
Daulatabad: a new study, JIH, v.17 (1938),
pp.159-80.

JIH

I-1093
Rudra, son of Ananta, fl.1596.
Rudrakavi's great poem of the dynasty of
Rastraudha, cantos 1-13 and 18-20, intro-
duced, translated and annotated by J.L.de
Bruyne. Leiden, E.J.Brill, 1968. (Orien-
talia Rheno-Traiectina, v.10). 173p.

(series)
Mul... ...k District
vvv
UofR

I-1094
Saletore, Bhasker Anand.
Ancient Karnataka. Poona, Oriental Book
Agency, 1936. Vol.1 - History of Tulva.
(Poona oriental series, no.53). 668p.

NUR
UoL

I-1095
Saletore, Bhasker Anand.
The authenticity of the Mudhol firmans,
NIA, v.2 (1939), pp.6-24.

year? *new Indian antiquary*

NIA

I-1100
Shejwalkar, Trymbak Shankar.
A few fragments of the Rahim Bakhar, IHRCP,
v.25 (1948), pp.52-53.

IHRC

I-1096
Saletore, G.N.
Two minor Kadamba dynasties, JBHS, v.6
(1941), pp.48-67.

JBHS

I-1101
Shende, Shankar Ramachandra.
How, whence and when Maharashtra came into
being? In: Siddha-Bharati...or, the rosary
of Indology. Presenting 108 original papers
on Indological subjects in honour of the
60th birthday of Dr.Siddheshwar Varma. Ed.
by Vishva Bandhu. Pt.II. Hoshiarpur, 1950.
pp.285-90.

*Bhandarkar Index-Comm
Orienta Afric Studies v16.*

I-1097
Saletore, R.N.
Abhiras in the Deccan, QJMS, v.30 (1939),
pp.147-62.

QJMS

I-1102
Sherwani, Haroon Khan, 1891-
Ascendency of Mahmud Gawan, IC, v.14 (1940),
pp.274-89.

II

I-1098
Seth, D.R.
Akbar and the Deccan, IC, v.30 (1956),
pp.126-38.

IC 8 56

I-1103
Sherwani, Haroon Khan, 1891-
The Bahmani kingdom. Bombay, National
Information & Pubs., 1947. 48p.

Lc

I-1099
Sharma, R.S.
Political institutions and social and economic history: Satavahana polity, IHCP, v.28
(1966), pp.81-93.

U 7 R

I-1104
Sherwani, Haroon Khan, 1891-
The Bahmani kingdom on Mahmud Gawan's
arrival at Bidar, IC, v.14 (1940), pp.1-16.

DS
36
I·2

II

I-1105
Sherwani, Haroon Khan, 1891-
The Bahmanis of the Deccan. Hyderabad,
Deccan, Manager of Pubs., 1953. 453p.

I-1106
Sherwani, Haroon Khan, 1891-
Cultural influences under Ahmad Shah Wali
Bahmani, IC, v.18 (1944), pp.364-77.

I-1107
Sherwani, Haroon Khan, 1891-
Deccani diplomacy and diplomatic usage in
the middle of the fifteenth century, JIH,
v.16 (1937), pp.27-49.

I-1108
Sherwani, Haroon Khan, 1891-
Establishment of the Bahmani kingdom, JIH,
v.20 (1941), pp.288-306.

(The reign of Alau'd-din Hasan Bahman Shah)

I-1109
Sherwani, Haroon Khan, 1891-
The council of regency during the minority
of the Bahmani Ahmad III and Muhammad III
(1461-1466), JIH, v.19 (1940), pp.45-55.

I-1110
Sherwani, Haroon Khan, 1891-
Gangu Bahmani, JIH, v.20 (1941), pp.95-99.

1. Bahmanids, Kings of Kulbarga, A.B.748-
933/A.D.1347-1526.

I-1111
Sherwani, Haroon Khan, 1891-
The independence of Bahmani governors, IHCP,
v.7 (1944), pp.256-62; IHCP, v.8 (1945), pp.
159-62.

I-1112
Sherwani, Haroon Khan, 1891-
Khwāja-i-Jahān Maḥmud Gāwān's campaigns in
the Mahārāshtra, IHCP, v.1,pt.2 (1935), pp.
28-41. Also in: JIH, v.16 (1937), pp.263-
73.

I-1113
Sherwani, Haroon Khan, 1891-
Mahmud Gawan, the great Bahmani wazir.
Allahabad, Kitabistan, 1942. 267p.

I-1114
Sherwani, Haroon Khan, 1891-
Mahmud Gawan's early life and his relations
with Gilan, IC, v.13 (1939), pp.306-12. Also
in: JIH, v.18 (1939), pp.179-87.

I-1115
    Sherwani, Haroon Khan, 1891-
      Muhammad I, organiser of the Bahmani kingdom,
    11.2.1358-23.3.1375. JIH, v.21 (1942), pp.173-
    97.

II

I-1116
    Sherwani, Haroon Khan, 1891-
      The reign of Sultan Humāyūn Shāh Bahmanī
    and his character. IHCP, v.3 (1939), pp.688-
    700.

II

I-1117
    Sherwani, Haroon Khan, 1891-
      The Riyādu'linshā as a source book of Deccan
    history, IHRCP, v.17 (1941), pp.170-77.

II

I-1118
    Sherwani, Haroon Khan, 1891-
      Some aspects of Bahmani culture, IC, v.17
    (1943), pp.25-35.

II

I-1119
    Sherwani, Haroon Khan, 1891-
      Tāju'd-din Fīrōz and the synthesis of Bah-
    mani culture, NIA, v.6 (1943-44), pp.75-89.

II

I-1120
    Siddiqi, Abdul Majeed.
      Feroz Shah Bahmani as a nation builder of
    the Deccan, IHCP, v.2 (1938), pp.286-96.

II

I-1121
    Siddiqi, Abdul Majeed.
      Makhduma-i-Jahan: a great ruler of the
    Deccan, IC, v.17 (1943), pp.265-72.

II

I-1122
    Siddiqi, Abdul Majeed.
      Malik Saifuddin Gori, the constitution-framer
    in the Bahmani kingdom, IHCP, v.3 (1939), pp.
    701-11.

II

I-1123
    Siddiqi, Abdul Majeed.
      Mīr Faḍlullāh Unjū, IC, v.22 (1948), pp.
    165-73.

II

I-1124
    Siddiqi, Abdul Majeed.
      The organisation of the central and
    provincial governments of the Deccan under
    the Bahmanides, AIOCPT, v.8 (1935), pp.463-81.

V-1 R

I-1125
Siddiqi, Abdul Majeed.
Shaikh Siraj Junaidi and his contributions
to the medieval history of Deccan, IHCP, v.6
(1943), pp.238-42.

I&CP

I-1126
Siddiqi, Abdul Majeed.
Sheik Azari and his contribution to the
history of the Bahmani Deccan, IHCP, v.8
(1945), pp.230-34.

II

I-1127
Sinha, Sri Krishna, 1920-
Mediaeval history of the Deccan. Hyderabad,
Govt.of Andra Pradesh, 1964- V.I - Bahmanids.
(Andra Pradesh Govt.Archaeological series,
no.18).

U of R

I-1128
Sircar, Dineschandra, 1907-
Date of Kadamba Mrgesavarman, JIH, v.14
(1935), pp.344-46.

JIH

I-1129
Sircar, Dineschandra, 1907-
Kadamba Mayurasarma, NIA, v.1 (1938), pp.
240-48.

NIA

I-1130
Sircar, Dineschandra, 1907-
The successors of the Satavahanas in lower
Deccan, Calcutta, University of Calcutta,
1939. 432p.

LC

I-1131
Sreenivasachar, P.
The Yadavas of Devagiri chronology, JOR,
v.12 (1938), pp.46-60.

Annual Bd. of Ind Hist
1938

I-1132
Srinivasachari, Chidambaram S., 1890-1951.
A great Maratha service to South India
in the pre-Shivaji epoch. In: Sardesai
Commemorative Volume. Ed.by Shripad R.
Tikekar. Bombay, 1938. pp.73-80.

II

I-1133
Subrahmanya Aiyer, Kandadai Vaidyanatha, 1875-
Historical sketches of ancient Dekhan.
Madras, Modern Print.Works, 1917-69. 3v.

U of R
PL 480, '69

I-1134
Subramanian, K.R.
The relations between the Rastrakutas and
the Eastern Chalukyas from 747 A.D. to 925 A.D.,
IHCP, v.2 (1938), p.247.

I HCP

I-1135
Subramanian, T.N.
The home of the Satavahanas. QJMS. v.13 (1923), pp.591-94.

GJMS

I-1136
Trivedi, H.V.
Singhana I/Simharaja Yadava (C 1105-1145 A.D.). IHCP. v.15 (1952), pp.378-79.

u of R

I-1137
Vaidyanathan, K.S.
Pallava Perunjinga and the Yadavas. QJMS. v.30 (1940), pp.381-85.

OJMS

I-1138
Vasconcellos Abreu, Guilherme de, 1842-1907.
Chand-Bibi, a sultana branca de Amenagara; lenda indiana fantasiada de tradição historica de seculo XVI. Lisboa, 1898. 93p.

I-1139
Venkataramanayya, N.
Muslim historians on Muhammad Shah Bahmany I's war with Vijayanagara. ABORI. v.28 (1947), pp.1-13.

I-1140
Venkataramanayya, N.
The Rastrakuta King Krsna II and Gurjara-Pratiharas of Kanauj. IHCP. v.6 (1943), pp.163-70.

IHCP

I-1141
Venkataramanayya, N.
An unknown incident in the history of the Rastrakutas of Malkhed. IHCP. v.9 (1945), pp.85-90.

IHCP

I-1142
Verma, Onkar Prasad.
Administrative machinery under the Yadavas. JOIB. v.17 (1967), pp.161-65.

I-1143
Verma, Onkar Prasad.
Jaitugi, a new Silāhāra king. NUJ. v.17 (1966), pp.5-7.

I-1144
Verma, Onkar Prasad.
Was Yādava Ramachandra a fratricide? NUJ. v.18 (1967), pp.67-69.

I-1145
Verma, Onkar Prasad.
    The Yādavas and their times. Nagpur, Vidarbha Samshodhan Mandal, 1970. 418p.

    1. Deccan, India - Hist.

LC

I-1146
Wajahat Husain, S.
    Mahmud Gawan, JASC, v.1 (1935), pp.81-102.

II

I-1147
Yazdani, Ghulam, 1885- ed.
    The early history of the Deccan. London, Oxford University Press, 1960. 2v.

                    Biography

I-1148
Abbott, Justin Edwards, 1853-1932.
    The 300th anniversary of the birth of the Maratha king Shivaji, JAOS, v.50 (1930), pp. 159-63.

I-1149
Altekar, Anant Sadashiv, 1898-
    Shivaji's visit to Benares, JEHS, v.2 (1929), pp.191-94.

I-1150
Apte, D.V.
    When did Sivaji start his career of independence?, IHRCP, v.17 (1940), pp.44-46.

I-1151
Bala-Krishna, 1882-
    Shivaji the Great. Kolhapur, The Arya Book Depot, 1940. 4v.

I-1152
Bendrey, Vasudeo Sitaram, 1896-
    Coronation of Shivaj the Great; or, the procedure of the religious ceremony performed by Gagabhatta for the consecration of Shivaji as Hindu king. Bombay, Pub.by J.S.Bhatt for P.P.H.Bookstall, 1960. 132p.

I-1153
Bhonsle, R.Krishnarao.
    The birth-date of Shivaji the Great, JAHRS, v.4 (1930), pp.233-34.

I-1154
Chowdhury, Jogindra Nath.
    Malik Ambar. Dacca, Dacca Univ., 1933.

I-1155
Chowdhury, Jogindra Nath.
    Malik Amber: a biography based on original
sources. Dacca, 1935. 202p.

IOL

I-1156
Deopujari, M.B.
    Jijabai, the inspirer of Shivaji, IHQ.
v.31 (1955), pp.267-72.

JaS 56

I-1157
Deopujari, M.B.
    The military genius of Shivaji, IHCP, v.26,
pt.2 (1964), pp.40-41.

U of R

I-1158
Deshpande, Gangadharrao Keshavrao, rao saheb.
    The deliverance or the excape of Shivaji
the Great from Agra. Poona, A.S.Gokhale,
1929. (Fragments from the history of the
Marathas, series, no.1) 1v.

U of R

I-1159
Deshpande, Yeshwant Khushal, 1884-
    Fresh light on the history of the family
of Shivaji's mother, IHRCP, v.18 (1942),
pp.233-35.

U of R

I-1160
Deshpande, Yeshwant Khushal, 1884-
    Historical families of Berar during the
Mughal period, IHRCP, v.14 (1937), pp.104-107.

IHRCP

I-1161
Dikshit, G.S.
    A new portrait of Shivaji and fresh light
on an incident in his Karnatak expedition.
In: Studies in Indian history, Dr. A.G.Pawar
felicitation volume. Ed.by V.D.Rao. Kolhapur, Y.P.Pawar, 1968. pp.19-24.

U of R

I-1162
Guarda, Cosme da.
    Vida, e acçoens do famoso, e felicissimo
Sevagy, da India Oriental. Escrita por
Cosme da Guarda...Lisboa Occidental, Na
Officina da musica, 1730. 177p.

1. Sivajee, Raja, 162?----?

I-1163
Hamid al-Din Khan, bahadur, supposed author.
    Anecdotes of Aurangzib. With a Life of
Aurangzib and historical notes, by
Sir Jadunath Sarkar. 3d ed., rev. and enl.
Calcutta, M.C.Sarkar, 1949. 128p.

U of R

I-1164
Joshi, P.S.
    Early life of Chhatrapati Rajaram, QRHS,
v.7 (1967-1968), pp.180-86.

Q RHS

I-1165
　Joshi, P.S.
　　The escape of chhatrapati Rajaram from
　Panhala to Jinji, QRHS, v.10 (1970/71),
　pp.91-98.

BAS 1970

I-1166
　Joshi, P.S.
　　The work of Chhatrapati Rajaram in
　Maharashtra, from Manchakarohana to the
　departure for Jinji, QRHS, v.8 (1968-69),
　pp.184-192.

Nat'l ... ...
BAS Sept 1970

I-1167
　Kamdar, Keshavlal Himatram, 1891-
　　The year of Shivaji's birth, 1627 or 1630?,
　JBHS, v.2 (1929), pp.90-95.

JBHS

I-1168
　Kanole, V.K.
　　Some light on the descendants of Netaji
　Palker, IHCP, v.25 (1963), pp.137-39.

U H R

I-1169
　Karaka, Dosoo Framjee, 1911-
　　Shivaji; portrait of an early Indian.
　Bombay, Times of India Press, 1969. 182p.

Burg.

I-1170
　Karkaria, Rustomji Pestonji, 1869-1919.
　　The death of Shivaji, ASBJ, v.21 (Extra
　no.) Pt.VII (1900-1905), pp.439-56.

ASBJ

I-1171
　Karkaria, Rustomji Pestonji, 1869-1919.
　　The death of Shivaji and other essays.
　Bombay, 1906.

Calcutta Nat'l Lib.

I-1172
　Keluskar, Krishnarao Arjun.
　　The life of Shivaji Maharaj, founder of
　the Maratha empire; by N.S.Takakhav. Adapted
　from the original Marathi work written by
　K.A.Keluskar. Bombay, Manoranjan Press, 1921.
　659p.

　　1. Sivājī, Rāja, 1627-1680. 2. Marathas. 3.
　India - Hist. - European settlements, 1500-1765.

U H R

I-1173
　Kincaid, Dennis, 1905-1937.
　　The grand rebel; an impression of Shivaji,
　Founder of the Maratha empire. London, Collins,
　1937. 329p.

　　1. Sivaji, raja, 1627-1680. 2. Mahrattas.
　3. India -

U H R

I-1174
　Krishnajī Anant Sabhāsad.
　　Life and exploits of Shivaji, trans.into
　English from unpublished Marathi manuscript
　by Jagannath Lakshuman. Alibag, 1884. 125p.

BM

I-1175
Krishnajī Anant Sabhasad.
Śiva Chhatrapati; being a translation of
Sabhāsad Bakhar with extracts from
Chiṭṇīs and Śivadigvijaya, with notes, by
Śurendranath Sen. Calcutta, Univ.of
Calcutta, 1920. (Extracts and documents
relating to Maratha history, v.1). 274p.

1. Shivaji, Raja, 1627 - 12. ◯
U of R

I-1180
Morrison, Barrie M.
A history of Shivaji (an 18th century
French account), JIH, v.42 (1964), pp.49-
76.

Ja S 64 ◯

I-1176
Kulkarni, Vaman Balaji.
Shivaji, the portrait of a patriot.
Bombay, Orient Longmans, 1963. 236p.

U of R ◯

I-1181
Muddachari, B., 1929-
Rise of Shahji, JMyU, v.18 (1959), pp.21-
34.

1. Sultanates of the Deccan. ◯
F I

I-1177
Mahaley, K.L., 1922-
Shivaji, the pragmatist. Nagpur, Vishwa
Bharati Prakashan, 1969. 205p.

LC ◯

I-1182
Orleans, Pierre Joseph d', 1644-1698.
Histoire des deux conquerans tartares
qui ont subjugué la Chine. Histoire du
Sevagi et de son successeur, nouveaux
conquerans dans les Indes. Paris,
C.Barbin, 1688. 356p.

NYPL ◯

I-1178
Majumdar, B.N.
The generalship of Shivaji the Great, AQ,
v.80 (1960), pp.65-70.

Ja S ◯

I-1183
Oturkar, Rajaram Vinayak, 1898-
Part played by Jijabai in the foundation of
the Maratha State, IHCP, v.21 (1958), pp.361-
64.

I HCP ◯

I-1179
Modi, Jivanji Jamshedji, 1854-1933.
Rustom Manock (1635-1721 A.D.), the broker
of the English East India Company (1699 A.D.)
and the Persian Qisseh (history) of Rustom
Manock: a study, ASBJ, n.s.,v.6 (1930), pp.
1-220.

JBUS ◯

I-1184
Oturkar, Rajaram Vinayak, 1898-
Shivaji, IAC, v.5 (1957), pp.376-404.

JAS ◯

I-1185
Oturkar, Rajaram Vinayak, 1898-
A study of the movements of Shahaji (Shivaji's father) during the period of 1624-30, IHCP, v.19 (1956), pp.271-74.

u d R

I-1186
Phadke, S.R.
Death of Shivaji, IHCP, v.21 (1958), p.401.

I H C P

I-1187
Pudumjee, Bomonjee D.
Notes on the subjects of Shivaji's sword. Shivaji's portrait and Shivaji's residence called Javhair Khana on Sinhghad Hill. 2d ed. Bombay, 1929. 34p.

I O L

I-1188
Puntambekar, Shrikrishna Venkatesh.
The role of Ramdas in the Maratha revolution of the 17th century. In: Professor K.V.Rangaswami Aiyangar Commemoration Volume. Essays and papers written by his friends, pupils and admirers...presented...on his 61st birthday. Ed.by Shashtiabdapurti Commemoration Committee. Madras, Benares printed, 1940. pp.95-105.

Bhandarkar Index . . .

I-1189
Raddi, Sheshadri Vasudev.
Shivaji. A short life sketch dispelling some misconceptions about the national hero of Maharashtra. Thana, the author, 1921. 315p.

Bom (Pres) Cat

I-1190
Ranade, Mahadev Govind, 1842-1901.
The tree blossomed. Shivaji as a civil ruler, ASBJ, v.19 (1895-97), pp.202-14.

ASBJ

I-1191
Rawlinson, Hugh George, 1880-
The life and work of Gerald Aungier, founder of Bombay, IHRCP, v.10 (1927), pp.30-35.

i. 1707

I H R C P

I-1192
Rawlinson, Hugh George, 1880-
Shivaji the Maratha, his life and times. Oxford, Clarendon Press, 1915. 125p.

Nur
L

I-1193
Rawlinson, Hugh George, 1880-
Some notes on the life and work of Gerald Aungier, founder of Bombay, IHCP, v.10 (1927), pp.30-35.

R B H Soc

I-1194
Saletore, Bhasker Anand.
The author of the Marathi Bharata - his age and importance. In: Bharata Kaumudi; Studies in Indology in honour of Dr.Radha Kumud Mookerji. Allahabad, Indian press, 1945-1947. pp.655-58.

Bhandarkar Index

I-1195
Saletore, Bhasker Anand.
Some unknown events in Venkoji's career.
IHRCP, v.17 (1940), pp.39-43.

IHRC

I-1200
Sardesai, Govind Sakharam, 1865-1959.
An unknown but daring project of King
Sambhaji. In: A volume of studies in
Indology presented to Prof.P.V.Kane...
Ed.by S.M.Katre and P.K.Gode. Poona,
Oriental Book Agency, 1941. (Poona
Oriental Series no.75), pp.390-94.

~~u~R

I-1196
Sardesai, Govind Sakharam, 1865-1959.
Blue prints of Shivaji's career - the
Chatrapati's titles. JUB, n.s.,v.25 (1957),
pp.17-21.

gab57

I-1201
Sardesai, Govind Sakharam, 1865-1959, ed.
Shivaji souvenir. Girgaum, 1927. 3v.

eM

I-1197
Sardesai, Govind Sakharam, 1865-1959.
Kavindra Paramanand - author of a sanskrit
poem describing Shivaji's life. IHRCP, v.16
(1939), pp.44-49.

IHRC

I-1202
Sarkar, Sir Jadunath, 1870-1958.
An early supporter of Shivaji. IHC, v.?
(1931), pp.362-64.

Ordu. de I HQ

I-1198
Sardesai, Govind Sakharam, 1865-1959.
Shahji's role in Maratha history. In:
Prof.C.S.Srinivasachari Sixty-first
Birthday Celebration Volume. Madras,
1950. pp.201-04.

I-1203
Sarkar, Sir Jadunath, 1870-1958.
The first printed life of Shivaji, 1688.
MR, v.35 (1924), pp.517-21.

MR

I-1199
Sardesai, Govind Sakharam, 1865-1959.
Shambhaji's widow. MR, v.21 (1917), p.237.

INMR

I-1204
Sarkar, Sir Jadunath, 1870-1958.
History of Shivaji, 1667-1670. MR, v.25
(1919), pp.400-409.

NYPL

I-1205
Sarkar, Sir Jadunath, 1870-1958.
History of the leading nobles of the
kingdom of Bijapur 1627-1686. In: Papers
on Indo-Iranian and other subjects written
by several scholars in honour of Shams-ul-
Ulama Dr.Jivanji Jamshedji Modi. Ed.by the
Dr.Modi Memorial Volume Editorial Board.
Bombay, 1930. pp.251-59.

Bhandarkar
Oriental Aff Studies

I-1206
Sarkar, Sir Jadunath, 1870-1958.
The last years and death of Shivaji,
MR, v.24 (1918), pp.471-77.

vrv MR

I-1207
Sarkar, Sir Jadunath, 1870-1958.
Life of Shivaji, trans.from the French
of Abbe Carre, BISMHM, (1928), pp.36-63.

NRU
JBHS (1925)

I-1208
Sarkar, Sir Jadunath, 1870-1958.
Malik Ambar; a new life, IHQ, v.9 (1933),
pp.629-44.

I.I

I-1209
Sarkar, Sir Jadunath, 1870-1958.
Rise of Shahji Bhonsle, MR, v.22 (1917),
pp.247-54.

MR

I-1210
Sarkar, Sir Jadunath, 1870-1958.
Shivaji, a study in leadership. Jullundar,
Dayanand Anglo-Vedic College, 1950. 67p.

Bom (Pres)Cat

I-1211
Sarkar, Sir Jadunath, 1870-1958.
Shivaji: his genius, environment and achieve-
ment, MR, v.41 (1927), pp.618-22.

MR

I-1212
Sarkar, Sir Jadunath, 1870-1958.
Shivaji and his times. 6th rev.ed. Calcutta,
M.C.Sarkar, 1961. 459p.

U of R

I-1213
Sarkar, Jagadish Narayan, 1907-
The rise of Mir Jumla, IHRCP, v.19 (1943),
pp.105-108.

I.I

I-1214
Saswadkar, Prabhakar Laxman.
Shivaji in Busatin-us-Salatin, IHCP, v.25
(1964), pp.143-49.

U of R

I-1215
  Sathianathaier, R.
    A vindication of Venkaji Bhonsle, IHCP, v.2
  (1938), pp.595-601.

I HCP

I-1216
  Sen, Surendra Nath, 1890-
    Life of the celebrated Sevagy (and History
  of Sevagy); a translation, CR, v.23 (1927),
  pp.101-15; v.25 (1927), pp.114-23; v.26
  (1928), pp.222-44; v.28 (1928), pp.411-20;
  v.29 (1928), pp.127-36, 337-57.

U of R

I-1217
  Sen, Surendra Nath, 1890-   ed.& tr.
    Foreign biographies of Shivaji. Calcutta,
  The Book Co., 1927. (Extracts and documents
  relating to Maratha history, v.2). 549p.

V of 2

I-1218
  Seth, D.R.
    The life and times of Malik Ambar, IC, v.31
  (1957), pp.142-55.

    1. Nizam Shahs of Ahmadnagar.

JJ

I-1219
  Seth, D.R.
    Malik Ambar: an estimate, IC, v.19 (1945),
  pp.347-51.

JJ

I-1220
  Sharma, Dasaratha.
    A contemporary record of Sivaji's birth,
  JBRS, v.20 (1934), pp.184-85.

✓✓✓ JBRS

I-1221
  Sharma, Shripad Rama, 1897-
    Shivaji. Bombay, National Information and
  Pubs., 1947. 48p.

LC

I-1222
  Shyam, Radhey.
    Life and times of Malik Ambar. Delhi, Mun-
  shiram Manoharlal, 1968. 169p.

U 3 R
PL 480 ⅞80 p272

I-1223
  Sivaji and the rise of the Mahrattas, by
    Richard Carnac Temple and others. Cal-
    cutta, Susil Gupta, 1953. 157p.

U of R

I-1224
  Tafazzul Daud Sayeed Khan, Saiyyid.
    The real Sevaji. Allahabad, Popular print-
  ing works, 1935. 238p.

Nat Lib Calcutta

I-1225
Tamaskar, Bhaskar Gopal.
An estimate of Malik Ambar, QRHS, v.8,no.4
(1968-69), pp.247-50.

QRHS

I-1226
Tamaskar, Bhaskar Gopal.
Malik Ambar and the Portuguese, JBRS,
v.33 (1947), pp.25-44. Also in: JAHRS,
v.16 (1945-46), pp.91-111.

JBRS ...

I-1227
Tamaskar, Bhaskar Gopal.
Malik Ambar's civil administration, QRHS,
v.8,no.1 (1968-69), pp.39-51.

Q RHS

I-1228
Tamaskar, Bhaskar Gopal.
Malik Ambar's defence arrangement, CR,
v.135 (1955), pp.49-55.

Chaudhuri

I-1229
Tamaskar, Bhaskar Gopal.
Malik Ambar's financial administration,
QJMS, v.44 (1953), pp.54-62; v.44 (1954),
pp.90-98; v.46 (1955), pp.156-63.

QJMS

I-1230
Thakur, Vasudeo V.
Life and achievements of Ramachandrapant
Amatya, Bawadekar, Hukmat-Panna, 1650-1720 A.D.,
IHRCP, v.17 (1940), pp.199-201.

IHRC

I-1231
Vaidya, Chintamana Vinayaka, 1861-1938.
Shivaji, the founder of Maratha Swaraj.
Poona, 1931. 418p.

BM

I-1232
Vaidya, Chintamana Vinayaka, 1861-1938.
Siva Bharata and the new date of Shivaji's
birth, JIH, v.6 (1927), pp.177-97.

JLHS

I-1233
Vaidya, G.M.
Raje Shiv Chhatrapati. Poona, Vidarbha
Marathwada, 1966. (Makers of India series,
8). 42p.

I-1234
Yazdani, Zubaida.
Malik Ambar, IC, v.34 (1960), pp.63-65.

II

General works

I-1235
  Bāla-Krishna, 1882-
    The European records on Shivaji, IHRCP,
    v.12 (1929), pp.40-48.

I-1236
  Bāla-Krishna, 1882-
    The nature of Sardeshmukhi during Shivaji's
    time, IHCP, v.3 (1939), pp.1189-93.

IHCP

I-1237
  Banhatti, Shrinivas Narayan, 1901-
    The social and political significance of
    the statecraft of Shivaji, IHCP, v.3 (1939),
    pp.1218-30.

LHCP

I-1238
  Basu, Kamal Krishna.
    The Bijapur-court letters, JBRS, v.27
    (1941), pp.255-62.

II

I-1239
  Behere, Narayan Keshav, 1890-1958.
    The background of Maratha renaissance
    in the 17th century; historical survey
    of the social, religious and political
    movements of the Marathas. Bangalore
    City, Bangalore press, 1946. (Rao
    Bahadur Bapurao Dada Kinkhede lecture
    series, 1934). 175p.

4/R.

I-1240
  Belekar N.L.
    The importance of the Bhonslas in Indian
    history, IHRCP, v.11 (1928), pp.67-72.

I-1241
  Bendrey, Vasudeo Sitaram, 1896-
    Mahārāshtra of the Shivashāhī period (seven-
    teenth century) Bombay, Phoenix Pubs., 1946.
    35p.

LC

I-1242
  Chaghtai, M.A.
    A contemporary copy of an Adil Shahi farman
    to Shahji Bhonsle, IHRCP, v.20 (1944), pp.11-
    12.

Adil Shahs of Bijapur

II

I-1243
  Chaghtai, M.A.
    A farman of Aurangzeb Alamgir to a zamin-
    dar in the province of Berar, IHRCP, v.23
    (1946), pp.8-9.

II

I-1244
  Chaghtai, M.A.
    A unique farman of Emperor Aurangzeb to a
    Maratha chief, IHRCP, v.18 (1942), pp.64-67.

IHRCP

I-1245
Commissariat, Manekshah Sorabshah, 1881-
Political and economic condition of Gujarat during the seventeenth century. IHRCP, v.3 (1921), pp.35-50.

IHRCP

I-1246
Deshpande, Yeshwant Khushal, 1884-
Revenue administration of Berar in the reign of Aurangzeb, IHRCP, v.12 (1929), pp.81-87. Also in: BPP, v.39 (1930), pp.43-48.

II

I-1247
Duarte, A.
Piracy in the Western seas in the reign of Aurangzeb, JUB, v.5 (1937), pp.1-30.

II

I-1248
English records on Shivaji. Poona, Shiva charitra karyalaya, 1931. (Shivaji tercentenary memorial series, 6) 2v.in 1.

U of R

I-1249
Gode, Parashuram Krishna, 1891-
Hari Kavi's contribution to the problem of the Bhavani sword of Shivaji the Great, NIA, v.3 (1940), pp.81-100.

IoL

I-1250
Gode, Parashuram Krishna, 1891-
The identification of Raghunatha, the protegé of Queen Dipabai of Tanjore and his contact with Saint Ramadas between A.D.1648 and 1682. Tanjore, 1942. (Reprint from the Journal of the Tanjore Sarasvati Mahal Library, v.3,no.1). 12p.

IoL

I-1251
Gode, Parashuram Krishna, 1891-
Parijata-dhvaja of the Maratha King Sambhaji. Calcutta, 1940. (Reprinted from the IHQ, v.16). 8p.

I-1252
Gokhale, Balkrishna Govind, 1919-
English trade with western India (1650-1700), JIH, v.42 (1964), pp.329-42.

JIH 64

I-1253
Gokhale, Balkrishna Govind, 1919-
English trade with western India (1600-1650), JIH, v.40 (1962), pp.269-86.

JIH 62

I-1254
Gupte, D.N.
Singarh or the rise of the Mahratta empire, NR, v.5 (1909), pp.233-42.

MR

I-1255
Hyderabad, India (State) Central Records Office.
Selected waqai of the Deccan 1660-1671. Ed.
by Yusuf Husain. Hyderabad, Central Records
Office, 1953. 343p.

SOAS

I-1256
Karandikar, Shivaram Laxman, 1899-1969.
The rise and fall of the Maratha power.
Vol.1: 1620-1689 (Shahaji, Shivaji, Sambhaji).
Poona, Sitabai Shivram Karandikar, 1969.
365p.

LC

I-1257
Kasinatha Tryambaka Telanga, 1840-1893.
Gleanings from Maratha chronicles,
QJPSS, v.15 (1892), pp.1-50.

QJSS

I-1258
Khan, Yar Muhammad.
Jahangir and the Deccan states, JASP, v.4
(1959), pp.97-112.

II

I-1259
Khan, Yar Muhammed.
The political relations of the Mughals with
the Deccan states (1556-1658 A.D.) London,
London Univ., 1958. 392p. *

SOAS

I-1260
Khan, Yusuf Husain.
The status of the Subedars and Diwans of the
Deccan in the time of Shah Jehan, IHCP, v.8
(1945), pp.273-76. Also in: IC, v.20 (1946),
pp.384-90.

II

I-1261
Krishna, M.H.
Shahaji's tomb at Hodigere, AIOCPT, v.10
(1940), pp.429-32.

U of R

I-1262
Kulkarni, Anant Ramchandra, 1925-
Encouragement to agriculture in Maharashtra
during Shivaji's period (1630-1680 A.D.),
IHCP, v.25 (1964), pp.182-85.

U of R

I-1263
Kulkarni, Anant Ramchandra, 1925-
Maharashtra in the age of Shivaji. Poona,
Deshmunkh, 1969. 308p.

History
BDCRI

I-1264
Kulkarni, Anant Ramchandra, 1925-
Population estimates of Shivaji's Maharashtra,
IHCP, v.23 (1960), p.258.

U of R

I-1265
Kulkarni, Anant Ramchandra, 1925-
  The position of women in Maharashtra in
Sivaji's times, JMaU, v.5 (1964), pp.71-77.

J MaU

I-1270
Kulkarni, Govind Trimbakrao.
  Maratha war of independence (1680 A.D.-1707
A.D.) Poona, Univ.of Poona, 1967. *

Jayakar Lib. #142

I-1266
Kulkarni, Anant Ramchandra, 1925-
  Protection to salt industry by Shivaji,
IHCP, v.24 (1961), pp.188-90.

44R

I-1271
Mavaji, Purushottama Vishrama, 1879-1929.
  Shivaji's Swarajya, ASBJ, v.22 (1908),
pp.30-42.

ASBJ

I-1267
Kulkarni, Anant Ramchandra, 1925-
  Rajgad: the first capital of Shivaji.
In: Studies in Indian history,
Dr.A.G.Pawar felicitation volume. Ed.
by V.D.Rao. Kolhapur, Y.P.Pawar, 1968.
pp.156-71.

44R

I-1272
Misra, Bankey Behari.
  The incident of Javli, JIH, v.15 (1936),
pp.54-70.

N YPL

I-1268
Kulkarni, Anant Ramchandra, 1925-
  Social and economic position of Brahmins in
Maharashtra in the age of Shivaji, IHCP, v.26,
pt.2 (1964), pp.66-74.

IHCP

I-1273
Pagdi, Setumadhava Rao, 1910-
  Administration of Maharashtra under the
Mughals: a study, JUB, v.30 (1961-1962),
pp.66-78.

JUB '62

I-1269
Kulkarni, Anant Ramchandra, 1925-
  Village life in the Deccan in the 17th
century, IESHR, v.4 (1967), pp.38-52.

*History
IESHR
EDCR, p. 35*

I-1274
Pissurlencar, Panduronga S.S.
  The extinction of the Nizamshahi. In:
Sardesai Commemorative Volume. Ed.by
Shripad R.Tikekar. Bombay, 1938.
pp.27-46.

[ ]

I-1275
Rāmacandra Nīḷakaṇṭha Bavadekara, d.1733.
    A royal edict on the principles of state
policy, and organization during the sixty
years' war of Maratha independence (A.D.1646-
1706) otherwise called Ramachandrapant Amatya's
Rajaniti, dated A.D.1716. Trans.into English
with an introduction, full notes and references,
by Shrikrishna Venkatesh Puntambekar. Madras,
Diocesan Press, 1929.

✓✓✓ Calcutta nat'l Lib

I-1276
Rao, Vasant Dinanath, 1913-
    Ajnyapatra re-examined, JIH, v.29 (1951),
pp.63-90.

JIH

I-1277
Rao, Vasant Dinanath, 1913-
    Shri Shiva Raj Rajyabhisheka Kalpataru.
In: Mahamahopadhyaya Prof.D.V.Potdar
sixty-first birthday commemoration
volume. Ed.by Surendra Nath Sen.
Poona, 1950. pp.352-68.

Birendeckav undex
Com m, vols.

I-1278
Rao, Vasant Dinanath, 1913-
    Side-light on the Maratha life from the
Bardic literature of the 18th century, IHCP,
v.3 (1939), pp.1194-1212.

IHCP

I-1279
Rawlinson, Hugh George, 1880-
    European tombs and graveyards of the 17th
century in western India, IHRCP, v.9 (1926),
pp.35-41.

IHRCP

I-1280
Sankara Rao, A.
    Hindu India from Talikota (1565) to Shivaji's
rise (1660), JAHRS, v.2 (1927), pp.50-57.

JBHS

I-1281
Sarkar, Sir Jadunath, 1870-1958.
    House of Shivaji; studies and documents of
Maratha history: royal period. 3d ed. Cal-
cutta, M.C.Sarkar, 1955. 343p.

uofR

I-1282
Sarkar, Sir Jadunath, 1870-1958.
    Shivaji letters, MR, v.3 (1908), pp.21-
25.

MR

I-1283
Sarkar, Jagadish Narayan, 1907-
    The Karnatak during Aurangzeb's Bijapur
campaign and the war of succession, IHCP,
v.9 (1945), pp.304-305.

IHCP

I-1284
Sen, Surendra Nath, 1890-
    Half a century of the Maratha navy, JIH,
v.10 (1931), pp.251-65; v.11 (1932), pp.17-
40.

NYPL

I-1285
Sen, Surendra Nath, 1890-
A note on the annexation of Jawli. In:
Sardesai commemorative volume. Ed.by
Shripad R.Tikekar. Bombay, 1939. pp.197-
201.

Bhandarkar Index to Comm Vols,

I-1286
Sen, Surendra Nath, 1890-
The revenue policy of Shivaji, JUC, v.4
(1921), pp.237-70.

NYPL

I-1287
Sharma, Shripad Rama, 1897-
The founding of Maratha freedom. Rev.ed.
Bombay, Orient Longmans, 1964. 467p.

1. Marathas - Hist.
Relations with European
Powers   Marathas - Foreign relations

I-1288
Dalvi, D.A.
The Khanderi affairs and Shivaji's relations
with the English factors at Bombay, IHCP, v.28
(1966), pp.180-87.

4 r/R

I-1289
D'Costa, Anthony.
Correspondence between Sivaji and the
government of Goa, 1678-1679. Indica, v.1
(1964), pp.187-97.

JAS '66

I-1290
De, J.C.
The immediate effects of the Maratha attack
on English trading interests at Surat, NIA,
v.2 (1940), pp.677-83.

N1A

I-1291
Desai, Walter Sadgun, 1892-
The relations of Bombay with the Marathas
during the Company's war with Aurangzeb, 1685-
1690, IHCP, v.2 (1938), pp.601-606.

II

I-1292
Gokhale, Balkrishna Govind, 1919-
Bombay and Sambhaji, ASBJ, n.s.,v.34/35
(1959/60), pp.59-67.

JAS '62

I-1293
Gokhale, Balkrishna Govind, 1919-
Bombay and Shivaji (1668-1680), ASBJ,
n.s.,v.33 (1958), pp.69-79.

JAS 61

I-1294
Hatalkar, V.G.
The relations between Shivaji and the French,
IHCP, v.9 (1945), pp.325-31.

IHCP

I-1295
Lobato, Alexandre.
Relações luso-Maratas, 1658-1737. Lisboa, Centro de Estudos Historicos Ultramarinos, 1965. (Estudos, memorias e documentos, para a historia des relações internacionais no Ultramar). 180p.

K

I-1296
Moraes, George Mark.
The causes of the Maratha-Portuguese War, 1683-84, IHRCP, v.18 (1942), pp.64-67.

I-1297
Moraes, George Mark.
The Maratha-Portuguese war of 1683-84, JUB, v.11 (1943), pp.31-47.

JUB

I-1298
Moraes, George Mark.
Portuguese diplomacy during the war of Maratha liberation. In: Indica (The Indian Historical Research Institute Silver Jubilee Commemoration Volume). Bombay, 1953. pp.274-78.

Bhandarkar Lib. Comm. vols.

I-1299
Moraes, George Mark.
A Portuguese embassy to Sambhaji - 1684, IHCP, v.22 (1959), pp.303-13.

IHCP

I-1300
Moraes, George Mark.
Shivaji and the Portuguese, ASBJ, n.s., v.34/35 (1959/60), pp.172-84.

JAS 62

I-1301
Nilakanta Sastri, Kallidaikurichi Aiyah Aiyar, 1892-
Sivaji's charters to the Dutch on the Coromandel Coast, IHCP, v.3 (1939), pp.1156-65.

U of R

I-1302
Oturkar, Rajaram Vinayak, 1898-
Sambhaji's relations with the sea powers in Konkan, IHCP, v.15 (1952), pp.254-58.

U of R

I-1303
Pissurlencar, Panduronga S.S.
The attitude of the Portuguese towards Shivaji during the campaign of Shaista Khan and Jai Singh, IHRCP, v.9 (1926), pp.109-115.

IHRCP

I-1304
Pissurlencar, Panduronga S.S.
A Portuguese embassy to Raigad in 1684, IHCP, v.1,pt.2 (1935), pp.66-77.

IHCP

I-1305
Pissurlencar, Panduronga S.S.
Portugueses e Maratas. I.Shivaji.
(With an appendix: O original do tratado
de 1667 confirmado por Shivaji...in the
original Marathi text). Nova Goa,
Boletim do Instituto Vasco da Gama, 1926.
(Separata do Boletim do Instituto
Vasco da Gama de Nova Goa, no.1). 53p.

SOAS

I-1306
Pissurlencar, Panduronga S.S.
Rajaram and the Portuguese, IHRCP, v.17
(1940), pp.222-27.

4 of R

I-1307
Powar, Appasaheb Ganapatrao, 1906-
The Sidi's incident and the Surat factory
demands in 1683, NIA, v.6 (1943-44), pp.1-6.

II

I-1308
Sarkar, Sir Jadunath, 1870-1958.
Portuguese-Maratha War, 1683-1684, JHAS,
v.5 (1919-1920), pp.1-32.

I-1309
Sarkar, Sir Jadunath, 1870-1958.
Shivaji and the English in Western India,
JBRS, v.4 (1918), pp.418-34.

JBRS

I-1310
Sen, Surendra Nath, 1890-
The Khanderi expedition of Charles Boone.
In: Dr.S.Krishnaswami Aiyangar Commemoration
Volume. Essays and papers presented to
Dr.Krishnaswami Aiyangar on his 66th birth-
day. Ed.by B.Bhattacharyya and others.
Madras, 1936. pp.138-42.

Bhandarkar Inter-
Comm vols.

I-1311
Sen, Surendra Nath, 1890-
Oxinden embassy, IHQ, v.3 (1927), pp.457-
69.

JBHS

I-1312
Tamaskar, Bhaskar Gopal.
The Carwar factory and Shivaji, PO, v.6
(1941), pp.217-29: v.7 (1942), pp.109-18:
165-76.

ABIHI v.5

I-1313
Tamaskar, Bhaskar Gopal.
The Dharangaon factory and Sivaji, QJMS,
v.33 (1942-43), pp.125-32.

QJMS

I-1314
Tamaskar, Bhaskar Gopal.
The English resettlement at Rajapore and
their relations with Sivaji, QJMS, v.35
(1945), pp.143-50, 193-98.

QJMS

I-1315
Tamaskar, Bhaskar Gopal.
The first encounter of Shivaji with the English, JIH, v.25 (1947), pp.84-120, 295-316.

NYPL

I-1316
Tamaskar, Bhaskar Gopal.
The policy of Shivaji and the English, NIA, v.4 (1941), pp.190-200,221-36.

NIA

I-1317
Tamaskar, Bhaskar Gopal.
Shivaji and the Europeans, JIH, v.25 (1947), pp.84-120.

JIH

Relations with Indian Powers

I-1318
Abbas, S.Ali.
Aurangzeb and the Mughal decline: a critical study, JPUHS, v.14 (1962), pp.1-25.

JPUHS '62

I-1319
Basu, Basanta Kumar.
Some notes on Aurangzib's expedition against Bijapur and the fortress of Golconda, BPP, v.40 (1930), pp.32-37.

I-1320
Chauhan, D.V.
Siddi Jauhar at Panhala, IHCP, v.25 (1963), pp.133-37.

4 MR

I-1321
Diskalkar, Dattatraya Balkrishna, 1892-
Shahji's relations with Vijayanagar. In: Vijayanagara sexcentenary commemorative volume. Ed.by Vijayanagara Empire Sexcentenary Association. Dharwar, 1936. pp.119-23.

Bhandarkar index to Comm. vols.

I-1322
Foster, Sir William, 1863-
Sivaji's raid upon Surat in 1664, IA, v.50 (1921), pp.312-21; v.51 (1922), pp.1-6.

II

I-1323
Goetz, Hermann, 1898-
Notes on the seige of Purandhar by Maharaja Jai Singh, PO, v.7 (1942), pp.181-86.

I-1324
Karkaria, Rustomji Pestonji, 1869-1919.
Pratapgad Fort, and the episode of Shivaji and Afzal Khan. Told from the original Maratha chronicles. Poona, Aryabhushan Press, 1896. 25p.

BM

I-1325
Khare, Ganesh Hari, 1901-
An Ādilshāhī farmān against Shivaji, the
Great, ABORI, v.25 (1944), pp.143-44.

Khare

I-1326
Krishna, M.H.
Sivaji and the Mysore Raj, QJMS, v.31
(1941), pp.380-83.

QJMS

I-1327
Krishnasvāmi Aiyangār, Sākkoṭṭai, 1871-
The rise of the Mahratta power in the south,
JIH, v.9 (1930), pp.173-217.

JIH

I-1328
Kulkarni, Anant Ramchandra, 1925-
Ram Singh and Shivaji's escape from Agra,
IHCP, v.28 (1966), p.169. Also in: JUP, v.31
(1969), pp.1-14.

U of R

I-1329
Kulkarni, Govind Trimbakrao.
Prince Muizz-ud-Din's siege of Panhala
(1692-1694): some unpublished information,
BIS, v.6 (July 1969), pp.59-63.

U of R

I-1330
Kunhan Raja, Chittenjoor, 1895-
Mirja Raja Jai Singh and Shivaji, IHQ,
v.22 (1946), pp.307-308.

Index to IHQ

I-1331
Kunte, B.G.
Aurangzeb's seige of Panhala. In: Studies in
Indian history, Dr. A.G.Pawar felicitation
volume. Ed.by V.D.Rao. Kolhapur, Y.P.Pawar,
1968. pp.172-89.

U of R

I-1332
Kunte, B.G.
Mughal Maratha conflict (1680-1707). A few
original documents, JUB, n.s.,v.33 (1964-
1965), pp.1-20.

JUB

I-1333
Moreland, William Harrison, 1868-1938, ed.
Relations of Golconda in the early seventeenth
century. London, Hakluyt Society, 1931. 109p.

U of R

I-1334
Muddachari, B., 1929-
The Mysore-Maratha relations in the 17th
century. Mysore, Prasaranga, Univ.of Mysore,
1969. 176p.

Mysore. Hist   Marathas hist
LC

I-1335
Mujib-ar-Rahman.
Shivaji and Afzul Khan. *IC*, v.12 (1938), pp.41-60.

II

I-1340
Powar, Appasaheb Ganapatrao, 1906-
An unrecorded Mughal campaign of the year A.D.1690-1691, *IHRCP*, v.22 (1945), pp.84-85.

II

I-1336
Pagdi, Setumadhava Rao, 1910-
Lectures on Maratha Mughal relations, 1680-1707. Nagpur, Nagpur University, 1966. 158p.

u of R

I-1341
Raja, C. Kunhan.
Mirja Raja Jaisingh and Shivaji, *IHC*, v.22 (1946), pp.307-08.

IHQ

I-1337
Phadke, S.R.
Rahimdad Khan, *IHCP*, v.23 (1960), pp.259-60.

UofR

I-1342
Saletore, R.N.
The beginnings of the Maratha revenue system in Karnataka, *ASBJ*, n.s.,v.15 (1939), pp.43-49.

I-1338
Potdar, Datto Vaman, 1890-
Afzakhan's invasion affects Vishalgad fort, *IHRCP*, v.16 (1939), pp.41-43.

IHRCP *Indial (Rep.) Indian Historical records committee proceedings*

I-1343
Saletore, R.N.
Sambhaji in Karnatak, *JOR*, v.13 (1939), pp.54-70.

JOR

I-1339
Powar, Appasaheb Ganapatrao, 1906-
An unrecorded Maratha victory of the year 1699 A.D., *IHCP*, v.6 (1943), pp.357-58.

IHCP

I-1344
Sarkar, Sir Jadunath, 1870-1958.
Aurangzeb's seige of Satara (as described in contemporary records), *IHRCP*, v.4 (1922), pp.2-11.

II

I-1345
    Sarkar, Sir Jadunath, 1870-1958.
    The Haft Anjuman of Udairaj alias Tale'yar
Munshi of Mirza Rajah Jai Singh, BPP, v.82
(1963), pp.65-73; v.83 (1964), pp.43-55;
v.84 (1965), pp.63-76.

II

I-1346
    Sarkar, Sir Jadunath, 1870-1958.
    The history of the Madras coast, 1680-
1690, JIH, v.3, pp.64-78.

JIH

I-1347
    Sarkar, Sir Jadunath, 1870-1958.
    How Jai Singh defeated Shivaji, MR, v.5
(1909), pp.287-94.

I-1348
    Sarkar, Sir Jadunath, 1870-1958.
    The last campaign of Aurangzib (1705),
JBRS, v.9 (1923), pp.353-68.

JBRS

I-1349
    Sarkar, Sir Jadunath, 1870-1958.
    The last campaign of Shivaji, IHQ, v.4
(1928), pp.605-11.

JBHS

I-1350
    Sarkar, Sir Jadunath, 1870-1958.
    Shahji Bhonsle in Mysore, MR, v.46 (1929),
pp.7-12.

MR

I-1351
    Sarkar, Sir Jadunath, 1870-1958.
    Shivaji in South Konkan and Kanara, JBRS,
v.5, no.1 (1919), pp.114-33.

V of R

I-1352
    Sarkar, Sir Jadunath, 1870-1958.
    Shivaji in the Madras Karnatak, MR, v.35
(1924), pp.149-55. Also in: IHRCP, v.6 (1924),
pp.20-28.

MR   IHRCP

I-1353
    Sarkar, Sir Jadunath, 1870-1958, ed.
    Rajasthani records: Shivaji's visit to
Aurangzib at Agra; a collection of con-
temporary Rajasthani letters from the
Jaipur state archives with an exhaustive
introduction and summary translations.
Calcutta, 1963. (Indian History Congress
Research Series, no.1). 1v.

V of R

I-1354
    Sarkar, Jagadish Narayan, 1907-
    Mir Jumla's diplomatic relations with Sri
Ranga Rayal and Shahuji Bhonsla, JBRS, v.30
(1944), pp.248-54. Also in: IHCP, v.7 (1944),
pp.360-65.

II

I-1355
Sarkar, Jagadish Narayan, 1907-
Mirza Rajah Jai Singh and Shivaji, JIH,
v.62 (1964), pp.251-64.

JIH 64

I-1360
Srinivasachari, Chidambaram S., 1890-1951.
Murari Rao Ghorepade (a Maratha adventurer
in the Carnatic), IHQ, v.15 (1939), pp.551-74.

I HQ

I-1356
Sarkar, Jagadish Narayan, 1907-
Recall of Mirza Raja Jai Singh and his death,
IHCP, v.28 (1966), pp.169-76.

U of R

I-1361
Srinivasachari, Chidambaram S., 1890-1951.
Shahaji and his achievment in the Carnatic,
AIOCPT, v.9 (1937), pp.777-88.

U of R

I-1357
Shejwalkar, Trymbak Shankar.
Shivaji's raid on Basrur, BDCRI, v.5,no.1
(1943), pp.1-12.

BDCRI

I-1362
Srinivasachari, Chidambaram S., 1890-1951.
A Tamil account of Shivaji's expedition
to the south and the Mughal siege of Gingee. In: Mahamahopadhyaya Prof.D.V.Potdar
sixty-first birthday commemoration volume.
Ed.by Surendra Nath Sen. Poona, 1950.
pp.1-8.

Bhandarkar Inst.
Com. v. vol's

I-1358
Srinivasachari, Chidambaram S., 1890-1951.
The Maratha occupation of Gingee and its
significance, IHCP, v.4 (1940), pp.297-305.

J HCP

I-1363
Tamaskar, Bhaskar Gopal.
The first plunder of Surat by Shivaji,
IHCP, v.5 (1941), pp.62-64.

U of R

I-1359
Srinivasachari, Chidambaram S., 1890-1951.
The Maratha occupation of Gingee and the
early years of their rule therein. In:
A volume of studies in Indology presented
to Prof.P.V.Kane, ed.by S.H.Katre and P.K.
Gode. Poona, Oriental Book Agency, 1941.
pp.456-68.

U of R

I-1364
Tamaskar, Bhaskar Gopal.
The second plunder of Surat by Shivaji,
IHCP, v.5 (1941), pp.64-66.

U of R

I-1365
Udairaj, Munshi, d.1675.
   The military despatches of a seventeenth
century Indian general; being an English
translation of the Haft Anjuman of Munshi
Udairaj, alias Tale'yar Khan by Jagadish
Narayan Sarkar. Calcutta, Scientific Books
Agency, 1969. 166p.

PL480,'69

I-1366
Verma, B.D.
   Shahaji's letter to a minister of Bijapur,
IHCP, v.5 (1941), p.100.

U Y R

I-1367
Wali, Abdul.
   Aurangzib's relations with Rajputs, Marhattas
and others. Side-lights from unpublished Persian correspondence, Islamica, v.1 (1925),
pp.428-53.

Biography   History - 1707-1858

I-1368
Abdul Ali, A.F.M.
   Mahadji Sindhia of Gwalior, MusR, v.4
(1929), pp.31-40. Also published in; IHCP,
v.12 (1929), pp.108-16; and BPP, v.33 (1930),
pp.3-11.

Case

I-1369
Agaskar, M.S.
   Mahadji Sindhia - a political career in
India, e.e. 1730-1794. Bombay, Univ.of
Bombay, 195- *

Case

I-1370
Agaskar, M.S.
   Mahadji Sindhia in the battle of Panipat,
Jan.14, 1761 A.D., IHCP, v.16 (1953), pp.
284-85.

U Y R

I-1371
   Authentic and faithful history of that
archpyrate Tulagee Angria, with a
curious narrative of the siege and taking
of the town and fortress of Geriah, and
the destruction of his whole naval force,
by Admiral Watson and Colonel Clive...
In a letter to a merchant in London,
from his brother, a factor at Bombay...
London, J.Cooke, 1756. 70p.

VVV NUC pre 1956

I-1372
   Authentic memoirs of Tippoo Sultaun, includ-
ing his cruel treatment of English prison-
ers; account of his campaigns with the
Mahrattas ... By an Officer in the East
India Company. Calcutta, 1819.

Calcutta Nat'l Lib.

I-1373
Banerjee, Anil Chandra, 1910-
   Peshwa Madhav Rao I. Calcutta, A.Mukherjee,
1943. 266p.

NUR
LC

I-1374
Banerjee, Anil Chandra, 1910-
   Peshwa Madhav Rao I and Raghunath Rao,
IHCP, v.4 (1940), pp.306-15.

I-1375
Banerjee, Anil Chandra, 1910-
Peshwa Madhav Rao I and the Nizam (1761-1763), JIH, v.20 (1938), pp.181-91.

Index Islam

I-1376
Banerji, R.D.
Balaji Baji Rao: an historical retrospect, IHQ, v.4 (1928), pp.431-46.

IHQ

I-1377
Basu, Basanta Kumar.
The side-light on the life of Daulat Rao Sindhia, Maharajah of Gwalior (1794-1824), BPP, v.39 (1930), pp.144-49.

Case

I-1378
Bell, Evans, 1825-1887.
Memoir of General John Briggs, of the Madras Army, with comments on some of his words and work. London, Chatto & Windus, 1885. 293p.

U of R

I-1379
Burway, Mukund Wamanrao.
Life of the Hon'ble rajah, Sir Dinkar Rao, Musheer-i-khas muntazim Bahadur, prime minister of Gwalior, 1858-59. Bombay, Tatva-Vivechaka Press, 1907. 255p.

pre 54 imprints

I-1380
Burway, Mukund Wamanrao.
Life of Ranoji Rao Sindhia, founder of the Gwalior state. Bombay, 1917. 73p.

CM

I-1381
Burway, Mukund Wamanrao.
Life of Subhedar Malhar Rao Holdar, founder of the Indore State, 1693-1766 A.D. Indore, Holder State Printing Press, 1930. (Indian history series) 314p.

BM

I-1382
Burway, Mukund Wamanrao and Burway, Ramkrishna Ganesh.
Life and times of Shivaji II. Indore City, M.W.Burway, 1932. 242p.

U of R

I-1383
Chitale, Vishnu Sitaram.
Assassination of Jayappa Shinde, IHCP, v.16 (1953), pp.347-48.

U of R

I-1384
Chitale, Vishnu Sitaram.
Raghunath Rao at Nasik, 1764, IHRCP, v.25 (1948), pp.58-62.

IHRC

I-1385
  Chitale, Vishnu Sitaram.
    Relations between Madhav Rao and Janoji
  Bhonsle. IHRCP. v.28 (1951), pp.13-18.

4 1 R

I-1386
  Colebrooke, Sir Thomas Edward, 4th bart.,
    1813-1890.
    Life of the Hon.Mountstuart Elphinstone.
  London, J.Murray, 1884. 2v.

LC

I-1387
  Cotton, Evan.
    Benoit de Boigne, BPP, v.33 (1927), pp.
  91-105. Also in: IHRCP, v.9 (1926), pp.8-
  21.

J BHS

I-1388
  Cotton, James Sutherland, 1847-1918.
    Mountstuart Elphinstone. Oxford,
  Clarendon Press, 1892. (Rulers of India
  series, v.14). 222p.

4 1 R

I-1389
  Datta, Kalikinkar, 1905-
    Gangadhar Shastri, IHRCP, v.27,pt.2 (1950),
  pp.38-46.

4 1 R

I-1390
  Deodhar, Y.N.
    Nana Phadavavis. Delhi, National Book
  Trust, India, 1968. (National biography
  series). 92p.

NUP
PL 480, '68

I-1391
  Deodhar, Y.N.
    Nana Phadnis and the external affairs of
  the Maratha empire. Bombay, Popular Book
  Depot, 1962. 247p.

    1. Nana Phadnis, 1742-1800. 2. Mahrattas -
  Hist.

4 1 R

I-1392
  Deodhar, Y.N.
    Nana Phadnis the man, Indica. v.4 (1967),
  pp.35-38.

I-1393
  Dighe, Vishvanath Govind.
    Kanhoji Angria. In: Sardesai commemorative
  volume. Ed.by Shripad R.Tikekar. Bombay,
  1938. pp.99-112.

Bhandarkar Index
its commemorative

I-1394
  Dighe, Vishvanath Govind.
    Peshwa Bajirao I and Maratha expansion.
  Bombay, Karnatak pub.house, 1944. 245p.

    1. Baji Rao, peshwa, 1700-1740. 2. Mahrattas.

M 1 R

I-1395
Dikshit, Moreshwar Gangadhar, 1915-
Early life of Peshwa Savai Madhav-rao (II),
BDCRI, v.7 (1946), pp.225-48.

Case

I-1400
Gokhale, Vithal.
Nana Phadnavis and the internal affairs
of the Maratha State, 1742-1800. Bombay,
Univ.of Bombay. *

Datta

I-1396
Dubey, R.K.
Downfall of Peshwa Narayan Rao, IHCP, v.30
(1968), pp.378-87.

U of R

I-1401
Gupta, Pratul Chandra, 1910-
Notes on Trimbakji Danglia, IHRCP, v.18
(1942), pp.85-86.

IHRC

I-1397
Elphinstone, Mountstuart, 1779-1859.
Life of Mountstuart Elphinstone, ER, v.160
(1884), pp.116-50.

Case

I-1402
Holcomb, James Foote.
Jhansi history and the Rani of Jhansi.
Madras, M.E.Press, 1904. 71p.

BM

I-1398
Elphinstone, Mountstuart, 1779-1859.
Mountstuart Elphinstone, CR, v.34 (1860),
pp.34-40.

Case

I-1403
Hutton, William Holden, 1860-1930.
The Marquess Wellesley. Delhi, S.Chand,
1961. (The Rulers of India series) 157p.

U of R

I-1399
Gode, Parashuram Krishna, 1891-
Keshavbhat Karve, a Poona banker of the
Peshwa period and his relations with the
Peshwa and Damaji Gaikwad, JUB, v.6 (1937),
pp.87-91.

Case

I-1404
Joshi, C.V.
Life and fortunes of Jeveram Jagadeesh,
IHRCP, v.18 (1942), pp.316-20.

U of R

I-1405
  Joshi, C.V.
    Rani Gahinabai of Baroda. IHRCP, v.22 (1945),
  pp.70-71.

IHRCP

I-1406
  Joshi, Shankar Narayan, 1890-
    Durgabai Bhosale of Savantwadi, IHCP, v.17
  (1954), p.381.

Chaudhuri

I-1407
  Joshi, Shankar Narayan, 1890-
    Shetye-Mahajan, IHCP, v.16 (1953), pp.
  287-88.

U of R

I-1408
  Karkhanis, M.D.
    The life and achievements of Samsher Bahadur,
  the son of Peshwa Bajirao I, IHCP, v.27 (1965),
  pp.307-12.

IHCP

I-1409
  Keene, Henry George, 1825-1915.
    Madhava Rao Sindia and the Hindu re-
  conquest of India. Oxford, Clarendon
  Press, 1901. (Rulers of India, 5).
  207p.

U of R

I-1410
  Khan, Yusuf Husain.
    Nizamu'l-Mulk, Asaf Jah I, founder of the
  Haiderabad state. Mangalore, Basel mission
  press, 1936. 322p.

  1 Haiderabad, India (State)
  Hist. 2 Mogul empire

I-1411
  Khandekar, Ganpatrao Gopal.
    Ganesh Sambhaji, IHCP, v.2 (1938), pp.579-
  87.

IHCP

I-1412
  Khandekar, Ganpatrao Gopal.
    Gopal Sambhaji, IHCP, v.3 (1939), pp.1283-
  90.

IHCP

I-1413
  Kishore, Brij, 1914-
    Tara Bai and her times. New York, Asia
  Pub.House, 1964. 232p.

  1. Tara Bai, d.1761. 2. Mahrattas - Hist.

U of R

I-1414
  Krishna, M.H.
    Memoirs of Hyder Ally from the year 1758 to
  1770 by Eloy Joze Correa Peixoto, IHCP, v.2
  (1938), pp.538-45.

IHCP

I-1415
Kulkarni, B.R.
A short note on Harkubai Holkar, IHCP, v.6
(1943), p.307.

IHCP

I-1416
The last of the Peishawas, MR, v.31 (1922),
pp.285-91; 438-46; 575-83.

MR

I-1417
MacDonald, Archibald.
Memoir of the life of the late Nana
Farnavis...Reprinted from the original
edition of 1851, together with an auto-
biographical memoir of the early life of
Nana Farnavis, trans.by Lieut.-Col.
John Briggs, etc. London, Oxford Univ.
Press, 1927. 184p.

BM

I-1418
Madhajee Sindia, CR, v.49 (1933), pp.49-82.

Case

I-1419
Malgonkar, Manohar, 1913-
Kanhoji Angrey, Maratha admiral; an account
of his life and his battles with the English.
New York, Asia Pub.House, 1959. 309p.

NUP.
LC

I-1420
Malgonkar, Manohar, 1913-
The Puars of Dewas Senior. Bombay, Orient
Longmans, 1963. 346p.

1.Puar family. 2. Dewas, Senior, India (State).
Hist.

U of R

I-1421
Mavaji, Purushottama Vishrama, 1879-1929.
The murder of Narayan Rao Peshwa.
Allahabad, Indian Press, 1907. (Reprinted
from the Modern Review). 6p.

BM

I-1422
Mehta, Makrand J.
Gangadhar Shastri Patwardhan, JIH, v.41
(1963), pp.223-26.

Case

I-1423
Mehta, Markand Nandshankar.
Nana Phadnavis. Bombay, Univ.of Bombay,
1894. 90p.

Calcutta Nat'l Lib

I-1424
Mukerjee, Satya Vrata.
Baji Rao: a study, MR, v.12 (1912), pp.
618-24.

MR

I-1425
Nagpur.
Sketch of the history of the Bhonsla family taken from an old female domestic of the palace together with an account of his administration. Nagpur, 1918. 33p.

SOAS

(

I-1426
Nana Furnawees. Memoir of the life of Balaji Janardhan Bhanu. Tr.by J.Brothers. Bombay? 1885. 112p.

on order

(

I-1427
Owen, Sidney James, 1827-1912.
Benoit de Boigne, EHR, v.3 (1888), pp.63-93.

EHR

(

I-1428
Pandit, V.P.
Trial of an impostor of Nanasahib Peshwa, IHRCP, v.30 (1954), pp.90-94.

IHRCP

(

I-1429
Paranjpye, Sai.
Nana Phadnavis. Bombay, India Book House, 1969.

(

I-1430
Pardhee, Prabhakar S.
Ibrahim Khan Gardi, BIS, v.5 (July 1968), pp.92-99.

U of R

(

I-1431
Pawar, Jaisingrao B
Queen Janakibai, QRHS, V.10 (1970-71), pp.224-26.

(

I-1432
Pearse, Hugh Wodehouse, 1855-
Memoir of the life and military services of Viscount Lake, baron Lake of Delhi and Laswaree, 1744-1808. Edinburgh, Blackwood, 1908. 440p.

U of R

(

I-1433
Phadke, N.V.
Maharaja Yeshwant Rao Holkar's critics, IHRCP, v.7 (1925), pp.76-78.

IHRCP

(

I-1434
Powar, Appasaheb Ganapatrao, 1906-
Nizam-ul-Mulk Asaf Jah I, IHCP, v.5 (1941), p.105.

U of R

(

I-1435
Powar, Appasaheb Ganapatrao, 1906-
A note on the date of Ramchandra Pant
Amatya's death, IHCP, v.4 (1940), pp.334-35.

IHCP

I-1436
Powar, Appasaheb Ganapatrao, 1906-
The reign of Shahu Chhatrapati, 1708-1749
A.D. London, London Univ., 1934. *

QJISS

I-1437
Prasad, Yadunath.
The life and career of Mir Qamaruddin
Nizamul Mulk Asaf Jah I. London, London
Univ., 1927. 2v. *

SOAS

I-1438
Qanungo, Sudhindra Nath.
Jaswant Rao Holkar; the golden rogue.
Lucknow, 1965. 351p.

IBP

I-1439
Qanungo, Sudhindra Nath.
Malhar Rao Holkar; the founder of the house
of Holkar, MR, v.115 (1964), pp.455-57.

MR

I-1440
Raghavendra Rao, V.
Private life of the Peshwas, QJMS, v.30
(1940), pp.339-44.

QJMS

I-1441
Rahman, Khalilur A.F.M.
Najib-ud-Daula, 1739-1770, BPP, v.62 (1942),
pp.1-24.

II

I-1442
Ramalingam, John A.
Persoji Bhonsla, IHQ, v.37 (1961), pp.192-
96.

Index to IHQ

I-1443
Ramanujam, Chidambaram Srinivasachari.
Was Nana the cause of Maratha downfall?,
JIH, v.39 (1961), pp.407-12.

insc

I-1444
Ramdas, Ravindranath Vaman.
Admiral Anandrao Dhulap, BIS, v.4 (April
1967), pp.103-106.

I.-tR

I-1445
Ramdas, Ravindranath Vamanrao.
Radhabai, the mother of Peshwa Bajirao,
IHCP, v.27 (1965), pp.286-87.

IHCP

I-1450
Saletore, Bhasker Anand.
Some prominent Parsis in the 18th century,
IHRCP, v.29 (1953), pp.164-67.

Case

I-1446
Ramdas, Ravindranath Vaman.
Raghuji Angre, BIS, v.5 (July 1968), pp.
72-76.

UofR

I-1451
Sardesai, Govind Sakharam, 1865-1959.
A life-sketch of Nana Fadnis, MR, v.48
(1930), pp.523-26.

Case

I-1447
Rao, Vasant Dinanath, 1913-
Ghashiram Kotwal, JUB, v.31 (1962-63), pp.
125-27.

JUB

I-1452
Sardesai, Govind Sakharam, 1865-1959.
The rise of Mahadji Sindhia, MR, v.75
(1944), pp.209-11.

Case

I-1448
Rao, Vasant Dinanath, 1913-
Historical setting of a grievous episode -
tragedy of Kastani, IHRCP, v.17 (1940), pp.
47-51.

I-1453
Sardesai, Govind Sakharam, 1865-1959.
The tragic career of a forgotten soldier,
MR, v.71 (1942), pp.233-37.

G ndi   name.   modern review

MR

I-1449
Rao, Vasant Dinanath, 1913-
Ramshastri. A re-valuation, IHQ, v.34 (1958),
pp.70-72.

IHQ

I-1454
Sarkar, Sir Jadunath, 1870-1958.
Account of the family of Mahadji Sindhia
translated from Berlin State Library Persian
Ms.Dr.III, BPP, v.88 (1969), pp.117-134.

Medical history - articles
BAS 1969

I-1455
Sarkar, Sir Jadunath, 1870-1958.
De Boigne. IHRCP, v.17 (1940), pp.1-3.

U of R

I-1456
Sarkar, Sir Jadunath, 1870-1958.
Life of Najib-ud-daulah, IC, v.8 (1934),
pp.237-57.

II

I-1457
Sarkar, Sir Jadunath, 1870-1958.
Mahadji Sindhia's end, MR, v.75 (1944),
pp.177-79.

Cael

I-1458
Sarkar, Sir Jadunath, 1870-1958.
Najib-ud-Daulah, Ruhela chief. A unique
Persian manuscript, IC, v.10 (1936),
pp.648-58.

Inex I:

I-1459
Sarkar, Sir Jadunath, 1870-1958.
The rise of Najib-ud-daula (from Brit.Mus.
Pers.Ms. 24,410), IHQ, v.9 (1933), pp.866-71.

Index to IHG

I-1460
Sarkar, Sir Jadunath, 1870-1958.
Zabita Khan, the Ruhela chieftain (from a
unique Persian MS.), IHQ, v.11 (1935), pp.
640-51.

Index to IHQ

I-1461
Sarkar, Upendra Nath.
A note on Raghunatha Angria, IHQ, v.28
(1952), pp.190-91.

Index to IHQ

I-1462
Sarkar, Upendra Nath.
Private property of Raghuji Angria, IHRCP,
v.30 (1954), pp.126-33.

IHRCP

I-1463
Sarkar, Upendra Nath.
Sambhaji Angria - a pretender to the Gadi
of Kolaba, IHRCP, v.29 (1953), pp.98-104.

IHRCP

I-1464
Saswadkar, Prabhakar Laxman.
Brahmendra Swami: his life and role in
Maratha history. Poona, Poona Univ., 1961.

Jayakar Lib # 1414

I-1465
Saswadkar, Prabhakar Laxman.
Last days of Peshwa Raghunathrao, IHCP,
v.28 (1966), pp.337-42.

U.M.R.

I-1466
Saswadkar, Prabhakar Laxman.
Sidelight on the life of Chatrapati
Ramraja under Nana Phadnis, IHCP, v.15 (1952),
pp.345-51.

U.M.R.

I-1467
Sen, Surendra Nath, 1890-
Early career of Kanhoji Angria and other
papers. Calcutta, Calcutta University, 1941.
237p.

U.M.R.

I-1468
Sen, Surendra Nath, 1890-
Sambhaji Angria: 1733-1741, NIA, v.1 (1939),
pp.118-26.

NIA

I-1469
Sen, Surendra Nath, 1890-
Tulaji Angria, JIH, v.25 (1947), pp.139-50.

JIH

I-1470
Shaikh, C.H.
Salabat Khan II, IHCP, v.5 (1941), pp.99-
100.

U.M.R.

I-1471
Sharma, Hira Lal.
Ahilyabai. New Delhi, National Book Trust,
1969. 123p.

PL 480, 2/70

I-1472
Shejwalkar, Trymbak Shankar.
The ancestors of the Rani of Jhansi, IHRCP,
v.24 (1948), pp.9-13.

Case

I-1473
Shejwalkar, Trymbak Shankar.
Early life of Naro Vishnu Apte. In:
Mahamahopadhyaya Professor D.V.Potdar
sixty-first birthday commemoration volume. Ed.by Surendra Nath Sen. Poona,
1950. pp.108-13.

Bhandarkar Index
to Comm'ls.

I-1474
Shejwalkar, Trymbak Shankar.
Haripant Phadke - the man he was, IHRCP,
v.23 (1946), pp.5-8.

U.M.R.

I-1475
Sinh, Raghubir, 1908-
Bapu Vitthal Mahadev - a Maharashtrian diplomat. In: Nehru Abhinandan granth, a birthday book, presented to Jawaharlal Nehur, Prime Minister of India on completion of his sixtieth year, Nov.14, 1949. Calcutta, V.More, 1949? pp.416-20.

I-1476
Sir John Malcolm. The life and correspondence..., BQR, v.6 (1857), pp.108-41.

I-1477
Srinivasachari, Chidambaram S., 1890-1951. Ayya Shastri - south Indian Chief Justice of the Maratha State, IHRCP, v.26 (1957), pp.19-20.

I-1478
Srinivasan, Chettur Krishnaswamy. Baji Rao I, the Great Peshwa. London, Asia Pub.House, 1961. 152p.

I-1479
Thakur, Vasudeo V. The Honourable Chief Justice Rama Shastri Prabhune of the Poona Supreme Court (1759-1789 A.D.), IHRCP, v.16 (1939), pp.206-10.

I-1480
Thakur, Vasudeo V. A short note on the charities of Devi Shri Ahilya Bai Holkar, IHRCP, v.13 (1930), pp.139-44.

I-1481
Trotter, Lionel James, 1827-1912. The bayard of India: a life of General Sir James Outram. London, J.M.Dent & co.; New York, E.P.Dutton & co., 1909. 255p.

I-1482
Vaidya, G.N. Ahalyadevi Holkar. Poona, Vidarbha Marathwada, 1965. (Makers of India series, 9) 32p.

I-1483
Vaidya, Suman G. The mystery of the murder of Gangadhar Shastri, BIS, v.5 (July 1968), pp.1-38.

I-1484
Vaidya, Sushila. Radhabai and the Peshwas (1700-1753), IHCP, v.27 (1965), pp.287-88.

I-1485
Vaidya, Sushila.
Role of Sakwarbai and Sagunabai - Queens
of Shahu in Maratha history 1730-49, IHCP,
v.28 (1966), pp.311-18.

U of R

I-1490
Basu, Santosh Kumar.
A premature attempt by the Bombay government
to set up a permanent naval and military
station at Aden, BPP, v.82 (1963), pp.26-30.

Jas '63

I-1486
Vaidya, Sushila.
Umabai Dabhade and Peshwa Bajirao I (1720-
40 A.D.), IHCP, v.26, pt.2 (1964), pp.185-
88.

General works

U of R

I-1492
Bhat, B.W.
Parwana relating to the Sanad of Sardesh-
mukhi, IHRCP, v.27, pt.2 (1950), pp.104-07.

I-1487
Advani, H.D.
History of India: the Moghuls and the
Mahrattas. Hyderabad, 1926. 45p.

ICL

I-1492
Bhave, Vasudeo Krishna, 1885-
Progress of Maharashtra under the Peshwas,
IHCP, v.2 (1938), pp.607-14.

IHCP

I-1488
Apte, H.D.
The nature and scope of the records from
Peshwa Daftar with reference to Zakat system,
IESHR, v.4 (1967), pp.369-79.

UVV IESHR

I-1493
Bombay (Presidency)
Correspondence illustrative of the practice
of the Peshwa's Government regarding adoptions
and the circumstances under which adopted sons
could succeed to property held from the state.
Bombay, Education Society's Press, 1856.
(Bombay Presidency. Selections from the
records, n.s., no.28).

I-1489
Banhatti, Shrinivas Narayan, 1901-
Colebrooke's observations about the state
of affairs - political, civil and military -
in the kingdom of the Bhonslas of Nagpur;
April 1799, IHRCP, v.22 (1945), pp.51-52.

IHRCP

I-1494
Bombay and Western India, AJ, v.9 (1820),
pp.609-10.

I-1495
 Bombay domestic annals, A.D.1800-1810. <u>CR</u>,
 v.96 (1893), pp.175-84; v.99 (1894), pp.
 49-74.

Case

I-1496
 Briggs, John, 1785-1875, tr.
 Secret correspondence of the court of the
 Peshwa, Madhu Rao, from the years 1761-1772;
 translated from the original Mahratta letters.
 London, 1830. 57p.

✓✓ pre '56 imprints

I-1497
 Broughton, Thomas Duer, 1778-1835.
 Letters written in a Mahratta camp during
 the year 1809, descriptive of the character,
 manners, domestic habits, and religious
 ceremonies, of the Mahrattas. New ed. Westminster [London] Constable & co., 1892.
 (Constable's Oriental miscellany of original
 and selected publications. Vol.IV). 304p.

1. Mahrattas.
LC

I-1498
 Bullock, H.
 Some colours of Bombay regiments, <u>JBHS</u>,
 v.2 (1929), pp.220-22.

U of R

I-1499
 Bullock, H.
 Some more colours of Bombay regiments,
 <u>JBHS</u>, v.3 (1930), pp.41-43.

I-1500
 Burton, Reginald George, 1864-
 History of the Hyderabad continent. Cal-
 cutta, Office of the Superintendent of Govt.
 Print., 1905. 331p.

BM

I-1501
 Cadell, Sir Patrick Robert, 1871-
 History of the Bombay Army. London, New
 York, etc., Longmans, Green & co., 1938.
 377p.

U of R

I-1502
 Chandra, Satish.
 Maratha activities in the Deccan, 1707-
 1712, <u>MIQ</u>, v.4 (1961), pp.36-43.

U of R

I-1503
 Chatterjee, Nondita.
 Administration of the last Rajah of Satara,
 <u>IHCP</u>, v.22 (1959), pp.426-29. Also in: <u>JIH</u>,
 v.38 (1960), pp.51-55.

HI
JaS '60

I-1504
 Chitale, Vishnu Sitaram
 The early phase of the struggle between the
 barbhais and Raghunath Rao, <u>IHRCP</u>, v. 24 (1948),
 pp. 18-22.

IHRCP

I-1505
Coats, Thomas.
Notes respecting the trial by Panchayat and
the administration of justice at Poona, under
the late Peshwa, LSBT, v.2 (1820-21), pp.273-
80.

Case

I-1506
Datta, Kalikinkar, 1905-
Factors in the eighteenth century history
of India, CR, v.62 (1937), pp.309-20.

Case

I-1507
Deopujari, M.B.
Maharashtradharma and the Peshwas, IHCP,
v.27 (1965), p.325.

IHCP

I-1508
Deshpande, Yeshwant Khushal, 1884-
Century old files of Marathi newspapers,
IHRCP, v.25 (1948), pp.121-24.

IHRC

I-1509
Deshpande, Yeshwant Khushal, 1884-
Contemporary chroniclers of the Nagpur
Rajahs, IHRCP, v.16 (1939), pp.137-39.

H M R

I-1510
Dhunjeebhoy, Hilla.
Popular agitation against Outram's dismissal
from Baroda, IHCP, v.5 (1941), pp.86-87.

H M R

I-1511
Dighe, Vishvanath Govind.
Decline of Maratha power. In: Maha-
mahopadgyaya. Prof.D.V.Potdar sixty-
first birthday commemoration volume. Ed.
by Surendra Nath Sen. Poona, 1950. pp.
219-28.

Bhandarkar Inder
Comm vols.

I-1512
Dighe, Vishvanath Govind.
Maratha political system: theory and
practice. In: Studies in Indian history;
Dr.A.G.Pawar felicitation volume. Ed.
by V.D.Rao. Kolhapur, Y.P.Pawar, 1968.
pp.5-18.

V-L R

I-1513
Dighe, Vishvanath Govind.
The problem of sovereignty in the Maratha
State, ASBJ, n.s.,v.34/35 (1959/60), pp.
84-90.

J A S '62

I-1514
East India Company (English)
Papers relating to pecuniary claims of
British subjects on the native Princes of
India, or of natives subject to the authority
of the East India Company. London, 1833.
2 pts.

F M

I-1515
Edwardes, Michael.
Glorious sahibs; the romantic as empire-builder, 1799-1838. N.Y., Taplinger, 1968. 248p.

1. India - Biog. 2. India - Hist. - 19th cent.

U of R

I-1516
Edwardes, Stephen Meredyth, 1873-1927.
The Marathas at the close of the 18th century as described by a soldier of fortune, IA, v.53 (1924), pp.69-77.

Case

I-1517
Firminger, Walter K.
The letters of a Governor of Bombay, 1839-1841, CR, v.128 (1909), pp.186-212; v.129 (1909), pp.309-53, 552-608; v.130 (1910), pp.49-79, 182-226.

I-1518
Fukazawa, Hiroshi.
Lands and peasants in the eighteenth century Maratha kingdom, HJE, v.6 (1965), pp.32-61.

I-1519
Gense, James H. and Banaji, Dady Rustomji, 1903-
The Gaikwads of Baroda; English documents. Bombay, D.B.Taraporevala, 1936-45. 10v.

U of R

I-1520
Gode, Parashuram Krishna, 1891-
The Bhagva Zenda of the Marathas between A.D.1685 and 1813. Poona, 1940. 3p.

IOL

I-1521
Gupta, Pratul Chandra, 1910-
The administration of Poona under Baji Rao II, IHRCP, v.16 (1939), pp.99-101.

U of R

I-1522
Gupta, Pratul Chandra, 1910-
Sir John Low's services at Bithur 1818-1825, NIA, v.5 (1942), pp.97-106. also in: IHCP, v.5 (1941), pp.495-503.

NIA

I-1523
Hope, John (late surgeon to the Court of Gwalior)
The house of Scindea: a sketch. London, 1863.

Calcutta Nat'l Lib

I-1524
Hyderabad, India (State) Central Records Office.
Poona Akhbars; Marathi text with summaries and introductions in English. Prep.by R.M.Joshi. Hyderabad, Deccan, 1953-3v.

SOAS

I-1525
India. Army.
Historical record of the 3rd Bombay Light
Infantry. Bombay, 1872.

Calcutta Nat'l Lib

I-1526
India. Army.
Historical record of the 21st Regiment, Bombay Native Infantry, or Marine Battalion. Bombay, 1875.

Calcutta Nat'l Lib

I-1527
India. Army.
Historical records of the 23rd Regiment
(2nd Battalion, Rifle Regiment) Bombay
Infantry, formerly the First Battalion,
12th Native Infantry. Comp.by Capt.W.A.M.Wilson. Bombay, Education Society's Steam
Press, 1894. 84p.

BM

I-1528
India. Army.
Historical records ... 8th regiment, Bombay
Infantry. Bombay, Printed at the Education
Society Press, 1894.

Calcutta Nat'l Lib

I-1529
Indus, pseud.
Bombay briberies; a tale of the present charter...Fourth edition, greatly enlarged, and containing the Author's Reply to L.R.Reid; together with a suppressed dispatch from Col.Outram. London, 1853.

BM

I-1530
Jacob, Sir George Le Grand, 1805-1881.
Western India before and during the mutinies:
pictures drawn from life. 2d ed. London, H.S.
King & Co., 1872. 270p.

1. India - Hist. - Sepoy Rebellion, 1857-
1858. 2. India - Hist. - British occupation,
1765-   3. India - Pol.& govt., 1765-

U of R

I-1531
Jha, Jata Shankar.
Some unpublished correspondence regarding
Nana Sahab's stay in Nepal in the State
Archives of Bihar, JIH, v.42 (1964), pp.532-
36.

Case

I-1532
Joshi, C.V.
Holkar to Gaikwad. IHRCP, v.23 (1946),
pp.58-59.

IHRC

I-1533
Joshi, C.V.
Social reform under Maharaja Anandrao
Gaikwad (1800-1820 A.D.), IHRCP, v.16 (1939),
pp.202-203.

U of R

I-1534
Joshi, Raghunath Muralidhar, 1904-
The Rajendras of Gangakhed and their records,
IHRCP, v.29 (1953), pp.64-68.

IHCP

I-1535
Joshi, Shankar Narayan, 1890-
The postal system under the Marathas (1761-1772), IHCP, v.15 (1952), pp.338-45.

U ≥ R

I-1536
Kale, Yadav Madhava, 1881-
An unpublished correspondence between Vyankoji Bhosla and Daulatrao Sindya, IHRCP, v.11 (1928), pp.85-88.

GBHS

I-1537
Kamdar, K.H.
The Maratha state of Baroda. In: Mahamahopadhyaya Prof.D.V.Potdar sixty-first birthday commemoration volume. Ed.by Surendra Nath Sen. Poona, 1950. pp.121-26.

Bhandarkar Orient. Comm nl.,

I-1538
Kamat, B.V.
Sir John Malcolm's impressions of his tour of southern Maratha country (March 1829), IHCP, v.27 (1965), pp.313-14.

IHCP

I-1539
Kamerkar, M.P.
An examination of the new policy of utilitarinism in the Bombay Presidency between 1827-1835, IHCP, v.28 (1966), pp.429-33.

IHCP

I-1540
Karkaria, Rustomji Pestonji, 1869-1919.
Lieut.-Col.Thomas Best Jervis (1796-1857) and his manuscript studies on the state of the Maratha people and their history, ASBJ, v.22 (1905-08), pp.43-66.

ASBJ

I-1541
Kibe, Madhav Vinayak, 1877-
An account of the Vrindawan of Peshwa Baji-rao I at Mauza Raverkhedi, IHRCP, v.12 (1929), pp.98-101.

IHRCP

I-1542
Kibe, Madhav Vinayak, 1877-
The cultural Indian empire of the saintly queen Ahilyabai Holkar, IHCP, v.3 (1939), pp.1330-33.

IHCP

I-1543
Kibe, Madhav Vinayak, 1877-
The foundations of Indore, IHRCP, v.25 (1948), pp.183-85.

IHRC

I-1544
Kibe, Madhav Vinayak, 1877-
Mahadaji Scindia and the Agra College. A peep into the records of the family of Gangadhar Shastri, IHRCP, v.23 (1946), pp.59-63.

case,

I-1545
Kibe, Madhav Vinayak, 1877-
Some financial matters of the Indore State in the 19th century, IHCP, v.15 (1952), pp. 388-90.

UofR

I-1550
Lal, Kasim Ali Sajan.
The Peshwa's money, IHCP, v.9 (1945), p.386.

IHCP

I-1546
Kothekar, Shanta.
1802 A.D.the year of crisis in the history of the Gaikwads, BIS, v.5 (July 1968), pp. 39-54.

UofR

I-1551
Landge, D.G., 1891-
Was Pandit Beniram Dubey a Marathi Brahmin?, IHRCP, v.36 (1961), pp.131-34.

UofR

I-1547
Krishnasvāmi Aiyangār, Śakkottai, 1871-
The Bakhair of Rama Raja, IHRCP, v.7 (1925), pp.54-62.

IHRCP

I-1552
The Mahratta history and empire - recent operations in the Kolapoor and Sawuntwaree countries, CR, v.4 (1845), pp.178-240.

Cal

I-1548
Kulkarni, B.R.
Nandurbar Desai daftar, IHRCP, v.30 (1954), pp.73-75.

IHRCP

I-1553
Malcolm, Sir John, 1769-1833.
A memoir of central India, including Malwa, and adjoining provinces. 2d ed. London, Kingsbury, Parbury, Allen, 1824. 2v.

1. India - Hist. 2. India - Statistics. 3. Malwa.

4 UR

I-1549
Lal, Kasim Ali Sajan.
Adoption under the Peshwa Baji Rao II, IHCP, v.9 (1945), pp.381-82.

IHCP

I-1554
Mandlik, Vishvanath Narayan, 1833-1889.
Adoption versus annexation, with remarks on the Mysore question. London, 1866. 58p.

ICL

I-1555
Martineau, Alfred Albert, 1859-
Le Général Perron, généralissime des
armées de Scindia et du Grand Mogol, 1753-
1834. Paris, 1931. 228p.

VRV
BM

I-1556
Mate, Madhukar Shripad.
Downfall of the Marathas. BDCRI, v.24
(1963-1964), pp.31-35.

gas 66

I-1557
Meade, M.J.
Gwalior, the capital of the Scindias, AR.
n.s.,v.22 (1926), pp.215-24.

NYPL

I-1558
Mitra, R.C.
Military strength of the Indian princes in
1784. IHRCP. v.24 (1948), pp.120-27.

IHRCP

I-1559
Murdeshwar, B.G.
Slavery under the Peshwas. In: Sardesai Comm-
emorative Volume. Ed.by Shripad R.Tikekar.
Bombay, 1938. pp.283-90.

Bhandarkar Inskep

I-1560
Origin of the Pindaries; preceded by historical
notices of the rise of the different Mahratta
states. By an officer in the service of the
Hon.East India Company. London, J.Murray,
1818. 176p.

LC

I-1561
Oturkar, Rajaram Vinayak, 1898-
Institution of watan and its influence on
the 18th century Maratha society. IHCP. v.9
(1945), pp.180-85.

IHCP

I-1562
Oturkar, Rajaram Vinayak, 1898-
Scope of state activity under the 18th
century Maratha rule. IHCP. v.13 (1950).
pp.202-204.

Cash

I-1563
Outram, Sir James, 1803-1863.
A few brief memoranda of some of the public
services rendered by Lieut.-Col.Outram. London, Privately printed, 1853.

BM

I-1564
Pagdi, Setumadhava Rao, 1910-
Eighteenth century Deccan. Bombay, Popular
Prakashan, 1963. 325p.

1. Deccan, India - Hist.

47R

I-1565
Pandya, Gangashanker Baldevshanker, 1915-1958.
Gaikwads of Baroda: Maharaja Sayajirao II,
A.D.1821 to A.D.1830; selections from the
Baroda Residency records. Baroda, Dept.of
History, Faculty of Arts, Maharaja Sayajirao
Univ.of Baroda, 1958. 282p.

U of R

I-1566
Patwardhan, R.P.
A problem about revenue accounts in the 18th
century. IHRCP, v.30 (1954), pp.94-98.

IHRCP

I-1567
Ranade, Mahadev Govind, 1842-1901.
Introduction to the Peshwa's diaries,
ASBJ, v.20 (1897-1900), pp.448-79.

Case

I-1568
Ranadive, R.K.
The navy of the Gaekwars, IHRCP, v.17
(1940), pp.184-90.

U of R

I-1569
Rao, Vasant Dinanath, 1913-
On the police in the city of Poona during
the period of Sawai Madhav Rao, JIH, v.36
(1958), pp.223-28.

J.a.s '58

I-1570
Rawlinson, Hugh George, 1880-
Some notes on the records in the Poona Daftar,
IHRCP, v.7 (1925), pp.44-49.

IHRCP

I-1571
Saksena, Banarsi Prasad, 1900-
Some unpublished news letters of the Court
of Holkar, IHRCP, v.34 (1958), pp.123-33.

IHRCP

I-1572
Saletore, R.N.
The policy of Maratha rulers towards wild
tribes. In: Sardesai Commemorative Volume.
Ed.by Shripad R.Tikekar. Bombay, 1938.
pp.89-98.

Bhandarkar Comm. Volume

I-1573
Sardesai, Govind Sakharam, 1865-1959.
The treaty of Kanakapur between Peshwa
Madhavrao I and Janoji Bhosle, IHRCP, v.11
(1928), pp.34-39.

JBHS

I-1574
Sarkar, Sir Jadunath, 1870-1958.
The noontide of Maratha power, MR, v.47
(1930), pp.421-31.

JBHS

I-1575
Saswadkar, Prabhakar Laxman.
The dawn of modernization in the Maratha state on the eve of its extinction, IHCP, v.29 (1967), pp.139-44.

IHCP

I-1576
Saswadkar, Prabhakar Laxman.
A note on the Kotwali of Poona in the last quarter of the eighteenth century, IHCP, v.24 (1961), pp.274-80.

I-1577
Saswadkar, Prabhakar Laxman.
Prohibition under the Peshwas in the latter half of the eighteenth century, IHCP, v.27 (1965), pp.326-28.

IHCP

I-1578
Sen, Sailendra Nath.
The strategic importance of Janjira (1761-87) - resident Farmer's policy, IHRCP, v.36 (1962), pp.121-23.

IHRC

I-1579
Sen, Surendra Nath, 1890-
Settlement of the Peshwa's territories, IHCP, v.3 (1939), pp.1256-64.

IHCP

I-1580
Shejwalkar, Trymbak Shankar.
Material for population estimates in the Peshwa Dafter, IHRCP, v.26 (1949), pp.16-18.

I-1581
Shejwalkar, Trymbak Shankar.
Nagpur Bhonsle Marathi papers, IHRCP, v.28 (1951), pp.87-89.

IHRCP

I-1582
Sindia and Dhar, CR, v.40 (1864), pp.102-23.

I-1583
Sinha, Har Narain, 1900-
An introduction to the rise of the Peshwas, JIH, v.7 (1928), pp.36-61, 185-216, 349-62.

JBHS

I-1584
Sinha, Har Narain, 1900-
The new foundations of Maratha power, IHCP, v.23 (1960), pp.230-40.

I-1585
Sinha, Har Narain, 1900–
Rise of the Peshwas. Allahabad, Indian
Press, 1931. 255p.

I L

I-1586
Sinha, Har Narain, 1900–
The rise of the Peshwas, JIH, v.8 (1929),
pp.182 ff; 299–322.

JI H

I-1587
Tambe, G.C.
The root cause of the financial distress of
Jhansi state during the years 1831 and 1841,
IHCP, v.15 (1952), pp.305–13.

4 7R

I-1588
Translated extract of a Persian manuscript
entitled memorandums and recent anecdotes
of the Southern Courts of Hindoostan, by
a Mussulman observer, in the year 1195–6
Hegree, A.D.1781–2, AAR, v.12 (1810–11),
pp.421–25.

AR

I-1589
Young, Marianne.
Western India in 1838. London, Saunders &
Otley, 1839. 2v.

LC

Mutiny and the Maratha
Participation

I-1590
Bajpai, S.C.
Later days of Nana Saheb of Bithur, JIH,
v.43 (1965), pp.647–55.

I-1591
Banerji, Brajendranath, d.1953.
The last days of Nana Sahib of Bithoor,
IHRCP, v.12 (1929), pp.59–62. Also in:
BPP, v.39 (1930), pp.150–52.

Cane

I-1592
Bhargava, K.P.
Two unpublished proclamations of Nana
Sahib, IHRCP, v.25 (1948), pp.36–37.

Ladendorf

I-1593
Bhargava, Yudhishthir, 1909–
Letters about the mutiny of 1857 in Madhya
Bharat, IHRCP, v.33 (1958), pp.39–43.

4 7R

I-1594
Browne, James, 1839–1896.
Cawnpore and the Nana of Bithoor. Cawnpore,
1890.

M Calcutta Natl Lib

I-1595
    Burn, R. and Cadell, Patrick.
      Rani Lakshmi Bai of Jhansi, RASGBIJ, ser.3
    (1944), pp.76-78.

Case

I-1596
    Chatterji, Nandalal, 1903–
      Lawless Brigands as soldiers of freedom in
    the great revolt of 1857, JIH, v.34 (1956),
    pp.209-10.

JIH

I-1597
    Dharairya, R.K.
      Did Tatya Tope pass his last days in
    Gujarat? JGRS, v.31 (1969), pp.266-70.

JGRS

I-1598
    Durand, Sir Henry Mortimer, 1850-1924.
      Central India in 1857. Being an answer to
    Sir John Kaye's criticisms on the conduct of
    the late Sir Henry Marion Durand whilst in
    charge of Central India during the Mutiny.
    London, 1876.

BM

I-1599
    Edwardes, Michael.
      Battles of the Indian Mutiny. London,
    Pan Books, 1970. (British battles series).
    225p.

History—modern—books
BM

I-1600
    Gupta, Pratul Chandra, 1910-
      Nana Sahib and the rising at Cawnpore.
    Oxford, Clarendon Press, 1963. 227p.

U of R

I-1601
    Gupta, Pratul Chandra, 1910-
      Nana Sahib at Bithur, BPP, v.77,pt.2 (1958),
    pp.61-82.

NRU

I-1602
    Husain, Agha Mahdi.
      Bahadur Shah II and the war of 1857 in
    Delhi with its unforgettable scenes. Delhi,
    Atma Ram, 1958. 526p.

        1. India - Hist. - Sepoy Rebellion, 1857-1858.
NUR
LC

I-1603
    Joshi, Purushottam Mahadeo, 1906-
      Material on Nana Saheb Peshva. Bombay,
    Department of Archives, Maharashtra, 1962.
    124p.

INB 1963
LC

I-1604
    Kincaid, Charles Augustus, 1870-
      Lakshmibai, Rani of Jhansi, RASGBIJ, ser.3
    (1943), pp.100-14.

ICL

I-1605
    Kincaid, Charles Augustus, 1870-
    Lakshmibai, Rani of Jhansi, and other essays.
London, the author, 1946. 102p.

        1. India - Hist. - Annecdotes.

                    (

LC

I-1606
    Lowe, Thomas.
    Central India during the rebellion of 1857
and 1858, a narrative of the operations of
the British Forces from the suppression of
mutiny in Aurungabad to the capture of
Gwalior, etc. London, 1860.

                    (

BM

I-1607
    Luniya, Bhanwarlal Nathuram, 1917-
    Complicity of the Maharaja Holkar with the
Mutineers, IHCP, v.18 (1955), pp.238-42.

IHCP   (

I-1608
    Luniya, Bhanwarlal Nathuram, 1917-
    The siege of Dhar (Oct.1857), IHCP, v.19
(1956), pp.321-27.

Uof R   (

I-1609
    Misra, Anand Swarup, 1908-
    Nana Saheb Peshwa and the fight for freedom.
Lucknow, Information Dept., Uttar Pradesh,
1961. 654p.

                    (

I-1610
    Mojumdar, Kanchanmoy.
    Later days of Nana Saheb, BPP, v.81 (1962),
pp.96-107.

                    (

Case

I-1611
    Pal, Dharm.
    Tatya Tope, the hero of India's first war
of independence, 1857-1859. New Delhi, Hindustan Times, 1957. 217p.

NUR
LC   (

I-1612
    Puntambekar, Shrikrishna Venkatesh.
    Rani Lakshmi Bai of Jhansi. In:
Dr.S.Krishnaswami Aiyangar Commemoration
Volume. Essays and papers presented to
Dr.Krishnaswami Aiyangar on his 66th
birthday. Ed.by B.Bhattacharyya and
others. Madras, 1936. pp.82-92.

Biographical Index
Commemorials.   (

I-1613
    The pursuit of Tantia Topee, BM, v.83 (1860),
pp.172-94.

Index Londra   (

I-1614
    Rawlinson, Hugh George, 1880-
    Two captures of Gwalior Fort, IHRCP, v.12
(1929), pp.18-20.

IHRCP   (

I-1615
  Rizawi, M.H.
    Tatya Tope in Bhopal. IHRCP, v.35 (1960),
  pp.168-70.

Ladendorf

I-1616
  Rogers, Alexander.
    The Rani of Jhansi, or, the widowed queen.
  Westminster, A.Constable and Co., 1895.
  126p.

BM

I-1617
  Sardesai, Govind Sakharam, 1865-1959.
    The last days of Nana-saheb of Bithur,
  MR, v.60 (1936), pp.508-10.

Case

I-1618
  Sareen, Tilak Raj.
    Gwalior under the mutineers, JIH, v.43
  (1965), pp.625-32.

Case

I-1619
  Savarkar, Vinayak Damodar, 1883-1966.
    The Indian war of independence, 1857.
  Bombay, Phoenix Pubs., 1947. 552p.

LC

I-1620
  Singh, B.K.
    Trial and execution of Tatya Tope, IHCP,
  v.28 (1966), p.379.

U of R

I-1621
  Smyth, Sir John George, bart., 1893-
    The rebellious Rani. London, Muller, 1966.
  223p.

    1. Lakshmi Bai, Rani of Jhansi, d.1858.

U of R

I-1622
  Tahmankar, Dattatraya Vishwanath.
    The Ranee of Jhansi. London, MacGibbon &
  Kee, 1958. 178p.

    1. India - History - Sepoy Rebellion, 1857-
  1858.

U of R

I-1623
  Taimuri, M.H.R.
    Some unpublished documents on the death of
  the Rani of Jhansi and the mutiny in Central
  India, IHRCP, v.29 (1953), pp.157-59.

Case

I-1624
  Thackeray, C.B.
    Indian leaders of the mutiny, CJ, v.20
  (1930), pp.549-53.

Ladendorf

I-1625
Vaidya, G.M.
Rani Lakshmibai. Poona, Vidarbha Marathwada,
1965. (Makers of India series, 10) 34p.

Marathas - Foreign Relations

Marathas - Foreign
Relations - General

I-1626
Abdul Ali, A.F.M.
The Pindaris. IC, v.11 (1937), pp.370-72.

I-1627
Askari, Syed Hasan.
Maratha activities as known from some
Persian literary works. In: Mahamahopad-
hyaya Prof.D.V.Potdar sixty-first birth-
day commemoration volume. Ed.by Surendra
Nath Sen. Poona, 1950. pp.88-103.

Bhandarkar Indiv
Com on vols.

I-1628
Askari, Syed Hasan.
Unpublished correspondence relating to
Maharaja Madho Singh of Jaipur and some
of his contemporaries, IHRCP, v.24 (1948),
pp.73-78.

IHRCP

I-1629
Charpentier, Karl.
Pindari, IA, v.59 (1930), pp.149-51.

JBHS

I-1630
Dikshitar, V.R.
Influence of Maratha rule, NR, v.15 (1949),
pp.54-60.

ABIHI y 5

I-1631
Joshi, Purushottam Mahadeo, 1906-
Selections from the Peshwa Daftar. New series.
Vol.I - Expansion of Maratha power, 1707-1761.
Bombay, Govt.Central Press, 1957.
Vol.III - Revival of Maratha power, 1761-1772.
Bombay, Govt.Central Press, 1962.

4 of R order

I-1632
Joshi, Shankar Narayan, 1890-
Maratha ambassadors during the reign of
Peshwa Madhavrao I (1761 to 1722 A.D.),
IHCP, v.14 (1951), pp.285-94.

Case

I-1633
Khare, Ganesh Hari, 1901-
A note on the family records of the Peshwas'
agents at Delhi, ABORI, v.23 (1942), pp.257-61.

U of R

I-1634
Khobrekar, Viththal Gopal.
Was there monetary gain in Sadashiv Rao
Bhau's first expedition?, IHCP, v.17
(1954), p.382.

Chaudhuri

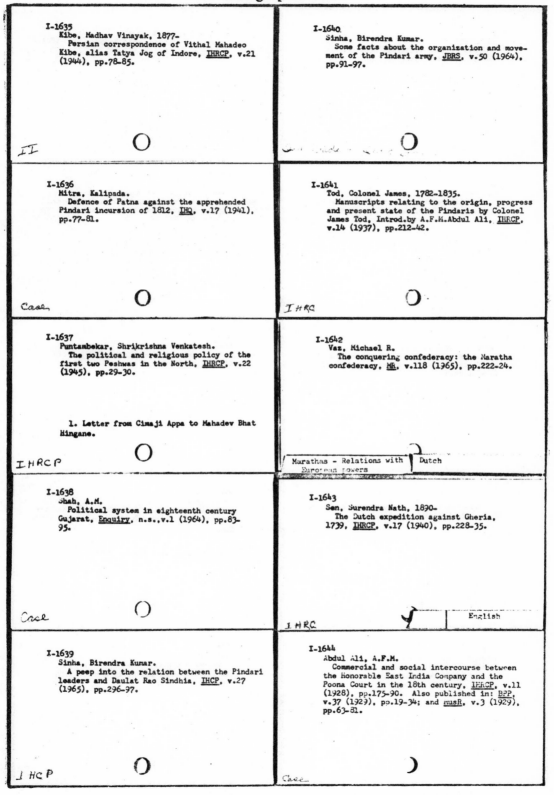

I-1635
Kibe, Madhav Vinayak, 1877-
Persian correspondence of Vithal Mahadeo Kibe, alias Tatya Jog of Indore, IHRCP, v.21 (1944), pp.78-85.

II

I-1636
Mitra, Kalipada.
Defence of Patna against the apprehended Pindari incursion of 1812, IHQ, v.17 (1941), pp.77-81.

Case

I-1637
Puntambekar, Shrikrishna Venkatesh.
The political and religious policy of the first two Peshwas in the North, IHRCP, v.22 (1945), pp.29-30.

1. Letter from Cimaji Appa to Mahadev Bhat Hingane.

IHRCP

I-1638
Shah, A.M.
Political system in eighteenth century Gujarat, Enquiry, n.s.,v.1 (1964), pp.83-95.

Case

I-1639
Sinha, Birendra Kumar.
A peep into the relation between the Pindari leaders and Daulat Rao Sindhia, IHCP, v.27 (1965), pp.296-97.

IHCP

I-1640
Sinha, Birendra Kumar.
Some facts about the organization and movement of the Pindari army, JBRS, v.50 (1964), pp.91-97.

I-1641
Tod, Colonel James, 1782-1835.
Manuscripts relating to the origin, progress and present state of the Pindaris by Colonel James Tod, Introd.by A.F.M.Abdul Ali, IHRCP, v.14 (1937), pp.212-42.

IHRC

I-1642
Vaz, Michael R.
The conquering confederacy: the Maratha confederacy, MR, v.118 (1965), pp.222-24.

Marathas - Relations with | Dutch
European powers

I-1643
Sen, Surendra Nath, 1890-
The Dutch expedition against Gheria, 1739, IHRCP, v.17 (1940), pp.228-35.

IHRC | English

I-1644
Abdul Ali, A.F.M.
Commercial and social intercourse between the Honorable East India Company and the Poona Court in the 18th century, IHRCP, v.11 (1928), pp.175-90. Also published in: BPP, v.37 (1929), pp.19-34; and MusR, v.3 (1929), pp.63-81.

Case

I-1645
Abdul Ali, A.F.M.
Early British relations with the Peshwa's
Durbar at Poona, IHCP, v.1,pt.2 (1935), pp.
42-45.

I-1650
Banerjee, Ashok Chandra.
British relations with Nagpur, 1798-1803,
JIH, v.28 (1950), pp.217-26.

JIH

I-1646
Atkinson, C.T.
A cavalry regiment of the Mahratta wars,
JSAHR, v.33 (1955), pp.80-87.

I-1651
Banerji, Brajendranath, d.1953.
A chapter of the East India Company and
diplomacy: the Begam of Sardhana, MR, v.37
(1925), pp.521-30.

I-1647
Banerjee, Anil Chandra, 1910-
A contemporary account of the origin of
the first Anglo-Maratha War, IHRCP, v.20
(1943), pp.31-33.

I-1652
Baqa'i, Irshad Husain.
The 'Ranger Snow' episode, IHRCP, v.18
(1942), pp.261-64.

I-1648
Banerjee, Anil Chandra, 1910-
A disputed article of the Treaty of Purandhar,
IHCP, v.21 (1958), pp.393-95.

I-1653
Bell, Evans, 1825-1887.
The English in India, letters from Nagpore,
written in 1857-58. London, J.Chapman, 1859.
205p.

1. India - Pol.& govt. - 1765-

I-1649
Banerjee, Anil Chandra, 1910-
Peshwa Madhav rao I's relations with the
English, IHCP, v.3 (1939), pp.1469-1507.

I-1654
Bell, Evans, 1825-1887.
Holkar's appeal: "the office" or the
Empire. London, privately printed, 1881.
102p.

I-1655
Bendrey, Vasudeo Sitaram, 1896-
Downfall of Angre's navy, BIS, v.4 (Oct. 1967), pp.1-41.

VVV
Uof R

I-1656
Bengal. Supreme Council.
Authentic abstracts of minutes in the Supreme Council of Bengal, on the late Contracts for draught and carriage bullocks, for victualling the European troops, and for victualling Fort William... and a remarkable Treaty, with the Ranah of Gohud, a Marratta. London, 1870. 100p.

SOAS

I-1657
Bennell, A.S.
The Anglo-Maratha confrontation of June and July 1803, RASGBIJ, series 3 (1962), pp.107-31.

I-1658
Bennell, A.S.
Factors in the Marquis Wellesley's failure against Holkar, 1804, BSOAS, v.28 (1965), pp.553-81.

I-1659
Bhandarkar, Devadatta Ramakrishna, 1875-
Capture of the Gwalior Fort in 1780, IHRCP, v.12 (1929), pp.49-53.

I HRCP

I-1660
Bhattacharya, Sukumar.
The second Anglo-Maratha War and Mewar, IHCP, v.22 (1959), pp.403-406.

I HCP

I-1661
Blacker, Valentine, 1778-1823.
Memoir of the operations of the British army in India, during the Maratta war of 1817, 1818, & 1819. London, Black, Kingsbury, Parbury, and Allen, 1821. 529p.

U of R

I-1662
Bombay (Presidency)
Report on the territory conquered from the Paishwa, submitted to the Supreme Government of British India, by Mountstuart Elphinstone. 2d ed. Bombay, 1838. 160p.

I-1663
Bombay (Presidency)
Treaties, Agreements and Engagements between the Honorable East India Company and the Native Princes, Chiefs and States in western India; the Red Sea; the Persian Gulf; &c. Also between Her Britannic Majesty's Government, and Persia, Portugal, and Turkey. Compiled under instructions... by R.Hughes Thomas. Bombay, 1851.

IOL

I-1664
Bordeaux, Henry, 1870-
Le comte de Boigne, général des Mahrattes, 1751-1830. Paris, Hachette, 1956. 223p.

1. Boigne, Benoît Le Borgne, comte de, 1751-1830.

I-1665
Boulger, Demetrius C.
The Murat of the Marathas, *AQ*, v.5 (1922),
pp.83-98.

Holkar . 1802-1805 .

Case

I-1666
Brief remarks on the Mahratta War, and on
the rise and progress of the French establishment in Hindostan, under Generals
De Boigne and Perron. London, 1804.

Calcutta Nat'l Lib

I-1667
Briggs, John, 1785-1875.
Statements of facts connected with the
capture of the Nassuck Jewels. London, 1828.

Calcutta nat'l Lib

I-1668
Burton, Reginald George, 1864-
The last Maratha war, *USIIJ*, v.30 (1900),
pp.93-116.

I-1669
Campbell, Lawrence Dundas.
A vindication of the justice and policy of
the late wars carried on in Hindostan and the
Deckan by Marquis Wellesley ... in conjunction
with H.H.the Peshwah Bajee Rao ... against the
subordinate Marhatta chieftains, Dowlut Rao
Scindiah, Ragajee Bhoonslah and Jesswunt Rao
Holkar. London, 1806. 112p.

IOL

I-1670
Central Provinces and Berar, India.
Collection of correspondence relating to the
escape and subsequent adventures of Appa Sahib, ex-
rajah of Nagpur, 1818-1840. Nagpur, Government
Printing, C.P. and Berar, 1939.

Nuc p~ 1956

I-1671
Chaplin, William.
A report exhibiting a view of the fiscal
and judicial system of administration introduced into the conquered territory above the
Ghauts, under the authority of the Commission-
ner in the Dekkan. Bombay, Courier Press,
1824. 161p.

U of R order

I-1672
Chatterjee, Nondita.
Anglo-Maratha relations during Maratha-
Mysore War (1785-1787), *JIH*, v.39 (1961),
pp.129-36.

Case

I-1673
Chatterji, Nandalal, 1903-
The failure of Anglo-Maratha negotiations
regarding the cession of Cuttack, *BPP*, v.61
(1939), pp.58-64.

Case

I-1674
Choksey, Rustom Dinshaw, 1914-
The aftermath, based on authentic records,
1818-1826; with select documents from the
Deccan Commissioner's files, Peshwa Daftar,
on the administrative and judicial organiza-
tion of Maharashtra by the British. Bombay,
New Book Company, 1950. 366p.

LC

I-1675
   Choksey, Rustom Dinshaw, 1914-
     A history of British diplomacy at the court
of the Peshwas 1786-1818; based on English
records of Mahratta history. Poona, R.D.
Choksey, 1951. 416p.

     1. Gt.Brit. - For.rel. - India. 2. Mahrattas.
3. India - For.rel. - Gt.Brit.

U 4R

I-1676
   Choksey, Rustom Dinshaw, 1914-
     The last phase: selections from the Deccan
Commissioner's files (Peshwa Daftar) 1815-
1818. Bombay, Phoenix publications, 1948.
270p.

     1. Gt.Brit. - For.rel. - India. 2. India -
For.rel. - Gt.Brit.

4 of R

I-1677
   Choksey, Rustom Dinshaw, 1914-
     Malwan residency; Savantvadi affairs,
1812-1819. Select documents from the
Ratnagiri collector's files, Peshwa
Daftar. Poona, R.D.Choksey, 1956. 154p.

UofR

I-1678
   Choksey, Rustom Dinshaw, 1914- comp.
     Period of transition (1818-1826). Poona,
R.D.Choksey, 1945. 250p.

4 of R

I-1679
   Choksey, Rustom Dinshaw, 1914- comp.
     Ratnagiri collectorate, 1821-1829. Poona,
R.D.Choksey, 1958. 221p.

U of R

I-1680
   Compton, Herbert Eastwick, 1853-1906, comp.
     A particular account of European military
adventurers in Hindustan from 1784-1803.
London, T.F.Unwin, 1893. (The adventure
series). 419p.

UofR

I-1681
   Cope, Capt.
     A new history of the East Indies ... With a
full account of the ... destruction of Tulagee
Angria, the pirate. London, 1758. 434p.

JIBOL

I-1682
   Das, Harihar.
     Peshwa Raghunath Rau's agents in England,
JIH, v.10 (1931), pp.27-28.

JIH

I-1683
   Datta, Sankar Kumar.
     The background of diplomatic contact be-
tween the Gaikwar and the East India Company,
IHCP, v.24 (1961), pp.205-206.

UofR

I-1684
   De Mauley, Lord.
     The Wellesleys' in India, AR, v.3 (1887),
pp.178-205.

AR

I-1685
Diskalkar, Dattatraya Balkrishna, 1892-
An English letter of Janardan Shivram, the Peshwa's vakil at Madras, to McCartney, the governor of Madras, *JIH*, v.11 (1932), pp.234-39.

G14

I-1686
Diskalkar, Dattatraya Balkrishna, 1892-
Maratha vakils with the British at Bombay, Calcutta and Madras. In: Dr.S.Krishnaswami Aiyangar Commemoration Volume. Essays and papers presented to Dr.Krishnaswami Aiyangar on his 66th birthday. Ed.by B.Bhattacharyya and others. Madras, 1936. pp.26-29.

Jul v3 p232

I-1687
Duncan, Jonathan.
Narrative of Gaikwar affairs from the unpublished manuscripts of the late J.Duncan, *RASGBIJ*, vol.4 (1837), pp.365-96.

. NRU

I-1688
East India Company (English)
A collection of treaties and engagements with the native Princes and States of Asia concluded, on behalf of the East India Co., by the British Governments in India. By the Govt.of Bengal from ... 1757 to 1809; by the Govt.of Fort St. George from ... 1759 to 1809; by the Govt.of Bombay from ... 1739 to 1808. London, 1812. 643p.

I-1689
East India Company (English)
Copies of papers relative to the restoration of the King of Tanjore, the arrest of the Rt.Hon.George Lord Pigot, and the removal of his lordship from the government of Fort St.George, by members of the council. London, 1777. 2v.

I-1690
East India Company (English)
Notes relative to the peace concluded between the British government ₍i.e. the East India Company₎ and the Marhatta chieftains ₍during 1804₎ and to the various questions arising out of the terms of the pacification. London, J.Stockdale, 1805. 109p.

BM

I-1691
East India Company (English)
Papers presented to the House of Commons relating to East India affairs - Dowlut Row Scindia and Jeswunt Rao Holkar. London, 1806. 295p.

CNL

I-1692
East India Company (English)
Papers respecting Pindarry and Mahratta wars ... Treaties and engagements with native princes and states in India, concluded for the most part in the years 1817 and 1818 at end. London, 1824. 617p.

UofR

I-1693
East India Company (English)
A state of the British authority in Bengal under the Government of Mr. Hastings, exemplified in the principles and conduct of the Marhatta War, and his negotiations with Moodajee Boosla, Rajah of Berar, etc. London, 1871.

I-1694
East India Company (English)
Treaty of perpetual friendship and alliance between the United Company of Merchants of England trading to the East Indies and the Marathaha ... completed ... the 24th of February 1783. Calcutta, 1783. 17p.

I-1695
    Elphinstone, Hon. Mountstuart, 1779-1859.
      Elphinstone correspondence, 1804-08:
ed.by R.M.Sinha, and A.Avasthi. Nagpur,
Nagpur Univ. Historical Society, 1961.
489p.

I-1700
    The first wars and treaties of the western
      presidency, <u>BQR</u>, v.4 (1856), pp.70-118.

NRU

I-1696
    Elphinstone, Mountstuart, 1779-1859.
      Selected minutes...1820-1827. Bombay,
1867. (Bombay Presidency, Selections from
the records, n.s.,no.104). 59p.

BM

I-1701
    Francis, Sir Philip, 1740-1818.
      Speeches in the House of Commons on the
war against the Marhattas. London, 1805.

BM

I-1697
    Elphinstone, Hon.Mountstuart, 1779-1859.
      Selections from the minutes and other official
writings of the Hon.Mountstuart Elphinstone,
governor of Bombay. London, R.Bentley, 1884.
588p.

    1. India - Hist. - British occupation, 1765-

I-1702
    Great Battles and the E.I.Co's Army, <u>CR</u>,
      v.23 (1854), pp.96-105.

I-1698
    Enthoven, Reginald Edward, 1869-
      The officials of the court of the king
of Satara, A.D.1822. In: B.C.Law Volume.
Ed.by D.R.Bhandarkar and others. Pt.II.
Poona, Bhandarkar Oriental Research
Institute, 1945-46. pp.2-7.

I-1703
    Gupta, Pratul Chandra, 1910-
      Baji Rao II and the East India Company,
1796-1818. 2d rev.ed. Bombay, N.Y., Allied
Pubs., 1964. 252p.

    1. India - History - British occupation,
1765-1947. 2. East India Company (English)

I-1699
    Fernandez, T.
      Negotiations between the Hon'ble East
India Company and the Bhonsla Rajahs regarding the establishment of a subsidiary
force in the Nagpur State, <u>IHRCP</u>, v.11
(1928), pp.72-79.

I-1704
    Gupta, Pratul Chandra, 1910-
      Baji Rao II and the East India Company,
1796-1818. London, H.Milford, Oxford Univ.
Press, 1939. 231p.

    1. India - History - British occupation -
1765-

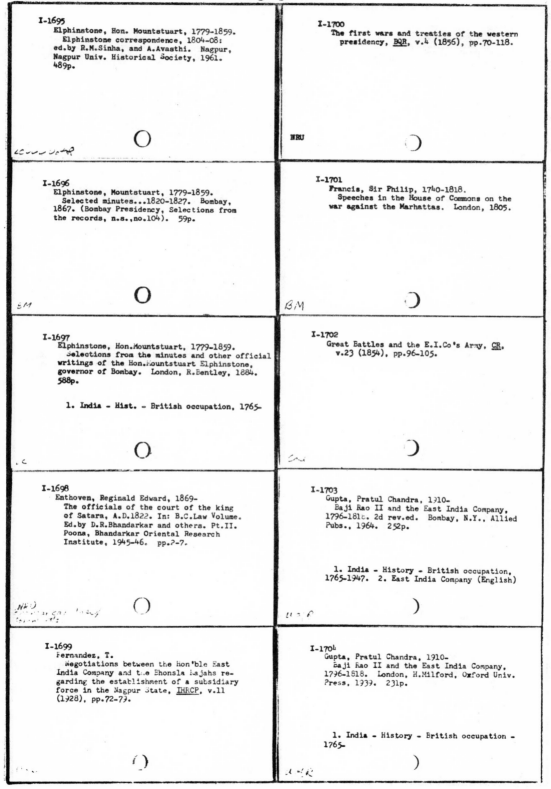

I-1705
    Gupta, Pratul Chandra, 1910-
        The commissioners at Bithur (1811-51), IHCP,
    v.6 (1943), pp.275-81.

Case

I-1706
    Gupta, Pratul Chandra, 1910-
        The last Peshwa Baji Rao II and the English
    commissioners, 1818-1851. Calcutta; S.C.
    Sarkar, 1944. 113p.

4 of R

I-1707
    Gupta, Pratul Chandra, 1910-
        Peshwa Bajee Rao II, the Gaikwad and the
    English, CR, v.54 (1935), pp.283-304.

Case

I-1708
    Gupta, S.S.
        The relations of Daulat Rao Sindhia with
    the British, from the treaty of Surji Arjan-
    gaon to the departure of Lord Wellesley,
    JUB, v.6 (1943), pp.316-18.

JUB

I-1709
    Hagar, Frederick Atwood.
        Richard Jenkins and the residency at
    Nagpur, 1807-1826. Berkeley, Univ.of
    California, 1960. 306p. *

I-1710
    Hough, William, d.1865.
        Political and military events in British
    India, from the years 1756-1849. London,
    W.H.Allen & Co., 1853. 2v.

SOAS

I-1711
    How the Marquess Wellesley ensnared the Peishwa,
    MR, v.28 (1920), pp.364-70;474-80;587-94.

MR

I-1712
    India. Army. General Staff Branch.
        The Mahratta and Pindari war. Comp.by R.G.
    Burton for General Stall, India. Simla,
    Govt.Monotype Press, 1910. 130p.

        1. Maratha War, 1816-1818.

4 of R

I-1713
    India. Army Dept.
        Wellingtons's campaigns in India, by R.G.
    Burton. Calcutta, Govt.of India, 1908.
    185p.

IOL

I-1714
    Indian annexation: British treatment of
        native princes, WR, v.79 (1863), pp.115-
    57.

Case

I-1715
Jeejeebhoy, Jeejeebhoy Rustomji Byramji,
1885-
The Duke of Wellington in Bombay, 1801
and 1804. Bombay, 1927. (Reprinted from
the Pateti Issue of the Sanj Vartaman,
1927). 16p.

/o↙

I-1716
Joshi, V.V.
Clash of three empires; a study of British
conquest of India with special reference to
Maratha people. Allahabad, Kitabistan, 1941.
207p.

1. Mahrattas. 2. India - Hist. - British
occupation, 1765-

LC

I-1717
Joshi, V.V.
Marquess of Wellesley and the conquest of
India. JUB, v.9 (1941), pp.8-48.

Case

I-1718
A journal of the march of the Bombay detach-
ment, across the Mahratta country, from
Culpee to Surat, in 1778; commanded by Lieut.-
Col.Goddard; together with the proceedings
of the Bombay Army, under Col.Egerton, in
their march towards Poonah. With a sketch of
Col.Goddard's route. London, 1779.

Cal rat< f.l

I-1719
Kale, Yadav Madhava, 1881-   ed.
Nagpur affairs, 1781-1820. Bombay, Govt.
Central Press, 1938. (English Records of
Maratha history. Poona Residency Correspondence,
v.5) 519p.

1. Nagpur, India (District) - Hist. 2.
India - Hist. - British occupation

LC

I-1720
Kaye, Sir John William, 1814-1876.
The life and correspondence of Major-
General Sir John Malcolm. London, Smith
Elder & co., 1856. 2v.

LC

I-1721
Khanna, D.D.
Supply system of Wellington's Army in
India. RUSIIJ, v.94 (1964), pp.195-99.

Caw

I-1722
Kibe, Madhav Vinayak, 1877-
The consolidation of the British supremacy
in Central India. CR, v.119 (1904), pp.336-73.

Case

I-1723
Kibe, Madhav Vinayak, 1877-
Glimpses of British correspondence regarding
Maharaja Jaswant Rao Holkar (1804-1810), IHRCP,
v.22 (1945), pp.76-78.

I HRCP

I-1724
Kibe, Madhav Vinayak, 1877-
Glimpses of the events that led to the fall
of the Maratha empire, IHCP, v.6 (1943), pp.
266-67.

I HC P

I-1725
  Kincaid, Charles Augustus, 1870-
    Ishtur Phakde, a gallant Englishman and
  other stories. Bombay, Times Press, 1917.
  142p.

LC

I-1730
  Malcolm, Sir John, 1769-1833.
    The political history of India, from 1784
  to 1823. London, J.Murray, 1826. 2v.

  1. India - Pol.& govt. - 1765-   2. India
  -Hist. - British occupation, 1765-

I-1726
  Machunn, Sir George Fletcher, 1869-1952.
    Battle of Kirkee, November 5, 1817, CM,
  v.65 (1928), pp.583-94.

I-1731
  .Malet, Sir Charles Warre, bart, 1752-1815.
    Selections from Sir C.W.Malet's letter-book
  (1780-1784). Ed.by R.Sinh. Bombay, 1953.
    (English records of Maratha history, extra
  volume)

I-1727
  Mahratta War, papers. 1804.

I-1732
  Mavaji, Purushottama Vishrama, 1879-1929.
    Sir Charles Malet, the first English
  resident at the Court of the Peshwa, MR,
  v.6 (1909), pp.68-75.

I-1728
  The Mahratta War: the origin, progress, and
  termination of the late war between the
  British government in India and the Mahratta
  Princes, Dowlut Rao, Scindeah, and Ragojee
  Bounsla, AAR, v.5 (1803), pp.1-77.

I-1733
  Mehta, B.N., 1904-
    How Warren Hastings bought off Mudaji
  (Mudhoji) Bhonsla, JIH, v.30 (1952), pp.
  77-86.

I-1729
  Malcolm, Sir John, 1769-1833.
    Instructions by Major-General Sir John Mal-
  colm ... to officers acting under his orders
  in Central India, A.D.1821. London, Parbury
  and Allen, 1824. 69p.

I-1734
  Mehta, B.N., 1904-
    Lord Wellesley's policy and its reversal,
  JIH, v.32 (1954), pp.171-90.

I-1735
　Misra, G.S., 1921-
　　British foreign policy and Indian affairs,
　1783-1815. N.Y., Asia Pub.House, 1963. 118p.

　　　1. Gt.Brit. - For.rel. - 1789-1820. 2.
　Gt.Brit. - For.rel. - India. 3. India -
　For.rel. - Gt.Brit.

U of R

I-1736
　Mukherji, Tarit.
　　Elliot's embassy, IHCP, v.14 (1951), pp.
　275-79.

I-1737
　Nagpur, India (Residency)
　　Selections from the Nagpur Residency
　records by Har Narain Sinha. Nagpur,
　Govt.Print., Madhya Pradesh, 1950-
　3v.

I-1738
　Nightingale, Pamela.
　　Trade and empire in western India, 1784-
　1806. Cambridge, Cambridge Univ.Press, 1970.
　(Cambridge South Asian studies, 9) 264p.

BAS 1970

I-1739
　Observations on the attack on mud forts; in
　which are noticed by way of illustration,
　occurences that took place at various
　sieges, particularly those of Bhurtpoor,
　and Deeg, in 1804-1805, by an officer of
　the Bengal army. Calcutta, P.Pereira, 1813.
　75p.

I-1740
　On home views of Indian affairs, BQR, v.7,no.
　14 (1858), pp.342-73.

U of R masthead

I-1741
　The origin and authentic narrative of the
　present Marratta war; and also, the late
　Rohilla war, in 1773 and 1774 ... to which
　is added, the unaccountable proceedings in
　the military storekeeper's office, in Ben-
　gal. London, J.Almon and J.Debrett, 1781.
　233p.

SOAS

I-1742
　Parasnis, Dattatraya Balwant, 1870-1926.
　　Original correspondence between the English
　and the Marathas, IHRCP, v.5 (1923), pp.91-
　99.

18th cent.

I-1743
　Pertsmakker, V.V.
　　Iz istorii bor'by Maratkhov s evropeïskimi
　zakhvatchikami (1698-1756), NAA, v.3 (1962),
　pp.73-82.

I-1744
　Poona, India (District) Commissioner.
　　Report on the territories, conquered from
　the paishwa. Submitted to the supreme govt.
　of British India, by the hon'ble Mountstuart
　Elphinstone, commissioner. Calcutta, Govt.
　Gazette Press, 1821. 182p.

　　　1. Mahrattas - Hist.

I-1745
Powar, Appasaheb Ganapatrao, 1906-
A forgotten Naval treaty between the
English and Raja Sambhaji's Governor
of Malwan 1739. In: A volume of studies
in Indology presented to Prof.P.V.Kane,
ed.by S.M.Katre and P.K.Gode. Poona,
Oriental Book Agency, 1941. pp.329-38.

I-1746
Prinsep, Henry Thoby.
History of the political and military trans-
actions in India under the administration of
the Marquess of Hastings. London, Kingsbury,
Parbury, 1825. 2v.

Cal Nat'l Lib.

I-1747
Qanungo, Sudhindra Nath.
Some sidelights on the battle of Indore
(14th October, 1801), UB, v.10 (1963), pp.
89-93.

I-1748
Ramalingam, John A.
The battle of Sitabaldi 26th and 27th,
November, 1817, IHQ, v.36 (1960), pp.227-
37.

IHQ

I-1749
Ramalingam, John A.
The consequences of the subsidiary alliance
which Appa Sahib had contracted with the
British Govt.on 27th May, 1816, IHCP, v.23,pt.2
(1960), pp.116-17.

I-1750
Rawlinson, Hugh George, 1880-
Anglo-Maratha negotiations, 1739, JIH, v.2
(1923), pp.206-21.

NYPL

I-1751
Rawlinson, Hugh George, 1880-
The battle of Kirkee. In: Sardesai Com-
memorative Volume. Ed.by Shripad R.Tikekar.
Bombay, 1938. pp.47-52.

Bhardarkar Index

I-1752
A retrospective view and consideration of
India affairs; particularly of the trans-
actions of the Mahratta war from its com-
mencement ot the month of October 1783.
London, J.Debrett, 1783. 112p.

Cal Nat Lib.

I-1753
Reu, Bisheshwar Nath, 1890-
Letters of British officers addressed to
Maharaja Man Singh of Jodhpur about the cap-
ture of Bhonsle of Nagpur, JBRS, v.33 (1947),
pp.20-24.

NRU
JBRS

I-1754
Review of the affairs of India, from 1798
to 1806, etc. London, T.Cadell and
W.Davies, 1807.

I-1755
Roy, Nirod Bhushan.
Marquess Wellesley's policy towards Sindia
in the war with Holkar (1804-05), IHRCP, v.16
(1939), pp.80-90.

4 JR

I-1756
Saletore, G.N.
The British expedition against Dhondji
Vagh, JUB, v.15 (1947), pp.5-17.

Case

I-1757
Sardesai, Govind Sakharam, 1865-1959.
The Poona Residency correspondence and
its value to history. In: Dr.S.Krishna-
swami Aiyangar Commemoration Volume.
Essays and papers presented to Dr.Krishna-
swami Aiyangar on his 66th birthday. Ed.
by B.Bhattacharyya and others. Madras,
1936. pp.118-21.

Bhandarkar Index
Common Vol.

I-1758
Sardesai, Govind Sakharam, 1865-1959, ed.
Poona affairs (Elphinstone's embassy).
Bombay, Printed at the Popular Press, 1950-
1953. (English records of Maratha history,
Poona residency correspondence, v.12 and 13).
2v.

NUR
LC

I-1759
Sardesai, Govind Sakharam, 1865-1959, ed.
Poona affairs, 1801-1810 (Close's embassy).
Bombay, Govt.Central Press, 1940. (Eng-
lish records of Maratha history. Poona resi-
dency correspondence,no.7). 612p.

LC

I-1760
Sardesai, Govind Sakharam, 1865-1959, ed.
Poona affairs, 1786-1797. (Malet's
Embassy). Bombay, Printed at the Govt.
Central Press, 1936. (English records of
Maratha history, Poona residency corres-
pondence, v.2). 596p.

U of R

I-1761
Sardesai, Govind Sakharam, 1865-1959, ed.
Poona affairs, 1797-1801. (Palmer's
embassy). Bombay, Printed at the Govt.
Central Press, 1939. (English records
of Maratha history, Poona residency correspondence, v.6). 727p.

U of R

I-1762
Sarkar, Sir Jadunath, 1870-1958.
The battle of Lakhere, 1793, or Campoo
versus Campoo, MR, v.75 (1944), pp.97-104.

Case

I-1763
Sarkar, Sir Jadunath, 1870-1958.
English residents with Mahadji Sindhia,
IHRCP, v.11 (1928), pp.10-14.

Case

I-1764
Sarkar, Sir Jadunath, 1870-1958.
Warren Hastings as seen by the Maratha
envoy, BPP, v.72 (1953), pp.30-38.

Case

I-1765
Sarkar, Upendra Nath.
Sketch of the battle of Dig, 13 November 1804. IndA. v.9 (1955), pp.113-20.

IndA

I-1766
Sen, Sailendra Nath.
Anglo-Maratha relations during the administration of Warren Hastings, 1772-1785. Calcutta, Firma K.L.Mukhopadhyay, 1961. 288p.

I-1767
Sen, Sailendra Nath.
Capture of Salsette by the English in 1774, IHCP, v.19 (1956), p.343.

U of R

I-1768
Sen, Sailendra Nath.
Origin of the first Anglo-Maratha War. IHCP, v.22 (1959), pp.400-402.

IHC

I-1769
Seth, D.R.
Wellington's Indian campaign, RUSIIJ, v.86 (1956), pp.190-98.

I-1770
Sharma, B.G.
The murder of Gangadhar Shastri and the role of Mountstuart Elphinstone, IHCP, v.27 (1965), pp.316-17.

I-1771
Shejwalkar, Trymbak Shankar.
The Surat episode of 1759, EDCRI, v.8 (1947), pp.173-203.

DS 401 J296

I-1772
Shejwalkar, Trymbak Shankar, ed.
Nagpur affairs. Poona, Deccan College Post-graduate and Research Institute, 1954- (Deccan College monograph series).

U of R

I-1773
Shrivastava, Rhudhayesh Kumar.
A critical examination of the relation of the Paramount power with the Gwalior State. Ujjain, Vikram Univ., 1970. *

Political science Hist + conditions

I-1774
Sinh, Raghubir, 1908-
Manuscript letter-book of Sir Charles Warre Malet, 1780-1784, IHRCP, v.14 (1937), pp.19-27. Also in: BPP, v.55 (1938), pp. 11-19.

U of I

I-1775
Sinh, Raghubir, 1908-   ed.
The treaty of Bassein and the Anglo-Maratha war in the Deccan, 1802-04. Bombay, Printed at the Sri Gouranga Press, 1951. (English records of Maratha history, Poona residency correspondence, v.10). 308p.

Vo*R

I-1780
Sinha, K.N.
Anglo-Maratha diplomacy during the residency of Colonel Palmer, IHCP, v.26, pt.2 (1964), pp.153-60.

IHCP

I-1776
Sinha, Har Narain, 1900-
The battle of Sitabaldi, IHCP, v.8 (1945), pp.369-72.

II

I-1781
Sinha, K.N.
British diplomacy in the court of the Peshwa during the residency of Col.B.Close, (1801-1804), IHCP, v.27 (1965), pp.287-94.

I-CP

I-1777
Sinha, Har Narain, 1900-
Capture and surrender of Gheria by the English, IHRCP, v.18 (1942), pp.226-32.

IHRC

I-1782
Sinha, K.N.
British relations with the Nagpur court (1799-1806), IHCP, v.28 (1966), pp.346-53.

I-1778
Sinha, Har Narain, 1900-
The embassy of H.T.Colebrooke at the Court of the Bhonsla Raghoai (sic) II, IHRCP, v.11 (1928), pp.62-67.

DS
451
B69 j
ENS

I-1783
Sinha, K.N.
Studies in Anglo Maratha relations. Jabalpur, Lok Chetana Prakashan, 1969. 132p.

I-1779
Sinha, K.N.
The Anglo-Bhonsla relations during the residency of Elphinstone, IHCP, v.29, pt.II (1967), p.34.

I-1784
Sinha, Ram Mohan.
An aspect of British-Bhonsla relations during the residency of Elphinstone, IHCP, v.14 (1951), pp.304-309.

I-1785
Smith, Lewis Ferdinand.
A sketch of the rise, progress, and termination of the regular corps formed and commanded by Europeans in the service of the native princes of India; with details of the principal events and actions of the late Mahratta war. Calcutta, Printed by J.Greenway, 1805. 93p.

BM

I-1786
Sovani, Nilkanth Vitthal.
British impact on India before 1850-57. JWH, v.1 (1954), pp.857-82.

Case

I-1787
Springer, William H.
The military apprenticeship of Arthur Wellesley in India, 1797-1805. New Haven, Conn., Yale Univ., 1963. *

Case

I-1788
Srinivasachari, Chidambaram S., 1890-1951.
Macartney, the Carnatic and Tanjore, IHRCP, v.28 (1951), pp.90-97.

Cases

I-1789
The struggle for empire with the Mahrattas. WR, v.91 (1869), pp.1-48.

Case

I-1790
Thompson, E.
The eve of the Anglo-Maratha War of 1803. In: Sardesai Commemorative volume. Ed.by Shripad R.Tikekar. Bombay, Keshav Bhikaji Dhawale, 1938. pp.53-58.

I I

I-1791
Thorn, Sir William, 1781-1843.
Memoir of the war in India conducted by Gen. Lord Lake, commander-in-chief, and Major General Sir Arthur Wellesley, duke of Wellington, from its commencement in 1803, to its termination in 1806, on the banks of the Hyphasis. London, T.Egerton, 1818. 533p.

1. Mahratta War, 1803.

UgR

I-1792
Varma, Shanti Prasad, 1910-
Anglo-Maratha relations, 1772-1783 A.D. (a study in Indian diplomacy of the late eighteenth century). Agra, Agra University, 1955. *

Case

I-1793
Varma, Shanti Prasad, 1910-
A study in Maratha diplomacy: Anglo-Maratha relations, 1772-1783. Agra, Shiva Lal Agrawala, 1956. 432p.

Ma   s.

U-rR

I-1794
Vindication of the justice and policy of the late wars carried on in Hindostan and the Deckan, by Marquis Wellesley, Governor General...in conjunction with His Highness the Peishwah Bajee Rao. Chief of the Marhatta states: against the subordinate Marhatta Chieftains Dowlut Rao Scindiah, Ragajee Bhoonslah, and Jesswunt Rao Holkar. London, John Stockdale, 1806. 113p.

Nat. Lib Cakutta

I-1795
   Wallace, Sir Robert, 1811-1890.
      The Guicowar and his relations with the
   British government. Bombay, Printed at the
   Education Society's Press, 1863. 712p.

      1. Baroda - Hist. 2. Baroda - For.rel. -
   Great Britain.

LC

I-1796
   Wellesley, Richard Colley Wellesley, marquis,
      1760-1842.
      History of all the events and transactions
   which have taken place in India; containing
   the negotiations of the British Government,
   relative to the glorious success of the late
   war. Trans.by J.Stockdale. London, 1805.

BM

I-1797
   Wellesley, Richard Colley Wellesley, marquis,
      1760-1842.
      Notes relative to the late transactions in
   the Marhatta empire. Fort William, 1803.
   1 vol. (various pagings)

ᴋᵃˢR

I-1798
   Wellesley, Richard Colley Wellesley, marquis,
      1760-1842.
      Notes relative to the peace concluded
   between the British government and the Marhatta chieftains and to the various questions
   arising out of the terms of the pacification.
   London, J.Stockdale, 1805. 109p.

IOL

I-1799
   Wills, Cecil Upton.
      British relations with the Nagpur state in
   the 18th century. An account based mainly on
   contemporary English records. Nagpur, Govt.
   Press, 1926. (Pubs.by the Dept.of Modern
   Indian history, Allahabad University, 3).
   274p.

NUR
SOAS

I-1800
   Wylie, John.
      Sketch of the column at Corygaum, with
   plan of the village, letters, the general
   orders, and despatch from court of directors,
   relating to the action, Jan.1, 1818. Madras,
   1843.

NYPL   French

I-1801
   Affaires de l'Inde, depuis le commencement de
      la guerre avec la France en 1756, jusqu'à
      la conclusion de la paix en 1783; contenant
      l'histoire des intérêts de l'Angleterre
      dans l'Indostan, les détails de deux guerres
      avec la France ... Préis historique sur
      les Marattes, compose en persan, par
      l'érivain Hameddin. Londres, 1788. 2v.

NYPL

I-1802
   Cultru, Prosper.
      Dupleix, Ses plans politiques: sa
   disgrace. Etude d'histoire coloniale.
   Paris, 1901. 392p.

Brit Mus

I-1803
   Hatalkar, V.G.
      French documents throwing fresh light on
   the embassy of M.de St.Lubin to the Maratha
   Court 1777-78, IHRCP, v.31 (1955), pp.45-49.

Cawe

I-1804
   Hatalkar, V.G.
      Relations between the French and Marathas
   (1668-1815). Bombay, T.V.Chidambaran,
   1958. (Originally submitted as Ph.D.
   thesis, Univ.of Bombay). 322p.

Unf

I-1805
Hatalkar, V.G.
Souillac's fresh approach to Maratha-Franco relations, IHRCP, v.32 (1956), pp.28-32.

I-1806
Khan, Mohibbul Hasan.
The policy of the French in the Maratha-Mysore War (1785-1787), IHRCP, v.25 (1948), pp.63-65.

I-1807
Sarkar, Sir Jadunath, 1870-1958.
Private correspondence of Montreau, a French officer in Maratha service, IHCP, v.10 (1947), pp.431-36.

I-1808
Sen, Siba Pada, 1914-
A "memoire" on Franco-Maratha negotiations from 1770-1783, IHRCP, v.28 (1951), pp.78-83.

I-1809
Sen, Siba Pada, 1914-
Private correspondence of Montreau, a French officer in Maratha service, IHCP, v.10 (1947), pp.431-35.

I-1810
Sen, Siba Padu, 1914-
A proposed treaty of alliance between the French and the Marathas (1782), IHCP, v.9 (1945), pp.349-57. Also in: CR, v.99 (1946), pp.67-74.

I-1811
Trilokekar, M.K.
Mons.de St. Lubin, a French adventurer at the Maratha Court, JBHS, v.3 (1930), pp.51-76.

Portuguese

I-1812
Costa, Diogo da.
Relaçam das guerras da India desde o anno de 1736 até o de 1740. Lisboa, 1741.

I-1813
Cunha Rivara, Joaquim Heliodoro da, 1809-1879.
A conjuração de 1787 em Goa, e varias cousas desse tempo. Memoria historica. Nova Goa, 1875. 282p.

I-1814
Dass, Dayal.
Some unpublished letters about Goa (1835 A.D.), UPHSJ, n.s.,v.3 (1955), pp.50-61.

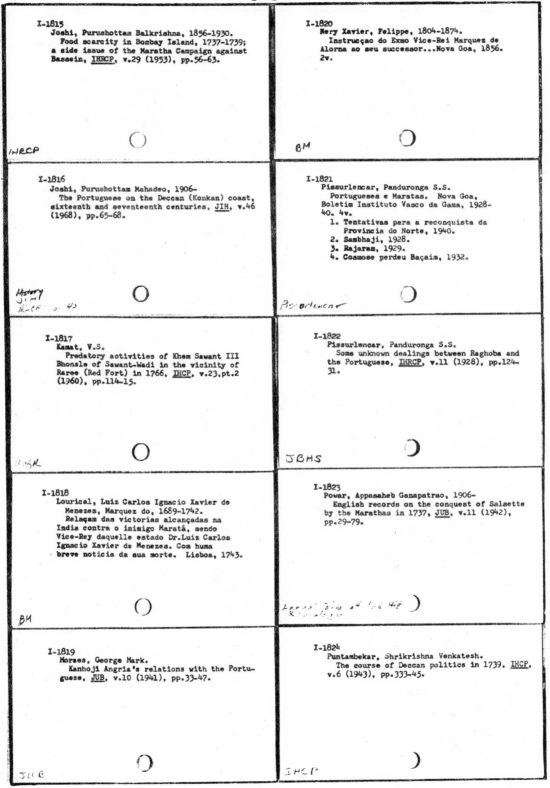

I-1815
Joshi, Purushottam Balkrishna, 1856-1930.
Food scarcity in Bombay Island, 1737-1739;
a side issue of the Maratha Campaign against
Bassein, IHRCP, v.29 (1953), pp.56-63.

IHRCP

I-1816
Joshi, Purushottam Mahadeo, 1906-
The Portuguese on the Deccan (Konkan) coast,
sixteenth and seventeenth centuries, JIH, v.46
(1968), pp.65-68.

History
JIH
IHRCP p. 45

I-1817
Kamat, V.S.
Predatory activities of Khem Sawant III
Bhonsle of Sawant-Wadi in the vicinity of
Raree (Red Fort) in 1766, IHCP, v.23,pt.2
(1960), pp.114-15.

I-1818
Lourical, Luiz Carlos Ignacio Xavier de
Menezes, Marquez do, 1689-1742.
Relaçam das victorias alcançadas na
India contra o inimigo Maratá, sendo
Vice-Rey daquelle estado Dr.Luiz Carlos
Ignacio Xavier de Menezes. Com huma
breve noticia da sua morte. Lisboa, 1743.

BM

I-1819
Moraes, George Mark.
Kanhoji Angria's relations with the Portu-
guese, JUB, v.10 (1941), pp.33-47.

JUB

I-1820
Nery Xavier, Felippe, 1804-1874.
Instrucçao do Exmo Vice-Rei Marquez de
Alorna ao seu successor...Nova Goa, 1856.
2v.

BM

I-1821
Pissurlencar, Panduronga S.S.
Portugueses e Maratas. Nova Goa,
Boletim Instituto Vasco da Gama, 1928-
40. 4v.
1. Tentativas para a reconquista da
Provincia do Norte, 1940.
2. Sambhaji, 1928.
3. Rajaram, 1929.
4. Cosmose perdeu Baçaim, 1932.

Pissurlencar

I-1822
Pissurlencar, Panduronga S.S.
Some unknown dealings between Raghoba and
the Portuguese, IHRCP, v.11 (1928), pp.124-
31.

JBHS

I-1823
Powar, Appasaheb Ganapatrao, 1906-
English records on the conquest of Salsette
by the Marathas in 1737, JUB, v.11 (1942),
pp.29-79.

I-1824
Puntambekar, Shrikrishna Venkatesh.
The course of Deccan politics in 1739, IHCP,
v.6 (1943), pp.333-45.

IHCP

Afghans and Panipat   Marathas - Relations with Indian powers

I-1825
Demetrius, J.G.
The last of the Panipats: a grim episode in India's history, MR, v.16 (1950), pp.52-62.

I-1826
Gupta, Hari Ram, 1902-   ed.
Marathas and Panipat. Chandigarh, Panjab University, 1961. 402p.

I-1827
Kasi Raja.
An account of the Battle of Panipat, and of the events leading to it. Written in Persian by Casi Raja Pundit, who was present at the battle, trans.by James Browne, AsiaRes, v.3 (1792), pp.91-139.

I-1828
Kasi Raja.
An account of the last battle of Panipat, and of the events leading to it; written in Persian by Casi Raja Pundit, who was present at the battle; trans.into English by Lieut.-Col.James Browne of Dinapore, 1st Feb., 1791; and now ed.with an introd., notes and appendices, by H.G.Ralinson. London, H.Milford, 1926. 78p.

I-1829
Pathakji, M.J.
Talikota and Panipat, IHCP, v.3 (1939), pp.1216-17.

I-1830
Raghavendra Rao, V.
Govind Pant Bundela and Panipat, AIOCPT, v.8 (1935), pp.527-31.

I-1831
Rao, Raghavendra V.
Panipat and the Nizam, IHCP, v.13 (1950), pp.204-206.

I-1832
Sardesai, Govind Sakharam, 1865-1959.
The battle of Panipat - its causes and consequences, MR, v.54 (1933), pp.269-74.

I-1833
Sarkar, Sir Jadunath, 1870-1958.
Battle of Panipat: the Victor's despatches, MR, v.79 (1946), pp.337-39.

I-1834
Sarkar, Sir Jadunath, 1870-1958.
The earliest Persian account of Panipat, 1761. In: Sardesai Commemorative volume. Ed.by Shripad R.Tikekar. Bombay, Keshav Bhikaji Dhawale, 1938. pp.257-60.

I-1835
Sarkar, Sir Jadunath, 1870-1958.
Events leading up to the battle of Panipat,
1761. IHQ, v.11 (1935). pp.547-58.

IHG

I-1840
Srivastava, Ashirbadi Lal.
The Marathas and Najib-ud-daulah (1757-
1760). IC, v.20 (1946). pp.49-57.

Bengal, Bihar and Orissa

I-1836
Sarkar, Sir Jadunath, 1870-1958.
An original account of Ahmad Shah Durrani's
campaigns in India and the battle of Panipat.
(From the Persian life of Najib-ud-daulah,
British Museum Persian MS 24,410). IC, v.7
pp.431-56.

Case

I-1841
Acharya, P.
An oriya letter from the Madalapanji rela-
ting to Raghuji Bhonsla's march to Orissa &
Bengal in 1743 A.D., IHRCP, v.24 (1948). pp.
115-18.

IHRCP

I-1837
Sarkar, Sir Jadunath, 1870-1958.
Panipat, 1761. IHQ, v.10 (1934). pp.258-73.

Case

I-1842
Bhattacharya, Sukumar.
Threat of Maratha invasion of Patna in
1738, plight of European merchants, IHRCP,
v.35 (1960). pp.49-50.

IH RC

I-1838
Shejwalkar, Trymbak Shankar.
Panipat: 1761. Poona, S.M.Katre for
Deccan College Postgraduate and Research
Institute, 1946. (Deccan College monograph
series, 1). 165p.

D.+R

I-1843
Datta, Kalikinkar, 1905-
The Marathas in Bengal after 1751. JIH,
v.15 (1936). pp.387-409.

Case

I-1839
Srivastava, Ashirbadi Lal.
The Maratha-Afghan diplomatic tussle on
the eve of Panipat. In: Sardesai Commem-
orative Volume. Ed.by Shripad R.Tikekar.
Bombay, 1938. pp.143-52.

Bhandarkar Inst-Copies

I-1844
Datta, Kalikinkar, 1905-
The Marathas in Bengal (1740-1765), JBHS,
v.3 (1930). pp.201-22; v.4 (1931), pp.1-10,
192-208.

Case

I-1845
Datta, Kalikinkar, 1905-
Social, economic and political effects of
the Maratha invasions between 1740 and 1764
on Bengal, Bihar and Orissa, AIOCPT, v.6
(1930), pp.181-98.

I-1846
Gaṅgārāma, 18th cent.
The Mahārāshtra Purāṇa; an 18th cent.
Bengali text. Trans.by E.C.Dimock.
Honolulu, Pub.for the Assoc.for Asian
Studies by East-West Center Press, 1965.
(Monographs of the Assoc.for Asian
Studies, no.12). 108p.

I-1847
Landge, D.G., 1891-
Did Khandoji Bhonsle of Nagpur ruling
family go to Bengal in 1764, IHRCP, v.33
(1958). pp.112-14.

I-1848
Majumdar, A.B.
"Bala Sahib" in North Bengal, JIH, v.47
(1969), pp.253-59.

I-1849
Mitra, Kalipada.
The defence of the frontier of Bihar and
Orissa against Maratha and Pindari incursions
(1800-1819), IHRCP, v.16 (1939), pp.150-57.

I-1850
Ray, Bhabani Charan.
British wishes for possession of Orissa
through diplomacy, IHCP, v.15 (1954), pp.332-37.

I-1851
Ray, Bhabani Charan.
Communication in Orissa during Maratha
rule, JAHRS, v.23 (1954-1956), pp.115-23.

I-1852
Ray, Bhabani Charan.
Orissa under Marathas; 1751-1803. Allaha-
bad, Kitab Mahal, 1960. 187p.

I-1853
Ray, Bhabani Charan.
Sadashiv Rao in Orissa, 1793-1803, IHCP, v.21
(1958). pp.336-39.

I-1854
Ray, Bhabani Charan.
Sheo Bhatt Sathe in Orissa, IHCP, v.20 (1957),
pp.229-35.

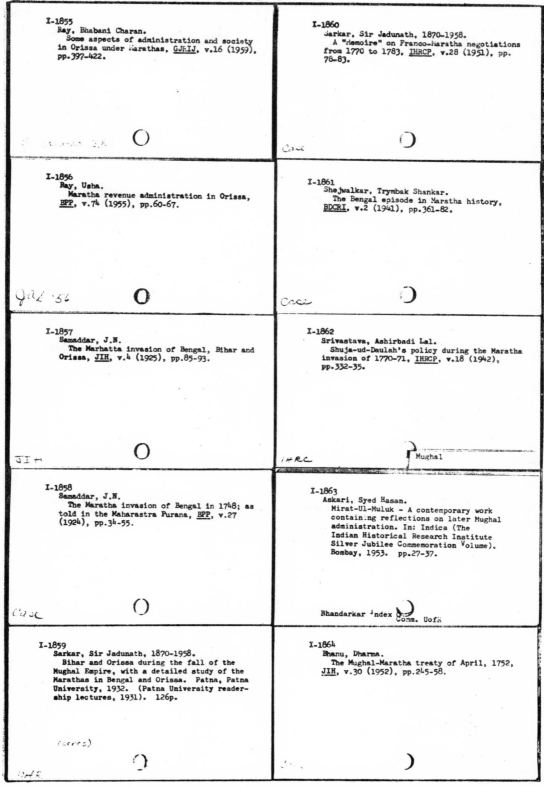

I-1855
Ray, Bhabani Charan.
Some aspects of administration and society in Orissa under Marathas, GJRIJ, v.16 (1959), pp.397-422.

I-1856
Ray, Usha.
Maratha revenue administration in Orissa, BPP, v.74 (1955), pp.60-67.

I-1857
Samaddar, J.N.
The Marhatta invasion of Bengal, Bihar and Orissa, JIH, v.4 (1925), pp.85-93.

I-1858
Samaddar, J.N.
The Maratha invasion of Bengal in 1748; as told in the Maharastra Purana, BPP, v.27 (1924), pp.34-55.

I-1859
Sarkar, Sir Jadunath, 1870-1958.
Bihar and Orissa during the fall of the Mughal Empire, with a detailed study of the Marathas in Bengal and Orissa. Patna, Patna University, 1932. (Patna University readership lectures, 1931). 126p.

I-1860
Sarkar, Sir Jadunath, 1870-1958.
A "memoire" on Franco-Maratha negotiations from 1770 to 1783, IHRCP, v.28 (1951), pp.78-83.

I-1861
Shejwalkar, Trymbak Shankar.
The Bengal episode in Maratha history, BDCRI, v.2 (1941), pp.361-82.

I-1862
Srivastava, Ashirbadi Lal.
Shuja-ud-Daulah's policy during the Maratha invasion of 1770-71, IHRCP, v.18 (1942), pp.332-35.

Mughal

I-1863
Askari, Syed Hasan.
Mirat-Ul-Muluk - A contemporary work containing reflections on later Mughal administration. In: Indica (The Indian Historical Research Institute Silver Jubilee Commemoration Volume). Bombay, 1953. pp.27-37.

Bhandarkar Index Comm. UofR

I-1864
Bhanu, Dharma.
The Mughal-Maratha treaty of April, 1752, JIH, v.30 (1952), pp.245-58.

I-1865
Burway, Mukund Wamanrao.
The struggle between the Mahrattas and the Moghuls. Bombay, 1914. 147p.

pre '56 imprints

I-1866
Chandra, Satish.
Baji Rao I and North India, IHCP, v.21 (1958), pp.370-75.

1 HCP

I-1867
Datta, Kalikinkar, 1905-
Delhi restoration, 1772, JIH, v.43 (1965), pp.71-86.

Case

I-1868
Gokhale, D.V.
A letter from the Maratha agent with the Mughal Vazir Safdarjang (1751 A.D.), IHRCP, v.23 (1946), pp.10-11.

47R

I-1869
Khare, Ganesh Hari, 1901-
Some Mughal-Maratha pacts between 1707-1750, AIOCPT, v.15 (1949), pp.301-303.

U M R

I-1870
Lauriston, Jacques Alexandre Bernard Law, Marquis de.
Mémoir sur quelques affaires de l'Empire Mogol 1756-1761. Paris, Publié par Alfred Martineau, 1913. 655p.

SOAS

I-1871
Parasnis, Dattatraya Balwant, 1870-1926.
The Maratha ambassadors at the Court of Delhi and their correspondence, IHRCP, v.8 (1925), pp.159-66.

II

I-1872
Powar, Appasaheb Ganapatrao, 1906-
The death of Aurangzib and after, IHRCP, v.18 (1942), pp.336-40.

II

I-1873
Powar, Appasaheb Ganapatrao, 1906-
Some documents bearing on imperial Mughal grants to Raja Shahu (1717-24), IHRCP, v.17 (1941), pp.204-15.

Case

I-1874
Sachdeva, Shri Krishan Lal.
Agra during the Mahratta regime (1785-1803), IHCP, v.19 (1956), pp.425-34.

U M R

I-1875
Sarkar, Sir Jadunath, 1870-1958.
Mughal-Maratha struggle for Madras, MR,
v.33 (1923), pp.17-25.

MR

I-1880
Sarkar, Sir Jadunath, 1870-1958, tr.
Delhi affairs, 1761-1788: news-letters
from Parasnis collection; translated with
notes by Jadunath Sarkar. Bombay, Director
of Archives, 1953. (Persian records of
Maratha history, 1).

IOL see
Persian catalogue

I-1876
Sarkar, Sir Jadunath, 1870-1958.
Sindhia as Regent of Delhi (1787 and
1789-91), Translated from the Persian
with notes, by Jadunath Sarkar. Bombay,
Director of Archives, Government of Bombay, 1954. (Persian records of Maratha
history, v.2). 78p.

Vof R

I-1881
Sarkar, Sir Jadunath, 1870-1958, tr.
Ibrat-namah by Faqir Khairuddin, MA, no.2
(1966), pp.1-102.

✓✓✓

I-1877
Sarkar, Sir Jadunath, 1870-1958.
The Mughal-Maratha contest for Malwa,
1728-1741, IC, v.6 (1932), pp.535-52.

II

I-1882
Sarkar, Sir Jadunath, 1870-1958, tr.
Tarikh-i-shah Alam by Munna Lal, MA, no.5
(1970), pp.7-46.

Mysore

I-1878
Sarkar, Sir Jadunath, 1870-1958, ed.
Daulat Rao Sindhia and north Indian
affairs 1794-1799. Bombay, Printed at
the Govt.Central Press, 1943. (English
records of Maratha history, Poona residency
correspondence, v.8). 311p.

1. India - Hist. - British occupation, 1765 - Sources,

LC

I-1883
Ali, B.Sheikh.
Cornwallis and the Mysore-Maratha War (1786-
1787), IHCP, v.26, pt.2 (1964), pp.148-51.

IHCP

I-1879
Sarkar, Sir Jadunath, 1870-1958, ed.
Mahadji Sindhia and north Indian affairs,
1785-94. Bombay, Printed at the Govt.
Central Press, 1936. (English records of
Maratha history, Poona residency corres-
pondence, v.1) 438p.

I-1884
Banerjee, Anil Chandra, 1910-
Peshwa Madhav Rao I's last Carnatic expedi-
tion, JIH, v.20 (supp.1941), pp.1-11.

JIH

I-1885
Baqa'i, Irshad Husain.
  Tipu's relations with the Nizam and the
Marathas during the period 1785-87. IC, v.17
(1943), pp.414-21.

I-1886
Dirom, Alexander, d.1830.
  A narrative of the campaign in India, which
terminated the war with Tippoo Sultan in 1792.
London, W.Faden [etc.] 1793. 312p.

  1. Tīpū Sultān, Fath 'Alī, nawab of Mysore,
1749-1799. 2. India - Hist. - British occupation, 1765-

I-1887
Gondker, Narayana Rao.
  Haider-Maratha relations, 1758-1782. Mysore,
Mysore Univ., 1961. 287p. *

I-1888
Krishna, M.H. and Rao, V.Raghavendra.
  Two Maratha documents from Mysore, IHRCP,
v.17 (1940), pp.182-83.

I-1889
Matthew, J.M.
  Nine letters from a very young officer serv-
ing in India, under the Marquis Cornwallis, ...
containing some particulars of the operations
of the army ... to which is added a ... sketch
of its subsequent movements and transactions
to the junction of the Marrattah army, on the
28th of May 1791. London, G.G.J. and J.Robin-
son, 1793. 59p.

I-1890
Moor, Edward, 1771-1848.
  A narrative of the operations of Captain
Little's detachment and of the Mahratta army,
commanded by Purseram Bhow; during the late
confederacy in India, against the Nawab Tippoo
Sultan Bahadur. London, Printed for the author
and sold by J.Johnson, 1794. 539p.

  1. Tipu Sultan Fath 'Ali, nawab of Mysore,
1749-1799. 2. India - Hist. - Brittish occupation, 1760-1947

I-1891
Muddachari, B., 1929-
  Maratha court in the Karnatak, IHCP, v.28
(1966), pp.177-79.

I-1892
Muddachari, B., 1929-
  The resistance of Mysore to the Maratha
expansion, 1726-1761. Mysore, Mysore,
University of Mysore, 1970. 199p.

I-1893
Narayana Rao, Gondker.
  The second invasion of Peşwa Madhava Rao
against Mysore, 1767, QJMS, v.37 (1947),
pp.171-89.

I-1894
Narayana Rao, Gondker.
  The third invasion of Peşwa Madhava Rao
against Mysore, 1769-1770. QJMS, v.39 (1948-
1949), pp.101-16, 172-86, 254-63.

I-1895
    Raghavendra Rao, V.
      Balaji Baji Rao and the south, QJMS, v.30
    (1940), pp.429-33.

QJMS

I-1896
    Raghavendra Rao, V.
      The end of Morari Rao of Gooty, 1776 A.D.,
    QJMS, v.30 (1939), pp.73-76.

QJMS

I-1897
    Raghavendra Rao, V.
      Haider Ali and the Mahratta War, 1779-82,
    QJMS, v.31 (1941), pp.415-20.

QJMS

I-1898
    Rau, N. Subba.
      Chikkadevaraja Wadeyar of Mysore and his
    successors (1673-1761). QJMS, v.23 (1932),
    pp.26-42.

I-1899
    Roy, Nirod Bhushan, ed.
      The allies' war with Tipu Sultan, 1790-1793.
    Bombay, Printed at the Govt.Central Press,
    1937. (English records of Maratha history,
    Poona residency correspondence, v.3). 734p.

V.+P

I-1900
    Shejwalkar, Trymbak Shankar.
      An unrecorded Canara campaign by the
    Marathas, BDCRI, v.5,no.3 (1943), pp.1-4.

BDC PI

I-1901
    Shejwalkar, Trymbak Shankar.
      Why Karnatak passed out of Maratha hands.
    In: Professor C.S.Srinivasachari sixty-
    first birthday celebration volume. Madras,
    1950. pp.216-24.

Bhandarkar Index to Comm vols.

I-1902
    Sinha, Narendra Krishna, 1903-
      Hyder Ali's relations with the Marathas,
    1769-70, IHQ, v.16 (1940), pp.719-26.

IHQ

I-1903
    Sinha, Narendra Krishna, 1903-
      Hyder Ali's relations with the Marathas
    (1766-67), IHQ, v.16 (1940), pp.1-8.

IHQ

I-1904
    Sinha, Narendra Krishna, 1903-
      Hyder Ali's relations with the Marathas,
    1763-65. IHRCP, v.16 (1939), pp.76-79.

IHRC

I-1905
Sinha, Narendra Krishna, 1703-
Peshwa Madhava Rao I and the first Anglo-
Mysore war. IHCP, v.3 (1939), pp.1334-39.

IHCP

I-1906
Srinivasan, Chettur Krishnaswamy.
Maratha rule in the Carnatic. Ed.by C.S.
Srinivasachari. Annamalainagar, Annamalai
University, 1944. 414p.

Nizam

I-1907
Chand Husain, Sh.
Salabat Khan II, IC, v.18 (1944), pp.187-
209.

II

I-1908
Chaudhuri, Nani Gopal.
British relations with Hyderabad. Calcutta,
Univ.of Calcutta, 1964. 336p.

1. Hyderabad, India (State) - Hist. 2.
British in Hyderabad, India (State)

I I

I-1909
Dighe, Vishvanath Govind.
The Edlabad meeting of the Peshwa and the
Nizam, IHCP, v.13 (1950), pp.325-27.

I I

I-1910
Dighe, Vishvanath Govind.
Nizam-ul-Mulk Asaf Jah I and the Marathas,
1721-1728, IHRCP, v.14 (1937), pp.107-13.

4 of R

I-1911
Dighe, Vishvanath Govind, ed.
...Maratha - Nizam relations, 1792-1795.
Bombay, Printed at the Government Central
Press, 1937. (English records of Maratha
history. Poona residency correspondence,
v.4). 358p.

4 of R

I-1912
Gujar, M.V.
The Peshwa Bajirao and Nizam-ul-Mulk Asaf
Jah, 1730-1738, IHCP, v.2 (1938), pp.614-23.

IHCP

I-1913
Hollingbery, William.
A history of his late highness Nizam Alee
Khaun, soobah of the Dekhan. Calcutta, J.
Greenway, 1805. 205p.

v of R
IC

I-1914
Khan, Yusuf Husain.
Why was Nasir Jang summoned to Delhi, IHCP,
v.5 (1941), pp.101-102.

4 of R

I-1915
Lal, Kasim Ali Sajan.
The battle of Kharda and its significance,
IHCP, v.3 (1939), pp.1340-59.

IHCP

I-1916
Lal, Kasim Ali Sajan.
The battle of Shrigonda, IHCP, v.5 (1941),
pp.102-103.

u of R

I-1917
Lal, Kasim Ali Sajan.
The battle of Shrigonda, 1761, NIA, v.6
(1943), pp.206-10.

NIA

I-1918
Lal, Kasim Ali Sajan.
Madhav Rao I's appeal to East India Company
for help at the battle of Shrigonda 1761,
NIA, v.5 (1942), pp.165-68.

NIA

I-1919
Lal, Kasim Ali Sajan.
Nizam Ali Khan and the Peshwa Madhav
Rao I and his successors, 1766-1774.
In: Prof.C.S.Srinivasachari Sixty-
first Birthday Celebration Volume.
Madras, 1950. pp.190-200.

I-1920
McAuliffe, Robert Paton.
The Nizam; the origin and future of the
Hyderabad state. London, C.J.Clay & sons;
Cambridge, University Press, 1904. 86p.

LC

I-1921
Mahajan, D.B.
The battle of Sakharkhelda (1724 A.D.),
IHCP, v.14 (1951), p.195.

u of R

I-1922
Mavaji, Purushottama Vishrama, 1879-1929.
Battle of Kharda, MR, v.2 (1907), pp.442-44.

VUMR

I-1923
Nizām 'Ali Khān, nizam of Hyderabad, 1732 or 3-
1803.
Diplomatic correspondence between Mir Nizam
Ali Khan and the East India Company (1780-
1798). Ed.by Yusuf Husain. Hyderabad, Central
Records Office, Govt.of Andhra Pradesh, 1958.
206p.

1. Hyderabad - Hist. - Sources. 2. India -
Hist. - British   occupation, 1765-1947 -
sources.

u of R

I-1924
Pagdi, Setumadhav Rao, 1910-
Ahwal-I-Khawaqin. In:Studies in Indian
history, Dr.A.G.Pawar felicitation volume. Ed.by V.D.Rao. Kolhapur, P.Y.Pawar,
1968. pp.207-52.

u of R

I-1925
Pagdi, Setumadhava Rao, 1910-
Anecdotes of Nizam-ul-Mulk, JIH, v.39 (1961),
pp.413-66.

JIH

I-1926
Pagdi, Setumadhava Rao, 1910-
Dismissal of the French from the court of
Nizam Salabat Jung. JMaU, v.3,no.1 (1962),
pp.86-97.

I-1927
Pagdi, Setumadhava Rao, 1910-
The first Nizam and the Marathas, Indica,
v.2 (1965), pp.131-39.

I-1928
Pagdi, Setumadhava Rao, 1910-
The letters of the Shah Navaz Khan, chief
minister of the Deccan, 1753-57, JIH, v.38
(1960), pp.57-75.

I-1929
Pagdi, Setumadhava Rao, 1910-
Maratha-Nizam relations. The Nasire Asafi
of Laxmi Narayan Shafiq Aurangabadi, JIH,
v.39 (1961), pp.53-78.

I-1930
Pagdi, Setumadhava Rao, 1910-
Maratha-Nizam relations - a Persian source,
the Tuzuke Asafia of Tajalli Shah, JUB, v.27
(1959), pp.1-25.

I-1931
Pagdi, Setumadhava Rao, 1910-
Maratha-Nizam relations (Nizam-ul Mulk's
letters), JIH, v.41 (1963), pp.131-50.

JIH

I-1932
Pagdi, Setumadhava Rao, 1910-
Maratha-Nizam relations; "the Kazana-i-
Amira" of Gulam Ali Bilgrami, JIH, v.38
(1960), pp.303-26.

I-1933
Pagdi, Setumadhava Rao, 1910-
Maratha-Nizam relations: the Mashiri Asafi
of Laxmi Nandivariman, from the Yapparunkala-
virutti, ALB, v.25 (1961), pp.123-30.

I-1934
Pagdi, Setumadhava Rao, 1910-
Maratha-Nizam relations; two Persian sources:
the Tarikhe Kahatafza and the Tarikh-e-Zafrah,
JUB, v.28 (1960), pp.1-35.

I-1935
  Sarkar, Sir Jadunath, 1870-1958.
    Salabat Jang's first war with the Peshwa,
    IC, v.11 (1937), pp.180-87.

Case   Rajput states

I-1940
  Parihar, G.R.
    Appasaheb Bhonsle in Marwar, JIH, v.45
    (1967), pp.521-34.

I-1936
  Gupta, Beni.
    Marathas and the states of Kota and Bundi
    from 1682-1818 A.D. Jaipur, Rajasthan Univ.,
    1963. *

Rajasthan Univ. Lit.

I-1941
  Parihar, G.R.
    Marwar and the Marathas, 1724-1843 A.D.
    Jodhpur, Hindi Sahitya Mandir, 1968. 332p.

    1. Jodhpur, India (State) - Hist. 2.
    Marathas - Hist.

U of R

I-1937
  Gupta, Krishna Swaroop.
    Mewar and the Maratha relations (1735-
    1818 A.D.) Jaipur, Rajasthan Univ., 1961. *

Rajasthan Univ. Lib.

I-1942
  Parihar, G.R.
    The political impact of the Marathas on
    Marwar, QRHS, v.6 (1966-1967), pp.148-52.

QRHS

I-1938
  Khare, Ganesh Hari, 1901-
    Some new records on the Mahratta-Jaipur
    relations, IHRCP, v.24 (1948), pp.5-8.

Case

I-1943
  Patkar, Madhukar Mangesh, 1907-
    Peshwa's relations with Jaipur rulers
    between A.D.1730 and 1761. In: Prin-
    cipal Karmarkar Commemoration Volume
    containing Essays on Numerous topics
    of Indology. Ed.by S.V.Dandekar,
    K.N.Watave, R.N.Gadre. Poona, 1948.
    pp.161-69.

Bhandarkar Index

I-1939
  Mehta, Prithvi Singh.
    Relations between the Mewar and the Marathas
    (1707-1818). Agra, Agra Univ., 1956. *

Case

I-1944
  The political impact of the Marathas on
    Marwar, QRHS, v.6 (1966-1967), pp.148-52.

I-1945
Reu, Bisheshwar Nath, 1890-
Maharaja Abhaisingh of Marwar and the Nizam,
IHRCP, v.16 (1939), pp.211-14.

4 of R

I-1946
Reu, Bisheshwar Nath, 1890-
Some more letters of Maharaja Abhaya Singh
of Marwar regarding Gujarat campaign, IHRCP,
v.24 (1948), pp.110-14.

IHRCP

I-1947
Reu, Bisheshwar Nath, 1890-
Maharaja Abhaysingh of Jodhpur and the
tactics of the Nizam, IHCP, v.3 (1939),
pp.1112-15.

4 of R

I-1948
Sarkar, Sir Jadunath, 1870-1958.
Mahadji Sindhia's Lalsot campaign 1787.
Ia: Sardesai Commemorative Volume. Ed.by
Shripad R.Tikekar. Bombay, 1938. pp.235-
48.

I-1949
Sarkar, Sir Jadunath, 1870-1958.
A proposal for a subsidiary alliance in
Rajputana in 1794, IHRCP, v.16 (1939),
pp.1-4.

IHRCP

I-1950
Sharma, G.N.
The document relating to Bapu Sindhia's
invasion of Mewar, IHRCP, v.22 (1945), pp.
79-80.

IHRCP   Sikhs

I-1951
Banerjee, S.N.
The Cis-Sutlej chiefs under Maratha rule,
IHRCP, v.23 (1946), pp.69-72.

IHRC

I-1952
Chahal, Darshan Singh.
The Maratha Sikh relations 1756 to 1818 A.D.
Bombay, Univ.of Bombay, 1970. *

I-1953
Kibe, Madhav Vinayak, 1877-
The lion of the Punjab and the Marathas,
IHCP, v.3 (1939), p.1291.

IHCP

I-1954
Shastri, R.P.
Zalim Singh and the Marathas from 1761 to
1818, IHCP, v.14 (1951), pp.322-26.

4 of R

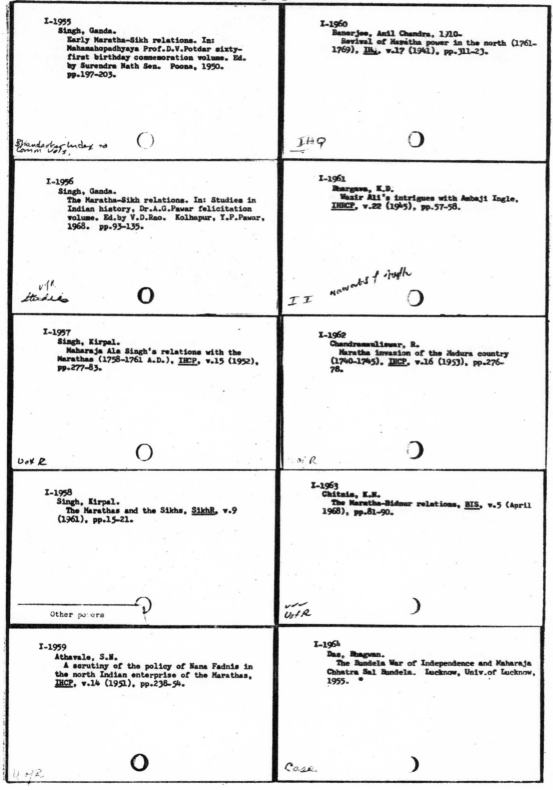

I-1955
  Singh, Ganda.
    Early Maratha-Sikh relations. In:
    Mahamahopadhyaya Prof.D.V.Potdar sixty-
    first birthday commemoration volume. Ed.
    by Surendra Nath Sen. Poona, 1950.
    pp.197-203.

Bhandarkar Index to
Comm Vols,

I-1956
  Singh, Ganda.
    The Maratha-Sikh relations. In: Studies in
    Indian history, Dr.A.G.Pawar felicitation
    volume. Ed.by V.D.Rao. Kolhapur, Y.P.Pawar,
    1968. pp.93-135.

v/R
Studies

I-1957
  Singh, Kirpal.
    Maharaja Ala Singh's relations with the
    Marathas (1758-1761 A.D.), IHCP, v.15 (1952),
    pp.277-83.

Dot R

I-1958
  Singh, Kirpal.
    The Marathas and the Sikhs, SikhR, v.9
    (1961), pp.15-21.

Other powers

I-1959
  Athavale, S.N.
    A scrutiny of the policy of Nana Fadnis in
    the north Indian enterprise of the Marathas,
    IHCP, v.14 (1951), pp.238-54.

I-1960
  Banerjee, Anil Chandra, 1710-
    Revival of Maratha power in the north (1761-
    1769), IH, v.17 (1941), pp.311-23.

IHQ

I-1961
  Bhargava, K.D.
    Wazir Ali's intrigues with Ambaji Ingle,
    IHRCP, v.22 (1945), pp.57-58.

I I   Nawabs of Oudh

I-1962
  Chandramouliswar, R.
    Maratha invasion of the Madura country
    (1740-1745). IHCP, v.16 (1953), pp.276-
    78.

Dot R

I-1963
  Chitnis, K.N.
    The Maratha-Bidnur relations, BIS, v.5 (April
    1968), pp.81-90.

Dot R

I-1964
  Das, Bhagwan.
    The Bundela War of Independence and Maharaja
    Chhatra Sal Bundela. Lucknow, Univ.of Lucknow,
    1955. *

Case

I-1965
Diskalkar, Dattatraya Balkrishna, 1892-
Mahdji Sindia's supersession of the Nabob
of Lucknow. UPHSJ, v.10 (1937), pp.17-29.

I-1970
Roy, Nirod Bhushan.
Daulat Rao Sindhia's affairs, 1804-09.
Bombay, Printed at the Govt.Central Press,
1943. (English records of Maratha history,
Poona residency correspondence, v.11). 492p.

I-1966
Kamath, Suryanath U.
Keladi Nayakas and Marathas, QJMS, v.61
(1970), pp.65-71.

I-1971
Saletore, R.N.
Relations between the Girassias and the
Marathas, NIA, Extra series 1 (1939) - A
volume of Eastern and Indian studies pre-
sented to Professor F.W.Thomas ... on his
72nd birthday. Ed.by S.M.Katre and P.K.
Gode. pp.215-25.

I-1967
Khandekar, Ganpatrao Gopal.
Papers relating to the protection afforded
by the House of Sindhia to the Khandekars of
Panth Piploda, IHRCP, v.12 (1929), pp.102-03.

I-1972
Sarkar, Sir Jadunath, 1870-1958, ed.
Daulat Rao Sindhia and North Indian
affairs, 1810-1818. Bombay, Printed at
the Modern India Press, Calcutta, 1951.
(English records of Maratha history.
Poona residency correspondence, v.14).
430p.

I-1968
Khare, Ganesh Hari, 1901-
A phase of north Indian policy of the Mara-
thas, PO, v.10 (1945), p.16.

I-1973
Shejwalkar, Trymbak Shankar.
Danger to Jhansi in 1774-75, IHRCP, v.27
(1950), pp.49-53.

I-1969
Rajayyan, K., 1929-
The Marathas at Trichinopoly; 1741-1743,
ABORI, v.51 (1970), pp.222-30.

I-1974
Sinh, Raghubir, 1908-
Malwa in transition; or a century of anarchy:
the first phase, 1698-1765. Bombay, D.B.Tara-
porevala, 1936. 406p.

I-1975
Sinh, Raghubir, 1908-
The Marathas in Malwa 1707-1719. In:
Sardesai Commemorative Volume. Ed.by
Shripad R.Tikekar. Bombay, 1938. pp.
59-72.

I-1980
Ajgaonkar, Gundu Phatu, 1919-
Senapati Bhonsale the I.N.A. chief and
father of National discipline scheme. English
version: D.G.Naik. Bombay, N.R.Ralkar, 1964.
77p.

1. Indian Nat'l army.

I-1976
Tambe, G.C.
The regime of Vinayak Ganesh Chandorkar as
the deputy governor of the Saugor territory
1795-1819. IHCP. v.14 (1951), pp.259-63.

I-1981
Akademiia nauk SSSR. Institut vostokovedi-
niia.
Tilak and the struggle for Indian freedom.
Edited by I.M.Reisner and N.M.Goldberg. New
Delhi, People's Pub.House, 1966. 682p.

History - 1858-   Biography &
Memoirs

I-1977
Aberigh-Mackay, George Robert, 1848-1881.
The chiefs of Central India. Calcutta,
Thacker, Spink, & co., 1879. 458p.

I-1982
Alva, Joachim.
Men and super men of Hindustan. Containing
pen sketches of India's political leaders.
Bombay, C.Murphy, Rampart Row, 1943. 403p.

I-1978
Aberigh-Mackay, George Robert, 1848-1881.
The native chiefs and their states in 1877.
Bombay, Times of India Steam Press, 1878.
94p.

I-1983
Ambedkar, Bhimrao Ramji, 1892-1956.
Ranade, Gandhi and Jinnah. Bombay, Thacker
and co., 1943. 90p.

I-1979
Adhikari, Gopala Govinda.
Life of Br. V.D.Savarkar. Bombay, Govardhan
Bhuvan, 1940. 44p.

I-1984
Ambekar, D.V.
Gopal Krishna Gokhale: a biographical
sketch. In: Gopal Krishna Gokhale, a
centenary tribute. Bombay, Printed at
the Government Central Press, 1966. pp.
3-24.

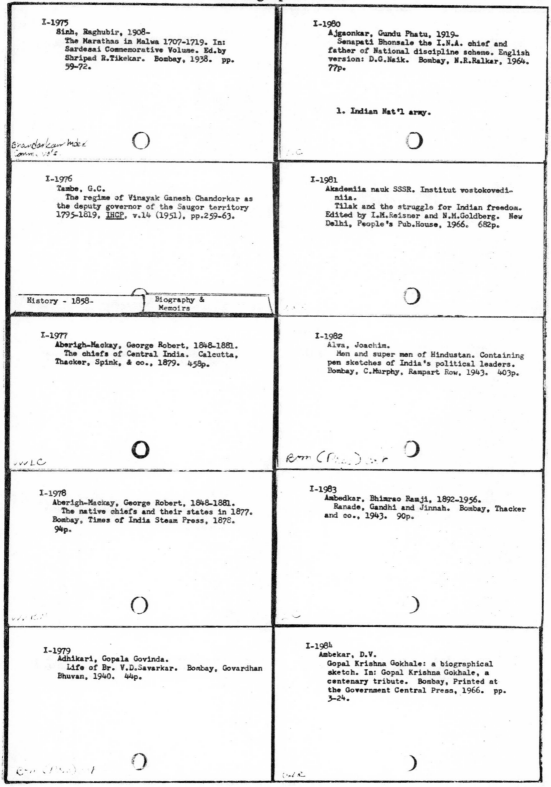

I-1985
    Athalye, D.V.
        The life of Lokamanya Tilak. Poona,
Annasahib Chiploonkar, 1921. 412p.

NUR
///ICL

I-1986
    Athavale, Parvatibai, 1870-1955.
        My story, the autobiography of a Hindu
widow, trans.by J.E.Abbott. London, Putnam's
sons, 1930. 163p.

UofR

I-1987
    Ayer, S.A. and Rao, G.K.
        Kher - A man of compassion, GM, v.1 (1957),
pp.250-55.

Case

I-1988
    Banerjee, Debendra Nath, 1895-
        India's nation builders. London, Headley
Brothers, Pubs., 1919. 234p.

    Includes articles on Tilak & Gokhale

RM

I-1989
    Banerjee, Kalyan Kumar.
        Dadabhai Naoroji: nestor of Indian politics,
CR, v.153 (1959), pp.229-41.

Case

I-1990
    Bapat, Purushottam Vishvanath, 1894-
        Prof.Dharmanand Kosambi, MR, v.83 (1948),
pp.134-37.

Case

I-1991
    Bapat, Sadshiv Vinayak, 1887-
        Reminiscences and anecdotes of Lokamanya
Tilak. Poona, 1928. 219p.

UofR

I-1992
    Bedekar, Dinkar Keshav, 1910-
        A leader of the renaissance in Maharashtra
[Gopal Hari Deshmukh], Quest, v.29 (1961),
pp.87-93.

JAS41

I-1993
    Bharill, Chandra.
        Experiences of an untouchable: glimpses of
Ambedkar's early life, PSR, v.5 (1966), pp.
323-31.

JAS9/48

I-1994
    Bhat, Vishwas G.
        Lokamanya Tilak, his life, mind, politics
and philosophy. Poona, Prakash, 1956.
115p.

NUR

I-1995
A biographical sketch of Sardar Mir
Abdul Ali Khan Bahadur, head of the
detective police, Bombay. By
Navaroji Manekji Dumasia. Bombay,
B.E.S.Press, 1896. 402p.

UofR

I-1996
Bose, Jogesh C.
Gopal K.Gokhale at a glance, MR, v.111
(1962), pp.473-77.

MR

I-1997
Bose, Jogesh C.
Lokmanya Bal Gangadhar Tilak, MR, v.106
(1959), pp.453-61.

QaL'59

I-1998
Bull, H.M. and Haksar, K.N.
Madhav Rao Scindia of Gwalior, 1876-1925.
Gwalior, the authors, 1926. 311p.

UofR

I-1999
Chandavarkar, Ganesh L.
A wrestling soul: story of the life of Sir
Narayan Chandavarkar. Bombay, Popular Book
Depot, 1955. 248p.

UofR

I-2000
Chandavarkar, Sir Narayan Ganesh, 1855-1923.
The speeches and writings of Sir Narayan
G.Chandavarkar. Ed.by L.V.Kaikini. Girgaon-
Bombay, Manoranjak grantha prasarak mandali,
1911. 654p.

UofR

I-2001
Chandra, Sudhir.
Badruddin Tyabji, BPP, v.62 (1968), pp.
190-98.

BPP

I-2002
Chandra, Sudhir.
Badruddin Tyabji: a reappraisal, IHCP,
v.27 (1965), pp.299-300.

IHCP

I-2003
Chatterji, Nandalal, 1903-
Lokamanya Balagangadhar Tilak; an apprecia-
tion, JIH, v.37 (1959), pp.161-65.

QaL'59

I-2004
Cox, Edmund Charles, bart., 1856-
The exploits of Kesho Naik, Dacoit. London,
Constable and Co., 1912. 302p.

BM

I-2005
    Dall, Caroline Wells (Healy), 1822-1912.
    The life of Dr. Anandabai Joshee, a
kinswoman of the Pundita Ramabai. Boston,
Roberts brothers, 1888. 199p.

    1. Ānandibāī, Joṣī, 1865-1887.

I-2006
    Damle, Prabhakar Ramkrishna.
    Three leaders; Tilak, Gokhale and Gandhi.
Poona, Kamalini Damle, 1962. 126p.

I-2007
    Deogirikar, Trimbak Raghunath, 1896-
    Gopal Krishna Gokhale (builders of modern
India). Delhi, Ministry of Information and
Broadcasting, Publications Division, 1964.
219p.

    1. Gokhale, Gopal Krishna, 1866-1915.

I-2008
    Deogirikar, Trimbak Raghunath, 1896-
    Twelve years in Parliament (democracy in
action) Poona, Chitrashala Prakashan, 1964.
366p.

    1. India - Hist - 1947-

I-2009
    Desai, Ramdatt W.
    Rao Bahadur Vasudev Jaganath Kirtikar. A
short sketch of the life of Rao Bahadur
Vasudev Jaganath Kirtikar. Bombay, B.N.
Gokhale, 1943. 11p.

I-2010
    Deshpande, Dattatraya Damodara.
    Life sketch of Senapati Bapat. Poona,
1935. 26p.

I-2011
    Dhananjaya Ramchandra Gadgil: making of the
    man. Poona, Gokhale Institute of Politics
and Economics; Bombay, N.Y., Asia Pub.
House, 1967. 57p.

I-2012
    Divatia, H.V.
    Balasaheb Kher-as I know him, GM, v.1
(1957), pp.237-40.

I-2013
    Diwakar, R.R.
    The Lokamanya and the Mahatma, GM, v.13
(1969), pp.188-195.

I-2014
    Dumasia, Navaroji Manekji.
    Short biographical sketch of the late Shet
Varjivandas Madhavdas. Bombay, Bombay
Gazette Steam Works, 1897. 188p.

I-2015
Dutt, K.Iswara.
Bal Gangadhar Tilak; a centenary tribute.
MarI, v.8 (1956), pp.12-15.

y...t...t

I-2016
Edwardes, Stephen Meredyth, 1873-1927.
Kharshedji Rustamji Cama, 1831-1909; a
memoire. London, Oxford Univ.Press, 1923.
164p.

Cama, Kharshedji Rustamji, 1831-1909.

u at K

I-2017
Gadgil, Dhananjaya Ramchandra, 1901-
Vaikunth L.Mehta - a brief appreciation.
MCQ, v.30 (1965), pp.148-50.

Dhananjaya

I-2018
Gai, Govind Swamirao, 1917-
A note on Tilaka and Kankana. In: Sushil
Kumar De felicitation volume. Ed.by N.G.
Kalelkar. Poona, 1960. pp.301-02.

fw 60

I-2019
Gandhi, Mohandas Karamchand, 1869-1948.
Gokhale, my political guru. Ahmedabad,
Navajivan Pub.House, 1958,c1955. 78p.

a y'i

I-2020
Gandhi, Mohandas Karamchand, 1869-1948.
The legacy of Mahatma Gokhale. In: Gopal
Krishna Gokhale, a centenary tribute.
Bombay, Printed at the Govt.Central Press,
1966. pp.157-72.

I-2021
Ghose, Aurobindo, 1872-1950.
Bankim-Tilak-Dayanand. 3d ed. Pondicherry.
S.A.Ashram, 1955. 66p.

u a/ K

I-2022
Gokhale, D.V.
The Tilak case. Poona, Pub.by the Manager.
Printing Agency, 1916. 192p.

R... (f...) ...t

I-2023
Gokhale, Gopal Krishna, 1866-1915.
Speeches and writings of Gopal Krishna
Gokhale. Editors: R.P.Patwardhan and D.V.
Ambekar. London, Asia Pub.House, 1962-
1967. 3v.

. a/R

I-2024
Gokhale, Gopal Krishna, 1866-1915.
The select Gokhale. Comp.& ed.by R.P.Pat-
wardhan. New Delhi, Maharashtra Information
Centre, 1968. 455p.

PL1/20 '68

I-2025
    Gokhale, Gopal Krishna, 1866-1915.
      Speeches of the honourable Mr. G.K.Gokhale.
3d ed. Madras, G.A.Natesan & co., 1920.
1287p.

BM

I-2026
    Gokhale: the man and his mission; Gopal
      Krishna Gokhale birth centenary lectures
      by C.P.Ramaswamy Aiyal and others. New
      York, Asia Pub.House, 1966. 131p.

U of R

I-2027
    Goldberg, N.M.
      Leader of the democratic wing in Maharashtra.
      In: Tilak and the struggle for Indian freedom.
      Ed.by I.M.Reisner and N.M.Goldberg. New Delhi,
      People's publishing house, 1966. pp.1-94.

I-2028
    Gopal Krishna Gokhale, a centenary tribute.
      New Delhi, Maharashtra Information , 1966.
      197p.

U of R

I-2029
    Gopalaswami, K., 1902-
      Gandhi and Bombay. Bombay, Bharitya Vidya
Bhawan, 1969. 581p.

I-2030
    Gupta, Chitra.
      Life of barrister Savarkar. Madras, B.G.
Paul & Co., 1926. 152p.

    1. Savarkar, Vinayak Damodar.

I-2031
    Gupta, R.Chandra.
      Bal Gangadhar Tilak, *Triveni*, v.33 (1964),
      pp.15-34.

JaS64

I-2032
    Hamilton, N.J.
      Ruling princes and chiefs of India. A brief
      historical record. Bombay, Times of India
      Press, 1930. 420p.

Bom(Pres)Cat

I-2033
    Harilal Savailal.
      Samaldas Parmananddas, a biographical sketch.
      Bombay, Tatvawivechak Press, 1912. 324p.

Bom (Pres) Cat

I-2034
    Houston, John.
      Representative men of Bombay Presidency. A
      collection of biographical sketches with por-
      traits of the princes, chiefs, philanthropists,
      statesmen and other leading residents of the
      Presidency. Philadelphia, C.B.Burrows, 1897.
      150p.

SOAS supp

I-2035
Hoyland, John Somervell, 1887-
Gopal Krishna Gokhale; his life and speeches.
Calcutta, Y.M.C.A.Pub.House, 1947. 165p.

U of R

I-2036
Hussain, M.Basheer.
Gokhale and Hindu-Muslim unity. PA. v.10
(1966), pp.256-64.

Ja S'66

I-2037
Jamnadas Dwarkadas, 1890-
Political memoirs. Bombay, United Asia Pubs.,
1969. 2 vols.

PL 480 '69

I-2038
Jayakar, Mukund Ramrao.
The story of my life. Bombay, Asia Pub.
House, 1958-1960. 2v.

U of R

I-2039
Jessawalla, Dosabhai Cowasji.
The story of my life. Bombay, the author,
1911. 509p.

Bom (Pres)cat

I-2040
Jhabvala, Shavakasha Hormusji, 1885-
Cowasji Dinshaw Adenwala. Bombay,
Published by the author, 1921. (Lives
of Eminent Parsis Series no.5). 15p.

disregard B688
Bom (Pres)cat

I-2041
Jhabvala, Shavakasha Hormusji, 1885-
Life sketches of the late Mr. Cowasji Dinshaw
and of Sir Hormusji Cowasji Dinshaw. 2d ed.
Bombay, the author, 1923. 29p.

Bom (Pres) cat

I-2042
Jog, Narayan Gopal.
Lokamanya Bal Gangadhar Tilak. Delhi, Pub.
Div., Ministry of Information and Broadcasting,
Govt.of India, 1962. (Builders of modern
India) 208p.

U of R

I-2043
Joshi, Ambelal Naranji.
Life and times of Chevalier Framroze
Dinshaw. Bombay, Brihad Gujarat Publication
House, 1950. 274p.

*SOAS
Supp*

I-2044
Joshi, Ambelal Naranji.
Life and times of Sir Hormusjee C.Dinshaw,
k.t., o.b.e., m.v.o. 1st ed. Bombay, D.B.
Taraporevala Sons, 1939. 300p.

U of R

I-2045
Joshi, Anandrao.
First Indian M.P. - Dadabhai Naoroji, MR,
v.72 (1942), pp.37-39.

I-2050
Kaji, Hiralal Lallubhai, 1886-
Life and speeches of Sir Vithaldas Thackersey. Bombay, D.B.Taraporevala, sons & co.,
1934. 581p.

I-2046
Joshi, Ganesa Venkatesa, rao bahadur, 1851-1911.
Writings and speeches of Hon.Rao Bahadur
G.S.Joshi. Poona, D.V.Joshi, 1912. 1263p.

I-2051
Kale, Baburao Balaji, 1925-
Man of crisis. Bombay, Sindhu Pubs., 1969.
126p.

I-2047
Joshi, Vishnu Shridhar.
Tilak and the revolutionaries, MR, v.117
(1965), pp.29-33.

I-2052
Karandikar, Shivaram Laxman, 1899-1969.
Lokamanya Bal Gangadhar Tilak; the Hercules
and Prometheus of modern India. Bombay,
Siddhamohan art printery, 1957. 655p.

I-2048
Joshi, Vishnu Shridhar.
Vasudeo Balvant Phadke: first Indian rebel
against British rule. Bombay, D.S.Marathe,
1959. 206p.

I-2053
Karanjia, B.K.
Rustom Masani: portrait of a citizen.
Bombay, Popular Prakashan, 1970. 224p.

I-2049
K.N.
Gopal Krishna Gokhale, MR, v.119 (1966),
pp.366-68.

I-2054
Karmarkar, Dattatraya Parashuram, 1902-
Bal Gangadhar Tilak: a study. 1st ed.
Bombay, Popular Book Depot, 1956. 307p.

I-2055
Karnik, Dwarkanath Bhagwant, 1912-
Y.B.Chavan; a political biography. Bombay,
United Asia Pubs., 1972. 164p.

I-2056
Karnik, V.B.
N.M.Joshi. Bombay, Asia Pub.House, 1973.
275p.

I-2057
Karve, Dattatraya Gopal, 1898-
Gokhale and Gandhi: spirituality in
public life, Triveni, v.35 (1966), pp.3-14.

I-2058
Karve, Dattatraya Gopal, 1898-
Gokhale and public life, PA, v.10 (1966),
pp.127-43.

I-2059
Karve, Dattatraya Gopal, 1898-
Gokhale and public life; Gokhale birth-
day centenary address. Bangalore,
Gokhale Institute of Public Affairs, 1966.
(Public affairs pamphlet 8). 23p.

I-2060
Karve, Dattatraya Gopal, 1898-
Ranade and Gokhale: piety and patriotism.
In: Gopal Krishna Gokhale, a centenary
tribute. Bombay, Printed at the government
central press, 1966. pp.142-156.

I-2061
Karve, Dattatraya Gopal, 1898-
Ranade, the prophet of liberated India.
Poona, Aryabhushan press, 1942. 263p.

I-2062
Kasinatha Tryambaka Telanga, 1840-1893.
Selected writings and speeches. Bombay,
Manoranjan Press, 1916-31. 2v.

I-2063
Kasinatha Tryambaka Telanga, 1840-1893.
Telang's Legislative Council speeches, with
Sir Raymond West's essay on his life. Edited,
with notes by D.W.Pilgamker. Bombay, Printed
at the Indian Printing Press, 1895. 146p.

I-2064
Keer, Dhananjay, 1913-
Dr. Ambedkar, life and mission. 2d ed.
Bombay, Popular Prakashan, 1962. 528p.

I-2065
Keer, Dhananjay, 1913-
Lokamanya Tilak, father of the Indian freedom struggle. 2d ed. Bombay, Popular Prakashan, 1969. 463p.

Biography - books
'R 7

LC

I-2066
Keer, Dhananjay, 1913-
Veer Savarkar. 2d ed. Bombay, Popular Prakashan, 1966. First ed.published in 1950 under title: Savarkar and his times. 579p.

Vol R

I-2071
Kellock, James.
Mahadev Govind Ranade: patriot and social servant. Calcutta, Association Press, 1926. (Builders of Modern India series). 215p.

LC

I-2070
Kelkar, Narsinha Chintaman, 1872-1947.
Life and times of Lokamanya Tilak. Trans. from the Marathi by D.V.Divekar. Madras, S.Ganesan, 1928-

I-2067
Kelkar, Narsinha Chintaman, 1872-1947.
Dadabhai Naoroji. Bombay, D.D.Sathaye, 1916. 17p.

Cat (Bom (Pres)

I-2072
Khandwala, Tuljaram Chunilal.
My life story. Bombay, V.S.Sohoni, 1941. 318p.

social life & customs
CT
1508
K45m
U of R

I-2068
Kelkar, Narsinha Chintaman, 1872-1947.
Full and authentic report of the Tilak trial. Poona, the author, 1908. 480p.

I-2073
Khare, Narayan Bhaskar, 1882-
My political memoirs; or, autobiography. Nagpur, J.R.Joshi, 1959. 643p.

1. India - Pol.& govt. - 1919-1947. 2. India - Pol.& govt. - 1947-

U of R

I-2069
Kelkar, Narsinha Chintaman, 1872-1947.
Landmarks in Lokamanya's life. Madras, 1924. 220p.

I-2074
Khosla, Kanshi Ram, 1882- comp.
His imperial majesty King George V and the princes of India and the Indian empire (historical-biographical), compiled by K.R.Khosla; ed.by R.P.Chatterjee. Lahore, Imperial Pub.Co., 1937. 902p.

NYPL

I-2075
Kibe, Madhav Vinayak, 1877-
In the public eye, H.H. The Maharaja Sayaji
Rao Gaekwar III, MR, v.68 (1936), pp.550-51.

JJJHR

I-2076
Kodanda Rao, Pandurangi, 1889-
Gokhale and Gandhi, GM, v.10 (1966), pp.101-
107.

gal'66

I-2077
Kodanda Rao, Pandurangi, 1889-
Gokhale and Sastri. Mysore, Prasaranga,
1961. 55p.

Ind Natl Rib.

I-2078
Kodanda Rao, Pandurangi, 1889-
Gokhale and the British connection, PA,
v.10 (1966), pp.184-89.

gal 66

I-2079
Krishnanath Raghunathji.
The story of Sundarabai. Bombay, Fort.Print.
Press, 1899. 37p.

Biography - Authors wife.

Com. (Pres) Cat

I-2080
Kulkarni, A.D.
N.C.Kelkar, MR, v.83 (1948), p.138.

MR

I-2081
Kulkarni, R.P. and Sarma, V.
Homi Bhabha; father of nuclear science in
India. Bombay, Popular Prakashan, 1969.
152p.

Indian Book Republic
I B '69 Feb 69

I-2082
Kunzru, H.N.
Gopal Krishna Gokhale: The man and his
mission. In: Gopal Krishna Gokhale, a
centenary tribute. Bombay, Printed
at the government central press, 1966.
pp.57-89.

voth

I-2083
Latthe, Annaji Babaji, 1878-
Memoirs of His Highness Shri Shahu Chhatra-
pati, Maharaja of Kolhapur. Bombay, The
Times Press, 1924. 2v.

NNU

I-2084
Life work of Mr. Gokhale - being anniversary
address of Professor V.K.Rajwade. Bombay,
N.D.Altekar, 1921. 8p.

Bombay (Presidency) Cat

I-2085
Loasby, Roland.
Lokamanya Bala Gangadhar Tilak, 1856-1920: his reorientation of the Gita tradition: a factor in the rise of Indian nationalism, 1918-1942. Los Angeles, Southern California Univ., 1957.

I-2086
McLeod, Marian B.
Gopal Krishna Gokhale: spokesman of Indian nationalism, UA, v.22,no.4 (1970), pp.201-18.

I-2087
Maharashtra, India (State) Maharashtra Information Centre.
Gopal Krishna Gokhale: a centenary tribute. New Delhi, 1966.

I-2088
Majumdar, Ramesh Chandra, 1888-
Rammohan Roy and Bal Gangadhar Tilak on social legislation. JIH, v.45 (1967), pp. 95-98.

I-2089
Mandlik, Vishvanath Narayan, 1833-1889.
Writings and speeches of the late Hon.Rao Sahib Vishvanath Narayan Mandlik. Ed.by Narayan Vishvanath Mandlik. Bombay, Native Opinion Press, 1896. 794p.

I-2090
Mankar, G.A.
Sketch of the life and works of the late justice M.G.Ranade. Bombay, Caxtan Printing Works, 1902. 2v.

I-2091
Hankekar, D.R.
Homi Mody, a many splendoured life; a political biography. Bombay, Popular Prakashan, 1968. 255p.

I-2092
Markhandikar, R.S.
G.G.Agarkar - a study in radical liberalism 1856-1896, MR, v.118 (1965), pp.518-23.

I-2093
Masani, Sir Rustom Pestonji, 1876-1966.
Dadabhai Naoroji. Delhi, Pub.Div., Ministry of Information and Broadcasting, Govt.of India, 1960. (Builders of Modern India). 195p.

I-2094
Masani, Sir Rustom Pestonji, 1876-1966.
Dadabhai Naoroji: the grand old man of India. London, G.Allen and Unwin, 1939. 567p.

I-2095
  Masani, Sir Rustom Pestonji, 1876-1966.
N.M.Wadia and his foundation. Bombay,
Popular Book Depot, 1961. 144p.

u of k

I-2096
  Mathur, Dwarka Bihari, 1932-
    G.K.Gokhale: the discerning liberal, PSR,
v.5 (1966), pp.304-14.

I-2097
  Mathur, Dwarka Bihari, 1932-
    Gokhale, a political biography; a study of
his services and political ideas. Bombay,
Manaktalas, 1966. 499p.

u of P.

I-2098
  Mathur, Dwarka Bihari, 1932-
    Gopal Krishna Gokhale and the impact of
the west, IJPS, v.22 (1961), pp.301-11.

I-2099
  Mathur, Dwarka Bihari, 1932-
    Gopal Krishna Gokhale's concept of demo-
cratic decentralisation, MR, v.113 (1963),
pp.455-59.

I-2100
  Mathur, Dwarka Bihari, 1932-
    Public life in India: the crisis in
character (a study of G.K.Gokhale's ideas
and services), PSR, v.2 (1963), pp.22-30.

case

I-2101
  Mehta, Pherozshah Merwanji, 1845-1915.
    The late Sir Pherozeshah Mehta: an
appreciation, HR, v.32 (1915), pp.472-78.

case

I-2102
  Mehta, Pherozshah Merwanji, 1845-1915.
    Some unpublished and later speeches and
writings. Ed.by J.R.B.Jeejeebhoy. Bombay,
"Commercial" Press, 1918. 500p.

I-2103
  Mehta, Pherozshah Merwanji, 1845-1915.
    Speeches and writings of the honourable
Sir Pherozeshah M.Mehta. Ed.by C.Y.Chinta-
mani. Allahabad, The Indian Press, 1906.

modern India - biography

I-2104
  Mehta, Vaikunth L.
    Vaikunth L.Mehta: tributes and reminiscences,
MQ, v.48 (1965), pp.139-73.

I-2105
Mody, Sir Hormasji Peroshaw, 1881-
Pherozeshah Mehta. Delhi, Pubs.Div.,
Ministry of Information and Broadcasting,
Govt.of India, 1967, c.1963. (Builders of
modern India) 219p.

4 of R

I-2106
Mody, Sir Hormasji Peroshaw, 1881-
Sir Pherozeshah Mehta, political biography.
1st ed., reprinted with minor amendments.
London, Asia Pub.House. 1963. 418p.

1. Mehta, Sir Pherozeshah Merwanji. 2. India-
Pol.& govt. - 1765-1947.

U of R

I-2107
Mody, Jehangir R.P.
Jamsetjee Jejeebhoy; the first Indian knight
and Baronet, 1783-1859. Bombay, 1959. 198p.

4 of R

I-2108
Moraes, Francis Robert, 1907-
Sir Purshotamdas Thakurdas, a biography.
Bombay, Asia Pub.House. 1957. 316p.

4 7 R

I-2109
Moraes, George Mark.
Dr.Jose Gerson da Cunha 1844-1900, ASBJ,
b.39/40 (1964/65), pp.1-50.

JAS 4/67

I-2110
Motivala, Bhavanidas Narandas.
Karsondas Mulji. A short sketch of a great
Indian social servant. In commemoration of
the Karsondas Mulji Centenary. Girgaum, 1934.
68p.

IOL

I-2111
Motivala, Bhavanidas Narandas.
Karsondas Mulji: a biographical study. Bombay, Karsondas Mulji Centenary Celebration Committee, 1935. 420p.

U of R

I-2112
Mukherjee, B.A.
H.H.Maharaja Sayaji Rao Gaekwar's diamond
jubilee, HR, v.68 (1936), pp.599-600.

HR

I-2113
Naidu, Sarojini (Chattopadhyay) 1879-1949.
Reminiscences of Gokhale. Ahmednagar, Ali
K.Irani, 1949. 32p.

Bom.(Pres)dnt

I-2114
Naidu, Sarojini (Chattopadhyay) 1879-1949.
Reminiscences of Mr. Gokhale. In: Gopal
Krishna Gokhale, a centenary tribute.
Bombay, Printed at the Govt.Central Press,
1966. pp.44-56.

4 7 R

I-2115
Naik, Vasant Narayan.
Gopal Ganesh Agarkar, a sketch. Bombay,
K.R.Mitra, 1916. 38p.

cat Rom (Pres)

I-2116
Naik, Vasant Narayan.
Gopal Krishna Gokhale: an anniversary
address delivered on the 19th Feb., 1919
under the auspices of the Bombay Branch of
the Servants of India Society. Bombay,
1919. 14p.

IOL

I-2117
Naik, Vasant Narayan.
Kashinath Trimbak Telang: an anniversary
address delivered at the Hindu Union Club
on the 25th Sept., 1920. Bombay, 1920. 37p.

IOL

I-2118
Nanda, B.R.
Gokhale's year of decision, JIH. v.43
(1965), pp.543-63.

Case

I-2119
Oke, Vinayak Kondadeo, 1840-1914.
Life of Mahadeo Govind Ranade. Bombay,
Nirnaya Sagar, 1901. 48p.

Rom (F...)

I-2120
Padhye, Damodar Ganesh.
Life and character of the late Dr. S.W.
Kane. Bombay, Indu Prakash, 1900. 17p.

Rom (Pres) cat

I-2121
Paranjpye, Sir Raghunath Purushottam, 1876-
Eighty-four, not out. Delhi, Govt.of
India, 1961. (A National Book Trust book)
184p.

47R

I-2122
Paranjpye, Sir Raghunath Purushottam, 1876-
Gopal Krishna Gokhale. 3d ed. Poona,
Aryabhushan Press, 1916. (Reprinted from
the Fergusson College magazine) 88p.

47R

I-2123
Paranjpye, Sir Raghunath Purushottam, 1876-
Gopal Krishna Gokhale: personal reminiscences. In: Gopal Krishna Gokhale, a
centenary tribute. Bombay, Printed at
the government central press, 1966. pp.
36-43.

UofR

I-2124
Paranjpye, Sir Raghunath Purushottam, 1876-
Selected writings and speeches of Dr. R.P.
Paranjpye. by B.M.Gore. Bombay, Karnatak
Printing Press, 1940. 270p.

UofR
Rom (Pr...)

I-2125
Parvate, Trimbak Vishnu, 1901-
Bal Gangadhar Tilak: a narrative and
interpretive review of his life, career
and contemporary events. Ahmedabad, Navajivan Publishing House, 1958. 559p.

South Asia Social Science.
Biography; Political Science

I-2126
Parvate, Trimbak Vishnu, 1901-
Gopal Krishna Gokhale; a narrative and
interpretative review of his life, career
and contemporary events. Ahmedabad, Navajivan Pub.House, 1959. 493p.

I-2127
Parvate, Trimbak Vishnu, 1901-
Influence of Gokhale's political thought
on present-day India. GM, v.10 (1966), pp.
145-50.

I-2128
Parvate, Trimbak Vishnu, 1901-
Mahadev Govind Ranade: a biography. Bombay.
Asia Pub.House, 1964, c1963. 336p.

I-2129
Parvate, Trimbak Vishnu, 1901-
Tilak and Gandhi. GM, v.11 (1967), pp.351-
64.

I-2130
Patwardhan, R.P.
Dadabhai Naoroji and Sir George Birdwood.
IHRCP, v.36 (1962), pp.1-9.

I-2131
Patwardhan, Rao Saheb.
Missionary of national freedom. In: Gokhale,
the man and his mission. Ed.by C.P.Ramaswamy
Aiyar, et al. Bombay, Asia publishing house,
1966. pp.11-23.

I-2132
Phadke, Vasudeo Balwant, 1845-1883.
Report of the trial of Vasudev Bulwant Pha-
dke, the notorious rebel leader before W.H.
Newnham Esq., Sessions Judge of Poona and a
jury, together with his diary and autobiography.
Poona, Daily Telegraph and Deccan Herald Press,
1879. 37p.

I-2133
Phatak, Narahara Raghunatha, 1894-
Gopalrao Deshmukh, "Lokahitawadi," 1823-
1892, Rationalists of Maharashtra. Calcutta,
Indian Renaissance Institute, 1962.

I-2134
Pollock, John.
The new political leaders in Maharashtra.
SAISR, v.11,no.4 (1967), pp.19-25.

I-2135
Pradhan, B.V.
The late Santaram Mahadeo Sonalkar. Jalgaon,
East Khandesh, R.K.Wani, 1932. 13p.

Cat. Bombay (Pw)

I-2136
Pradhan, G.P., 1922-
Gopal Ganesh Agarkar, 1856-1895.
Rationalists of Maharashtra. Calcutta,
Indian Renaissance Institute, 1962.

I-2137
Pradhan, G.P., 1922-   and Bhagwat, A.K., 1918-
Lokamanya Tilak; a biography. Bombay, Jaico
Pub.House, 1959. 380p.

I-2138
Pradhan, G.P., 1922-   and Bhagwat, A.K.
Lokamanya Tilak; the politician and the
reformer. Quest. v.2 (1956), pp.43-48.

Jaipur

I-2139
Prasad, Madho, 1902 or 3-1964.
A Gandhian patriarch; a political and
spiritual biography of Kaka Kalelkar.
Bombay, Popular Prakashan, 1965. 388p.

NUR
LC

I-2140
Pratapsing Rao Gaekwar, Maharaja of Baroda,
1908-
His Highness Maharaja Pratapsinh Gaekwar: a
life-sketch and speeches, by Chakrawak. 2d ed.
Baroda, V.P.Nene, 1939. 90p.

U or R

I-2141
Rajarama Maharaj, Chhatrapati of Kolhapur,
d.1870.
Diary of the late Rajah of Kolhapoor
during his visit to Europe in 1870. Ed.
by E.W.West. London, 1872.

BM

I-2142
Ram Gopal, 1912-
Lokamanya Tilak: a biography. New York,
Asia Pub.House, 1965,c1956. 481p.

U or R

I-2143
Ramaswami Aiyar, Sir Chetpat Pattabhirama,
1879-1966.
Liberalism of Gokhale. In: Gokhale, the
man and his mission. Ed.by C.P.Ramaswamy
Aiyar, et al. Bombay, Asia publishing
house, 1966. pp.1-10.

2 different spellings of Ramaswami in
volume.

I-2144
Ranade, Mahadev Govind, 1842-1901.
The miscellaneous writings. Bombay, Manora-
jan Press, 1915. 331p.

I-2145
Ranade, Mahadev Govind, 1842-1901.
The wisdom of a modern rishi, writings and
speeches of Mahadev Govind Ranade; with an
address on Rishi Ranade, by Right Hon'ble
V.S.Srinivasa Sastri, ed.by T.N.Jagadisan.
Madras, Rochouse and sons, 1942. 197p.

Cal Nat Lib.

I-2146
Ranade, Ramabai.
Himself; the autobiography of a Hindu lady.
Trans.by K.van Akin Gates. New York, Long-
mans, Green & co., 1938. 253p.

LC

I-2147
Ranade, Ramabai.
Ranade: his wife's reminiscences. Trans.
by Kusumavati Deshpande. Delhi, Pubs.
Division, Ministry of Information and
Broadcasting, Govt.of India, 1963. 232p.

I-2148
Ranade, Vinayak Govind.
Life of His Highness Raja Shreemant Sir
Raghunathrao S., alias Babasaheb Pandit
Pant Sachiv, Raja of Bhor. Poona, V.G.
Ranade, 1951. 412p.

I-2149
Rangiah, R.
Gokhale, the Parliamentarian, PA, v.10
(1966), pp.206-12.

I-2150
Rao, R.Kodanda.
Gokhale and Sastri. In: Gopal Krishna
Gokhale, a centenary tribute. Bombay,
Printed at the Govt.Central Press, 1966.
pp.125-41.

I-2151
Rao, Vasant Dinanath, 1913-
A maker of modern Maharashtra: Dadoba Pandurang (1814-1882). IHCP, v.28 (1966), pp.442-
48.

I-2152
Rao, Vasant Dinanath, 1913-
A maker of modern Maharashtra; Hon'ble
Shri Jugannath Sunkersett (February 10,
1803 to July 31, 1865). JIH, v.43 (1965),
pp.201-17.

I-2153
Rao Bahadur R.N.Mudholkar; a sketch of his
life and his services to India. Madras,
G.A.Natesan, 1912. (Biographies of
eminent Indians) 46p.

I-2154
Reisner, Igor Mikhailovich, 1895-1958.
Social and political contribution of Bal
Gangadhar Tilak. In: Tilak and the struggle
for Indian freedom. Ed.by I.M.Reisner and N.M.
Goldberg. New Delhi, People's publishing
house, 1966. pp.627-62.

I-2155
Rice, Stanley Pitcairn, 1869-
    Life of Sayaji Rao III, maharaja of Baroda.
London, Oxford University Press, 1931. 2 vols.

4 *of* R

I-2156
Rothermund, Dietmar.
    Emancipation or re-integration. The politics
of Gopal Krishna Gokhale and Herbert Hope
Risley. In: Soundings in modern South Asian
history. Berkeley, Univ.of California Press,
1968. pp.131-58.

I-2157
Saggi, Parshotam Das, 1913-   ed.
    Life and work of Lal, Bal, and Pal, a
nation's homage. New Delhi, Overseas Pub.
House, 1962. 363p.

4 *of* R

I-2158
Sapru, P.N.
    Gokhale as a statesman. In: Gokhale, the
man and his mission. Ed.by C.P.Ramaswamy
Aiyar, et al. Bombay, Asia publishing
house, 1966. pp.24-40.

U₀+R

I-2159
Sarin, L.N.
    Studies of Indian leaders. Delhi, Atma
Ram, 1963. 130p.

    1. Statesmen, East Indian.

U₀§R

I-2160
Sastri, Valangiman Sankaranarayana Srinivasa,
    1869-1946.
    Gokhale: the less known aspects. In:
Gopal Krishna Gokhale, a centenary
tribute. Bombay, Printed at the government central press, 1966. pp.25-35.

U₀+R

I-2161
Sastri, Valangiman Sankaranarayana Srinivasa,
    1869-1946.
    Life of Gopal Krishna Gokhale. Bangalore,
Bangalore Print.and Pub.Co., 1937. 138p.

NUR
IOL

I-2162
Sastri, Valangiman Sankaranarayana Srinivasa,
    1869-1946.
    My master Gokhale. Ed.by T.N.Jagadisan.
Madras, Model publications, 1946. 287p.

Calcutta Nat'l Lib

I-2163
Satghar, Shripad Narayan.
    A saintly soul; an appreciation of the
life, career and mission of Govind Janardan
Borkar, astrologer. Bombay, Pub.by the
author, 1933. 44p.

h a *of* R

I-2164
Savarkar, Vinayak Damodar, 1883-1966.
    Hindu Rashtra darshan: a collection of the
presidential speeches delivered from the
Hindu Mahasabha platform. Bombay, L.G.
Khare, 1949. 309p.

IOL

I-2165
Savarkar, Vinayak Damodar, 1883-1966.
Hindu rashtravad; being an exposition of
the ideology and immediate programme of
Hindu rashtra. Collected and Ed.by Satya
Parkash. Rohtak, S.Parkash, 1945. 218p.

NYPL

I-2166
Savarkar, Vinayak Damodar, 1883-1966.
Historic statements. Bombay, G.P.Parchure,
1967. 248p.

UofR

I-2167
Savarkar, Vinayak Damodar, 1833-1966.
Samagra Savarakara Vannaya. Vol. 5 & 6 -
English writings. Poona, Maharashtra Prantik
Hindusatha, 1963-65.

I-2168
Savarkar, Vinayak Damodar, 1883-1966.
The story of my transportation for life.
trans.by V.N.Naik from the original Marathi.
Mājhī Janmathepa. Bombay, Sadbhakti Pubs.,
1950. 576p.

1. Political crimes and offences - India.

UofP

I-2169
Savyasachi.
Acharya Kakasaheb Kalelkar - literateur,
educationalist, parliamentarian; fifty-five
years of public service. MR, v.115 (1964),
pp.360-64.

I-2170
Sayaji Rao Gaekwar III, maharaja of Baroda,
1863-
Speeches and addresses of His Highness
Sajaji Rao III, maharaja of Baroda, 1877-
1927. London, Macmillan, 1928. 533p.

1. India. 2. India - Soc.condit.

UofR

I-2171
Sergeant, Philip Walsingham, 1872-
The ruler of Baroda, an account of the life
and work of the Maharaja Gaekwar. London,
J.Murray, 1928. 320p.

UofR

I-2172
Shah, Amritlal B., 1920-
Gopal Krishna Gokhale and the contemporary
crisis in Indian politics, HumR, v.2 (1970),
pp.301-15.

I-2173
Shah, Amritlal B., 1920-   and Aiyar, S.P.
Gokhale and modern India; centenary lectures.
Bombay, Manaktalas, 1966. 104p.

LC

I-2174
Shah, Chandulal M., 1913-
Yeshwantrao Chavan. Bombay, Vidya Pub.
House, 1963. 107p.

LC

I-2175
Shah, P.G.
Sir Rustom Pestonji Masani, *JASB*, v.12, no.1
(1966), pp.1-4. Also in: *JGRS*, v.27 (1965),
pp.4-6.

u og a

I-2180
Shay, Theodore L.
Tilak, Gandhi, and Arthaśastra. Evanston,
Illinois, Northwestern Univ., 1955. *

Case

I-2176
Shahani, Dayaram Gidumal.
Behramji M.Malabari; a biographical sketch.
London, T.Fisher Unwin, 1892. 269p.

1. Malabari, Behramji M., 1853-1912.
2. India - Soc.condit.

U of R

I-2181
Shri Guruji, the man and his mission, on the
occasion of his fifty-first birthday. Delhi,
B.N.Bhargava, 1956. 96p.

*1.Golwalkar, Madhav Sadashiv. 2.Rastriya
Swayam Sevak Sangh.*

U of R

I-2177
Shahani, Tejumal Karamchand.
Gopal Krishna Gokhale, a historical biogra-
phy. Bombay, R.K.Mody, 1929. 396p.

U of R

I-2182
Shriman Narayan.
Vinoba: his life and work. Bombay,
Popular Prakashan, 1970. 370p.

Biography - books

I-2178
Shaikh, A.U.
The development of Anglo-Indian biographical
literature. Bombay, Univ.of Bombay, 1944. *

Case

I-2183
Singh, Jogendra Sardar, 1877-
B.M.Malabari: rambles with the pilgrim
reformer. London, G.Bell, 1914. 202p.

U of R

I-2179
Sharma, S.P.
Mr. Gokhale as a financier, *HR*, v.68 (1936),
pp.728-36.

H P

I-2184
Singh, Nihal.
Mr. Tilak's work in England, *MR*, v.26
(1919), pp.367-73.

Case

I-2185
Stewart, Cosmo.
A great Indian prince and reformer. BM,
v.224 (1928), pp.831-48.

shahu chhatrapati

Case

I-2186
Strachey, Sir Arthur, 1858-1901.
Charge to the jury in the case of the Queen-
Empress vs. Bal Gangadhar Tilak and Keshav
Mahadev Bal in the High Court of Bombay. Rev.
ed. Bombay, Thacker & co., 1897. 119p.

BM

I-2187
Tahmankar, Dattatraya Vishwanath.
Lokamanya Tilak, father of Indian unrest
and maker of modern India. London, J.Murray,
1956. 352p.

U M R

I-2188
Talwalkar, Govind.
Naoroji to Nehru. Bombay, Majestic Book
Depot, 1969. 288p.

I.B '49

I-2189
Tilak, Bal Gangadhar, 1856-1920.
All about Lok.Tilak. A collection of Tilak's
speeches and writings, preceded by press notices
and appreciations, and by a biographical sketch
by S.Airavatam. Madras, V.R.Sastrulu and sons,
1922. 805p.

BM

I-2190
Tilak, Bal Gangadhar, 1856-1920.
Full and authentic report of the Tilak trial,
1908. Being the only authorized verbatim account of the whole proceedings with introduction and character sketch of B.G.Tilak together
with a press opinion. Bombay, N.C.Kelkar,
1908. 576p.

Lc

I-2191
Tilak, Bal Gangadhar, 1856-1920.
His writings and speeches, [with]
appreciation by Aurobindo Ghose. Madras,
Ganesh and co., 1918. 395p.

IOL

I-2192
Tilak, Bal Gangadhar, 1856-1920.
The late Gopalrao Gokhale. In: Gopal Krishna
Gokhale, a centenary tribute. Bombay, Printed
at the government central press, 1966. pp.
173-178.

U M R

I-2193
Tilak, Bal Gangadhar, 1856-1920.
Letters of Lokamanya Tilak. Ed.by Mahadeo
Dhondo Vidwans. Poona, Kesari Prakashan,
1966. 301p.

u of R

I-2194
Tilak, Bal Gangadhar, 1856-1920.
Tilak's master-piece: a verbatim report of
his address to the jury. Surat, M.M.Raeji,
1908. 147p.

Bom (Pres) Cat

I-2195
  Tilak, Bal Gangadhar, 1856-1920.
    Tilak's speeches. Ed.by Mahadeo Narayan
  Kavade. Poona, Hari Raghunath Bhagwat, 1908.
  108p.

Bom (Pres) cat

I-2196
  The Tilak case, being a summary of the
  arguments for the defence. Poona, N.C.
  Kelkar, 1908. 86p.

Bom (Pres) cat

I-2197
  Tilak-Paranjpe controversy: as it appeared in
  the Bombay Chronicle. Correspondence that
  passed between Mr. Tilak and Prof.Paranjpe
  on the subject of the giving of an address
  to Tilak on behalf of all the citizens of
  Poona, Bombay, Vaibhav Press, 1920.

Bom. (Pres) cat

I-2198
  Tucker, Richard Philip.
    M.G.Ranade and the moderate tradition in
  India, 1842-1901. Cambridge, Harvard Univ.,
  1966. 551p. *

Shulman #603

I-2199
  Tucker, Richard Philip.
    Ranade and the roots of Indian nationalism.
  Chicago, Univ.of Chicago Press, 1972.
  Micro-fiche.

U of R

I-2200
  Tyabji, Husain Badruddin, 1873-
    Badruddin Tyabji; a biography. Bombay,
  Thacker, 1952. 410p.

    1. Tyabji, Badruddin, 1844-1906.

U of R

I-2201
  Ugrankar, Venkatrao Lakshaman.
    A brief biographical sketch of Shamrao
  Vithal Kaikini. A Saraswat patriot and
  philanthropist. Bombay, G.N.Kulkarni,
  1911. 16p.

Bom (Pres) cat

I-2202
  Vaidya, D.G.
    The inner life of Sir Narayan Chandavarkar.
  bR, v.42 (1927), pp.26-30.

V of MR

I-2203
  Varma, Vishwanath Prasad.
    The economic and social activities of
  Lokamanya Tilak, PUJ, v.15 (1960), pp.27-
  39. Also in: Mankind, v.5 (1960), pp.19-
  32.

Case

I-2204
  Varma, Vishwanath Prasad.
    Lokamanya Tilak and early Indian nationalism,
  1881-1896. PUJ, v.16 (1961), pp.1-35.

Case

I-2205
    Wacha, Dinsha Edulji, 1844-1936.
        Premchand Roychand. His early life and career.
    Bombay, Times Press, 1913. 234p.

Row (Madras)

I-2210
    Abhyankar, Ganesh Raghunath.
        Native states and post-war reforms. Poona,
    Aryabhushan Press, 1917. 85p.

I-2206
    Wacha, Dinsha Edulji, 1844-1936
        Reminiscences of the late Hon. Mr.G.K.
    Gokhale. Bombay, H.T.Anklesaria, 1915.
    52p.

BM

I-2211
    An address of welcome to his excellency the
    Honourable Sir Richard Temple, K.S.C.I.
    Governor of Bombay, QJPSS, v.2,no.2 (1879),
    pp.95-102.

QJPSS

I-2207
    Wacha, Dinsha Edulji, 1844-1936.
        Speeches and writings. Madras, G.A.Natesan
    and co., 1920. 550p.

Bombay - Madras

I-2212
    Anderson, Hugh Stark
        Historical records of the services of the
    First Regiment Bombay Infantry, Grenadiers.
    Poona, 1885. 73p.

IOL

I-2208
    Wedderburn, William, 1838-
        Allan Octavian Hume, father of the Indian
    National Congress, 1829 to 1912. London,
    1913. 188p.

I-2213
    Anderson, MacClesfield Heptenstall.
        The Poona Horse (17th Queen Victoria's
    own Cavalry), 1817-1931. London, United
    Service Institution, 1933. 2v.

BM

I-2209
    Wolpert, Stanley A.
        Tilak and Gokhale: revolution and reform
    in the making of modern India. Berkeley,
    Univ.of California Press, 1962. 370p.

    1. Tilak, B.G.

I-2214
    Bhattacharya, Sukumar.
        An intercepted letter of Keir Hardie to
    Bal Gangadhar Tilak, IHCP, v.21 (1958), pp.
    554-57. Also in: JIH, v.37 (1959), pp.81-
    84.

I-2215
  Bhutani, Viney Chander.
    The administration of Lord Curzon: socio-
    economic policies. New Delhi, Univ.of New
    Delhi, 1966. *

BAS 1970

I-2216
  Bombay (Presidency) Committee on the Riots
    in Poona and Ahmednagar.
    Report of the Committee on the Riots in
    Poona and Ahmednagar, 1875. Bombay, 1876.
    2v.in 3.

Brit Mus

I-2217
  Bombay (Province) Riots Inquiry Committee.
    Report. Bombay, 1929.

I-2218
  Bombay Tilak day prosecution, notes, MR, v.48
    (1930), p.356.

M R

I-2219
  Broomfield, John H.
    The regional elites: a theory of modern
    Indian history, IESHR, v.3 (1966), pp.279-
    91.

I-2220
  Cashman, Richard Ian.
    The political recruitment of God Ganapati,
    IESHR, v.7 (1970), pp.347-73.

I-2221
  Cashman, Richard Ian.
    The politics of mass recruitment: attempts
    to organize popular movements in Maharashtra,
    1891-1908. Durham, N.C., Duke Univ., 1969.
    261p. *

Shulman #537

I-2222
  Chakrabarti, Jadab Chandra.
    The native states of India. Calcutta, S.K.
    Shaw, 1895. 287p.

I-2223
  Chapman, John.
    Baroda and Bombay, their political morality:
    a narrative drawn from the papers laid before
    Parliament in relation to the removal of Lt.-
    Col.Outram from the Office of resident at the
    court of the Gaekwar. London, J.Chapman,
    1853. 178p.

I-2224
  Chatterji, Nandalal, 1903-
    The Congress session of 1907, JIH, v.38
    (1960), pp.131-38.

I-2225
  Chatterji, Nandalal, 1903–
    The cult of violence and India's freedom
  movement. JIH, v.35 (1957). pp.1-6.

JIH

I-2226
  Chatterji, Nandalal, 1903–
    How the first split came in the Indian Nation-
  al Congress. IHCP, v.21 (1958), pp.543-48.

IHCP

I-2227
  Chavda, V.K.
    Gaekwads and the British; a study of their
  problems 1879-1920. Delhi, Univ.Pubs., 1967?
  196p.

I-2228
  Cheragh Ali, Maulavi.
    Hyderabad (Deccan) under Sir Salar Jung.
  An account of the Civil Military and Public
  Works Depts. Bombay, 1885-86. 4 vols.

I-2229
  Chicherov, A.I.
    Tilak's trial and the Bombay political strike
  of 1908. In: Tilak and the struggle for
  Indian freedom. Ed.by I.M.Reisner and N.M.Gold-
  berg. New Delhi, People's publishing house,
  1966. pp.545-626.

I-2230
  Chirol, Valentine, 1852-1929.
    Indian Unrest. A reprint, rev.and enl.,
  from "The Times," with an Introd.by Alfred
  Lyall. London, Macmillan, 1910. 387p.

*1 India Pol + govt - 1765-1947
2. Education - India   3 India -
Soc conditions*

I-2231
  Costa, Manuel de Oliveira Gomes da.
    A revolta de Goa e a campanha de 1895/1896.
  Lisboa, 1939.

Scholberg Portuguese

I-2232
  Crawford, Arthur Travers, 1835-1911.
    Our troubles in Poona and the Deccan.
  Westminster, A.Constable, 1897.   273p.

    1. Poona, India (District) 2. Gt.Brit. -
  Colonies - India.

I-2233
  Campston, Mary.
    Some early Indian nationalists and their
  allies in the British Parliament, 1851-1906,
  EHR, v.76 (1961), pp.279-97.

I-2234
  Das, Manindra Nath.
    Impact of liberal victory in Britain on
  Indian politics:1905-06, JIH, v.41 (1963),
  pp.619-29.

I-2235
Desai, Akshayakumar Ramanlal.
    Social background of Indian Nationalism.
4th ed. Bombay, Popular Prakashan [1966]
480p.

    1. India - Soc.condit. 2. India - Econ.
condit. 3. Nationalism - India.

UqR

I-2236
Deshpande, Gangadharrao Keshavrao, rao saheb.
    A call to arms. An appeal to the Marathas and
the nation. Amraoti, R.A.Deshpande, 1918. 32p.

Bom (Pres) cat

I-2237
Deshpande, Yeshwant Khushal, 1884-
    Do-amli or the dual control over Berar.
IHRCP, v.13 (1930), pp.159-60.

I HRCP Dibu. 1.

I-2238
Dighe, Vishvanath Govind.
    The renaissance in Maharashtra: the first
phase (1819-1870), ASBJ, v.36/37, n.s.
(1961/62), pp.23-31.

case

I-2239
Great Britain. India Office.
    Correspondence regarding the claim of the
Nizam of Hyderabad to the restoration of the
province of Berar. London, H.M.S.O., 1925.
90p.

IOL

I-2240
Haig, Sir Wolseley, 1865-1938.
    The Berar question again, NC, v.95 (1924),
pp.592-98.

Case

I-2241
Hambly, G.R.G., ed.
    Mahratta Nationalism before Tilak; two
unpublished letters of Sir Richard Temple
on the state of the Bombay Deccan, 1873,
RCASJ, v.49 (1962), pp.144-60.

Case

I-2242
Hardas, Balshastri.
    Armed struggle for freedom; ninety years
war of Indian independence, 1857 to
Subhash, rendered into English by S.S.Apte.
Poona, Kal Prakashan, 1958. 480p.

LC

I-2243
India (Republic) Office of the Accountant-
    General, Bombay.
    History of services, state of Bombay.
Nagpur, Government Press, 1962. 8v.

UqR

I-2244
Kamerkar, M.P.
    Some aspects of national activity in the
Bombay province between 1870-1880, IHCP, v.23
(1960), pp.122-23.

UqR

I-2245
Kelkar, Narsinha Chintaman, 1872-1947.
A passing phase of politics. Poona City,
S.W.Awati, 1925. 276p.

1. India - Pol.& govt. - 1919-

I-2246
Khan, Nasrullah Nawabzada.
The ruling chiefs of Western India and the
Rajkumar College. Bombay, 1898. 207p.

IOL

I-2247
Khobrekar, Viththal Gopal.
How Baroda became a problem state during
1870 to 1874 A.D., IHCP, v.30 (1968), pp.267-
73.

I-2248
Krishnaswamy, S.
A riot in Bombay, August 11, 1893: a study
in Hindu-Muslim relations in western India
during the late nineteenth century. Chicago,
Univ.of Chicago, 1966. 276p.

I-2249
Kumar, Ravinder.
The Deccan Riots of 1875, JAS, v.24
(1965), pp.613-35.

I-2250
A letter to the government of Bombay review-
ing the report of the Deccan Riots Commission, QJPSS, v.1,no.3 (1878), pp.35-43.

I-2251
The Mahomedan and Hindu riots in Bombay,
August 1893. 3rd ed. (Bound with "Times
of India"-The Bombay riots of August,
1893). Bombay, The Bombay Gazette
Steam Press, 1894. 66p.

IOL
under Bombay Gazette
p.400

I-2252
Majumdar, Bimanbehari, 1900-
The inner circle of the Congress in the
pre-Gandhian era, QRHS, v.5 (1965/66),
pp.38-51.

I-2253
Majumdar, Bimanbehari, 1900-
Militant nationalism in India and its socio-
religious background, 1897-1917. Calcutta,
General Printers & Publishers, 1966. 209p.

I-2254
Majumdar, Ramesh Chandra, 1888-
Three phases of India's struggle for freedom.
Bombay, Bharatiya Vidya Bhavan, 1961. 61p.

1. India - Hist. - Brittish occupation, 1765-
1947. - Addresses,essays,lectures. 2. Nationalism - India.

I-2255
  Manshardt, Clifford, 1897-   ed.
    Bombay; today and tomorrow; eight lectures.
  Bombay, D.B.Taraporevala sons & co., 1930.
  127p.

LC

I-2256
  Manshardt, Clifford, 1897-   ed.
    Bombay looks ahead; eight lectures ...
  Bombay, D.B.Taraporevala sons & co., 1934.
  114p.

IOL

I-2257
  Masselos, James C.
    Liberal consciousness, leadership and
  political organization in Bombay and Poona,
  1867-1895. Bombay, Univ.of Bombay, 1964. *

Indica v2, no 2

I-2258
  Mehrotra, S.R.
    The Poona Sarvajankik Sabha: the early
  phase (1870-1880), IESHR, v.6 (1969), pp.
  293-321.

Notice articles
BAS Sept 1970

I-2259
  Mr. Gokhale's Servants of India Society and
  its work, MR, v.25 (1919), pp.623-25.

I-2260
  Mukerji, K.
    The Renaissance in Bengal and Maharashtrian
  thought from 1850 to 1920, AV, v.4 (1962),
  pp.331-42.

I-2261
  Naoroji, Dadabhai, 1825-1917.
    Baroda administration in 1874. A statement
  in reply to the remarks in the Baroda Blue
  Book of 1875, concerning Dadabhai Naoroji
  and his colleagues. London, 1875.

I-2262
  Perry, Sir Thomas Erskine, 1806-1882.
    Sir Erskine Perry's notes on the Deccan
  Riots Report of 1875, QJPSS, v.1 (1878),
  pp.1-12.

Case

I-2263
  Potdar, Datto Vaman, 1890-
    Mind of the Maharashtra, JUP, v.9 (1958),
  pp.57-64.

I-2264
  Prasad, Bimla.
    The Indian National Congress and the
  problem of poverty, 1885-90, PUJ, v.17
  (1962), pp.35-44.

I-2265
Raghavendra Rao, Kurukundi, 1928-
The early phase of Indian nationalism,
1878-1897. JKU, v.5 (1961), pp.43-61; v.6
(1962), pp.115-27.

gas 63

I-2266
Rao, Vasant Dinanath, 1913-
The beginning and growth of nationalism
in Maharashtra in the nineteenth century.
QRHS, v.4 (1965-66), pp.222-30.

gas '66

I-2267
Rao, Vasant Dinanath, 1913-
Ideas motivating political and social
evolution in Maharashtra during the nineteenth century. JUB, n.s.,v.32 (1963-1964),
pp.1-18.

I-2268
Regani, Sarojini.
The cession to Berar, IHCP, v.20 (1957),
pp.252-59.

IH C P

I-2269
Setlur, S.Shrinivasiyengar and Deshpande,
Kesava Ganesa, eds.
A full and authentic report of the trial
of the Hon.Mr. Bal Gangadhar Tilak. Bombay,
Education Society's Press, 1897. 393p.

BM

I-2270
Simcox, Arthur Henry Addenbrooke.
A memoir of the Khandesh Bhil corps, 1825-
1891; comp.from original records. Bombay,
Thacker, 1912. 281p.

Lc

I-2271
Singh, Pardaman.
The Indian National Congress - Surat split.
BPP, v.84 (1965), pp.121-39.

gas

I-2272
Taleyarkhan, Dinshah Ardeshir.
The riots of 1874; their true history and
philosophy, tracing the origin of the Moslem
fanaticism throughout Asia and ascertaining
its real and thorough remedies. Bombay, 1874.
70p.

IOL

I-2273
Thombre, R.K.
The sovereignty over Berar and the question
of the retrocession of Berar to the Nizam, MR,
v.82 (1947), pp.31-35.

*NRD
case*

I-2274
Tucker, Richard Philip.
The proper limits of agitation; the crisis
of 1879-80 in Bombay Presidency, JAS, v.28
(1969), pp.339-355.

*Modern history articles
EAS Sept 1970*

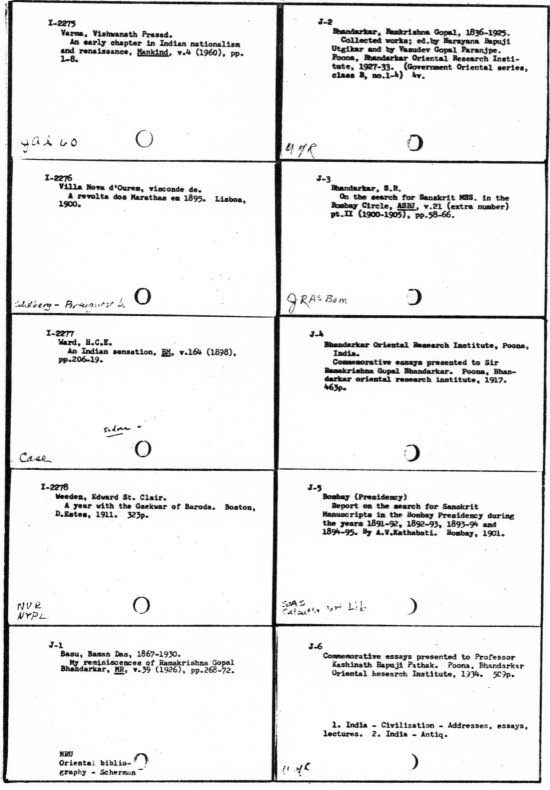

I-2275
Varma, Vishwanath Prasad.
An early chapter in Indian nationalism and renaissance. <u>Mankind</u>, v.4 (1960), pp. 1-8.

ya260

I-2276
Villa Nova d'Ourem, visconde de.
A revolta dos Marathas em 1895. Lisboa, 1900.

Schilberg - Portuguese b.

I-2277
Ward, H.C.E.
An Indian sensation. <u>BM</u>, v.164 (1898), pp.206-19.

salme -

Case

I-2278
Weeden, Edward St. Clair.
A year with the Gaekwar of Baroda. Boston, D.Estes, 1911. 323p.

NUB
NYPL

J-1
Basu, Baman Das, 1867-1930.
My reminiscences of Ramakrishna Gopal Bhandarkar, <u>MR</u>, v.39 (1926), pp.268-72.

NRU
Oriental biblio-
graphy - Scherman

J-2
Bhandarkar, Ramkrishna Gopal, 1836-1925.
Collected works; ed.by Narayana Bapuji Utgikar and by Vasudev Gopal Paranjpe. Poona, Bhandarkar Oriental Research Institute, 1927-33. (Government Oriental series, class B, no.1-4) 4v.

UYR

J-3
Bhandarkar, S.R.
On the search for Sanskrit MSS. in the Bombay Circle, <u>ASBJ</u>, v.21 (extra number) pt.II (1900-1905), pp.58-66.

RAS Bom

J-4
Bhandarkar Oriental Research Institute, Poona, India.
Commemorative essays presented to Sir Ramakrishna Gopal Bhandarkar. Poona, Bhandarkar oriental research institute, 1917. 463p.

J-5
Bombay (Presidency)
Report on the search for Sanskrit Manuscripts in the Bombay Presidency during the years 1891-92, 1892-93, 1893-94 and 1894-95. By A.V.Kathabati. Bombay, 1901.

SOAS
Calcutta Uni Lib

J-6
Commemorative essays presented to Professor Kashinath Bapuji Pathak. Poona, Bhandarkar Oriental Research Institute, 1934. 509p.

1. India - Civilization - Addresses, essays, lectures. 2. India - Antiq.

UYR

J-7
Dandekar, Ramchandra Narayan, ed.
Progress of Indic studies, 1917-1942. Bhandarkar Oriental Research Institute. Silver jubilee. Poona, 1942. 406p.

J-8
Das Gupta, Nalini Nath.
D.R.Bhandarkar (eminent Indian historians series), QRHS, v.5 (1965/66), p.37.

J-9
Gajendragadkar, S.N.
Prof.H.D.Velankar: An appreciation. In: H.D. Velankar commemoration volume. A volume of Indological studies by his students presented to Prof.H.D.Velankar on the occasion of his seventy-second birthday on 3rd October 1965. Ed.by S.N.Gajendragadkar and S.A.Upadhyaya. Bombay, Prof.H.D.Velankar, Commemoration volume committee, 1965. pp.1-3.

J-10
Gajendragadkar, S.N.
Professor Hari Damodar Velankar, ASBJ, v.41/42 (1966/67), pp.1-7.

J-11
Gode, Parashuram Krishna, 1891-
The chronology of Raghunatha Sastri Parvate and his works - between A.D.1821 and 1859. In: Raja Sir Annamalai Chettiar Commemorative Volume. Ed.by B.V.Narayanaswamy Naidu. Annamalainagar, 1941. pp.197-206.

J-12
Gode, Parashuram Krishna, 1891-
The date of the Kāyastha Parabhūdharmādarśa of Nīlakaṇṭha Śūri and identification of its author in contemporary records, JOR, v.13 (1939), pp.129-39.

J-13
Gode, Parashuram Krishna, 1891-
Harikavi alias Bhanubhatta a court-poet of King Sambjai and his works, ABORI, v.16 (1934), pp.262-91.

J-14
Gode, Parashuram Krishna, 1891-
Identification of Dalpat Rai mentioned in Burhan-i-Masir with Dalpatiraja the author of the Dharmashastra work called the Nrsimhaprasad, IHCP, v.2 (1938), pp.313-18.

J-15
Gode, Parashuram Krishna, 1891-
The identification of Raghunatha, the protegé of Queen Dipabai of Tanjore and his contact with Saint Ramadas between A.D.1648 and 1682.

J-16
Gode, Parashuram Krishna, 1891-
The influence of Jagannatha Panditaraja on some Deccani authors of the seventeenth century, QJMS, v.33 (1942), pp.29-37.

J-17
Gode, Parashuram Krishna, 1891-
Raghava Apakhandekar of Punyastambha, his
work and descendants (from A.D.1750 to 1942),
ABORI, v.24 (1943), pp.27-44.

Bhan.O.R.I.

J-22
K.R.Cama Oriental Institute golden jubilee
volume.
(Commemorative volume issued on the occasion
of the golden jubilee of the institute founded
in the memory of Kharshedji Rustomji Cama,
1831-1909; collection of articles, chiefly on
ancient Indian and Iranian culture and literature). Bombay, K.R.Cama Oriental Institute,
1969. 270p.

Acc. list Feb 1978,
p. 78

J-18
Gode, Parashuram Krishna, 1891-
The Samayanaya of Gāgābhaṭṭa, composed for
the Maratha King Sambhaji in A.D.1680-1681,
IHCP, v.3 (1939), pp.1166-71.

NRU
IHCP

J-23
Karambelkar, Vinayak Waman, 1912-
Gangadhara Kavi and his works, ABORI, v.30
(1950), pp.31-42.

J-19
Gode, Parashuram Krishna, 1891-
Some verses about the Kayastha-Parabhus
composed by Kesava Pandita by the order of
King Sambhaji, son of Shivaji, c.A.D.1675,
ABORI, v.20 (1939), pp.235-48.

A B O R I

J-24
Kielhorn, Franz, 1840-1908.
Report on the search for Sanskrit mss. in
the Bombay Presidency, during the year 1880-
81. Bombay, Govt.Central Book Depot, 1881.
117p.

E M

J-20
Gode, Parashuram Krishna, 1891-
Vanchesvara alias Kutti Kavi and his contact
with the Patvardhan Sardars of the southern
Maratha country, ABORI, v.20 (1938), pp.9-20.

Bhan CRI

J-25
Panse, Murlidhar Gajanan, 1918-
Jyotisaratnamala of Sripatibhatta, BDCRI,
v.17 (1956), pp.237-502.

J-21
Gode, Parashuram Krishna, 1891-
Visvanatha Mahadeo Ranade, a Chittpavan
court-poet of Raja Ramsing I of Jaipur and
his works between A.D.1650 and 1700, ASBJ,
n.s.,v.17 (1941), pp.43-55.

ASBJ

J-26
Paradkar, M.D.
Kavindracarya Saraswati - a native of
Maharashtra, GJRIJ, v.25 (1969), pp.381-
95.

Lib.

J-27
Paranjpe, Vasudev Gopal, 1887-
The late Dr.Sir R.G.Bhandarkar. An appreciation, ABORI, v.7 (1925-26), pp.153-56.

NRU
~~Inventor Delis.~~
~~Schram~~

J-32
Sarma, K.V.
Dr.S.K.Belvalkar, VIJ, v.5 (1967), pp.114-16.

Biog articles
BAS Sept 1969

J-28
Peterson, Peter.
Detailed report of operations in search of Sanskrit MSS. in the Bombay Circle, August 1882-March 1883, ASBJ, v.16 (1883-85), pp.1-72.

NRU
ASBJ

J-33
Sarma, K.V.
Pandit S.D.Satwalekar, VIJ, v.6 (1968), pp.135-137.

biography articles
BAS Sept 1970

J-29
Phadke, H.A.
R.G.Bhandarkar. New Delhi, National Book Trust, 1968. (National biography series). 96p.

PL 480 '69

J-34
Tope, Trimbak Krishna.
Modern sage: a brief sketch of the life and learning of M.M. Dr. P.V.Kane, national research professor of Indology. Bombay, Brahman Sabha, 1960. 139p.

LC

J-30
Poleman, Horace Irvin, 1905-
A census of Indic manuscripts in the United States and Canada. New Haven, Conn., American Oriental Society, 1938. New York, Kraus Reprint Corp., 1967. (American Oriental series, v.12) 571p.

4 HP

J-35
Upadhyaya, S.A.
Prof. H.D.Velankar (1893-1967), VIJ, v.5 (1967), pp.209-210.

biography articles
BAS Sept 1970

J-31
Professor H.D.Velankar Commemoration Volume Committee.
H.D.Velankar commemoration volume. Editors: S.N.Gajendragadkar and S.A.Upadhyaya. Bombay, 1965. 222p.

1. Sanskrit philology - Addresses, essays, lectures. 2. Velankar, Hari Damodar.

LC

J-36
Zimmerman, Robert.
R.G.Bhandarkar, ZDMG, v.80 (1926), pp. 328-35.

Journalism & Press

K-1
Ahluwalia, M.M.
Press--and India's struggle for freedom,
1858-1909. JIH, v.38 (1960), pp.599-604.

K-2
Bhuraney, Phagun Haricmal.
Anglo-Indian journalism in Bombay upto
1900. Bombay, Univ.of Bombay, 1956. *

Journalism
BDD

K-3
Gupta, Anirudha.
Indian newspaper press and national movement
till 1920. VBQ, v.27 (1961), pp.150-62.

Case

K-4
Kulkarni, Vinayak Yeshwant.
Nirnayasagar; a century of type-casting,
printing and publishing. New Delhi, Maharashtra Information Centre, 1969. 26p.

1. Chaudhari, Jawaji Dadaji, 1839-1892 - Biog.

P-480 2/70

K-5
The oldest paper in India: the Bombay
Samachar. CR, v.106 (1898), pp.218-36.

Case

K-6
Parvate, Trimbak Vishnu, 1901-
Marathi journalism. New Delhi, Maharashtra
Information Centre, 1969. 38p.

P: 480, 2/70

K-7
Ramachandra Rao, T.S.
The journalist in Gokhale. PA, v.10
(1966). pp.277-82.

g q 8'66

K-8
Sanial, S.C.
The Father of Indian journalism Robert
Knight - his life-work. CR, v.19 (1926),
pp.287-325; v.20 (1926), pp.28-63, 305-49.

Bibliography & reference | Language, Linguistics and Literature

L-1
Abbott, Justin Edwards, 1853-1932.
A catalogue of Marathi Christian literature
during eighty years, 1813-1892. Bombay,
Jawaji Dadaji's Nirnaya Sagar Press, 1892.

L-2
Bombay (Presidency) Educational Department.
Gramaphone records of languages and
dialects spoken in the Bombay Presidency.
Translations and transcripts. Madras, 1923.

Brit Mus

L-3
British Museum. Dept.of Oriental Printed Books and Manuscripts.
Catalogue of Marathi and Gujarati printed books in the library of the British Museum. By J.F.Blumhardt ... Printed by order of the Trustees of the British Museum. London, B. Quaritch [etc.] 1892. 237p. Supplement, 1915. 259p.

L-4
Calcutta. National Library.
A bibliography of dictionaries and encyclopaedias in Indian languages. Calcutta, Librarian, National Library, 1964. 175p.

L-5
Haig, J.S.
Classified catalogue of Marathi Christian literature, at the close of the 19th century. 1902.

L-6
India Office Library.
Accessions in modern Indian languages. Marathi. 1954-

L-7
Jain, Sushil Kumar, comp.
Indian literature in English, a bibliography; being a check-list of works of poetry, drama, fiction, autobiography, and letters written by Indians in English, or translated from modern Indian languages into English. Tenterden, Kent, Eng., Pub.Priv., copies can be had from Sushil Jain Pub., 1965-67. 3v.

L-8
Kelekar, Ravindra, ed.
A bibliography of Konkani literature in Devanagari, Roman and Kannada characters. Goa, Gomant Bharati Pubs., 1963. 87p.

L-9
Pattanayak, Devi Prasanna, 1931-   comp.
Indian languages bibliography. New Delhi, Educational Resources Center, Printed at Crescent Printing Works Private Limited, 1967. 84p.

L-10
Raeside Ian.
A bibliographical index of Mahanubhava works in Marathi, *BSOAS*, v.23,no.3 (1960), pp.464-507.

L-11
Rangachar, H.N.
Indo-English literature; a historical bibliography, *ILib*, v.14 (1959), pp.67-69.

Language & linguistics

L-12
Abbott, Justin Edwards, 1853-1932.
The Katkari language (a preliminary study), *ASBJ*, v.21 (1900-05), Extra no. part II, pp.78-126.

L-13

Bhagwat, Madhuri.
A study of Varhadi dialect in the neighbourhood of Akola. Poona, Univ.of Poona,
1967-68. *

Linguistics
BDCRI.

L-14

Bhagwat, Shriram Vasudeo.
Phonemic frequencies in Marathi and
their relation to devising a speed-script.
Poona, 1961. (Poona University and Deccan
College. Publication in linguistics,1).
208p.

linguistics LC

L-15

Bloch, Jules, 1880-1953.
La formation de la langue marathe. Paris,
E.Champion, 1919. 447p.

LC

L-16

Bloch, Jules, 1880-1953.
The formation of the Marathi language.
Tr.by Dev Raj Chanana. Delhi, Motilal
Banarsidass, 1970. 430p.

L-17

Chavan, Viththal Pandurang.
The Konkan and the Konkani language. Bombay,
1924. 81p.

L-18

Chitnis, Vijaya Shridhar.
The Khandeshi dialect as spoken by farmers
in the village of Mahadi. Poona, Univ.of
Poona, 1964-65. *

Linguistics
BDCRR

L-19

Consonantal germination in Konkani, IL,
v.26 (1965), pp.237-39.

L-20

Dalgado, Sebastiao Rodolpho, 1855-1922.
...Dialecto indo-português de Gôa.
Reimpressão fac-simile; ... Rio de Janeiro,
J.Leite & co., 1922.

Scholberg — Portuguese b.

L-21

Dandekar, V.P.
Where Marathi meets Gujarathi, AIOCPT, v.7
(1933), pp.931-35.

L-22

Gajendragadkar, S.N.
Marathi affricates. In: Studies in Indian
linguistics; Professor M.B.Emeneau Saṣṭi-
pūrti volume. Ed.by Bhadriraju Krishnamurti. Annamalainagar, Centres of Advanced
Study in Linguistics, Deccan College,
Poona Univ.and Annamalai Univ., 1968.
pp. 81-94.

L-23
  Ghatage, Amrit Madhav, 1913-
    Cochin. Bombay, State Board of Literature
    and Culture, 1967. (Survey of Marathi dialects,
    4) 144p.

4k of R

L-24
  Ghatage, Amrit Madhav, 1913-
    Konkani of Kankon. Bombay, State Board
    for Literature and Culture, 1968. (Survey
    of Marathi dialects, 5) 154p.

11 of R

p^{pe}
2317
r154

L-25
  Ghatage, Amrit Madhav, 1913-
    Konkani of South Kanara. Bombay, State
    Board for Literature and Culture, 1963.
    (Survey of Marathi dialects, 1) 144p.

4 of R

L-26
  Ghatage, Amrit Madhav, 1913-
    Kudali. Bombay, State Board for Literature
    and Culture, 1965. (A survey of Marathi
    dialects, 2) 153p.

Kudali dialect

4 of R

L-27
  Ghatage, Amrit Madhav, 1913-
    Kunabi of Mahad. Bombay, State Board
    for Literature and Culture, 1966. (A
    survey of Marathi dialects, 3). 150p.

1 Kunabi dialect

4 of R

L-28
  Ghatage, Amrit Madhav, 1913-
    Marathi linguistics, IL, v.23 (1962), pp.
    49-59.

JAS 63

L-29
  Ghatage, Amrit Madhav, 1913-
    Marathi of Kasargole, IL, v.31 (1970),
    pp.138-44.

Language + linguistics
BAS 1970

L-30
  Ghatage, Amrit Madhav, 1913-
    Marati of Kasargod. Bombay, State Board
    for Literature and Culture, 1970. (Survey
    of Marathi dialects, 6) 172p.

4 of R

L-31
  India. Linguistic Survey.
    Linguistic survey of India. Calcutta, Office
    of the Superintendent of Govt.printing, India,
    1903-1928. 11 vols.
    Vol.7 - Indo-Aryan family. Southern group.
    Specimens of the Marathi language. Comp.& ed.
    by G.A.Grierson. 1905.

4 of R

L-32
  James, A.Lloyd and Kanhere, S.G.
    The pronunciation of Marathi, BSOAS, v.4
    (1926-28), pp.791-801.

BSOAS

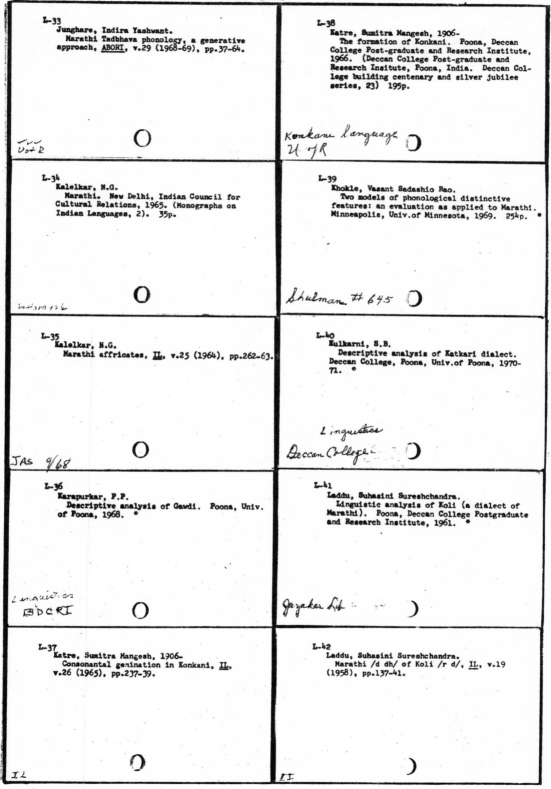

L-33
Junghare, Indira Yashwant.
Marathi Tadbhava phonology, a generative approach, ABORI, v.29 (1968-69), pp.37-64.

ᴜᴜ
Uₒ+R

L-34
Kalelkar, N.G.
Marathi. New Delhi, Indian Council for Cultural Relations, 1965. (Monographs on Indian Languages, 2). 35p.

intro 956

L-35
Kalelkar, N.G.
Marathi affricates, IL, v.25 (1964), pp.262-63.

JAS 9/68

L-36
Karapurkar, P.P.
Descriptive analysis of Gawdi. Poona, Univ. of Poona, 1968. *

Linguistics
BDCRI

L-37
Katre, Sumitra Mangesh, 1906-
Consonantal gemination in Konkani, IL. v.26 (1965), pp.237-39.

IL

L-38
Katre, Sumitra Mangesh, 1906-
The formation of Konkani. Poona, Deccan College Post-graduate and Research Institute, 1966. (Deccan College Post-graduate and Research Insitute, Poona, India. Deccan College building centenary and silver jubilee series, 23) 195p.

Konkani language
U of R

L-39
Khokle, Vasant Sadashio Rao.
Two models of phonological distinctive features: an evaluation as applied to Marathi. Minneapolis, Univ.of Minnesota, 1969. 254p. *

Shulman # 645

L-40
Kulkarni, S.B.
Descriptive analysis of Katkari dialect. Deccan College, Poona, Univ.of Poona, 1970-71. *

Linguistics
Deccan College

L-41
Laddu, Suhasini Sureshchandra.
Linguistic analysis of Koli (a dialect of Marathi). Poona, Deccan College Postgraduate and Research Institute, 1961. *

Jayakar Lib

L-42
Laddu, Suhasini Sureshchandra.
Marathi /d dh/ of Koli /r d/, IL, v.19 (1958), pp.137-41.

II

L-43
Maurya, Raj Narayan.
    Descriptive analysis of the Hindi language
of Namadeva. Poona, Univ.of Poona, 1963. *

L-44
Miranda, Rocky Valerine.
    Synchronic and historical phonology of six
Konkani dialects. Ithaca, Cornell Univ.,
1971. 112p. *

L-45
Nitenson, Edward.
    Military typesetting equipment and systems
for Indo-Aryan and Dravidian languages, Hindi,
Marathi and others, 1961-63. Natick, Mass.,
U.S.Army Natick Laboratories, Mechanical
Engineering Div., 1964. 86p.

L-46
Panse, Murlidhar Gajanan, 1918-
    Nominal stem-formants in old Marathi,
BDCRI, v.17 (1955), pp.98-115.

L-47
Paranjpe, V.W.
    Karhadi. Poona, Univ.of Poona, 1970. *

L-48
Patil, Gajanan M.
    Dialect atlas of Marathi - a direction,
ASBJ, v.39-40 (1964-1965), pp.243-46.

L-49
Patil, Gajanan M.
    Sibilants in Wadwal dialect, JMaU, v.4,no.
2 (1964), pp.28-32.

L-50
Pavie, Theodore Marie, 1811-1896.
    Quelques observations sur le Gouzerati et
le Maharatti, JA, 3d ser.,v.11 (1841), pp.
193-214.

L-51
Sardesai, Vidyadhan Nahar.
    Some problems in the nasalisation of Marathi,
RASGBIJ, n.s.(1930), pt.3, pp.537-65.

L-52
Silva, Severine.
    Konkani language, GJMS, v.54 (1964),
pp.132-43.

L-53
Sinclair, William F.
On the boundaries of the Marathi language,
<u>IA</u>, v.3 (1874), p.250.

Pinge ◯

L-54
Stevenson, John, 1798-1858.
An essay on the language of the aboriginal
Hindus, <u>ASBJ</u>, v.1 (1842), pp.103-26.

Pinge ◯

L-55
Stevenson, John, 1798-1858.
Observations on the Marathi language,
<u>ASBJ</u>, v.7 (1843), pp.84-91.

Deccan, vol. 9-10 ◯

L-56
Thompson, Charles S.
Rudiments of the Bhili language. Ahmedabad,
United Printing Press, 1895. 347p.

1. Bhil language.

LC ◯

L-57
Turner, R.L.
The Indo-Germanic accent in Marathi,
<u>RASGBIJ</u>, ser.3 (1916), pp.203-51.

A.R.L. ◯

L-58
Walimbe, S.G.
Descriptive analysis of Mangi Marathi in
Malwa (M.P.) Poona, Univ.of Poona, 1964-
65. *

Dictionaries, glossaries ◯

L-59
Athale, Bhikadeva Vasudeva.
A Marathi English dictionary. Bombay,
Asiatic Press, 1871. 230p.

◯

L-60
Belsare, Khanderao Bhikaji.
The English and Marathi school dictionary,
with pronunciation & etymology. Bombay, Laxman Pandurang Nagawekar, 1904. 1252p.

LC ◯

L-61
Bhide, Vidyadhar Vaman, 1861-1936.
English into Marathi dictionary. Bombay,
Damodar Savalaram and Co., 1910. 664p.

BM ◯

L-62
Bidvai, Mahadev Vinayak.
The handy pronouncing dictionary, English and
Marathi. Bombay, Education Society's Press,
1906. 827p.

◯

L-63
Bidvai, Mahadev Vinayak.
The pronouncing and etymological student's English and Marathi dictionary with syllables, accents, phrases, etc. 2d ed. Bombay, Education Society's Press, 1905. 688p.

marathi grantha suci

L-64
Canan, H.A.
A Marathi and English vocabulary. Bombay, The American Mission Press, 1951.

marathi grantha suci

L-65
Carey, William, 1761-1834.
Dictionary of the Mahratta language. Serampore, 1810.

1. Marathi language - Dictionaries - English.
2. English language - Dictionaries - Marathi.

LC

L-66
Dalgado, Sebastião Rodolpho, 1855-1922.
Diccionario portuguez-komkani. Lisboa, Imprensa nacional, 1905. 938p.

UofR

L-67
Date, Yashwant Ramkrishna, 1891-
English Indian dictionary of scientific terminology. ¿Sastriya paribhasa kosa¿ Poona, Maharastra kosa mandala, 1948. 650p.

SOAS

L-68
Deva, Gajanana Cintamana, d.1932.
Marathi ingraji kosh. 2d ed. Poona, the author, 1916.

Pitta raipt

L-69
Dias, D.F.X.
A vocabulary in five languages, English, Portuguese, Goa, Marathi and Hindustani, printed in Roman character. Satara, 1878. 208p.

BM

L-70
Francisco Xavier, de Santa Anna.
Diccionario purtuguez-concani, composto por um missionario italiano. Nova-Goa, Imprensa nacional, 1868. 280p.

LC

L-71
Ghumre, Bhagwantrao Wasudewji.
A dictionary of English and Marathi synonyms. Bombay, 1872. 1076p.

IOL

L-72
Hivale, Bhaskar P.
Marathi synonyms explained. Bombay, the author, Tatvavivechak, 1917.

marathi grantha suci

L-73
Homem, Paulo Mario.
Novo vocabulario em Portuguez, Concanim,
Inglez e Hindustani co-ordenado alpha-
beticamente paro o uso seus Tatricios
que percorres a India Ingleza, tomo 1.
Assagão, Bombay, Printed at the reporters'
press, 1874. 104p.

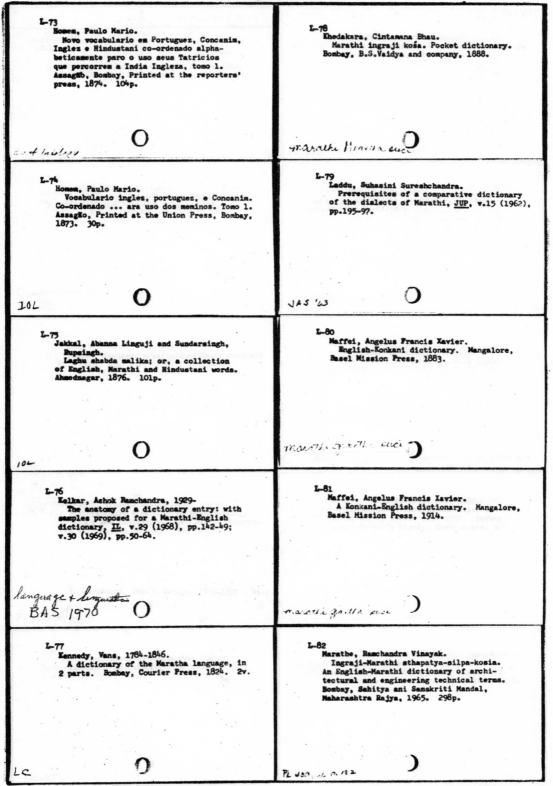

L-78
Khedakara, Cintamana Bhau.
Marathi ingraji kośa. Pocket dictionary.
Bombay, B.S.Vaidya and company, 1888.

L-74
Homem, Paulo Mario.
Vocabulario inglez, portuguez, e Concanim.
Co-ordenado ... ara uso dos meminos. Tomo 1.
Assagão, Printed at the Union Press, Bombay,
1873. 30p.

L-79
Laddu, Suhasini Sureshchandra.
Prerequisites of a comparative dictionary
of the dialects of Marathi, JUP, v.15 (1962),
pp.195-97.

L-75
Jakkal, Abanna Linguji and Sundarsingh,
Rupsingh.
Laghu shabda malika; or, a collection
of English, Marathi and Hindustani words.
Ahmednagar, 1876. 101p.

L-80
Maffei, Angelus Francis Xavier.
English-Konkani dictionary. Mangalore,
Basel Mission Press, 1883.

L-76
Kelkar, Ashok Ramchandra, 1929-
The anatomy of a dictionary entry: with
samples proposed for a Marathi-English
dictionary, IL, v.29 (1968), pp.142-49;
v.30 (1969), pp.50-64.

L-81
Maffei, Angelus Francis Xavier.
A Konkani-English dictionary. Mangalore,
Basel Mission Press, 1914.

L-77
Kennedy, Vans, 1784-1846.
A dictionary of the Maratha language, in
2 parts. Bombay, Courier Press, 1824. 2v.

L-82
Marathe, Ramchandra Vinayak.
Ingraji-Marathi sthapatya-silpa-kosia.
An English-Marathi dictionary of archi-
tectural and engineering technical terms.
Bombay, Sahitya ani Samskriti Mandal,
Maharashtra Rajya, 1965. 298p.

L-83
  Molesworth, James Thomas, 1795-1872.
    A compendium of Molesworth's Marathi and
  English dictionary; by Baba Padmanji. 3d
  rev.ed. Bombay, Education Society Press,
  1882. 645p.

cxi Tat pil

L-88
  Pandita, Visnu Parasuramasastri, 1827-1876.
    Ingreji ani Marathi kosa. Bombay, Education
  Department, 1864.

Marathi Grantha suci

L-84
  Molesworth, James Thomas, 1795-1872.
    A dictionary Murat,hee and English, comp.
  for the Govt.of Bombay by Capt.James Thomas
  Molesworth, assisted by Lts. Thomas and George
  Candy. Bombay, Printed by the compilers, 1831.
  1180p.

u of p.

L-89
  Patankar, B.R. and Padhye, Damodar Ganesh.
    Student's new modern dictionary, English-
  English-Marathi. Bombay, 1961. 752p.

IOL

L-85
  Navaroji Dosabhai Kasinatha.
    The bright Marathi and English dictionary.
  Bombay, 1904. 320p.

r

L-90
  Pinto, Jose Manoel.
    Concania-inglez dictionar. Bombay, 1916.
  190p.

IOL

L-86
  Padmanji, Baba, 1831-1906.
    A comprehensive dictionary, English and
  Marathi. Bombay, Printed at the Education
  Society's Press, 1870. 680p.

L-91
  Pocket school dictionary, English and Marathi,
    with syllables, accents, etc. Bombay, D.V.
  Sadhale & co., 1901. 682p.

IOL

L-87
  Padmanji, Baba, 1831-1906.
    Sabdaratnavali. Marathi-Marathi and Marathi-
  English. Bombay, Thomas Graham Press, 1860.

L-92
  Poona, India (City) University.
    Bhu-sastriya paribhasha. A vocabulary of
  geological terms: Marathi-English. Poona,
  1965. 34p.

L-93
The pronouncing pocket dictionary. English and Marathi. By Gajanana Chintaman Deva. Poona, Shrisamarth Press, 1893. Pt.1

MBM

O

L-94
Rajadikṣa, Suryaji Ananda, 1828-1888.
Mahārashtra Portuguese kośa. Nova Goa, 1879.

Marathi Granthasuci

O

L-95
Ranade, Nilakantha Babaji.
The twentieth century English Marathi dictionary. Pronouncing, etymological, literary, scientific and technical dictionary. Bombay, Western India Pub.Co., 1903-1916.

BM

O

L-96
Sexton, J.J.O'B
A short Marathi-English vocabulary. Bombay, Nirnaya Sagar Press, 1899. 58p.

Rev. (President)

O

L-97
Sirodakara, Gajeśa Sadaśiva.
Marāṭhī-Portugīja Sabdasaṅgraha. Nāya-baṅdara, Sadānanda, 1912.

O

L-98
Sleeman, William Henry, 1788-1856.
Ramaseeana: or, a vocabulary of the peculiar language used by the thugs, with an introduction and appendix, descriptive of the system pursued by that fraternity and of the measures which have been adopted by the supreme government of India for its suppression. Calcutta, G.H. Huttmann, Military Orphan Press, 1836. 792p.

    1. Thugs.

u

O

L-99
Sojwal, Madhukar Ramchandra, 1923-
English Marathi theological glossary. Poona, 1966. 128p.

NR

O

L-100
Stevenson, John, 1798-1858.
Comparative vocabulary of non-Sanskrit primitives in the vernacular languages of India, pt.II, ASBJ, v.4,no.17 (1853), pp. 319-39.

Pune

O

L-101
Stevenson, John, 1798-1858.
A comparative vocabulary of the non-Sanskrit vocables of the vernacular languages of India, pt.I, ASBJ, v.4,no.15 (1852), pp.117-31.

O

L-102
Students' English and Marathi dictionary, with syllables, accents, phrases, appendix, etc. Bombay, D.V.Sadhale & co., 1900. 453p.

IOL

O

L-103
    Suryanarayana Rao, V.
      An English Marathi vocabulary. Madras, G.W.
    Taylor, 1893. 132p.

OC v.7

L-104
    Talekar, Shrikrishna Raghunathshastri, 1826-
    1880.
    A school dictionary; English and Marathi.
    4th ed. Bombay, Govt.Central Book Depot, 1874.
    389p.

      1. Marathi language - Dictionaries - English.

U M R

L-105
    Tulpule, Shankar Gopal, 1914-
      Two glossarial works, JTSML, v.10 (1955),
    pp.3-8.

      1. Akārādi Prākṛta Bhāshā-Nighantu and Bhāshā-
Prakāsh by Rama Kavi.

JTSML

L-106
    Vaze, Shridhar Ganesh.
      The Arya-Bhusan school dictionary, Marathi-
    English, specially intended for the use of
    students in high schools. Bombay, 1928.
    579p.

L-107
    Virkar, H.A.
      The popular modern dictionary (English-
    English-Marathi). 2d rev.ed. Bombay, Edu-
    cational Pub.Co., 1965. 912p.

LC

L-108
    Virkar, Krishnaji Bhaskar.
      The student's concise modern dictionary.
    English into English and Marathi. Bombay,
    1938. 936p.

IOL

Etymology & words studies

L-109
    Avalikar, Dattatreya Narhar, 1931-
      Some Kannada words in old Marathi, JKU,
    v.5 (1961), pp.148-52.

JKU '61

L-110
    Harshe, Ramkrishna Ganesh, 1900-
      Some sumero Marathi correspondences, BDCRI,
    v.14 (1952), pp.16-32.

BDCRI

L-111
    Joshi, C.N.
      A few thoughts on Kanarese and some other
    words from Jñāneśvar, AIOCPT, v.7 (1933),
    pp.937-50.

L-112
    Karandikar, Maheshwar Anant, 1909-
      The elements of Marathi vocabulary. Bombay,
    Univ.of Bombay, 1940. *

L-113
Katre, Lalita S.
Konkani kinship terms, IL, v.31 (1970),
pp.145-61.

Language & linguistics
BAS 1970

L-114
Katre, Sumitra Mangesh, 1906-
"Cheap" vs. "dear" in Konkani, IL, v.25
(1964), p.264.

JAS 4/68

L-115
Katre, Sumitra Mangesh, 1906-
A comparative etymological index to "Formation of Konkani", BDCRI, v.3 (1941), pp.291-
348.

BDCRI

L-116
Katre, Sumitra Mangesh, 1906-
Marathi and Gujarati words for 'week'. In:
Munshi Indological felicitation volume. A
volume of Indological studies by eminent
scholars of India and other countries presented to Dr.K.M.Munshi on his completion
of 75 years in December 1962. Bombay,
1963. p.395.

SOAS xerox

L-117
Katre, Sumitra Mangesh, 1906-
Notes on Marathi etymology, NIA, v.1 (1938),
pp.399-403.

NIA

L-118
Katre, Sumitra Mangesh, 1906-
On some kinship terms in Konkani. In:
Studies in Indian linguistics; Professor
M.B.Emeneau Sastipurti volume. Ed.by
Bhadriraju Krishnamurti. Annamalainagar,
Centres of Advanced Study in Linguistics,
Deccan College, Poona Univ.and Annamalai
Univ., 1968. pp.164-65.

u of R

L-119
Katre, Sumitra Mangesh, 1906-
On the caste name Naito in Konkani, BSOAS,
v.20 (1957), pp.365-66.

Etymology
Fuller

L-120
Kelkar, Ashok Ramchandra, 1929-
Marathi kinship terms: a lexicographical
study, TLCD, (1962), pp.1-22.

L-121
Master, Alfred, 1883-
Kolt or Dharalo, etc., BSOAS, v.9 (1937-
1939), pp.1009-1013.

BSOAS

L-122
Panse, Murlidhar Gajanan, 1918-
Old Marathi Avasvara and Vedic Avasvr,
BDCRI, v.18 (1957), pp.47-54.

JAS

L-123
    Patil, Gajanan M.
        Persian 'Mavis' in Marathi, IL, v.19
    (1958), pp.169-71.

L-128
    Apte, Mahadeo Laxman.
        The nominal endocentric constructions in
    Marathi. In: Studies in Indian linguistics;
    Professor M.B.Emeneau Ṣaṣṭipūrti volume.
    Ed.by Bhadriraju Krishnamurti. Annamalai-
    nagar, Centres of Advanced Study in
    Linguistics, Deccan College, Poona Univ.
    and Annamalai Univ., 1968. pp.20-29.

L-124
    Patwardhan, Madhav Trimbak, 1894-1939.
        Persian and Arabic words in Marathi, AIOCPT,
    v.1 (1919), pp.461-70.

L-129
    Apte, Mahadeo Laxman.
        A sketch of Marathi transformational
    grammar. Madison, Univ.of Wisconsin,
    1962.

L-125
    Raeside, Ian.
        Marathi kinship terms: a lexicographical
    study, Lingua, v.13 (1964), pp.75-76.

L-130
    Beames, John, 1837-1902.
        A comparative grammar of the modern Aryan
    languages of India: to wit, Hindi, Panjabi,
    Sindhi, Gujarati, Marathi, Oriiya and Ben-
    gali. Delhi, Munshiram Manoharlal, 1966.
    3 vols.

        1. Indo-Aryan langauges, Modern - Grammar.

L-126
    Rao, H.Narain.
        Etymological research in Kanarese and
    Marathi, ASBJ, v.25,no.73 (1917-21),
    pp.491-97.

L-131
    Bellairs, Henry Spencer Kenrick and Askhed-
    kar, Laxman Yadava.
        A grammar of the Marathi language. Bombay,
    Education Society's Press, 1868. 90p.

Grammar

L-127
    Agarkar, Gopal Ganesh, 1856-1895.
        Inquiry into the nature of sentences with
    analysis of them. Poona, Hari Narayan
    Gokhale, 1888. 120p.

L-132
    Burgess, Ebenezer, 1805-1870.
        Grammar of the Marathi language. Bombay,
    American Mission Press, 1854. 190p.

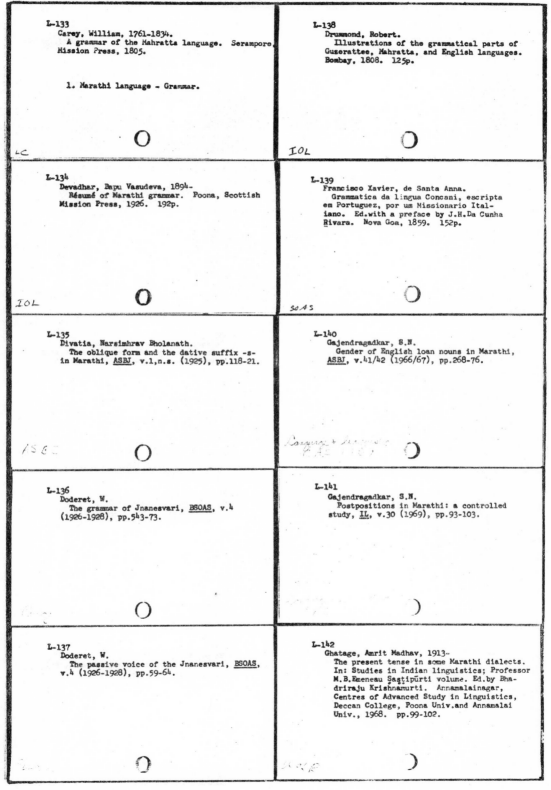

L-133
    Carey, William, 1761-1834.
      A grammar of the Mahratta language. Serampore, Mission Press, 1805.

    1. Marathi language - Grammar.

LC

L-134
    Devadhar, Bapu Vasudeva, 1894-
      Résumé of Marathi grammar. Poona, Scottish Mission Press, 1926. 192p.

IOL

L-135
    Divatia, Narsimhrav Bholanath.
      The oblique form and the dative suffix -s- in Marathi, ASBJ, v.1,n.s. (1925), pp.118-21.

ISBS

L-136
    Doderet, W.
      The grammar of Jnanesvari, BSOAS, v.4 (1926-1928), pp.543-73.

L-137
    Doderet, W.
      The passive voice of the Jnanesvari, BSOAS, v.4 (1926-1928), pp.59-64.

L-138
    Drummond, Robert.
      Illustrations of the grammatical parts of Guzerattee, Mahratta, and English languages. Bombay, 1808. 125p.

IOL

L-139
    Francisco Xavier, de Santa Anna.
      Grammatica da lingua Concani, escripta em Portuguez, por um Missionario Italiano. Ed.with a preface by J.H.Da Cunha Rivara. Nova Goa, 1859. 152p.

SOAS

L-140
    Gajendragadkar, S.N.
      Gender of English loan nouns in Marathi, ASBJ, v.41/42 (1966/67), pp.268-76.

L-141
    Gajendragadkar, S.N.
      Postpositions in Marathi: a controlled study, IL, v.30 (1969), pp.93-103.

L-142
    Ghatage, Amrit Madhav, 1913-
      The present tense in some Marathi dialects. In: Studies in Indian linguistics; Professor M.B.Emeneau Ṣaṣṭipūrti volume. Ed.by Bhadriraju Krishnamurti. Annamalainagar, Centres of Advanced Study in Linguistics, Deccan College, Poona Univ.and Annamalai Univ., 1968. pp.99-102.

L-143
Godbole, Krishna Shastri, 1831-1886.
   A new grammar of the Marathi language.
2d ed. Bombay, Ganpat Krishnaji's Press,
1874. 362p.

   1. Marathi language - Grammar.

NYPL

L-144
Grammatica da lingua concani no dialecto
   do norte, composta no secula XVII, por
   hum missionario portuguez (with a
   preface by J.H.da Cunha Rivara). Nova
   Goa, Imprensa Nacional, 1858. 188p.

SOAS

L-145
Joshi, Krishnaji Keshav, 1881-1933.
   Declension of nouns in Marathi as seen
in Dnyaneshwar's works. Inaugural
Dissertation...der...Universität Würzburg
zur Erlangung der Doktorwürde...Februar
1914, von Krishnaji Joshi. Leipzig,
G.Kreysing, 1914. 56p.

   1. Marathi language-grammar.

VVV SOAS

L-146
Joshi, Ramachandra Bhikaji.
   A comprehensive Marathi grammar. 1st English
ed. Poona, Aryabhushan Press, 1900. 568p.

L-147
Kelkar, Ashok Ramchandra, 1929-
   The category of case in Marathi study in
method. IL, v.20 (1959), pp.131-39.

Pattanayak.

L-148
Kelkar, Ashok Ramchandra, 1929-
   Marathi baby talk, Word, v.20 (1964), pp.40-
54.

gql '66

L-149
Kelkar, Ashok Ramchandra, 1929-
   Marathi English: a study in foreign accent,
Word, v.13 (1957), pp.268-282.

L-150
Kelkar, Ashok Ramchandra, 1929-
   The phonology and morphology of Marathi.
Ithaca, Cornell Univ., 1958. 207p. *

4 gR

L-151
Kelkar, Gopal Jivaji.
   Handbook of the Marathi grammar. Bombay,
Asiatic Society, 1875.

L-152
Konow, Sten, 1867-
   Note on the past tense in Marathi, RASGBIJ,
n.s., pt.2 (1902), pp.417-21.

RASGBIJ

L-153
Leddu, Tukarama Krishna.
    Genitive-accusative in Marathi, RASGHIJ,
(1911), pp.819-21.

L-154
Lesny, Vincenc.
    The construction of genitive-accusative in
Marathi, RASGHIJ, ser.3 (1910), pp.481-84.

L-155
Lesny, Vincenc.
    Further note on the genitive-accusative
construction in Marathi, RASGHIJ, ser.3
(1911), pp.179-82.

Deccan Coll. v.9-10

L-156
Maffei, Angelus Francis Xavier.
    A Konkani grammar. Mangalore, Basel Mission
Press, 1882.

Cal + at Pub

L-157
Makba, Mohammed Ibrahim.
    A grammar of the Mahratta language. Bombay,
Courier, 1825.

L-158
Master, Alfred, 1883-
    A grammar of old Marathi. Oxford, Clarendon
Press, 1964. 186p.

4 of R

L-159
Master, Alfred, 1883-
    Some parallelisms in Indo-Aryan and
Dravidian with special reference to Marathi,
Gujarati and Kanarese, ASBJ, n.s.,v.5 (1929),
pp.95-140; v.8 (1932), pp.29-68.

L-160
Modi, Jivanji Jamshedji, 1854-1933.
    The baby language among the Parsees, JASB,
v.13 (1926), pp.410-11.

Surer

L-161
Morais, Graciano.
    Gramatica Concani; sintaxe Kônkanni veakoro:n:
vakiorochna. Lisboa, Agência-Geral do Ultramar,
1961. 389p.

LC

L-162
Nadkarni, Mangesh Vithal.
    NP-embedded structures in Kannada and
Konkani. Los Angeles, Univ.of California,
1970. 320p. *

Shulman #652

L-163
    Navalkar, Ganpatrao Raghunath, 1837-1912.
    The analysis and synthesis of Marathi sen-
    tences. Bombay, Mistry Printing Works, 1900.
    24p.

Rom (Prec) cat (

L-164
    Navalkar, Ganpatrao Raghunath, 1837-1912.
    An introduction to Marathi grammar. Bombay,
    Education Society Press, 1891.

(

L-165
    Navalkar, Ganpatrao Raghunathi, 1837-1912.
    Lectures on some peculiar Marathi grammati-
    cal forms. Kolhapur, 1912.

(

L-166
    Patil, Gajanan M.
    Adverbial compounds in Marathi, JMaU, v.1,
    no.1 (1961), pp.83-87.

(

L-167
    Patwardhan, Madhav Trimbak, 1894-1939.
    Chhandorachana; an investigation into the
    fundamentals of Marathi metrics and of allied
    subjects and a compilation of metres brought
    up to date. Bombay, Bombay University, 1938.*

(

L-168
    Pereira, Jose.
    Gaspar de S.Miguel O.F.M.Arte de Lingoa
    Canarim Parte 2a Sintaxis Copiosissima na
    lingoa bramana e polida, a syntax of standard
    Konkani, JUB, v.36,pt.2 (1967), pp.1-155.

lang & ling. article (
BAS 1969

L-169
    Phadke, Gangadarshastri.
    Grammar of Marathi language. Bombay, Ganpat
    Krishnaji, 1849.

Pattarayak (

L-170
    Pires, Phillipe Neri.
    Grammatica Maratha, explicada em lingua
    Portugueza compilada das mais abalizadas
    que ate o presente se tem dado a luz.
    Bombaim, Na typographia da missao Americana,
    1854. 137p.

Cal Nat. Lib (

L-171
    Raeside, Ian.
    The Marathi compound verb, IL, v.19 (1958),
    pp.237-48.

IL (

L-172
    Saldanha, Mariano.
    História de gramática concani, BSOAS,
    v.8 (1936), pp.715-35.

(

L-173
Sidgwick, L.J.
The genitive-accusative construction in
Marathi, RASGBIJ, (1911), p.821.

L-178
Vale, Ramchandra Narayan.
An introduction to verbal composition in
Marathi, AIOCPT, v.13 (1946), pp.224-27.

11 of R

L-174
Southworth, Franklin C., 1922-
The Marathi verbal sequences and their
co-occurences, Language, v.37 (1961), pp.
201-208.

L-179
Vale, Ramchandra Narayan.
Kriyāsamāsas in Marāthi, EDCRI, v.22
(1961-1962), pp.175-99.

9°244

L-175
Stephens, Thomas.
Grammatica da lingua Concani, composta
pelo padre T.Estevao, e accrescentada por
outros padres da Companhia de Jesus. Secunda
impressão...annotada: a que precede como
introducçao a memoria sobre a distribuição
geographica das principaes linguas da India
por Sir E.Perry, e o Ensaio historico da
Lingua Concani pelo editor, J.H.da Cunha Rivara. Nova-Goa, 1857. 539p.

BM SOAS

L-180
Vale, Ramchandra Narayan.
Verbal composition in modern Indo-Aryan.
Poona, Deccan College, 1948. (Deccan College
dissertation series, 6) 336p.

L-176
Stevenson, John, 1798-1858.
Observations on the grammatical structure
of the vernacular languages of India, ASBJ,
v.3 (1849), pp.71-76; v.3 (1850), pp.1-7;
v.3 (1851), pp.196-202; v.4 (1852), pp.15-20.

Pinge

L-181
Velankar, Hari Damodar, 1893-
Apabhramśa and Marathi metres, NIA, (1938),
pp.215-28.

Annual bib of ling ling 1938

L-177
Stevenson, John, 1798-1858.
The principles of Murathee grammar. 3d ed.
Bombay, Collett & co., 1850. 185p.

SOAS

L-182
Wilberforce-Bell, Harold, 1885-
Grammatical treatise of the Marathi language.
Bombay. Tract and Book Society, 1914.

History

L-183
Abhyankar, K.V.
Mahārāṣṭrī Prākrit, APORI, v.36 (1955),
pp.373-76.

L-184
Apte, H.N.
Marathi: its sources and development. Wilson
philological lectures, 1915. Poona, Aryabhushan, 1922.

L-185
Ballantine, Henry.
On the relations of the Marathi to the
Sanskrit, JAOS, v.3 (1853), pp.367-85.

L-186
Chauhan, D.V.
Origin of the consecutive conjunction ki
in Marathi: an historical search, IL, v.30
(1969), pp.85-89.

Lang + ling - articles
BAS 1970

L-187
Da Cunha, Joseph Gerson, 1842-1900.
The Konkani language and literature.
Bombay, Govt.Central Press, 1881. 51p.

LC

L-188
Doderet, W.
Further light on the archaic Marathi आ
genitive, BSOAS, v.5 (1928-1930), pp.251-52.

BSOAS

L-189
Ghatage, Amrit Madhav, 1913-
Maharashtri language and literature, JUB,
v.4 (1936), pp.19-70.

JUB

L-190
Ghatage, Amrit Madhav, 1913-
Narrative literature in Jain Maharastri,
ABORI, v.16 (1934-35), pp.26-43.

ABORI

L-191
Gokhale, Vasudeo Damodar.
Sanskrit loan words in Marathi. Poona,
Deccan College Postgraduate and Research
Institute, 1957. *

Jeyakar Lib

L-192
Jahagirdar, R.V.
Kanarese influence on old Marathi with
special reference to Jnanesvari, ABORI,
v.11 (1930), pp.374-97.

ABORI

L-193
Kelkar, S.V.
Marathi terminology used in the teaching of geometry; some thoughts, JAS, v.37 (1963), pp.250-52, 249.

JAS '63

L-194
Konow, Sten, 1867-
Maharashtri and Marathi, IA, v.32 (1903), pp.180-92.

Pinge

L-195
Kulkarni, K.B.
Text books in Marathi in the 19th century, their authors and their effects on the structure of the Marathi language. Bombay, Univ.of Bombay, 1953. *

Case

L-196
Kulkarni, S.B.
An experiment in estimating transfer of information among some Marathi dialects, IL, v.30 (1969), pp.73-76.

languages & linguistics
BAS 1970

L-197
Master, Alfred, 1883-
The development of the Marathi language up to A.D.1300. London, Oxford Univ., 1961-1962. *

Q.5JS5

L-198
Meersman, Achilles.
Gaspar de São Miguel - a Konkani scholar, Indica, v.6 (1969), pp.101-104.

Indica

L-199
Mirashi, Vasudev Vishnu, 1893-
The original name of the Gathasaptaśati, AIOCPT, v.13 (1946), pp.370-74.

UoR

L-200
Saldanha, Jerome Anthony.
Origin of the Konkani people and language, QJMS, v.16 (1926), pp.233-39.

QJMS

L-201
Sastri, P.Seshadri.
A note on the Saptasati of Hala, IHCP, v.10 (1947), pp.195-96.

IHCP

L-202
Soares, Anthony X.
The Portuguese heritage to the East or the influence of Portuguese on the languages of the East with special reference to the languages of the Bombay Presidency, ASBJ, v.26 (1921-23), pp.11-39.

ASBJ

L-203
　Tulpule, Shankar Gopal, 1914-
　　Marathi element in three pre-Gommata plates,
　　JUP, v.7 (1956), pp.1-13.

JUP

L-208
　Wilson, John.
　　Indian comparative philology. Notes on
　　the constituent elements, the diffusion and
　　the application of the Marathi language...,
　　BQR, v.7,no.13 (1858), pp.26-55.

Phrase books, proverbs

L-204
　Tulpule, Shankar Gopal, 1914-
　　A philological study of old Marathi in
　　Yadav period. Bombay, Univ.of Bombay, 1940.

L-209
　Apte, Vasudeo Govind, 1871-1930.
　　Idioms and proverbs in Marathi language.
　　Poona, G.Ramchandra, 1910.

L-205
　Upadhye, A.N.
　　Marathi elements in a Prakrit drama, IL,
　　v.16 (1955), pp.147-52.

L-210
　Bombay (Presidency) Educational Department.
　　A collection of English phrases, by
　　H.Green...with their idiomatic Marathi
　　equivalents. Bombay, 1879. 2d ed.

IOL

L-206
　Vaidya, Visvanath P.
　　Gujarati in relation to Marathi, AIOCPT,
　　v.7 (1933), pp.1075-83.

L-211
　Chavan, Viththal Pandurang.
　　The Konkani proverbs. Bombay, Ramchandra
　　Govind Ani Mandali, 1928.

Kart

L-207
　Vyas, Kantilal Baldevram, 1910-
　　Intimate borrowing between Gujarati and
　　Marathi, JGRS, v.20 (1958), pp.1-6.

L-212
　Chavan, Viththal Pandurang.
　　Proverbs in Konkani language, JASBen, v.13
　　(1924-27), p.297, 497-583.

Sen Gupta

L-213
Dalgado, Sabastião Rodolpho, 1855-1922.
Florilegio de Proverbios Concanis; tradu-
sidos, explicados, comentados e comparados
com os de linguas asiáticas e europeias.
Coimbra, Imprensa da Universidade, 1922.
355p.

NYR
NYPL

L-218
Ballantyne, James Robert, 1813-1864.
A grammar of the Mahratta language. For the
use of the East India College at Hayleybury.
London, sold by J.Madden & co., 1839. 53p.

L-214
Konow, Sten, 1867-
A Marathi idiom. IL, v.4 (1934), pp.545-
52.

IL

L-219
Belsare, Dattatraya Malhar.
The romanized Marathi and Hindustani self-
helper; or a manual of four languages: English,
Marathi, Hindustani and German. Bombay, 1909.
85p.

SOAS

L-215
Manwaring, Alfred, comp. & tr.
Marathi proverbs. Oxford, The Clarendon
Press, 1899. 271p.

LC

L-220
Bhide, Ganesa Hari.
Marathi-English primer, part I. 2d ed.
Bombay, the author, Induprakasha, 1901.
157p.

SOAS

L-216
Mule, G.S.
Handbook of Marathi phrases and proverbs
explained in English. Bombay, the author,
1911.

Kirk.

L-221
Bombay (Presidency) Educational Department.
Idiomatic sentences, English and Marathi.
By Thomas Candy. Bombay, 1876.

IOL

L-217
Pendase, Sitarama Vasudeva, d.1931.
A companion to the study of Marathi.
Marathi proverbs and phrases with English
equivalents. Baroda, Vyapari Press, 1911.

Marathi Council...

L-222
Damle, Kamalini.
Teaching of Marathi and phonetics, PE,
v.40 (1966), pp.291-96.

L-223
Darby, Alfred.
A primer of the Marathi language, for the use of adults. 3d ed. Bombay, Tatva-Vivechaka Press, 1933. 229p.

BM

L-224
Easy lessons in reading with an English and Marathi vocabulary. Bombay, 1851. 217p.

IOL

L-225
Fairbank, Edward.
A start in Marathi. 3d ed. Poona, 1922. 234p.

BM

L-226
Godbole, N.T.
English Marathi reading series. Poona, 1933. 31p.

IOL

L-227
Kanitkar, B.M.
Marathi without tears: a book of self instruction in Marathi. Poona, International Book Service, 1952. 122p.

4 of R

L-228
Kavadi, Naresh Bhikaji, 1922-   and Southworth, Franklin C., 1922-
Spoken Marathi. Book 1: First-year intensive course. Philadelphia, Univ.of Pennsylvania, 1965. 252p.

1. Marathi language - Spoken Marathi.

4 3 R

L-229
Kher, Appaji Kasinatha, d.1903.
A higher Anglo-Marathi grammar. 2d ed. Bombay, Education Society's Press, 1899. 870p.

BM

L-230
Lambert, Hester Marjorie.
Marathi language course. Calcutta, Oxford Univ.Press, 1943.

MGS

L-231
Marathi grammar explained in English. Bombay, D.V.Sadhale & co., 1891. 119p.

IOL

L-232
Navalkar, Ganpatrao Raghunathi, 1837-1912.
Student's Marathi grammar. 3d ed. Bombay, 1894. 388p.

BM

L-233
Patankar, Kamal Arvind.
Teaching Marathi as a regional language
to non-Marathi speaking pupils studying in
standard III in Anglo-Indian and the English
schools in the city of Bombay and its neighbourhood: a critical study of the present
plan, the course and the books prescribed.
Bombay, Univ.of Bombay, 1965. *

Elementary education O

L-234
Seddon, Charles Norman, 1870-
An elementary Marathi grammar for English
beginners. Bombay, H.Milford, Oxford Univ.
Press, 1931. 70p.

LC O

L-235
Tulpule, Shankar Gopal, 1914-   ed.
An old Marathi reader. With grammatical in-
troduction, English trans., notes and glossary.
Poona, Venus Prakashana, 1960. 278p.

U of R O

L-236
Wilson, John, 1804-1875.
Idiomatical exercises, illustrative of the
phraseology and structure of the English and
Marathi languages. 2d ed. Bombay, 1839.
330p.

Literature		Drama	

L-237
Bhate, Govind Chimnaji, 1870-
A modern Marathi dramatist (Ram Ganesh
Gadkari), AL, n.s.,v.2 (1929), pp.106-10.

zelliot O

L-238
Nadkarni, Jnaneshvar Ganpat, 1928-
Modern Marathi drama, UA, v.10 (1958),
pp.116-19.

Jas O

L-239
Nadkarni, Jnaneshvar Ganpat, 1928-
The temperament of Marathi drama, SH, v.2
(1966), pp.63-73.

zelliot O

L-240
Naik, B.S.
A century of Marathi drama, MP, v.1,no.2
(1968), pp.19-24.

zelliot O

L-241
Yajnik, Ramanlal Kanaiylal, 1895-
The influence of British drama on the
Indian stage, with reference to western
India. London, London University, 1931-32.

Bloomfield		Fiction	

L-242
Apte, Mahadeo Laxman.
Contemporary Marathi fiction: obscenity or
realism?, JAS, v.29,no.1 (1969), pp.55-66.

BAS 1969

L-243
Chitre, Dilip.
Alienation in four Marathi novels, HumR,
v.1,no.2 (1969), pp.161-75.

L-244
Deshpande, Nirmala, 1929-
Chingling. 1st ed. Rajghat, Sarva Seva Sangh
Prakashan, 1966. 244p.

U a/R

L-245
Gokhale, Balkrishna Govind, 1919-
Shivaram Mahadeo Paranjape: nationalism
and the uses of the past, JIH, v.48 (1970),
pp.259-74.

L-246
Karandikar, Maheshwar Anant, 1909-
Hari Narayan Apte. New Delhi, National
Book Trust, India, 1968. (National
Biography series). 91p.

L-247
Krasnodembskaya, N.G., ed.
Zamorskaya kuritsa. Novellui pisatelei
Macharashtrui. A collection of stories by
writers of Maharashtra; translated into
Russian from Marathi by various translators.
Compiled and edited by N.G.Krasnodembskaya.
Moskva, Izdatel'stvo Nauka, 1967.
(Institut narodov Azii: AN SSSR). 120p.

L-248
Kulkarni, Hemant.
Hari Narayan Apte. Hyderabad, Marathi Sahitya
Parishad, Andhra Pradesh, 1965. 31p.

L-249
Madgulkar, Vyankatesh Digambar, 1927-
The village had no walls. Trans.by Ram
Deshmukh from the Marathi novel Bangarwadi.
N.Y., Asia Pub.House, 1958. 170p.

L-250
Pendse, Shripad Narayan, 1913-
Wild Bapu of Garambi. Garambica Bapu.By
Shripad Narayan Pendse. Trans.from the Marathi
by Ian Raeside. New Delhi, Sahitya Akademi,
1969. (UNESCO collection of representative
works. Indian series). 264p.

L-251
Pundlik, Vidyadhar.
Post-1945 revolutions in the Marathi novel,
IWT, v.3,no.1 (1964), pp.47-50.

L-252
Raeside, Ian.
Early prose fiction in Marathi, 1828-1885,
JAS, v.27 (1968), pp.791-808.

L-253
Rege, Purushottam Shivram, 1910-
Savitri and Avalokitā. Trans.by Kumud
Mehta. Bombay, Thacker and Co., 1969.
174p.

L-254
Sardesai, Gargi.
V.S.Khandekar: a social humanist, ILit,
v.11 (1968), pp.92-97.

L-255
Tikekar, Shripad Ramchandra, 1900-
Swami-a discussion of Ranjit Desai's novel,
IP.E.N., v.33 (1967), pp.39-41.

History & crit.

L-256
Altekar, M.D.
Marathi. In: The Indian literatures of
today: a symposium. Ed.by Bharatan Kuma-
rappa. Bombay, International Book House,
1957. pp.105-12.

L-257
Bedekar, Dinkar Keshav, 1910-
Contemporary Marathi literature, IWT, v.1,
no.2 (1967), pp.49-54.

L-258
Bedekar, Dinkar Keshav, 1910-
Five Mahabharata studies, IWT, v.2,no.4
(1968), pp.24-29.

L-259
Bedekar, Dinkar Keshav, 1910-
Marathi: widening the mental horizon, ILit,
v.9,no.4 (1966), pp.66-71.

L-260
Bhate, Govind Chimnaji, 1870-
History of modern Marathi literature, 1800-
1939. Poona, Aryabhushan Press. 1939. 753p.

L-261
Bhave, Sadashiv S.
Marathi: some good books, nothing spectacular,
(Survey of 1967), ILit, v.11,no.4 (1968), pp.
60-65.

L-262
Bruce, Henry James.
The literary work of the American Marathi
Mission 1813-1881. Bombay, Education Society's
Press, 1882. 76p.

L-263
   Dandekar, V.P.
     Literature and drama; Marathi. In:
   Modern India and the West; a study of
   the interaction of their civilizations.
   Ed. by L.S.S.O'Malley. London, Oxford
   University Press, 1941. pp.498-505.

HofR

L-264
   Davtar, Vasant.
     The literary scene in Marathi in 1968,
   ILit, v.13,no.2 (1970), pp.67-75.

literature-articles
BAS 1970

L-265
   Deshmukh, Mahadeo Gopal, 1913-
     An investigation of the principles of
   poetics underlying the works of the chief
   Saint-Poets in Maharashtra from Jñaneshwar
   to Ramdas. Nagpur, Nagpur Univ., 1941. *

Lit PhD Thesis

L-266
   Deshpande, J.S.
     Notes on research in ancient Marathi
   literature, ASBJ, v.43/44 (1968/69), pp.
   119-22.

BAS 1970

L-267
   Deshpande, Kusumavati, 1904-
     Marathi. In: Indian literature: short
   critical surveys of twelve major Indian
   languages and literatures. Ed. by Nagendra.
   Agra, Lakshmi Narain Agarwal, 1959. pp.
   233-94.

Zelliot ....

L-268
   Deshpande, Kusumavati, 1904-
     Marathi literature. In: Literatures in
   the modern languages. Ed. by Vinayak Krishna
   Gokak. New Delhi, Ministry of Broadcasting
   and Information, 1957. pp.223-34.

Zelliot

L-269
   Deshpande, Kusumavati, 1904-
     Marathi sahitya; review of the Marathi
   literature up to 1960. New Delhi,
   Maharashtra Information Center, 1966. 107p.

PL 470/... p 8
Uof Reader

L-270
   Deshpande, Kusumavati, 1904-
     Tagore and the Marathi literature, CIL,
   v.2 (1962), pp.6-7.

JAS '65

L-271
   Dixit, M.S.
     Marathi literature in 1961, CIL, v.2
   (1962), pp.6-7.

JAS'65

L-272
   Gode, Parashuram Krishna, 1891-
     References to tobacco in Marathi literature
   and records between A.D.1600 and 1900, PO,
   v.20 (1955), pp.20-30.

JAS 56

L-273
Gokhale, D.N.
Dr. S.V.Ketkar: a study, <u>JUP</u>, v.1 (1953),
pp.167-71.

Case

L-278
Kulkarni, Waman Lakshman, 1911-
Little reviews in Marathi, <u>IWT</u>, v.3,no.4
(1969), pp.33-43.

Literature
BAS 1970

L-274
Hatkanagalekar, M.D.
New trends in Marathi criticism, <u>IWT</u>, v.2,
no.3 (1968), pp.37-43.

u of R

L-279
Lad, Shrikant.
Trends in Marathi literature, <u>CIL</u>, v.7
(1967), pp.7-8, 23-26.

JAS 9/68

L-275
Kulkarni, Krishnaji Pandurang, 1893-
Presidential address, <u>AIOCPT</u>, v.13 (1946),
pp.203-15.

marathi literature

U of R

L-280
Lamshukov, V.K.
On the periodization of Marathi literature,
<u>NAA</u>, v.2 (1965), pp.111-18.

CIiL

L-276
Kulkarni, V.D.
New trends in Marathi literary criticism,
<u>IWT</u>, v.2,no.3 (1968), pp.44-52.

u of R

L-281
Machwe, Prabhakar Balvant, 1917-
1857 and Indian literature, <u>ILit</u>, v.1
(1957), pp.53-59.

Case

L-277
Kulkarni, Waman Lakshman, 1911-
Humour in modern Marathi literature, <u>JMaU</u>,
v.4,no.1 (1963), pp.27-36.

JMaU

L-282
Machwe, Prabhakar Balvant, 1917-
Modern Marathi literature, <u>IFR</u>, v.3
(1966), pp.14-15.

JAS '66

L-283
   Marathi literature, MarI, v.11 (1959), pp.42-45, 47.

L-284
   Mehta, Kumud A.
      Shakespeare's Marathi translators, ASBJ, v.41/42 (1966/67), pp.241-50.

L-285
   Mitchell, John Murray, 1815-1904.
      Marathi works composed by the Portuguese, ASBJ, Pt.I, v.3,no.12 (1849), pp.132-57.

L-286
   Mukherjee, B.A.
      Marathi literature and its present needs, HR, v.68 (1936), pp.665-71.

L-287
   Nadkarni, Jnaneshvar Ganpat, 1928-
      Consolidation of earlier gains, a review of Marathi writing in 1966, ILit, v.10 (1967), pp.49-55.

L-288
   Nadkarni, Jnaneshvar Ganpat, 1928-
      Marathi ("on stage"), Seminar, no.32 (1962), pp.28-31.

L-289
   Nadkarni, Jnaneshvar Ganpat, 1928-
      Marathi literature: a review of current Indian writing, ILit, v.1 (1957), pp.65-136.

L-290
   Nadkarni, Jnaneshvar Ganpat, 1928-
      Marathi literature: a review of current Indian writing, ILit, v.6 (1963), pp.100-103.

L-291
   Nadkarni, Jnaneshvar Ganpat, 1928-
      Marathi literature [1962], ILit, v.6 (1963), pp.100-105.

L-292
   Nadkarni, Jnaneshvar Ganpat, 1928-
      Marathi literature (survey of 1963), ILit, v.7 (1964), pp.64-70.

L-293
Nadkarni, Jnaneshvar Ganpat, 1928–
Marathi writer and his commitment, Quest,
no.39 (1963), pp.32-42.

L-298
Pradhan, G.P., 1922–
Marathi literature, ILit, v.3,no.1 (1959-
60), pp.78-84.

L-294
Nadkarni, Jnaneshvar Ganpat, 1928–
The Marathi writer and the film, IP.E.N.,
v.30 (1964), pp.304-309.

L-299
Priolkar, Anant Kakba, 1897–
Old literature in various dialects of
Marathi, JUB, n.s.,v.30 (1961), pp.106-17.

L-295
Nadkarni, Jnaneshvar Ganpat, 1928–
Modern trends in Marathi literature,
IP.E.N., v.28 (1962), pp.167-69.

L-300
Priolkar, Anant Kakba, 1897–   and
Deshpande, Kusumavati, 1904–
Marathi literature, MarI, v.3,no.3 (1959),
pp.42-45,47.

L-296
Panse, Murlidhar Gajanan, 1918–
Rajwade; text of Sripati's Jyotisa-Ratna-
Mala?, BDCRI, v.14 (1952), pp.195-207.

L-301
Rajadhyaksha, Mangesh Vitthal, 1913–
Marathi literature. In: Contemporary Indian
literature, a symposium. Delhi, Sahitya
Akademi, 1957. pp.150-70.

L-297
Panse, Murlidhar Gajanan, 1918–
Sripati's Marathi commentary on his own
Jyotisa-ratna-mala. In: P.K.Gode Commem-
oration volume 3. Ed.by the late Dr.H.L.
Hariyappa...&Dr.M.M.Patkar. Poona, Oriental
Book Agency, 1960. (Poona oriental series,
no.93). pp.151-56.

L-302
Rajadhyaksha, Mangesh Vitthal, 1913–
Shakespeare in Marathi, ILit, v.7 (1964),
pp.83-94.

L-303
Ranade, Mahadev Govind, 1842-1901.
A note on the growth of Marathi literature,
ASBJ, v.20 (1897-1900), pp.78-105.

Case

L-304
Ranade, Ramachandra Dattatraya, 1866-1957.
Pathway to God in Marathi literature.
Bombay, Bharatiya Vidya Bhavan, 1961.
(Bhavan's book university, 89). 337p.

V of R

L-305
Ranganathan, Shiyali Ramamrita, 1892-
Classification of Marathi literature.
Poona, N.K.Pub.House, 1945. (Kaikhushru
Taraporewala Memorial Series in Library
Science, no.8). 44p.

IBL

L-306
Sahasrabuddhe, Purushottam Ganesh, 1904-
The development of the art of character-
isation in Marathi (Swabhavalekhana) literature from 1865-1938. Bombay, Univ.of Bombay, 1939. *

Bib PH D thesis

L-307
Sant, D.K.
Women in Marathi literature of the British
period (1818-1947). Bombay, Univ.of Bombay,
1953. *

Case

L-308
Sardessai, Manohar.
Contemporary Konkani literature; a brief
survey, IWT, v.2,no.4 (1968), pp.16-19.

Literature articles
& 1969

L-309
Sarma, K.V.
Raghunatha Navahasta and his contribution to
Sanskrit and Marathi literature, VIJ, v.7
(1969), pp.69-82.

L-310
Shikhare, Damodar Narhar, 1903-
Impact of Gandhism on Marathi literature,
GM, v.4 (1960). pp.253-57. 337-42.

Case

L-311
Stevenson, John, 1798-1858.
An essay on the vernacular literature of
the Marathas, ASBJ, v.1 (1841), pp.1-10.

Pinge

L-312
Wammali, V.R.
Marathi literature: A review of current Indian
writing, IIdt, v.2 (1958-1959), pp.86-163.

NPu
SAS 39

Poetry

L-313
Achwal, Madhav.
Contemporary Marathi poetry, IWT, v.3,no.3 (1969), pp.28-33.

L-314
Acworth, Harry Arbuthnot, 1849-1933.
On the Marathi ballad written on the Suttee of Ramabai, widow of Madhavrao Peshwa, JASB, v.2 (1889-1892), pp.179-92.

Kirk

L-315
Acworth, Harry Arbuthnot, 1849-1933, ed.& tr.
Ballads of the Marathas, rendered into English verse from the Marathi originals.
New York, Longmans, Green, 1894. 167p.

1. Marathi ballads & songs. 2. English poetry - Trans.from Marathi. 3. Marathi poetry-Trans.from English.

NUR

L-316
Bha'u-Daji
Notes on Mukunda Raja, ASBJ, v.9,no.5 (1867-70), pp.166-67.

NRU
JRASBom

L-317
Bh'u-Daji.
Notes on the age and works of Hemadri, ASBJ, v.9,no.25 (1868), pp.158-65.

L-318
Bhave, Sadashiv S.
The new poetic idiom, IWT, v.2 (1969), pp. 62-64.

L-319
Bhave, Shrikrishna Sakharam, 1903-
The changing idiom in modern Marathi poetry, IWT, v.1,no.2 (1967), pp.19-23.

U of R

L-320
Chitre, Dilip.
A tribute to Keshavsut, Quest, no.51 (1966), pp.45-49.

Quest no.51

L-321
Chitre, Dilip, ed.
An anthology of Marathi poetry, 1945-65.
Bombay, N.Sadanand, 1967. (Centre for Indian writers. Contemporary Indian poetry, 1). 204p.

NUR

L-322
Da Gama, F.C.
Narayan Waman Tilak, poet, patriot and preacher, MR, v.112 (1962), pp.230-34.

Cace

L-323
Damale, Krshnāji Keśava, 1866-1905.
The trumpet. Trans.from the Marathi by
Sarojini and Suniti Namjoshi, PI, v.2,no.
2 (1967), pp.41-42.

L-324
Dasopanta-charitra.
Dasopant Digambar. Translation of the
Dasopant Charitra...By Justin E.Abbott.
Poona, N.R.Godbole, 1928. (The poet-
saints of Maharashtra, no.4). 194p.

L-325
Deshpande, J.S.
Notes on ancient Marathi poems, ASBJ,
v.39-40 (1964/65), pp.247-48.

L-326
Deshpande, L.V.
Cangadeva Pancasasti - a reply to Changadeo
in stanzas sixty-five by Jnanadeva, ASBJ,
v.43/44 (1968/69), pp.123-28.

L-327
Edwards, James Fairbrother.
Dnyaneshwar, the out-caste Brahmin.
Poona, United Theological College of
Western India, 1941. (The poet-saints of
Maharashtra, 12). 525p.

L-328
Ekanatha, ca.1548-ca.1609.
Bhikshugita; the mendicant's song, the
story of a converted miser; a trans.of the
23rd chapter of the Eknathi Bhagavata by
J.Abbott. Poona, Scottish mission industries,
1928. (The poet-saints of Maharashtra,
no.3). 260p.

L-329
Fraser, James Nelson, 1869-1918 and Edwards,
James Fairbrother.
The life and teachings of Tukārām. Madras,
Christian literature Society for India, 1922.
347p.

1. Tukārāma, Marathi poet, ca.1608-ca.1649.

L-330
Gadkari, Ram Ganesh.
Poems of Govindagraj [translated by]
Sarojini Namjoshi and Suniti Namjoshi.
Calcutta, Writers Workshop, 1968. 19p.

L-331
Kale, Pramod.
P.S.Rege: universal-personal, BA, v.43
(1969), pp.513-20.

L-332
Kanekar, Anant.
Post independence Indian poetry: Marathi.
In: Indian writers meet. Proceedings of
the 8th All-India Writers' Conference,
Chandigarh, 1966. Ed.by Iqbal Monani.
Bombay, The P.E.N.All-India Centre, 1966.
pp.17-24.

L-333
Kanhere, Sadashiv Govind.
Waman Pandit: scholar and Marathi poet
(17th century), BSOAS, v.4 (1927), pp.305-
14.

L-334
Kantak, S.G., tr.
Some Marathi dramatic songs. A book containing
an English rendering of some Marathi dramatic
songs. Bombay, Shree Laxmi Narayan Press,
1934. 15p.

L-335
Kincaid, Charles Augustus, 1870-
The poet Mahipati, AL, n.s.,v.2 (1928),
pp.43-49.

L-336
Machwe, Prabhakar Balvant, 1917-
Keshavsut. New Delhi, Sahitya Akademi,
1966. 64p.

L-337
Macnicol, Nicol, 1870-1952.
The Indian poetry of devotion, HJ, v.16
(1917-1918), pp.74-88.

L-338
Macnicol, Nicol, 1870-1952, tr.
Psalms of Maratha saints; one hundred
and eight hymns translated from the
Marathi. Calcutta, Association press;
London, N.Y., etc., Oxford university
press, 1920. (The heritage of India).
101p.

L-339
Mahipati, 1715-1790.
Bhanudas; translation from Mahipati's
Bhaktavijaya, chapters 42 and 43, by
Justin E.Abbott. Poona, Scottish Mission
Industries Co., ltd., 1926. (The poet-
saints of Maharashtra, no.1). 119p.

L-340
Mahipati, 1715-1790.
Eknath; a translation from the
Bhaktalilāmrta by Justin E.Abbott. Poona,
Scottish Mission Industries Co., ltd.,
1927. (The poet-saints of Maharashtra, no.2).
299p.

L-341
Mahipati, 1715-1790.
Nector from Indian saints; trans.from
Bhaktalilāmrta, by Justin E.Abbott, N.R.
Godbole, and J.F.Edwards. Poona, J.F.
Edwards, 1935. (The poet-saints of
Maharashtra, no.11)

L-342
Mahipati, 1715-1790.
Ramdas; trans.from Santavijaya by Justin
E.Abbott, and R.Godbole. Poona, N.R.Godbole,
1932. (The poet-saints of Maharashtra, no.
8) 434p.

L-343
Mahipati, 1715-1790.
Stories of Indian saints; trans.from
Bhaktavijaya, by Justin E.Abbott. Poona,
Narhar R.Godbole, 1933-34. (The poet-saints
of Maharashtra, no.9, 18) 2v.

4 7 R

L-344
Mahipati, 1715-1790.
Tukaram; trans.from Mahipati's Bhaktali-
lamrta, chapters 25-40, by Justin E.Abbott.
Poona, Scottish Mission Industries Co., ltd.,
1930. (The poet-saints of Maharashtra, no.7)
366p.

47R

L-345
Mardhekar, Bal Sitaram.
Poems. Trans.from the Marathi by Dilip
Chitre, PI, v.1,no.1 (1966), pp.49-58.

24 7 R

L-346
Mehta, Kumud A.
Creative principle in P.S.Rege, ILit, v.11
(1968), pp.97-102.

zelliot

L-347
Mitchell, John Murray, 1815-1904.
The chief Marathi poets, ICOP, v.9,pt.1
(1892), pp.782-96.

4 4 R

L-348
Nemade, Bhalchandra.
Towards a definition of modernity in modern
Marathi poetry: a perspective on contemporary
Marathi verse, Mahfil, v.6,no.2/3 (1970),
pp.71-82.

Lit- articles
BAS 1970

L-349
Padhye, Prabhakar.
Mardhekar's critique of Aristotle, JKU,
v.13, Humanities (1969), pp.82-92.

Philosophy & Religion—articles
BAS Sept 1970

L-350
Pandit, R.V.
Wedding. Trans.from Konkani by Harindranath
Chattopadhyaya, PI, v.1,no.2 (1966), pp.31-
32.

lit

PR
9769.5
A1P7
v.1 no.2

L-351
Patankar, R.B.
Mardhekar's contribution to aesthetics and
criticism. In: Critical essays on Indian
writing in English, presented to Armando
Menezes. Ed.by M.K.Naik, S.K.Desai and
G.S.Amur. Dharwar, Karnatak Univ.; [sole
distributors, Macmillan, Madras] 1968.
pp.296-316.

lit R

L-352
Rao, Vasant Dinanath, 1913-
The Maratha bardic poetry, MR, v.124
(1969), pp.749-52.

Literature - articles
BAS 1969

L-353
  Rege, Purushottam Shivram, 1910-
    Four poems. Trans.from the Marathi by
  Dilip Chitre, PI, v.2,no.2 (1967), pp.37-
  40.

a of R

L-354
  Rege, Sadananda Santarama, 1923-
    Poems. Trans.from the Marathi by Indrasen
  M.Jayakar, PI, v.1,no.4 (1966), pp.14-15.

U of R

L-355
  Sardar, Gangadhar Balkrishna, 1908-
    The saint-poets of Maharashtra (Their impact
  on society). Rendered into English from their
  original Marathi, by Kumud Mehta. New Delhi,
  Orient Longmans, 1969. 160p.

U of R

L-356
  Shahane, V.A.
    B.S.Mardhekar, a modern Marathi poet,
  IIJ, v.6 (1962), pp.141-50. Also in:
  Quest. v.28 (1961), pp.42-48.

*g a b 62
    61*

L-357
  Tukarama, Marathi poet, ca.1608-ca.1649.
    Poems of Tukarama, translated and re-arranged
  with notes and introduction by J.Nelson Fraser.
  London, Madras, Christian Literature Society,
  1909-1915. 3 vols.

L C

L-358
  Tukarama, Marathi poet, ca.1608-ca.1649.
    Psaumes du pèlerin; traduction, introduction
  et commentaires de G.A.Deleury. 2d ed. Paris,
  Gallimard, 1956. (Connaissance de l'orient;
  collection UNESCO d'oevres représentatives).
  220p.

L C

L-359
  Tukarama, Marathi poet, ca.1608-ca.1649.
    Songs. Trans.from the Marathi by Arun
  Kolhatkar, PI, v.1,no.1 (1966), pp.21-29.

U of R

L-360
  Tukarama, Marathi poet, ca.1608-ca.1649.
    Tukaram: twenty five poems translated from
  Marathi by Prabhakar Machwe, Mahfil, v.5,
  no.1/2 (1968-69), pp.61-69.

*marathi literature
    BAS 1969*

L-361
  Tukarama, Marathi poet, ca.1608-ca.1649.
    Village songs of western India; translations
  from Tukaram by John S.Hoyland. London, Allen-
  son & co., ltd., 1934. 86p.

L C

L-362
  Tulpule, Shankar Gopal, 1914-
    Madhavaswamy, the great Tanjore poet,
  AIOCPT, v.13 (1946), pp.228-37.

U of R

L-363
Vaidya, G.M.
Sri Sant Tukaram. Poona, Vidarbha Marathwada, 1965. (Makers of India series, 7)
37p.

Short stories

L-368
Bhave, Purushottaman Bhaskara, 1910-
The justice. Trans.by Vasant N.Joshi and Carlo Coppola, Mahfil, v.3,pt.2-3 (1966), pp.16-31.

L-364
Vaswani, Thanwardas Lilaram.
Tukaram; poet and prophet. Poona, Gita Pub. House, 195-? 80p.

LC

L-369
Bhave, Sadashiv S.
The story. Trans.by Gauri Deshpande, Mahfil, v.4,pt.4 (1970), pp.9-16.

L-365
Velankar, Hari Damodar, 1893-
Prince Sambhaji as a poet, ASBJ, n.s.,v.1 (1925), pp.252-58.

L-370
Gadgil, Gangadhar, 1923-
To tell you the truth. Trans.by Gauri Deshpande, Mahfil, v.4,pt.4 (1970), pp. 1-7.

L-366
Wilberforce-Bell, Harold, 1885-
Some translations from the Marathi poets with copious notes in English and Marathi. Bombay, Times Press, 1913. 213p.

L-371
Gokhale, Arvind Vishnu, 1919-
Kamalana. Short stories in Marathi. Bombay, Popular, 1952. 172p.

L-367
Winslow, John Copley, 1902-
Narayan Vaman Tilak: the Christian poet of Maharashtra. Calcutta, Association Press (YMCA), 1930. 137p.

L-372
Gokhale, Arvind Vishnu, 1919-
The unmarried widow and other stories. Trans.from Marathi by Smt.Snehprabha Pradhan. Bombay, Jaico Pub.House, 1957. 121p.

L-373
  Joshi, Ramachandra Bhikaji.
    Marathi short story and its development.
  In: Indian writers at Chidambaram. Pro-
  ceedings of the 3rd All-India Writers'
  Conference, Annamalainagar, 1954. Ed.by
  Hilla Vakeel. Bombay, The P.E.N.All-
  India Centre, 1957. pp.179-89.

M-1
  Asiatic Society of Bombay.
    A narrative of the development and
  achievement of the Bombay Branch, Royal
  Asiatic Society, compiled by V.D.Muzumdar.
  Bombay, G.C.Jhala, 1954. 50p.

L-374
  Kavadi, Naresh Bhikaji, 1922-
    One hand's clapping. Trans.by Maxine Berntsen,
  Mahfil, v.3,pt.2-3 (1966), pp.32-54.

M-2
  Bhonsle, R.Krishnarao.
    A note on the Tanjore Palace Library and
  the Historical Records pertaining to the
  administration of the Tanjore Kingdom by the
  Maratha rulers of Tanjore, *IHRCP*, v.13 (1930),
  pp.121-28.

L-375
  Raeside, Ian, tr.
    The rough and the smooth; short stories trans.
  from Marathi. Bombay, N.Y., Asia Pub.House,
  1966. 189p.

M-3
  Bombay Natural History Society.
    The Bombay Natural History Society, 1883-
  1933; printed in commemoration of the golden
  jubilee of the society, 1933. Bombay, 1933.
  103p.

L-376
  Shinde, B.G., ed.
    Modern Marathi short stories. Bombay,
  Pub.by B.G.Shinde, Saroj Prakashan, 194?
  127p.

M-4
  Ganapathy, K.P., 1912-
    Library movement in Maharashtra, *HLS*, v.3
  (1954), pp.194-98.

L-377
  Sixteen modern Marathi short stories. Bombay, Kutub-Popular, 1961. 236p.

M-5
  Holmes, William Robert and Raj Gopal, S.
    Research facilities in Bombay, Calcutta
  and Madras. Delhi, Printed by Graphic
  Aids at Cambridge Print.Works, 1968. 167p.

M-6
Indian Association of Special Libraries and
Information Centres.
   Directory of special and research libraries
in India. 1st ed. Calcutta, sole selling
agent: Oxford Book and Stationery Co., 1962.
285p.

M-7
Karve, C.G.
   Manuscript-curatorship under the Marathas.
In: Professor P.K.Gode commemoration volume.
Ed.by H.L.Hariyappa and M.M.Patkar. Poona,
Oriental Book Agency, 1960. pp.199-202.

M-8
Marshall, D.N.
   Bombay University Library, LH, v.6 (1963),
pp.143-53.

M-9
Men of library science and libraries in India.
New Delhi, Premier Publishers, 1967-

M-10
Priolkar, Anant Kakba, 1897-
   The origin and development of the library
movement in the Bombay Presidency, IHCP, v.10
(1947), pp.500-16.

M-11
Scott, Rev.H.R.
   History of the society, ASBJ, v.21 (extra
number) pt.I (1900-1905), pp.15-29.

NRD
ASBJ

M-12
Shreemati Nathibai Damodar Thackersey Women's
University, Bombay. Library.
   Directory of libraries, publishers and
booksellers in the city of Bombay. Ed.by
Vidyut K.Khandwala, and M.K.R.Naidu. Bombay,
S.N.D.T.Women's University, 1965. 76p.

M-13
Students' Literary and Scientific Society,
Bombay.
   Students' Literary and Scientific Society.
1848-49 to 1947-48. Bombay, S.B.Raikar,
1950. 96p.

LC Accession - 1969, p.22

M-14
Waknis, Trimbak Dinkar, 1902-
   Libraries in Bombay City, ILib, v.16
(1961), pp.138-42.

Numismatics   Bibliography & reference

N-1
Bal Krishan.
   Ancient Indian coinage; a select bibliography.
[With a foreword by C.Sivaramamurti] New
Delhi, Research Institute of Ancient Scien-
tific Studies (1968), 53p.

N-2
Rodgers, Charles James, 1838-1898.
Catalogue of the coins of the Indian Museum.
Calcutta, 1893-1896. 4v.

BM

N-3
Singhal, C.R.
Bibliography of Indian coins. Ed.by A.S.
Altekar. London, Arthur Probsthain, 1950-
52. 2v.in 1.

General

N-4
Abbott, Justin Edwards, 1853-1932.
A preliminary study of the Shivarai, or
Chhatrapati copper coins, ASBJ, v.20 (1897-
1900), pp.109-30.

ASBJ

N-5
Biddulph, C.H.
Bronze medallions issued by the mint at
Bombay, JNSI, v.26 (1964), pp.276-77.

JNSI
99 8 45

N-6
Biddulph, C.H.
The Marathas in southern India and their
coinage, JNSI, v.25 (1963), pp.217-37.

99 8 63

N-7
Bird, James.
Notice by the secretary of the Society, on
ten Hindu gold coins, found at the village
of Hewli, in the Southern Konkan...also on
a collection of gold Zodiac coins of the
Emperor Jehangir, ASBJ, v.2 (1844), pp.
63-65.

ASBJ

N-8
Chakravarti, S.N.
A new find of silver punch-marked coins
from the Bombay Presidency, ASBJ, n.s.,
v.20 (1944), pp.83-87.

N-9
Clunes, John.
Maratha coins in the early ninteenth
century, INC, v.4 (1965-66), pp.26-37.

INC

N-10
Codrington, Oliver, 1837-
Notes on the cabinet of coins of the Bombay Branch, Royal Asiatic Society, ASBJ,
v.18 (1890-94), pp.30-38.

NR 4

N-11
Codrington, Oliver, 1837-
On some old silver coins found near Wai,
ASBJ, v.12 (1876), pp.400-403.

ASBJ

N-12
Codrington, Oliver, 1837-
On the seals of the late Satara kingdom,
ASBJ, v.16 (1883-85), pp.126-66.

N-13
Dikshit, K.N.
A note on some rare coins in the cabinet
of the Bombay Branch of the Royal Asiatic
Society, ASBJ, v.24 (1915-1917), pp.382-84.

N-14
Dikshit, Moreshwar Gangadhar, 1915-
Coins from the Tripuri excavations, JNSI,
v.16 (1954), pp.65-71.

N-15
Dikshit, Moreshwar Gangadhar, 1915-
A note on the Honas of Chatrapati Sivaji,
INC, v.4 (1965-66), pp.29-31. Also in: JNSI,
v.29 (1967), pp.50-51.

N-16
Dikshit, Moreshwar Gangadhar, 1915-
Padma-tankas of Yadava Bhillama IV, JNSI,
v.29 (1967), pp.46-48.

N-17
Dikshit, Moreshwar Gangadhar, 1915-
Punch-marked coins from Nevari, Umrer;
Dist.Nagpur, JNSI, v.26 (1964), pp.91-94.

N-18
Gupta, Parmeshwari Lal, 1914-
Coins from Brahmapuri excavations (1945-
1946), BDCRI, v.21 (1960/61), pp.38-84.

N-19
Gupta, Parmeshwari Lal, 1914-
The punch-marked coins from Hyderabad,
JNSI, v.16 (1954), pp.51-54.

N-20
Iyengar, Srinivasa R
Some old Maratha gold coins: fanams of
Rama Raja, AIOCPT, v.2 (1922), pp.291-94.

N-21
Kamat, V.S.
Historical seals of Satara raja; a summary,
IHCP, v.25 (1964), pp.282-83.

N-22
Katare, Sant Lal.
King Sātavāhana of the coins, IHQ, v.27
(1951), pp.210-14.

Index to IHQ

N-23
Kaus, Hurmaz.
Copper coins of Shivaji, NumCir, v.63
(1955), pp.267-70.

Opus '36

N-24
Khandalavala, Karl.
Brahmapur: a consideration of the metal
objects found in the Kundangar hoard, LK,
v.7 (1960), pp.29-75.

JaS 15

N-25
Khare, Ganesh Hari, 1901-
Some coins of the Peshwas, JNSI, v.4 (1942),
pp.73-77.

ACIHI v5

N-26
Khare, Ganesh Hari, 1901-
Some more information on the lions of Muhammad
Adilshāh, JNSI, v.16 (1954), pp.13C-31.

Khare

N-27
Khatun, Monira.
Some observations on Maratha coins,
JNSI, v.22 (1960), pp.221-24.

JAS '62
DS 50

N-28
Krishna, C.
Discovery of a pallava coin(?) at Nagar,
district Bhandara, Maharashtra, JNSI, v.26
(1964), pp.240-43.

N-29
Kukuranov, L.M.
Gandahar of Deccan, a likely mint of Shāh-
jahān, JNSI, v.17 (1955), pp.102-105.

Chaudhuri

N-30
Marsden, William, 1754-1836.
Marsden's Numismata Orientalia. A new
edition. Ed.by Edward Thomas. Trüber,
1874-86. 3v.

BM

N-31
Mirashi, Vasudev Vishnu, 1893-
A large hoard of Sātavāhana coins, IHQ, v.16
(1940), pp.503-505.

Index to IHQ

N-32
  Mirashi, Vasudev Vishnu, 1893-
    A problem raised by the finds of coins in
    Vidarbha, <u>JNSI</u>, v.24 (1962), pp.188-89.

ga & 63

N-33
  Pai, M.Govind.
    The Vilivayakuras and Sivalakura of the
    Kolhapur coins, <u>ABORI</u>, v.23 (1942), pp.319-
    29.

a BORI

N-34
  Phatak, D.M.
    On certain copper coins minted by the Bombay
    mint authorities, <u>JNSI</u>, v.29 (1967), pp.55-57.

International Guide to Indic Studies

N-35
  Ranade, Mahadev Govind, 1842-1901.
    Currencies and mints under Mahratta
    rule, <u>ASBJ</u>, v.20 (1897-1900), pp.191-200.

CASE

N-36
  Ranade, P.V.
    A copper coin of Wima Kadaphises discovered
    in Aurangabad, <u>JNSI</u>, v.26 (1964), pp.228-31.

ga & '65

N-37
  Ranade, P.V.
    A silver coin of Jajna Shri Satkarni, <u>JMaU</u>,
    v.4,no.1 (1963), pp.55-59.

jmaU

N-38
  Rode, V.P.
    The coin collection in the central museum,
    Nagpur, <u>JNSI</u>, v.23 (1961), pp.488-90.

ga & '62

N-39
  Sankalia, Hasmukhlal Dhirajlal, 1908-
    Coins from Nasik excavations, <u>JNSI</u>, v.5
    (1953), pp.1-8.

JNSI

N-40
  Scott, Rev.H.R.
    The Nasik (Joghaltembhi) hoard of
    Nahapāna's coins, <u>ASBJ</u>, v.22 (1906-08),
    pp.223-44.

*NRU
ASBJ*

N-41
  Scott, Rev.H.R.
    Traijutaka coins from the Poona (Indapur)
    district, <u>ASBJ</u>, v.23 (1909-14), pp.1-7.

*NRU
ASBJ*

N-42
 Sherwani, Haroon Khan, 1891-
    Antecedents of the Bahmani kingdom, IHCP,
 v.4 (1940), pp.208-19.

IHCP

N-43
 Sherwani, Haroon Khan, 1891-
    Bahmani coinage as a source of Deccan
 history. In: Mahamahopadhyaya Prof.D.V.Potdar
 sixty-first birthday commemoration volume.
 Ed.by Surendra Nath Sen. Poona, 1950. pp.204-
 218.

Bhanderkar Index on
comm Vols.

N-44
 Siddiqui, A.H.
    A copper coin of Jahandar Shah of Sholapur
 mint, JNSI, v.26 (1964), pp.255-56.

✓✓✓ JNSI
Ja 8 65

N-45
 Siddiqui, A.H.
    Copper coins of Burhan Nizam Shah III,
 JNSI, v.26 (1964), pp.262-66.

JNSI

N-46
 Siddiqui, A.H.
    A new legend on a copper coin of Ibrahim
 Barid, JNSI, v.28 (1966), pp.82-83.

Current Guide to Indic Studies

N-47
 Siddiqui, A.H.
    A new type copper coin of Muhammad Quli
 Qutub Shah, JNSI, v.26 (1964), pp.258-61.

JNSI

N-48
 Siddiqui, A.H.
    A note on copper coins of Feroz Shah Bahmani,
 JNSI, v.28 (1966), pp.79-82.

Internat Guide to Indic Studies

N-49
 Siddiqui, A.H.
    Note on some legends of the Bahmani coins,
 JNSI, v.26 (1964), pp.267-71.

✓✓✓ JNSI
Ja 8 65

N-50
 Siddiqui, A.H.
    A note on some Satavahana coins, JNSI, v.28
 (1966), pp.54-57.

Internat Guide to Indic Studies

N-51
 Siddiqui, A.H.
    A note on the copper coins of Murtaza Nizam
 Shah II, JNSI, v.28 (1966), pp.84-86.

Current Guide to Indic Studies

N-52
Siddiqui, A.H.
  On the coins of Jahangir and Shah Jahan of
Ahmadnagar, <u>JNSI</u>, v.28 (1966), pp.87-89.

Internat Guide to Indic Studies

N-53
Siddiqui, A.H.
  Some dateless copper coins of the Bahmani
kings, <u>JNSI</u>, v.26 (1964), pp.271-75.

N-54
Sohoni, Nirmala.
  Some notes on Maratha coinage, <u>INC</u>, v.4
(1965-66), pp.38-40.

INC

N-55
Sohoni, Shridhar V.
  Feudatory coinage in Maratha period, <u>INC</u>,
v.4 (1965-66), p.32.

N-56
Sohoni, Shridhar V.
  Notes on Sātavāhāna bust coinage, <u>JNSI</u>,
v.17 (1955), pp.100-03.

N-57
Sohoni, Shridhar V.
  Reference to Satavahana coinage in Gatha
Saptaśati, <u>JBRS</u>, v.42 (1955), pp.329-31.

N-58
Talvalkar, V.R.
  History of Baroda coins: and mint names
1766 to 1800, <u>IHCP</u>, v.1,pt.2 (1935), pp.88.

N-59
Tarapore, P.S.
  Is the name of Tahamtan or Eahman Shah
found on the coins of Ghiyasuddin Shah of the
Bahmani Dynasty? <u>JNSI</u>, v.16 (1954), pp.256-59.

N-60
Taylor, George P.
  The coins of Surat, <u>ASBJ</u>, v.22 (1908),
pp.245-72.

N-61
Thomas, Edward.
  The coinages of the East India Company, at
Bombay, under the charters of Charles II, with
a note on the Indian exchanges of the period,
<u>IA</u>, v.11 (1882), pp.313-19.

IA

N-62
Tiwari, G.S.
Padmatankas of Yadava king Singhana from
Nimar. JNSI, v.28 (1966), pp.214-15.

Bibliography & Reference | Political patterns

O-1
Alexandrowicz-Alexander, Charles Henry.
A bibliography of Indian law. Madras,
New York, Indian Branch, Oxford Univ.Press,
1958. 78p.

O-2
Barfivala, Chunilal Damodardas, 1889-
Directory of local self-government in India
with special reference to the Bombay Province.
Bombay, 1941. 1134p.

O-3
Directory of local self-government in
Maharashtra State. Bombay, All-India
Institute of Local Self-government,
1962. 566p.

O-4
Garde, D.K. and Apte, P.P.
Bibliography of political thought and
institutions in ancient and medieval India,
JPU, v.31 (1969), pp.87-124.

O-5
Garde, D.K. and Vakil, Mitra R.
Bibliography of Centre-State relations in
India (1952-1967), JUP, v.29 (1969), pp.103-
50.

O-6
Gautam, Brijendra Pratap, 1933-
Researches in political science in India;
a detailed bibliography. Comp.by Brijendra
Pratap Gautam, with a foreword by A.V.Rao.
Kanpur, Oriental Pub.House, 1965. 123p.

O-7
Harrington, E.
An index to, and analytical digest of Morris's
reports of the Sudder Foujdaree Adawlat, from
1854 to 1858. Bombay, 1860. 510p.

O-8
India (Republic) Parliament. Council of States.
Who's who. New Delhi, Rajya Sabha Secre-
tariat, 1st- 1952-

O-9
India (Republic) Parliament. House of the
People.
Who's who. New Delhi, Lok Sabha Secretariat
[etc.] 1st- Lok Sabha; 1952-

O-10
Iswara Dutt, Kunduri, 1898-
Congress cyclopaedia: the Indian National
Congress, 1885-1920. New Delhi, 1967-
v.1: The pre-Gandhian Era.

O-11
Jain, Hem Chandra, 1933-
Indian legal materials; a bibliographical guide. Bombay, N.M.Tripathi; Dobbs Ferry, N.Y., Oceana Publications, 1970. 146p.

47R

O-12
Jaipur, India (Rajasthan) University of Rajasthan Library.
A select bibliography on electoral and party behavior in India. Institute on the Study of Electoral and Party Behaviour in India, December 1-10, 1966. Jaipur, 1966. 163p.

4.4R

O-13
Jaipur, India (Rajasthan) University of Rajasthan Library.
A select bibliography on Indian government and politics [comp.by N.N.Gidwani for the] Seminar on State Politics in India, December 6-15, 1965. Jaipur, 1965. 75p.

O-14
Jaipur, India (Rajasthan) University of Rajasthan Library.
A select bibliography on panchayati raj, planning and edmocracy. Jaipur, 1964. 75p.

47R

O-15
Maharashtra, India (State) Bureau of Economics and Statistics.
Municipal year book, Maharashtra State. Bombay, 1961?- annual.

O-16
Maharashtra, India (State) Legislature. Legislative Council.
List of members. Bombay, Maharashtra Legislature Secretariat. irregular.

47R

O-17
Maharashtra, India (State) Legislature. Secretariat.
List of members of the Maharashtra Legislative Assembly. Bombay. irregular.

47R

O-18
Singh, Baljit, comp.& ed.
India, government and politics; a selected bibliogrphy. East Lansing, Michigan State University, 1964. 74p.

4 4R

O-19
Wilson, Patrick, 1927-
Government and politics in India and Pakistan 1885-1955; a bibliography of works in western languages. Berkeley, South Asia Studies, Institute of East Asiatic studies, Univ.of California, 1956. (California Univ.Inst.of East Asiatic Studies. South Asia Studies, Modern India Project, Bibliographic studies, no.2) 356p.

Constitutional history
& administration

O-20
Abdul Ali, A.F.M.
Phases of early British administration in Bombay, EPP, v.40 (1930), pp.18-26. Also in: MusR, v.4 (1930), pp.10-20.

0-21
   Administrative reforms in the Bombay Presidency. QJPSS, v·4 (1881), pp.1-56.

PSS

0-22
   Aggarwala, Rama Nand.
      National movement and constitutional development of India. 6th ed. Delhi, Metropolitan Book Co., 1967. 536p.

VVU of R

0-23
   Alexandrowicz-Alexander, Charles Henry.
      The discriminatory clause in South Asian treaties in the seventeenth and eighteenth centuries. IYBIA, v.6 (1957), pp.126-42.

0-24
   Ambedkar, Bhimrao Ramji, 1892-1956.
      States and minorities, what are their rights and how to secure them in the constitution of free India. Bombay, 1947. 81p.

IOL

0-25
   Aundh, India (State)
      The annual administration report of the Aundh state. 1930-46.

NYPL

0-26
   Bhargava, S.P.
      Some aspects of the administration of the C.P. and Berar from 1861 to 1920. Nagpur, Nagpur Univ., 1952. *

Public administration
not ...
BDD

0-27
   Bhor, India (State).
      Administration report. Annual. For years 1936/37 to 1944/45.

LC.

0-28
   Bombay (Presidency)
      History of services of Gazetted officers in the Civil Department serving in the Bombay Presidency. Corrected up to 1st July 1884 (-1908) Bombay, 1884-1908. 17v.

BM

0-29
   Bombay (Presidency)
      Minutes by H.E.Sir Richard Temple, 1877-80. Bombay, 1878-80. 3v.

0-30
   Bombay (Presidency) General Department.
      Bombay...A review of the administration of the province...1859/60- Bombay, 1861-

LC

O-31
    Bombay (Presidency) Judicial Department.
      Police report of the Northern and Southern
    Divisions of the Bombay Presidency for:
    1. 1868-69. By D.Havelock and A.Rogers.
    2. 1870. By L.R.Ashburner and D.Havelock.
    3. 1871. By D.Havelock.
    4. 1872. By D.Havelock.
    Bombay, 1870-73.

10L

O-32
    Bombay (Presidency) Political Department.
      Minute on the Revenue and Judicial Admin-
    istration of the southern Maharata country.
    (By Sir John Malcolm dated Bombay, 23 April
    1829). Bombay, 1829(?).

O-33
    Bombay (Presidency) Western Bhil Agency.
      Annual report on the working of the Western
    Bhil Agency, Khandesh, 1883-84-1905-06. Bom-
    bay, 1885-1907.

O-34
    Bombay (State) Backward Class Department.
      Report on the working of the backward
    class department for the years 1947-48,
    1948-49, and 1949-50. Poona, Yeravda
    Prison Press, 1952.

O-35
    Bombay (State) Directorate of Publicity.
      Separation of executive and judicial
    functions in Bombay State, second directive
    principle implemented. Bombay, 1953.

O-36
    Bombay government resolution anent the dis-
    tribution of seats in the council, QJPSS,
    v.16,no.1 (1893), pp.12-22.

O-37
    Broomfield, Robert Stonehouse, 1882-
      Report by the Hon'ble Mr. Justice R.S.
    Broomfield, I.C.S., on the firing by the
    Bombay City police at the Chhota Qabrastan
    on the 1st August 1939. Bombay, Printed at
    the Govt.Central Press, 1940. 25p.

        Bombay - Riots, 1939.

O-38
    Chakravarty, Sasadar.
      The evolution of representative government
    in India, 1884-1909, with reference to the
    Central and Provincial Legislative Councils.
    London, University of London, 1954. *

O-39
    Copland, I.F.S.
      The Bombay political service, 1863-1924.
    Oxford, Univ.of Oxford, 1969. *

O-40
    Crawford, Arthur Travers, 1835-1911.
      The plighted word of a British Government:
    the proceedings of a public meeting of the
    citizens of Poona ... to express their ...
    thanks to the Bombay Government conducting
    the Crawford Inquiry, etc. London, 1889.

O-41
Deputation to his excellency the Governor of
Bombay requesting the distribution of seats
in the New Legislative Council, with reply.
QJPSS, v.16,no.1 (1893), pp.1-11.

P55

O-42
Dewas, Junior, India (State)
Administration report of the Dewas State
(Junior branch) for the year 1935/36-1938/39.

NYPL

O-43
Dhar, India (State)
Report on the administration of the Dhar
State. 1917/20-1926/31; 1936/37-1944/45.

NYPL

O-44
Dubey, N.P.
Working of provincial autonomy in Central
Provinces and Berar from 1937 to 1949.
Gour Nagar, Sagar, Univ.of Saugar, 1964. *

O-45
Five years' administration of Sir James
Fergusson, QJPSS, v.7 (1884), pp.44-
66.

O-46
Ghauri, Iftikhar Ahmad.
Central structure of the kingdom of Bijapur,
IC, v.44 (1970), pp.19-33.

O-47
Gribble, James Dunning Baker, d.1906.
The native states and the paramount power
in India, AR, v.9 (1890), pp.466-69.

OR

O-48
Gupta, Amitkumar.
The policy of Sir James Fergusson as Governor
of Bombay Presidency, 1880-1885. London, Univ.
of London, 1967. *

O-49
Hunter, Sir William Wilson, 1840-1900.
Bombay 1885-1890: a study in Indian administration. London, Henry Frowde; B.M.Malabari,
1892. 511p.

1. Bombay (Presidency) - Pol.& govt. 2.
Gt.Brit. - Colonies - India.

LC

O-50
Ilbert, Sir Courtenay Peregrine, 1841-1924.
The government of India: a brief historical
survey of Parliamentary legislation relating
to India. Oxford, Clarendon Press, 1922.
152p.

1. India - Pol.& govt. - 1765-

0-51
Indian Institute of Public Administration.
Maharashtra Regional Branch.
Organisation of government in Maharashtra.
Bombay, Popular Prakashan, 1965. 485p.

4 7 R

0-56
Lely, Sir Frederic Styles Philpin, 1846-
Suggestions for the better government of
India, with special reference to Bombay
Province. London, Alston Rivers, 1906.

Wilson

0-52
Jeejeebhoy, Jeejeebhoy Rustomji Byramji, 1885-
An account of some unfortunate officials of
the Bombay government, IHCP, v.10 (1947), pp.
481-95.

IHaP
Case

0-57
Maharashtra, India (State)
History of services. Bombay, Printed at the
Govt.Central Press, 1961-
Pt.1 - General administration
Pt.2 - Judicial

N u C

0-53
Kale, D.V.
Development of constitutional ideas in the
history of the Marathas, JUB, v.2 (1934),
pp.239-51.

Case

0-58
Maharashtra, India (State) Administrative
Reorganisation Committee.
Report. Bombay, Printed at the Govt.Central
Press, 1968. 367p.

BAS 1949

0-54
Keith, Arthur Berriedale.
Bombay and English constitutional law, IHQ,
v.11 (1935), pp.57-69.

I HQ

0-59
Maharashtra, India (State) Backward Class
Welfare Wing.
Annual administration report on the welfare
of backward classes. Bombay, Director, Govt.
Print& Stationery, 1960/61-

N u C

0-55
Kolhapur, India (State)
Kolhapur administration report. Kolhapur,
1933-46. annual. 1934-47.

N Y L

0-60
Malet, H.P.
Poonah administration, a rejoinder, AR,
v.8 (1889), pp.105-16.

0-61
Mavaji, Purushottama Vishrama, 1879-1929.
   Native administrative genius of the 19th
century. Bombay, Nirnaya Sagar Press, 1905.
48p.

Bom (Pres) cat

0-62
Miraj, Junior, India (State)
   The annual administration report of the
Miraj Junior State. Budhgaon, 1901-43.

NYPL

0-63
Miraj, Senior, India (State)
   Report on the administration of the Miraj
Senior State. Miraj, 1921-46.

NYPL

0-64
Misra, J.P.
   The Crawford case, IHCP, v.30 (1968), pp.
273-76.

K o/R   DS Mol I WISP   v. 30

0-65
Murty, E.S.
   Sir John Lawrence's difficulties with the
government of Bombay, IHCP, v.30 (1968),
pp.358-67.

a o/ R

0-66
Naik, G.D. and Latthe, Annoji Babaji, 1878-
   Backward classes in the Bombay Deccan and
Indian constitutional reform proposals. Poona,
V.B.Kothari, Deccan Ryots Association, 1918.
8p.

Bom (Pres) cat

0-67
Nowrozjee Furdoonjee.
   On the civil administration of the Bombay
Presidency. London, John Chapman, 1853.
93p.

NJ NLC

0-68
The political department in Bombay, CR,
   v.56 (1873), pp.288-302.

case

0-69
Prasad, Bisheshwar.
   Origins of provincial autonomy; being a
history of the relations between the central
government and the provincial governments
in India from 1860 to 1919. 2d ed. Delhi,
Atmaram, 1960. 288p.

   1. India - Pol.& govt. - 1765-1947. 2.
India - Constitutional history.

LC

0-70
The proceedings of a public meeting of the
   citizens of Poona, held on the 1st
September, 1889...Rao Bahadur K.L.Nulker
in the Chair. London, 1889. 48p.

√√ Calcatta Nat'l Lib
   QRHS + 9

0-71
Reply of the government of Bombay to the
memorial of the Sabha on the proposed
provincial service scheme. CJPSS, v.17,
no.2 (1894), pp.22-24.

NED
CJPSS

0-72
Representation on local self-government in
the Bombay Presidency. QJPSS, v.5,no.1
(1882), pp.1-16; v.5,no.2 (1882), pp.17-
34; v.5,no.3 (1882), pp.35-52.

QJPSS

0-73
A representation to his excellency the
Governor-General in council regarding the
distribution of seats in the new legislative council. QJPSS, v.16,no.1 (1893),
pp.22-33.

QJPSS

0-74
The representations to the government of
Bombay regarding the New Council's Act of
1892; No.37 of 1893; No.162 of 1893. QJPSS,
v.15,no.4 (1892), pp.59-73.

QJPSS

0-75
Sangli, India (State)
Annual administration report of the
Sangli state. 1919-

0-76
Sawantwadi, India (State)
Administration report of the Sawantwadi
State. Sawantwadi, 1900-1942. annual.

NYPL

0-77
Sharma, B.A.V.
Public personnel administration in India
with special reference to Maharashtra.
Bombay, Univ.of Bombay, 1966. *

Public administration
Personnel
BDD

0-78
Sharma, Indra Datt, 1909-
The government and administration at Baroda
(1881-1938). Lucknow, Univ.of Baroda, 1949. *

CnC

0-79
Singh, Gurmukh Nihal, 1895-
Landmarks in Indian constitutional and
national development. 2d ed. Delhi, Atma
Ram, 1950-

0-80
Sinha, Ram Mohan.
Nagpur State in the 19th century: a study
in some aspects of its administrative system
1818-1854. Nagpur, Nagpur Univ., 1956. *

Public administration
Hist. + conditions

0-81
Venkataraman, K.R.
A Maratha leaven in the administrative and
cultural history of Pudukkottai. In: Mahamahopadhyaya Prof.D.V.Potdar sixty-first birthday
commemoration volume. Ed.by Surendra Nath Sen.
Poona, 1950. pp.44-49.

Elections

0-82
Badhe, G.S. and Rao, M.U.
Bombay civic election of 1968, JUB, v.37
(1968), pp.287-307.

U of P.

0-83
Dange, Shripad Amrit, 1900-
Report on the general elections in Bombay.
Bombay, 1957. 24p.

Elections - Bombay (State)

0-84
Dastur, Aloo J.
Election organization cutting across party
lines: North Bombay constituency. In:
Indian voting behavior; (studies of the
1962 general elections) Ed.by Myron Weiner
and Rajni Kothari. Calcutta, Mukhopadhayay,
1965. pp.106-22.

0-85
Dastur, Aloo J.
Menon vs. Kripalani: North Bombay election,
1962. Bombay, University of Bombay, 1967.
149p.

0-86
Dastur, Aloo J. and Mehta, Usha H.
General election in greater Bombay, PSR,
v.2 (1963), pp.i-x.

0-87
Fisher, Margaret Welpley, 1903-
Indian experience with democratic elections.
Berkeley, University of California, 1956.
(Indian Press Digests-Monograph series, no.3).
200p.

0-88
Halappa, G.S., 1922-   et al.
The first general elections in Goa.
Dharwar, Karnatak Univ., 1964. (Karnatak
University, Dharwar, India. Political
series, no.2) 136p.

1. Elections - Goa. 2. Goa - Pol.& govt.

0-89
India (Republic) Election Commission.
Report of the first General Elections in
India, 1951-52. Delhi, Manager of Publications,
1955. 2 vols.

0-90
India (Republic) Election Commission.
Report on the fourth general elections
in India, 1967. New Delhi, 1968. 2vols.

0-91
India (Republic) Election Commission.
Report of the second general elections
in India, 1957. New Delhi, Government
of India Press, 1959.

0-92
India (Republic) Election Commission.
Report of the third general election in
India, 1962. Delhi, Manager of Publications,
1963-66. 2v.

0-93
India votes, a source book on Indian elections.
Ed.and comp.by R.Chandidas [and others]
Bombay, Popular Prakashan, 1968. 727p.

0-94
Joshi, Ram.
General elections in Goa, AS, v.4 (1964),
pp.1093-1101.

0-95
Kogekar, S.V.
Bombay. In: Reports on the Indian general
elections, 19 1-52, by S.V.Kogekar and Richard
L.Park. Bombay, Popular Book Depot, 1956.
pp.37-44.

0-96
Kulkarani, Anant Ramachandra, 1925-
Second general election in Sholapur.
Sholapur, Institute of Public Administration,
1958. 38p.

0-97
Maharashtra, India (State) General Administration Dept.
1961 census population figures; delimitation
of parliamentary and assembly constituencies.
Nagpur, Govt.Press, 1964-

0-98
Mehta, Usha H.
The second general elections in greater
Bombay. IJPS, v.19 (1958), pp.151-60.

0-99
Palmer, Norman D.
The 1962 election in North Bombay. PacA,
v.36 (1963), pp.120-37.

0-100
Sharma, B.A.V. and Jangam, R.T.
The Bombay Municipal Corporation; an election study. Bombay, Popular Book Depot, 1962.
170p.

1. Elections - Bombay. 2. Bombay - Pol.&
govt.

O-101
Shrader, Lawrence L. and Joshi, Ram.
Zilla Parishad elections in Maharashtra
and the district political elite, AS, v.3
(1963), pp.143-56.

gal '63

O-102
Sirsikar, V.M.
General elections in Maharashtra, 1962,
PSR, v.2 (1963), pp.25-32.

gal 63

O-103
Sirsikar, V.M.
Party loyalties versus caste and communal
pulls: Poona constituency. In: India voting
behaviour; studies of the 1962 general
elections. Ed.by Myron Weiner and Rajni
Kothari. Calcutta, Firma K.L.Mukhopadhaya,
1965. pp.35-46.

4 gR

O-104
Sirsikar, V.M.
Political behavior in India; a case study of
the 1962 general elections. Bombay, Manaktalas, 1965. 274p.

4 gR

O-105
Sirsikar, V.M.
Study of voting behavior in India: limita-
tion and problems, PSR, v.2 (1963), pp.54-
59.

O-106
Sirsikar, V.M.
Traditional techniques of propaganda: as
observed in the 1962 elections in Poona,
JUP, v.19 (1964), pp.101-105.

gal '64

O-107
Suri, Surindar.
1962 elections: a political analysis. New
Delhi, Sudha Pubs., 1962. 201p.

1. Elections - India.

4 gR

O-108
Venkatarangaiya, Mamidupudi, 1889-
Bombay City. In: Reports on the Indian
general elections, 1951-52. By S.V.Kogekar
and Richard L.Park. Bombay, Popular Book
Depot, 1956. pp.45-67.

votR

O-109
Venkatarangiaya, Mamidipudi, 1889-
The general elections in the city of Bombay
1952. Bombay, Vora, 1953. 177p.

Judiciary, laws, statutes,
etc.

O-110
Atkinson, George.
Commentaries on the laws of British India
as administered in the Bombay Presidency. Ed.
by R.M.Patell. Bombay, 1887. 373p.

WVI SL

O-111
Bombay (Presidency)
Report of the commission appointed for framing a code of laws adapted to the Parsee community, with accompanying documents. Bombay, 1862.

BM

O-112
Bombay (Presidency) Laws, General Collections. Bombay Acts and Regulations, with notes, decisions, notifications, etc. Ed.by Jamietram Nanabhai ... and ... Chimanlal Harilal Setalvad. Bombay, Ripon Printing Press, 1894. 3v.

O-113
Bombay (Presidency) Laws, General Collections. The Bombay Code, etc. Ed.by D.G.Khandekar. Poona, D.G.Khandekar, 1909-11. 4v.

O-114
Bombay (Presidency) Laws, General Collections. Local rules and orders made under enactments applying to Bombay ... Corrected up to the 31st December 1895 (30th June 1897). Bombay, 1896. 2v.

O-115
Bombay (Presidency) Laws, statutes, etc. The Bombay Acts (civil, criminal and revenue), 1827-1923. By P.Hari Rao. Bombay, 1924.

O-116
Bombay (Presidency) Laws, statutes, etc. The Bombay code; consisting of the unrepealed Bombay regulations, acts of the Supreme Council relating solely to Bombay, and acts of the Governor of Bombay in Council. 3d ed. Calcutta, Office of the Superintendent of Govt. Print., India, 1907-1909. 4v.

LC

O-117
Bombay (Presidency) Laws, statutes, etc. The Bombay Hereditary Offices Act, no.III of 1874, as amended by Act V. of 1886. With full notes and rulings. By Hanumant Seshagiri Phadnis. Bombay, Ramchandra Govind, 1897.

BM
1c

O-118
Bombay (Presidency) Laws, statutes, etc. A compilation of laws relating to the administration of criminal justice, revenue, etc.in force within the town and island of Bombay. By Frederick Lindemann Brown. Bombay, 1855.

BM

O-119
Bombay (Presidency) Laws, statutes, etc. A digest of the criminal rulings of the High Court of Bombay from July 1890 to December 1894. By Balvant Vithal Harolikar. Chikodi, Dnyan Prasarak press, 1895.

BM

O-120
Bombay (Presidency) Laws, statutes, etc. Digest of the unreported printed judgements and criminal rulings of the High Court of Bombay from 1869-1896. By Jamietram Nanabhai and Chimanlal Harilal Setalvad. Bombay, Ripon Printing Press, 1897.

O-121
    Bombay (Presidency) Laws, statutes, etc.
      Interpretations of the Bombay regulations.
    Bombay, 1939.

Cal nat'l Lib

O-122
    Bombay (Presidency) Laws, statutes, etc.
      The manual of Bombay Acts and regulations.
    By D.G.Khandekar. Poona, 1922-28. 2v.

BM

O-123
    Bombay (Presidency) Laws, statutes, etc.
      The regulations of the Government of Bombay
    in force at the end of 1850; to which are
    added, the acts of the government of India
    in force in that presidency. London, Printed
    by J.& H.Cox, 1851.

O-124
    Bombay (Presidency) Legislative Department.
    Local rules and orders made under enactments
    applying to Bombay. Bombay, 1896-98. 2v.

O-125
    Bombay (Presidency) Sadr Diwani Adalat.
    Reports of Civil cases adjudged by the
    Court of Sudur Udalut for the Presidency
    of Bombay, between...A.D.1800 and A.D.1824...
    with an appendix. Compiled by H.Borradaile.
    Bombay, 1825. 2v.

Bri- Mus

O-126
    Bombay (Presidency) Sadr Diwani Adalat.
      Reports of Civil Cases determined in the
    Court of Sudder Dewanee Adawlut of Bombay.
    Compiled by A.F.Bellasis...1840-48. Bombay,
    Education Society's Press, 1850.

Bri- Mus

O-127
    Bombay (Presidency) Sadr Diwani Adalat.
      Reports of selected cases (1820-40) decided
    by the Sudder Dewanee Adawlut, Bombay. Bombay, 1843.

O-128
    Bombay (Presidency) Sadr Diwani Adalat.
      Selected decisions of the Court of
    Sudder Dewanee Adawlut of Bombay. Compiled
    by James Morris. Bombay, Education
    Society's Press, 1853.

Bri - Mus

O-129
    Bombay (Presidency) Sadr Faujdari Adalat.
      Reports of criminal cases determined in the
    Court of Sudder Foujdaree Adawlut, of Bombay
    (1827 to 1846) Comp.by A.F.Bellasis. Bombay,
    1849.

EM

O-130
    Branson, Reginald Montague Auber, comp.
      Digest of cases reported in the Indian
    Law reports, Bombay, Times of India
    Steam Press, 1879. 309p.

O-131
Code of Gentoo laws, or, Ordinations of the
Pundits, from a Persian translation, made
from original, written in the Shanscrit
language, trans.by Nathaniel Brassey Halhed.
London, 1777. 405p.

Law, Hindu.

O-132
Correspondence with the Bombay Government, in
connection with the creation of benches of
Honorary magistrates for Poona, QJPSS, v.12,
no.1 (1889), pp.1-15.

PSS

O-133
Cranenburgh, D.E., comp.
A handbook of criminal cases containing
a verbatim reprint of all criminal cases
reported in vols.I to XXIII, Bombay series,
I.L.R. (1875-1899). Calcutta, B.Baral, 1901.
1380p.

O-134
Dadyburjor, Sorab B.
Cases referred from the Bombay Court of
Small Causes for the opinion of the High
Court of Bombay, 1899-1927. Bombay, 1927.
343p.

O-135
Dighe, Vishvanath Govind.
Penal code of the Peshwas, IHCP, v.10 (1947),
pp.448-53.

Case

O-136
East India Company (English).
The code of civil procedure of the
courts of the East India Company. Calcutta,
1854.

O-137
East India Company (English)
The regulations of the government of Bombay
in force at the end of 1850. Prepared by
Richard Clarke. London, 1851. 815p.

BM

O-138
East India Company (English).
Regulations passed by the Governor in
Council of Bombay, from the year 1799
to 1816 inclusive; also police regulations,
denominated rules, ordinances, and regulations from...1812 to 1816 inclusive. London,
1822. 635p.

BM

O-139
Erskine, William.
Diaries of Sir William Erskine, ASBJ, v.25,
no.72 (1917-1921), pp.373-409.

O-140
Fawcett, Sir Charles, 1869-
The first century of British justice in
India; an account of the Court of Judicature
at Bombay, established in 1672 ... Oxford,
Clarendon Press, 1934. 290p.

O-141
Gajendragadkar, Pralhad Balacharya, 1901-
Chief Justice Gajendragadkar: his life,
ideas, papers and addresses, by Vidya Dhar
Mahajan. Delhi, S.Chand, 1966. 356p.

1. Law - India - Addresses, essays, lectures.

U of R

O-142
Gandhi, Kalidasa Vandravanadasa.
A manual of Hindu law as administered in
the Bombay Presidency. Bombay, Eastern
Printing Press, 1895. 154p.

LOL

O-143
Gune, Vithal Trimbak.
The judicial institutions of the Marathas,
JUB, v.18 (1950), pp.101-104.

JUB

O-144
Gune, Vithal Trimbak.
The judicial system of the Marathas; a
detailed study of the judicial institutions
in Maharashtra from 1600-1818A.D., based
on original decisions called mahzars,
nivadpatras and official orders. Poona,
Deccan College, Post-Graduate and Research
Institute, 1953. (Deccan College dissertation series, 12). 426p.

U of R

O-145
Jahangir, Rustam Pestanji.
The truth about the Bombay opium defamation
cases, based on the facts ascertained during
the trial. Bombay, Jehangir B.Marzban and Co.,
1894. 149p.

BM

O-146
Kamat, V.S.
How civil disputes were settled in the Deccan
during the regime of the last Peshwa. IHCP, v.22
(1959), pp.351-53.

IHCP

O-147
Kane, Pandurang Vaman, 1880-
History of Dharmaśastra (ancient and mediae-
val religious and civil law) Poona, Bhandar-
kar Oriental Research Institute, 1941-
(Government Oriental series. Class B, no.6)

1. Dharma. 2. Hinduism - Sacred books.

U of R

O-148
Kemp, Norman Wright.
The law of costs and practice of taxation in
the Bombay High Court. Bombay, Mssrs. N.M.
Tripathi and Co., 1922. 424p.

LC

O-149
Knox, George Edward.
The criminal law of the Bombay Presidency.
Calcutta, 1873. 2v.

IOL

O-150
Kohler, J.
Die gewohnheitsrechte der Provinz Bombay,
ZVR, v.34 (1892), pp.23-117.

fürer

O-151
Kotewal, Bejanji Ruttonji.
The practice of the Bombay court of small
causes. Bombay, 1876. 233p.

IOL

O-152
Kothari, G.L.
Industrial relations law in Maharashtra,
Gujarat and former Madhya Pradesh; law and
practice. Delhi, Metropolitan Book Co.,
sole agents: N.M.Tripathi, Bombay, 1963.
560p

1. Labor laws & legislation - Maharashtra,
India (State) 2. Labor laws & legislation -
Madhya Pradesh, India. 3. Labor laws & legis-
lation - Gujarat, India (State)

LC

O-153
Law, Bimala Churn, 1892- and Mookerjee, B.L.
Rent acts, Calcutta, Bombay and Rangoon.
Calcutta, 1924. 107p.

IOL

O-154
Maharashtra, India (State) High Court of
Judicature.
High Court of Bombay, 1862 to 1962. Bombay,
Govt.Central Press, 1962. 186p.

O-155
Maharashtra, India (State) Laws, statutes,
etc.
Maharashtra local acts, unified and regional
laws, 1827-1966, civil, criminal, revenue,
with rules, regulations and orders, commentary
and up-to-date case law. Agra, Wadhwa, 1967.
7v.

O-156
Malabari, Phirozshah Behramji Merwanji, 1853-
1912.
Bombay in the making, being mainly a history
of the origin and growth of judicial institutions in the Western Presidency, 1661-1726.
London, T.Fisher Unwin, 1910. 507p.

1. Justice, Administration of - Bombay. 2.
Bombay - Hist.

U & R

O-157
Mirams, A.E.
An address to the members of municipality
and citizens of Poona on the Bombay tour planning act of 1915. Poona, Yeravda Prison Press,
1916. 27p.

Cal nat'l Lib

O-158
Mitra, Avinasacandra.
Hindu law of adoption with leading cases
decided by the Privy Council, the Sudder Court
and High Courts of Calcutta, Bombay, Madras
and Allahabad from 1813 to 1889. Calcutta,
Central Press, 1890. 84p.

BM

O-159
Munshi, Kanaiyalal Maneklal, 1887-
Bombay High Court; half a century of
reminiscences. Bombay, Bharatiya Vidya
Bhavan, 1963. (Bhavan's book university.
Rupee series, 10). 43p.

1. Lawyers - India - Correspondence, reminiscences,
etc.

LC

O-160
Natekar, Papu Narayan.
The Dekkan Agriculturists' Relief Act:
no.XVII of 1879 (as amended by Acts XXI
of 1881, XXII of 1882 and XXIII of 1886)
with copious notes and full index. Poona,
1888. 210p.

IOL

O-161
Nery Xavier, Felippe, 1804-1874.
Colleccao de bandos, e outras differentes providencias que seriem de leis regulamentares para o Governo...das provincias demoninadas Novas Conquistas, etc. Nova Goa, 1840-51. 3v.

Rules & regulations

BM

O-162
Perry, Sir Thomas Erskine, 1806-1882.
Cases illustrative of oriental life, and the application of English law to India, decided in H.M.Supreme Court at Bombay. London, S.Sweet, 1853. 617p.

1. Las - India.

LC

O-163
Pradhan, Manohar Waman.
A treatise on the law relating to minors together with commentary on Central and Bombay Acts concerning children. Bombay, N.M.Tripathi, 1948. 355p.

LC

O-164
Rana, Frawji Ardsher.
Parsi law, containing the law applicable to Parsis as regards succession and inheritance, marriage and divorce. Bombay, Examiner Press, 1902. 185p.

BM

O-165
Ranade, Mahadev Govind, 1842-1901.
Statistics of criminal justice in the Bombay Presidency, to which are appended observations on the minute of the Hon.Mr. Fitzjames Stephen on the administration of justice in India. Bombay, Times of India Exchange Press, 1847. 54p.

O-166
Ratanlal, Ranchhoddas.
Unreported criminal cases of the High Court of Bombay, 1862-1898. Bombay, The Bombay Law Reporter Office, 1901. 1129p.

Col Nat Lib

O-167
The reign of law in the Bombay Presidency, QJPSS, v.2,no.2 (1879), pp.1-42.

GJPSS

O-168
Saldanha, Jerome Anthony.
Philology and ethnology and their bearing on customary law in the Bombay Presidency, ASBJ, v.25,no.71 (1917-21), pp.1-5.

ASBJ

O-169
Shivdasni, Tahilram Lilaram.
The Dekhan Agriculturist's Relief Act of 1879 as ammended up to the 15th July, 1901, and annotated with all the rulings of the Bombay High Court, etc. Hyderabad, Kauseria Press, 1901. 72p.

IO

O-170
Sinha, Ram Mohan.
Judicial administration under the Nagpur Bhonslas before the advent of British power in 1818, JIH, v.47 (1969), pp.95-114.

O-171
Steele, Arthur.
   Summary of the law and customs of Hindoo
castes within the Dekhun provinces subject
to the Presidency of Bombay, chiefly affecting civil suits. Bombay, Printed at the
Courier Press, 1827. 434p.

U of R

O-176
Argal, Rajeshwar Prasad.
   Municipal government in C.P. and Berar.
Nagpur, Nagpur Univ., 1949. *

Local govt - urban areas
BDD

O-172
Vachha, Phirozeshah Bejanji.
   Famous judges, lawyers and cases of Bombay:
a judicial history of Bombay during the British
period. Bombay, N.M.Tripathi, 1962. 374p.

LC

O-177
Arjun Rao Devashankar.
   Gram panchayat in Maharashtra, QJLSGI,
v.36 (1965), pp.201-209.

JaS '65

O-173
West, Sir Raymond, 1832-1912 and Bühler,
   Johann Georg, 1837-1898.
   A digest of the Hindu law from the replies
of the Shastris in the several courts of the
Bombay Presidency. 2d ed. Bombay, 1878.
711p.

BM

O-178
Barfivala, Chunilal Damodardas, 1889-
   The Bombay Village Panchayats Act, 1933,
and the rules thereunder (as amended up to
March 31, 1944) a study. QJLSGI, v.14 (1944),
pp.341-434: v.15 (1944-45), pp.1-18,19-42,
43-74: v.16 (1945-46), pp.75-90, 91-110.

Case

O-174
West, Sir Raymond, 1832-1912 and Bühler,
   Johann Georg, 1837-1898.
   A digest of the Hindu law of inheritance,
partition and adoption, embodying the replies
of the Sastries in the courts of the Bombay
Presidency. With introduction and notes by
Raymond West and Johann Georg Bühler. 3d ed.
Bombay, Printed at the Education Society's
Press, Byculla, 1884. 1v.

Local government

O-179
Barfivala, Chunilal Damodardas, 1889-
   Cases on local self-government acts; Bombay
and Gujarat, 1900-1963. Bombay, All India
Institute of Local Self-Government, 1964.
1236p.

U of R

O-175
All-India Institute of Local Self-Government.
   Poona municipal corporation. Bombay, 1953.
(Its series, no.1,pub.no.12). 29p.

U of R

O-180
Bombay. Local Self-Government Institute.
   Poona municipal corporation. Bombay, All-
India Institute of Local Self-government,
1953.

O-181
Bombay (Presidency)
Memorandum on municipal conservancy in the districts of the Bombay Presidency, Sind and Sattara. By E.Pratt. Bombay, 1856. (Bombay Presidency. Selections from the records, n.s.,no.27)

IOL

O-182
Bombay (State) Laws, Statutes, etc.
The bombay village Panchayat Act, 1958, by D.H.Chaudhari. Poona, N.R.Bhalerao, 1959.

1. Municipal corporations - Bombay (State)
2. Local government - Bombay (State)

O-183
Bombay marches on ... local self-government. QJLSGI, v.22 (1951), pp.275-77.

O-184
Carras, Mary Calliope.
The dynamics of political factions: a study of district councils (Zilla Parishads) in the State of Maharashtra. Philadelphia, Univ.of Pennsylvania, 1969. 485p. *

Shulman # 707

O-185
Dharmendra Nath.
The Delhi Municipal Corporation: a study of its structure in comparison to that of Calcutta, Bombay and Madras. Lucknow, Univ.of Lucknow, 1969. *

Local govt - urban areas

O-186
Inamdar, Narayan Raghunath.
Functioning of village panchayats.
Bombay, Popular Prakashan, 1970. 368p.

District Gov't & Panchayats Raj-books
BAS 1970

O-187
Inamdar, Narayan Raghunath and Pendse, Vinayak Vishwanath.
Panchayat leadership: a case study, JUP, no.15 (1962), pp.188-93.

Village of Dedu
JUP

O-188
Letter to Bombay government, forwarding the draft of a bill prepared by the Poona arbitration court to legalize trial by Panchayat court in civil suits, QJPSS, v.13,no.2 (1890), pp.70-78.

QJPSS

O-189
Local self-government in the Bombay Presidency, QJPSS, v.5,no.2 (1882), pp.12-63; v.6,no.2 (1883), pp.27-76; v.6,no.3 (1883), pp.23-61.

QJPSS

O-190
Maharashtra, India (State) Committee of Democratic Decentralisation.
Report. Bombay, Co-operation and rural development Dept., Govt.of Maharashtra, 1961. 304p.

1. Local govt. - Maharashtra, India (State)
2. Villages - India - Maharashtra (State)
3. Panchayat - Maharashtra, India (State)

NUR
LC

O-191
Maharashtra, India (State) Laws, statutes, etc.
The Bombay village panchayats act, 1958,
with rules (Bombay act no.III of 1959) by D.H.
Chaudhari, assisted by A.D.Chaudhari. Jalgaon,
D.H.Chaudhari, 1966. 502p.

O-192
Maharashtra, India (State) Laws, statutes, etc.
The Maharashtra zilla parishads and panchayat
samitis manual. Bombay, Director, Govt.Print.,
and Stationery, 1965. 2v.

1. Panchayat - Maharashtra, India (State)
2. Local government - Maharashtra, India (State)

O-193
Mangudkar, Manik Padmanna.
The constitutional development of local
self-government in India during the last
100 years. QJLSGI, v.25 (1955), pp.629-39.

case

O-194
Mangudkar, Manik Padmanna.
Municipal government in Poona, 1882-1947:
a case study. Poona, Univ.of Poona, 1957. *

O-195
Masani, Sir Rustom Pestonji, 1876-1966.
Evolution of local self-government in
Bombay. London, N.Y., H.Milford, Oxford
Univ.Press, 1929. 439p.

Bombay - Pol.& govt.

O-196
Masani, Sir Rustom Pestonji, 1876-1966.
The law and procedure of the municipal corporation of Bombay. Bombay, Times Press,
1921. 333p.

BM

O-197
Michael, L.W., comp.
The history of the municipal corporation
of the city of Bombay. Bombay, Union Press
(printers) 1902.

Col nath Lib.

O-198
Muley, D.S.
Working of village panchyats in Bhandara
District. Nagpur, Nagpur Univ., 1966. *

O-199
Muley, D.S.
Working of village panchayats in Bhandara
District. QJLSGI, v.37 (1967), pp.391-412;
v.38 (1968), pp.313-37; v.39 (1969), pp.
324-32.

O-200
Municipal corporation of Greater Bombay.
QJLSGI, v.26 (1955), pp.1-33.

O-201
Nayak, B.J.
An analytical study of the Bombay
Local Boards Act, 1923 (Act VI of 1923),
QJLSGI, v.28 (1957), pp.128-96, 369-414.

O-206
Proceedings of the Bombay Provincial Conference of 1888, QJPSS, v.11,no.2 (1888),
pp.1-25.

— Gort d pol .. local gort.

QJPSS

O-202
Pande, Vinayak Krishnarao.
Constitutional growth of municipalities
in Marathwada, JMaU, v.1,no.1 (1961), pp.
111-18.

O-207
Proceedings of the 2nd Bombay Provincial Conference held in May 1889, QJPSS, v.12,no.1
(1889), pp.1-116.

local. Gort

JMaU

QJPSS

O-203
Pherwani, Shewaram N.
Municipal efficiency, with special reference
to the Bombay Presidency. Hyderabad, Sind,
Blavatsky Press, 1926. 404p.

O-208
Representations on the Bombay local self-
government bills, JQPSS, v.6,no.3 (1883),
pp.29-54; v.6,no.4 (1883), pp.55-68.

Bom (Presid)

QJPSS

O-204
Pradhan, R.G.
Local self-government in the Bombay Presi-
dency, QJPSS, v.20,no.2 (1916), pp.86-100.

O-209
Rosenthal, Donald B.
The limited elite; politics and government
in two Indian cities. Chicago, Chicago
Univ.Press, 1970. 360p.

QJPSS

Municipal outsurban scw oppor
BAS 1970

O-205
Proceedings of a public meeting of the inhabitants of Poona, QJPSS, v.2,no.1 (1879),
pp.78-94.

O-210
Samant, Sitaram Vishwanath.
Village Panchayats with special reference
to Bombay State. Bombay, Local Self Government Institute, 1957. 224p.

panchayat

QJPSS

O-211
　Sastry, S.M.Y.
　　Studies in municipal administration of Greater
　Bombay. Bombay, All India Institute of Local
　Self Govt., 1969. 87p.

PL480/70

O-212
　Shah, Rasikchandra G.
　　The growth of local self-government in the
　presidency since 1858, QJLSGI, v.11 (1940),
　pp.71-138, 267-312.

Case

O-213
　Shah, Rasikchandra G.
　　The growth of local self-government in the
　province of Bombay since 1858. Bombay, C.D.
　Barfivala, 1955. 142p.

　　1. Local government - Bombay.

u.-'K

O-214
　Shaikh, R.C.
　　A critical study of administration of
　Ahmednagar Municipality, 1854-1962. Poona,
　Univ.of Poona, 1969. *

O-215
　Thakore, J.M.
　　Development of local self-government in
　Bombay and Saurashtra, QJLSGI, v.27 (1956),
　pp.159-206.

Case

O-216
　Thakore, J.M.
　　Development of local self-government in
　Bombay and Saurashtra, with an appendix on
　principles of local self-government. Bombay,
　C.D.Barfivala, 1957. 158p.

LC

O-217
　Thorner, Daniel.
　　The village Panchayat as a vehicle of
　change, EDCC, v.2 (1953), pp.209-15.

f urir

O-218
　Tinker, Hugh Russel.
　　Local government in India and Burma, 1908
　to 1937; a comparative study of the evolution
　and working of lacal authorities in Bombay,
　the United Provinces and Burma. London,
　London Univ., 1951. 456p. *

SOAS

O-219
　Wacha, Dinsha Edulji, 1844-1936.
　　Rise and growth of Bombay Municipal Govern-
　ment. Madras, G.A.Natesan & co., 1913. 467p.

　　1. Bombay - Pol.& govt.

LC

O-220
　Yajnika, Javerilala Umashankar.
　　Note on local self-government in the
　Bombay Presidency. Bombay, 1882. 61p.

NYPL

Politics & government

0-221
Baker, Donald Edward Uther.
Politics in a bilingual province: the
Central Provinces and Berar, India, 1919-
1939. Canberra, Australian National Univ.,
1969. *

0-222
Bombay (Presidency) Legislative Council.
Proceedings of the Council of the Governor
of Bombay assembled for the purpose of
making laws and regulations, 1894(-1920).
Bombay, 1895-1920.

Brit Mus

0-223
Bombay (Presidency) Legislature. Legislative
Assembly.
Debates. Official report. Vols.1-July
19,1937-1939. Bombay, Printed at the
Govt.Central Press, 1937-1939. 7v.

0-224
Bombay (Presidency) Legislature. Legislative
Council.
Bombay Legislative Council debates ...
official report, 1921-36. Bombay, Printed
at the Government Central Press, 1922-37.
45v.

Brit Mus.

0-225
Bombay (Presidency) Legislature. Legislative
Council.
Debates. Bombay, 1937-1939. 8v.

0-226
Bombay (Presidency) Legislature. Legislative
Council.
Proceedings of the legislative council of
the Governor of Bombay. Bombay, Printed at
the Government Central Press, 1912.

0-227
Bombay (State)
What Bombay government said and did.
Bombay, 1950-1960.

Singh

0-228
Bombay Representative Conference, 1922.
A report of the Proceedings ... Bombay,
1922.

0-229
Hart, Henry C.
Bombay politics: pluralism or polarization?.
JAS, v.20 (1961), pp.265-97.

0-230
Indian National Congress. Bombay Legislature
Congress Party.
Position of the minorities under the Congress
Government in Bombay, 21st July 1937-4th Nov.
1939. Bombay, The Hon.Secretaries, Bombay
Legislature Congress Party, 1939?

Wilson

O-231
Joshi, Ram.
Maharashtra. In: State politics in India,
ed.by Myron Weiner. Princeton, N.J.,
Princeton Univ.Press, 1968. pp.177-212.

O-232
Kini, N.G.S.
Caste as a factor in state politics: A case
study of the political behaviour of Kostis
of Nagpur City. In: State Politics in India.
Ed.by Iqbal Narain. Meerut, Meenakshi Prakashan, 1967. pp.562-74.

O-233
Kogekar, S.V.
The Bombay Presidency 1937-39: an interlude.
IJPS, v.2 (1941), pp.324-39.

O-234
Maharashtra, India (State) Legislature.
Maharashtra legislature manual. 5th ed.
Bombay, Director, Govt.Print.& Stationery,
1967. 265p.

1. Maharashtra, India (State) Legislature -
Rules & practice. 2. Maharashtra, India
(State) Legislature - Salaries, pensions, etc.

O-235
Maharashtra, India (State) Legislature. Legis-
lative Assembly.
Debates; official report. Bombay, Director,
Govt.Print.& Stationery, Maharashtra State.
v.1-   July 7, 1960-

O-236
Maharashtra, India (State) Legislature.
Legislative Council.
Debates; official report. Bombay,
Director, Govt.Print.and Stationery.
v.1-July 13, 1960-   Irregular.

O-237
Maharashtra, India (State) Legislature. Legislative Council.
Maharashtra Legislative Council rules. 4th
ed. Bombay, Director, Govt.Print.& Stationery, Maharashtra State, 1967. 190p.

1. Maharashtra, India (State) Legislature.
Legislative Council - Rules & practice.

O-238
Naik, Babu.
Who should rule Samyukta Maharashtra or
its caste pattern, Mankind, v.4 (1960),
pp.73-78.

O-239
Sirsikar, V.M.
Politics in Maharashtra: problems and pros-
pects. In: State politics in India. Ed.by
Iqbal Narain. Meerut, Meenakshi Prakashan,
1967. pp.192-202.

O-240
Wilson, Lawrence Bertell.
The Bombay Legislature, 1946-52: a study in
structure, composition and work. Bombay,
Univ.of Bombay, 1953. *

Political theory

O-241
Ambedkar, Bhimrao Ramji, 1892-1956.
Federation versus freedom. Bombay,
R.K.Tatnis, 1939. (Tracts for the times,
no.3). 161p.

1. India. Constitution   2. India - Polegout - 1919 -

O-242
The Ambedkar plan, MR, v.77 (1945), pp.252-
53.

Cool

O-243
Basu, Kamal Krishna.
Medieval kingship in the Deccan, JBRS,
v.31 (1945), pp.236-43.

JBPS index

O-244
Bharill, Chandra.
Social and political ideas of Dr.B.R.
Ambedkar: a study of his life, services,
social and political ideas. Jaipur, Univ.
of Rajasthan, 1970. *

Political science Biog

O-245
Brown, Donald Mackenzie, 1908-
The white umbrella; Indian political
thought from Manu to Gandhi. Berkeley,
University of California, 1953. 220p.

DNR

O-246
Gadgil, Dhananjaya Ramchandra, 1901-
The federal problem in India. Bombay,
1947. (Gokhale Institute of Politics and
Economics, Pub.no.15). 201p.

1. State governments - India   2. Federal government - India   DNR

O-247
Gadgil, Dhananjaya Ramchandra, 1901-
The formation of new provinces. Poona,
Samyukta Maharashtra Parishad, 1946.

Dhananjaya

O-248
Garde, D.K.
Social and political thought of the saints
of Maharashtra from Jnaneshwara to Ramdas
with special reference to Ramdas. Allahabad,
Univ.of Allahabad, 1958. *

O-249
Ghare, P.S.
Political thought in Maharashtra 1600-
1818. Poona, Univ.of Poona, 1969. *

Philosophy theory

O-250
Goyal, O.P.
Political ideas of Justice M.G.Ranade,
IJPS, v.23 (1962), pp.258-67.

0-251
Goyal, O.P.
Political thought of Gokhale. Allahabad,
Kitab Mahal, 1965. 143p.

UofR

0-252
Goyal, O.P.
Studies in modern Indian political thought;
the moderates and extremists. Allahabad,
Kitab Mahal, 1964. 119p.

UofR

0-253
Gundappa, D.V., 1889-
Gokhale: exponent of the citizen's Dharma,
PA, v.10 (1966), pp.107-12.

0-254
Gundappa, D.V., 1889-
Gokhale for today; liberalism restated,
Triveni, v.29 (1958), pp.42-61)

0-255
Inamdar, Narayan Raghunath.
Political thought in journals in Maharashtra
during 1818-1873, JUP, v.27 (1968), pp.37-55.

0-256
Inamdar, Narayan Raghunath.
Political thought of Balshastri Jambhekar
(1812-1846), the pioneer of renaissance in
Maharashtra, IJPS, v.21 (1960), pp.321-30.

casa

0-257
Inamdar, Narayan Raghunath.
Political thought of Vishnushastri Chip-
lunkar, JPU, v.31 (1969), pp.15-24.

*Modern history — articles
1969*

0-258
Jatava, Daya Ram, 1933-
Political philosophy of B.R.Ambedkar. Agra,
Phoenix Pub.Agency, 1965.

vvv LC ⁶³/₆₇

0-259
Joshi, Tukaram Dattaram.
Social and political thoughts of Ramdas.
1st ed. Bombay, Vora, 1970. 176p.

*Political science —
Biography
BAS 1970*

0-260
Kashikar, S.G.
The political thought of Samarth Ramlas
Swami, IJPS, v.24 (1963), pp.148-52.

0-261
Kher, V.
Contribution of Maharashtra to Indian political thought from 1885 to 1920. Gour Nagar, Sagar, Madhya Pradesh, Univ. of Saugar, 1964. *

Political science — Philosophy & theory
BDD

0-262
Kuber, Waman Narayan.
A critical study of the social and political thought of Dr.B.R.Ambedkar. Poona, Univ.of Poona, 1968. *

...ical science - ...
BDD

0-263
Mangudkar, Manik Padmanna.
Liberal thought in Maharashtra, JUP, v.9 (1958), pp.77-86.

South Asia Social Science Bibliography : Political Science | p. 11

0-264
Nim Hoti Lal.
Thoughts on Dr. Ambedkar. Agra, Siddhartha Educational and cultural Society, 1969. 107p.

JB 69

0-265
Oturkar, Rajaram Vinayak, 1898-
Theory of sovereignty in Maratha state, IHCP, v.23 (1960), pp.240-42.

UMR

0-266
Patil, A.P.
Social and political ideas of Mahatma Phule. Poona, Univ.of Poona, 1969. *

Political science.
BDD   Biog

0-267
Rajasekhariah, A.M.
Dr.B.R.Ambedkar: a study of his contribution to the political and constitutional evolution of India. Dharwar, Karnatak Univ., 1967. *

... ...
BDD

0-268
Rao, Vasant Dinanath, 1913-
Socio-political thought of Jotiba Phooley, IHCP, v.27 (1965), pp.333-38.

J HC P

0-269
Reddy, V.Narayan Karan.
Sarvodaya ideology and Acharya Vinoba Bhave. Hyderabad, Andhra Pradesh Sarvodaya Mandal, 1963. (World-integration series). 116p.

(series)

LC

0-270
Sapru, P.N.
The political philosophy of Gokhale, GM, v.10 (1966), pp.123-30.

O-271
Sarkar, Benoy Kumar.
The Maratha political ideas of the 18th century. IHQ, v.12 (1936), pp.88-103.

O-272
Sarkar, Benoy Kumar.
The political philosophy of Ramdas, CR, v.57 (1935), pp.157-68.

O-273
Shay, Theodore L.
The legacy of the Lokamanya: the political philosophy of Bal Gangadhar Tilak. Bombay, Indian Branch, Oxford University Press, 1956. 235p.

O-274
Suda, Jyoti Prasad.
Main currents of social and political thought in modern India. Meerut, Jai Prakash Nath, 1963.
Vol.1 - The liberal and national traditions.

1. Political science - Hist. - India.

O-275
Varma, Vishwanath Prasad.
Political philosophy of Lokamanya Tilak, IJPS, v.19 (1958), pp.15-24.

O-276
Badhe, G.S. and Rao, M.U.
Political parties in municipal level, JUB, v.39 (1970), pp.250-67.

O-277
Biographical sketch. In: Our Doc, tributes to comrade Gangadhar Akhikari on his seventieth birthday. Ed.by M.B.Rao and Mohit Sen. New Delhi, New Age Printing Press, 1968. pp.1-10.

O-278
Carras, Mary Calliope.
Congress factionalism in Maharashtra: a case study of the Akola Zilla Parishad, AS, v.10,no.5 (1970), pp.410-26.

O-279
Chari, Dilshad.
Dr.Adhikari. In: Our Doc, tributes to comrade Gangadhar Adhikari on his seventieth birthday. Ed.by M.B.Rao and Mohit Sen. New Delhi, New Age Printing Press, 1968. pp.52-55.

O-280
Curran, Jean A., Jr.
RSS militant Hinduism, FES, v.19 (1950), pp.93-98.

O-281
Dastur, Aloo J. and Mehta, Usha H.
Congress rule in Bombay 1952 to 1956.
Bombay, Popular Book Depot, 1958. 219p.

u of R

O-282
Desai, M.G.
Dr.Gangadhar Adhikari, Ph.D. In: Our
Doc, tributes to comrade Gangadhar
Adhikari on his seventieth birthday.
Ed.by M.B.Rao and Mohit Sen. New Delhi,
New Age Printing Press, 1968. pp.24-32.

U of R

O-283
Gandhi, Mohandas Karamchand, 1869-1948.
Address to Congress workers in Maharashtra,
Aundh, 1944. 6p.

IOL

O-284
Ghate, S.V.
Most human comrade. In: Our Doc, tributes
to comrade Gangadhar Adhikari on his
seventieth birthday. Ed.by M.B.Rao and
Mohit Sen. New Delhi, New Age Printing
Press, 1968. pp.11-14.

U of R

O-285
Grover, B.L.
The genesis of the Indian National Congress.
JIH, v.41 (1963), pp.607-18.

O-286
Josh, Sohan Singh.
'Our Doc'. In: Our Doc, tributes to
comrade Gangadhar Adhikari on his
seventieth birthday. Ed.by M.B.Rao and
Mohit Sen. New Delhi, New Age Printing
Press, 1968. pp.15-23.

U of R

O-287
Joshi, Ram.
Political parties in Maharashtra. In:
State Politics in India. Ed.by Iqbal
Narain. Meerut, Meenakshi Prakashan,
1967. pp.475-84.

O-288
Joshi, Ram.
The Shiv Sena: a movement in search of
legitimacy, AS, v.10,no.11 (1970), pp.967-
78.

*Buddhism
BAS 1970*

O-289
Kapilacharya.
Siva Sena speaks. Bombay, Bal K.Thackeray,
1967.

O-290
Katdare, L.A.
On the occasion of Dr.Adhikari's birthday.
In: Our Doc, tributes to comrade
Gangadhar Adhikari on his seventieth
birthday. Ed.by M.B.Rao and Mohit Sen.
New Delhi, New Age Printing Press, 1968.
pp.48-51.

U of R

O-291
    Kelkar, Narsinha Chintaman, 1872-1947.
      Presidential address, AIOCPT, v.10
    (1940), pp.654-63.

UofR

O-292
    Krishnan, N.K.
      Comrade Adhikari. In: Our Doc, tributes
    to comrade Gangadhar Adhikari on his
    seventieth birthday. Ed.by M.B.Rao and
    Mohit Sen. New Delhi, New Age Printing
    Press, 1968. pp.41-44.

UofR

O-293
    Kulkarni, Atmaram Ganesh.
      Study of political parties in Maharashtra
    with special reference to the period 1947-62.
    Poona, Poona Univ., 1968.

Jayakar List # 1433

O-294
    Our Doc; tributes to Comrade Gangadhar Adhi-
    kari on his seventieth birthday. Ed.by
    M.B.Rao & Mohit Sen. New Delhi, Communist
    Party of India, 1968. 63p.

U of R

O-295
    Pardiwala, H.R.
      The Shiv Sena, Why? and Why not? Bombay,
    Popular Prakashan, 1968.

O-296
    Pareek, Udai Narain, 1925- comp.
      Studies in rural leadership. Delhi, Behavi-
    oral Sciences Centre, 1966. 116p.

      1. Leadership. 2. Comunity development -
    India. 3. India - Rural condit.

LC

O-297
    Rahudkar, Wasudeo B.
      The relationship of certain personal
    attributes to the success of village level
    workers, IJSW, v.23 (1963), pp.319-26.

So. Asia Soc. Sci. Bib.

O-298
    Rao, C. Rajeswara.
      Ideal comrade. In: Our Doc, tributes to
    comrade Gangadhar Adhikari on his
    seventieth birthday. Ed.by M.B.Rao and
    Mohit Sen. New Delhi, New Age Printing
    Press, 1968. pp.33-34.

UofR

O-299
    Rao, M.B.
      Working with Doc. In: Our Doc, tributes
    to comrade Gangadhar Adhikari on his
    seventieth birthday. Ed.by M.B.Rao and
    Mohit Sen. New Delhi, New Age Printing
    Press, 1968. pp.56-59.

UofR

O-300
    Rosenthal, Donald B.
      Factions and alliances in two Indian
    cities, NYSPSAP, (1966), pp.44-59.

JAS 5/68

0-301
Sardesai, S.G.
To whom a generation of communists owes so much. In: Our Doc, tributes to comrade Gangadhar Adhikari on his seventieth birthday. Ed.by M.B.Rao and Mohit Sen. New Delhi, New Age Printing Press, 1968. pp.35-40.

UotR

0-302
Sen, Mohit.
Scientific temper. In: Our Doc, tributes to comrade Gangadhar Adhikari on his seventieth birthday. Ed.by M.B.Rao and Mohit Sen. New Delhi, New Age Printing Press, 1968. pp.60-64.

UotR

0-303
Sinha, D.P.
An underground human being! In: Our Doc, tributes to comrade Gangadhar Adhikari on his seventieth birthday. Ed.by M.B.Rao and Mohit Sen. New Delhi, New Age Printing Press, 1968. pp.45-47.

4 gR

0-304
Sirsikar, V.M.
Leadership patterns in rural Maharashtra, AS. v.4 (1964), pp.929-39.

ga864

0-305
Sirsikar, V.M.
The rural elite in a developing society: a study in political sociology. New Delhi, Orient Longmans, 1970. 227p.

BAS 1970

0-306
Sirsikar, V.M.
A study of political workers in Poona, JUP. v.13 (1961), pp.77-159.

ga861

0-307
Srinivasan, R.
Maharashtra and the Congress Party, 1962-67. JUB. v.37 (1968), pp.254-77.

ua R

0-308
Ambedkar, Bhimrao Ramji, 1892-1956.
Maharashtra as a linguistic province. Statement submitted to the Linguistic Provinces Commission. Bombay, Thacker & co., 1948. 41p.

10L

0-309
Aney, Madhav Shrihari.
Memorandum submitted to the States Reorganization Commission. Yeotmal, Yeotmal District Association, n.d.

VVV Stern

0-310
Antulay, A.R., 1929-
Mahajan report uncovered. Bombay, New York, Allied Publishers, 1968. 192p.

0-311
    Bombay Citizens' Committee.
        Case for Bombay: a brief summary. Bombay,
    1955? 11p.

0-312
    Bombay Citizens' Committee.
        Memorandum submitted to the States Reorgani-
    sation Commission...re: reorganisation of the
    states. Bombay, 1954. 92p.

0-313
    Bombay Provincial Congress Committee.
        Memorandum submitted to Linguistic
    Provinces Commission...re: regrouping of
    provinces. Bombay, 1948. 29p.

0-314
    A case for the formation of a new province,
    "United Maharashtra." Trans.into English by
    T.V.Patwate. Poona, Shri Shankarrao Deo,
    1948. 128p.

0-315
    Dave, Rohit.
        Regionalism in Maharashtra-an outsider's
    appreciation, JUP, v.9 (1958), pp.131-37.

0-316
    Discussion, JUP, v.9 (1958), pp.146-57.

        (Maharashtra & regionalism with several
    participants)

0-317
    Gadgil, Dhananjaya Ramchandra, 1901-
        The future of Bombay City. Poona, Samyukta
    Maharashtra Parishad, 1948. 34p.

0-318
    Gadgil, Dhananjaya Ramchandra, 1901-
        Some observations on the report of the
    states reorganization commission. Poona,
    Samyukta Maharashtra Parishad, 1956.

0-319
    Gadgil, Dhananjaya Ramchandra, 1901-
        Unification of Maharashtra. Poona, Samyukta
    Maharashtra Parishad, 1946.

0-320
    Gujarat Pradesh Congress Committee.
        Memorandum, presented by Gujarat Pradesh
    Congress Comm. to the States Reorganization
    Commission. Ahmedabad, Nanubhai Derasary, 1954.
    72p.

0-321
 Halappa, G.S., 1922-   and Jangam, R.T.
  The Mahajan Commission and after; a study of
 elite response, *JKU*, v.4 (1968), pp.9-17.

[handwritten notation]

0-322
 India (Republic) States Reorganisation Commission.
  Report. Delhi, Manager of Publications,
 1955. 273p.

uzjk

0-323
 Iyengar, M.A.S.
  Regionalism and Maharashtra: an outsider's
 appreciation, *JUP*, v.9 (1958), pp.138-45.

South Asia Social Science
Bibliography; Political
Science, p. 22

0-324
 Kothurkar, Vasudeo Krishna.
  Content analysis of some pro and anti- Samyukta Maharashtra news-paper materials, *JUP*,
 no.9 (1958), pp.99-104.

JUP

0-325
 Lincoln Institute of Social Research and
 Public Opinion, Dharwar, India. Research
 Unit.
  The moving frontiers of Maharashtra; an
 objective analysis of the border disputes
 between Maharashtra and Mysore. Dharwar,
 1967. (Current affairs pamphlet series, 3).
 63p.

1. Maharashtra, India (State) - Bound. - Mysore 2 Mysore -
Bound, - Maharashtra,   India (State)
uof 2

0-326
 Linguistic provinces and the Karnatak problem.
  A detailed statement by the Karnatak Provin-
 cial Congress Committee and the Karnatak
 Ekikaran Mahasamiti. Hubli, A.J.Dodmetti,
 1948. 76p.

Bom (Pres) cat

0-327
 Maharashtra, India (State)
  Maharashtra and Mysore. Facts relating to
 border dispute. Bombay, 1966. 70p.

Prabhu

0-328
 Maharashtra, India (State)
  Memorandum on Maharashtra-Mysore border
 dispute to the Commission on Maharashtra-
 Mysore-Kerala boundary disputes. Bombay,
 1967. 256p.

uuu
Prabhu
Uof R order

0-329
 Maharashtra, India (State)
  Supplementary memorandum submitted by the
 Gvernment of Maharashtra to the commission
 on Maharashtra-Mysore-Kerala boundary dispute.
 Bombay, 1967. 55p.

prabhu

0-330
 Mukerji, Krishna Prasanna, 1901-   , Ramaswamy,
 Suhasini.
  Reorganization of Indian states. Bombay,
 Popular Book Depot, 1955. 91p.

  1. Bombay (State) Boundaries. 2. India -
 Pol.& govt. - 1947-

uof F

O-331
　　Munshi Kanaiyalal Maneklal, 1887-
　　　　Linguistic provinces and the future of
　　Bombay. Bombay, Nat'l Information & Pubs.,
　　1948. 72p.

u ⋋R

O-332
　　Nadkarni, Anand S.
　　　　Regionalism in Maharashtra and democracy,
　　JUP, v.9 (1958), pp.72-76.

South As a Social Science
Bibliography political survey
2Ik

O-333
　　Quaerens Veritatem, pseud.
　　　　Justice shall prevail; the struggle for
　　Samyukta Maharashtra. Poona, J.S.Tilak,
　　1958. 107p.

LC

O-334
　　Rama Rao, D.V.
　　　　Linguistic units and bilingual areas,
　　Triveni, v.25 (1954), pp.35-44.

NYPL

O-335
　　Rege, D.V.
　　　　Bilingual Bombay State and border dispute,
　　MR, v.106 (1959), pp.204-206.

JVVMR

O-336
　　Samyukta Maharashtra Parishad.
　　　　A case for the formation of a new province:
　　"United Maharashtra". Poona, Samyukta Maha-
　　rashtra Parishad, 1949. 124p.

U ⋋R micra

O-337
　　Samyukta Maharashtra Parishad.
　　　　Reorganization of States in India with
　　particular reference to the formation of
　　Maharashtra, being the memorandum submitted
　　to the States Reorganization Commission.
　　Bombay, Topiwalla Mansion, 1954.　110p.

LC Accessions 1957, p.637

O-338
　　Stern, Robert W.
　　　　Maharashtrian linguistic provincialism
　　and Indian nationalism, PacA, v.37 (1964),
　　pp.37-49.

ga&64

O-339
　　Tikekar, Shripad Ramachandra, 1900-
　　　　Trouble over Bombay, IAR, v.2 (1956), pp.
　　4-6.

Social Science Bibliography
India 1956 - Political Science,
p 26

O-340
　　Times of India, Bombay.
　　　　Claim of Samyukta Maharashtra over Bombay:
　　from "illogical" to "reprehensible". A picture
　　of deterioration. Bombay, C.L.Gheewala, Hon.
　　Secretary, Bombay Citizens Committee, 1955?
　　11p.

LC Accessions 1957 p 578

O-341
Windmiller, Marshall.
The politics of states reorganization in India: the case of Bombay, FES, v.25 (1956), pp.129-43.

State formation & boundaries

Public hygiene & sanitation

P-1
Aitken, Russel.
Report on the main drainage of Bombay. Bombay, 1866. 35p.

Bom (Pres) cat

P-2
Ambrose, L.F.
Pandharpur plague 1911. Nasrapur, the author, 1912. 21p.

P-3
Bentley, Charles Albert.
Report of an investigation into the causes of Malaria in Bombay and the measures necessary for its control. Bombay, Printed at the Govt.Central Press, 1911. 182p.

1. Malarial fever - Bombay. 2. Malarial fever - Prevention. 3. Mosquito.

LC

P-4
Bombay (City) Municipal Commissioner.
Report ... on the plague in Bombay for the year ending 31st May 1900. Bombay, 1900-1901. 2v.

IOL

P-5
Bombay (Presidency).
The Bombay plague, being a history of the progress of plague in the Bombay presidency from Sept.1896 to June 1899. By Condon. Bombay, Printed at the Education Society's Press, 1900. 396p.

1. Plague - Bombay. 2. Bombay (Presidency - Sanitary affairs.
Check in LC

LC

P-6
Bombay (Presidency)
Leprosy and its control in the Bombay Presidency. Bombay, 1941. 4p.

BM

P-7
Bombay (Presidency)
On the supply of water to Bombay. Bombay, 1854. (Bombay Presidency. Selections from the records, n.s.,no.1).

IOL

P-8
Bombay (Presidency)
Report on the sanitary state and sanitary requirements of Bombay, with appendices; by H.Conybeare. Bombay, 1885. (Bombay Presidency. Selections from the records, n.s.,no.11). 145p.

Brit. Mus.
Ind. Off Lib

P-9
Bombay (Presidency)
Report on the sanitary state of the city of Poona. By A.H.Leith. Bombay, 1864. (Bombay Presidency. Selections from the records, n.s., no.79). 145p.

IOL

P-10
    Bombay (Presidency)
       Report on the sanitary state of the island
    of Bombay. By A.H.Leith. Bombay, 1864.
    (Bombay Presidency. Selections from the
    records, n.s.,no.80) 50p.

IOL

P-11
    Bombay (Presidency) Bombay Plague Committee.
       Report...on the plague in Bombay, for the
    period extending from the 1st July, 1897 to
    the 30th April, 1898. Bombay, 1898. 2v.

BM

P-12
    Chakrabarti, M.C.
       A statistical study of the data collected
    at the health centre at Khar, Bombay, JGRS,
    v.16 (1954), pp.149-57.

P-13
    Chandrachud, C.N.
       Memories of an Indian doctor. Bombay,
    Popular Prakashan, 1970. 240p.

P-14
    Compulsary vaccination in the Bombay Presi-
       dency, QJPSS, v.14,no.3 (1891), pp.1-16.

P-15
    Dhurandhar, K.V.
       The sanitary conditions of the towns and
    villages in the Bombay Presidency and the
    means for improving the same, QJPSS, v.14,
    no.1 (1891), pp.1-16.

P-16
    James, C. Carkeet.
       Forty Years' sanitary progress in
    Bombay, AR, n.s.,v.12 (1917), pp.282-92.

P-17
    Joshi, Raghunath Muralidhar, 1904-
       Diseases, medicines and physicians during
    the Peshwa regime (1713-1818), IJHM, v.3
    (1958), pp.25-32.

P-18
    Kantawala, S.T.
       The second report of health, economic and
    nutrition survey of 55 families at Khar
    (Greater Bombay), JGRS, v.16 (1954), pp.124-41.

P-19
    Maharashtra, India (State) Directorate of
       Publicity.
       Progress and problems of health in Maharash-
    tra. 4th ed. Bombay, 1962. 84p.

       1. Hygiene, Public - Maharashtra, India (State)

P-20
    Mehta, Chamanlal.
        Rural medical relief in Bombay Province,
    JGRS, v.10 (1948), pp.209-13.

u of R

P-21
    Menant, Delphine, 1850-
        Un sanatorium dans l'Inde: Mahableshvar,
    TdM, n.s., v.13 (1907), pp.97-120.

CB

P-22
    Morison, J.
        The causes of monsoon diarrhoea and dysen-
    tery in Poona, IJMR, v.2 (1915), pp.950-76.

I OL

P-23
    Narde, A.D.
        Problem of tuberculosis control in Bombay,
    IJSW, v.17 (1956), pp.21-29.

P-24
    Pai, D.N.
        Socio-economic and health survey of
    Narli-Agripada village; a preliminary
    report, JGRS, v.25 (1963), pp.189-220.

u of R

P-25
    Poona, India (City) University.
        A report on health status and level of
    living in Kolhapur Community project, by
    Vasudeo Kothurkar and others. Poona, 1969.
    142p.

U of R
PL480 4/70

P-26
    Pottinger, D.
        A clinical survey of the intestinal infec-
    tions of Poona, Deccan, 1925-27. Edinburgh,
    Edinburgh University, 1929. *

Bloomfield

P-27
    Preliminary report of health screening con-
    ducted at Health Research Institute, Khar
    from July 1959 to April 1960, JGRS, v.22
    (1960), pp.261-67.

P-28
    Raman, K.S.
        Bombay City's water supply, CA, v.10
    (1963), pp.25-29.

P-29
    Raman, K.S.
        Bombay cries out for more water, CA,
    v.13 (1966), pp.25-30.

P-30
    Representation to the Bombay government on
        the district vaccination bill, QJPSS, v.14,
        no.4 (1891), pp.31-34.

QJPSS

P-31
    Sanitary aspects of Bombay, BQR, v.7,no.14
        (1858), pp.219-51.

b.yR manufacture

P-32
    Sowerby, William.
        Remarks on the drainage of Bombay. Bombay,
    Printed at Education Society's Press, 1869.
    40p.

P-33
    Viegas, A.G.
        Bubonic plague in Bombay, etc. Bombay,
    Tattvavivechaka Press, 1897. 67p.

BM

P-34
    Waters, G.
        Plague in Bombay, JASB, v.5 (1901), pp.282-
    96.

Case

P-35
    World bank aid for Bombay's water supply
        plans, CA, v.16,no.4 (1969), pp.35-38.

*Foreign aid Nulvestment -
articles;
BAS 1969*

P-36
    Yodh, B.B.
        Health Research Institute at Khar, JGRS,
    v.21 (1959), pp.187-90.

*APU
LC Accessions 1960 - 2*

P-37
    Yodh, B.B.
        In search of positive health further re-
    ports of multiphasic surveys by the Health
    Research Institute. JGRS, v.23 (1961), pp.
    203-05.

Recreation &   Bibliography & Reference
performing arts

Q-1
    Mehta, Chandravadan Chimanlal, 1901-
        Bibliography of stageable plays in Indian
    languages. Comp.by C.C.Mehta with the help
    of V.Raghavan [and others] and arranged in
    the alphabetical order of the languages:
    Gujarati, Hindi, Kashmiri, Marathi, Punjabi,
    Sanskrit, Telugu, Urdu. New Delhi, Pub.under
    the joint auspices of M.S.University of
    Baroda and Bharatiya Natya Sangha, 1963-

U of R

Q-2
    Rangoonwalla, Firoze.
        Indian films index: 1912-1967. Compilation
    work: Vishwanath Das. Bombay, J.Udeshi,
    1968. 130p.

General works

Q-3
Agarkar, Achyut Jagannath.
Folk dance of Maharashtra. Bombay,
Popular Book Depot, 1950. 172p.

Social anthropology

Q-4
Arte, S.B.
Mr. D.G.Phalke and his 'Hindusthan Cinema
Films', MR, v.23 (1918), pp.516-19.

Q-5
Barnouw, Erik, 1908-   and Krishnaswamy, S.
Indian film. New York, Columbia Univ.Press,
1963. 315p.

LC

Q-6
Burton, Reginald George, 1864-
Sport and wild life in the Deccan: an
account of big-game hunting during nearly
40 years of service in India, with much
interesting information on the habits of the
wild animals in that country. London, Seeley,
Service & co.ltd. 282p.

1. Hunting- India - Haidarabad (State) 2.
Hunting - India - Haidarabad assigned districts.
3. Zoology - India - Haidarabad (State) 4.
Zoology - India -   Haidaradab assigned
districts.

LC

Q-7
Damle, S.V.
A short history of the origin, growth and
activities of the Maharashtriya Mandal, Poona
City. Poona, S.V.Damle, 1934. 16p.

Cat. Bom (Ind)

Q-8
Daniélou, Alain.
A catalogue of recorded classical and
traditional Indian music. Introd.on
Indian musical theory and instruments.
Paris, UNESCO, 1952. (Archives of
Recorded Music, ser.B., Oriental music,
v.1). 235p.

LC

Q-9
Day, Charles Russell, 1860-1900.
The music and musical instruments of
Southern India and the Deccan. London,N.Y.,
Novello, Ewer & co., 1891. 190p.

1. Music - India. 2. Musical instruments -
India.

LC

Q-10
Deshpande, Vamanrao.
Maharashtra's contribution to music. New
Delhi, Maharashtra Information Centre, 1973?

2

Statesmens Weekly 11-2, 73

Q-11
Joshi, N.V.
The influence of Marathi stage on music,
SN, no.15 (1970), pp.48-56.

BAS 1970

Q-12
Kabunkar, G.S.
Pandit Bhatkhande, HR, v.68 (1936), pp.417-
22.

HR

Q-13
Kale, Keshav Narayan, 1904–
Theatre in Maharashtra. New Delhi,
Maharashtra Information Centre, Govt.of
Maharashtra, 1967. 23p.

Q-18
Mehta, Kumud A.
Bombay's theatre world: 1860–1880, ASBJ,
v.43/44 (1968/69), pp.251–78.

Q-14
Khanapurkar, D.P.
Tamasha, EA, v.7 (1953), pp.19–36.

Q-19
Mehta, Kumud A.
English drama on the Bombay stage towards
the turn of the century – 1880–1900, ASBJ,
n.s., v.39–40 (1964/65), pp.205–24.

Q-15
Lobo, Ansthen.
The history and evolution of Goan music,
Marg, v.8 (1954), pp.59–61.

Q-20
Modi, Rusi.
Cricket forever. Bombay, 1964. 128p.

1. Cricket – India.

Q-16
Lupi, Nita.
Musica e alma da India Portuguesa. Lisboa,
Agência Geral do Ultramar, Divisão de Publica-
ções e Biblioteca, 1956. 191p.

Q-21
Mujawar, Isak.
Maharashtra, birthplace of Indian film
industry. New Delhi, Chief Information
Officer, Maharashtra Information Center,
1969. 156p.

Q-17
The Marathi theatre, 1843–1960. Bombay, Pub.
for Marathi Natya Parishad by Popular Book
Depot, 1961. 78p.

1. Theater – Maharashtra, India (State)
2. Maharathi drama – Hist. & crit.

Q-22
Nadkarni, Jnaneshvar Ganpat, 1928–
The experimental theatre in Maharashtra,
MP, v.1 (1968), pp.16-18.

Q-23
Nadkarni, Jnaneshwar Ganpat, 1928-
Marathi Tamasha yesterday and today, SN,
no.12 (1969), pp.19-28.

music, dance, drama
RAS 1969

Q-24
Nadkarni, Jnaneshwar Ganpat, 1928-
New directions in the Marathi theatre.
New Delhi, Chief Information Officer,
Maharashtra Centre, 1967. 53p.

NuR
PL480 '68

Q-25
Nakhooda, Zulie.
Leisure and recreation of society. Allahabad,
Kitab Mahal, 1961. 361p.

1. Leisure. 2. Recreation. 3. Bombay -
Soc.condit.

Q-26
Pavri, Merwanji Erachji.
Parsi cricket. Bombay, Jame Jamshed Print.
Works, 1901. 196p.

Rem.(Pra.) cat

Q-27
Pereira, Jose and Martins, Micael.
Representative examples of the classical
and vocal music of Goa, Marg. v.8 (1954),
pp.64-89.

KNX

Q-28
Ranade, Ganesh Hari.
Gayanacharya Pandit Mirashibuwa, SN, v.14
(1969), pp.50-64.

Biog- artist
RAS 1970

Q-29
Ranade, Ganesh Hari.
Music in Maharashtra. New Delhi, Maharashtra
Information Centre, 1967. 60p.

PL480 '69

Q-30
Ranade, Ganesh Hari.
Powada, a folk music form of Maharashtra,
JMAM, v.13 (1942), pp.71-73.

Filer

Q-31
Ranade, Ganesh Hari.
The tamasha: a form of open-air opera of
Maharashtra, JMAM, v.33 (1962), pp.140-41.

Q-32
Shah, Panna.
The Indian film. Bombay, Motion Picture
Society of India, 1950. 305p.

Sociology leisure
Recreation

Q-33
Shapurji Sohrabji.
Chronicle of cricket amongst parsis and the
struggle polo versus cricket. Bombay, Ripon
Print.Press, 1897. 128p.

kcm (Bres, cat

R-1
Dr. C.P.Ramaswami Aiyar Research Endowment
Committee.
A bibliography of Indian philosophy.
Madras, 1963-

Q-34
Sheppard, Samuel Townsend, 1880-
The Byculla Club, 1833-1916; a history.
Illustrated by Cecil L.Burns. Bombay,
Bennett, Coleman, 1961. 188p.

u of 2

R-2
Encyclopedia of Indian philosophies. By
Sibajiban Bhattacharya and others. Delhi,
Pub.for American Institute of Indian
Studies by Motilal Banarsidass, 1970-
v.1 - Bibliography of Indian philosophies.
Comp.by Karl L.Potter.

V of P

Q-35
Vaidya, Sudhir, 1938-
Vinoo Mankad. Bombay, Thacker, 1969. 169p.

PL 480 9/70

R-3
India. Imperial Record Dept.
An alphabetical list of the feasts and
holidays of the Hindus and Muhammedans.
Calcutta, Superintendent, Government
Printing, 1914. 131p.

Q-36
Vishnu Digambar Paluskar, DMJ, v.6 (1970),
pp.42-44.

Burg - Articles
BAS 1970

R-4
International bibliography of the history of
religions. Bibliographie internationale de
l'histoire des religions. 1952-

M of R

Q-37
Yajnik, Ramanlal Kanaiylal, 1895-
The Indian theatre, its origins and its
later development under European influence,
with special reference to western India.
New York, E.P.Dutton & co., 1934. 3 pts.

1. Theater - India. 2. Shakespeare, Wm. -
India, appreciation.

Lc

R-5
Jain, Chhote Lal.
Jaina bibliography: with a foreword by
Kalidas Nag. Calcutta, Bharati Jaina
Parisat, 1945. (Jaina bibliography series,
no.1) 387p.

4 of R

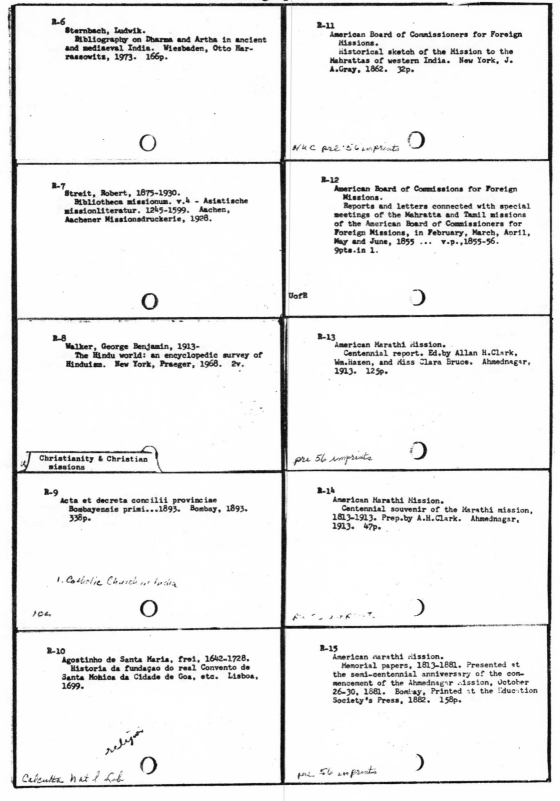

R-6
Sternbach, Ludwik.
    Bibliography on Dharma and Artha in ancient
and mediaeval India. Wiesbaden, Otto Har-
rassowitz, 1973. 166p.

R-7
Streit, Robert, 1875-1930.
    Bibliotheca missionum. v.4 - Asiatische
missionliteratur. 1245-1599. Aachen,
Aachener Missionsdruckerie, 1928.

R-8
Walker, George Benjamin, 1913-
    The Hindu world: an encyclopedic survey of
Hinduism. New York, Praeger, 1968. 2v.

Christianity & Christian
missions

R-9
Acta et decreta concilii provinciae
    Bombayensis primi...1893. Bombay, 1893.
    338p.

1. Catholic Church in India

104

religion

Calcutta Nat'l Lib

R-10
Agostinho de Santa Maria, frei, 1642-1728.
    Historia da fundaçao do real Convento de
Santa Mohica da Cidade de Goa, etc. Lisboa,
1699.

R-11
American Board of Commissioners for Foreign
    Missions.
    Historical sketch of the Mission to the
Mahrattas of western India. New York, J.
A.Gray, 1862. 32p.

NUC pre '56 imprints

R-12
American Board of Commissions for Foreign
    Missions.
    Reports and letters connected with special
meetings of the Mahratta and Tamil missions
of the American Board of Commissioners for
Foreign Missions, in February, March, April,
May and June, 1855 ... v.p.,1855-56.
9pts.in 1.

UofR

R-13
American Marathi Mission.
    Centennial report. Ed.by Allan H.Clark,
Wm.Hazen, and Miss Clara Bruce. Ahmednagar,
1913. 125p.

pre 56 imprints

R-14
American Marathi Mission.
    Centennial souvenir of the Marathi mission,
1813-1913. Prep.by A.H.Clark. Ahmednagar,
1913. 47p.

pre 56 imprints

R-15
American Marathi Mission.
    Memorial papers, 1813-1881. Presented at
the semi-centennial anniversary of the commencement of the Ahmednagar Mission, October
26-30, 1881. Bombay, Printed at the Education
Society's Press, 1882. 158p.

pre 56 imprints

R-16
Ashley-Brown, William, 1887-
On the Bombay coast and Deccan; the origin
and history of the Bombay diocese, a record
of 300 years' work for Christ in western
India. London, Society for promoting Christian Knowledge. 1937. 288p.

1. Church of India, Burma & Ceylon. Bombay
(Diocese) - Hist. 2. India - Missions.

NUR
LC

R-17
Bardwell, Horatio.
Anecdotes of the Bombay mission for the
conversion of the Hindoos. London, 1836.
(Reprint of Memoir of G.Hall, Andover, Mass.,
1834). 257p.

R-18
Bardwell, Horatio.
Memoir of Reverend Gordon Hall, A.M. one
of the first missionaries of the American
Board of Commissioners for Foreign Missions,
at Bombay. Andover, Mass., 1834. 260p.

R-19
Barros Gomes, Henrique de, 1843-1898.
O padroado da Coroa de Portugal nas
Indias orientaes e a concordata de 23 de
Junho de 1886 Discurses proferidos na
Camara dos Senhores Deputados nas
sessões de 5,6 e 7 de maio de 1887.
Lisboa, 1887. 107p.

BM

R-20
Berduda, Claudio Legrange Monteiro de,
1803-45.
Instruçoes com que El-Rei D.Jose Imandou
passar ao Estado do India o Governador e
Capitao General e o Ciroebispo Primas
Orients no anno de 1774. 2d ed. Nova Goa,
1903.

R-21
Bombay (Presidency) All Saints Bombay
Missionary Association.
From Bombay to the Deccan. With a preface
by the Rev.O.D.Watkins, etc. London, A.R.
Mowbray & Co., 1914.

Brit Mus

R-22
Bombay Auxiliary Bible Society.
Jubilee commemoration at Bombay of the
British and Foreign Bible Society, 21st
December, 1853. Bombay, 1854.

R-23
Bouhours, Dominique.
The life of St.Francis Xavier. Trans.by
Mr.Dryden. London, for Jacob Tonson, 1698.
787p.

BM

R-24
Bowen, George, 1816-1888.
George Bowen of Bombay, missionary, scho-
lar, mystic, saint; a memoir by Robert E.
Speer. N.Y., Missionary review of the world,
1938. 376p.

NUR
LC

R-25
Boxer, Charles Ralph, 1904-
The problem of the native clergy in
Portuguese India, 1518-1787, HT, v.17
(1967), pp.772-80.

R-26
Bragança Pereira, Antonio Bernardo de.
    Historia religiosa de Goa. Nova Goa, 1937-

SOAS

R-27
Bruce, Helen E.
    In memoriam. Satara, Columbian Press, 1894.
8p.

1. Christian Missions - Satara.

Bom (Pres) Sat

R-28
Bruce, Henry James.
    In memoriam - a brief life of the Reverend
Ruttonji Nowroji. Panchgani, the author,
1912. 21p.

Bom (Pres) Sat

R-29
Bruce, Henry James.
    Letters from India. Satara, 1897. 202p.

R-30
Bruce, Henry James.
    The natural history of the Marathi
Bible...Calcutta, Calcutta advertiser
press, 1886.

R-31
Bruce, Henry James.
    The orphanage at Satara, India. Satara,
Columbia Press, 1901. 12p.

R-32
Calcutta Missionary Conferences.
    Statistical tables of Protestant missions
in India, Burma, and Ceylon. Calcutta, 1882.

R-33
Camps, Arnulf.
    Jerome Xavier, S.J.and the Muslims of the
Mogul Empire; controversial works and
missionary activity. Schöneck, Nouvell
revue de science missionaire Suisse, 1957.
(Neue Zeitschrift für Missionswissenschaft
Supplementa, 6) 278p.

R-34
Carey, Eustace, 1791-1855.
    Memoir of William Carey, D.D., late mission-
ary to Bengal; professor of Oriental languages
in the college of Ft.William, Calcutta.
Hartford, Canfield & Robins, 1837. 468p.

LC

R-35
Casimiro, Augusto.
    S.Francisco de Xavier e os Portugueses.
Lisboa, Agência geral do ultramar, Divisão
de publicações e biblioteca, 1954. 539p.

R-36
Chaplin, Ada C.
Our gold mine, the story of American
Baptist missions in India. Boston,
W.G.Corthell, 1877.

Syracuse Univ. Lib.

R-37
Chatterton, Eyre, bp.of Nagpur, 1863-
A history of the Church of England in India
since the early days of the East India Company. London, S.P.C.K., 1924. 379p.

L C

R-38
Christovao de Nazareth, Casimiro.
Mitras lusitanas no oriente: catalogo
chronologico-historico dos superiores das
missoes do norte e sul de Goa, e das
diocese de Crabganor, Cochim, Meliapor,
Malaca, Macao e Moçambique, Pte.I,II.
Bombay, 1887-88. 263p.

R-39
Clark, Alden Hyde, 1878-
India on the march. New York, Missionary
Education movement of the United States and
Canada, 1930. 208p.

4 y R

R-40
Clutterbuck, George W.
In India (the land of famine and of plague);
or Bombay the beautiful, the first city of
India, with incidents and experiences of
pioneer mission work in western India. 3d ed.
London, Ideal Pub.Union, 1899. 331p.

Pre '56 imprints

R-41
Colaco, Denis.
The christian missions in the kingdom of
the maratha rajas of Tanjore, MangR, v.11
(1930), pp.58-71.

PS
401
B69J

JBHS

R-42
Coleridge, Henry James, 1822-1893.
The life and letters of St.Francis Xavier.
New ed. London, Burns and Oates, 1881.
2v.in 1.

4 y R

R-43
Conversion of two Parsis and prosecution
of the Reverend John Wilson, D.D.
Bombay, 1839.

R-44
Cronin, Vincent.
Pearl to India; the life of Roberto de
Nobili. London, R.Hart-Davis, 1959. 297p.

4 y R

R-45
Da Cunha, Joseph Gerson, 1842-1900.
The diary of a French missionary in
Bombay, from November 8th, 1827 to May
12th, 1828, ASBJ, v.18 (1890-1894), pp.
350-69.

case

R-46
Da Cunha, Joseph Gerson, 1842-1900.
M. Dellon and the inquisition of Goa,
ASBJ, v.17,pt.2,no.47 (1887-89), pp.55-62.

ASBJ

R-47
Dawson, Edwin Collas, ed.
In and out of Chanda: being an account of
the mission of the Scottish Episcopal
Church to the city and district of Chanda;
together with Papers on the religions and
customs of the people, by the Rev. Alex
Wood and Indian folk-lore stories, translated by the Rev.Alex Wood. With a
preface by the Bishop of St.Andrews.
Edinburgh, Foreign Mission Board, 1906.
76p.

LC

R-48
D'Costa, Anthony.
The christianisation of the Goa Islands,
1510-1567. Bombay, 1965. 240p.

U of R

R-49
Dellon, Gabriel, b.ca.1649.
Account of the inquisition at Goa, trans.
from the French by H.Wharton. London, Hull,
1812. 198p.

v. India Cffee.Po.

R-50
Dellon, Gabriel, b. ca. 1649.
History of the Inquisition as it is
excercised at Goa. London, J.Knapton,
1688.

Scholberg-Portuguese

R-51
Dellon, Gabriel, b.ca.1649.
Relation de l'inquisition de Goa. Paris,
Chez Daniel Horthemels, 1688. 278p.

LC main

R-52
Dixon, James.
The sword of the Lord in the Indian crisis.
A fast day sermon. London, Manchester Printed,
1857.

BM

R-53
Dongre, Rajas Krishnarao and Patterson,
Josephine E.
Pandita Ramabai; a life of faith and prayer.
Madras, Christian Literature Society, 1963.
116p.

LC

R-54
Duff, Alexander, 1806-1878.
Missions: the chief end of the Christian
church; also the qualifications, duties,
and trials of an Indian missionary. Edinburgh, 1839. 177p.

IM

R-55
Dyer, Helen S.
Pandita Ramabai: her vision, her mission and
triumph of faith. London, Pickering and
Inglis, 1923. 173p.

U of R

R-56
　Elwin, Edward Fenton.
　　Indian Jottings, from 10 years' experience
in and around Poona city. London, J.Murray,
1907. 325p.

R-57
　Elwin, Edward Fenton.
　　Thirty-four years in Poona City: being the
history of the Panch Howds Poona City Mission.
London, H.R.Mowbray & co., 1911. 113p.

NUK

R-58
　Elwin, Edward Fenton.
　　Thirty nine years in Bombay city: being the
history of mission work of the Society of St.
John the Evangelist in that city. London, A.
R.Mowbray and Co., 1913. 138p.

NUK

R-59
　Evanglische missionsgesellschaft, Basel.
　　Report of the German mission in the Southern
Mahratta, Canara, and Malabar Provinces.
Madras, Printed at the American mission Press,
18-- annual.

　　1. Missions - India.

R-60
　Fernandes, Braz A.
　　Bandra, its religious and secular history.
Bombay, 1927. 150p.

R-61
　Ferreira Martins, José Frederico, 1874-
　　Historia da Mesericordia de Goa.
Nova-Goa, Imprensa Nacional, 1910-14.
3v.

R-62
　Francisco Xavier, Saint, 1506-1552.
　　Lettres de Saint François-Xavier de la
Compagnie de Jésus ... tr.par m.Léon Pages
... Paris, 1855. 2 vols.

R-63
　Garcia, Francisco, 1641-1685.
　　Vide y de San Francisco Xavier, apostal de
las Indias. Madrid, 1676.

R-64
　Gardner, Charles Edwyn.
　　Life of Father Goreh. Ed.by R.M.Benson.
London, Longman, Green & Co., 1900. 421p.

BM

R-65
　Greenfield, William, 1799-1831.
　　A defence of the Serampore Mahratta version
of the New Testament: in reply to animadver-
sions of an anonymous writer in the Asiatic
Journal for September 1829. London, 1830.

BM

R-66
Gribble, James Dunning Baker, d.1906.
History of freemasonry in Hyderabad (Deccan).
Madras, Higginbotham and co., 1910. 294p.

BM

R-67
Grierson, George Abraham, 1851-
The early publication of the Serampore
Missionaries. IA, v.32 (1903), pp.241-54.

Pinge

R-68
Guzman, Luis de.
Historia de las missiones qve han hecho los
religiosos de la Conpañia de Iesvs, para
predicar el sancto euangelio en la India
oriental, y en los reynos de la China y
Iapon ... Alcala, Biuda de I.Gracian, 1601.
2v.

LC

R-69
Hart, Frank.
Rahator of Bombay, the apostle to the
Marathas. London, The Epworth press, 1936.
189p.

Missions card.

U of R

R-70
Hough, James.
History of Christianity in India, from the
commencement of the Christian era. London,
1839-60. 5 vols.

BM

R-71
Hull, Ernest R.
Bombay mission-history with a special study
of the Padroado question. Bombay, The Examiner
Press, 1927-30. 2 vols.

R-72
Ingham, Kenneth.
Reformers in India, 1793-1833; an account of
the work of Christian missionaries on behalf
of social reform. Cambridge, Cambridge Univ.
Press, 1956. 160p.

U of R

R-73
Ipsen, P.
Pandita Ramabai. Ein Werkzeug Gottes zur
Befreiung der indischen Frau. Nach dem Engl.
Breklum, Christl. Buchh. in Komm., 1911.
56p.

R-74
Jervis, William Paget.
Thomas Best Jervis, as Christian, soldier,
geographer & friend of India, 1796-1857. A
centenary tribute by his son ... London, E.
Stock, 1898. 544p.

LC

R-75
Kamoji, D.C.
The christian missions in Bombay, 1870-
1885, JIH, v.44 (1966), pp.839-52.

R-76
    Karmarkar, Sumant Vishnu.
       Famine relief by missionaries at Ahmednagar.
Bombay, Nirnaya Sagar Press, 1900. 12p.

Com (Pres) cat

R-77
    Karmarkar, Sumant Vishnu.
       Present famine relief by American mission-
aries in the Ahmednagar district. Bombay,
Nirnaya Sagar Press, 1900. 12p.

Com (Pres) cat

R-78
    Lucena, Joao de, 1548-1600.
       Vida do Padre Francisco Xavier. Trans.into
Spanish by Alonso de Sandoval. Sevilla, 1619.

Burnell

R-79
    M.D'sa.
       History of the Catholic Church in India.
Bombay, B.X.Furtado & sons, 1910.
    v.1 - 52 A.D.-1652 A.D. 259p.

Bom (Pres) cat

R-80
    Macnicol, Nicol, 1870-1952.
       Pandita Ramabai. Calcutta, Association
Press, Y.M.C.A., 1926. (Builders of Modern
India) 154p.

LC

R-81
    Marshman, John Clark, 1794-1877.
       The life and times of Carey, Marshman and
Ward, embracing the history of the Serampore
Mission. London, Longman, Brown, Green,
Longmans, and Roberts, 1859. 2v.

U of R

R-82
    Marshman, John Clark, 1794-1877.
       The story of Clark, Marshman, and Ward, the
Serampore missionaries. London, J.Heaton &
son, 1864. 333p.

U of R

R-83
    Meersman, Achilles.
       The Franciscans in Bombay; history of the
Franciscans in the territory comprised within
the boundaries of the present Archdiocese of
Bombay. Bangalore, Everybody's St.Anthony,
1957. 297p.

NUC

R-84
    Memorial papers of the American Marathi Mission,
1813-1881: presented at the semi-centennial
anniversary of the commencement of the Ahmednagar Mission, Oct.26-30, 1881. Bombay,
1882. 158p.

IOL

R-85
    Mitchell, John Murray, 1815-1904.
       In western India: recollections of my
early missionary life. Edinburgh, D.Douglas,
1899. 417p.

BM

R-86
Mitchell, John Murray, 1815-1904.
   Memoir of the Rev.Robert Nesbit, Missionary
of the Free Church of Scotland, Bombay.
London, Edinburgh, 1858.

West Mus

R-87
Modak, Manorama Ramkrishna.
   The world is my family; biography of Rev.
Ramkrishna Shahu Modak. Bombay, Thackers,
1970. 276p.

UofR maharashtra-bio.
& Christianity.

R-88
Moraes, George Mark.
   History of Christianity in India from early
times to St. Francis Xavier: A.D.52-1542.
Bombay, Manaktalas, 1964. 320p.

   1. India - Church Hist.   2. Catholic Church
in India.

LC

R-89
Moulton, Joseph Langdon
   Faith for the future: the American Marathi
Mission, India sesquicentennial, 1963. New
York, United Church Board for World Ministries,
1967. 247p.

R-90
Munshi, Rustamji Nasarvanji.
   An inquiry as to how a bell in the
Portuguese church at Borivli came to be
transferred to a Hindu temple at Nasik,
ASBJ, v.23 (1914), pp.328-48.

UofR

R-91
Munshi, Rustamji Nasarvanji.
   The life-story of the old Portuguese bell
in the National Dabul Church at Girgaum,
Bombay, ASBJ, v.25,no.71 (1917-1921),
pp.134-52.

NRO
JR ASBom

R-92
Nayak, Gregory and Rul-Lan, Gasper.
   Our Catholic boy; survey of his religious
attitudes in the last three years at school.
Poona, Catechetical Centre, De Nobili College,
1963. 172p.

Ind nat'l bib '63

R-93
Nowroji, R.
   The recollections of an old Indian mission-
ary being an account of mission work in India.
Poona, Scottish Mission Industries Co., 1908.
40p.

Rom (Presbyt)

R-94
Padmanji, Baba, 1831-1906.
   An autobiography, ed.by J.Murray Mitchell.
Madras, 1892. 107p.

R-95
Pandita Ramabai: her search for God. In:
   AB, v.2,no.3 (1970), pp.42-45.

R-96
Pathak, Sushil Madhava.
American missionaries and Hinduism; a study of their contacts from 1813 to 1910. With a foreword by Norman D.Palmer. Delhi, Munshiram Manoharlal, 1967. 283p.

Christianity, Christian missions books
BAS Sept 1970

R-97
Pedro da Costa, Antonio.
Relatorio da nova diocese de Damao. Bombaim, 1892.

Calcutera-Portuguesa b.

R-98
Perumalil, Rev. A.C.
The apostles of Kalyana (Bombay), *JIH*, v.22 (1943). pp.71-92.

JIH

R-99
Priolkar, Anant Kakba, 1897-
The Goa Inquisition, being a quatercentenary commemoration study of the Inquisition in India. Bombay, 1961. 310p.

R-100
Queyroz, Fernaõ de, 1617-1688.
Historia da vida do veneravel irmaõ Pedro de Basto, coadjutor temporal da Companhia de Jesus, etc. Lixboa, Miguel Deslades, 1689. 504p.

R-101
Ramabai Sarasvati, pundita, 1858-
A testimony. 3d ed. Kedgaon, the author. 1912. 54p.

Rom (PRS) cat

R-102
Ramabai Sarasvati, pundita, 1858-
Trying to be saved by their own merit: a christian tract. Kedgaon, the author, 1910. 38p.

Rom (Roscat

R-103
Read, Hollis, 1802-1887.
The Christian Brahmun; or, memoirs of the life, writings and character of the converted Brahmun, Babajee. Including illustrations of the domestic habits, manners, customs, and superstitions of the Hindoos; a sketch of the Deckan and an account of the American mission at Ahmednuggur. New York, Leavitt, Lord, 1836. 2 vols.

R-104
Rego, Antonio da Silva, 1905-   ed.
Documentação para a história das missões do Padroado Português do Oriente. Lisboa, Divisão de Publicações e Biblioteca, Agência Geral das Colónias, 1947-1959. 12v.

1. Missions-Asia.
LC

R-105
Rego, Antonio da Silva, 1905-
Le patronage portugais de l'Orient; aperçu historique. Traduit du portugais par J.Haupt. Lisbõa, Agéncia Geral do Ultramar, 1957. 376p.

subject
PADROAD. LC

R-106
Richter, Julius, 1862-
A history of missions in India; tr.by Sydney H.Moore. N.Y., Chicago, Flemming H. Revell co., 1908. 477p.

1. Missions - India.

u of R

R-107
The romance of the Wesleyan Marathi Mission, by A.Y. Wright. Bombay, Tatva-Vivechaka Press, 1926. 8p.

R-108
Saldanha, Jerome Anthony.
The first Englishman in India and his works, especially his Christian Puran, ASBJ, v.22 (1906-08), pp.209-21.

NRU
ASBJ

R-109
Satthianadhan, Krupabai.
Saguna: a story of native Christian life. 2d ed. Madras, Srinivas Varadachari, 1895. 259p.

1. Maharashtra - Soc.life - Christians.
2. Maharashtra - Soc.hist.

L OL

R-110
Schurhammer, Georg.
Some documents on the Bassein mission in the possession of the Society of Jesus, JBHS, v.2 (1929), pp.195-200.

R-111
Sherring, Matthew Atmore, 1826-1880.
The history of Protestant missions in India from their commencement in 1706 to 1881. New ed. revised by Rev.Edward Storrow. London, The Religious tract society, 1884. 478p.

u of P

R-112
Sinclair, William F.
On the Catholics of Western India, IA, v.4 (1875), p.21.

R-113
Sinha, Ram Mohan.
Glimpse into the activities of christian missions under the Nagpur Bhonslas, IHCP, v.16 (1953), pp.322-26.

R-114
Smith, George, 1833-1919.
The life of John Wilson, D.D.,F.R.S., for fifty years philanthropist and scholar in the East. 2d ed. London, J.Murray, 1879. 391p.

U of R

R-115
Society for the Propagation of the Gospel. Diocesan Committee, Bombay.
Rise and progress of the Indo-British mission in Bombay, and of the Guzerat mission: report of the Bombay Diocesan Committee, 1838 to 1844. London, 1846. 34p.

R-116
Souza, Francisco de.
Oriente conquistado a Jesus Christo pelos
padres da Companhia de Jesus da Provincia
de Goa. Bombaim, 1881-86. 2v.

IOL

R-117
Stock, Eugene, 1836-1928.
History of the Church Missionary Society,
its environment, its men and its work. London,
Church Missionary Society, 1899-1916. 4 vols.

LC

R-118
Suau, Pierre.
Les bienheureux martyrs de Salsette.
Rodolphe d'Acquaviva et ses compagnons
de la compagnie de Jésus... Lille, Bruges,
1893. 206p.

BM

R-119
Temple, Sir Richard Carnac, 1850-1931.
Superstition and the inquisition at
Bombay in 1707, IA, v.39 (1910), p.224.

IA

R-120
Tilak, Lakshmibai (Gokhale), 1873-1936.
From Brahma to Christ, the story of Narayan
Waman Tilak and Lakshmibai, his wife. London,
United Society for Christian Literature, 1956.
95p.

U of R ordered

R-121
Tilak, Lakshmibai (Gokhale), 1873-1936.
I follow after; an autobiography. Trans.by
E.Josephine Inkster. Madras, Oxford Univ.
Press, 1950. 353p.

U of R

R-122
United Free Church of Scotland, India.
Our Church's work in India: the story of the
missions of the United Free Church of Scotland
in Bengal, Santalia, Bombay, Rajputana and
Madras. By various authors. Edinburgh, 1909.

Col nat Lib

R-123
Valignano, Alessandro, 1538-1606.
Historia del principio y progresso de la
Compañia de Jesus en las Indias Orientales,
1542-1564... Roma, 1944. (Bibliotheca
Instituti historici, S.I.,v.2). 618p.

DY

R-124
Venn, Henry.
The missionary life and labours of Francis
Xavier, taken from his own correspondence.
London, 1862. 333p.

BM

R-125
Weld, Arthur.
The suppression of the Society of Jesus
in the Portuguese dominions. London, 1877.
428p.

IOL

Hinduism & Various sects

R-126
    Abbott, John.
      The keys of power; a study of Indian ritual
and belief. London, Methuen, 1932. 560p.

religion

R-127
    Abbott, Justin Edwards, 1853-1932.
      Stotramālā, a garland of Hindu prayers.
Poona, Scottish Mission Industries Co.,
ltd., 1929. (The poet-saints of Maharashtra,
no.6) 330p.

4 a/R

R-128
    Adriel, Jean.
      Avtar, the life story of the perfect master
Meher Baba. Santa Barbara, J.F.Rowny Press,
1947. 284p.

BElliott

R-129
    Agaskar, M.S.
      The analytical study of Hanumant Swami's
chronicle of Ramdas, IHCP, v.14 (1951),
pp.176-83.

4 7 R

R-130
    Ahuja, Ram.
      Religion of the Bhils: a sociological
analysis, SB, v.14 (1965), pp.21-33.

Ja 8 65

R-131
    Amladi, D.R., 1922-
      Tulajapur Bhavani. Bombay, Director,
Govt.Print.,Publishers and Stationery,
Maharashtra State, 1961. (Government
of Maharashtra. State Board for Historical
Records and Ancient Monuments. Monograph
series, no.2). 14p.

LC

R-132
    Another unwritten chapter - the saints and
prophets of Maharastra, QJPSS, v.17,no.4
(1894), pp.1-19.

R-133
    Apte, Shivaram Shankar, 1907-
      Samarth Ramdas, life and mission. Bombay,
Vora and Co., 1965. 265p.

Ramadasa, 6.16...

4 7 R

R-134
    Baden, W.
      Tukarama, ein Dichter und Gottsucher aus
dem Mahrattavolke, EMM, v.53 (1868), pp.
427-32, 485-89.

O B

R-135
    Bahini, ca.1528-ca.1700.
      Bahina Bai, a translation of her auto-
biography and verses by Justin E.Abbott.
Poona, Scottish Mission Industries Co.,ltd.,
1929. (The poet-saints of Maharashtra, no.5).
313p.

U t R

R-136
Bahirat, Balchandra Pandharinath, 1904-
The philosophy of Jñanadeva. 2d ed.
Bombay, Popular Book Depot, 1961. 289p.

UofR

R-137
Bal, Sharayu Ganesh.
Study of the philosophy of Ekanātha with
special reference to his Bhāgavata and the
influence of Sankara's 'advaitism' on it.
Poona, Poona Univ., 1959. *

R-138
Belsare, Kesava Vishnu, 1909-
Shri Ram, the Saint of Gondawali, or the
life and sayings of Shri Brahma Chaitanya.
Poona, Y.G.Joshi, 1961. 328p.

L.C.

R-139
Belsare, Kesava Vishnu, 1909-
Tukaram. New Delhi, Maharashtra Information
Centre, 1967.

R-140
Belvalkar, Shripad Krishna, 1880-   and
Ranade, Ramachandra Dattatraya, 1886-1957.
History of Indian philosophy, v.7: Mysticism
in Maharashtra. Poona, Aryabhushan Press,
1933.

Ferguson College

R-141
Brown, Donald Mackenzie, 1908-
The philosophy of Bal Gangadhar Tilak:
Karma vs. Jñana in the Gita Rahasya, JAS.
v.17 (1958), pp.197-208.

R-142
Chavan, Viththal Pandurang.
Vaishnavism of the Gowd Saraswat Brahmin
Shaivites with some notes on the two sects
of Vaishnavism and the Shaivism, JASB, v.13
(1924-28), pp.470-91.

R-143
Chitgupi, B.B.
Vithal and Abhang, JUB, v.27 (1958-59),
pp.1-24.

R-144
Dandekar, Shankar Vaman, 1896-1968.
Dnyanadeo. New Delhi, Chief Information
Offices, Maharashtra Information Centre,
1969. 94p.

PL 480 1969

R-145
Deleury, G.A.
Cult of Vithoba. Poona, Deccan College
Postgraduate and Research Institute, 1952. *

R-146
Delfendahl, Bernard.
Les dieux champêtres d'un village du Maharashtra (Inde). Paris, Université de Paris, 1969. *

religion & philosophy
— village gods.

Silverman # 803

R-147
Deming, Wilbur Stone, 1889-
Eknāth, a Marātha bhakta. Bombay, Karnatak Printing Press, 1931. 117p.

BM

R-148
Deming, Wilbur Stone, 1889-
Ramdas and the Ramdasis. Calcutta, Assoc.Press (Y.M.C.A.). London, New York, H.M.Milford, Oxford University Press, 1928. (The religious life of India). 239p.

UofR

R-149
Deshpande, Gauri.
A journey towards understanding Irawati Karve's Yugant, IWT, v.4,no.3 (1970), pp. 127-33.

mahabharata - biog.

Literature

R-150
Deshpande, Manohar Sriniwas, 1899-
Dr. Ranade's life of light. Bombay, Bharatiya Vidya Bhavan, 1963. (Bhavan's book university, 109). 281p.

LC

R-151
Dingre, Gajanan Vithalrao.
Study of a temple town and its priesthood. Poona, Deccan College Postgraduate and Research Institute, 1968. *

Jayakar List. # 1523

R-152
Gajendragadkar, K.V.
The mystical life and teachings of the late Sri Gurudeva Dr. R.D.Ranade, JKU, v.4 (1960), pp.14-25.

Case

R-153
Ghurye, Govind Sadashiv, 1893-
Gods and men. Bombay, Popular Book Depot, 1962. 310p.

1. India - Religion - Hist.

LC

R-154
Gilder, Charles.
On Hinduism, and the principal Hindu deities worshipped in the Bombay Presidency; a lecture, etc. Bombay, 1855.

NLC

R-155
Gode, Parashuram Krishna, 1891-
The history of the Jaṭāsaṁkara temple at Nandurbar. JUB, v.15 (1946), pp.1-13.

JUB

R-156
Gode, Parashuram Krishna, 1891-
My reminiscences of the late R.D.Ranade,
PO, v.21 (1956), pp.1-11.

Case

R-157
Hanumanta Rao, S.
Hindu religious movements in medieval Deccan,
JIH, v.15 (1936), pp.103-13.

JIH

R-158
Irani, Meherwanji Sheheriyarji, 1894-
Shri Meher Baba: his philosophy and
teachings, comp.from his own dictations
by A.K.Abdulla. Nasik, R.K.S.Irani, 1933.
112p.

1. Yoga ...

NYPL

R-159
Jagannath Rao, N.V.
Sant Namadev as a social educationist,
MR, v.760 (1970), pp.301-304.

R-160
Jayakar, R.S.
The Hindu god Ganesh, JASB, v.7 (1906),
pp.479-91.

Zelliot

R-161
Jñanadeva, fl.1290.
Amrtamubhav. Trans.by Narayan Visanji Thakkur.
Bombay, Gujarati Printing Press, 1915. 349p.

Bib of Ind Lit

R-162
Jñanadeva, fl.1290.
Amritanubhava. Translated from Jñanadeva by
B.P.Bahirat. Bombay, Popular Prakashan, 1963.
93p.

LC

R-163
Jñanadeva, fl.1290.
Bhavartha-Dipika, otherwise known as
Dnyaneshwari, being an illuminating
commentary in Marathi on Bhagwad-Gita by
the celebrated poet-saint, Shri Dnyandev.
Rendered into English by R.K.Bhagwat.
Poona, Pub.by B.R.Bhagwat for Dnyaneshwari
English Rendering Pub.Assoc., 1953-54. 2v.

NYPL

R-164
Jñanadeva, fl.1290.
Gita explained by Dnyaneshwar Maharaj. Trans.
by Manu Subedar. 3d ed. Bombay, Manu Subedar,
1945. 318p.

SOAS

R-165
Jñanadeva, fl.1290.
Jnaneshvari (Bhavarthadipika); translated
from the Marathi by V.G.Pradhan, edited and
with an introduction by H.M.Lambert. London,
Allen & Unwin, 1967-69. (UNESCO collection
of representative works: Indian series). 2v.

Vol 2

R-166
Joshi, Purushottam Balkrishna, 1856-1930.
The duties of Brahmans: being the substance
of a lecture delivered by Rao Saheb P.B.Joshi
condemning anarchy as quite foreign to the
spirit of Hindu religion. Bombay, the author,
1910. 16p.

Rom(Pres) ...t

R-167
Joshi, Purushottam Balkrishna, 1856-1930.
On the household and village gods of the
Maharashtra, JASB, v.2 (1887-92), pp.132-58.

Surer

R-168
Joshi, Tukaram Dattaram.
Saint Ramdas' idea of Ramrajya, JGRS, v.32
(1970), pp.125-28.

Literature
BAS 1970

R-169
Kalekar, Narayan Govind, 1909-
La secte Mânbhâv. Paris, Paris Univ.,
1952. *

La Librairie Français

R-170
Kannabhiran Moodaliar, V.
Namadev: an Indian Saint. Triplicane (Madras),
1910.

OB under 1. Kannapiran Mudali

R-171
Karve, Irawati (Karmarkar) 1905-
Yuganta, the end of an Epoch. Poona,
Deshmukh Prakashan, 1969. 270p.

R-172
Khare, Ganesh Hari, 1901-
Khandoba, a popular deity of the south, IHCP,
v.21 (1958), pp.126-28.

IHCP

R-173
Khare, Ganesh Hari, 1901-
Krishnadevaraya of Vijayanagara and the
Vitthala image of Pandharapur. In: Vijaya-
nagara Sexcentenary Commemorative volume.
Ed.by Vijayanagara Empire Sexcentenary
Association. Dharwar, 1936. pp.191-95.

Chandarkar Index
comm. ...ols

R-174
Khare, Ganesh Hari, 1901-
Mahalakshmi of Kolhapur throuth the ages,
IHCP, v.18 (1955), pp.97-93.

Chaudhuri

R-175
Kincaid, Charles Augustus, 1870-
The Hindu Gods, and how to recognize them.
Bombay, Times Press, 1917. 44p.

1. Brahmanism.   2. India - Religion.   3. Gods.

LC

R-176
  Kotnis, Anant Narsinha.
    Life sketch of Sant Tatyasaheb Kotnis.
  Sangli, India, 1963. 105p.

LC

R-181
  Lederle, M.R.
    Philosophical trends in modern Maharashtra.
  Poona, Poona Univ., 1964. 2v.

Gupta Lib. #1371

R-177
  Krishnanath Raghunathji.
    A list of the Hindu godlings of Bombay, IA,
  v.29 (1900), p.308.

Fürer

R-182
  Ledrus, Michel.
    L'Inde Profonde: Toukaram. Louvain, 1933.

NLC

R-178
  Kulkarni, Krishnaji Rangrao, 1912-
    The saint of Shegaon; a book of poems on
  the life of Shri Gajanan Maharaj. Nagpur,
  1969. 194p.

PL480 5/70

R-183
  Mahipati, 1715-1790.
    Bhaktivijaya, or the triumph of devotion.
  Trans.from original Marathi. Bombay,
  Dubhashi and Co., 1892. 99p.

R-179
  Kulkarni, P.D.
    Were Jñanesvara and Namadeva contemporaries?
  ABORI, v.6 (1924-1925), pp.67-74.

ABORI

R-184
  Mahipati, 1715-1790.
    Tales of the saints of Pandharpur by C.A.
  Kincaid. Bombay, H.Milford, Oxford Univ.
  Press, 1919. 120p.

LC

R-180
  Kulkarni, Shridhar Rangnath, 1916-
    Saint Eknath. New Delhi, Mahrashtra Infor-
  mation Centre, 1968. 28p.

R-185
  Mandlik, Vishvanath Narayan, 1833-1889.
    Sangameshwara Mahatmya and Linga worship,
  ASBJ, v.11 (1876), pp.99-114.

R-186
Mandlik, Vishvanath Narayan, 1833-1889.
Serpent worship in western India: the
Nagapanchami holiday as it is now observed;
serpent worship: the Nagas and Sarpas, ASBJ,
v.9 (1867-70), pp.169-200.

Furer

R-187
Mandlik, Vishvanath Narayan, 1833-1889.
The shrine of the River Krishna at the
village of Mahabales'vara, ASBJ, v.9
(1867-68), pp.250-61.

ASBJ

R-188
Mitchell, John Murray, 1815-1904.
Notes of a visit of Jejuri. Bombay, 1855.
30p.

R-189
Mitchell, John Murray, 1815-1904.
Pandharpūr, IA, v.11 (1882), pp.149-56.

IA

R-190
Mitchell, John Murray, 1815-1904.
The story of Tukarama. From the Marathi
Prakit, ASBJ, Pt.I,v.3.,no.12 (1849), pp.1-
29.

R-191
Mitchell, John Murray, 1815-1904.
Tukārām, IA, v.11 (1882), pp.57-66.

IA

R-192
Modi, Jivanji Jamshedji, 1854-1933.
A visit to Nasik on the opening days of
the present Sinhast Pilgrimage, JASB, v.12
(1921-1924), pp.306-22.

R-193
Munge, P.R.
Inspirations of Saint Tukaram. With a
short sketch of his life, 1930. 47p.

R-194
Naik, A.V.
Cult-characteristics of the Hindu temples
of the Deccan, BDCRI, v.11 (1950-51), pp.83-
119.

R-195
Nandre, Brahm Nath.
Living force Shri Saibaba. Poona, the author,
1965. 487p.

R-196
Narasimha Swami, B.V.
Life of Saibaba. Madras, All India Sai
Samaj, 1955. 366p.

Ind Nat'l Bib '??

R-197
Narasimha Swami, B.V.
Saibaba's apostles and mission. Madras,
All India Sai Samaj, 1956. 424p.

Ind Nat'l Bib '58

R-198
Narasimha Swami, B.V. and Subbarao, S.
Sage of Sakuri. 4th ed. Sakuri, Maharashtra,
Shri Upasani Kanya Kumari Sthan, 1966. 212p.

U of K

R-199
Osborne, Arthur, 1906-
The incredible Sai Baba. London, Rider,
1958. 128p.

LC

R-200
Padhye, K.A.
The Warkari sect of the Deccan: an offshoot
of the Mahayana Buddhism, MB, v.50 (1941),
pp.28-31.

R-201
Panse, Murlidhar Gajanan, 1918-
Religion and politics in the early medieval
Deccan, JIH, v.45 (1967), pp.673-87.

JIH

R-202
Patkar, Madhukar Mangesh, 1907-
Brahmendraswami, a political Maratha
saint, MR, v.62 (1937), pp.45-47.

MR

R-203
Pendse, Shankar Damodar, 1897-
Jñaneśwara and Yogavasistha, AIOCPT, v.13
(1946), pp.238-39.

R-204
Pendse, Shankar Damodar, 1897-
The philosophy of Jnaneshwar. Nagpur,
Nagpur University, 1939.*

Bib PhD theses

R-205
Pradhan, Manohar Waman.
Sri Sai Baba of Shirdi. Bandra, A.Turkhud,
1933. 48p.

Bom (Pres) Cat

R-206
  Raeside, Ian.
    The Panduranga. Mahatmya of Sridhar, <u>BSOAS</u>,
  v.28 (1965), pp.81-100.

B SO AS

R-207
  Rāmadāsa, b.1608.
    Dasabodha. English version by V.S.Kanvinde.
  Nagpur, Jayashree Prakashan, 1963. 216p.

LC

R-208
  Ramdas, Swami, 1884-1963.
    God-experience. Bombay, Pub.for
  Anāndashram by Bharatiya Vidya Bhavan,
  1963. (Bhavan's book university, 107).
  25p.

LC

R-209
  Ranade, Mahadev Govind, 1842-1901.
    Religious and social reform; a collection
  of essays and speeches; comp.by M.B.Kolasker.
  Bombay, Gopal Narayan & co., 1902. 367p.

Cal Nat Lib.

R-210
  Ranade, Ramachandra Dattatraya, 1886-1957.
    Essays and reflections, comp.by B.R.Kulkarni.
  Bombay, Bharatiya Vidya Bhavan, 1964. 194p.

JAS 64

R-211
  Mistau, Hiltrud.
    Die philosophischen anschauungen Swami
  Vivekanandas und Lokamanya Bal Gangadhar
  Tillaks. Berlin, Humboldt Universität,
  1966. 370p.

Shulman #906

R-212
  Sankalia, Hasmukhlal Dhirajlal, 1908-
    Vitthala and Hari, <u>JUB</u>, v.21 (1953), pp.
  10-11.

JUB

R-213
  Saraswati, Baidyanath.
    Temple organization in Goa, <u>MI</u>, v.43
  (1963), pp.131-40.

fürer

R-214
  Savarkar, Vinayak Damodar, 1883-1966.
    Hindutva ...; with a foreword by Shri Bhai
  Parmananda. New Delhi, 1938. 189p.

R-215
  Sedgwick, Leonard John.
    Bhakti, <u>ASBJ</u>, v.23 (1914), pp.119-34.

R-216
Sharma, Shripad Rama, 1897-
Focus on Tukaram from a fresh angle. Bombay, Popular Book Depot, 1962. 106p.

U of R

R-217
Sharma, Shripad Rama, 1897-
Ranade; a modern mystic. Translation and adaption of Pra.R.D.Ranade, Caritra ani tatvajñana, by S.G.Tulpule. Poona, Venus Prakashan, 1961. 227p.

R-218
Sharma, Shripad Rama, 1897-
Teachings of Jnanadeva. Bombay, Bharatiya Vidya Bhavan, 1965. (Bhavan's book university. Rupee series, 59). 47p.

R-219
Sharma, Shripad Rama, 1897-
Tukaram's teachings. Bombay, Bharatiya Vidya Bhavan, 1964. (Bhavan's book university. Rupee series, 25). 67p.

LC

R-220
Sharma, Sri Ram, 1900-
The Arya Samaj and its impact on contemporary India in the nineteenth century. Una, Inst. of Public Administration, 196- 28p.

LC

R-221
Sykes, William Henry, 1790-1872.
An account of the origin of the living god at the village of Chinchore, near Poona, LSBT, v.3 (1823), pp.64-72.

R-222
Tilak, Bal Gangadhar, 1856-1920.
The Hindu philosophy of life, ethics and religion. Om-tat-sat, srimad Bhagavadgita rahasya: or, Karma-yoga-sastra, including an external examination of the Gita, the original Sanskrit stanzas, their English translations, commentaries on the stanzas, and a comparison of eastern with western doctrines, etc. Trans. by Balchandra Sitaram Sukthankar. Poona, J.S.Tilak & S.S.Tilak, 1965. 2 vols.

U of R

R-223
Tipnis, Shantaram Narayan.
Contribution of Upasani Baba to Indian culture. Sakuri, Shri Upansani Kanya Dumari Sthan, 1966. 250p.

U of R

R-224
Tulpule, C.A.
In search of the divine; or, mysticism in Maharashtra. Poona, 1931. 53p.

R-225
Underhill, Muriel Marion.
The Hindu religious year. Calcutta, Association Press, 1921. 194p.

R-226
Upadhyaya, Baldeva.
Vārakarī: the foremost Vaiṣṇava sect of
Mahārāṣṭra, IHQ, v.15 (1939), pp.265-77.

I-5

R-227
Vaidya, G.M.
Shri Sant Dnyaneshwar. Poona, Vidarbha
Marathwada, 1965. (Makers of India series,
4) 37p.

Indian Nat'l Bib.

R-228
Varma, Vishwanath Prasad.
Tilak's interpretation of the Bhagavadgita,
JBRS, v.43 (1957), pp.299-322.

LC accessions 1960 p.451
Buddhism, Jainism & Islam

R-229
Ahir, D.C.
Buddhism and Ambedkar. New Delhi, Ajay
Prakashan, 1968. 184p.

NUC 1973

R-230
Ahmad, Aziz.
Dar al-islam and the Muslim kingdoms of
Deccan and Gujarat, JWH, v.7 (1963), pp.
787-93.

R-231
Bird, James.
Historical researches on the origin and
principles of the Bauddha and Jaina religions;
embracing the leading tenets and their system,
as found prevailing in various countries: illustrated by descriptive accounts of the sculptures
in the caves of western India, with translations
of the cave inscriptions from Kanari, Ajanta,
Ellora, Nasik, etc.indicating the connection
of these caves with the Topes and Caves of the
Panjab & Afganistan, ASBJ, v.2 (1844), pp.
71-108.

ASBJ

R-232
Birdwood, Sir George Christopher Molesworth,
1832-1917.
The Muharram in Bombay, RSAJ, v.58 (1909),
pp.1013-22.

R-233
Dikshit, Moreshwar Gangadhar, 1915-
A new Buddhist sect in Kanheri, IHQ, v.18
(1942), pp.60-63.

R-234
Jatava, Daya Ram, 1933-
Ambedkar's Buddhism and science, ICQ,
v.26 (1970), pp.1-8.

R-235
Khaja Khan.
Sufi orders in the Deccan, MW, v.18 (1928),
pp.280-85.

R-236
Miller, Beatrice Diamond.
    Revitalization movements: theory and
    practice as evidenced among the Buddhists
    of Maharashtra. In: Anthropology and
    archaeology; essays in commemoration of
    Verrier Elwin, 1902-64. Ed.by M.C.Pradhan
    [and] others. Bombay, Indian Branch,
    Oxford Univ.Press, 1969. pp.108-26.

Buddhism
2 of R

R-241
Sengupta, Sudha.
    Buddhism in western India. MB, v.63 (1955).
    pp.243-47.

Chaudhari

R-237
Miller, Robert J
    Background to Buddhist resurgence: India and
Ceylon. SOA, v.7 (1966), pp.39-48.

R-242
Wilkinson, T.S. and Thomas, M.M.
    Ambedkar and the Neo-Buddhist movement.
    Madras, Christian Literature Society for the
    Christian Institute for the Study of Religion
    and Society, Bangalore, 1972. 163p.

R-238
Miller, Robert J.
    They will not die Hindus: the Buddhist con-
    version of Mahar ex-untouchables, AS, v.7
    (1967), pp.637-44.

BAS 65-70

R-243
Zelliot, Eleanor Mae.
    Background of the Mahar Buddhist conversion,
    SOA, v.7 (1966), pp.49-63.

R-239
Niyogi, M.B.
    Problem of Nava Buddha in Maharashtra,
    SSQ, v.38 (1963), pp.97-105.

Social Science quarterly

R-244
Zelliot, Eleanor Mae.
    Buddhism and politics in Maharashtra. In:
    South Asian politics and religion. Ed.by
    Donald Eugene Smith. Princeton, N.J.,
    Princeton University Press, 1966. pp.191-
    212.

Uof R

R-240
Robbin, Jeannette, 1938-
    Dr. Ambedkar and his movement. Hyderabad,
Dr. Ambedkar Pubs.Society, 1964. 180p.

LC

R-245
Zelliot, Eleanor Mae.
    Dr.Ambedkar and the Mahar Movement. Phila-
delphia, Univ.of Pennsylvania, 1969. 357p. *

R-246
Zelliot, Eleanor Mae.
   Mahar and non-Brahman movements in
Maharashtra, <u>IESHR</u>, v.7 (1970), pp.397-
415.

EAS 1970   O

R-251
Kennedy, Robert E., Jr.
   The Protestant Ethic and the Parsis,
<u>AJS</u>, v.68 (1962-63), pp.11-20.

N.L.
Furer

R-247
Zelliot, Eleanor Mae.
   The revival of Buddhism in India, <u>Asia</u>,
no.10 (1968), pp.33-45.

Buddhism
Zelliot   Zoroastrianism

R-252
Masani, Sir Rustom Pestonji, 1876-1966.
   The religion of the good life, Zoroastrianism.
London, G.Allen & Unwin, ltd., 1938. 189p.

LC

R-248
Bilimoria, Ardesir Nasarvanji and Alpaivala,
Dinshah D.
   The excellence of Zoroastrianism (the re-
ligion of the Parsis) Bombay, Jamsetjee
Petit Parsi Orphanage Captain Prtg.Works,
1898. 274p.

re skin puts   O

R-253
Modi, Jivanji Jamshedji, 1854-1933.
   The disa-pothi and the nam-grahan of the
Parsis, a summary, <u>AIOCPT</u>, v.2 (1922), pp.
167-69.

UofR

R-249
Chattopadhyaya, Nisikanta.
   Lecture on Zoroastrianism. Bombay, Educa-
tion Society's Steam Press, 1894. 20p.

BM   O

R-254
Modi, Jivanji Jamshedji, 1854-1933.
   The Persian Rivayats of the Parsis and
the Smrtis of the Hindus and the Talmud of
the Hebrews; a summary, <u>AIOCPT</u>, v.2 (1922),
pp.109-18.

Wife

R-250
Hodivala, Shahpurshah Hormasji.
   Jadi Rana and the Kissah-i-Sanjan, <u>ASBJ</u>,
v.23 (1909-14), pp.349-70.

ASBJ

R-255
Parrinder, E.G.
   The Parsis. In: Worship in the world's reli-
gions. Ed.by Edward Geoffrey Simons Parrinder.
London, Faber & Faber, 1961. pp.84-94.

Furer

R-256
  Patell, Bombanji Byramji.
    Notes on the towers of silence in India.
    JASB, v.2 (1870-1892), pp.55-64.

εμιλ

R-257
  Sanjānā, Dārābjī Peshotanjī.
    The collected works of the late Das-
    tur Darab Peshotan Sanjana. (Selection
    from the English works, consisting prin-
    cipally of translations of works by German
    authors. Edited by J.C.Tarapore. With a
    portrait). Bombay, British India Press,
    1932. 530p.

BM

R-258
  Wilson, John, 1804-1875.
    The Parsi religion as contained in the Zand-
    Avestá, and prepounded and defended by the Zora-
    strians of India and Persia, unfolded, refuted
    and contrasted to Christianity. Bombay, Ameri-
    can Mission Press, 1843. 600p.

    1. Zorastrianism. 2. Avestá

Index

E

Pilgamkar, D. W.   I2063
Pillay, K. K.   I373
Pina de Mello, Francisco de
   I374
Pinder, D. A.   I123
Pingree, David   C133
Pinkerton, John   I124
Pinto, Jose Manoel   L90
Pinto Pereira, Antonio   I375
Pires, Phillipe Neri   L170
Pires, Thome   I125
Pissurlencar, Panduronga S. S.
   I376, I627-I629, I658,
   I1274, I1303-I1306, I1821-
   I1822
Pithawalla, Maneck Bejanji
   B504, B591, F47
Pitt, R. B.   E501, E516, E522-
   E523, E535, E540, E542-E543,
   E545-E546, E554
Plan for Poona metropolitan
   region: some broad features
   of draft plan...   B741
Planning at state level - Ma-
   harashtra's experience...
   E249
Playfair, J. W.   E61
Playne, Somerset   I377
Plowden, G.   I777
Pocket school dictionary, Eng-
   lish and Marathi, with
   syllables, accents, etc....
   L91
Pogson, Wredenhall Robert   I378
Pointon, A. C.   E844
Poleman, Horace Irvin   J30
The political department in
   Bombay...   O68
The political impact of the
   Marathas on Marwar...   I1944
Pollock, John   I2134
Pondicherry   I379
Poona, India (City)   F122, I794
Poona, India (City) Municipal
   Corporation   E747

Poona, India (City) University
   L92, P25
Poona, India (City) University.
   Department of Mathematics
   and Statistics   F137
Poona, India (City) University.
   Evaluation Committee to ex-
   amine the Community Develop-
   ment Project, Kolhapur   E748
Poona, India (District) Commis-
   sioner   I1744
Poona municipal corporation.
   See All India Institute of
   Local Self-Government.
Potdar, Datto Vaman   I126, I795,
   I1338, I2263
Potter, Karl L.   R2
Pottinger, D.   P26
Powar, Appasaheb Ganapatrao
   I1307, I1339-I1340, I1434-
   I1436, I1745, I1823, I1872-
   I1873
Prabhu, Pandharinath. See Va-
   lavalkar, Pandharinath Hari.
Pradhan, B. V.   I2135
Pradhan, G. P.   I2136-I2138,
   L298
Pradhan, Gopinath Ramchandra
   E439-E440
Pradhan, Kusum   B700
Pradhan, Manohar Waman   O163,
   R205
Pradhan, R. G.   O204
Pradhan, Snehprabha   L372
Pradhan, V. G.   R165
Prasad, Bimla   I2264
Prasad, Bisheshwar   O69
Prasad, Jagdish   E24
Prasad, Madho   I2139
Prasad, Ram Chandra   I127
Prasad, Yadunath   I1437
Prasanna, Kumud   G63
Pratapsinh Rao Gaekwar, Maha-
   raja of Baroda   I2140
Pratinidhi, Bhavanarao   C134
Pratt, E.   O181

V